Softcover reprint of the hardcover 1st edition 2006

Pro SQL Server 2005 Replication

Sujoy P. Paul

Apress®

Pro SQL Server 2005 Replication

Copyright © 2006 by Sujoy Paul

Softcover reprint of the hardcover 1st edition 2006

ISBN   978-1-4842-2028-3   ISBN   978-1-4302-0313-1   (eBook)
DOI 10.1007/978-1-4302-0313-1

Lead Editor: Jim Sumser
Technical Reviewer: Judith Myerson
Editorial Board: Steve Anglin, Ewan Buckingham, Gary Cornell, Jason Gilmore, Jonathan Gennick,
    Jonathan Hassell, James Huddleston, Chris Mills, Matthew Moodie, Dominic Shakeshaft,
    Jim Sumser, Keir Thomas, Matt Wade
Project Manager: Sofia Marchant
Copy Edit Manager: Nicole Flores
Copy Editor: Andy Carroll
Assistant Production Director: Kari Brooks-Copony
Production Editor: Ellie Fountain
Compositor: Dina Quan
Proofreader: Linda Seifert
Indexer: Carol Burbo
Artist: Kinetic Publishing Services, LLC
Cover Designer: Kurt Krames
Manufacturing Director: Tom Debolski

Distributed to the book trade worldwide by Springer-Verlag New York, Inc., 233 Spring Street, 6th Floor, New York, NY 10013. Phone 1-800-SPRINGER, fax 201-348-4505, e-mail orders-ny@springer-sbm.com, or visit http://www.springeronline.com.

For information on translations, please contact Apress directly at 2560 Ninth Street, Suite 219, Berkeley, CA 94710. Phone 510-549-5930, fax 510-549-5939, e-mail info@apress.com, or visit http://www.apress.com.

The source code for this book is available to readers at http://www.apress.com in the Source Code section. You will need to answer questions pertaining to this book in order to successfully download the code.

Dedicated to my parents, Subhendu and Kavita Paul

Contents at a Glance

Contents

▇CHAPTER 9   **Configuring Transactional Replication Using T-SQL**..... 301

About the Author

SUJOY PAUL has a bachelor's degree in chemical engineering from the University of Toronto, Canada, and a postgraduate degree in the same discipline from the University of Strathclyde, Glasgow, UK. Since then, he has moved on to the software industry and has gained extensive experience in database management systems, such as Microsoft SQL Server 2000, Sybase ASA, and Sybase ASE; data modeling; and case-based tools like PowerDesigner and ERWIN. His background includes expertise in database replication, with a special interest in two-way replication, backup and recovery, performance and tuning, and troubleshooting. He is a Microsoft Certified Professional on SQL Server 2000. His other professional interests include knowledge management, semantic web, and bioinformatics, in which he also has a postgraduate diploma. Currently, he is working for a major consulting company in Toronto, Canada.

He is an avid fan of soccer and tennis. In his spare time he plays squash and enjoys reading literature, and he has also published poetry. He can be reached at sujoyp@hotmail.com.

About the Technical Reviewer

JUDITH M. MYERSON is a systems architect and engineer. Her areas of interest include middleware technologies, application development, web development, software engineering, network management, servers, security management, information assurance, standards, RFID technologies, and project management. Judith holds a Master of Science degree in engineering, and is a member of the IEEE organization. She has reviewed/edited a number of books, including *Hardening Linux, Creating Client Extranets with SharePoint 2003*, and *Microsoft SharePoint: Building Office 2003 Solutions*.

Acknowledgments

First of all, I would like to thank Mr. Jim Sumser, without whose constant encouragement and support this book would not have been possible. I would also like to thank Mr. Andy Carroll, Ms. Ellie Fountain, Ms. Kylie Johnson, Ms. Sofia Marchant, Ms. Judith Myerson, and the rest of the Apress team for their unending patience and superb professionalism in constantly striving for excellence. They also gave me sufficient time even when the deadlines had elapsed. I sincerely appreciate that.

I would like to thank my parents for helping me in pursuing my dreams, and my sister, Manashi, who taught me how to dream and helped develop the savoir faire in me. I would also like to thank Didi, Ajoyda, Mohor, Gogol, Ma, Anjanda, Shweta, and my dear friend Bob for being there for me. Finally, I would like to thank my wife, Aditi, who suffered the most during this venture. Her tireless support in proofreading my writing, editing the figures every day and night, and bearing all of this with a smile on her face made it all the more worthwhile.

CHAPTER 1

■ ■ ■

Introduction: Distributed Data

MS SQL Server 2005 distributes data to remote or mobile users by replication either over the Internet or over the local area network (LAN). Throughout this book I will focus on how the different types of replication can be used in distributing data and database objects. I will discuss the fundamentals, the implementations, the architectures, and the topologies of replication and demonstrate them with real-world examples.

Before we look at replication as one of the methods of distributing data, however, I will explain what distributing data means. In this chapter, I will outline the different kinds of distributed data and the methods and considerations for distributing data. Then we'll look at replication as a method of distributing data.

On completing this chapter, you will be able to describe the following:

- Various methods of data distribution

- Eager replication

- Lazy replication

Distributed Data

Companies nowadays have multiple copies of data distributed across various locales. These data can be in different formats, employ different relational database management systems (RDBMSs), and often reside on multiple servers. Depending on the business logic, it may be necessary to access the data residing either on a local machine or at a remote site using either the LAN or the company's wide area network (WAN). At other times it may be essential to integrate the distributed data available across the network. The purpose in all these cases is to bring the data closer, to allow autonomy of data, and to reduce conflicts for the users. In subsequent chapters, I will discuss some business considerations in designing a distributed environment for replication.

Distributed databases are loosely connected databases stored on multiple servers distributed over a network. These databases are logically interrelated. Figure 1-1 shows the representation of a distributed database system where databases residing in Paris, Montreal, London, and Boston can cooperate with each other via the company's network. Distributed systems can be found in any organization that has a decentralized structure, such as the travel and airline industries, hotel and retail chains, and hospitals.

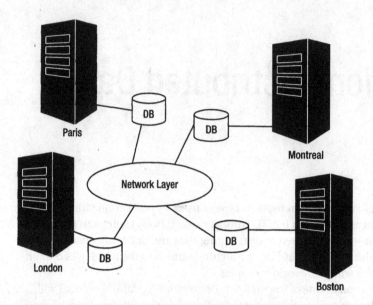

Figure 1-1. *Configuring a distributed database system*

■**Note** The terms *distributed databases* and *distributed processing* are often used interchangeably. Distributed processing involves applications that share the resources among the members of the network. The client-server system would be an example of distributed processing.

Information systems are sometimes distributed because of the evolution of the companies that create them. As companies grow, they often become decentralized, and different sites might want to remain autonomous and design databases that cater to their particular needs. Therefore, depending on the business requirements, it may be imperative to add servers in a particular site or to a centralized site to share the workload. You can also use failover clustering for high availability. The distribution of all these heterogeneous sources, like processors, networks, operating systems, and data, opens up new opportunities in scalability as well as creating challenges in security, transactional consistency, and transparency. Distributed computing systems are systems in which several autonomous processes interconnected in a computer network cooperate to perform a specific task. Distributed databases are parts of this much bigger distributed computing picture.

■**Note** For more information on distributed computing, refer to M. Tamer Özsu and Patrick Valduriez, *Principles of Distributed Database Systems,* second edition.

Consider the challenges of a distributed system such as a distributed data environment. In a distributed data environment, like a replication environment, the various sites are autonomous and can be online when needed. As such, scalability is allowed. Transactions are atomic, meaning that either the whole of a transaction is committed, or all of it is rolled back. Although latency is an integral factor in replication, the consistency of the transactions is still maintained. Data entry users can look at the system as a whole—they do not have to be concerned about the logistics of the data. This means data can be relocated from one place to another with minimal impact to the user or the application. In a distributed environment, each of the components is independent of each other, so they can also function independently.

Databases in a distributed system can either be homogeneous, such as when using all SQL Server databases, or heterogeneous, using databases like DB2, Oracle, or Sybase residing on different servers. Homogeneous databases in a distributed environment provide tight coupling, such as the close interaction between the SQL Server client and the SQL Server database server. Heterogeneous databases provide looser coupling due to the autonomous nature of each of the sites. For example, using replication in SQL Server, you can transmit data from the SQL Server databases to remote servers running Oracle or DB2 databases. SQL Server provides access to heterogeneous databases by using the ODBC or OLE DB drivers. These drivers are included on the SQL Server 2000 CD. The Microsoft OLE DB provider for SQL Server (SQLOLEDB) is installed automatically with SQL Server 2005. The other OLE DB providers that are installed with SQL Server 2005 are

- Microsoft OLE DB Provider for ODBC

- Microsoft OLE DB Provider for Jet

- Microsoft OLE DB Provider for Oracle

For a list of OLE DB providers, please refer to http://msdn2.microsoft.com/en-us/library/ms187072.aspx.

Note Throughout this book, the term "SQL Server" refers to SQL Server 2005.

Although each of the databases in a distributed database system is distinct, users can use applications that access the distributed database system as if they were connected to a single database. Such applications can execute transactions that read or modify the data in different databases. SQL Server users can execute distributed queries across data in several instances of SQL Server and across OLE DB–enabled heterogeneous data sources by the use of a linked server, as shown in Figure 1-2.

Tip The OpenQuery function can be used to execute the query on the remote server. This way the processing can be done on the remote server and the result set is returned to the local server.

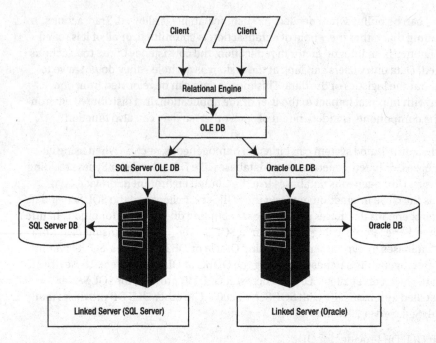

Figure 1-2. *SQL Server using OLE DB to communicate with heterogeneous data sources*

■**Note** Heterogeneous databases and heterogeneous replication are discussed in Chapter 20.

Linked servers enable users to access remote servers and allow remote data to be retrieved and joined with local data. A linked server facilitates the execution of the queries locally, and since data is retrieved from the remote sites and transferred across the network to the local server, it can cause significant overhead and have an impact on system performance.

■**Note** For more information on linked servers, refer to SQL Server 2005 Books Online (BOL). You can install the BOL when you install SQL Server 2005.

SQL Server Management Studio (SSMS) can be used in the configuration of linked servers. The configuration of a linked server is shown in Figure 1-3. A linked server configuration can issue distributed queries, updates, commands, and transactions.

Now suppose an application issues a transaction, in the linked server configuration of Figure 1-3, and the transaction is processed on Server A but needs some data from the Oracle database. In this configuration, it is not important to Server B where the transaction request comes from. Server B simply communicates with the Oracle database and processes the transaction's request, returning the results to wherever the request came from—in this case, Server A.

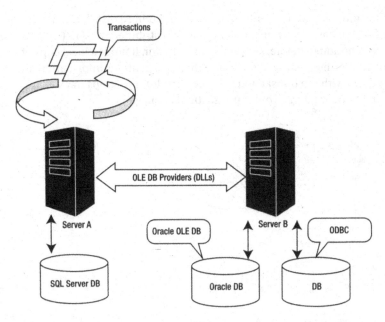

Figure 1-3. *Configuring linked servers*

Methods of Distributing Data

There are two methods of distributing data in SQL Server: distributed transactions and replication. It is possible to maintain multiple copies of current data in the same environment using both of these methods. It is also possible to implement either of these methods in a distributed environment. In transactional replication with queued updates, you can transmit data by using the Microsoft Distributed Transaction Coordinator (MS DTC). Although, the focus of this book is on replication, I will explain distributed transactions here, and the differences between the two methods.

Distributed Data Transactions

Distributed transactions are transactions that span two or more servers. These servers are called *resource managers*, and the coordination of these transactions across resource managers is done by *transaction managers*. MS DTC is a transaction manager that coordinates transaction-processing requests from databases, message queues, and file systems either on a local machine or distributed across the network. By employing the two-phase commit (2PC) protocol, MS DTC guarantees the completion of the transaction at all sites at the same time.

For example, suppose you have two databases—one storing customer accounts and the other containing the sales history of the customers—residing on two different servers, and you want to find out the account information and sales history of a particular customer. The distributed transaction in this example would therefore involve the execution of data manipulation language (DML) statements on both the databases. Therefore, databases like those in SQL Server are regarded as resource managers when an application gets, stores, or manipulates a distributed transaction.

The configuration of the different components involved in executing a distributed transaction is shown in Figure 1-4. Typically the application initiates a distributed transaction, and the transaction manager, as mentioned before, acts as the coordinator. It holds a local copy of the MS DTC log, which maintains the identity of the transaction and contains information on any resource managers enlisted with the transaction manager. The log also keeps track of any transactions that are coming from or going to other transactional managers.

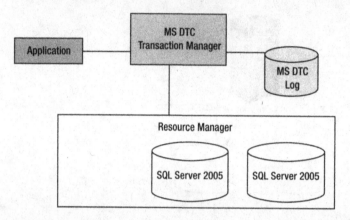

Figure 1-4. *MS DTC components executing a distributed transaction*

So, in effect, a distributed transaction can traverse several nodes, where each node consists of a MS DTC. This is illustrated in Figure 1-5.

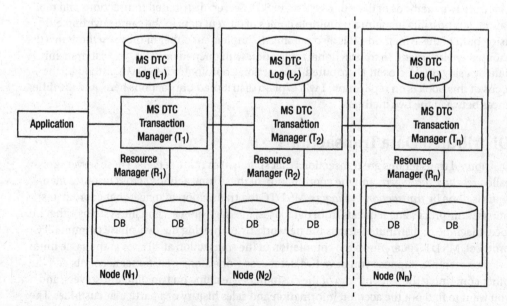

Figure 1-5. *Transmitting a distributed transaction through several nodes*

Caution The MS DTC transaction manager cannot be started without the log file. It is therefore best to keep a backup copy of the log file on a separate machine.

SQL Server manages distributed transactions internally. When these transactions connect to two or more servers, these servers are called *resource managers*. To a user, it looks as if the transaction is being executed locally.

First, the application initiates a transaction by calling the BeginTransaction method on the MS DTC, which is a transaction manager. A transaction object is created, and it acts as the representative of the transaction. The log file keeps a record of all the transactions, and the resource manager for each node checks whether such a transaction exists. The transaction object then binds to the connection object of the Open Database Connectivity (ODBC) interface by calling the SQLSetConnectAttr method. The ODBC layer is an intermediary layer that sits on top of the database layer. ODBC facilitates the movement of the transaction between the transaction manager and the resource manager. The transaction will either update or read the data or will perform both operations. At the end of the transaction, the application will normally either call the Rollback method or complete the transaction by calling the Commit method. This is illustrated in Figure 1-6.

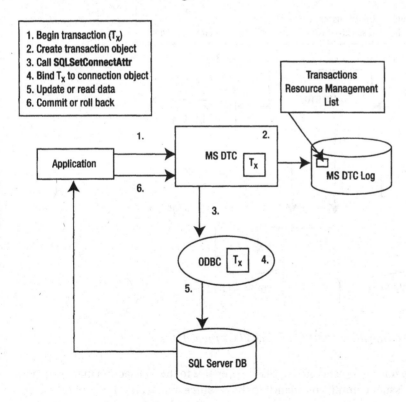

Figure 1-6. *Transferring distributed data*

If the application fails, the MS DTC aborts the command. However, if the application issues a COMMIT command, the MS DTC needs to accommodate all possible scenarios. For example, some of the resource managers might successfully complete the transaction and others might not. Or there might be a disruption in the network traffic that impedes the completion of the transaction. You can resolve these problems by using the two-phase commit (2PC) protocol. The transaction manager ensures that all the resource managers either issue a COMMIT command fully to the transaction or, in the event of one transaction failing, the transactions are aborted.

The 2PC protocol consists of two phases: prepare and commit. The prepare phase starts off with the MS DTC broadcasting a message to all the resource managers asking them whether they are prepared to accept the transactions. At this stage, any transactions in the buffers are written to disk. The resource managers then reply to the broadcast by sending out either a success or failure notification to the MS DTC. If any of the resource managers report a failure, the MS DTC sends a rollback command to each of the resource managers, including those successful transaction operations, and the transaction is aborted. The process is shown in Figure 1-7.

1. Application issues a **Commit** command
2. MS DTC broadcasts message to resource managers
3. Transactions are flushed to disk
4. Resource managers notify MS DTC of success or failure
5. If there are any failures, MS DTC sends a **Rollback** command to all resource managers

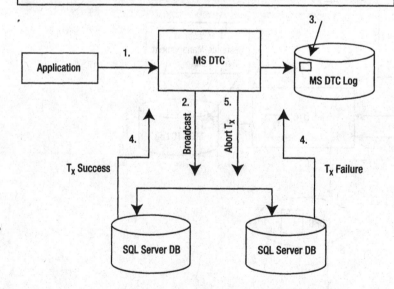

Figure 1-7. *Diagram showing the prepare phase in a 2PC protocol*

If all the resource managers send out successful prepares to the transaction manager, the transaction manager issues commit commands to the resource managers. The resource managers then proceed to commit the commands, as shown in Figure 1-8.

1. Application issues a **Commit** command
2. MS DTC broadcasts message to resource managers
3. Resource managers notify MS DTC of all successes
4. MS DTC issues a **Commit** command to all resource managers

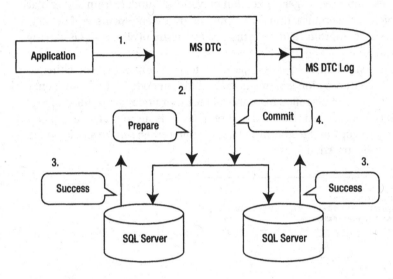

Figure 1-8. *Commit phase of the 2PC protocol*

Once the transaction manager has sent the commit or rollback messages to the resource managers, it sends a success or failure notification to the application.

Replication

Now that you know what a distributed data transaction is, I will explain what replication is and what the different types are. Replication, as described by BOL, is a "set of technologies" that can move data and database objects from one database to another and across different platforms and geographic locales. This allows users to work with a local copy of the database, and any changes they make are transferred to one or more remote servers or mobile users across the network. The consistency of the database is maintained by the process of synchronization.

The advantages of replicating databases are the physical separation of the databases and the normal latency of the data. For example, sales staff working in the field can enter their orders or changes on their portable devices and transfer the data automatically to the head office while maintaining database consistency at each site.

The question is how to distribute data using replication, and the answer depends on when, where, and how data is propagated. There are two kinds of replication: eager and lazy replication.

Eager Replication

Eager replication is also known as *synchronous replication*. In this method, an application can update a local replica of a table, and within the same transaction it can also update other replicas of the same table. No concurrency anomalies occur, since synchronous replication gives serializable execution. Any anomaly in concurrency is detected by the locking method. If any of the nodes are disconnected, eager replication prevents the update from taking place. Furthermore, the atomicity of the transactions is guaranteed by the employment of the 2PC method. However, there is a compromise in performance as a result of all the updates being carried in a single transaction.

Eager replication consists of the following steps: execute, transmit, notify, and either commit or rollback. An executed transaction is transmitted to different nodes, and in the event of failure in one node, the transaction is rolled back and all the other nodes are notified of the failure. The transaction is then aborted in all nodes. If replication is successful in all the nodes, a commit is broadcast and a copy of the committed transaction is then sent to all the nodes. This type of replication is illustrated in Figure 1-9.

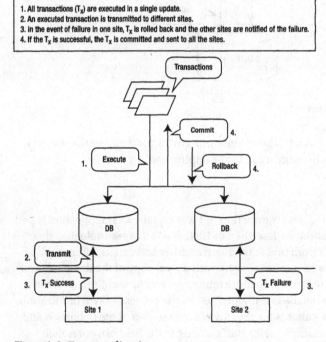

Figure 1-9. *Eager replication*

SQL Server 2005 BOL does not mention eager replication explicitly, so you may wonder why you would want to use it. Suppose you want to have a real-time copy of the master database so that you have a ready backup in the event of a failure. The synchronous nature of data transfer in eager replication facilitates real-time data transfer and in this situation it would be useful. However, eager replication is not a good choice for a remote or mobile environment, since it reduces update performance. Also, in a mobile environment the nodes are not always connected.

Note If you are interested in knowing the research trends in eager replication, a good article to read is "Database Replication Techniques: A Three Parameter Classification," by M. Weismann, F. Pedone, A. Schiper, B. Kemme, and G. Alonso. This paper describes the eight classes of eager replication protocols.

Lazy Replication

Lazy replication is also known as *asynchronous replication*. In this case, if the transactions are committed, they are sent to the different sites for the updates to occur. However, if they are rolled back, the changes will not be transmitted to the different sites. Thus, the very nature of asynchronous replication allows the updates of committed transactions to be sent to disconnected sites, as in the case of handheld sets or mobile devices. This is shown in Figure 1-10.

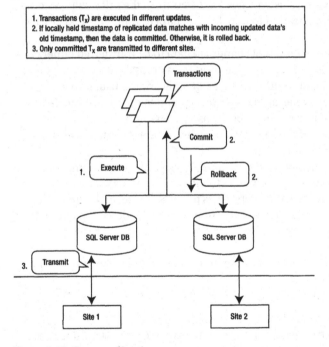

Figure 1-10. *Lazy replication*

With this type of replication, it is possible for two different sites to update the same data on the same destination site. This will lead to a conflict in the updating of the data. Such update conflicts need to be resolved in lazy replication, and this is done by associating timestamps with each of the transaction objects. Each object carries the timestamp associated with the previous update of that data. So when a transaction is sent to the destination site, it first checks to see whether the timestamp associated with the local copy of the replicated data matches the incoming transaction's old timestamp for that data. Only if they match will the changes, including the transaction's new timestamp, be applied. If the timestamps do not match at the initial stage, the updated transaction is rejected. SQL Server has a conflict-resolution viewer that deals with updates, inserts, and deletes.

> ■**Note** For an excellent discussion of the theoretical aspects of both eager and lazy replication, including the mathematical formulations of transactions, see "The Dangers of Replication and a Solution," by J. Gray, P. Helland, P. O'Neil, D. Sasha.

Replication in SQL Server

SQL Server follows asynchronous (lazy) replication. It permits three different kinds of asynchronous replication: snapshot, transactional, and merge replication.

Snapshot replication makes a copy of the data and propagates changes for the whole set of data rather than individual transactions, thereby making it a discontinuous process and entailing a higher degree of latency. For example, suppose a bookstore chain offers discounts once or twice a year. The regional bookstores only need to be aware of the price changes occasionally, so you could use snapshot replication to transfer the changes from the head office to the regional bookstores.

Transactional replication allows incremental changes to data to be transferred either continuously or at specific time intervals. Transactional replication is normally used where there is a high volume of inserts, updates, and deletes. This type of replication is usually used in a server-to-server environment. For example, auto repair shops need to have real-time data about inventory in their warehouses and other shops. By using transactional replication across all stores, it is possible for each of the shops to know the current inventory, and stock shortages can be anticipated ahead of time.

Merge replication permits a higher degree of autonomy. It allows the subscribing servers to make changes and then it propagates those changes to the publishing servers, which in turn transfer the changes to other subscriber servers. Sales people working in the field can enter their orders or changes once the transactions are complete. The updated data from different sales people can lead to conflicts, which can be resolved by setting up a conflict policy in merge replication. The Conflict Policy Viewer in SQL Server 2005 helps you track the conflicts. Point of sales applications, like sales force automation, are situations where you can use merge replication.

> ■**Note** Snapshot replication is discussed in Chapters 4 through 7, transactional replication is discussed in Chapters 8 through 10, and merge replication is discussed in Chapters 11 through 14.

Benefits of Replication

Managing replication can be a challenging task to even a seasoned database administrator, so why would we want to use it? Scalability, fault-tolerance, autonomy of sites, and compatibility with various platforms such as handheld devices, are some of the benefits of using replication in a business environment.

The next question is when you would use replication. The BOL lists several scenarios in which you would be likely to use replication in a distributed data environment:

- Data applications that need to be used either in online or offline environments

- Situations where you need to copy and distribute data to different sites on a scheduled basis

- Environments in which changes are made by multiple users at multiple sites, and you need to merge the data modifications, resolving any potential conflicts

- Web applications that allow users to browse large volumes of data

So what are the differences between replication and distributed transactions? In the case of replication, there can be a time lag in the propagation of data, depending on the type of replication used. In the case of distributed transactions, all copies of the data must be synchronized at all times. Each server that is included in the transaction must be available online at all times and must be able to commit its part of the transaction. Failure of the transaction on any of the servers causes the transaction to be aborted. Hence, distributed transactions have a lower latency compared to asynchronous replication.

Unlike replication, distributed transactions are not scalable. With replication, the servers do not need to be online all the time, so autonomy of the sites is supported, allowing more scalability in the process.

Figure 1-11 shows the degree of the autonomy and latency in the different methods of distributed data. As you can see, distributed transactions have the lowest latency, while merge replication has the highest latency and maximum autonomy.

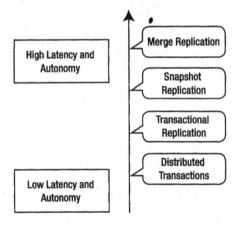

Figure 1-11. *Degree of autonomy and latency in the different methods of distributing data*

Transactional replication has a lower latency and autonomy compared to both snapshot and merge replication. In transactional replication, incremental data changes need to be updated at both the source and the destination.

Merge replication allows remote sites to make autonomous changes to data, and changes from all the sites are then merged either at a scheduled time or on demand. This means conflicts can occur, but the method allows for the latency and autonomy of the sites.

Snapshot replication makes a snapshot of the data and database objects at a specific point in time and does not monitor the specific changes in the data. The autonomy and latency of snapshot replication lies between transactional and merge replication.

SQL Server 2005 Tools

We'll start looking at the fundamentals of replication in Chapter 2, but first let's look at the tools introduced in SQL Server 2005. We will be making use of them in the following chapters to configure, administer, and adjust performance of the different types of replication.

SQL Server Configuration Manager

The SQL Server Configuration Manager is a new management tool in SQL Server 2005. It is a one-stop interface that allows administrators to configure and manage the services of SQL Server, SQL Server agent, SQL Server Analysis Services, and MS DTC. It can be integrated with other Microsoft Management Console (MMC) applications. The different configurations of the server are shown in Figure 1-12.

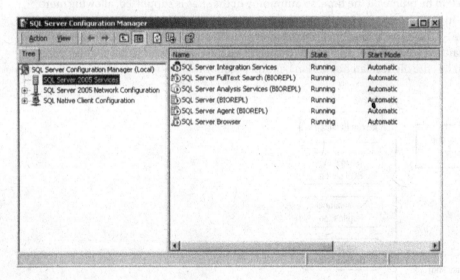

Figure 1-12. *Different SQL Server services*

By right-clicking on the name of a service, you can start, stop, or check the properties of that service. The SQL Server Configuration Manager is installed with SQL Server 2005. It combines the functionality of the Service Manager, the Server Network Utility, and the Client Network Utility of SQL Server 2000.

SQL Server Management Studio

The SQL Server Management Studio (SSMS) integrates the functionalities of Enterprise Manager, Analysis Manager, and Query Analyzer in SQL Server 2000. It also allows for the administration of services like Reporting Services, Integration Services, Notification Services, and Replication. The features that were available in SQL Server 2000 for each of the preceding components have now been incorporated into SSMS. This is shown in Figure 1-13.

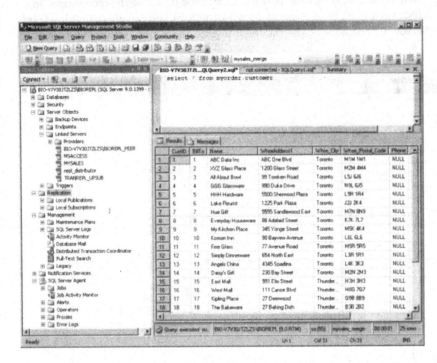

Figure 1-13. *SQL Server Management Studio and the integration of the different components*

The Object Explorer is a component of the SSMS, and it allows you to view lists of the objects for a particular instance of SQL Server like a Database Engine, Analysis Service, Notification, and Integration Services. It lists the System and user databases, the linked servers, Replication, and SQL Server agent.

■**Note** The pubs and the Northwind sample databases in previous versions of SQL Server have been replaced. The new sample database, AdventureWorks, can be installed either with SQL Server or afterwards.

If you want to execute a query, the Object Explorer will also allow you to open the Query Editor. The alternate way is to open a new Database Engine Query and connect to the server. You can then execute T-SQL (Transact SQL) statements as shown in Figure 1-13.

■**Tip** If you want to check the veracity of the T-SQL syntax in the Query Editor, you can highlight the statement and press Shift+F1. It will take you directly to the online help.

Database Engine Tuning Advisor

The Index Tuning Wizard in SQL Server 2000 has been replaced with the Database Engine Tuning Advisor. It helps you to optimize the performance of the databases by recommending the optimal set of indexes and types of physical design structures. You can also use this wizard to optimize SQL Server 2000 databases. The Database Engine Tuning Advisor is shown in Figure 1-14.

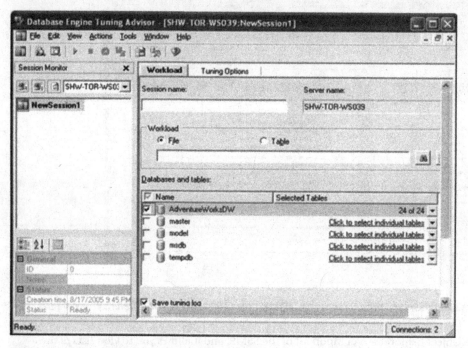

Figure 1-14. *Database Engine Tuning Advisor*

This advisor is also integrated with the SSMS.

Replication Monitor

The Replication Monitor lists the status of the publications and subscriptions, as shown in Figure 1-15. While a number of warnings are issued by default, it is possible to enable warnings for other conditions. Thresholds can also be set that will trigger alerts.

The Replication Monitor can also monitor the performance of transactional and merge replication by allowing you to set warnings and thresholds, view detailed synchronization statistics of merge replication, and view transactions and delivery times for transactional replication. It is also possible to check replication agent profiles, such as the Distributor, Snapshot, and Merge Agents in the Replication Monitor by selecting Action ➤ Agent Profiles as shown in Figure 1-16.

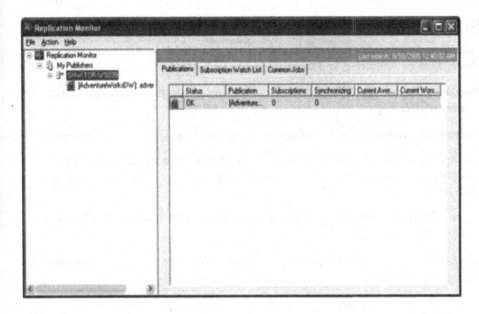

Figure 1-15. *Replication Monitor*

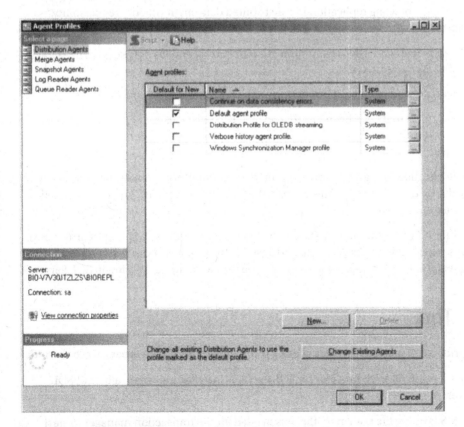

Figure 1-16. *Different agent profiles in the Replication Monitor*

Summary

This chapter introduced replication and the different tools available in SQL Server for configuring, administering, monitoring, and troubleshooting replication.

- Databases that are logically interrelated and connected over the network are called distributed databases.

- There are two methods of distributing data: distributed transactions and replication.

- Distributed transactions are coordinated by the MS DTC. The transaction manager coordinates the distribution of the transaction with the resource managers and the MS DTC log.

- The two-phase commit protocol is employed by the MS DTC to successfully execute distributed transactions.

- Replication is the process by which copies of distributed data can be sent to remote sites.

- There are two kinds of replication: synchronous and asynchronous replication.

- SQL Server supports asynchronous replication.

- The benefits of using replication in a distributed data environment are scalability, performance, and autonomy of the sites.

- SQL Server uses OLE DB to communicate with heterogeneous data sources like Oracle by using the linked server.

- Replication has a higher autonomy and latency than distributed transactions.

- The new tools that have been introduced in SQL Server 2005 are SQL Server Management Studio, the Database Engine Tuning Advisor, and the SQL Server Configuration Manager.

- The Replication Monitor allows the monitoring of publications and subscriptions. It can also be used to monitor the performance of snapshot, merge, and transactional replication.

In Chapter 2, I will introduce the Publisher-Subscriber model. We will look at articles, publications, subscriptions, distribution, and agents, which will help you better understand the fundamentals of replication. I will also show you how to set up replication in SQL Server.

Quick Tips

- Distributed processing involves sharing resources among the members of the network.

- The Microsoft OLE DB provider for SQL Server is installed automatically with SQL Server.

- The MS DTC log file is a binary file. It is needed for the transaction manager to start.

CHAPTER 2

■■■

Replication Basics

In the previous chapter, I introduced replication as a method of distributing data. I described what asynchronous replication is and outlined the replication types available in SQL Server. We are now ready to look at the details of replication. In this chapter, I will explain the Publisher-Subscriber model that is used to represent the several components involved in replication: the Distributor, Publisher, Subscriber, publications, articles, subscriptions, and agents. In addition, you will also learn how different agents are used in transferring the data.

On completing this chapter, you will be able to do the following:

- Describe the Publisher-Subscriber model

- Identify replication components

- Apply agent types to different kinds of replication

- Compare physical replication models

Publisher-Subscriber Model

The Publisher-Subscriber model is based on a metaphor from the publishing industry. This metaphor is a logical representation of the architecture the software industry has followed in database replication.

Imagine you want to buy a couple of books on replication and SQL Server from a publisher that publishes several books and magazines on database topics. The *publisher* packages the books you order and sends them to the distributor. The *distributor* distributes these books and magazines, which are then picked up by the different *agents* whose job is to sell them to you—the *subscriber*. When you buy a book from a publisher, you are buying a *publication*. Each of the chapters inside the book is an *article* of the publication. This is shown in Figure 2-1.

Replication ensures the consistency and integrity of the databases at different server locations. Data is synchronized initially. For example, the Publisher server propagates the changes or updates to the subscribing servers, albeit with a certain time lag. Any conflicts that arise are resolved either programmatically or by the mechanisms provided by SQL Server. The corollary to this is that changes made by the Subscriber servers can be sent back to the Publisher server or republished to other subscribing servers.

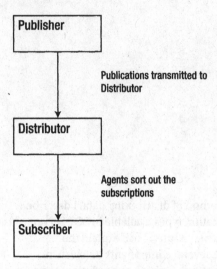

Figure 2-1. *The publisher-subscriber metaphor used in replication*

■ **Note** The paradigm of bidirectional replication has also been used with transactional replication, in which data is replicated between tables on two servers. Each server has a copy of the table, and changes made in one table get copied to the other server. Each server acts as both a Publisher and a Subscriber server to the other server.

Components of Replication

These are the different components of replication:

- Distributor

- Publisher

- Subscriber

- Publication

- Article

- Subscriptions

- Agents

Distributor

The Distributor server is the common link that enables all the components involved in replication to interact with each other. It contains the distribution database, and it is responsible for the smooth passage of data between the Publisher servers and the Subscriber servers.

If the Distributor server is located on the same machine as the Publisher server, it is known as the *local* Distributor server, but if it is on a separate machine from the Publisher server, it is called the *remote* Distributor server. In large-scale replication, it is better to house the Distributor server on a remote server. This will not only improve performance but will also reduce I/O processing and reduce the impact of replication on the Publisher server.

Note The optimization of the three types of replication is discussed in Chapters 17 through 19.

The role of the Distributor server varies depending on the type of replication:

- In snapshot and transactional replication, the distribution database in the Distributor server stores the replicated transactions temporarily and also stores the metadata and the job history. The replication agents are also stored in the Distributor server, except in cases where the agents are configured remotely or pull subscriptions are used. (A pull subscription is one in which the Subscriber server asks for periodic updates of all changes made at the publishing server.)

- In merge replication, unlike in snapshot and transactional replication, the distribution database in the Distributor server stores the metadata and the history of the synchronization. It also contains the Snapshot Agent and the Merge Agent for push subscriptions. (A push subscription is a subscription in which the Publisher server propagates the changes to the subscribing servers without any specific request from the subscribing server.)

The distribution database is a system database that is created when the Distributor server is configured. You should not drop the distribution database unless you want to disable it. It not only stores information about replication but also the metadata, job history, and transactions.

SYSTEM DATABASES

The four system databases—master, model, msdb and tempdb—are created when SQL Server is installed. If you open Windows Explorer, you will find the data files (.mdf files) listed in the following directory, assuming that you installed SQL Server in the same directory as I did: C:\Program Files\Microsoft SQL Server\MSSQL.1\MSSQL\Data\. However, in the same directory you will notice that there is another data file called Mssqlsystemresource.mdf. It does not show up in the list of system databases in the SQL Server Management Studio (SSMS). In fact, this is the data file for the Resource database that has been added in this version. If you try to add this, then you will get the following error message:

You cannot perform this operation for the resource database. (Microsoft SQL Server, Error: 4616)

The Resource database is a read-only system database. According to the Books Online (BOL), if you want to make the upgrade procedure to newer versions of SQL Server easier and faster, you only need to copy this file to the local server, since it contains all the system objects.

Publisher

While the Distributor server manages the data flow, the Publisher server ensures that data is available for replication to other servers. The Publisher is the server that contains the data to be replicated. It can also identify and maintain changes in data. Depending on the type of replication, changes in data are identified and periodically time-stamped. You can see the list of Publisher servers on the machine in the Replication Monitor.

Subscriber

The Subscriber server stores replicas and receives updates from the Publisher server. Periodic updates made on the Subscriber server can then be sent back to the Publisher server. It may also be necessary for the Subscriber server to act as a Publisher server and republish the data to other subscribing servers.

Publication

The Publisher server contains a collection of articles in the publication database. This database tells the Publisher server which data needs to be sent to other servers or to the subscribing servers. In other words, the publication database acts as the data source for replication.

Any database that is used as a source of replication therefore needs to be enabled as a Publisher server. In SQL Server you can achieve this by using the Create Publication Wizard, the Configure Publishing and Distribution Wizard, or the sp_replicationdboption system stored procedure.

The database that is published can contain one or more publications. A publication is a unit that contains one or more articles that are sent to the subscribing servers.

■**Caution** You cannot publish msdb, tempdb, model databases, or the system table in the master database.

Article

An article is any grouping of data to be replicated; it is a component of a publication. It may contain a set of tables or a subset of tables. Articles can also contain a set of columns (vertical filtering), a set of rows (horizontal filtering), stored procedures, views, indexed views, or user-defined functions (UDFs).

■**Note** The Subscriber servers subscribe to publications only. They do not subscribe to individual articles.

Subscriptions

Subscriber servers must define their subscriptions for a particular set of publications in order to receive the snapshot from the Publisher server. For all three types of replication, snapshot files are made of the schema and initial data files of the publication and are stored in the snapshot folder. Subsequent changes to the data or the schema are transferred from the Publisher server to the Subscriber server. This process is known as synchronization.

The subscriptions map the different articles to the corresponding tables in the Subscriber server. They also specify when the Subscriber servers should receive the publications from the publishing servers.

■**Caution** Subscriptions need to be synchronized within a specific period of time, which depends on the replication and subscription types used. If they are not synchronized in time, the Distribution clean up job can deactivate them.

There are two methods by which data changes made on the publication can be sent to subscriptions in SQL Server: *anonymous subscriptions* and *named subscriptions*. In an anonymous subscription, no information about the subscribing server or the subscription is stored on the Publisher server. It is the responsibility of the subscribing servers to keep track of the history of the data and the subscriptions. These details are then passed on to the Distribution Agent at the time of the next synchronization. Named subscriptions are those in which the Subscriber servers are explicitly enabled in the Publisher server. There are two kinds of named subscriptions: push subscriptions and pull subscriptions. (In fact, anonymous subscription is a kind of pull subscription.) Which subscription type you use depends on where you want the administration of the subscription and the agent processing to take place.

Push subscriptions are created at the Publisher server, as shown in Figure 2-2. The Publisher server retains control of the subscriptions and can propagate the changes either on demand, or continuously, or at scheduled intervals. However, synchronization in push subscriptions is typically transmitted continuously, whenever changes occur in the publication, without waiting for the Subscriber server to make a request. In this case, there is no need to administer individual subscribing servers—the Distribution or the Merge Agent that resides on the Distributor server implements the scheduling. The Subscriber server must be explicitly enabled in the Publisher server for this type of replication to function.

For pull subscriptions, the Subscriber servers must be enabled explicitly in the Publisher server, just as for push subscriptions. In pull subscriptions, however, the subscriptions are created at the Subscriber server. The Subscriber server requests changes in the publication from the Publisher server, and the data is synchronized either on demand or at a scheduled time.

1. Subscribers created on the Publisher server
2. Subscriptions created on the Publisher server
3. Publisher enables the Subscriber and the subscriptions
4. Publisher transmits changes in publications to Distributor server
5. Distribution Agent in the Distributor server gets the replicated data
6. Distribution Agent stores the job history and log in distribution database
7. Distribution Agent then moves the transactions and the snapshot to the appropriate Subscribers

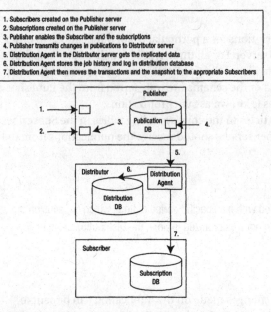

Figure 2-2. *Publishing with a push subscription*

The implementation of a pull subscription is done by the Distribution or the Merge Agent, but the agent synchronization is done on the Subscriber server. The changes are administered by the Subscriber server. This is shown in Figure 2-3.

1. Subscribers created on the Subscriber server
2. Subscriptions created on the Subscriber server
3. Publisher enables the Subscribers and the subscriptions
4. Publisher gets information on Subscribers and subscriptions
5. Subscriber requests data
6. Distributor sends the request to the Publisher
7. Publisher looks up the information
8. Publisher gets a response indicating whether the information is available or not
9. If the information is available, the Publisher sends the publications to the Distributor
10. Publisher sends error messages and data history to the Distributor, and the distribution
    database stores the transactions and the log updates
11. Distributor sends the transactions to the Subscriber

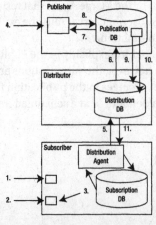

Figure 2-3. *Publishing with a pull subscription*

Agents

So where do the agents fit in, and what purpose do they serve? They are the workhorses in the group. The agents collate all the changes and perform the necessary jobs in distributing the data.

These agents are the executables, which, by default, run as jobs under the SQL Server Agent folder in the SQL Server Management Studio (SSMS). Bear in mind, though, that the SQL Server Agent needs to be running in order for the jobs to do their work! The executables are located under Program Files\Microsoft SQL Server\90\COM, and they can be run from the command prompt.

There are five different types of agents:

- Snapshot Agent

- Log Reader Agent

- Queue Reader Agent

- Distribution Agent

- Merge Agent

Note These agents are grouped differently in the Replication Monitor. Snapshot, Log Reader, and Queue Reader Agents are associated with subscriptions in the Replication Monitor. Distribution and Merge Agents are associated with publication in the Replication Monitor.

There are also other miscellaneous jobs that perform maintenance and servicing for replication. The Distribution clean up job is one such example.

Snapshot Agent

The name of the Snapshot Agent executable is snapshot.exe. This agent usually resides in the Distributor server.

The Snapshot Agent is used in all replications, particularly at the time of initial synchronization. It makes a copy of the schema and the data of the tables that are to be published, stores them in the snapshot file, and records information about synchronization in the distribution database.

Log Reader Agent

The name of the Log Reader Agent executable is logread.exe. This agent is used in transactional replication.

The Log Reader Agent monitors the transaction logs of all databases that are involved in transactional replication. The agent copies any changes in the data that are marked for replication in the transaction log of the publication database and sends them to the Distributor server where they are stored in the distribution database. The transactions are held there until they are ready to be sent to the Subscriber servers.

▪Note Transactional replication is discussed in Chapters 8 through 10.

Distribution Agent

The name of the Distribution Agent executable is `distrib.exe`. Both snapshot and transactional replication use this agent.

The Distribution Agent is responsible for moving the snapshot and the transactions held in the distribution database to the subscribing servers. In the case of push subscriptions, the Distribution Agent resides on the Distributor server, as shown in Figure 2-2. In the case of pull subscriptions, it resides on the Subscriber server, as shown in Figure 2-3.

Merge Agent

The name of the Merge Agent executable is `replmerg.exe`. This agent is used with merge replication.

The Merge Agent applies the initial snapshot to the Subscriber servers. Incremental changes subsequent to the initial synchronization are monitored and merged to the Subscriber servers by the Merge Agent. The agent also resolves the update conflicts.

Each of the databases taking part in the process has one Merge Agent. Like the Distribution Agent, the Merge Agent runs on the Distributor server in push subscriptions, and on the Subscriber server in the case of pull subscriptions.

▪Note Merge replication is discussed in Chapters 11 through 14.

Queue Reader Agent

The name of the Queue Reader Agent executable is `qrdsvc.exe`. In transactional replication, there is an option to either immediately update the messages or store them in a queue, using either the SQL Server queue or the Microsoft Messaging queue. If the updated messages need to be sent immediately, there needs to be a constant connection between the Publisher and the Subscriber servers. However, if you are going to store the messages in the queue, you do not need a constant connection; you can send the messages whenever the connection is available. In such cases, the Queue Reader Agent takes the messages from the queue and applies them to the publishing server.

The Queue Reader Agent is multithreaded and runs on the Distributor server. There is only one instance of this agent for a given distribution database, and it services all the publications and Publisher servers.

▪Note Snapshot replication is discussed in Chapters 4 through 7.

Physical Replication Models

Now that we have looked at the logical architecture and the different components involved in replication, it's time to see the physical implementations of the logical model. There are four physical models for replication:

- Publisher/Distributor–Subscriber model

- Central Publisher–Multiple Subscribers model

- Central Subscriber–Multiple Publishers model

- Multiple Publishers–Multiple Subscribers model

Publisher/Distributor–Subscriber Model

In the Publisher/Distributor–Subscriber model, you place the Distributor server along with the Publisher server in one physical server, and the Subscriber server in another physical server, as shown in Figure 2-4. This is the simplest of all the models. Data is replicated from the Publisher server to the Subscriber server.

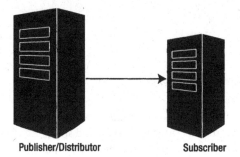

Publisher/Distributor   Subscriber

Figure 2-4. *Simple Publisher/Distributor–Subscriber model*

Central Publisher–Multiple Subscribers Model

The Central Publisher–Multiple Subscribers model is actually an extension of the previous model. In this one, you have one Publisher server publishing data that is sent to several Subscriber servers. For example, the publisher publishes a book, and you and others want to read several chapters. In this case, each of you buys the book, and each of you is a subscriber. Each chapter constitutes an article, but you have to buy the whole book—the publication—to read either all or some of the chapters.

The Publisher server is a central Publisher that is distributing data to multiple Subscriber servers, as shown in Figure 2-5. The Distributor server can reside on the same physical server as the Publisher server, or on a different one.

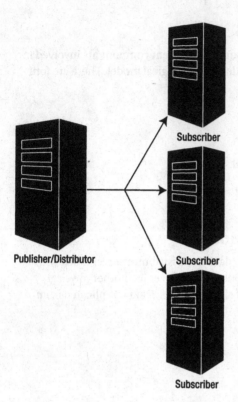

Publisher/Distributor   Subscriber

Subscriber

Subscriber

Figure 2-5. *Central Publisher/Distributor–Multiple Subscribers model*

Typically this model is used when you want the Subscribers to have read-only permission. The Distributor server processes the changes in data from the Publisher server, and sends them to the Subscriber servers. As such, the administrator needs to ensure that SELECT permissions have been granted to the Subscriber servers.

When you put the Distributor server on another physical server, you are essentially offloading the work of replication. This may be done to take advantage of a high-speed network connection or to optimize the performance of replication. Either way, you want to take advantage of the powerful network at your disposal. You might implement this model if, for example, the regional sales people working in the field do not have access to retrieve data from the central publishing server.

The Publisher server partitions the data and only sends out data that is relevant to the subscribing servers. The distributing server receives all the data from the publishing server and transmits the subscriptions to the subscribing servers at the regional level. Instead of logging on to the main publishing server, the sales people log on to the local Subscriber server and retrieve the data set. This is shown in Figure 2-6.

■**Note** You need to have separate installations of SQL Server when you use this model—one for the Distributor server and one for the Publisher server.

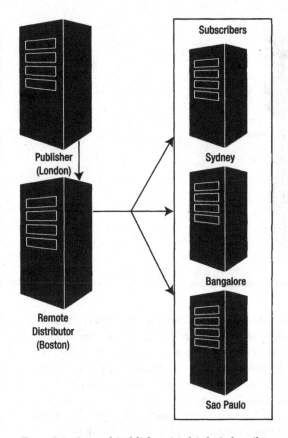

Figure 2-6. *Central Publisher–Multiple Subscribers model with Remote Distributor*

■**Caution** The replication process might be disrupted if there is only one remote Distributor server in the network and it fails.

Central Subscriber–Multiple Publishers Model

The Central Subscriber–Multiple Publishers model is commonly used in situations where data from multiple sites needs to be consolidated at a central location while providing access to the local site with local data. Data warehousing is a typical example. A diagram of this model is shown in Figure 2-7.

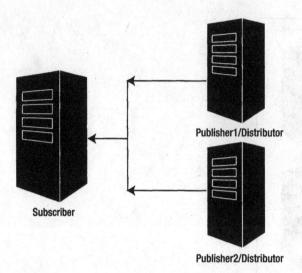

Figure 2-7. *Central Subscriber-Multiple Publishers model*

The multiple Publisher servers replicate their data to the same subscription table, and this poses a unique problem. For example, suppose regional product orders are tracked by consolidating them in an inventory database at a central location. The Publisher servers publish a table called Products, which contains the following columns: productid, product_name, and quantity. Because data from the Products table on each Publisher server is being published to the same subscription table, data from one Publisher server runs the risk of being overwritten by another. One way to resolve this issue is to create a unique local identifier for each Publisher server. This can be done by adding a column called region_id in the Products table and assigning each Publisher server a unique number for region_id. This means the two columns, productid and region_id, are a composite key.

Multiple Publishers–Multiple Subscribers Model

The Multiple Publishers–Multiple Subscribers model allows the Publisher in one server to also act as a Subscriber. When using such a model, you need to consider consistency in data and any potential update conflicts.

For example, suppose three or more shops belong to the same manufacturer of refrigerator parts. Each of the shops keeps a record in the Parts table of ice-maker kits, water inlet valves, o-rings, and so on. If a shop owner knows the inventory of the parts in the other stores, they will be able to get inventory from the other shops if they run out of the parts in any store.

This is made possible by implementing the Multiple Publishers–Multiple Subscribers model using transactional or merge replication. Each shop is a Publisher server of the Parts table to the other two subscribing servers, and it is also a Subscriber server to the same table. Any time the data in the table is updated, it can be replicated by transactional replication. And if you want to ensure that other shops know each other's inventory, you can use transactional replication with updateable subscriptions. This is shown diagrammatically in Figure 2-8.

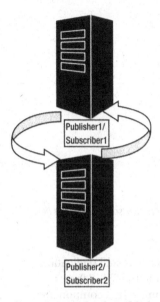

Figure 2-8. *Multiple Publishers–Multiple Subscribers model*

Installing and Configuring Replication

Now that you have an understanding of the logical representation and the physical implementation of replication, it is time to look at the procedure for installing and configuring the different replication components.

Installing SQL Server Replication

When you install SQL Server, you have the option to select the different components of SQL Server as shown in Figure 2-9. By default, when you choose to install the SQL Server Database Services, it also installs the objects for replication.

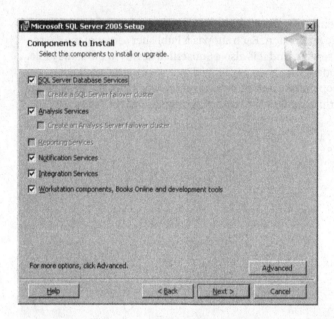

Figure 2-9. *Replication is one of the default components installed when you select SQL Server Database Services*

As you can see in Figure 2-10, you only need 31 MB of disk space to install replication. When you install replication, you will see under the Object Explorer in the SSMS that the Replication and SQL Server Agent objects are installed. However, some of the components that are involved in replication, like the distribution database, are not installed. You have to manually configure the Distributor server in the SSMS before the distribution database is installed. Next, using the SSMS, you need to configure the Publisher server and then set up the publications and subscriptions before you can start replicating data.

I earlier mentioned that agents are actually jobs by default. If you open the SSMS, you will see that even though the SQL Server Agent is running, there are no agents running under the Jobs folder. This is because the Distributor server has yet to be configured; once it is, you will see that the agents are also installed.

You can run both the SQL Server database engine and the SQL Server Agent as services, which are Windows operating system applications that run in the background. You can start these services manually or automatically, or you can disable them.

When you install SQL Server 2005, the service to start the SQL Server Agent is disabled by default, but the service for the SQL Server engine is set to start automatically. If you open the SQL Server Configuration Manager, expand SQL Server Services, and select SQL Server engine, you will see under the Start Mode column that the engine has been set to Automatic. (This is shown later in Figure 2-13.) The Start Mode column can be set to manual, automatic, or disabled.

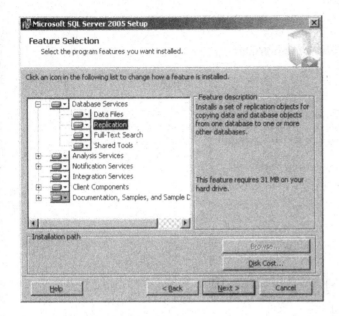

Figure 2-10. *Installation of Replication requires 31 MB of disk space*

■**Note** In order to enable the SQL Server Agent service to run automatically, open the SQL Server Configuration Manager, right-click on the SQL Server Agent, select Properties, select the Service tab, and set the Start Mode to Automatic. Once you have enabled the Start Mode, go back to the Configuration Manager, right-click on the SQL Server Agent services and select Start.

Now we need to configure the Distributor server, the distribution database, and the Publisher server. There are two ways to accomplish this: use the graphical user interface (GUI) that comes with the SSMS or write T-SQL code. I will show you both methods.

Configuring with the GUI

To configure the Distributor server with the GUI, select the Replication object in the SSMS. Right-click on Replication and select Configure Distribution. This will start the Configure Distribution Wizard. This wizard will not only guide you in setting up the Distributor server but will also help you set up the Publisher server, as shown in Figure 2-11.

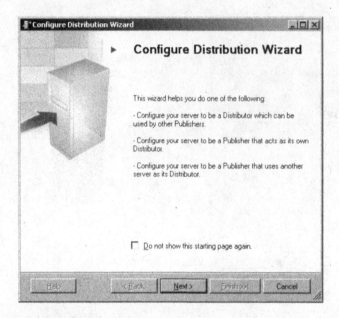

Figure 2-11. *Starting the Configure Distribution Wizard*

Click Next in the initial page of the Configure Distribution Wizard, and it will ask you to select the server that will be used as a Distributor. By default, it will select the local server, as you can see in Figure 2-12.

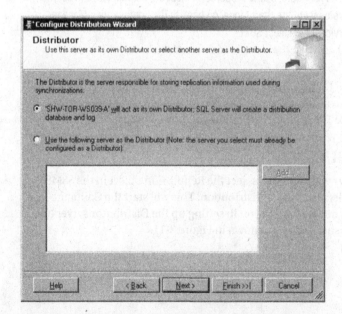

Figure 2-12. *Setting up Distributor servers in the local server*

At this stage you can also select any other remote servers that you want to use as Distributor servers. However, you should note that you need to install SQL Server on each remote machine that you want to use as a Distributor server. In Figure 2-12, the focus is primarily set on the local server to act as the Distributor.

Note You can go back and forth in this wizard, so if you want to change something during the process, you can do so easily.

Click Next and the wizard will ask you whether you want to configure the SQL Server Agent to start automatically. This is shown in Figure 2-13. Set the SQL Server Agent service to start automatically, and ensure that you have the right permissions, as mentioned in the figure.

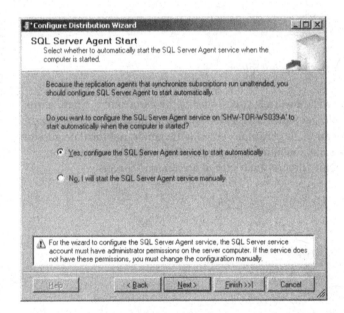

Figure 2-13. *Setting the SQL Server Agent to start automatically as a service*

Click the Next button, and the wizard will ask you where you want to place the snapshot folder, as shown in Figure 2-14. This snapshot folder will contain the snapshot of the publications to be accessed by the Distribution and Merge Agents. By default, the folder is placed in the following path: C:\Program Files\Microsoft SQL Server\MSSQL.1\MSSQL\ReplData. You must ensure that you have permissions to the folder where you store the snapshot files.

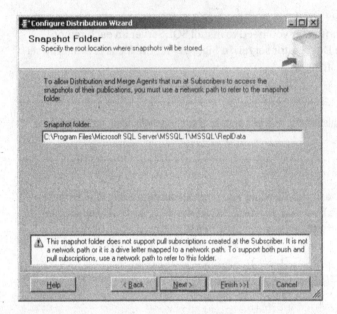

Figure 2-14. *Specifying a location for the Snapshot folder*

Click the Next button, and the wizard will ask you to specify the name and the path of the distribution database and the log files, as shown in Figure 2-15. Sometimes, it might be necessary to set the files in a different location. For example, you might want to put the data and the log files on a separate drive on the same machine for performance reasons. In production environments, the data and the log files are normally stored on separate servers.

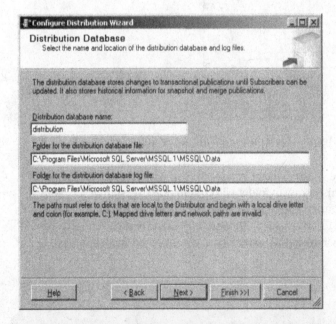

Figure 2-15. *Specifying the location of the data and the log files for the distribution database*

Note Performance and optimization are discussed in Chapters 17 through 19.

Because I selected the local server as the Distributor, the wizard does not allow me to select a network drive. For the purpose of this configuration, we will keep the location of the data and log files as shown in Figure 2-15.

The next wizard page enables you to set the Publisher, as shown in Figure 2-16. I am using the current server to act as the Publisher and have enabled it to use the distribution database that I configured in Figure 2-15. The wizard also allows you to add any other registered instances of SQL Server or an Oracle server as a Publisher. By clicking on the ellipsis button beside the distribution database, you can set the security parameters for the Publisher server and also change the location of the snapshot folder.

Figure 2-16. *Enabling the Publisher server with the distribution database*

By default, SQL Server uses Impersonate the agent process account (essentially the Windows account) as the Agent Connection Mode. Agents use this connection to connect to the Publisher server. Alternatively, it is possible to use SQL Server Authentication to connect to the Publishers. This is shown in Figure 2-17. You can also see that I have kept the default location for the snapshot folder.

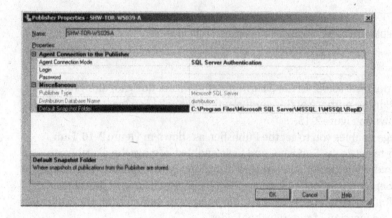

Figure 2-17. *Setting the Agent Connection Mode property for the Publisher server*

On clicking the Next button, the wizard will ask you whether you want to configure distribution and whether you want to generate a script file for all these configuration steps. You can see this in Figure 2-18.

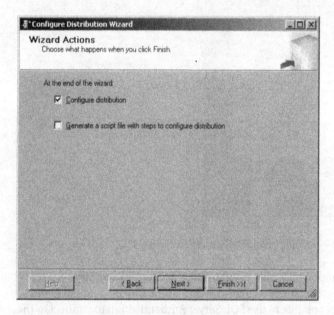

Figure 2-18. *Setting the final wizard options*

If you do not choose to generate a script file (a SQL file), the wizard will take you to the Complete the Wizard page (shown in Figure 2-20). But if you do, the wizard will take you to the page shown in Figure 2-19, where you can specify a location for the script file. You can choose to append the script to an existing file or to overwrite it.

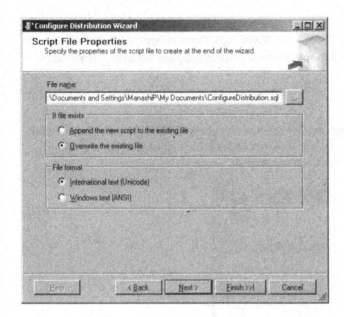

Figure 2-19. *Setting a location for the script file*

Whether you generate a script or not, you will end up at the Complete the Wizard page, shown in Figure 2-20. The wizard summarizes the actions that it will take to configure the Distributor server, the location of the snapshot folder, the distribution database, and the options set for configuring the distribution.

Figure 2-20. *The configuration options for the Distributor server and the distribution database*

■**Note** If you do not click Finish in the Complete the Wizard page (shown in Figure 2-20), the next time you try to configure the Distributor server, it will remember your previous setup and will immediately go to the Complete the Wizard page.

Finally, the wizard goes through the configuration process and tells you whether or not it has succeeded, as shown in Figure 2-21. It also lists each of the actions taken by the wizard. The figure shows that the process has been successful.

Figure 2-21. *Configuring the Distributor, enabling the Publisher, and generating a script file*

Configuring Database Properties

Once you have configured the Distributor and Publisher servers, whether with the GUI or T-SQL, you can go back to the SSMS, and you will find the distribution database listed under the system databases, as shown in Figure 2-22.

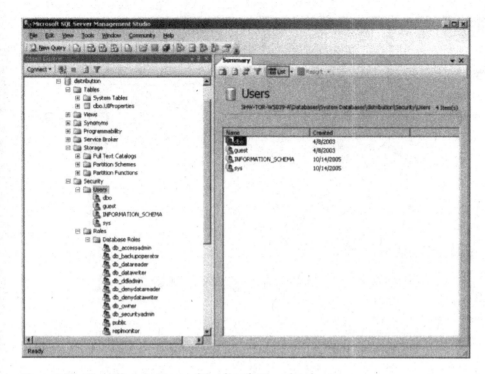

Figure 2-22. *The different objects of the distribution database*

Distribution Database Properties

Like the other system databases, the Users and Roles of the distribution database are located in the Security folder, as shown in Figure 2-22. Right-click on the distribution database and select Properties to open the window shown in Figure 2-23.

Here you can see the type of collation sequence used and the recovery model, which in this case is Simple. This is the default recovery model used in the distribution database. If you check the properties of the other system databases, except the model database, you will also find that the recovery model is set to Simple by default. The recovery model for the model database is set to Full.

Note Backup and recovery of the databases used in a replicated environment are discussed in Chapters 15 and 16.

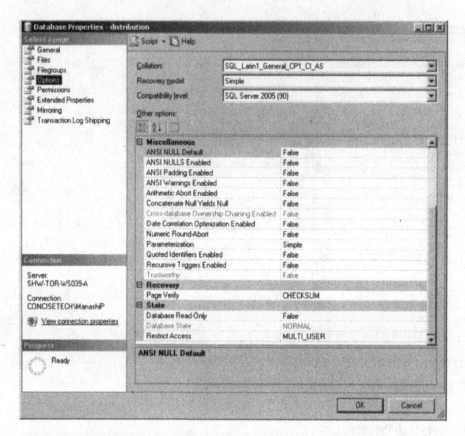

Figure 2-23. *The different properties of the distribution database*

At the bottom of Figure 2-23, you can see that the database is not set to read-only. If the Database Read-Only option were set to True, users could not modify the distribution database—the cylinder icon for the distribution database would be disabled and marked Read-Only in the SSMS. In this case, I set Database Read-Only to False and did not restrict any users because I am the only person accessing the machine. Depending on your business environment, you may need to prevent users from modifying the distribution database.

If you select the Files page in the Database Properties window, as shown in Figure 2-24, you will see the initial size of the data and log files for the distribution database. When we configured the database, we did not have an option to set the initial size of the data and log files, so this is the time for you to reset it if you need to, or to change the Autogrowth option.

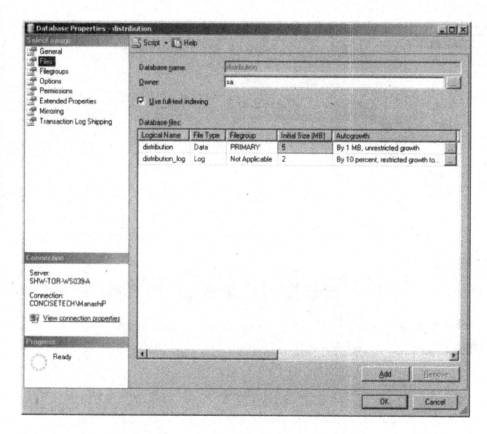

Figure 2-24. *File size specifications for the distribution database's data and log files*

Distributor Server Properties

Since you have already configured the Distributor and Publisher servers, you can now check the properties of both these servers by right-clicking on the Replication object in the Object Explorer and then selecting Distributor properties, and it will open the page shown in Figure 2-25.

This page shows the name of the Distributor server and the user connection. You can also see that the distribution database is tied to this Distributor server. The retention period of transactions, and the history in the distribution databases have also been set.

Remember that subscriptions need to be synchronized or they will be deactivated. So if there are changes in the distribution database, and the transactions have not been delivered to the subscribing server within the retention period, which by default is 72 hours, the subscription will be marked as deactivated by the Distribution clean up job. You will then have to reinitialize the subscription.

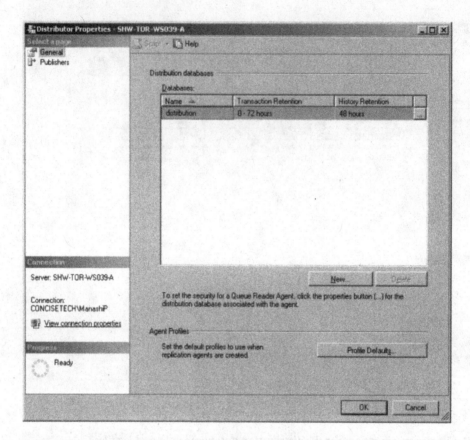

Figure 2-25. *Displaying the Distributor server properties*

The history retention parameter keeps a record of the agent history, and this parameter has been set to 48 hours. You can change the retention time of the transactions and the agent history by clicking on the ellipsis button beside the history retention time.

Distribution Agent Profiles

To see the profile of the agents, click on the Profile Defaults button at the bottom of the Distributor Properties page (shown in Figure 2-25), and you will see the page shown in Figure 2-26. You can select one profile for each of the agents listed by clicking a check box in the Default for New column. Whenever an agent is executed, it uses the parameters that have been set in the agent profile.

If you click on the ellipsis button beside the Type column for the Distribution Agent profile, it will display the parameters for the profile, as shown in Figure 2-27. You can similarly view the different profiles for each of the agents.

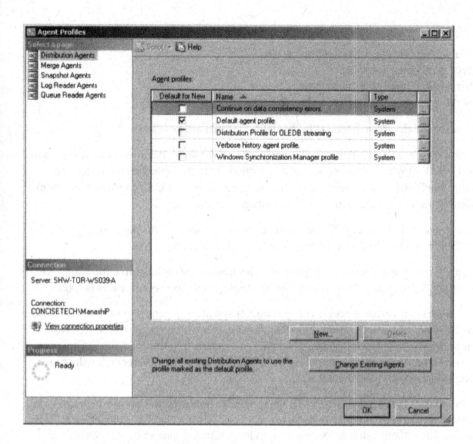

Figure 2-26. *Displaying all the agent profiles for the Distribution Agent*

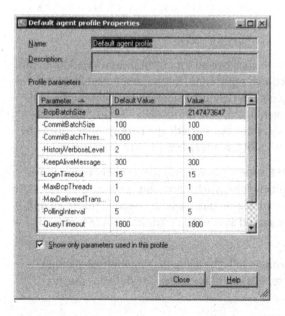

Figure 2-27. *Viewing the parameter settings for the default Distribution Agent profile*

The syntax to start the Distribution Agent is as follows:

```
distrib -Publisher server_name[\instance_name]
-PublisherDB publisher_database
-Subscriber server_name[\instance_name]
-SubscriberDB subscriber_database [-parameters]
```

The parameters that have been set in the default profile are as follows:

Distrib [-BcpBatchSize]: This specifies how many rows are to be copied when you want to send a bulk copy to the server as one transaction. This also specifies the number of rows that the Distribution Agent logs before it is processed as a bulk copy program (bcp). The default value is 0, which means that messages are not logged.

Distrib [-CommitBatchSize]: This specifies how many transactions need to be sent to the Subscriber server before they are committed. The default value is 100.

Distrib [-CommitBatchThreshold]: This specifies how many replication commands are issued to the Subscriber server before they are committed. The default value is 1000.

Distrib [-HistoryVerboseLevel]: This parameter specifies the amount of history logged during the distribution operation. The default value is 2, which means that the previous information will be removed. Setting the value to 1 means that the previous information will be updated. A setting of 3 (the maximum value) means that new records will always be inserted except for idle messages.

Distrib [-KeepAliveMessageInterval]: This specifies how long the agent will wait before the history thread checks whether there are any connections waiting for a response from the server. The default value is 300 seconds. In long-running batch processes, you may have to reduce the value for performance reasons.

Distrib [-LoginTimeout]: This parameter specifies the timeout in seconds for login sessions. The default time is 15 seconds. If you do not log in within the specified time, the session will be logged out.

Distrib [-MaxBcpThreads]: This parameter specifies how many bulk copy operations can be run in parallel. In the case of transactional replication, this parameter can be passed to both the Snapshot and Distribution Agents. The default value is 1. Bear in mind that this parameter can affect the Distribution Agent in copying the snapshot to the Subscriber server. Increasing this parameter to a high value can degrade the performance, since the processors will have to manage the number of threads specified by this parameter.

Distrib [-MaxDeliveredTransactions]: This sets the maximum number of transactions that are sent to the subscribing server during one synchronization. A value of 0 means an infinite number of transactions can be sent. We should consider resetting this to an optimum value, such as 1000, to shorten the period after which transactions are sent, and hence improve performance.

Distrib [-PollingInterval]: This parameter tells the agent at what interval it should query the distributed database for any replicated transactions. The default value is 5 seconds.

`Distrib [-QueryTimeout]`: This parameter ensures that queries are executed within the stipulated time. The default is 1800 seconds.

`Distrib [-TransactionsPerHistory]`: This parameter specifies how many transactions are to be committed before the history is logged. The default value is 100.

We will discuss the other agents in Chapter 3. The profile parameters can be set differently depending on the situation or the type of replication used, or for troubleshooting purposes. You can also create your own agent profile and run it as a job.

Publisher Server Properties

In the Distributor Properties window (see Figure 2-25), select Publishers in the left pane. As you can see in Figure 2-28, both the Publisher and the Distributor reside on the same server. The name of the Distributor server is shown beside the Distributor Properties, while the name of the Publisher server is given under the Publisher column. It also shows you that the distribution database is enabled with this Publisher server.

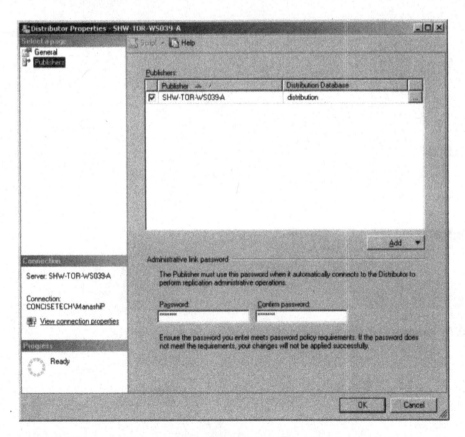

Figure 2-28. *The Publisher server is enabled with the Distributor server*

At the bottom right of the window shown in Figure 2-28, you can reset the password if you want to. If you click on the ellipsis button beside the distribution database, you can see the agent connection mode of the Publisher server, which was set during the configuration (see Figure 2-17).

Now go back to the Object Explorer, right-click on the Replication object, and select Publisher Properties. If you select General in the left pane, it will tell you explicitly that this server acts as both the Distributor and the Publisher. If you now select Publication Database in the left pane, you will find that there are no databases configured for replication, as shown in Figure 2-29.

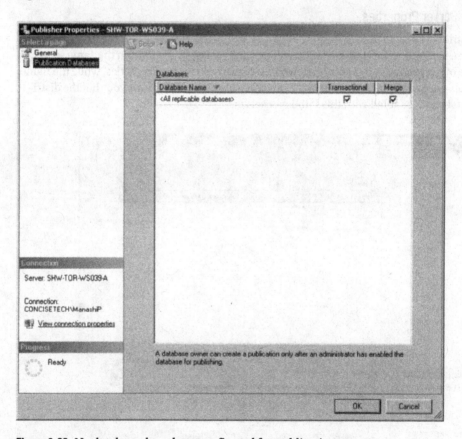

Figure 2-29. *No databases have been configured for publication yet*

Replication Agents

By right-clicking on the Replication object in the Object Explorer again, you can launch the Replication Monitor, shown in Figure 2-30.

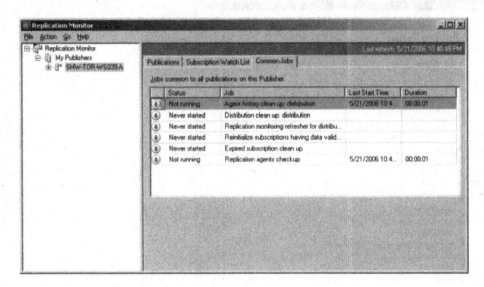

Figure 2-30. *The miscellaneous jobs listed in the Common Jobs tab in the Replication Monitor*

The Replication Monitor in SQL Server 2000 was a part of the Enterprise Manager, but in SQL Server 2005 it is a stand-alone program. You can use it to monitor the status of the subscriptions, and you can also see a list of jobs in the Common Jobs tab. The Publications tab displays all the publications for a specified Publisher server. The Subscription Watch List tab shows all the subscriptions for all the publications of a specified Publisher server. Since we have not yet configured the publications and the subscriptions, they will not be displayed in the Publications and the Subscription Watch List tabs.

Now click on the SQL Server Agent object in the SSMS's Object Explorer, and you will see the Jobs object. Remember that before we configured the Distributor server, the Jobs object folder was empty. If you click on the Jobs object now, you will see the list of miscellaneous jobs, as shown in Figure 2-31. This is similar to what we saw in the Replication Monitor (Figure 2-30). The miscellaneous jobs are essentially cleanup agents that are used for the routine maintenance of replication. The miscellaneous jobs and their actions are described in Table 2-1.

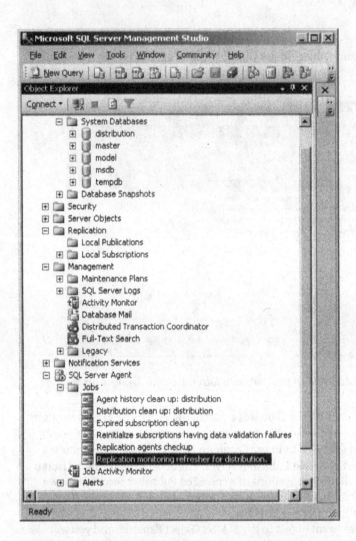

Figure 2-31. *The miscellaneous jobs listed in the Jobs object*

Table 2-1. *The Miscellaneous Cleanup Jobs and Their Actions for Replication*

Job	Description of Job
Agent history clean up: distribution	This job removes agent history from the distribution database.
Distribution clean up: distribution	This job removes any replicated transactions. It also deactivates any subscriptions that have not been synchronized within the maximum retention time.
Expired subscription clean up	This job detects and removes any expired subscriptions from the publication database.

Job	Description of Job
Reinitialize subscriptions having data validation failures	This job does looks for any subscriptions that have failed to validate. Once one is detected, the job then marks it for reinitialization so that the next time the Distribution or Merge Agent runs, a new snapshot will be provided to the Subscriber server.
Replication agents checkup	This job checks whether replication agents are logging their history. If they are not and a job step fails, the Replication agents checkup job will write to the event log in Windows.
Replication monitoring refresher for distribution	This job refreshes any cached queries.

In the Jobs object folder, some of the jobs are highlighted in blue and some are grayed out. If you right-click on the Replication agents checkup job, you will see the Job Properties window, as shown in Figure 2-32.

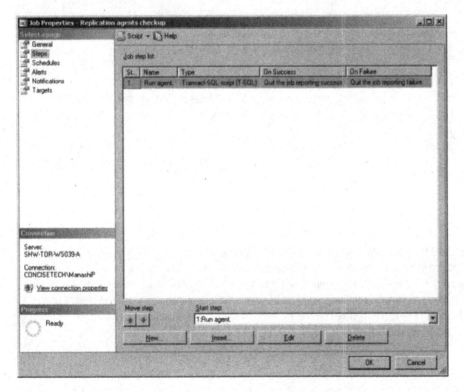

Figure 2-32. *The job properties of the Replication agents checkup job*

On the General page, you will see that this job is enabled, and hence is highlighted in blue. Jobs that are disabled are grayed out, which means that the job will not run in response to a schedule or an alert. You can, however, manually start a job using the sp_start_job stored procedure.

On the Steps page, shown in Figure 2-32, you will see the job steps listed. Click the Edit button, and you will be able to see the T-SQL script for the job.

TO GUI OR NOT TO GUI

Whether you choose to configure using the GUI method or the T-SQL method, the underlying objects will still be generated by SQL Server. If you have used the GUI method to configure the Distributor and Publisher servers and now want to follow the T-SQL method shown next, you need to drop the Publisher server, then the distribution database, and finally the Distributor server. The following script does so, assuming that you have set up the Distributor and Publisher servers as I explained. This script can be executed using the SQL Query Editor using the SSMS.

```
/* Declare variable to store name of Publisher */
set @publisher_name =(select name from msdb..MSdistpublishers where
name=@@servername);
print @publisher_name;

/*Drop the Publisher */
exec sp_dropdistpublisher @publisher=@publisher_name,@no_checks=0;

declare @distributiondb as sysname;
set @distributiondb =(select name from sys.sysdatabases where name
='distribution');
/*Drop the distribution database */
exec sp_dropdistributiondb @distributiondb;

/*Remove the local Distributor */
exec sp_dropdistributor;

go
```

This script first checks for the existence of the Publisher server from the MS_distpublishers table, which is located in the msdb database. It then drops the Publisher server using the sp_distpublisher stored procedure. The @no_checks parameter is set to 0, which ensures that there are no publication or distribution objects on the local server. It then gets the name of the distribution database and drops it using the sp_dropdistributiondb stored procedure. Finally, it drops the Distributor server using the sp_distributor stored procedure.

Configuring with T-SQL

I will now use the T-SQL method to configure the Distributor server, the distribution database, and the Publisher server. Once you have finished the configuration with T-SQL, you should go back to the "Configuring Database Properties" section and follow the steps described there to ensure that the configuration using T-SQL is similar to the GUI method.

Listing 2-1 shows the T-SQL code that configures the Distributor and the distribution database. The code that configures the Publisher on the local server is shown in Listing 2-2.

Note In order to run Listing 2-1, the SQL Server Agent must be running as a service.

Listing 2-1. *Configuring the Distributor Server and the Distribution Database*

```
Use master
go
/* Declare the variables */
declare @distributor as sysname;
declare @distributorserver_msg as varchar(50);

/*Get the default instance of the name of the server
and use that as the Distributor */

set @distributor = (select convert (sysname,serverproperty('servername')));

/*Set the name and then print the name of the Distributor server */

set @distributorserver_msg='The name of the Distributor server:';
print @distributorserver_msg + ' ' +@distributor;
/* Add the Distributor */
exec sp_adddistributor @distributor=@distributor;

/* Install the distribution database on the default directory
 and use Windows Integrated Authentication*/

declare @distributiondb as sysname;
set @distributiondb ='distribution';
exec sp_adddistributiondb @database =@distributiondb,@security_mode=1;
go
```

In Listing 2-1, the variables are declared first. The sysname data type is equivalent to varchar(30). After the variables are declared, we need to know the instance name of the server, so that it can be used as the Distributor. You can retrieve the name of the server with the following code:

```
Select convert (sysname, serverproperty('servername'))
```

The output of this query is as follows:

```
SHW-TOR-WS039\SQLSERVER
```

Once we know the name of the server, we can assign it to the distributor variable and print out the name of the Distributor server. We then use the sp_adddistributor system stored procedure to add the name of the Distributor on the local server.

SERVERPROPERTY OR @@SERVERNAME

You can easily use the @@servername function to find the name of the server instead of using serverproperty. However, any change in the name of the computer on the network is immediately recognized by serverproperty. This is not possible with the @@servername function.

The code then adds the distribution database on the Distributor server. This is done by assigning the name of the distribution database to the database variable, and then using the sp_adddistributiondb system stored procedure to add the database.

I have used the default settings for adding the distribution database. This means that the data and log files will be stored in the following folder: C:\Program Files\Microsoft SQL Server\MSSQL.1\MSSQL\Data\. You can also see that I have set the security_mode parameter to 1. This means that Windows Integrated Authentication will be used when I log in, which is what I want. If you want to use SQL Server Authentication, you should set the parameter to 0.

The output of Listing 2-1 is as follows:

```
The name of the Distributor server: SHW-TOR-WS039\SQLSERVER
```

Having configured the Distributor server, it is now time to configure the Publisher server. This is shown in Listing 2-2.

Listing 2-2. *Configuring the Publisher Server*

```
/* Declare the variables */
declare @distributor as sysname;
declare @publisher as sysname;
declare @publisherserver_msg as varchar (50);

/*Get the default instance of the name of the server and
 use that as the Distributor */

set @distributor = (select convert (sysname,serverproperty('servername')));


/*Set the name and then print the name of the Publisher server.
The Publisher and the Distributor are residing on the same server */
```

```
set @publisher =@distributor;
set @publisherserver_msg='The name of the publisher server:';
print @publisherserver_msg +' '+ @publisher;


/*Now add the Publisher to the same Distributor as
installed locally --- remember that sp_adddistpublisher can
be used for snapshot, transactional and merge replication*/

use distribution

declare @distributiondb as sysname;
set @distributiondb ='distribution';
exec sp_adddistpublisher @publisher, @security_mode=1,
@distribution_db=@distributiondb,
@publisher_type = 'MSSQLSERVER';
go
```

Again, in this code the variables are declared first and then the name of the server is retrieved and assigned to the distributor variable. Since the Publisher and the Distributor are to be on the same server, I assign the value of the distributor to the publisher variable and print out the name of the Publisher server. The code then assigns the name of the distribution database to the distributiondb variable. In order to add the Publisher, we use the sp_adddistpublisher system stored procedure.

You can see that I have added the same Windows Integrated Authentication by setting the security_mode parameter to 1. Also, note the type of the Publisher in the publisher_type parameter. I have assigned MS SQL Server as the Publisher server, and this is the default value. In case of heterogeneous replication, you can use another RDBMS, like Oracle, as the Publisher server.

The output of Listing 2-2 is as follows:

```
The name of the publisher server: SHW-TOR-WS039\SQLSERVER
```

Now that we have configured the Distributor server, the distribution database, and the Publisher server, let's look into the changes made in the system tables. The metadata stores information about replication, such as subscription expiration, publication retention period, and agent profiles, in the subscription, publication, and distribution databases.

■ **Note** Catalog views act as the interface to the catalog metadata used by the SQL Server database engine. Although they look into the metadata, catalog views do not contain any information about replication.

We first want to find out whether the Distributor server is registered in any of the system tables. Listing 2-3 shows how we can find out.

Listing 2-3. *Remote Server Link*

```
use master
go
/* Declare the table variable */

declare @servername_dist table
(
serverid smallint,
servername sysname);

/* We want the names of the server id and the corresponding server names from the
sys.sysservers and then insert into the table variable */

insert into @servername_dist (serverid, servername) select srvid, srvname from
sys.sysservers;

/* We then retrieve the name of the server from the table variable */

select * from @servername_dist;
go
```

The code in Listing 2-3 first creates a table variable that will store the ID and name of the server, which will be retrieved from the sys.sysservers system table. The column of interest in the system table is the server name. I have used the table variable, because it is stored in memory—it does not make use of the tempdb to store the data temporarily, so the processing is faster. It has a well-defined scope that lasts for the duration of the batch, in this case, so we do not have to clean up by issuing a drop table statement. The code inserts the value of the server name into the column of the table variable and then queries the table variable to display the result.

The output of Listing 2-3 is as follows:

```
(2 row(s) affected)
serverid servername
------------------------------------------------- ------------
1        repl_distributor
0        SHW-TOR-WS039\SQLSERVER
```

In the result set you can see the name of the SQL Server instance whose server ID is 0. But what is the server named repl_distributor for server ID 1? This is a remote server that is created automatically during configuration for security reasons. It ensures the connection between the Publisher and Distributor servers and communicates with the distribution database regardless of whether the Distributor server is installed locally, as in this case, or set up on a remote server.

When the Distributor server is configured locally, repl_distributor generates a random password. The Distributor server uses this password to authenticate that the Publisher server is registered with the Distributor server, and to validate any stored procedure that is used for replication before it is executed.

Now that we know for sure that the Distributor server has been configured and that SQL Server used its built-in features to provide the security link, we need to see what happens to the distribution database. Listing 2-4 checks the category type of the distribution database.

Listing 2-4. *Retrieving the Category Type of the Distribution Database*

```
use master
go
/* Declare the table variable */

declare @databasename_dist table
(
dbname sysname,
categorytype int,
databaseid smallint
);

/* We want the names of the database, the database id and the category type
from the  sys.sysdatabases and then insert into the table variable */

insert into @databasename_dist(dbname,databaseid,categorytype) select name,
dbid,category from sys.sysdatabases;

/* We then retrieve the name, the id and the category type of the database
from the table variable */

select databaseid, dbname, categorytype from @databasename_dist order by
databaseid;
go
```

As in Listing 2-3, this code declares a table variable that houses the ID, name, and category type of the databases that are set up in the server. This information is retrieved from the sys.sysdatabases system table and inserted into the table variable. The column of interest from the system table is category.

■**Note** You cannot use the sys.databases catalog view instead of the sys.sysdatabases system table, since catalog views do not contain any information on replication.

The output of Listing 2-4 is shown here:

```
(7 row(s) affected)
databaseid dbname                                      categorytype
---------- -------------------------------------- ------------
1          master                                          0
2          tempdb                                          0
3          model                                           0
4          msdb                                            0
5          AdventureWorksDW                                0
6          AdventureWorks                                  0
7          distribution                                   16
```

In the output you can see that all the system databases, except for the distribution database, have a value of 0 for categorytype. So do the sample databases. The distribution database has a categorytype value of 16, which indicates that only this database is being used for replication. This is correct, since we cannot use any of the system databases for replication while there is no database set up for publications.

Now we need to see the security mode and the type of the Publisher server in the system table. Listing 2-5 retrieves this information.

Listing 2-5. *Retrieving the Type of the Publisher and the Security Mode of the Login*

```
use msdb
go
/* Declare the table variable */

declare @publishertype_dist table
(
servername sysname,
distdb sysname,
security int,
publishertype sysname
);
/* We want the names of the server, the database, the security mode and
the Publisher type from the  MSdistpublishers and then insert into the
table variable */

insert into @publishertype_dist(servername,distdb,security,publishertype)
select name, distribution_db,security_mode,publisher_type from
MSdistpublishers;

/* We then retrieve the names of the server, the database, the security
mode and the Publisher type from the table variable */

select servername,distdb,security,publishertype from @publishertype_dist;
go
```

This code saves the security_mode and the publisher_type from MSdistpublishers in a table variable as in the previous two listings. They are then retrieved from the table variable.

The output of Listing 2-5 is shown here:

```
(1 row(s) affected)
servername                     distdb          security    publishertype
---------------------------------------------------------------------------
SHW-TOR-WS039\SQLSERVER        distribution    1           MSSQLSERVER
```

In the output, you can see that security is set to 1. This confirms that Windows Integrated Authentication has been set. Note that the type of the Publisher listed in the output is MSSQLSERVER.

Listing 2-6 retrieves the agent profiles that I described earlier in the chapter.

Listing 2-6. *Retrieving Descriptions of the Agent Profiles*

```
use msdb
go
/* Retrieve data from MSagent_profiles to see the agent definition */

select profile_id,
profile_name,
agent_type,
type,
description,
def_profile
from MSagent_profiles;
go
```

The output of Listing 2-6 is shown in Figure 2-33.

	profile_id	profile_name	agent_type	type	description	def_profile
1	14	Continue on data consistency errors.	3	0	Agent profile for skipping data consistency errors. It can be used only by SQL Server Subscribers.	0
2	1	Default agent profile	1	0	NULL	1
3	2	Default agent profile	2	0	NULL	1
4	4	Default agent profile	3	0	NULL	1
5	6	Default agent profile	4	0	NULL	1
6	11	Default agent profile	9	0	Agent profile for replicated queued transaction reader.	1
7	16	Distribution Profile for OLEDB streaming	3	0	Distribution agent profile enabled for the processing LOB data using OLEDB streaming.	0
8	15	High Volume Server-to-Server Profile	4	0	Merge agent profile optimized for the high volume server-to-server synchronization scenario.	0
9	13	Rowcount and checksum validation profile	4	0	Profile used by the Merge Agent to perform rowcount and checksum validation.	0
10	12	Rowcount validation profile.	4	0	Profile used by the Merge Agent to perform rowcount validation.	0
11	7	Slow link agent profile.	4	0	Agent profile for low bandwidth connections.	0
12	3	Verbose history agent profile.	2	0	Agent profile for detailed history logging.	0
13	5	Verbose history agent profile.	3	0	Agent profile for detailed history logging.	0
14	8	Verbose history agent profile.	4	0	Agent profile for detailed history logging.	0
15	9	Windows Synchronization Manager profile	4	0	Profile used by the Windows Synchronization Manager.	0
16	10	Windows Synchronization Manager profile	3	0	Profile used by the Windows Synchronization Manager.	0

Figure 2-33. *Output of the code in Listing 2-6*

Earlier, in Figure 2-25, we looked at the different profiles for the Distribution Agent in the Distributor Properties window. The type column in the preceding output tells you whether the profile is custom-made or generated by the system. A value of 0 indicates that it is generated by the system. Now take a look at the agent_type column. You will see the values are 1, 2, 3, 4, and 9, which correspond to agent types of *Snapshot, Log Reader, Distribution, Merge,* and *Queue Reader Agent* respectively. Check that the profile_name of the Distribution Agent for the preceding output matches with the Name column in the Agent Profiles window of Figure 2-26.

Summary

In this chapter, I have discussed the publisher-subscriber metaphor that is the logical representation of replication. By now you should have a clear understanding of the different components of replication and a grasp of the fundamentals of the physical models of replication. I have shown you how to configure replication and how to set up the Distributor server, the Publisher server, and the distribution database locally. You should feel comfortable setting them up using either the GUI method or the T-SQL method. You also now have a understanding of the internals of some of the system tables.

- The publisher-subscriber metaphor is the logical representation of replication.

- The different components of replication are the Distributor, the Publisher, publications, articles, agents, the Subscriber, and subscriptions.

- There are three different kinds of subscriptions: push, pull, and anonymous subscriptions.

- Both push and pull subscriptions must be enabled at the Publisher server.

- The Publisher and Distributor can be installed locally on the same server.

- The Distributor server can also be installed on a remote server.

- The distribution database is a system database that is installed after replication is configured.

- The installation of replication requires 31 MB of disk space.

- There are five different kinds of agents: the Distribution Agent, the Snapshot Agent, the Merge Agent, the Log Reader Agent, and the Queue Reader Agent.

- There are other maintenance agents, such as the Distribution clean up job, that are run as jobs.

- There are four different physical models for implementing replication: the Publisher/Distributor–Subscriber model, the Central Publisher–Multiple Subscriber model, the Central Subscriber–Multiple Publishers model, and the Multiple Publishers–Multiple Subscribers model.

- The Distributor server, the distribution database, and the Publisher server can be configured either by using the GUI or the T-SQL method.

- The SQL Server Agent needs to run before you can set up replication.

- SQL Server installs `repl_distributor` after the configuration of replication. It generates a password that the Distributor server uses to authenticate the registration of the Publisher server on the Distributor server.

- The master, model, msdb, and tempdb system databases cannot be replicated.

- When configuring replication, set up the Distributor server first, followed by the distribution database. Then configure the Publisher server.

- When using T-SQL, use the `sp_adddistributor` stored procedure to set up the Distributor server. Use the `sp_adddistributiondb` stored procedure to set up the distribution database. Then use the `sp_adddistpublisher` stored procedure to configure the Publisher server.

In the next chapter, I will show you how to set up the publication database, the subscriptions, and the Subscriber server. First, though, I will further explain the different types of replication: snapshot, transactional, and merge replication, which I introduced in Chapter 1. The different physical models of replication can be implemented with any of these types of replication.

Quick Tips

- The service for SQL Server Agent is disabled by default at the time of installation. Use the SQL Server Configuration Manager to start the service automatically.

- Synchronize the subscriptions within a specific period of time to prevent them being deactivated by the Distribution clean up job.

CHAPTER 3

■■■

Types of Replication

In Chapter 2, I introduced the publisher-subscriber metaphor that is the logical representation of replication and the various physical models of replication. But knowing the replication design alone is not enough. You need to understand the functionality and how to administer it, which means you need to know all about the different kinds of replication. This chapter discusses the replication types that you will be using.

On completion of this chapter, you will be familiar with the following:

- The different types of replication

- The workings of snapshot replication and when it is used

- The workings of transactional replication and when it is used

- The workings of merge replication and when it is used

Snapshot Replication

A snapshot is an instantaneous photograph, and that is exactly what happens in snapshot replication. The Snapshot Agent makes a bulk copy of all the objects and data to be published, and it transfers them to the Distributor server; the Distribution Agent then processes them to send to the appropriate Subscriber servers.

There is a high degree of latency involved, since publications do not need to be updated often. Also, since data is distributed exactly at the scheduled time, there is no need to continuously monitor the updates, which means there is very low overhead. This offers a high degree of autonomy—even if a particular Subscriber server is not connected to the Publisher server, you can always transfer the publications the next time it is connected.

Tip The amount of data and objects transferred in snapshot replication can cause significant overhead at the time of replication. You should consider the frequency and the timing for transferring with snapshot replication (perhaps choosing off-peak hours).

In what situations would you use snapshot replication? There are quite a few, and the SQL Server Books Online (BOL) gives an overview:

- When data changes are infrequent

- When you do not need to have the data in sync with the Publisher server all the time

- When you are replicating small volumes of data

- When you need to replicate large volumes of data within a short period of time

- When site autonomy for Subscriber servers is required

- When you want data to be read-only

So what would be a likely scenario for implementing snapshot replication? Consider a bookstore chain where the prices of the books are fixed, and that special offers are made once a year during the holiday season. Since each of the bookstores needs to know this one-time offer only once a year, the updates occur infrequently, and snapshot replication can be used.

Snapshot replication involves complete synchronization of the data and objects. The initial synchronization generated by the Snapshot Agent is, by default, also implemented by both transactional and merge replication. Figure 3-1 shows how it works.

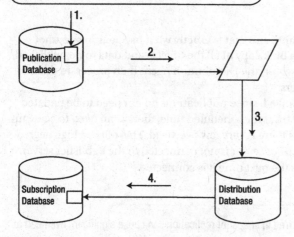

Figure 3-1. *The snapshot replication process*

The Snapshot Agent generates the snapshot files, containing the schema and the bulk copy of the data, from the publication and stores them in the snapshot folder. This folder is normally stored in the distribution database on the Distributor server, which also keeps a history of the transaction. Next, in the case of snapshot and transactional replication, the

Distribution Agent reads the database objects and the data from the snapshot files in the snapshot folder and moves them to the appropriate Subscriber servers. The Distribution Agent runs on the Distributor server for push subscriptions, and on the Subscriber server for pull subscriptions. In merge replication, it is the responsibility of the Merge Agent to distribute the snapshot files. The Merge Agent runs on the Distributor server for push subscriptions and on the Subscriber server for pull subscriptions. (Push and pull subscriptions were discussed in the "Subscriptions" section in Chapter 2.)

While it is true that you can store the snapshot folder at the Distributor server, it is possible to keep it at an alternative location, compress the snapshot files, or even write them on a CD. Since the location of the snapshot folder is a property of the Publisher server, it is possible for the Distribution and Merge Agents to find the locations. However, once you specify the location of the snapshot folder and generate the synchronization process, you should not change the location.

The Snapshot Agent Profile

In the "Distribution Agent Profiles" section of Chapter 2, we looked at the different profiles for the Distribution Agent. As you can see in Figure 3-2, the Snapshot Agent has only one default profile.

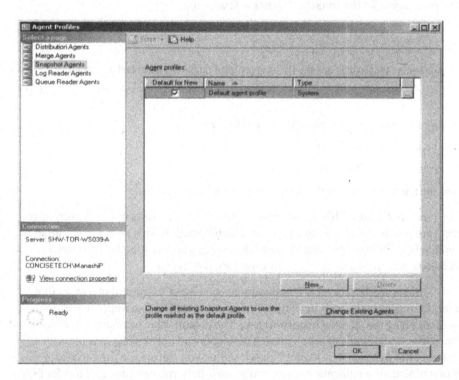

Figure 3-2. *The Snapshot Agent's one default profile*

As was mentioned in Chapter 2, understanding the parameters for the default profile will help you troubleshoot and create your own profiles. The parameters for the Snapshot Agent's default profile are shown in Figure 3-3.

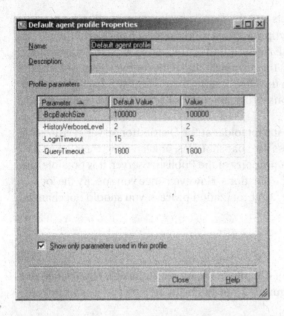

Figure 3-3. *The parameters for the Snapshot Agent's default profile*

■**Note** The components of replication and the Distribution Agent profile are described in Chapter 2.

The syntax for starting the Snapshot Agent is as follows:

```
snapshot -Publisher server_name[\instance_name]
-Publication publication_name [-parameters]
```

These are the parameters set in the Snapshot Agent's default profile:

Snapshot [-BcpBatchSize]: This parameter specifies how many rows in a bulk copy operation (bcp) are sent to the Distributor server as one transaction. This is also the number of rows that the Distribution Agent logs before it logs a bcp progress message. The default value is 100000; a value of 0 means that messages are not logged.

Snapshot [-HistoryVerboseLevel]: This parameter specifies the amount of history that is logged for the snapshot replication. Setting the value to 1 will help to improve performance by minimizing the effect of history logging. The default value of 2 means that the Snapshot Agent updates idle or long-running messages and only inserts new messages. Initially it is better to have all the history logged so that you can ensure the successful completion of snapshot replication. Once you are satisfied, you can change it to 1 for performance reasons. If you set the value to 3, new records will always be inserted, except for idle messages.

Snapshot [-LoginTimeout]: The default timeout for login sessions is 15 seconds. This is the same as for the Distribution Agent.

Snapshot [-QueryTimeout]: This parameter ensures that the queries are executed within the stipulated time. The default value is 1800 seconds.

How Snapshot Replication Works

Now that you know some of the parameters of the Snapshot Agent, the next question is how it works. Initially the Snapshot Agent establishes a connection between the Distributor server and the Publisher server. Then, for snapshot replication and at the initial phase of the transactional replication, it puts a lock on all the tables that are to be published (this does not happen in the case of merge replication).

The agent then generates the schema of the tables and writes them to a file with an .sch extension in the snapshot folder on the Distributor server. It also generates script files for each of the stored procedures, indexes, views, functions, and other database objects that need to be replicated.

The Snapshot Agent then bulk copies the data from the publication database and, like the schema files, stores it in the snapshot folder. It also makes entries in the distribution database about the location of the script and data files. (The Distribution Agent will later read the location of these files from the MSrepl_commands system table in the distribution database.) Finally, the locks that were held on the publication tables are released. This process is shown in Figure 3-4.

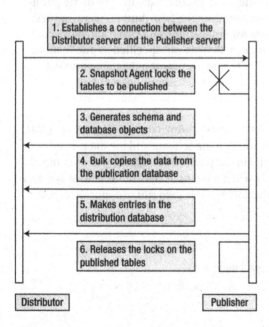

Figure 3-4. *How the Snapshot Agent works*

You cannot make changes to the schema of the publication tables during snapshot generation. You can, however, see the files in the Windows Explorer after they are generated.

■**Note** In Chapter 7, I will show you how the Snapshot Agent works behind the scenes. Chapters 4 through 7 all discuss snapshot replication.

Transactional Replication

Before you can start with transactional replication, you need to synchronize the initial database objects, the schema, and the dataset with the subscribing servers. This is done by taking an initial snapshot using the Snapshot Agent and then distributing it to the subscribing servers via the Distribution Agent.

Once the synchronization procedure is done, any incremental changes made at the Publisher server are transferred to the Subscriber server at the same time the changes are made at the Publisher server. As such, there is minimal latency in transactional replication. Since only committed data changes are applied in transactional replication, you are guaranteed transfer of data, and you can rest assured about the consistency of the data. The atomicity of data means that any transactions that are rolled back are not replicated.

While the initial synchronization of the schema and the dataset is often performed with the Snapshot and Distribution Agents, another option is to make a backup copy of the publication database and restore it at the Subscriber servers; then the Distribution Agent applies the necessary stored procedures and the metadata for replication. Since a backup has a copy of the entire schema and the dataset, including objects that are not specified as publications, it is the responsibility of the database administrator to remove unwanted database objects. Subsequent synchronizations will ensure that data is replicated according to the specifications. This method might be faster, since the overhead costs associated with the transfer across the network is eliminated.

Another option is to copy the initial dataset of the publication database by attaching it at the Subscriber servers. In that case, you must ensure that the schema and the dataset are properly synchronized and that there is no activity in the publication database at the time. If there is, data changes in the publication database will not be replicated at the time of synchronization. As with the backup method, the Distribution Agent is then run to copy the stored procedures and the metadata for replication.

■**Note** Transactional replication is discussed in Chapters 8 through 10.

So when would you use transactional replication?

- When you want to transfer incremental changes from the Publisher server to the Subscriber server

- When you want minimal latency

- When you want the transactions at the Subscriber server to be read-only

- When the network connections between the Publisher server and the various Subscriber servers are reliable

- When the Publisher server has a high volume of data modifications

- When you want to use heterogeneous databases as a Publisher server

Likely scenarios for implementing transactional replication would definitely include online transaction processing (OLTP), with changes made at the central Publisher server being updated at the various regional offices. It is also useful if you need to use data marts or you want to keep updated information from the production database in another location as a possible backup. Since most of the subscriptions in transactional replication are read-only, there is little possibility of any conflicts or lost updates.

How Transactional Replication Works

The process of transactional replication is shown in Figure 3-5. Transactional replication makes use of the Snapshot Agent, the Log Reader Agent, and the Distribution Agent.

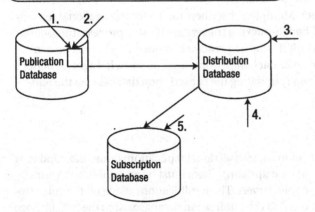

1. Transactions are written in the transaction log of the publication database
2. Log Reader Agent reads only committed transactions from the publication database
3. Log Reader Agent writes committed transactions in the distribution database
4. Distribution Agent reads from MSrepl_transactions
5. Distribution Agent transfers data to the subscription database

Figure 3-5. *How transactional replication works, following the initial synchronization*

The synchronization process is completed by the Snapshot Agent and the Distribution Agent as mentioned before, but the locking employed in transactional replication is not the same as in snapshot replication. In case of snapshot replication, all tables to be published share a lock, so you cannot make any changes during the snapshot generation. In transactional replication there are no shared locks in place during the snapshot generation, so you can work unhindered while replication is generating the initial snapshot files in the background. This process, known as *concurrent snapshot processing*, is the default for transactional replication.

Once synchronization is complete, the Log Reader Agent scours the transaction logs for each published database that is configured for transactional replication. If the agent notices any data modifications in the log files, it copies the committed transactions that are marked for replication, and forwards them in batches to the distribution database. The Log Reader Agent uses the sp_replcmds internal stored procedure to get the next set of commands for transactions marked for replication. The distribution database then becomes, in SQL Server parlance, a *store-and-forward* queue. Once the distribution database receives the entire batch of transactions, they are committed in the distribution database.

Next, the Log Reader Agent goes back to the publication databases and executes the sp_repldone stored procedure to mark the completion of the replication. The agent then tells the transaction log that it is ready for the replicated rows to be purged. Any rows that have not yet been replicated will not be purged.

The Distribution Agent then copies the transactions from the distribution database and sends them to the appropriate subscribing servers. The transactions are stored in the distribution database until all the transactions have been sent to the subscribing servers or the maximum retention time has elapsed.

Immediate Updating and Queued Updating Subscriptions

Although the subscriptions for transactional replication are set to be read-only by default, horizontal and vertical partitioning of tables makes it possible for different servers to subscribe to different sets of data. It is also possible for transactional replication to update the data at the subscribing servers with either *updatable subscriptions* or *peer-to-peer transactional replication*. With peer-to-peer transactional replication, you can either read or modify the data at both the publishing and the subscribing servers.

You can use the Central Publisher–Multiple Subscribers model for transactional replication with updatable subscriptions. Change-tracking triggers are used to process transactions, and the 2PC protocol is used to transmit the messages across a network that must be constantly connected, so there might be an impact on performance. As such, it might be better to use this option when you are occasionally updating the subscription database on the Subscriber servers.

Immediate Updating Subscriptions

There are two ways to update subscriptions in transactional replication: immediate updating and queued updating. In case of immediate updating, there must be an established connection between the Publisher and Subscriber servers. The modifications made on the subscription database are immediately transferred to the publication database using the 2PC protocol, as you can see in Figure 3-6. Notice that the updates issued at the subscriptions do not go via the Distributor server. The changes in data bind directly to the Publisher server using the MS DTC. So how does this work?

Note For a quick review of the 2PC protocol, see the "Distributed Data Transactions" section of Chapter 1.

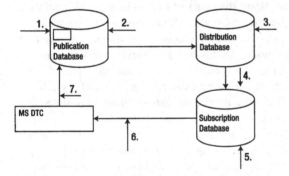

1. New column, MSrepl_tran_version, created in each of the published tables
2. Log Reader Agent reads only committed transactions from the publication database
3. Log Reader Agent writes committed transactions in the distribution database
4. Distribution Agent transfers data to the subscription database
5. Insert, update, and delete triggers are added to the subscription database
6. Changes in the subscription database are propagated to the Publisher server using MS DTC
7. RPC and 2PC calls are made

Figure 3-6. *The immediate updating subscription option for transactional replication*

When you create publications for transactional replication, you have the option of immediate updating or queued updating. If you set up immediate updating subscriptions, a new MSrepl_tran_version column is created in each of the tables in the publication database. Changes in this column and possible conflicts are tracked by the Log Reader Agent. New change-tracking triggers, such as insert, update, and delete triggers, are added for each of the published tables in the subscription database, and they are marked with NOT FOR REPLICATION. Insert, update, and delete stored procedures are also created for each of the tables in the publication.

The change-tracking triggers are known as replication triggers, and they are different from the DML triggers that are used to enforce business rules when data changes occur. In the case of replication triggers, the execution of the triggers is not replicated. For example, if the user performs an insert operation, the insert trigger will be fired to change the data, but if the insert data is going to be replicated, the Distribution Agent will not execute the trigger for any changes that are going to be sent to the Subscriber server. This prevents any unnecessary rows from being added to the replicated table. Replication triggers also monitor the identity and the timestamp columns in the subscription database. Values for these columns are entered in the publication database in the Publisher server and are sent to the Subscriber server using the 2PC protocol.

■**Note**   Replication triggers can coexist with the application triggers, and they don't interfere with each other's capabilities.

Any changes in the subscription database cause the appropriate replication trigger to issue a remote procedure call via the MS DTC to the appropriate stored procedure to make the necessary changes. If there are no conflicts, the changes are committed in the publication database in the Publisher server using the 2PC protocol through the MS DTC, and they are then replicated to other Subscriber servers through the Distribution Agent. If there are any conflicts, the transaction is aborted.

Queued Updating Subscriptions

If you decide to use queued updating subscriptions, the changes to data in the subscription database are applied to the publishing database occasionally, when the network is available. The updates that you make in the subscription database are placed in the queue, and since the queued transactions are applied asynchronously in the Publisher server, conflicts can occur that need to be resolved. Detecting and resolving conflicts in transactional replication is discussed in Chapter 10, but for now you should know that you can set the conflicts to be resolved either by allowing the Publisher server to follow the *publisher win policy* or the Subscriber server to follow the *subscriber win policy*.

As with immediate updating subscriptions, a new MSrepl_tran_version column is created in each of the tables in the publication database for tracking changes in the column. The change-tracking triggers are also created for the each of the published tables in the subscription database, and stored procedures are created for each of the tables in the publication database.

In the subscription database, the MSreplication_queue system table is created, and any changes made in the subscription database are logged in this table. The Queue Reader Agent picks up the changes from this table and applies the queued transactions to the publication database by using the requisite stored procedures. If it detects any conflicts, it resolves them by following the conflict policy, and it sends the necessary commands to the distribution database, which in turn sends them to the other Subscriber servers. It also posts conflict information to the Publisher server by calling the appropriate stored procedure. This is shown in Figure 3-7.

1. Changes are marked in the MSrepl_tran_version column in each of the published tables
2. Log Reader Agent reads only committed transactions from the publication database
3. Log Reader Agent writes committed transactions in the distribution database
4. Distribution Agent transfers data to the subscription database
5. Changes are stored in the MSreplication_queue system table
6. Queue Reader Agent reads changes from the MSreplication_queue system table

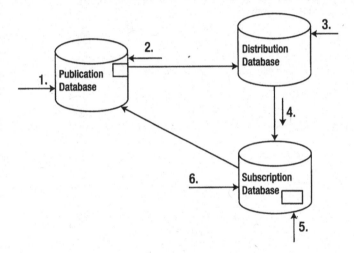

Figure 3-7. *The queued updating subscription option for transactional replication*

Note It is possible to switch between immediate updating and queued updating subscriptions. You must enable the publication and the subscription for both modes before you can select either one. This is done on the Subscriber server.

The Queue Reader Agent, like the Log Reader Agent, runs in the Distributor server. It is multithreaded and thread-safe. However, you can only run one instance of the Queue Reader Agent, which means that it services all the publishing servers. Its job is to take the messages from the queue and send them to the appropriate Publisher server. These messages are either stored in the SQL Server queue or in the Microsoft Messaging queue.

Tip Use the SQL Server queue whenever possible, as the processing is faster. This is the default.

The Log and Queue Reader Agent Profiles

Now that you know what the Log Reader and Queue Reader Agents do in transactional replication, let's look at the parameters of their profiles.

The Log Reader Agent has two profiles: the default agent profile and the verbose history agent profile, as shown in Figure 3-8.

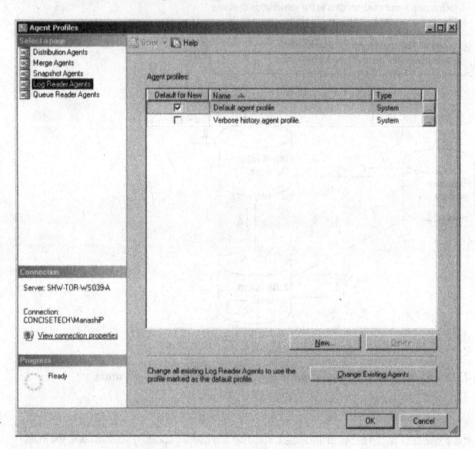

Figure 3-8. *The two profiles of the Log Reader Agent*

The syntax for starting the Log Reader Agent is as follows, and the parameters used in the default profile are shown in Figure 3-9:

```
logread -Publisher server_name[\instance_name]
-PublisherDB publisher_database [-parameters]
```

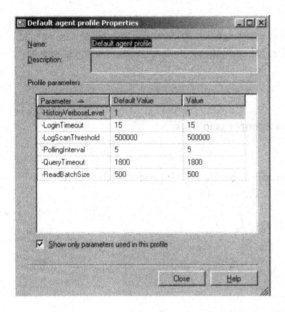

Figure 3-9. *The parameters of the Log Reader Agent's default profile*

These are the parameters set for the Log Reader Agent's default profile:

Logread [-HistoryVerboseLevel]: This parameter specifies the amount of history that is logged for the log reader operation. The default value is 1, which improves performance by minimizing the effect of history logging. If you set the value to 2, it will update the previous records for idle or long-running jobs; otherwise it will insert the new history records.

Note The HistoryVerboseLevel parameter for the Distribution Agent can have values of 1, 2, or 3, whereas for the Log Reader Agent it has values of 1 or 2.

Logread [-LoginTimeout]: This parameter sets the timeout for login sessions. The default is 15 seconds.

Logread [-PollingInterval]: This parameter specifies how often the Log Reader Agent reads the transaction log for replicated transactions. The default value is 5 seconds.

Logread [-LogScanThreshold]: The SQL Server BOL lists this parameter as being for internal use only.

Logread [-QueryTimeout]: This parameter specifies the time limit for the Log Reader Agent to execute its query before it times out. The default is 1800 seconds.

Logread [-ReadBatchsize]: This parameter sets the maximum number of transactions read by the Log Reader Agent from the log for every batch. The default size is 500 transactions.

Tip The default profile does not contain the packet size parameter. By increasing the packet size, you can improve the performance for transactional replication over the network. Performance and tuning of transactional replication is discussed in Chapter 18.

The syntax for starting the Queue Reader Agent is as follows:

```
qrdrsvc -[-parameters]
```

The Queue Reader Agent has only one profile generated by the system—the default profile. The parameters for this profile are shown in Figure 3-10.

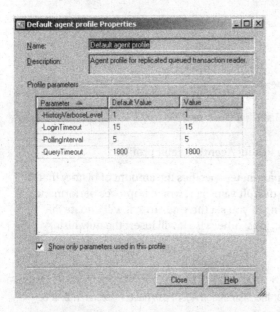

Figure 3-10. *The parameters for the Queue Reader Agent's default profile*

These are the Queue Reader Agent's parameters:

Qrdsvc [-HistoryVerboseLevel]: This parameter specifies the amount of history that is logged for the queue reader operation. The possible values are from 0 to 3. The default value of 1 will improve performance by minimizing the effect of history logging. A value of 0 means that no history will be logged, while a value of 2 means that new history records will be inserted, including those for idle and long-running job messages. For further details when you are troubleshooting, you can use a value of 3.

Qrdsvc [-LoginTimeout]: The default timeout for login sessions is 15 seconds. This is the same as for the Distribution Agent.

Qrdsvc [-PollingInterval]: This parameter specifies how often the Queue Reader Agent reads the messages that use SQL Server–based queues. The default value is 5 seconds.

Qrdsvc [-QueryTimeout]: This parameter specifies the time limit for the Queue Reader Agent to execute its query before it times out. The default value is 1800 seconds.

Tip By reducing the polling interval of both the Log Reader and Queue Reader Agents, you can improve the latency of transactional replication.

Peer-to-Peer Transactional Replication

So far, I have discussed two approaches in transactional replication. In the first case, data is replicated from the primary source, the Publisher server, to the secondary source, the Subscriber server, which can also act as a Publisher server to the subscribing servers, which are usually read-only. In the second case, data is transferred from the primary source to the secondary source, the Subscriber server, which can also republish the data back to the primary source. The primary source then sends the modified data to the remaining leaf-node Subscriber servers. Both of these systems are hierarchical in nature, as illustrated in Figure 3-11.

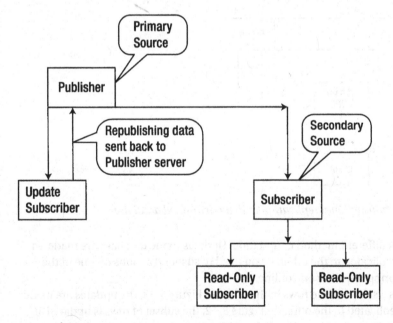

Figure 3-11. *Hierarchy of transactional replication*

SQL Server gives you another option, where the different nodes in the topology are peers: peer-to-peer transactional replication. The relationship between the nodes in peer-to-peer transactional replication is equal, so each node contains identical schema and data.

You might use this type of replication if your business needs a hot backup. Another scenario would be an online business application that needs to read or modify data and the databases participate in replication. You can improve the performance of the queries by spreading them out across multiple databases, and in the event of one database failing, you can route the traffic to other servers since each will have an identical database copy.

In this topology, both the Publisher and Subscriber servers are of the same node, which means they contain the same schema and data. Changes made in one are reflected in the other. However, SQL Server recognizes that data modifications in one node should not be cycled back again.

Figures 3-12 and 3-13 show how data can be distributed across multiple databases in peer-to-peer replication environment. In both cases, there is load balancing of the data. However, in Figure 3-12 the database is partitioned between the two servers. For example, by partitioning, a client application can update a subset of rows for a published table to one node and update another subset of rows to the second node. The updated data is replicated from one node to the other. If one of the servers or the database goes down, you can easily connect your application to the other one, since it will have the latest copy of the data.

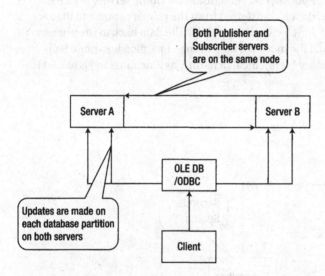

Figure 3-12. *Peer-to-peer transactional replication with a partitioned database*

Figure 3-13 shows a different method of updating. Updates to the database are made on a single node, and it is replicated to the other. If you need to suspend actions on one of the servers, you can easily bring the other one online.

Partitioning creates a subset of the rows in the table. In Figure 3-13, the updates are made in one node and then replicated to the other. In Figure 3-12, the subset of rows is updated at two different nodes, and the updates are then replicated to the other node. While both these methods can be used for peer-to-peer replication, the type of replication shown in Figure 3-13 is used for standard transactional replication. Standard transactional replication is hierarchical, and the subscriptions are read-only. In peer-to-peer replication the nodes for all the servers are equal, and any updates in one node can lead to data conflicts. Since peer-to-peer replication does not have the means to deal with data conflicts, it is necessary to partition the data either horizontally or vertically.

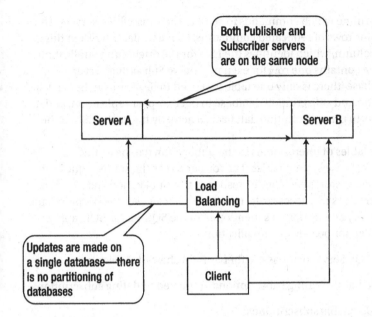

Figure 3-13. *Peer-to-peer transactional replication with no partitioning of the database*

ONLINE OR OFFLINE

In a peer-to-peer replication, you sometimes need to be online, and at other times you can go offline. During online sessions you can perform data modifications and issue the ALTER COLUMN and ADD COLUMN DDL commands. When you take any of the nodes offline, you are rendering the system inactive. The system is said to be *quiesced*, which means that all activity on all the published tables at all nodes has been suspended, and it ensures that each of the nodes have received all the changes from the other nodes.

■**Note** A horizontal partition contains a subset of the columns of a table, while a vertical partition contains a subset of rows.

In peer-to-peer replication, the two agents at work are the Log Reader Agent and the Distribution Agent. In peer-to-peer transactional replication, the agents behave much as in standard transactional replication. The Log Reader Agent processes the transactions from the Publisher server and sends them to the Distributor server. The Distribution Agent then sends them to the required subscriptions. It is up to the Subscriber servers to decide whether they want to apply the changes.

There are three tables in the distribution database that keep track of the metadata for peer-to-peer transactional replication: MScached_peer_lsns, MSrepl_commands, and MSrepl_originators. The MScached_peer_lsns table tracks the log sequence number (LSN) in the transaction log to determine which commands to send to the subscribing servers. The `MSrepl_commands` table contains rows of replicated commands. Of particular interest in this table is the `originator_lsn` column, which identifies the LSN for the originating publication. The `MSrepl_originators` table contains one row for each updatable Subscriber server.

In the subscription database, there is only one table you need to be aware of: `MSpeer_lsns`. It is added to every publication and subscription database in peer-to-peer replication, and it maps each of the transactions to the subscription database. It actually tracks the LSN of the originating publication.

There are also two other tables of interest to us in the publication database: the `MSpeer_request` and `MSpeer_response` system tables. The former tracks the status requests for a given publication, while the latter stores each node's response to a publication status request.

Simply having two servers does not necessarily mean that you can use peer-to-peer transactional replication. The following conditions, as mentioned in the SQL Server BOL, apply when the publication is enabled for peer-to-peer replication:

- You cannot have non-SQL Server databases either as Publishers or Subscribers

- You cannot have immediate updating subscriptions or queued updating subscriptions

- You cannot have transformable subscriptions

- You cannot have the `-SubscriptionStreams` parameter for the Distribution Agent

- You cannot have the `-MaxCmdsInTran` parameter for the Log Reader Agent

- You cannot have the SQL call format for `sp_addarticle`

- You cannot use columns with timestamps

By now you should have a basic understanding of snapshot and transactional replication. Next let's look at the third type of replication: merge replication.

■**Note** Snapshot replication is discussed in Chapters 4 through 7, transactional replication is discussed in Chapters 8 through 10, and merge replication is covered in Chapters 11 through 14.

Merge Replication

In merge replication, like transactional replication, the Snapshot Agent makes a snapshot of the schema and data during the initial synchronization. Subsequently, incremental data modifications can either be made at the Publisher server, the Subscriber servers, or both. Changes made at all sites are then combined, or *merged*, into a single uniform result set. The Merge Agent performs the subsequent synchronization, and it can either be asked to run on demand or at a scheduled time.

Merge replication allows autonomous changes to be made at multiple nodes or different sites, and this can cause problems—notably update conflicts. At other times there may be constraint violations, and changes may not be propagated to other sites.

SQL Server offers four ways of reconciling the conflicts:

- Default priority-based conflict resolver

- Business logic handler

- COM-based custom resolver supplied by Microsoft

- COM-based custom resolver

Conflict resolution in merge replication is done at the article level. The type of conflict resolver that you choose is determined during the configuration of merge replication. When a conflict arises, the Merge Agent invokes the necessary resolver. If you use the default priority-based conflict resolver, the Merge Agent will establish which sites will accept the data, and what type of data, according to the priority values that have been set. The last three resolvers are known as *article resolvers*. If you select any of the article resolvers, you need to set the resolver property for the article on the Publisher server.

If the default resolver is used, it behaves according to the type of subscription you choose. A subscription can be either a client or a server subscription, and priority values are assigned to the subscriptions accordingly. If you have a republishing Subscriber server, you choose the server subscription; otherwise you must choose the client subscription. A client subscription has the same priority value as the Publisher server after synchronization, while the priority values for the server subscription range from 0.00 to 0.99. In case of client subscriptions, the Subscriber server that makes the first change wins the conflict for that particular row or column.

■**Note** The configuration of conflict resolvers in merge replication using the GUI and T-SQL is discussed in Chapters 11 and 13.

If you want to assign priority values to the Subscriber servers in the default priority-based conflict resolver, any changes in the row for the subscription will also include the priority value of the Subscriber servers when they are propagated. This ensures that Subscriber servers with a higher priority value do not lose out to the Subscriber servers with a lower priority value.

■**Note** A subscription with a priority value assigned at the Publisher server is referred to as a *client sub-scription*; if the priority value is assigned on the Subscriber server, the subscription is known as a *server subscription*.

The business logic handler is a framework that implements the logic specific to the business rules to resolve the conflict. You can write code that responds to data changes, conflicts, and errors during the synchronization process. When you invoke the custom-made business-rule handler for data change, you can either reject or accept the data or apply custom data to override specific values in the data.

The COM-based custom resolvers provided by Microsoft are installed with SQL Server. The resolvers can handle insert, update, and delete conflicts. They can handle column conflicts, and most of them can handle row conflicts.

Tip If you run the `sp_enumcustomresolvers` stored procedure, SQL Server will list all the conflict resolvers that are registered in the distribution database.

The COM-based custom resolvers also implement logic specific to the business rules in the resolution of the conflict. They are essentially drivers, and you have to program conflict-resolution code in a language like Visual Basic.

You could use merge replication if you have several subscribing servers updating information that is transferred to the Publisher server, which then directs that information to other subscribing servers. The autonomous nature of merge replication and the latency involved should be considered. Sales force automation (SFA) is another application that can make use of merge replication. Sales people working in the field can update the data in laptops and then forward the updated data to the central database in the Publisher server. In this situation, you might also consider partitioning the database so that each of the sales people will receive filtered data from the Publisher servers. If data is filtered and partitioned, you should not expect as many conflicts arising, but you will have to allow for and resolve the conflicts.

The process of merge replication is shown in Figure 3-14.

> 1. Publication database contains articles in the Publisher server
> 2. Conflict tables, change-tracking tables, and triggers are present in publication and subscription databases
> 3. Merge Agent transfers data
> 4. Merge Agent writes history in the MSmerge_history table in the distribution database

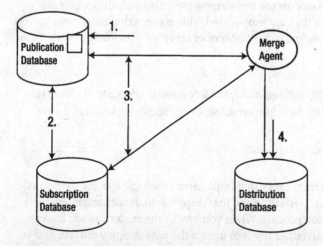

Figure 3-14. *The process of merge replication*

I mentioned previously that the initial synchronization is done by the Snapshot Agent, as in snapshot and transactional replication. However, in merge replication the Snapshot Agent makes some changes in the schema. It adds a ROWGUID column in every published table, unless there is already a column with a uniqueidentifier data type that has been set with the ROWGUIDCOL property, in which case it will use that column. Next it adds the following objects in all the published tables in the publication database under the dbo schema:

- Insert, update, and delete triggers that track changes. These triggers have names of the form MSmerge_ins_<GUID>, MSmerge_upd_<GUID>, and MSmerge_del_<GUID>. The sysmergearticles system table provides the values for the GUID entry.

- Stored procedures are created to handle the insert, update, and delete statements for the published tables.

- Views are created to filter the data and DML statements.

- Conflict tables are created that match the schema of the published tables. You will see in Chapters 11, 13, and 14 that these table names are in the form MSmerge_conflict_ <Publication>_<Article>.

The Merge Agent then takes up the responsibility of transferring all these objects and the data to the subscriptions in the initial synchronization. Once the synchronization is complete, the Merge Agent then tracks the data changes in the publication.

The Merge Agent resides in the Distributor server if you have configured push subscriptions. If you are running pull subscriptions, it resides in the Subscriber servers.

■**Note** SQL Server allows for the peaceful coexistence of development triggers and triggers created during merge replication.

The Merge Agent Profile

Now that we have looked at the purpose of the Merge Agent, let's look at its parameters. They are shown in Figure 3-15.

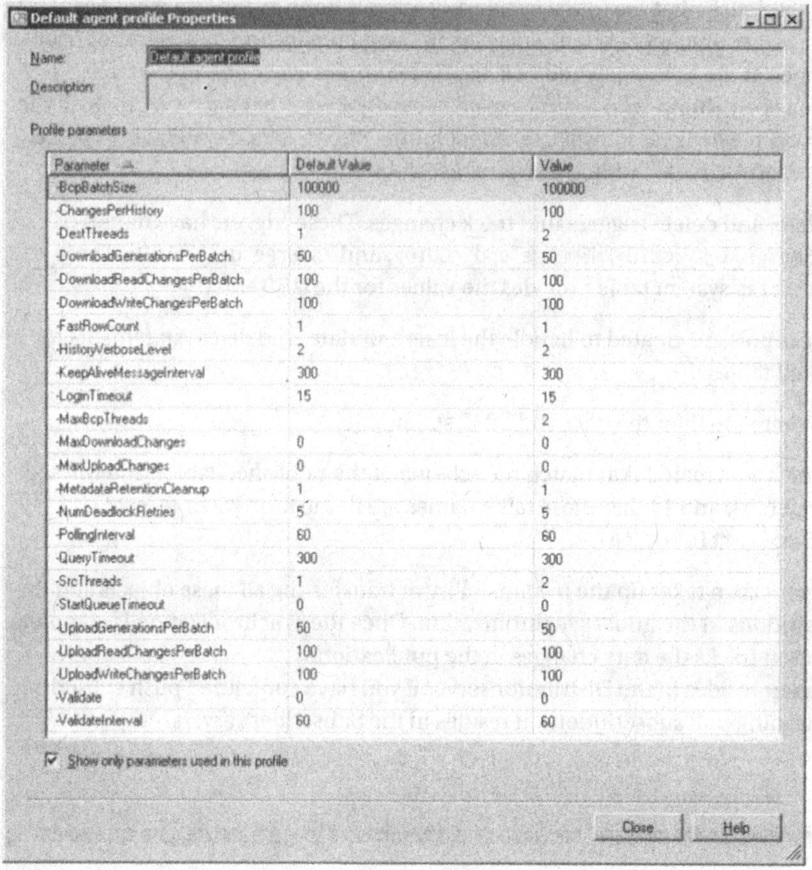

Parameter	Default Value	Value
BcpBatchSize	100000	100000
ChangesPerHistory	100	100
DestThreads	1	2
DownloadGenerationsPerBatch	50	50
DownloadReadChangesPerBatch	100	100
DownloadWriteChangesPerBatch	100	100
FastRowCount	1	1
HistoryVerboseLevel	2	2
KeepAliveMessageInterval	300	300
LoginTimeout	15	15
MaxBcpThreads		2
MaxDownloadChanges	0	0
MaxUploadChanges	0	0
MetadataRetentionCleanup	1	1
NumDeadlockRetries	5	5
PollingInterval	60	60
QueryTimeout	300	300
SrcThreads	1	2
StartQueueTimeout	0	0
UploadGenerationsPerBatch	50	50
UploadReadChangesPerBatch	100	100
UploadWriteChangesPerBatch	100	100
Validate	0	0
ValidateInterval	60	60

Figure 3-15. *Parameters for the Merge Agent's default profile*

The syntax for starting the Merge Agent is as follows:

```
replmerg -Publisher server_name[\instance_name]
-PublisherDB publisher_database
-Publication publication
-Subscriber server_name[\instance_name]
-SubscriberDB subscriber_database [-parameters]
```

These are the parameters for the Merge Agent's default profile:

`Replmerg [-BcpBatchSize]`: This parameter specifies how many rows of data can be sent when you perform a bulk copy operation (`bcp`). The default value is `100000`. By controlling the batch size, you can optimize the performance in merge replication.

`Replmerg [-ChangesPerHistory]`: This parameter specifies the threshold value beyond which the uploaded and downloaded messages will be logged.

`Replmerg [-DestThreads]`: This parameter specifies how many threads are used to process the articles either at the Publisher or the Subscriber server. The default value is `1`.

Replmerg [-DownloadGenerationsPerBatch]: A logical group of changes per article is called a *generation*, and this parameter specifies the number of generations that are processed in a single batch when downloading from a Publisher to a Subscriber server. By increasing the value for frequent updates, the performance can be optimized. The default value is 100.

Note A batch is a group of one or more T-SQL statements that are executed as a command.

Replmerg [-DownloadReadGenerationsPerBatch]: This parameter sets the number of generations that are read when downloading from the Publisher server to the Subscriber server. The default value is 100.

Replmerg [-DownloadWriteGenerationsPerBatch]: This parameter sets the number of generations that are written when downloading from the Publisher server to the Subscriber server. The default value is 100.

Replmerg [-FastRowCount]: This parameter specifies the type of rowcount calculation method that should be used for the validation of rowcount. The default value is 1.

Replmerg [-HistoryVerboseLevel]: This parameter specifies the amount of history that is logged for merge replication; the value can be from 0 to 3. A value of 1 will improve performance by minimizing the effect of history logging. The default value is 2, which means that the incremental session results, the errors, and the agent status messages are logged.

Replmerg [-KeepAliveMessageInterval]: This parameter specifies a time after which the history thread checks whether there is any connection left waiting for a response from the server. The default value is 300 seconds.

Replmerg [-LoginTimeout]: The default timeout for login sessions is 15 seconds. This is the same as for the other agents.

Replmerg [-MaxBcpThreads]: This parameter specifies how many bulk copy operations can be run in parallel. The default value is 1.

Replmerg [-MaxDownloadChanges]: This specifies the maximum number of rows changed during the download process. The default value is 0.

Replmerg [-MaxUploadChanges]: This specifies the maximum number of rows changed during the upload process. The default is 0.

Replmerg [-MetadataRetentionCleanUp]: This parameter specifies whether the agent will clean up the metadata based on the setting of the publication retention period. The default value is 1, which indicates that cleanup should occur. The tables that hold the metadata are MSmerge_genhistory, MSmerge_contents, and MSmerge_tombstone.

Replmerg [-NumDeadlockRetries]: This parameter specifies how many times the Merge Agent will try to process the change if it encounters a deadlock. The default value is 5.

Replmerg [-PollingInterval]: This parameter specifies at what interval the agent should query the publication database or the subscription database for any changes. The default value is 60 seconds.

Replmerg [-QueryTimeout]: This parameter specifies a time limit for queries to be executed within. The default is 300 seconds for the Merge Agent.

Replmerg [-SrcThreads]: This parameter specifies how many threads are used to process the articles at the source. The source can be a Publisher server during upload or a Subscriber server during download.

Replmerg [-StartQueueTimeout]: This parameter specifies how long the Merge Agent will wait until the other Merge Agents have completed processing. The default value of 0 indicates that the Merge Agent will wait for an indefinite time. It is better to reset this to some other value for optimum performance.

Replmerg [-UploadGenerationsPerBatch]: This parameter specifies the number of generations that are processed in a single batch when uploading articles from a Subscriber to the Publisher server. By increasing the value for frequent updates, the performance can be optimized. The default value is 100.

Replmerg [-UploadReadGenerationsPerBatch]: This parameter specifies the number of generations that are read when uploading from the Subscriber server to the Publisher server. The default value is 100.

Replmerg [-UploadWriteGenerationsPerBatch]: This parameter specifies the number of generations that are written when uploading from the Subscriber server to the Publisher server. The default value is 100.

Replmerg [-Validate]: This parameter specifies whether, at the end of the merge session, validation for the subscriptions for a particular publication should be performed or not. It also specifies the type of validation that should be carried out. The default value of 0 means that there is no validation.

Replmerg [-ValidateInterval]: This parameter specifies how often the subscription is validated in a continuous mode. The default value is 60 minutes.

Summary

In this chapter, I have discussed the different types of replication—snapshot, transactional, and merge—and the scenarios in which you would most likely consider using them. You should now have a clear understanding of the different agents used for each type of replication and the parameters used in the default profiles. You should also have a basic knowledge of the workings of the different types of replication.

- There are three types of replication in SQL Server: snapshot, transactional, and merge replication.

- Snapshot replication involves the bulk copying of database objects and data from the Publisher server to the Distributor server. This is carried out by the Snapshot Agent.

- The Snapshot Agent generates the database objects and the data, and stores them in a snapshot folder on the Distributor server or at a remote site.

- The Distribution Agent then transfers the data to the required subscriptions.

- There is a high degree of latency involved in snapshot replication.

- Snapshot Agent is used by both transactional and merge replication during the initial synchronization process.

- In transactional replication, only committed transactions are replicated from the Publisher server to the Subscriber servers.

- Standard transactional replication involves the use of the Snapshot, Log Reader, and Distribution Agents.

- There are two ways to update subscriptions: immediate updating subscriptions or queued updating subscriptions.

- Immediate updating subscriptions require the use of MS DTC and remote procedure calls for the subscriptions to be updated immediately to the Publisher server before they are transferred to the other subscribing servers.

- Queued updating subscriptions do not require a network connection all the time. Updates are placed in the message queue and are transferred once the network connection is established.

- For queued updating, the updates are placed in a message queue. It can either be a SQL Server queue or a Microsoft Messaging queue.

- In the case of queued updating, the Queue Reader Agent processes the message from the queue before it is sent to the Publisher server.

- Replication that involves the transfer of data from the primary to the secondary source is hierarchical in nature.

- Peer-to-peer transactional replication involves nodes that are equal.

- Peer-to-peer replication cannot be used with non-SQL Server databases.

- Merge replication involves modifications of data both at the Publisher server and at multiple Subscriber servers.

- Data modifications can be made either online or offline. The Subscriber servers can then synchronize the data changes.

- Merge replication is performed by the Snapshot and Merge Agents. The autonomous nature of merge replication can lead to update conflicts.

- The Merge Agent resides in the Distributor server for push subscriptions and in the Subscriber servers for pull subscriptions.

- The update conflicts are resolved based on the principle of first priority.

- There are four types of conflict resolvers: the default priority-based conflict resolver, the business logic handler, the COM-based custom resolver provided by Microsoft, and the COM-based custom resolver.

In the next chapter, I will show you how to set up snapshot replication. I will also show you how to configure the publication database, subscriptions, and Subscriber server for snapshot replication using the GUI method.

Quick Tips

- Consider the frequency and the timing of synchronization with snapshot replication. This type of replication causes significant overhead when transferring data, and you may want to do this in off-peak hours.

- Files generated by snapshot replication can be viewed in the Windows Explorer.

- The schema of the publications cannot be changed during snapshot replication.

- It is possible to switch between the immediate updating and the queued updating subscriptions, but you must first enable the publication and the subscription for both modes first.

- Use the SQL Server queue for queued updating, as the processing is fast.

- Increase the packet size in the Log Reader Agent for faster processing when sending messages across the network.

- If you execute the sp_enumcustomresolvers stored procedure, SQL Server will show the different resolvers installed.

CHAPTER 4

■ ■ ■

Configuring Snapshot Replication Using the GUI

In Chapter 3 I explained how snapshot, transactional, and merge replication work. In this chapter, and Chapters 5 to 7, I will focus on snapshot replication. The SQL Server products that support snapshot replication are listed in Table 4-1.

Table 4-1. *SQL Server Products That Support Snapshot Replication*

SQL Server Product	Supports Snapshot Replication (Y/N)
SQL Server Workgroup Edition	Y (limited publication)
SQL Server Enterprise Edition	Y
SQL Server Standard Edition	Y
SQL Server Express Edition	Y

In this chapter, I will show you how to configure and implement snapshot replication using the GUI method (Chapter 5 will cover the T-SQL method). I will show you how to configure the publication and the different subscriptions. The generation of the snapshot will be discussed in Chapter 6, and the internal workings of snapshot replication will be covered in Chapter 7.

Before you proceed with this chapter, however, you need to install the database script from Source Code/Downloads at http://www.apress.com. The Entity-Relationship (E-R) diagram for the database is shown in Appendix A, and the SQL code for the database is given in Appendix B.

Tip The topic of replication is replete with jargon that can be confusing, but it is important to be comfortable with the terminology. Chapter 2 discusses in detail the terms used in replication. Do familiarize yourself with the terms, if you are a beginner.

On completing this chapter, you will be able to do the following using the GUI:

- Configure snapshot replication

- Configure publication

- Configure both push and pull subscriptions

- Use Windows Synchronization Manager to pull subscriptions

Configuring Publication

If you are reading this book sequentially, you have already learned how to configure the Distributor server, the Publisher server, and the distribution database in Chapter 2. In this section, I will show you how to configure the publication.

To begin, open the Microsoft SQL Server Management Studio (SSMS). I have already configured the publication, so it is listed under the Local Publications object, as you can see in Figure 4-1. Since you haven't done so yet, your Local Publications list will be blank in the Object Explorer, although the Publisher server has been configured. If you expand the Jobs object under the SQL Server Agent, you will notice that the Snapshot Agent is not in the list of agents. This makes sense, since we have not yet configured snapshot replication.

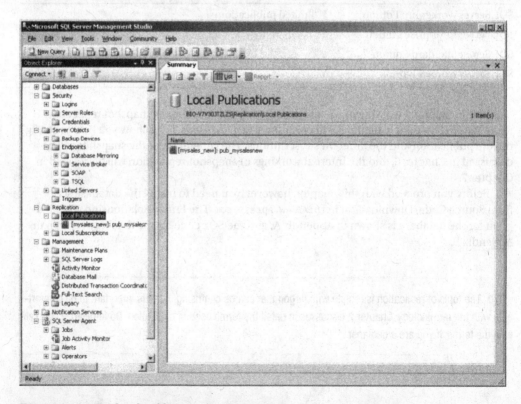

Figure 4-1. *Viewing local publications in the SSMS*

■**Note** The types of miscellaneous jobs and their functions for monitoring replication are discussed in Chapter 2.

Right-click on the Local Publications object under the Replication folder in the left pane, and select New Publication from the menu. The wizard for configuring new publications will open, as shown in Figure 4-2.

Figure 4-2. *Starting the New Publication Wizard*

This wizard guides you through the creation of the publication. Click Next in the first page of the New Publication Wizard, and you will see the page in Figure 4-3. Choose the database that contains the data or objects you want to publish, and click Next.

■**Note** Throughout the book, the mysales database has been given different names to illustrate the different publications of all three types of replication (in this case, mysales_new). The database structures and the E-R diagrams are similar. They can be found in Appendixes A and B.

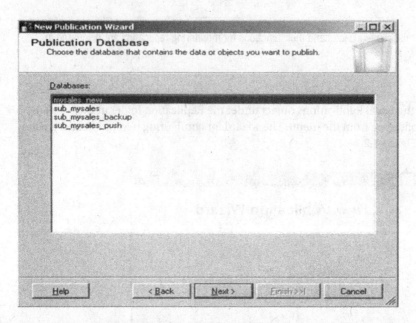

Figure 4-3. *Selecting the database whose data and objects you want to publish*

In the next page, shown in Figure 4-4, the wizard lists the different types of publications, such as snapshot publication, transactional publication, transactional publication with updatable subscriptions, and merge publication. At the bottom of the page, it describes the different publication types. Select Snapshot publication and click Next.

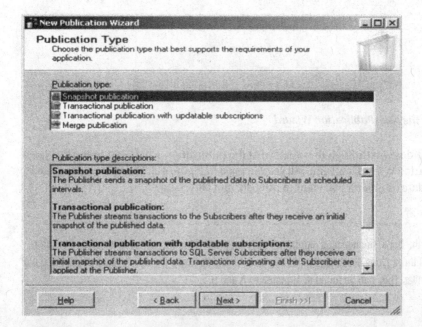

Figure 4-4. *Selecting snapshot publication*

Note It is possible to have different types of replication within the same publication.

The next page displays the list of objects in the database that you can publish as articles. This can be seen in Figure 4-5. Select the objects you want to publish, and click Next.

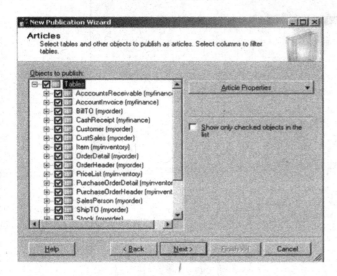

Figure 4-5. *Selecting the articles that you want to publish*

In the next page, shown in Figure 4-6, the wizard asks whether you want to filter the rows horizontally for the articles. You can click Add to choose horizontal partitioning; otherwise click Next.

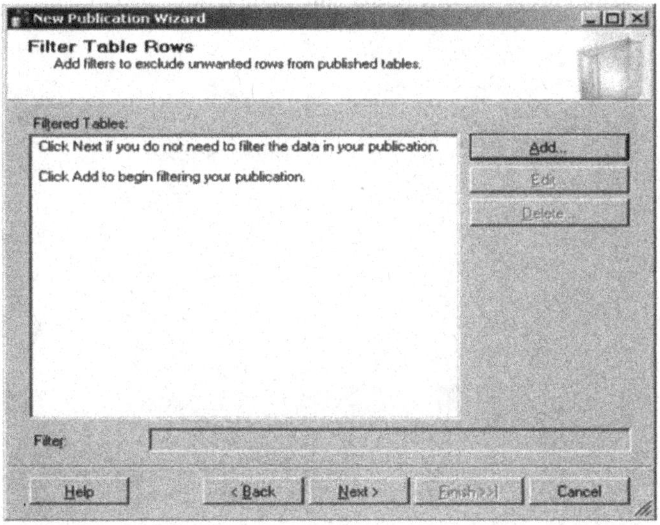

Figure 4-6. *Choosing whether you want to exclude unwanted rows from published tables*

If you click the Add button, the wizard displays the Add Filter page shown in Figure 4-7. To add a filter, first use the drop-down list to select the table from which you want to filter rows. Then, in the Columns box, choose the columns you want to include in the SQL query, and check if the query has been properly formulated in the right pane.

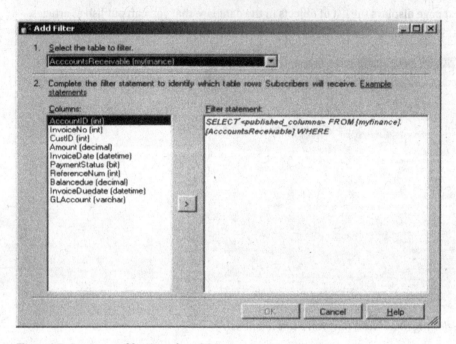

Figure 4-7. *Setting up filtering of a table's rows with a SQL query*

If you chose to ignore the horizontal filtering in Figure 4-6, and you clicked Next, you will see the Snapshot Agent page shown in Figure 4-8. As you can see, I have specified that the Snapshot Agent should create a snapshot for the publications immediately, and also that it should run at the scheduled times.

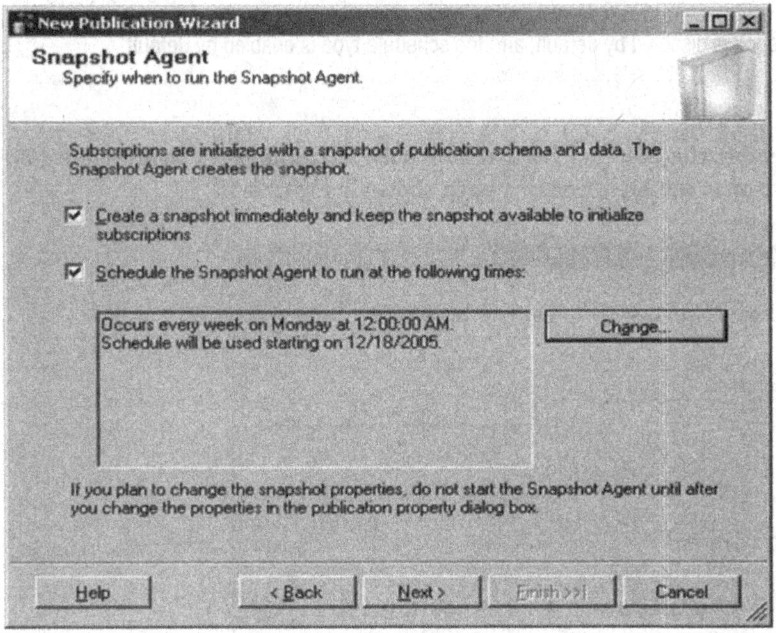

Figure 4-8. *Specifying the tasks and the scheduling of the Snapshot Agent*

To set up the Snapshot Agent's schedule, click the Change button in Figure 4-8. Doing so will display the page shown in Figure 4-9. In this example, I have scheduled the Snapshot Agent to run once every week at midnight on Monday—the wizard summarizes the schedule at the bottom of the screen.

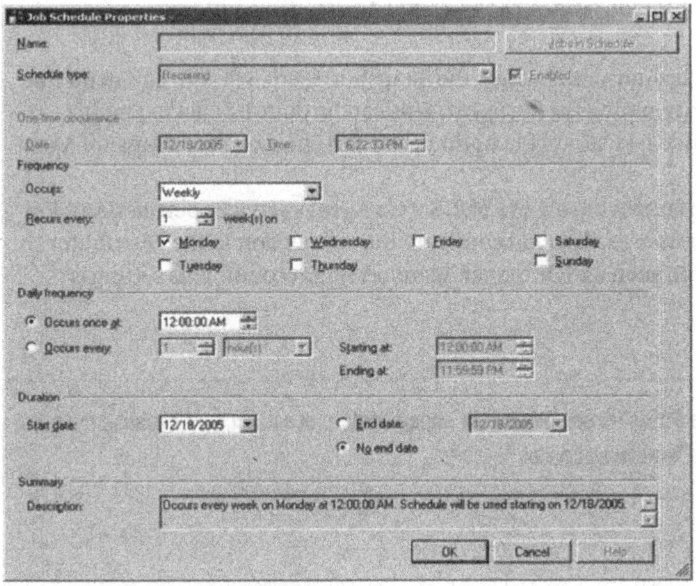

Figure 4-9. *Scheduling the frequency and the duration of the execution of the Snapshot Agent*

Note The name of the job is disabled by default, and the schedule type is enabled by default.

Once you have set the schedule, click OK to return to the Snapshot Agent page (Figure 4-8), and click Next to move on to the Agent Security page, shown in Figure 4-10.

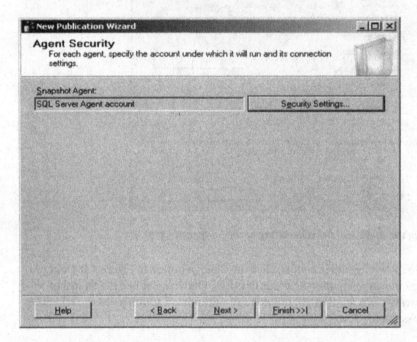

Figure 4-10. *The security account under which the Snapshot Agent will run*

You need to specify the account under which the Snapshot Agent will run, and to do this you need to specify the security settings of the agent. This can be done by clicking on the Security Settings button. Figure 4-11 shows the options you can choose to set Snapshot Agent security.

Although it is possible to connect using the SQL Server Agent's services permissions, it is recommended, for security purposes, that you configure the connection to the Distributor server using a domain account, such as SQL Server Agent service account. This setting is shown in Figure 4-11.

Note When you connect to the Publisher server, use the impersonate process account because the security credentials are checked in the Windows account.

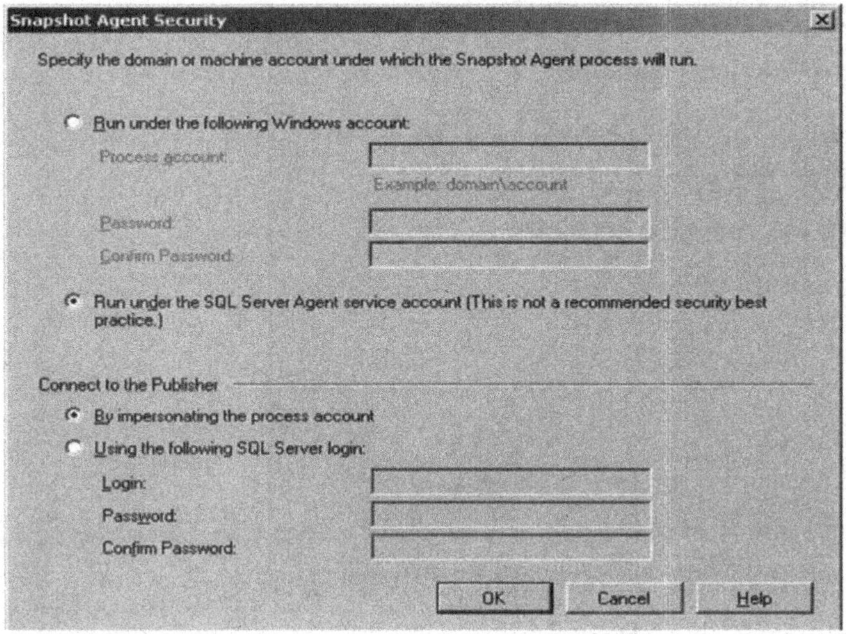

Figure 4-11. *Specifying Snapshot Agent security settings*

The Snapshot Agent resides on the Distributor server and also establishes a connection to the Publisher server, so you need to have a second connection setting for the Snapshot Agent. In Chapter 3, I mentioned that the Snapshot Agent needs to establish a connection to the publication server during the snapshot process to lock the tables that are being published. As you can see in the lower part of the page in Figure 4-11, the Snapshot Agent connects to the Publisher server by impersonating the process account, which is essentially the Windows account.

Note Chapter 3 describes the three different types of replication. The "How Snapshot Replication Works" section explains how the Snapshot Agent connects to the Publisher server and establishes a lock.

Once you have set the security settings, click OK to return to the Agent Security page of the wizard (Figure 4-10), and click Next. You'll see the Wizard Actions page, shown in Figure 4-12.

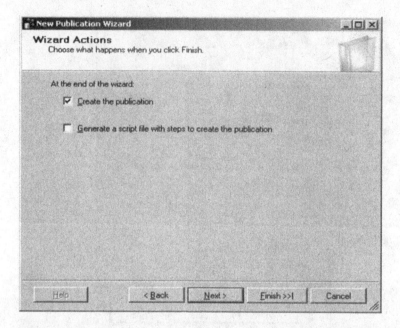

Figure 4-12. *Choosing to create a publication*

Check the box for creating the publication, as shown in the figure. You can also choose to generate a script file for the publication. If you set up the publication in a test environment, you can then use this script to load it on a production environment by selecting File ➤ Open ➤ File in SSMS.

When you're done, click Next to go to the last page of the wizard, where you can give a name to the publication, as shown in Figure 4-13.

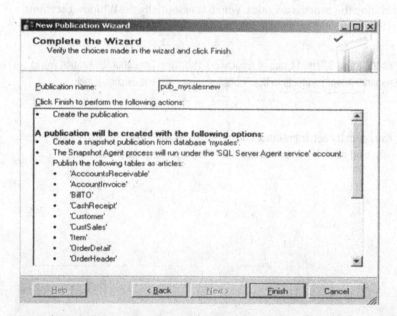

Figure 4-13. *Setting a name for the publication*

The wizard asks you to verify the list of tables that are being published, the account under which the Snapshot Agent will run, and the type of replication that you want to publish. Ensure that the right articles for publication, the domain account for the Snapshot Agent, and the type of publication are correct before you click the Finish button. Otherwise, you will have to drop the publication and recreate it. If you need to change any of the properties, you can use the Back button to return to previous pages in the wizard.

After checking that you have made the right selections, click the Finish button. The next wizard page you will see confirms the success in creating the publication, as shown in Figure 4-14.

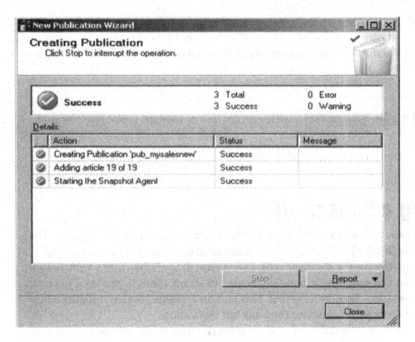

Figure 4-14. *The successful creation of the publication and the articles*

As you can see, the New Publication Wizard lists its success in creating the publication, the number of articles created for the publication, and its success in executing the Snapshot Agent.

In case you want to interrupt the wizard while the publication and articles are being created, you can do so by clicking the Stop button. The Stop button is disabled once the process is successful, as shown in Figure 4-14.

Should any of the actions listed in Figure 4-14 fail, you can click the Report button to check whether there are any error messages. Figure 4-15 shows the report for the successful creation of the publication.

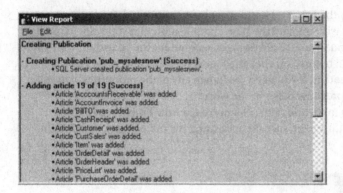

Figure 4-15. *The report for the publications created can be saved in a file*

■**Tip** Save the report in a file. In the event of a failure, you can then go back and troubleshoot any error messages.

Configuring a Subscription

Now that you know how to create a publication, the next step is to create a subscription. The Snapshot Agent generates the publications that are stored in the snapshot folder, and the Distribution Agent distributes the database objects and data to the Subscriber server. Before the Distribution Agent can send the data to the Subscriber server, though, you need to create a subscription database on a Subscriber server. This section explains how to configure a Subscriber server and a subscription database for snapshot replication.

In Chapter 2, I explained the different types of subscriptions: push, pull, and anonymous subscriptions. All three can be used in snapshot, transactional, and merge replication. In this section, I will show you how to configure push and pull subscriptions. An anonymous subscription is a type of pull subscription.

■**Note** The configuration of anonymous subscriptions using T-SQL is covered in Chapter 5.

Configuring Push Subscriptions

To configure push subscriptions, right-click the Local Subscriptions object under the Replication folder in the SSMS and select New Subscriptions from the menu. The New Subscription Wizard will open, as shown in Figure 4-16.

Figure 4-16. *Starting the New Subscription Wizard*

As the wizard's first page explains, you can have multiple subscriptions for the same publication, and you can specify when and where the agents for the synchronization process run. Depending on the type of subscription, the Distribution Agent can either run on the Distributor server for push subscriptions, or on the Subscriber server for pull or anonymous subscriptions. Click Next to go to the next page, shown in Figure 4-17.

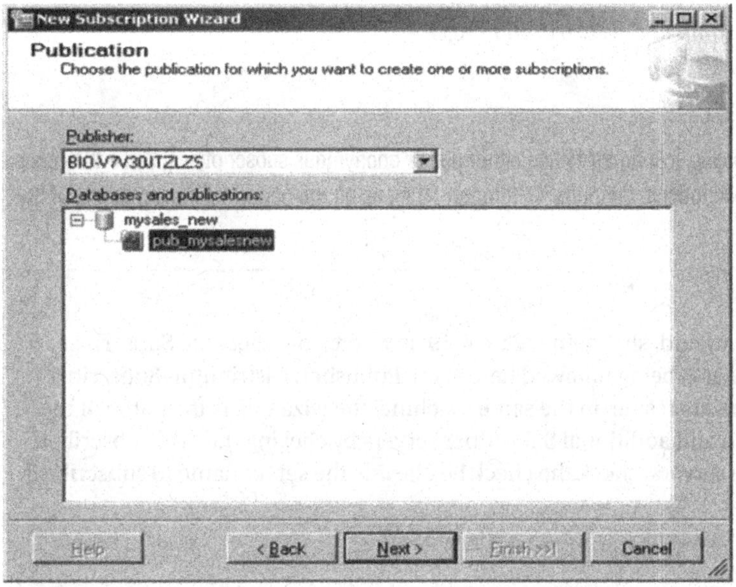

Figure 4-17. *Selecting the publication to subscribe to*

From the Publisher drop-down box, select the name of the Publisher server that you want to associate with the subscriptions. Once you do so, the wizard will list the database that is used for publications. Select the name of the publication by highlighting it, as shown in Figure 4-17, and click Next.

In the next page, shown in Figure 4-18, the wizard asks for the location of the Distribution Agent. For this example, I have selected the option to run the Distribution Agent at the Distributor server (a push subscription), since I want to push through the snapshot of the whole database to the Subscriber server. Click Next to go to the next page.

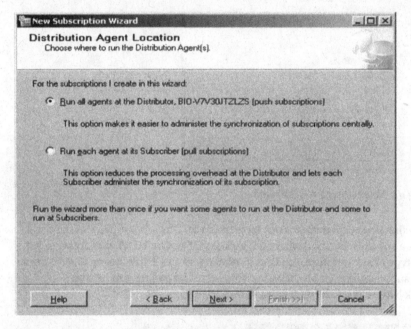

Figure 4-18. *Setting the location of the Distribution Agent*

■**Tip** For performance purposes, it is better to use either pull or anonymous subscriptions, since they cause less overhead than push subscriptions. Chapters 17 through 19 focus on the performance and tuning of the three types of replication.

The next page of the wizard, shown in Figure 4-19, is where you select the Subscriber server. Since the model that is being followed here is the Publisher/Distributor–Subscriber model, where all three servers reside on the same machine, the wizard lists the name of the Subscriber server. You can add additional Subscriber servers by clicking the Add Subscriber button; once you add the servers, check the check box beside the server name to subscribe it.

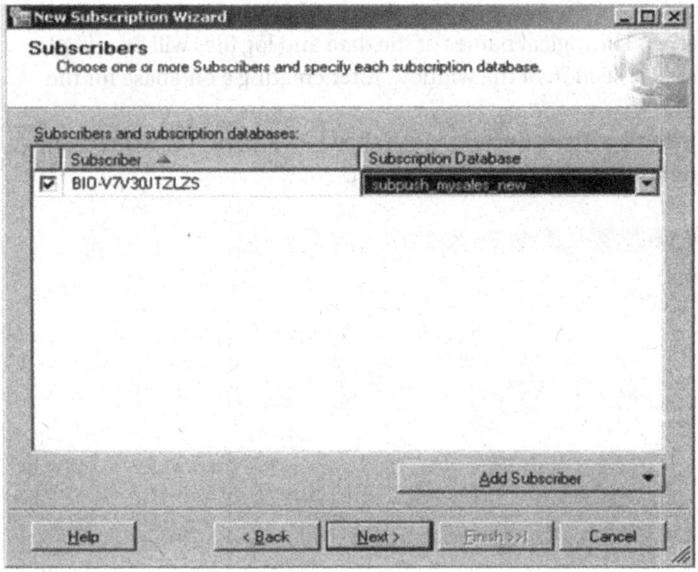

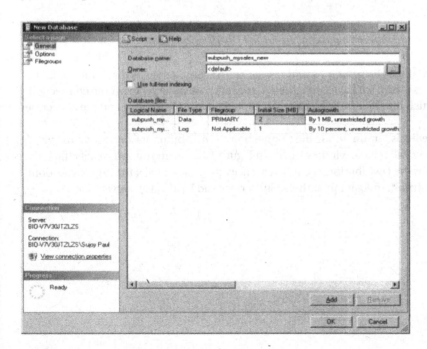

Figure 4-19. *Choosing a Subscriber server*

Now we need to attach a subscription database to the Subscriber server. Since none have been created yet, open the drop-down list under the Subscription Database, and click New database to create a database for the subscription. You will see the New Database window shown in Figure 4-20.

Figure 4-20. *Creating the subscription database*

In the Database name field, enter the name of the subscription database that you want to attach to the Subscriber server. The logical names of the data and log files will be added automatically in the Database files section of the window. After creating a database for the subscription, click Next.

The next page is the Distribution Agent Security page shown in Figure 4-21, where you can set the connection parameters for the Distribution Agent.

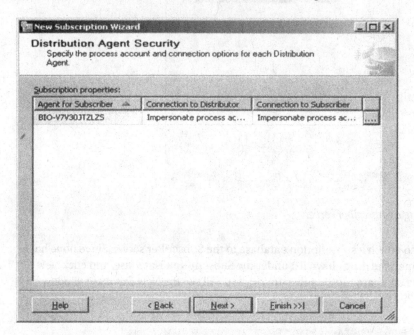

Figure 4-21. *Setting the connection parameters for the Distribution Agent*

You can see that the Distribution Agent resides on the same server as the Publisher and the Subscriber. This is how we have configured it. However, we have yet to set the connection parameters by which the Distribution Agent can connect to the Distributor and the Subscriber servers.

Click on the ellipsis button beside the Connection to Distributor or Connection to Subscriber column. You will see the window shown in Figure 4-22 where you can specify the security settings for the Distribution Agent. For security purposes, I used the process account to connect the Distribution Agent to both the Subscriber and Distributor servers.

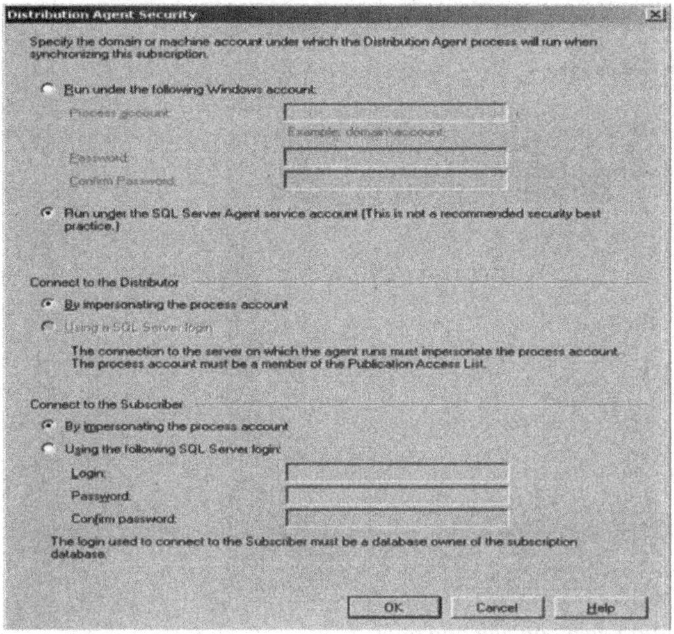

Figure 4-22. *Specifying security settings for the Distribution Agent*

Tip It is essential that when the agent impersonates a process account, the process account itself be a member of the Publication Access List (PAL). You can check whether the process account is a member of PAL by selecting the Publication Access List in the Publication Properties of the publication object. This is further discussed in the "Publication Access List" section in Chapter 7.

Click OK and the wizard will take you back to the Distribution Agent Security page (Figure 4-21). The connection settings for the Distributor and Subscriber servers will now be listed in the respective columns. Click the Next button.

In the next wizard page, you can schedule the synchronization process as you can see in Figure 4-23.

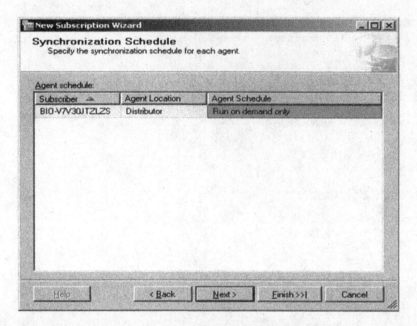

Figure 4-23. *Running the Distribution Agent on demand only*

I have scheduled the Distribution Agent to execute on demand only, but it is also possible to ask the agent to run continuously. If you do so, the agent will run immediately after the execution of the snapshot and will not stop unless you stop the agent services manually. I will discuss this further in Chapter 7 where I explain the steps in the execution of the agents. Click Next to continue.

In the next page, shown in Figure 4-24, you can specify when you want to initialize the subscriptions. You have two options: immediately or at first synchronization. When you select the latter, the Distribution Agent reapplies the snapshot on the Subscriber server so that you have data consistency between the publication and the subscription databases. In this case, set the synchronization to start immediately, and click Next.

Tip Although the initial synchronization of the subscription database is set immediately, subsequent synchronization for snapshot replication usually occurs on schedule.

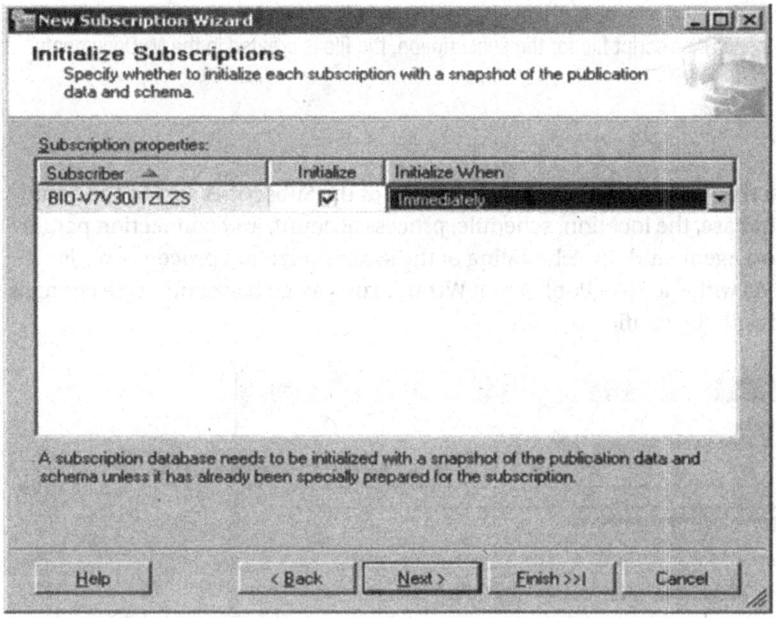

Figure 4-24. *Initializing the subscription immediately*

The next step is to specify the wizard's actions, as shown in Figure 4-25. Check the box to create the subscription. You can also create a script file for the subscription and keep it as a backup that you can load on the subscription database later. Click Next.

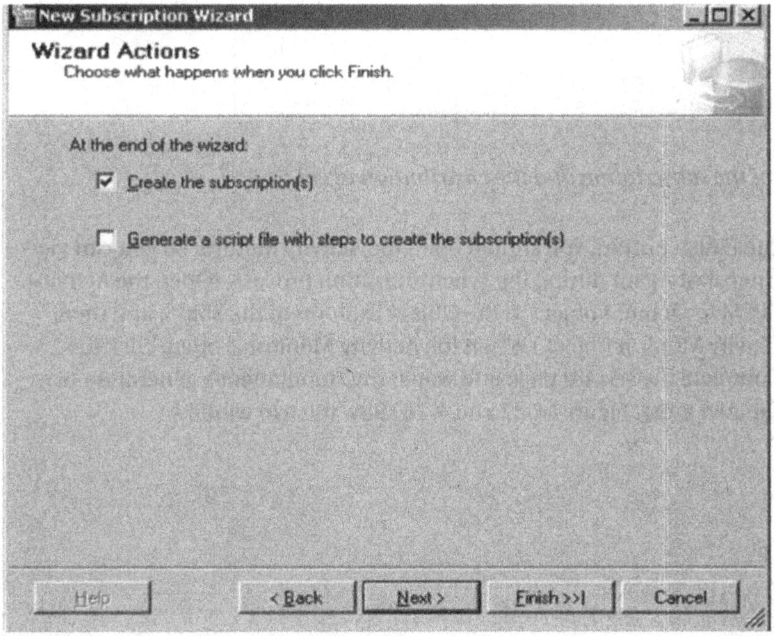

Figure 4-25. *Setting the wizard to create the subscription*

■Note If you choose to generate a script file for the subscription, the file is created in the MyDocuments folder by default.

The next wizard screen summarizes the configuration of the Subscriber server, the name of the subscription database, the location, schedule, process account, and connection parameters of the Distribution Agent, and the scheduling of the synchronization process. This is shown in Figure 4-26. As with the New Publication Wizard, you can go back and make changes if you are not satisfied with the configuration.

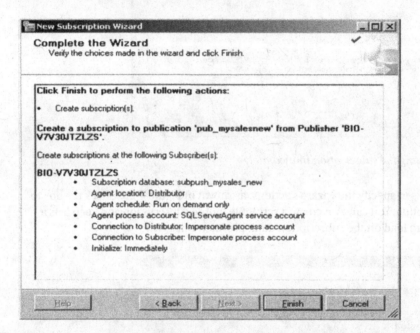

Figure 4-26. *Summary of the subscription and the Distribution Agent*

Before you click the Finish button, you should open the Activity Monitor so you can view the locks held by the Snapshot Agent during the synchronization process. (Open the Activity Monitor by opening the Management object in the Object Explorer of the SSMS, and then double-clicking the Activity Monitor object.) When the Activity Monitor is open, click the Finish button of the Complete the Wizard page and watch the simultaneous generation of the snapshot and the shared locks. Figures 4-27 and 4-28 show the two windows.

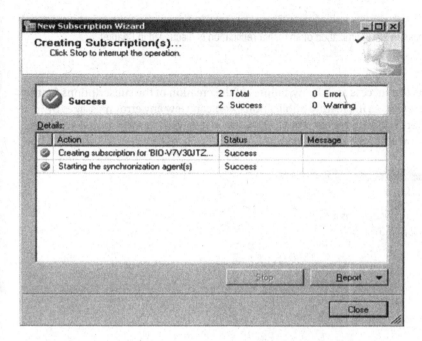

Figure 4-27. *Successful creation of the subscriptions*

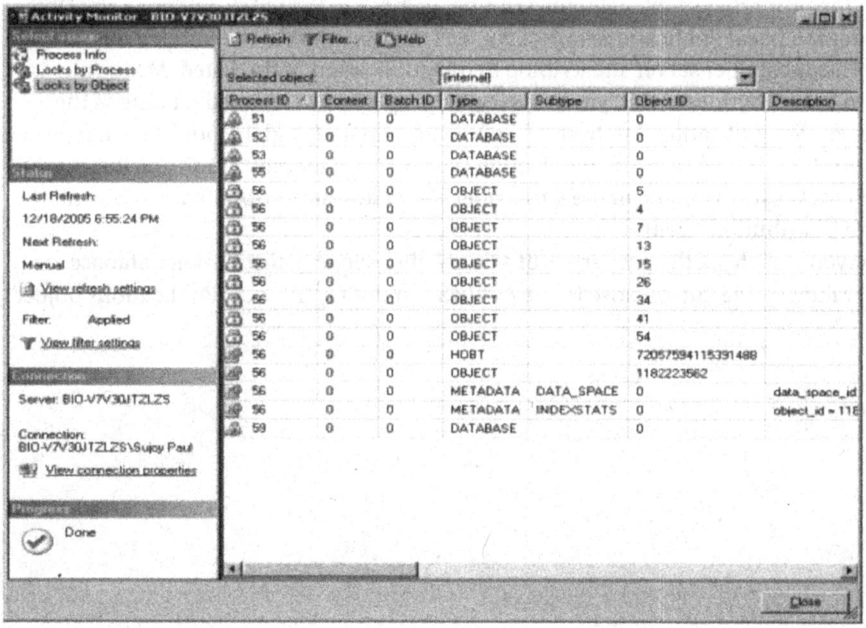

Figure 4-28. *The shared locks held on the database objects by the Snapshot Agent*

Note The use of locks in the optimization of snapshot replication is discussed in Chapter 17.

The wizard lists the success and, if any, failures of the creation of the subscriptions for the publication (Figure 4-27). As in creating publications, you can view any error messages by clicking on the Report button. Save the report, shown in Figure 4-29, in a file so that you have it available later for troubleshooting purposes.

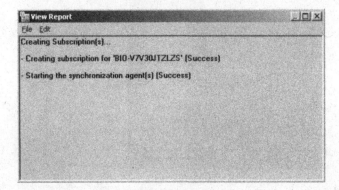

Figure 4-29. *Viewing the report on the creation of the subscription*

To check the properties of the new subscription, go back to the SSMS and open the Object Explorer. Under the Local Publications object you will see the name of the publication that you created. The Subscriber server subscribing to the publication is also listed. Move your cursor close to the subscription, and you will see a pop-up window listing the name of the Publisher server, the publication database, the publication name, and the publication type, as shown in Figure 4-30. In this case, the publication type is snapshot replication. Furthermore, the pop-up window lists the name of the Subscriber server and subscription database and the location of the Distribution Agent.

Similarly, you can check the properties of a Subscriber server, subscription database, or publication by moving the cursor close to the publication under the Local Publications object.

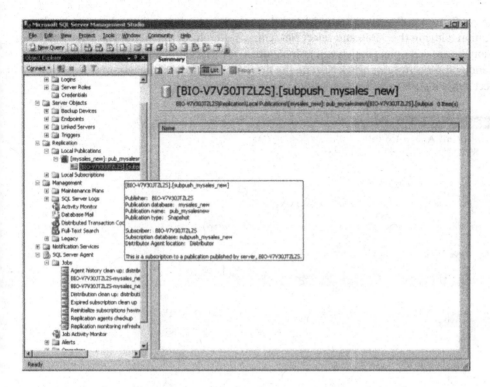

Figure 4-30. *Verifying the properties of a subscription*

Configuring Pull Subscriptions

In the case of push subscriptions, the Publisher server retains control of the distribution of the changes in data. This is not the case with either pull or anonymous subscriptions—for these subscriptions, it is the Subscriber server that requests the Publisher server send the replicated data either at a stipulated time or when required.

Another difference is that the Distribution Agent does not reside on the Distributor server in pull subscription—it resides on the Subscriber server. This causes a significant reduction in the overhead for processing the data changes.

Pull subscriptions also allow each Subscriber server the flexibility to administer the changes. The New Subscription Wizard will remind us of this when we configure a subscription using the GUI method.

To configure a pull subscription, right-click on the Local Subscriptions object under the Replication folder in the SSMS and select New subscription from the menu. The New Subscription Wizard will open (shown earlier in Figure 4-17). The same wizard is used for both push and pull subscriptions. Click Next on the first wizard page, and the wizard will ask you to select either a push or pull subscription, as shown in Figure 4-31.

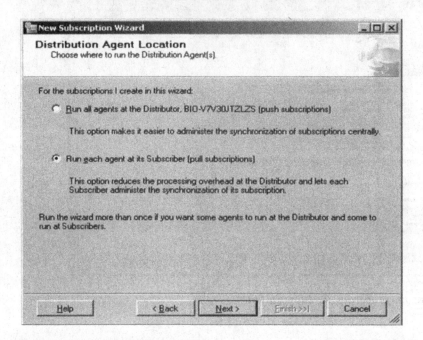

Figure 4-31. *Choosing to use a pull subscription*

The wizard tells you where the Distribution Agent resides, depending on the type of subscription. For this example, choose the pull subscription and click Next.

In the next page, the wizard asks you to select the Subscribers and their corresponding subscription databases, as shown in Figure 4-32. Once you have selected a Subscriber server, the Subscription Database drop-down box identifies the different databases residing on that particular Subscriber.

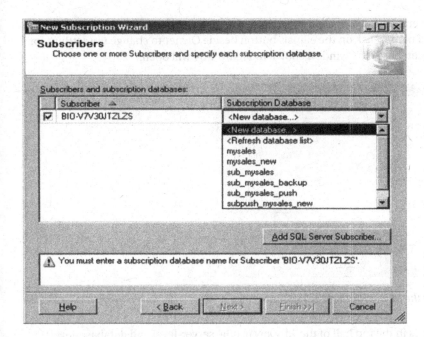

Figure 4-32. *Selecting a subscription database*

Select the New database option to create a new subscription database. The wizard will display the New Database page shown in Figure 4-33 so you can create the new database.

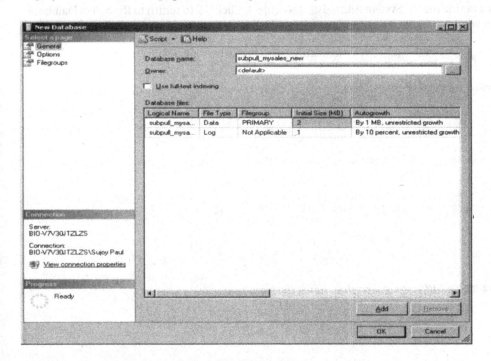

Figure 4-33. *Creating and setting the properties for the new database*

Select the General page and the wizard will ask you for the name of the database. Once you have entered a name, click on the ellipsis button beside Owner to change the settings for the owner for the database. The window shown in Figure 4-34 will open.

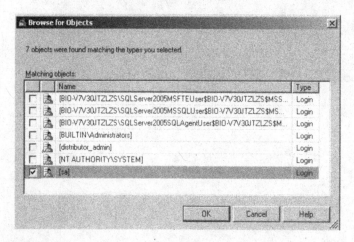

Figure 4-34. *Setting the owner for the new database*

The object types in the top half of the window list the server-level and database-level security settings for the SQL Server. You can select the type of object owner that you want for the database, which in this example is Logins.

In the lower half of the window, click the Browse button. The window shown in Figure 4-35 will open, listing the names of the objects that match the Login type. Scroll down and check the box beside the sa (System Administrator) object. Click OK to return to the Select Database Owner window (Figure 4-34).

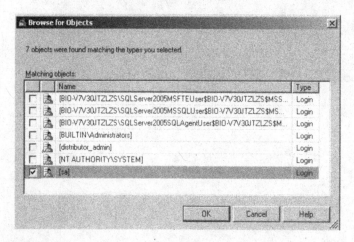

Figure 4-35. *The different objects that match the login type*

In the Select Database Owner window, you will now see that the "sa" object is in the list. Click OK, and the wizard will take you back to the New Database window (Figure 4-33) where you can now see that the database owner is "sa."

If you select the Options page in the New Database window, as shown in Figure 4-36, and scroll to the bottom of the page, you will see that the database allows you to do both read and write operations—the Database Read-Only property has been set to False.

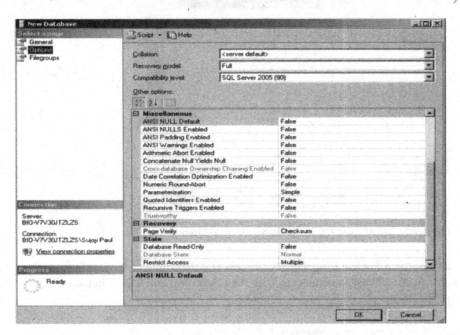

Figure 4-36. *Setting the Database Read-Only option to True will make the database read-only for Subscriber servers*

For subscribing servers using snapshot replication, if read-only and latency are integral parts in the design, you would set Database Read-Only to True. However, in my case, I am the only one who has access to the database, so I set it to False. Click OK to return to the Subscribers page of the New Subscription Wizard (Figure 4-32).

In the Subscribers page, you will now see that the name of the subscription database is listed, as shown in Figure 4-37. If you wish, you can add additional Subscribers by clicking the Add SQL Server Subscriber button. Click Next to continue to the next wizard page.

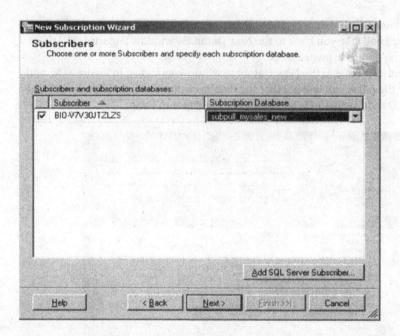

Figure 4-37. *The newly added subscription database is now listed*

The wizard will now ask you to specify the process and the connection parameters that the Distribution Agent will use to connect to both the Distributor and Subscriber servers, as shown in Figure 4-38.

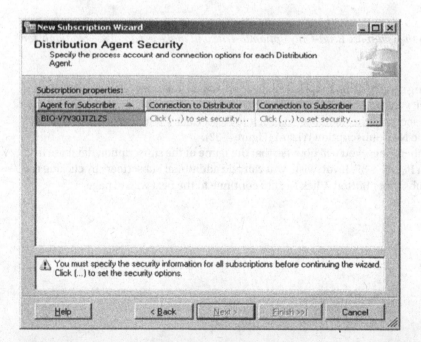

Figure 4-38. *Configuring the security settings for the Distribution Agent to communicate with the Distributor and the Subscriber servers*

In this case, the Publisher, Distributor, and Subscriber servers all reside on the same machine, and the Distribution Agent is on the Subscriber server. Click the ellipsis button beside the Connection to Subscriber column to access the connection settings shown in Figure 4-39.

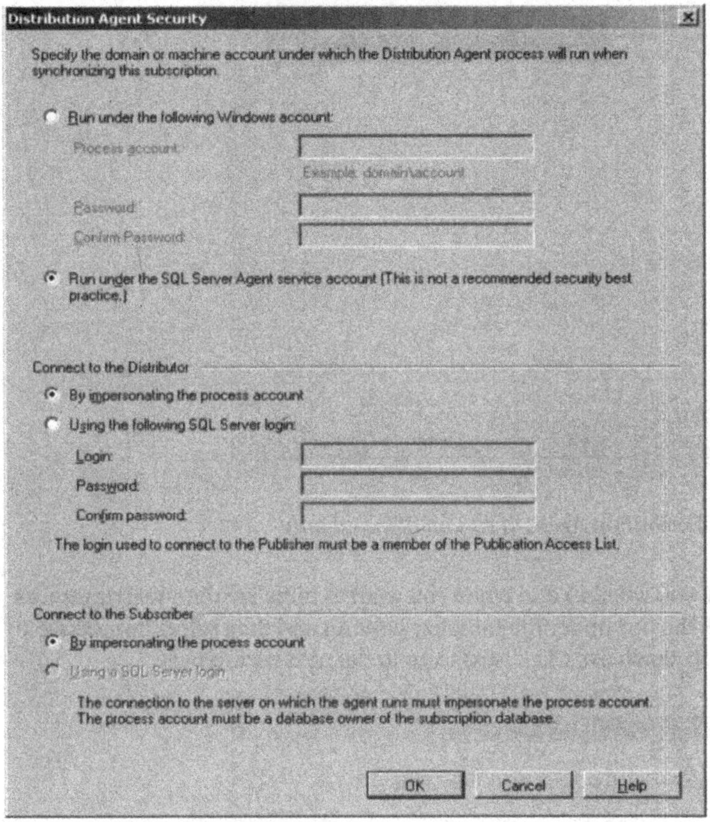

Figure 4-39. *Setting the connection parameters for the Distribution Agent to communicate with the Distributor and Subscriber servers*

Configure the settings as shown in the figure, and click OK. You will see the changed security settings reflected in the Distribution Agent Security wizard page (Figure 4-38). Click Next to continue.

The wizard will now ask you to schedule the synchronization process. Select the option to have the agent run on demand only, as shown in Figure 4-40. Click Next to continue.

Tip In the earlier section on push subscriptions, the Distribution Agent was located on the Distributor server, and in pull subscriptions it is on the Subscriber server. You can see this difference by comparing Figures 4-23 and Figure 4-40.

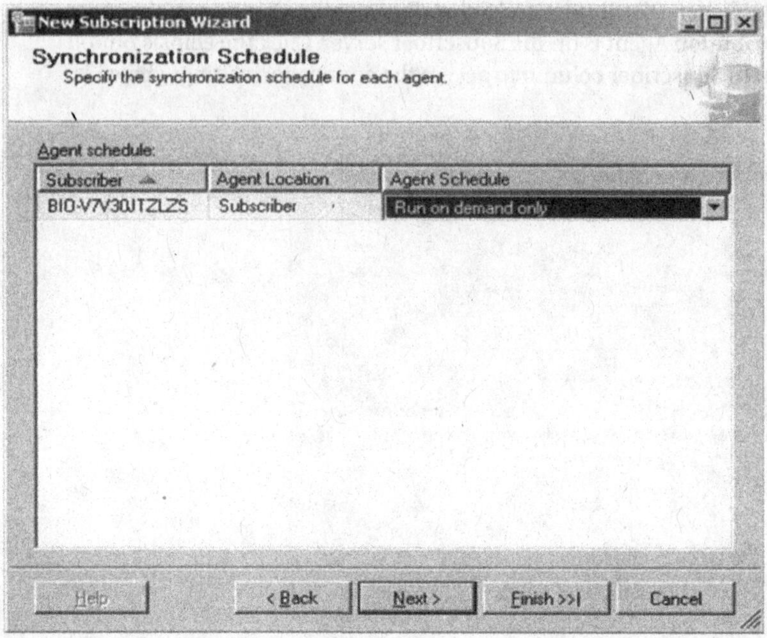

Figure 4-40. *Scheduling the Distribution Agent to run on demand only*

The wizard will now ask you whether and when you want to initialize the subscription, as shown in Figure 4-41. Check the box under the Initialize column and then select Immediately from the Initialize When drop-down list. Click Next to go to the next wizard page.

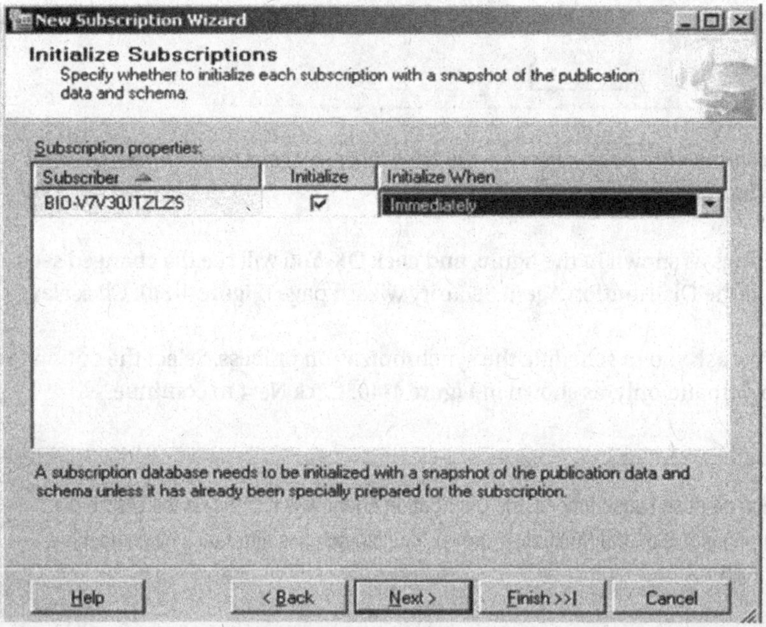

Figure 4-41. *The wizard asks you to create the synchronization immediately*

Note The Distribution Agent does not start to run until the initial synchronization process has started.

In the Wizard Actions page, you can specify what the wizard will create, as shown in Figure 4-42. Check the box to create the subscription. You can also create a script file and save it so that you can either use it as a backup or for troubleshooting purposes. Click Next when you are done.

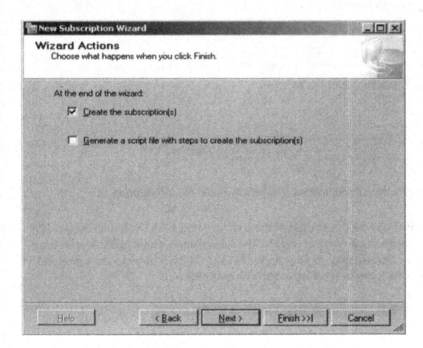

Figure 4-42. *Creating the pull subscription*

The wizard will now summarize the actions it will take to configure the pull subscription, as you can see in Figure 4-43. If need be, you can click the Back button and make any necessary changes.

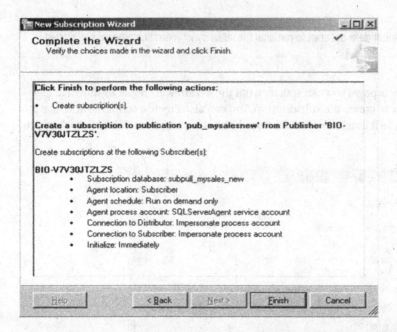

Figure 4-43. *Checking the actions the wizard will take to create the subscription*

Once you are satisfied with the settings of the configuration, click the Finish button. The wizard will churn through the process of creating the subscription, and it will also start the synchronization agent immediately. As you can see in Figure 4-44, it displays the status and any error messages, which can be used for diagnostic purposes.

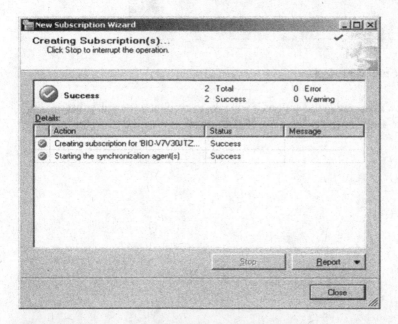

Figure 4-44. *The successful creation of the subscription*

You can click the Report button to view the report, and you can save it as a file or send it by e-mail. I find it is always better to save it as a file so that, in the event of a failure, I can compare the successful creation of subscriptions with those that failed and identify the problems. Figure 4-45 shows how a report is viewed.

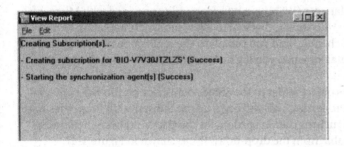

Figure 4-45. *Viewing the report for the successful creation of a subscription*

Starting Synchronization for Pull Subscriptions

Now that we have configured a pull subscription and synchronized the schedule for the snapshot, how can you start the synchronization at your discretion? There are a couple of ways to do this: with the GUI using the SSMS or with T-SQL. In this section, I will show you how to use the GUI method.

Note Chapter 5 focuses on the configuration of snapshot replication using T-SQL, including how to start synchronization for pull subscriptions.

First, expand the Local Subscriptions object in the SSMS, and right-click on the pull subscription that has just been configured. Select View Synchronization Status in the menu. This will open the window shown in Figure 4-46. You can now start the synchronization process by clicking the Start button.

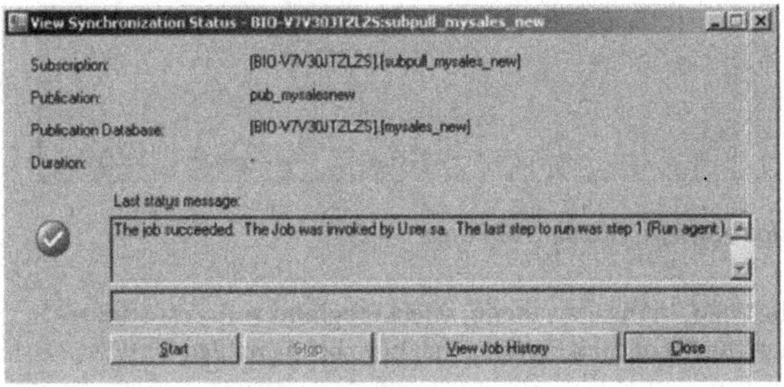

Figure 4-46. *Starting the synchronization process for pull subscription*

You can also synchronize pull subscriptions using a built-in Windows tool, the Windows Synchronization Manager (WSM), as discussed next.

Starting Pull Subscriptions Using the WSM

The Windows Synchronization Manager (WSM) is a Windows utility provided with Microsoft Windows 2000 and later versions. You can use this tool to allow the synchronization of pull subscriptions according to your schedule, and you can allow the replication of data updates before you shut down the computer, or when you log in. You will also see how you can reinitialize or even delete subscriptions.

From the Local Subscriptions object folder in the SSMS, right-click on the pull subscription that you created and select Properties. This will open up the Subscription Properties page for the pull subscription. In the Synchronization section, for the Use Windows Synchronization Manager property, select Enable from the drop-down list as shown in Figure 4-47.

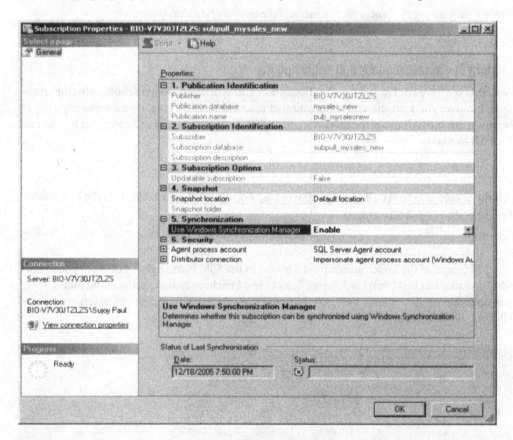

Figure 4-47. *Enabling the Windows Synchronization Manager*

Now you need to open the WSM. In the Start menu, select Programs ➤ Accessories ➤ Synchronize. Figure 4-48 shows the list of subscriptions that have been enabled for WSM.

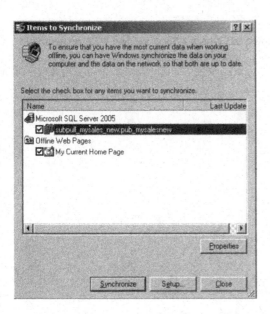

Figure 4-48. *The list of pull subscriptions that have been enabled for WSM*

If you select a subscription and click the Properties button, the window in Figure 4-49 will be displayed. The Identification tab displays the name of the Subscriber server, the subscription database, the Publisher server, the name of the publication, the publication database, and the name of the Distributor server. It also displays the publication type.

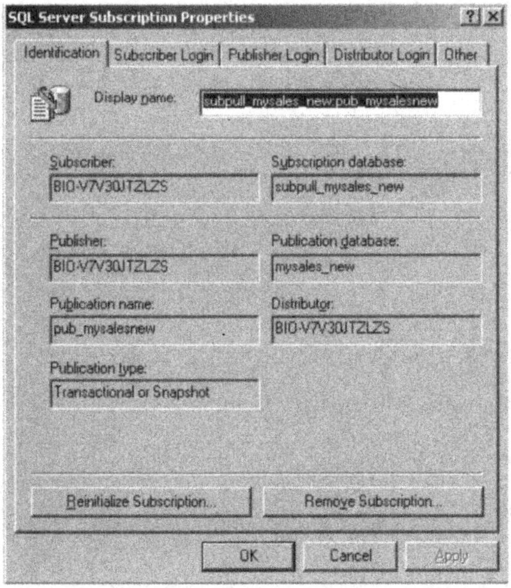

Figure 4-49. *Pull subscription properties*

You can also see the security settings for the Subscriber, Publisher, and Distributor servers by selecting the Login tabs for each. They are shown in Figures 4-50, 4-51, and 4-52, respectively.

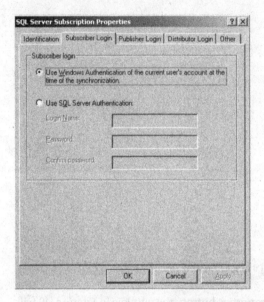

Figure 4-50. *Displaying the Subscriber server's login settings*

Note In addition to displaying the login properties in the WSM, you can also change them.

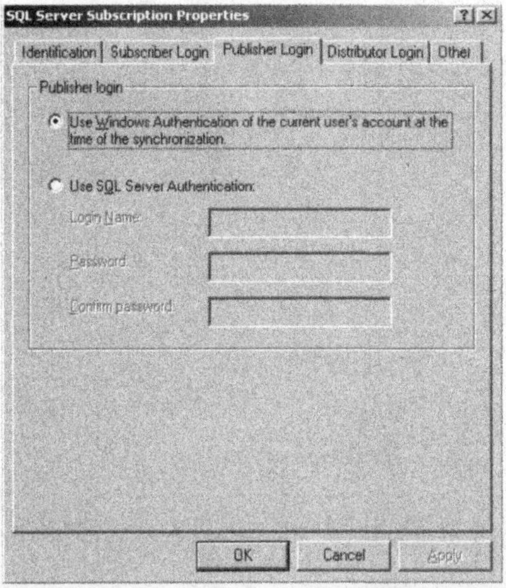

Figure 4-51. *Displaying the Publisher server's login settings*

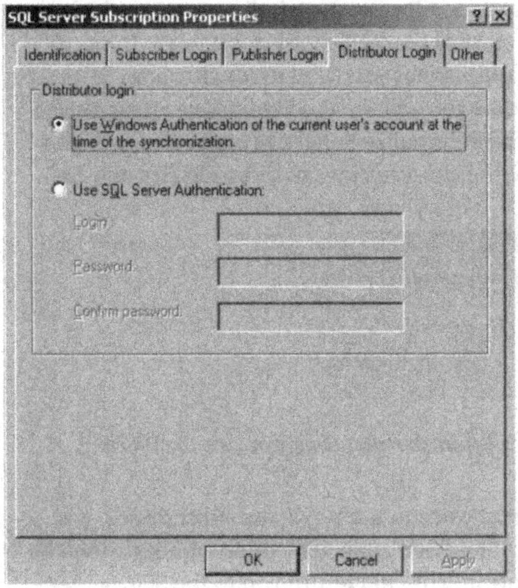

Figure 4-52. *Displaying the Distributor server's login settings*

If you select the Other tab, you will see the login and the query timeout settings for the Distribution Agent, as shown in Figure 4-53. As you can see in the figure, both the update modes, immediate updating and queued updating, have been disabled for the Subscriber server.

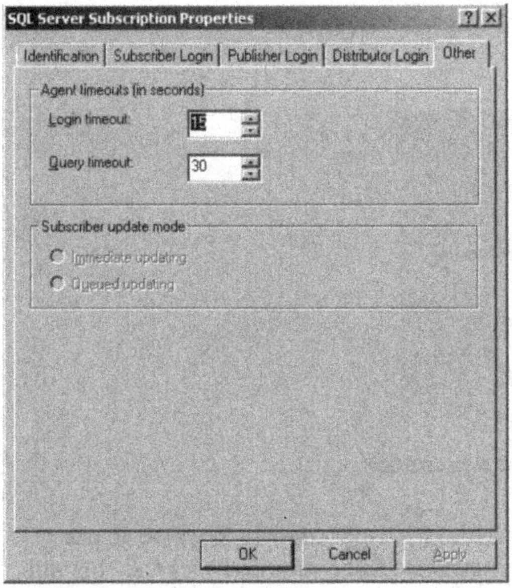

Figure 4-53. *Displaying the agent timeouts and Subscriber server update mode*

Click the OK button in the SQL Server Subscription Properties window to get back to the Items to Synchronize window (Figure 4-48). If you click on the Setup button in the Items to Synchronize window, you can select the subscriptions that you want to synchronize. Select the Identification tab, and at the bottom of the window you will see the Reinitialize Subscription and Remove Subscription buttons. If you click the Reinitialize Subscription button, a dialog box will ask you whether you want to reinitialize the subscription, as shown in Figure 4-54.

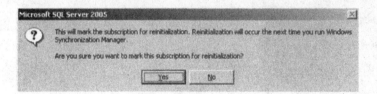

Figure 4-54. *Clicking Yes will reinitialize the subscription the next time you run the WSM*

If you click Yes in this dialog box, the next time you run the WSM, the subscription will reinitialize. If no new articles have been added, the subscription will not reinitialize. Since we have not added any new articles, click the No button. This will return you to the SQL Server Subscription Properties window (Figure 4-49).

■**Note** For snapshot replication, any changes made at the Subscriber server due to reinitialization will be overwritten the next time you run the Snapshot Agent.

Now click the Remove Subscription button. This will display the window shown in Figure 4-55.

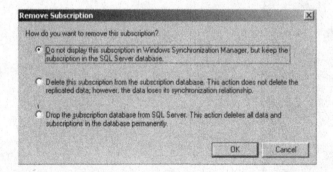

Figure 4-55. *You have three options for removing a subscription*

You can see that there are three options for removing a subscription. Since we do not want to delete the subscription from the WSM, choose the first option and click OK. This will return you to the Items to Synchronize window (Figure 4-48).

Now click the Setup button. The Synchronization Settings window shown in Figure 4-56 will be displayed. As you can see, you can set the synchronization to happen when you log on or off or when the machine is idle, or you can change the schedule of the WSM.

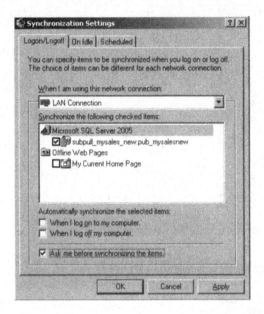

Figure 4-56. *Specifying which subscription you want to synchronize*

Now that we have specified the settings, the subscriptions are ready to pull the data from the publication. Select the Scheduled tab to start the Scheduled Synchronization Wizard of Figure 4-57. Schedule the synchronization and click Next.

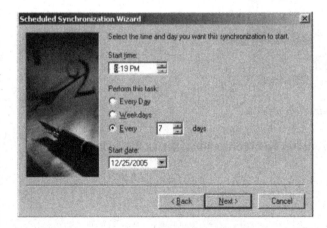

Figure 4-57. *Scheduling the subscription to run on a weekly basis*

You will now be asked to enter a name for the synchronization, as shown in Figure 4-58. Enter a name and click Next.

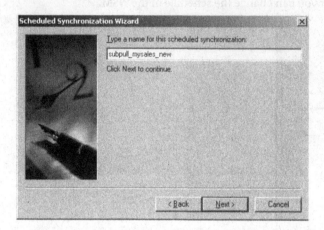

Figure 4-58. *Give a name that you will remember for the scheduled synchronization*

The wizard summarizes the synchronization process as shown in Figure 4-59.

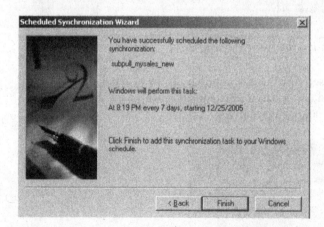

Figure 4-59. *Summary of the synchronization process*

Click Finish and you will see the current synchronization tasks, as shown in Figure 4-60. Click OK.

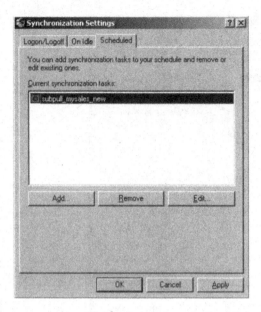

Figure 4-60. *Gives you the current status of the synchronization process*

Now that we have finished configuring the WSM for the pull subscription, go back to the Items to Synchronize window (Figure 4-48) and click the Synchronize button to start the synchronization process.

Adding and Deleting an Article

In the "Configuring Publication" section earlier in this chapter, I showed you how to select the articles in a publication that will be transmitted to the subscribing servers. In this case, both the publishing and the subscribing servers are synchronized so that the data integrity is maintained. Now suppose you needed to add an article to the publication after the synchronization is done. Or maybe you need to drop an article due to some business considerations. This section explains how to add or delete an article once the initial synchronization is complete.

First, select the publication from the Local Publications folder under the Replication object in the SSMS. Then right-click on the publication you want to add the article to or drop the article from, and select Properties. This will open the Publication Properties window shown in Figure 4-61.

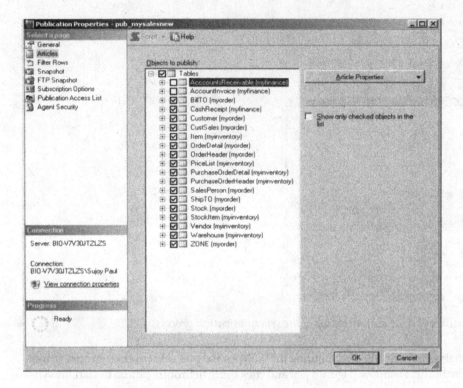

Figure 4-61. *Adding and deleting the articles in a publication*

Select Articles from the left pane and you will see the Objects to Publish list, as shown in the figure. To add an article to the publication, simply uncheck the box that says Show only checked objects in the list. This will list the articles that are not included in the publication, and you can simply check the box beside the tables you want to publish.

If you want to delete any of the articles, just uncheck the box beside the appropriate tables. A dialog box will be displayed, asking you whether you want to drop the article, as shown in Figure 4-62. Click Yes, and the wizard will reinitialize the subscription.

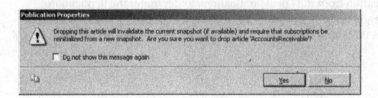

Figure 4-62. *Dropping the articles from a publication requires you to reinitialize the subscription*

Summary

In this chapter, I showed you how to configure a publication for snapshot replication and how to set up push and pull subscriptions for snapshot publication using the GUI. I also discussed setting up pull subscriptions using the WSM.

- All the different editions of SQL Server support snapshot replication.

- You first configure the publication, then the Subscriber server, and finally the subscription.

- By default, when you configure a subscription, the wizard selects a push subscription.

- You can also use the GUI to configure pull subscriptions.

- Only after the synchronization has been initialized will the Distribution Agent run.

- The Windows Synchronization Manager (WSM) allows the synchronization of subscriptions. This allows pull subscriptions to call for updates from publications at scheduled times.

- Pull subscriptions reduce the overhead associated with push subscriptions.

- The Use Windows Synchronization Manager option must be enabled in the Subscription Properties window for the pull subscription.

- It is possible to add or delete articles after the initial synchronization.

In the next chapter, I will show you how to use T-SQL to configure the publication and push and pull subscriptions, and to add and drop articles. Understanding the configuration of the publication and the subscription using the GUI method is important, as it will help you better understand the implementation of the publication and subscription of snapshot replication using T-SQL.

Quick Tips

- The Snapshot Agent makes two connections: one to the Publisher server and the other to the Distributor server.

- You can check whether the process account is a member of PAL by selecting the Publication Access List in the Publication Properties of the publication object in the SSMS.

- Save the reports on the success or failure of creating both publications and subscriptions. This will help in future troubleshooting.

■ ■ ■

CHAPTER 5

Configuring Snapshot Replication Using T-SQL

Both transactional and merge replication use the Snapshot Agent for the initial synchronization, which is essential for maintaining database consistency and integrity on both the Publisher and Subscriber servers. It is crucial that you understand the steps involved in snapshot replication regardless of which type of replication you are using.

Chapter 4 showed how to configure snapshot replication with the GUI, so in this chapter we will first use T-SQL to drop the publications and subscriptions that were configured in Chapter 4. We will then configure publications and subscriptions using the T-SQL method.

On completing this chapter, you will know how to use T-SQL to do the following:

- Drop subscriptions and publications

- Configure snapshot replication

- Configure publication

- Configure both push and pull subscriptions

Dropping Subscriptions and Publications

If you are reading this book sequentially, you probably have configured the publication and the subscriptions using the GUI method described in Chapter 4. If you now want to use the T-SQL method on the same set of publications for the same set of subscriptions, you will need to drop those publications and subscriptions. Alternatively, you can use T-SQL to configure the publications and subscriptions on an alternate set of articles.

I am assuming that you have set up the Distributor and Publisher servers as I configured them in Chapter 2. I explained how to drop the Publisher, then the distribution database, and finally the Distributor server in Chapter 2 (in the "To GUI or Not to GUI" sidebar). In the following sections, I will show you how to drop publications and subscriptions for snapshot replication.

You need to drop the subscriptions first and then the publications. If the publication has one or more subscriptions, you will not be able to drop the publication.

Dropping a Pull Subscription

To drop a pull subscription, you essentially need to execute two steps. The third is optional.

1. Execute the sp_droppullsubscription stored procedure on the subscription database on the Subscriber server.

2. Execute the sp_dropsubscription stored procedure on the publication database on the Publisher server.

3. Optionally, drop the Subscriber server using the sp_dropsubscriber stored procedure, specifying the name of the Subscriber server for the @subscriber parameter.

■**Note** In this case, I do not want to drop the Subscriber server, so I did not follow the third step. However, this is the stored procedure to use if you need to.

Now that you know what's involved in dropping a pull subscription, look at Listing 5-1, which performs the first two steps in the preceding list. As you can see from the listing, the script needs to be executed from the distribution database initially.

Listing 5-1. *Dropping a Pull Subscription*

```
/* Execute this on the Distributor server on the distribution database.
The Distributor server is on the same machine as the Publisher server */

use distribution
go

/*Declare a table variable */

declare @subscription_pull table
(publisher_id smallint,
publisher_db sysname,
subscriber_db sysname,
subscription_type int,
sync_type tinyint,
status tinyint);

/* Insert data into the table variable from the MSsubscriptions table in the
distribution database */

insert into @subscription_pull select
publisher_id,
publisher_db,
subscriber_db,
subscription_type,
```

```
sync_type,
status from distribution..MSsubscriptions
where subscription_type=1 and status =2

/* Check the data of the @subscription_pull table variable */

select * from @subscription_pull

/* Declare table variable that will store the Publisher, the publication database,
the type of publication, and the name of the publication
using sp_helpsubscription_properties */

declare @subscriberinfo table
(publisher sysname,
publisher_db sysname,
publication_type int,
publication sysname);

/* Insert the data into the @subscriberinfo table variable */

insert into @subscriberinfo
exec sp_helpsubscription_properties

/* Check the data for the @subscriberinfo table variable */
select * from @subscriberinfo

/* Execute on the Subscriber on the subscription db - use the name of the Publisher,
the publication database, and the name of the publication*/

exec sp_droppullsubscription 'BIO-V7V30JTZLZS','mysales_new','pub_mysalesnew'

/* Finally, on the Publisher server on the publication database, remove the
subscription for the Publisher*/

exec sp_dropsubscription 'pub_mysalesnew','all', 'BIO-V7V30JTZLZS'
go
```

What this script does is create a table variable called @subscription_pull that will retain the information from the MSsubscriptions table in the distribution database. This table contains a row for each of the published articles in a subscription that is serviced by the local Distributor server. The information we want is the name of the publication database and the subscription database, the type of subscription, the synchronization type, and the status of the subscriptions. In this case, you can see that I set the subscription_type to 1, which indicates a pull subscription, and the status to 2, which means that the subscription is still active. We want to delete active, pull subscriptions. Then the script ensures that the data for the publisher_id, publisher_db, subscriber_db, subscription_type, sync_type, and status is correct by retrieving all of them from the @subscription_pull table variable.

Next, we need to know the name of the Publisher server, the publication database, and the name of the publication for snapshot replication. A table variable called @subscriberinfo retrieves this data by using the sp_helpsubscription_properties stored procedure. The script then drops the subscription by executing the sp_droppullsubscription stored procedure on the subscription database on the Subscriber server. The parameters that we need to specify are the names of the Publisher server, the publication database, and the publication to which the subscription is enabled.

Now that we have dropped the subscription from the Subscriber server, we need to remove the subscription that is enabled on the Publisher server. This is done by executing the sp_dropsubscription stored procedure on the publication database on the Publisher server, specifying the name of the publication and the name of the Subscriber server. To delete all the articles, use a value of all for the @article parameter. Since we are executing this on the publication database, we do not need to specify the name of the Publisher server.

So what are the security permissions for executing all these stored procedures? In the case of sp_droppullsubscription, you need to be a member of the sysadmin fixed server role or the user who created the pull subscription. If you are a member of the db_owner fixed database role, you can execute it only if you also created the pull subscription. To execute the sp_dropsubscription stored procedure, you have to be either a member of the sysadmin fixed server role, the db_owner fixed database role, or the user who created the subscription. To execute the sp_helpsubscription_properties stored procedure, you need to be either a member of the sysadmin fixed server role or the db_owner fixed database role.

Dropping a Push Subscription

Dropping a push subscription is quite similar to dropping a pull subscription. You only have to take a single step to delete a push subscription: Execute the sp_dropsubscription stored procedure on the publication database on the Publisher, specifying the name of the publication and the name of the Subscriber server.

Listing 5-2 shows you how to delete a push subscription.

Listing 5-2. *Dropping a Push Subscription*

```
/* Execute this on the Distributor server on the distribution database. The
Distributor server is on the same machine as the Publisher server */

use distribution
go

/*Declare a table variable */

declare @subscription_push table
(publisher_id smallint,
publisher_db sysname,
subscriber_db sysname,
subscription_type int,
sync_type tinyint,
status tinyint);
```

```
/* Insert data into the table variable from the MSsubscriptions table in
the distribution database */

insert into @subscription_push select
publisher_id, publisher_db, subscriber_db, subscription_type, sync_type,
status from distribution..MSsubscriptions
where subscription_type=0 and status =2

/* Check the data of the @subscription_push table variable */

select * from @subscription_push

/* Declare table variable that will store the Publisher and the
Subscriber information from the MSSubscriber_info table */

declare @subscriberinfo table
(publisher sysname,
subscriber sysname);

/* Insert the data into the @subscriberinfo table variable */

insert into @subscriberinfo
select publisher, subscriber from distribution..MSsubscriber_info

/* Check the data for the @subscriberinfo table variable */
select * from @subscriberinfo

/* Finally, on the Publisher server on the publication database
remove the subscription for the Publisher*/

exec sp_dropsubscription 'pub_mysalesnew','all', 'BIO-V7V3OJTZLZS'
go
```

The steps in this script are pretty much the same as in Listing 5-1. The first part of the script is executed on the distribution database to find all the publications that support push subscription. Notice the difference in the value for the subscription_type parameter, which here is set to 0, for push subscriptions.

Listing 5-1 used sp_helpsubscription_properties, and in this case we use MSsubscriber_info from the distribution database to find the names of the Publisher and Subscriber servers and store them in a table variable. The MSsubscriber_info table stores a row for each pair of Publisher and Subscriber servers, and the Distribution Agent (in the local Distributor server), pushes the subscriptions to the Subscriber server.

We then execute the sp_dropsubscription stored procedure on the publication database on the Publisher server.

> **Tip** To remove the replication metadata for a subscription dropped at a Subscriber server, you can use the `sp_subscription_cleanup` stored procedure on the subscription database. The parameters that you must specify are the names of the publication database and the publication. If you do not specify the name of the publication database, you will get an error message.

The next step in the process is to drop the publication.

Dropping a Publication

Now that we have dropped the subscriptions, we need to drop the required publications. In this case, I will use `sp_droppublication` to remove one publication at a time.

There is only one step to removing a publication with `sp_droppublication`, as shown in Listing 5-3.

Listing 5-3. *Dropping a Publication*

```
/* Use the distribution database to find the name of the publication */

Use distribution
Go

Select * from MSpublications
Go

/* Use the publication database */
Use mysales_new
Go

/* Finally drop the publication */
sp_droppublication 'pub_mysalesnew'
```

As you can see, this script retrieves the names of the publications to be dropped from the MSpublications system table in the distribution database. It then drops the publication by executing the stored procedure on the publication database. If the MSpublications system table contained a list of several publications, and you wanted to drop all the publications, you would have to execute the `sp_removedbreplication` stored procedure.

> **Note** Deleting a publication does not remove the published objects from the subscription database or the publication database. That is why the subscription was dropped before the publication. If you removed the publication first, and then wanted to drop the objects in the publication database, you would need to use the DROP <object> statement.

Configuring a Publication Using T-SQL

As you will recall, these are the steps in preparing for snapshot replication:

- Create a Distributor server.
- Create a distribution database.
- Create a Publisher server.
- Create one or more publications.
- Add articles to the publications.
- Create a Subscriber server.
- Create one or more subscriptions.

Chapter 2 covered the configuration of the Distributor server, distribution database, and Publisher server. Chapter 4 then explained how to configure the publication and subscription using the GUI method; this chapter will show you how to configure them using the T-SQL method.

These are the steps involved in binding the publication database to the Publisher server:

1. Create a publication using the sp_addpublication stored procedure.

2. Create an agent for the publication—in this case, a Snapshot Agent—by using sp_addpublication_snapshot.

3. Grant publication access to the users with the sp_grant_publication_access stored procedure.

4. Create articles for publication using sp_addarticle.

Creating a Publication

The script in Listing 5-4 enables the database for replication using the sp_replicationdboption stored procedure, and then adds the publication to the Publisher server.

Listing 5-4. *Creating a Snapshot Publication*

```
/* Enable the database for replication */

use master
exec sp_replicationdboption @dbname = 'mysales_new',
@optname = 'publish',
@value = 'true'
go
```

```
/* Add the snapshot publication */

use [mysales_new]

exec sp_addpublication @publication = 'pub_mysalesnew',
@description = 'Snapshot publication of database ''mysales_new''
from Publisher ''SHW-TOR-WS039''.',
@sync_method = 'native',
@repl_freq = 'snapshot',
@status = 'active',
@allow_push = 'true',
@allow_pull = 'true',
@allow_anonymous = 'false',

@immediate_sync = 'false',
@allow_sync_tran = 'false',
@autogen_sync_procs = 'false',
@retention = 336,
@allow_queued_tran = 'false',
@snapshot_in_defaultfolder = 'true',
@compress_snapshot = 'false',
@allow_dts = 'false',
@allow_subscription_copy = 'false',
@add_to_active_directory = 'false',
@replicate_ddl=1
go
```

This script first uses the sp_replicationdboption stored procedure to set up the database for replication. The @value parameter is set to true to enable the database to publish all the publications. The @optname parameter specifies the kind of replication—I assigned it the value publish so that all the publications can be used. Bear in mind that you need to be a member of the sysadmin fixed server role to execute this stored procedure. You can execute it either on the Publisher server or on the Subscriber server.

Next, the script adds the publication by executing the sp_addpublication stored procedure. You can execute it in the publication database on the Publisher server. The script first assigns a name to the publication that is unique to the database using the @publication parameter. The @sync_method parameter is set to native mode, which tells the bcp utility to use the native format for generating the data from the tables. This is appropriate if you are using SQL Server on both the Publisher and Subscriber servers.

Tip For non-SQL Server Publishers, like Oracle, you need to use the character format for the @sync_method parameter.

The @repl_freq parameter specifies how frequently the replicated data will be sent. This parameter can have two values: continuous and snapshot. For snapshot replication, the frequency is set to snapshot, which means that the Publisher server will forward the transactions when the synchronization is scheduled. You can also see that the @status parameter is set to active, which means that the data is immediately available for replication.

This publication can also be used for both push and pull subscriptions, since both the parameters @allow_push and @allow_pull have been set to true. The subscription server will not be using anonymous subscriptions, so the @allow_anonymous parameter is set to false. The @immediate_sync parameter has also been set to false, which means that the synchronization files will not be created every time the Snapshot Agent runs—they will be generated only if new subscriptions are created. This is what we want, because snapshot generation creates significant overhead and affects performance.

Tip If @immediate_sync is set to true, you also need to run a stand-alone Distribution Agent for the publication by setting the @independent_agent parameter to true. Setting the @independent_agent parameter to false (the default) means the publication will use a shared agent rather than a stand-alone Distribution Agent. A stand-alone Distribution Agent serves only one subscription, whereas a shared agent serves many subscriptions.

Note that the retention time is 336 hours, which is the default for subscription activity. Setting it to 0 sets the retention time to infinity, and the Distribution Agent will not clean up the messages if the Subscriber servers do not pick them up.

The script also specifies that the snapshot is stored in the default folder by setting the @snapshot_in_defaultfolder parameter to true. If you want the snapshot to be stored in another location in addition to the default location, you can use the @alt_snapshot_folder parameter and specify the other location. A snapshot stored at an alternative location like this can be compressed by setting the @compress_snapshot parameter to true; snapshots in the default location cannot be compressed. There is a limit to how much you can compress a snapshot when using the CAB format, and you can only do so if the total size of the snapshot does not exceed 2 GB. The use of CAB format in generating snapshots is discussed in Chapter 6.

Note Compressed snapshots are uncompressed where the Distribution Agent is located. So in the case of pull subscriptions, the uncompressing is done at the Subscriber server.

The @replicate_ddl parameter in the script is set to 1, which means that changes in the schema in the publication database can be replicated—this is the default value for SQL Server. Note that you can disable this setting on the fly by setting the parameter to 0. If you were to set the parameter to 0, you would not be able to replicate any schema changes.

So, if you want to see whether the publication has been configured to replicate any schema changes, right-click on the publication in the Local Publication object in the SSMS, and select Properties. This will open the Publication Properties window. Select the Subscription Options page, and you will see that the Replicate schema changes option has been set to True, as shown in Figure 5-1.

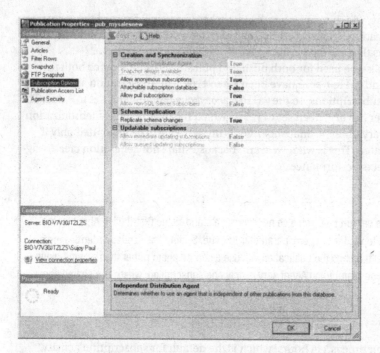

Figure 5-1. *The replication of schema changes is enabled by default.*

Creating a Snapshot Agent

Once you have run the script in Listing 5-4 and created a publication on the Publisher server, it is time to create the Snapshot Agent for the publication. This is done by executing the sp_addpublication_snapshot stored procedure on the publication database. Listing 5-5 shows you how.

Listing 5-5. *Creating the Snapshot Agent*

```
/* Execute the stored procedure under the current publication database*/

use [mysales_new]

exec sp_addpublication_snapshot @publication = 'pub_mysalesnew',
@frequency_type = 8,
@frequency_interval = 4,
@frequency_relative_interval = 1,
@frequency_recurrence_factor = 1,
@frequency_subday = 1,
@frequency_subday_interval = 1,
@active_start_time_of_day = 0,
@active_end_time_of_day = 235959,
@active_start_date = 0,
@active_end_date = 0,
```

```
@job_login = null,
@job_password = null,
@publisher_security_mode = 1
go
```

This stored procedure creates a Snapshot Agent for the specified publication. Again, the name of the publication is specified using the @publication parameter. The @frequency_type parameter specifies when the agent is executed—the value of 8 means that the Snapshot Agent is run on a weekly basis. Table 5-1 lists the frequency types for the execution of the Snapshot Agent.

Table 5-1. *Frequency Type for the Snapshot Agent*

Value	Description
1	Run once
4	Run daily
8	Run weekly
16	Run on a monthly basis
32	Run monthly, relative to the frequency interval
64	Whenever the SQL Server Agent starts
128	Run whenever the computer is idle

The @frequency_interval parameter specifies the days on which the agent will run. This value for @frequency_interval is dependent on the frequency set by the @frequency_type parameter. The @frequency_type in this case has been set to run weekly. If the @frequency_type is set to 8, the values for @frequency_interval can be 1 (Sunday), 2 (Monday), 4 (Tuesday), 8 (Wednesday), 16 (Thursday), 32 (Friday), or 64 (Sunday). Here the @frequency_interval has been set to 4, meaning that it will run every Tuesday. The @frequency_relative_interval parameter specifies the date the Snapshot Agent runs, depending on the value that has been set for @frequency_interval.

Note For a complete description of the parameters for the creation of the Snapshot Agent, type **sp_addpublication_snapshot** on BOL.

The frequency with which the execution of the Snapshot Agent recurs is set by @frequency_recurrence_factor, which has been set to 1. The @frequency_recurrence_factor is determined by the value of the @frequency_type parameter.

The @frequency_subday parameter can have values of 1, 2, 4, or 8, which correspond to once, second, minute, and hour, respectively. The parameter has been set to 1, which means that it will run only once. The @frequency_subday_interval is the number of intervals for the @frequency_subday between each execution of the agent, which specifies the interval for the frequency sub-day.

The time when the Snapshot Agent starts is specified by the `@active_start_time_of_day` parameter, which is set to 0 in this script, meaning that the schedule starts at 12:00 a.m. Sunday. The schedule ends at 11:59:59 p.m., which is equivalent to the value of 235959 set for the `@active_end_time_of_day` parameter. The date on which the Snapshot Agent first runs is specified by the `@active_start_date` parameter, and the date when it ends by the `@active_end_date` parameter.

The `@job_login` and the `@job_password` parameters have been set to null for the Snapshot Agent, which means it uses the Windows account (`@publisher_security_mode = 1`). If the `@publisher_security_mode` is set to 0, it means that the Snapshot Agent is using the SQL Server authentication to connect to the Distributor server.

■**Note** Do not specify the login parameters in the script file for security reasons. It is recommended that you prompt the user for the login and the password. I have specified the values for the `@job_login` and `@job_passwords` in Listing 5-5 to exemplify the process.

Granting Publication Access

Having set up the Snapshot Agent, we now need to grant publication access to the users by using the `sp_grant_publication_access` stored procedure. This is shown in Listing 5-6.

Listing 5-6. *Granting Publication Access to the Users*

```
/* Grant access to the current publication database and execute
on the publication database*/

exec sp_grant_publication_access @publication = 'pub_mysalesnew',
@login = 'distributor_admin'
go
exec sp_grant_publication_access @publication = 'pub_mysalesnew',
@login = 'sa'
go
```

This stored procedure adds a login to the publication access list (PAL). As you can see, this script gives login permissions to sa and distributor_admin for the specified publication. This stored procedure is executed on the publication database on the Publisher server, and to execute it you need to be a member of the sysadmin fixed server role or have a db_owner fixed database role.

Creating Articles for Publication

Now that we have finished setting up the publication on the Publisher server, have added the Snapshot Agent, and have granted publication access to the users, we need to add the articles to the publication.

The `sp_addarticle` stored procedure is executed on the publication database in the Publisher server. It creates an article and then adds it to the publication. Listing 5-7 demonstrates how you can use it.

Listing 5-7. *Adding the Articles to the Publication*

```
/* Adding each of the articles in the current publication */

use [mysales_new]
exec sp_addarticle @publication = 'pub_mysalesnew',
@article = 'AccountsReceivable',
@source_owner = 'myfinance',
@source_object = 'AccountsReceivable',
@type = 'logbased',
@description = null,
@creation_script = null,
@pre_creation_cmd = 'drop',

@destination_table = 'AccountsReceivable',
@destination_owner = 'myfinance',
@vertical_partition = 'false'
go

use [mysales_new]
exec sp_addarticle @publication = 'pub_mysalesnew',
@article = 'AccountInvoice',
@source_owner = 'myfinance',
@source_object = 'AccountInvoice',
@type = 'logbased',
@description = null,
@creation_script = null,
@pre_creation_cmd = 'drop',

@destination_table = 'AccountInvoice',
@destination_owner = 'myfinance',
@vertical_partition = 'false'
go

use [mysales_new]
exec sp_addarticle @publication = 'pub_mysalesnew',
@article = 'BillTo',
@source_owner = 'myorder'
@source_object = 'BillTo',
@type = 'logbased',
@description = null,
@creation_script = null,
@pre_creation_cmd = 'drop',

@destination_table = 'BillTo',
@destination_owner = 'myorder',
@vertical_partition = 'false'
go
```

Note For the purposes of brevity, I haven't included all of the articles in Listing 5-4.

This script first specifies a unique name for the article that will be used in the publication. This is set with the `@article` parameter. Then the owner of the source is specified with the `@source_owner` parameter. The `@source_object` parameter identifies the database object to be published.

Note The `@source_object` parameter has replaced the `@source_table` parameter.

The `@type` parameter specifies that the article is `logbased`, which is the default because no description has been entered for the article.

The `@creation_script` parameter tells you whether you want an optional script that contains the article schema to be executed in creating the article in the subscription. In that case you have to specify the path and the name of the script. Since we do not need it, we set it to `null`. The `@pre_creation_cmd` parameter specifies what the system should do if the object already exists on the Subscriber server. In this case, it will drop the object; the other values that you can specify are `none`, `delete`, and `truncate`.

The `@destination_owner` parameter specifies the name of the subscription owner, and `@destination_table` indicates to which subscription table it should be sent.

Finally, setting the `@vertical_partition` parameter to `false` specifies that there is no vertical filtering and that all columns will be published.

DROPPING AN ARTICLE

In the earlier sections of the chapter, I showed you how to drop a subscription and a publication. Similarly, it is also possible to drop a single article from a snapshot publication. However, you cannot drop an article if a subscription exists for that article.

You can drop an article by executing the `sp_droparticle` stored procedure on the publication database on the Publisher server. The syntax for the code is as follows:

```
sp_droparticle @publication, @article, @ignore_distributor,
@force_invalidate_snapshot, @publisher, @from_drop_publication
```

The @force_invalidate_snapshot parameter is used to invalidate the snapshot. If you drop an article, the snapshot will obviously be invalidated, so setting the value of @force_invalidate_snapshot to 1 will mark the existing snapshot as obsolete if there are existing subscriptions that require a new snapshot. This will cause a new snapshot to be generated for that subscription. Setting the parameter to 0 means that the snapshot will not be invalidated for changes in the article. Should the stored procedure detect any changes that require generating a new snapshot, an error will be generated if a subscription exists and no changes will be made.

The @ignore_distributor and @from_drop_publication parameters are used for internal purposes, and the @publisher parameter is used for non-SQL Server publishers only. As with the other stored procedures, you need to be a member of the sysadmin fixed server role or the db_owner fixed database role to run it.

Dropping an article does not mean that the object (such as a table) will be dropped from the publication and the subscription database. As when dropping a publication, you have to manually drop the database object.

Starting the Snapshot Agent

Now that we have configured the publication, granted users the permissions to access the publication, and added the snapshot and articles, we have one more thing to do before we can generate the snapshot. We need to start the Snapshot Agent. You do this by executing the sp_startpublication_snapshot stored procedure as shown in Listing 5-8.

Listing 5-8. *Starting the Snapshot Agent Job*

```
/* Start the Snapshot Agent and execute this on the publication database*/

exec sp_startpublication_snapshot 'pub_mysalesnew'
```

This stored procedure is executed on the publication database in the Publication server, and it generates the first snapshot for the publication. You have to be a member of the sysadmin fixed server role or db_owner fixed database role in order to execute the stored procedure.

Keep in mind that you can also use this stored procedure to generate the initial snapshot for the other replication types.

Alternatively, you can execute the script shown in Listing 5-9 to find out the name and the replication type for the publication, and then execute the Snapshot Agent.

Listing 5-9. *Running the Snapshot Agent Executable*

```
/* Execute on the distribution database */

use distribution
go

declare @distpub sysname;
set @distpub =(select convert(sysname, serverproperty('servername')))
declare @publisherdatabases table
(pub_id smallint,
pubdb sysname,
id int)
insert into @publisherdatabases(pub_id,pubdb, id)
select publisher_id, publisher_db, id from MSpublisher_databases

if (select top 1 publication_type from MSpublications)<>1
begin
print 'this is not snapshot replication'
end
else
begin
declare @pubname sysname;
declare @pubdb sysname;
declare @cmd varchar(4000);
set @pubname=
(select top 1 b.publication
from @publisherdatabases a, MSpublications b where a.pub_id
=b.publisher_id)
set @pubdb= (select pubdb from @publisherdatabases)
/*end */

/* Execute the Snapshot Agent */
set @cmd=
'"C:\Program Files\Microsoft SQL Server\90\COM\snapshot.exe"
-Publication @pubname -Publisher @distpub -Distributor @distpub
 -DistributorSecurityMode 1'
exec xp_cmdshell '@cmd'
end
```

ENABLING XP_CMDSHELL

Before you run the script in Listing 5-9, you need to enable xp_cmdshell (an extended stored procedure) as follows:

```
/*Execute this on the master database */
Use master
Go

Exec sp_configure 'show advanced options', 1
Go
Reconfigure with override
Go
Exec sp_configure 'xp_cmdshell', 1
Go
Reconfigure with override
Go
```

This script first checks whether xp_cmdshell is enabled or not by executing the sp_configure stored procedure and setting show advanced options to 1. Then it enables xp_cmdshell if it is not already. You can then check whether it is enabled by executing sp_configure again.

The script in Listing 5-9 initially declares a variable that will store the name of the server that houses both the Distributor and the Publisher servers; then it retrieves the name of the server using the serverproperty function.

Next, a table variable is declared that will store the ID of the Publisher server and the name of the publisher database. These values are retrieved from the system table, MSpublisher_databases, which is in the distribution database. This system table stores one row for each Publisher server and corresponding publication database that is serviced by the local Distributor server. Since both the Publisher and Distributor servers reside on the same machine, we can use this system table.

The system tables used in the distribution database for snapshot replication are discussed in Chapter 7.

Now the script ensures that the publication is used for snapshot replication by retrieving the value for the publication_type column in the MSpublications system table, which is also in the distribution database. This table contains a row for each of the publications that is replicated by the Publisher server. If the value for the publication_type is not set to 1, the publication is not used for snapshot replication, and the script prints out a message to that effect. The publication_type values and the corresponding types of replication are shown in Table 5-2.

Table 5-2. *The Values for the* `publication_type` *Column in the* `MSpublications` *Table*

Value	Replication Type
0	Transactional
1	Snapshot
2	Merge

If the publication is indeed used for snapshot replication, the script then selects the name of the publication.

Finally, the path for the Snapshot Agent and the necessary parameters are stored in the @cmd variable, and it is then run with the xp_cmdshell extended stored procedure.

Notice in the listing that if you knew the name of the publication database and the corresponding name of the Publisher and Distributor servers, you could have simply executed the following code from the command prompt:

```
"C:\Program Files\Microsoft QLServer\90\COM\snapshot.exe" -Publication @pubname
-Publisher @distpub -Distributor @distpub -DistributorSecurityMode 1
```

Ensure that this command is written in one single line.

Configuring a Subscription Using T-SQL

I have shown you how to configure the publication and bind it to the Publisher server, and how to add the articles to the publication and run the Snapshot Agent. In this section, I will show you the next step of the replication process: how to configure the subscription using T-SQL.

As mentioned earlier, there are two kinds of subscriptions: push and pull. We will look at push subscriptions first.

Configuring Push Subscriptions

Push subscriptions are created on the Publisher server, and it is the Publisher that monitors the changes in the publication and propagates them to the Subscriber servers. As such, you need to configure the subscriptions in the Publisher server.

To do this, you essentially need to perform two steps:

1. Add the subscription in the publication database on the Publisher server using the sp_addsubscription stored procedure.

2. Execute the sp_addpushsubscription_agent stored procedure in the publication database on the Publisher server.

Before you do either of these steps, though, it is good practice to verify whether the publication supports push subscriptions. You can check the MSpublications system table in the distribution database, as shown in Listing 5-10.

Listing 5-10. *Checking the Status of the Type of Subscriptions for the Publication*

```
/* Check the allow_push column to see whether the subscription supports
push subscriptions. Execute this on the distribution database*/

use distribution
go
Select publication, publisher_db, publication_type, allow_push from MSpublications
```

The script in Listing 5-10 will produce output like this:

publication	publisher_db	publication_type	allow_push
pub_mysalesnew	mysales_new	1	1

```
(1 row(s) affected)
```

Adding a Subscription to the Publication Database

Now that we have verified that the publication supports push subscriptions, we need to configure the subscription. The first thing to do is add the subscription, as shown in Listing 5-11.

Listing 5-11. *Adding the Push Subscription*

```
/* Run the stored procedure on the publication database that supports
push subscription */

use mysales_new
go

exec sp_addsubscription @publication = 'pub_mysalesnew'
@subscriber = 'BIO-V7V30JTZLZS',
@destination_db ='subpush_mysales_new',
@subscription_type = 'Push',
@sync_type = 'automatic',
@article = 'all',
@update_mode = 'read only',
@subscriber_type = 0
```

The sp_addsubscription stored procedure adds a subscription to the publication so that it is aware of the subscription status. As mentioned earlier, push subscriptions are executed from the Publisher server, which is why this stored procedure is executed on the publication database in the Publisher server. You need to be a member of the sysadmin fixed server role to execute the stored procedure.

This script first specifies the name of the publication (@publication) to be published and the name of the Subscriber server (@subscriber). The name of the subscription database is then assigned using the @destination_db parameter, and the type of subscription—Push—is set in the @subscription_type parameter.

The @sync_type parameter has been set to automatic, which indicates that the schema and the data for the publication are to be sent first to the Subscriber server. All the articles are to be transmitted, as set in the @article parameter.

The @update_mode parameter has been set to read only, which means that the subscription is read-only and that changes made at the Subscriber server are not allowed to be sent back to the Publisher server.

The @subscriber_type parameter is set to the default value of 0, which means that all the subscribing servers are using SQL Server databases. Table 5-3 shows the values and corresponding types of subscribers.

Table 5-3. *Values for the* subscriber_type *Parameter*

Values	Description
0	SQL Server
1	ODBC data source
2	Microsoft Jet database
3	OLE DB provider

Adding a Scheduled Agent Job on the Publisher

Now that we have enabled the subscription on the Publisher server, we need to execute the sp_addpushsubscription_agent stored procedure, as shown in Listing 5-12.

Listing 5-12. *Executing the Agent*

```
/*Execute this code on the publication database */

exec sp_addpushsubscription_agent @publication = 'pub_mysalesnew',
@subscriber = 'BIO-V7V30JTZLZS',
@subscriber_db = 'subpush_mysales_new',
@job_login = null,
@job_password = null,
@subscriber_security_mode = 1,
@frequency_type = 1,
@frequency_interval = 0,
@frequency_relative_interval = 0,
@frequency_recurrence_factor = 0,
@frequency_subday = 0,
@frequency_subday_interval = 0,
@active_start_time_of_day = 0,
@active_end_time_of_day = 0,
@active_start_date = 0,
@active_end_date = 19950101,
@enabled_for_syncmgr = 'False',
@dts_package_location = 'Distributor'
```

This stored procedure is executed on the publication database in the Publisher server. As usual, you need to have either the sysadmin fixed server role or the db_owner fixed database role to run it.

As in previous scripts, the name of the publication is assigned, as are the names of the Subscriber server and subscription database that are to be used for push subscription.

The @job_login and @job_password parameters specify, with default values of null, that the Windows account is used to run the agent and connect to the Distributor server. The @subscriber_security_mode parameter has been set to 1, which indicates that it uses Windows Authentication to connect to the Subscriber server. You can give a name to the job by using the @job_name parameter, provided you are using an existing job, but this script is not.

The @enabled_for_syncmgr parameter has been set to False, which means that the WSM will not be used to synchronize the subscription. The @dts_package_location parameter specifies that the DTS package is located on the Distributor server.

The @frequency_type, @frequency_interval, @frequency_relative_interval, @frequency_recurrence_factor, @frequency_subday, @frequency_subday_interval, @active_start_time_of_day, @active_end_time_of_day, @active_start_date, and @active_end_date parameters are the same as in Listing 5-5, except that here they are applicable to the Subscriber server—see the explanation of these parameters in the "Creating a Snapshot Agent" section. The other difference is that the @frequency_type parameter, in this script, is for the Distribution Agent, whereas in Listing 5-5 it is for the Snapshot Agent.

Configuring Pull Subscriptions

Pull subscriptions are created on the Subscriber server, and the subscriptions must be enabled on the Publisher server. The monitoring of the process is done on the Subscriber server, so the synchronization is done on demand only. This is particularly helpful for Subscriber servers that are not always online, such as sales agents working in the field—they can pull the data down from the central Publisher to their laptop database when they have the opportunity.

Configuring pull subscriptions involves the following steps:

1. Execute the sp_addpullsubscription stored procedure on the Subscriber server to create a pull subscription.

2. Use the sp_addpullsubscription_agent stored procedure to add an agent job to synchronize the pull subscription for the publication.

3. Register the subscription on the Publisher server by using the sp_addsubscription stored procedure.

As in push subscription, it is best to check whether the publication supports pull subscriptions. You can do this by executing the sp_helppublication stored procedure on the Publisher server as shown in Listing 5-13.

Listing 5-13. *Checking Whether the Publication Supports Pull Subscriptions*

```
/*Execute it on the publication database */

sp_helppublication 'pub_mysalesnew'
```

If, on executing this stored procedure, each of the allow_push and allow_pull columns return a value of 1, the publication allows both push and pull subscriptions.

Creating a Pull Subscription and Adding a Scheduled Agent Job on the Subscriber

Now that we know the publication allows pull subscriptions, we need to set the name of the publication, the publication database, and the Publisher server on the Subscriber server. We then need to add the pull subscription and a scheduled agent job to synchronize the pull subscription on the Subscriber server. Listing 5-14 describes the process.

Listing 5-14. *Enabling the Names of the Publication, Publication Database, and Publisher Server on the Subscriber Server*

```
/* Execute the code on the Subscriber server.  Execute this on the
subscription database */

declare @publisher sysname;
declare @publication sysname;
declare @pbdb sysname;

set @publisher='BIO-V7V30JTZLZS';
set @publication = 'pub_mysalesnew';
set @pbdb ='mysales_new';

/* Add the pull subscription on the Subscriber server. Execute this on the
subscription database */

exec sp_addpullsubscription
@publisher=@publisher,
@publication=@publication,
@publisher_db=@pbdb,

@update_mode='read only'

/* Add the Distribution Agent to synchronize the pull subscription.  Execute this
on the subscription database*/

exec sp_addpullsubscription_agent
@publisher=@publisher,
@publication=@publication,
@publisher_db=@pbdb,
@distributor=@publisher
@job_login=null,
@job_password=null
```

After executing the stored procedure shown in Listing 5-13, we know that the publication, pub_mysales_new, supports pull subscription since it returned a value of 1 for the allow_pull column. As a result, in Listing 5-14 we first declare variables that will store the names of the publication, the publication database, and the Publisher server, and then we assign their values.

The sp_addpullsubscription stored procedure then adds the pull subscription. As you can see, this stored procedure is executed on the Subscriber server on the publication database, which is where the pull subscription is to be created. You need to have either the sysadmin fixed server role or the db_owner fixed database role to execute the procedure.

The stored procedure receives the name of the Publisher server, the publication database, and the publication through the @publisher, @publisher_db, and @publication parameters. As for the earlier push subscription, this subscription has been set to read-only.

Now that we have added the pull subscription, we need to synchronize the subscription using the sp_addpullsubscription_agent stored procedure, which is executed on the subscription database. As for the sp_addpullsubscription stored procedure, the names of the Publisher server, the publication database, and the publication are passed through the @publisher, @publisher_db and @publication parameters. Since the Distributor server and the Publisher server reside on the same machine, we can assign the value of the Publisher server to the variable @distributor. The agent is using Windows Authentication. The @job_login and the @job_password parameters are set to null. The values for the parameters correspond to the Windows account under which the agent is running. This was covered in the "Adding a Scheduled Agent Job on the Publisher" section.

Enabling the Subscriptions on the Publisher

The next step in the process is to enable the subscriptions on the Publisher server. This is done by executing the sp_addsubscription stored procedure on the Publisher server as shown in Listing 5-15. I have already discussed the details of using sp_addsubscription in Listing 5-11.

Listing 5-15. *Enabling the Subscriptions on the Publisher Server*

```
/* Execute this on the Publisher server. Execute on the publication database */
/*declare the variables first */

declare @subscriber sysname;
declare @publication sysname;
declare @subdb sysname;
set @subscriber= 'BIO-V7V30JTZLZS';
set @publication ='pub_mysalesnew';
set @subdb ='subpull_mysales_new';

/* Now register the pull subscription */

exec sp_addsubscription
@publication=@publication,
@subscriber=@subscriber,
@destination_db=@subdb,
@article='all',
@subscription_type='pull',
@subscriber_type=0,
@update_mode='read only'
```

Compared to Listing 5-11, the only difference in the use of sp_addsubscription here is that the @subscription_type parameter has been set to pull.

Synchronizing a Pull Subscription

We already know that pull subscriptions usually synchronize on demand. You set up the synchronization by executing the Distribution Agent either from the command prompt or from the SSMS. Listing 5-16 shows you how you can execute the Distribution Agent.

Listing 5-16. *Synchronizing the Pull Subscription Using the Distribution Agent*

```
declare @subscriber sysname;
declare @subdb sysname;
declare @publisher sysname;
declare @pbdb sysname;
declare @distributor sysname;
declare @cmd varchar(1000);

set @subscriber='BIO-V7V30JTZLZS';
set @subdb ='subpull_mysales_new';
set @publisher='BIO-V7V30JTZLZS';
set @distributor = @publisher;
set @pbdb ='mysales_new';
/* Execute the Distribution Agent */

set @cmd=
'"C:\Program Files\Microsoft SQL Server\90\COM\distribution.exe"
-Subscriber @subscriber -SubscriberDB @subdb -Publisher @publisher
-PublisherDB @pubdb -Distributor @distributor -DistributorSecurityMode 1 -Continuous
-SubscriptionStreams 4'
exec xp_cmdshell '@cmd'
go
```

In this script, the variables are set with the values of the Publisher server, the Subscriber server, and their corresponding publication and subscription databases. Next, the same values are set for the Distributor server, since both the Publisher and Distributor servers are on the same machine in this example.

Then, the parameters for the Distribution Agent are stored in a variable called @cmd. The first parameter is Continuous, which means that the Distribution Agent will poll the transactions continuously from the source at intervals, even if there are no transactions waiting to be replicated. The SubscriptionStreams parameter is set to 4, which means there are four connections for the Distribution Agent running in parallel to the Subscriber server.

Finally, the agent is executed using the xp_cmdshell extended stored procedure.

Configuring Anonymous Subscriptions

An anonymous subscription is a kind of pull subscription, so like the pull subscription, the anonymous subscription must be enabled on the Publisher server. These are the steps in configuring an anonymous subscription:

1. Execute the sp_addpullsubscription stored procedure on the Subscriber server to create the anonymous subscription.

2. Schedule the Distribution Agent on the Subscriber server to synchronize the anonymous subscription for the publication by using the sp_addpullsubscription_agent stored procedure.

3. Register the subscription on the Publisher server using the sp_addsubscription stored procedure.

Listing 5-17 shows you how to do all three of these steps.

Listing 5-17. *Configuring an Anonymous Subscription*

```
/* Execute the code on the Subscriber server; execute this on the
subscription database*/

declare @publisher sysname;
declare @publication sysname;
declare @pbdb sysname;

/* Assign values to the variables */

set @publisher='BIO-V7V3OJTZLZS';
set @publication ='pub_mysalesnew_anon';
set @pbdb ='mysales_new';

/* Add the pull subscription on the Subscriber server; execute this on the
subscription database */

exec sp_addpullsubscription
@publisher=@publisher,
@publication=@publication,
@publisher_db=@pbdb,

@update_mode='read only'

/* Add the agent to synchronize the pull subscription; execute this
on the subscription database*/
```

```
exec sp_addpullsubscription_agent
@publisher=@publisher,
@publication=@publication,
@publisher_db=@pbdb,
@distributor=@publisher,
@job_login=null,
@job_password=null

/* Execute sp_addpublication on the Publisher server on the publication database;
execute this on the publication database*/

use mysales_new
go

exec sp_addpublication
@publication='pub_mysalesnew_anon',
@allow_pull='true',
@allow_anonymous='true',
@immediate_sync='true',
@independent_agent='true'
```

The coding for anonymous subscriptions is similar to that for pull subscriptions (see the earlier "Configuring Pull Subscriptions" section), except for the sp_addpublication stored procedure in this listing. The @allow_pull, @allow_anonymous, and @immediate_sync parameters need to be set to true for anonymous subscriptions. When you set the @immediate_sync parameter to true, it means that the synchronization files are created each time the Snapshot Agent runs. You can then run the Distribution Agent at a scheduled time.

Snapshot Replication Stored Procedures

Before closing this chapter, I will summarize the stored procedures and parameters for each type of configuration as a reference.

Table 5-4 lists the stored procedures and parameters for configuring the publication.

Table 5-4. *Procedures for Configuring Publications for Snapshot Replication*

Stored Procedure	Parameters
sp_replicationdboption	@dbname, @optname, @value
sp_addpublication	@publication, @repl_freq =snapshot
sp_addpublication_snapshot	@publication, @frequency_type, @frequency_interval, @job_login, @job_password. For SQL Server Authentication, set @publisher_security_mode=0 and specify @publisher_login and @publisher_password
sp_grant_publication_access	@publication, @login
sp_addarticle	@publication, @article, @type, @source_object, @source_owner
sp_startpublication_snapshot	@publication

Table 5-5 lists the stored procedures and parameters for configuring a push subscription.

Table 5-5. *Procedures for Configuring Push Subscriptions for Snapshot Replication*

Stored Procedure	Parameters
sp_helppublication	@publication
sp_addsubscription	@publication, @subscriber, @destination_db, @subscription_type=push
sp_addpushsubscription_agent	@subscriber, @subscriber_db, @publication, @job_login, @job_password

Table 5-6 lists the stored procedures and parameters for configuring a pull subscription.

Table 5-6. *Procedures for Configuring Pull Subscriptions for Snapshot Replication*

Stored Procedure	Parameters
sp_helppublication	@publication
sp_addpullsubscription	@publisher, @publication
sp_addpullsubscription_agent	@publisher, @publication, @publisher_db, @job_login, @job_password
sp_addsubscription	@publication, @subscriber, @destination_db, @subscriber_type=pull

Table 5-7 lists the stored procedures and parameters for configuring an anonymous subscription.

Table 5-7. *Procedures for Configuring Anonymous Subscriptions for Snapshot Replication*

Stored Procedure	Parameters
sp_addpullsubscription	@publisher, @publication
sp_addpullsubscription_agent	@publisher, @publication, @publisher_db, @job_login, @job_password
sp_addpublication	@publication, @allow_pull, @allow_anonymous, @immeditate_sync
sp_addsubscription	@publication, @subscriber, @destination_type, @subscriber_type=pull

Summary

In this chapter, you learned to use T-SQL to drop both publications and subscriptions that were configured using the GUI method in Chapter 4. You also learned to configure the publication and pull, push, and anonymous subscriptions using the T-SQL method.

By now you should be comfortable using both the GUI and T-SQL methods for configuring snapshot replication. While you can configure snapshot replication and other types of replication using the GUI method, T-SQL will offer you more flexibility, as you have seen in this chapter.

- Drop the pull subscription using the sp_droppullsubscription stored procedure, and drop the push subscription using the sp_dropsubscription stored procedure.

- Drop the publication using the sp_droppublication stored procedure.

- Dropping the publication does not drop the corresponding objects, either in the publication database or in the subscribing database.

- When you drop the subscription, you can clean the replication metadata using the sp_subscription_cleanup stored procedure.

- Publication is configured using the sp_addpublication, sp_addpublication, sp_addpublication_snapshot, sp_grant_publication_access, and sp_addarticle stored procedures.

- The snapshot is uncompressed wherever the Distribution Agent is located. In the case of pull subscriptions, the snapshot is therefore uncompressed in the Subscriber server.

- Pull subscriptions are configured using the sp_addpullsubscription and sp_addpullsubscription_agent stored procedures. Then on the Publisher server you need to register the subscription using the sp_addsubscription stored procedure.

- Anonymous subscriptions are configured using the sp_addpullsubscription stored procedure on the Subscriber server.

- On executing sp_addpullsubscription_agent, the stored procedure creates a scheduling job for synchronization of anonymous subscription, a type of pull subscription.

- Finally, on the Publisher server, you need to register the subscription using the sp_addsubscription stored procedure.

In the next chapter, I will show you how to generate different snapshot types. You will need this added flexibility to circumvent the overhead costs associated with the initial synchronization with snapshot replication.

Quick Tips

- Use the sp_helppublication stored procedure to check whether the publication supports push or pull subscription.

- Dropping a publication or an article does not mean that the corresponding objects are dropped from the publication or the subscription database. You need to manually drop those database objects.

- After dropping the subscription, use the sp_subscription_cleanup stored procedure to remove the replication metadata from the subscription database.

CHAPTER 6

■ ■ ■

Snapshot Generation

Snapshot Agent is used in all three types of replication (snapshot, merge, and transactional), since the initial snapshot is essential for the synchronization between the publication and subscription databases. However, as I have mentioned, heavy network traffic can significantly affect the performance of the generation of the snapshot, which can be alleviated by having large network bandwidth.

To avoid performance problems with snapshot replication, you need to consider the following factors:

- Where snapshot folders are created

- What kind of snapshot folders—default or alternative

- What kind of network you have

- How the snapshots are transmitted and stored

- When the Snapshot Agent should be optimally scheduled

In this chapter, I will explore methods for generating snapshots without causing unnecessary performance problems.

On completing this chapter you will know much more about the following:

- Creating snapshot folders

- Security considerations for snapshot folders

- Different formats of snapshot folders

- Generating snapshots

Locating the Snapshot Folder

The snapshot folder is created by default at the local path of `C:\Program Files\Microsoft SQL Server\MSSQL.1\MSSQL\repldata` when you configure the Distributor server using either the Configure Distribution Wizard or the New Publisher Wizard. The default location for the snapshot folder is on the Distributor server.

To locate your snapshot folder in the Windows Registry Editor, open the Windows Start menu and select Run. Then run the executable Registry Editor by typing **regedt32**. In the left pane, select and open the following entries in the directory tree: HKEY_LOCAL_MACHINE, SOFTWARE, Microsoft, Microsoft SQL Server, 90, MSQL.1, and finally Replication. Select Replication in the left pane, and the right pane will display the path for the snapshot folder in the WorkingDirectory entry, as shown in Figure 6-1.

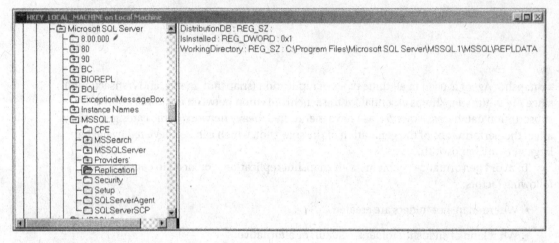

Figure 6-1. *Locating the snapshot folder in the registry*

■**Caution** Do not alter any portion of the registry. Correct registry entries are essential for the proper functioning of the software.

Securing Snapshot Data

The snapshot folder stores the snapshot of the publication. Hence, you must ensure that the appropriate privileges are granted to both the Distribution Agent and the Snapshot Agent.

The Snapshot Agent should have Write privileges, since it needs to perform write operations when it makes a snapshot of the publication. On the other hand, you should give Read permissions to the Distribution Agent, as it needs to read the files generated by the Snapshot Agent in the snapshot folder so that it can transmit the messages to the Subscriber server.

■**Note** If you are using a remote Distributor server or a pull subscription, you need to specify a shared directory that follows the Universal Naming Convention (UNC) path. The path name in that case will be \\computer name\folder name.

To grant permissions to the folder in the local path, right-click on the snapshot folder in Windows Explorer and select Properties. Then open the Security tab. Click the Advanced button to see the permissions granted to the users, as shown in Figure 6-2. You will need to confer with your System Administrator about assigning the appropriate privileges.

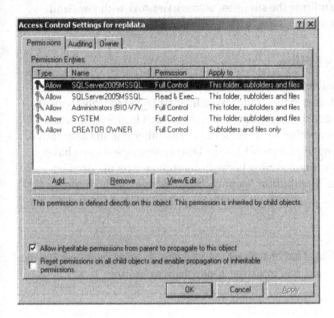

Figure 6-2. *Granting permissions to use the snapshot folder*

If you are specifying permissions for the network path, you can do so by right-clicking on the snapshot folder in Windows Explorer and selecting Properties. Then select the Sharing tab to grant the necessary permissions.

Be aware that if you decide to drop any publications at any stage, SQL Server will try to remove the snapshot folder using the permissions provided under the security context of the SQL Server Services. If the local path is specified, SQL Server will not be able to drop the folder if it does not have Modify privileges. If you are using the network share, then you need to grant Full Control.

Transmitting and Storing Snapshots

You know where the snapshot files are, and now you need to bear in mind the amount of disk space that you will need for all the snapshot files. This will depend on the following:

- The number of articles involved in the publication

- Whether the files are compressed

- Whether the files are placed on remote servers

- The amount of space available in the folder

Once you have decided where the snapshot files should be (which is usually on the Distributor server), you can decide how to move the contents of the folder. You can use the Snapshot Agent to transfer the snapshot, but the overhead costs associated with generating the snapshot from the Publisher server in a default folder and then relocating the folder can be high, particularly if you are transmitting the snapshot across a network with low bandwidth. Fortunately there are alternatives.

Transferring Compressed Files

One option is to compress the writeable snapshot files in the CAB format. However, you cannot compress files that exceed 2 GB, and to use compressed files, you need to store them at alternative locations, since you cannot compress the files in the default location. Alternative locations can be a network drive, on another server, or a CD. (Remember that the alternative folder location is a property of the publication to which the Distribution Agent must have access.) Compressing a file can be time consuming because additional work needs to be done by the Snapshot Agent and the Distribution Agent (or by the Merge Agent for merge replication).

■**Note** If you are storing the snapshot files at both the default and alternative locations, remember that you must store files first in the default location and then copy them to the alternative location.

To compress the files in the folder, open the Local Publications object in the SSMS, right-click on the snapshot publication that you created, and select Properties from the menu. In the Publication Properties window, select the Snapshot page, as shown in Figure 6-3. As you can see in the figure, I have unchecked the default folder so the files will not be compressed in that location. I have instead checked the "Put files in the following folder" check box. Checking the "Compress snapshot files in this folder" check box will compress the files.

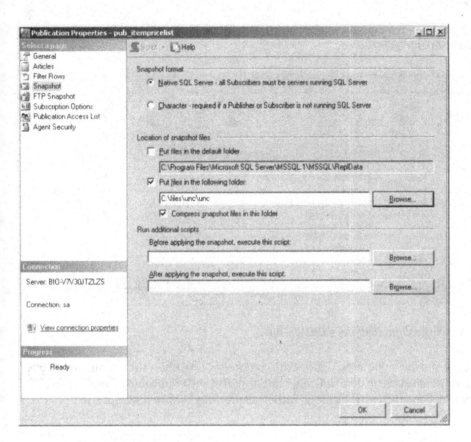

Figure 6-3. *Setting the snapshot folder in CAB format to be compressed*

Click OK, and the dialog box shown in Figure 6-4 will inform you that after the changes are saved you can start the Snapshot Agent to generate a new snapshot. Click Yes, if you want to generate a new snapshot.

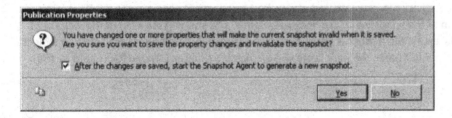

Figure 6-4. *Confirming the changes to the snapshot*

Now if you open WinZip, you will be able to see a list of the compressed files in CAB format, as shown in Figure 6-5.

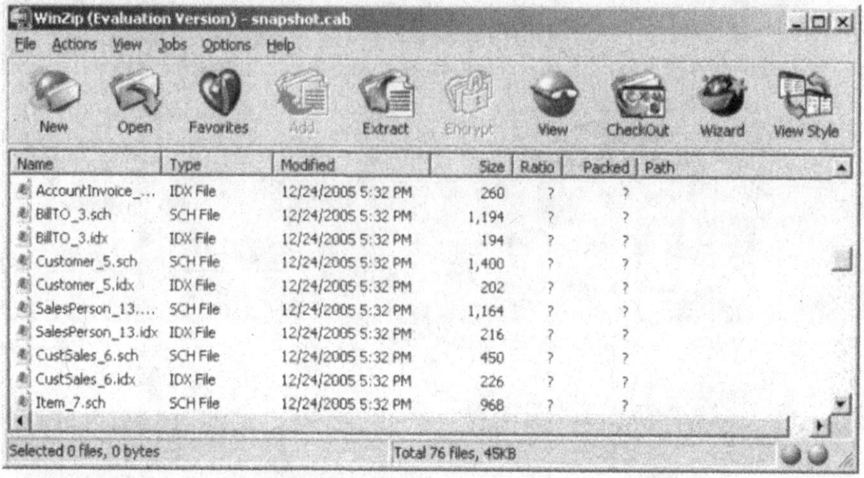

Figure 6-5. *Viewing compressed files with WinZip*

Normally, you use a pull subscription with compressed snapshots since it can extract the data from the publication on demand only. The Subscriber server uncompresses them in a temporary folder and then extracts the snapshots in the order they were compressed.

■**Caution** If the alternative location of the folder is changed after the initial snapshot is created, subsequent generations of snapshots may not be directed to the new alternative location, and the Distribution Agent might not find them. This will cause a breakdown in synchronization and the loss of valuable data.

Open the Activity Monitor (located under the Management object in the SSMS) during the generation of the snapshot by the Snapshot Agent, and you will see a list of the locks held by the objects, each with a process ID, as shown in Figure 6-6. If you select the Locks by Object page in the upper left pane, the right pane will display the different shared locks held by the objects.

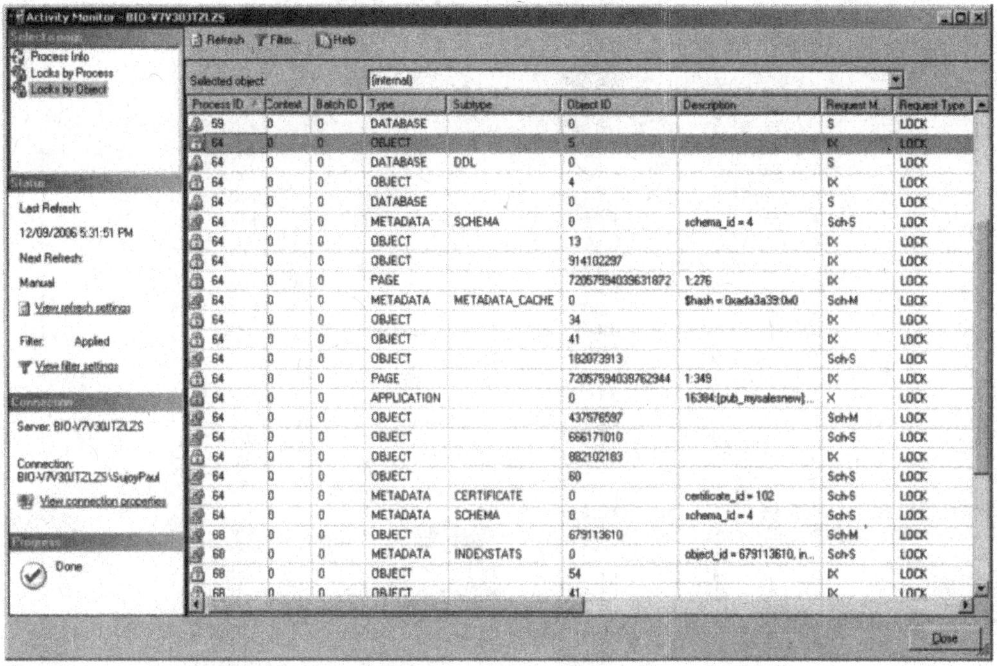

Figure 6-6. *Activity Monitor showing locks by objects*

Alternatively, if you execute the sp_lock stored procedure on the publication database when the snapshot is generated by the Snapshot Agent, you will see a series of locks. Listing 6-1 shows you how to do it.

Listing 6-1. *Executing the* sp_lock *Stored Procedure*

```
/*Execute this on the publication database */

Use mysales
Go

Exec sp_lock
```

The output of Listing 6-1 is shown in Figure 6-7.

spid	dbid	Objld	Indld	Type	Resource	Mode	Status
51	8	0	0	DB		S	GRANT
52	4	0	0	DB		S	GRANT
52	4	277576027	0	TAB		IS	GRANT
52	4	277576027	1	KEY	(3c0211b45aba)	S	WAIT
52	4	133575514	0	TAB		IS	GRANT
52	4	325576198	0	TAB		IS	GRANT
52	4	1589580701	0	TAB		Sch-S	GRANT
52	4	261575970	0	TAB		IS	GRANT
52	4	277576027	1	PAG	0.445138889	IS	GRANT
52	4	421576540	0	TAB		IS	GRANT
52	4	309576141	0	TAB		IS	GRANT
53	11	0	0	DB		S	GRANT
54	8	0	0	DB		S	GRANT
54	8	0	0	APP	16384:[BIO-V7V3C	X	GRANT
56	4	0	0	DB		S	GRANT
57	5	0	0	DB		S	GRANT
57	1	1115151018	0	TAB		IS	GRANT
59	4	0	0	DB		S	GRANT
61	5	0	0	DB		S	GRANT
61	8	0	0	DB		S	GRANT
61	4	0	0	DB		S	GRANT
61	4	629577281	0	TAB		IX	GRANT
61	4	421576540	3	KEY	(3c03051f4757)	X	GRANT
61	4	277576027	2	KEY	(9c0b16ffc334)	X	GRANT
61	8	933578364	1	KEY	(d406f5745666)	X	GRANT
61	4	421576540	1	KEY	(3f029426a753)	X	GRANT
61	5	882102183	1	PAG	0.163888889	IX	GRANT
61	4	0	0	MD	29(68:0:0)	Sch-S	GRANT
61	8	933578364	1	PAG	0.216666667	IX	GRANT
61	4	629577281	1	KEY	(47027b0e1396)	X	GRANT
61	4	421576540	1	KEY	(3e02f1411beb)	X	GRANT
61	4	421576540	1	KEY	(3d021feeaef9)	X	GRANT
61	4	421576540	3	KEY	(ec0223d07852)	X	GRANT

spid	dbid	Objld	Indld	Type	Resource	Mode	Status
61	5	882102183	1	KEY	(03000d8f0ecc)	X	GRANT
61	4	421576540	3	KEY	(f4025649e2e9)	X	GRANT
61	4	421576540	2	KEY	(ec07149afbea)	X	GRANT
61	4	277576027	0	TAB		IX	GRANT
61	32767	0	0	MD	29(66:0:0)	Sch-S	GRANT
61	4	277576027	1	KEY	(3c0211b45aba)	X	GRANT
61	4	277576027	2	PAG	0.446527778	IX	GRANT
61	4	309576141	0	TAB		IX	GRANT
61	4	517576882	1	KEY	(0b00e2a7ba09)	X	GRANT
61	4	421576540	2	KEY	(3604961441d7)	X	GRANT
61	4	277576027	3	KEY	(4b02e814ab25)	X	GRANT
61	4	421576540	0	TAB		IX	GRANT
61	4	421576540	1	PAG	0.509027778	IX	GRANT
61	4	277576027	4	KEY	(3d02bac5a818)	X	GRANT
61	4	309576141	2	KEY	(3f02ca1fe87b)	X	GRANT
61	4	309576141	1	KEY	(3d02d04a0d1d)	X	GRANT
61	4	277576027	1	PAG	0.445138889	IX	GRANT
61	4	277576027	4	PAG	0.449305556	IX	GRANT
61	4	277576027	3	PAG	0.447916667	IX	GRANT
61	4	421576540	1	PAG	0.451388889	IX	GRANT
61	4	421576540	3	PAG	0.454166667	IX	GRANT
61	4	421576540	2	PAG	0.452777778	IX	GRANT
61	4	421576540	2	KEY	(cf07ad1f42c7)	X	GRANT
61	4	629577281	1	PAG	0.456944444	IX	GRANT
61	4	0	0	MD	29(100:0:0)	Sch-S	GRANT
61	4	517576882	1	PAG	0.455555556	IX	GRANT
61	4	309576141	2	PAG	0.459722222	IX	GRANT
61	4	309576141	1	PAG	0.458333333	IX	GRANT
61	8	933578364	0	TAB		IX	GRANT
61	5	882102183	0	TAB		IX	GRANT
61	4	517576882	0	TAB		IX	GRANT

Figure 6-7. *The output of the* sp_lock *stored procedure as run in Listing 6-1*

You can see from this result set that there is a shared lock on the database and that most of the tables have intent-exclusive locks (IX) held by the Snapshot Agent in snapshot replication. This means that the agent intends to place an exclusive lock on some of the resources that are subordinate in the locking hierarchy. Once the snapshot generation is completed, the locks will be released automatically.

Note How the Snapshot Agent works is discussed in Chapter 7. The Snapshot Agent does not hold any locks for merge replication; for transactional replication, the locks are held during the initial phase of the snapshot generation.

This stored procedure is being deprecated, however, and is being used only for backward compatibility. Let's try the new feature: Dynamic Management View. Using the sys.dm_tran_locks dynamic management view, you can find out the mode, status, type of resources, and addresses of the active locks.

You can access this feature through the sys.dm_tran_locks dynamic management view. Listing 6-2 shows how I executed it.

Listing 6-2. *Viewing Manager Resources of Active Locks Held by the Publication Database*

```
/* Execute this on the publication database */
Use mysales
Go

Select * from sys.dm_tran_locks
```

Transferring a Snapshot with Other Methods

You can also transfer the snapshot by attaching the publication database to the subscription database on the Subscriber server. The database can be attached for pull subscriptions once the database is attached on the Subscriber in SQL Server 2000. However, this feature has been deprecated in SQL Server 2005.

Another way of transferring the snapshot is to make a backup copy of the publication database using the full backup method. Once you have backed up the data and the log files, you then restore the snapshot to the subscription database.

Note Backing up and restoring publication databases for snapshot replication is discussed in Chapter 15.

You can also use the File Transfer Protocol (FTP) to transfer the snapshot and store it on a server dedicated for the purpose. In that case, Subscriber servers using pull subscriptions on demand make the request for updates at the Publisher server. This is discussed later in the "Transmitting Snapshots Using FTP" section of this chapter.

Locating the Snapshot Files

In Chapter 2, you saw how to set the location for the snapshot folder using the wizard, and the "Locating the Snapshot Folder" section of this chapter showed how to identify that location. However, if you do not remember the location when you are configuring the Distributor server (see the "Configuring with the GUI" section in Chapter 2), there is another way of finding it.

■**Note** Chapter 2 discusses the configuration of the Distributor server, the distribution database, and the publisher.

In the Object Explorer of the SSMS, right-click on the publication that you created for push subscription, and select Properties. On the Snapshot page of the Publication Properties window, you will see the location of the folder, as shown in Figure 6-8.

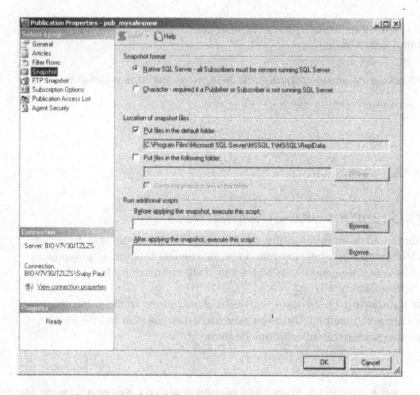

Figure 6-8. *Showing the default location of snapshot files for a push subscription*

■**Note** The user in the above figure has sa permissions.

Remember that the Snapshot Agent must have Write permissions on this folder, and the Distribution Agent must have Read permissions. In Figure 6-8, since we are using a push subscription, you can specify the path name for the snapshot folder as shown. If you were using a pull subscription, or if you were running the Distributor server on a remote location, you would need to use the Universal Naming Convention (UNC).

■**Tip** In merge replication, the Merge Agent must also have Read permissions on the snapshot folder. For security purposes, you need to grant Write permissions on the folder to the account using the Snapshot Agent. Give only Read permissions on the folder to the Windows account that uses the Distribution Agent.

Determining the Types and Size of Snapshot Files

If you open the Windows Explorer and go to the directory where you have asked the Snapshot Agent to generate the snapshot files, you will see a list of files with different extensions, as shown in Figure 6-9.

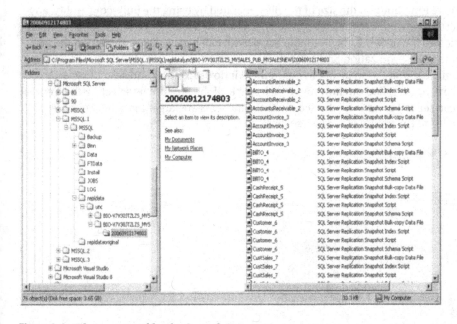

Figure 6-9. *Files generated by the Snapshot Agent*

In Figure 6-9, the Snapshot Agent generated four types of files for each of the articles in the publication. Since there were no triggers in the articles, and the snapshot was not compressed, files with .trg and .cab extensions were not generated. Table 6-1 lists the different file types a Snapshot Agent generates.

■**Tip** You can open each of the files in a text editor and see the contents of the schema and the index files.

Table 6-1. *File Types Generated by the Snapshot Agent*

File Extension	Description
.sch	Schema for each of the database objects
.bcp	Data of the snapshot to the target tables in bulk copy program files
.idx	Indexes of the snapshot to the target tables
.cab	Compressed snapshot files
.trg	Trigger files
.pre	Referential integrity constraints on the target tables

■**Note** If the snapshot is interrupted and reinitialized, it will send those files that need to be synchronized. The Snapshot Agent will not regenerate the files it has already created.

While there is no limit on the size of the file generated by using the bulk-copy utility, anything over 10 GB has a considerable overhead cost associated with it. On top of that, if you are sending data over the network, the available bandwidth can have a major impact on the performance of the synchronization process.

If you right-click on the snapshot folder in the Windows Explorer and select Properties from the menu, you can find out how much disk space all the files use by selecting the General tab. As you can see in Figure 6-10, the accumulated file sizes are larger than the database size—this is due to the nature of the sparse files.

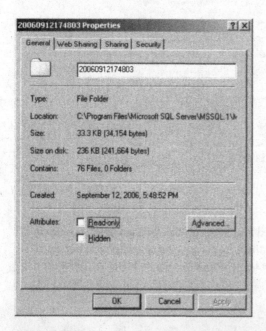

Figure 6-10. *Viewing the total size of the files generated by the Snapshot Agent*

You can also find out the maximum size each of the sparse files can grow to. Listing 6-3 shows you how.

Listing 6-3. *Getting Size Information for Sparse Files in the Current Database File*

```
/* Need to run from the current publication database */
/* Declare the variables */
declare @dbname sysname
declare @fileid int
declare @dbid smallint

/* Get the name of the current database */
set @dbname =(select db_name(db_id()));

/* Get the current database id */
set @dbid = (select db_id());

/* Get the ID of the data file for the current database.
 Type=0 from the sys.database_files correspond to the
data file while type=1 correspond to the log file */

set @fileid= (select file_id from sys.database_files where type=0);

/*Get the maximum bytes on the disk for the current data file and the corresponding
SQL Server pages from fn_virtualfilestats */

select db_name(db_id()) as currentdatabase,
bytesondisk,
(bytesondisk/8192)as pages
from
fn_virtualfilestats (@dbid,@fileid)
```

Here is the output for the script in Listing 6-3:

Currentdatabase	bytesondisk	pages
adventureworks_subpull	177536	11008

The script in Listing 6-3 first declares the variables that will store the name of the current database and its corresponding database ID and file ID. It then uses the db_id() function to first retrieve the id of the database and then extract the name of the database using the dbname() function. Since we are only interested in finding the size of the sparse file for the data file for the current database used in the publication, the script only selects the file_id column from the sys.database_files view by matching with the value of 0 for the type column. A value of 1 for the type column means that it is a database log file. The file_id is now stored in the fileid variable.

Now that the script has the database and the file ID of the current database, it calls the system table-valued function, fn_virtualstats, which returns statistical information on database files and log files. The two columns that we are interested in are dbid and bytesondisk. The bytesondisk specifies the maximum number of bytes on the disk for the data file corresponding to the database ID (dbid). We also want to know the number of SQL Server pages that the number of bytes corresponds to, and this can be calculated by dividing the number of bytes on the disk by 8,192. The parameters that are passed to the function are the dbid and fileid variables.

■**Note** The user needs View Server State permission on the server to use the fn_virtualstats function.

SPARSE FILES

Sparse files are a feature of the NTFS file system, and they are created at the time of database creation. SQL Server 2005 makes use of sparse files to reduce contention by allocating the appropriate disk space as necessary. Snapshot replication uses one or more sparse files to store data during the generation of the snapshot. Initially a sparse file is empty since no user data has been entered and disk space has not been allocated to the sparse file for the user data. The amount of disk space that is allocated for the sparse file is larger, but the disk space consumed by the sparse file is nil. With the addition of data, sparse files grow, and the expansion of the sparse files, like database files, can be fast. As more data is added to the data file, and as more pages are added to the database, the size of the sparse file will grow in 64 KB increments. NTFS allocates disk space gradually, and a sparse file can grow considerably in size.

Transmitting Snapshots Using FTP

As mentioned earlier, you can use the File Transfer Protocol (FTP) to retrieve the snapshot files for pull subscriptions. Once you set up an FTP account for the publication, any subscribing servers that use that particular publication will, by default, use FTP to pull the subscriptions. In this section, I will show you how to use FTP to deliver the snapshot.

Don't forget the security considerations. Retrieving the snapshot over FTP is not the same as transmitting the snapshot over the network using the Distribution Agent. The replication agents in SQL Server run under the security context of either the Windows Authentication account or the SQL Server account. The Distribution Agent impersonates the user account at the Distributor server. SQL Server 2005 also allows you to use the FTP share to store the snapshot folder. However, when FTP share is used, passwords for the FTP server are stored and sent to the Subscriber servers in plain text. Hence, you need to take into consideration the password that you would use to connect to the Subscriber servers. You can use Windows Authentication for this purpose.

■**Caution** Do not grant anonymous logins to the Subscriber servers.

Setting Up the Snapshot Folder

In order to transmit the snapshot using FTP, you need to have the FTP server set up and running. In this case, I will assume that you have Microsoft Internet Information Services (IIS) installed on your machine. Once you install IIS, it will also host the web and the FTP site by default.

Note You need to confer with your network administrator to set up the FTP server.

If you are not sure where the default FTP site is, go to the Start menu and select Settings ➤ Control Panel ➤ Administrative Tools ➤ Computer Management. At the bottom of the Computer Management console, under the Services and Applications tree, you will find Internet Information Services. The default FTP site has been configured for you, as shown in Figure 6-11.

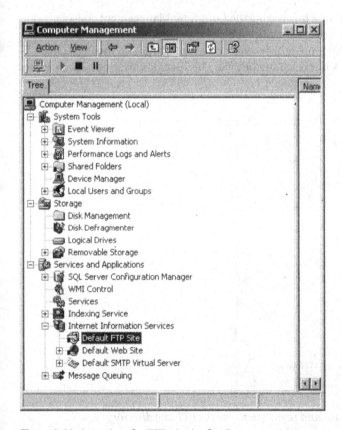

Figure 6-11. *Locating the FTP site in the Computer Management console*

Note If you do not have IIS installed on your machine, you can install it by selecting Add/Remove Windows Components in the Add/Remove Programs of the Control Panel.

In order to enable the subscribing servers to download files from the FTP site, select a publication (one whose snapshot you want to download from FTP) from the Local Publications object in the Object Explorer section of the SSMS. Right-click on the object and select Properties. Select the FTP Snapshot page in the left pane, and in the right pane check the "Allow Subscribers to download snapshot files using FTP" check box.

The next step is to set up user accounts and passwords so that the Subscriber servers can access the snapshot files from the FTP server—don't allow anonymous logins. Make sure the port number for the FTP server is the default 21.

Tip To see the FTP server's port number, open the Computer Management console. Then select Internet Information Services, right-click on the Default FTP Site, select Properties, and choose the FTP Site tab.

You can see your FTP site directory by opening the Computer Management console, selecting Internet Information Services, and right-clicking on the Default FTP Site. Next select Properties, and select the Home Directory tab. As you can see in Figure 6-12, the Read check box is checked, and the Write check box is left unchecked. This means Subscribers can read or download the files.

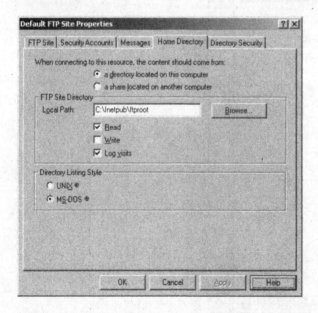

Figure 6-12. *Specifying the logical path and permissions for the FTP site directory*

Having ensured the logical path and permissions for the FTP site directory are correct, go back to the FTP Snapshot page of the Publication Properties window, shown in Figure 6-13. In the right pane, the "Path from the FTP root folder" property specifies the path where the Subscriber will look for the snapshot files. So if the FTP server root is \\Intepub\ftproot (as shown Figure 6-12), and you want to store the snapshot files at \\Intepub\ftproot\snapshot, you'll need to specify \snapshot\ftp for the property. You need not specify the ftp folder, because replication will automatically append it. You should ensure that the Snapshot Agent has Write permissions for the snapshot folder and that you use a UNC name for the path to the snapshot folder for the pull subscription.

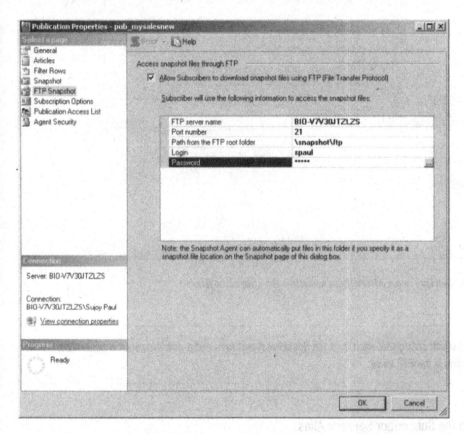

Figure 6-13. *Specifying where Subscriber servers can retrieve the snapshot files*

Now you need to specify that the Snapshot Agent writes to the FTP root folder, so select the Snapshot page in the left pane, as shown in Figure 6-14. Here you can set the location for the snapshot files. You basically have two options: to put them in the default folder, or to place them in the alternative location, which is where the ftp folder is located. Check the "Put files in the following folder" check box, and specify the location of the FTP folder as shown.

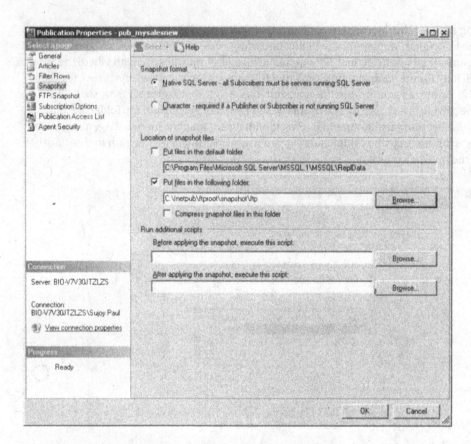

Figure 6-14. *Specifying an alternative location for snapshot files*

■**Note** It is worth noting that each time the Snapshot Agent runs and a new snapshot is generated, it will update the files in the FTP folder.

Setting Up the Subscriber Server's Alias

We have configured the publication and set up the path for the snapshot folder in the FTP server. The next step is to make sure the Subscriber and SQL Server can talk to each other. The default port number for FTP is 21, and SQL Server uses the default port number of 1433, so we need to set up an alias for the Subscriber to facilitate communication between the two.

Start by opening the SSMS and selecting SQL Native Client Configuration, as shown in Figure 6-15. You will see two objects, Client Protocols and Aliases, belonging to the SQL Native Client Configuration.

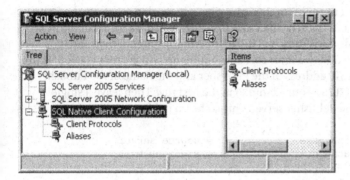

Figure 6-15. *Showing aliases under SQL Native Client Configuration*

Right-click on Aliases, and select New Alias, which opens the window shown in Figure 6-16. Enter a name for the alias that matches the name of the Publisher server. (Right-click on the Replication object in SSMS and select Publisher Properties, and you will find the name of the Publisher server under Connection.) You can then enter the default port number for SQL Server (1433), select the TCP/IP protocol, and the name of the server you want the Subscriber to connect to.

Figure 6-16. *Configuring the alias for the Subscriber server*

Now that we have configured the alias for the Subscriber, we need to associate the Publisher server's NETBIOS with that of TCP/IP. Open the Hosts file, which is located in the `WINNT\ system32\drivers\etc` folder. This file is used by TCP/IP for Windows and it maps the IP addresses to the host names. The first two lines contain comments, which are preceded by the # character. You need to place the IP address of the Publisher and the name of the Publisher server (`localhost` or `BIO-V7V30JTZLZS` in our example) in the first row. Then leave a single space and specify the name of the Publisher server. This is shown in Figure 6-17.

```
#       102.54.94.97        rhino.acme.com          # source server
#        38.25.63.10        x.acme.com              # x client host

127.0.0.1          localhost
24.141.XX.XX       BIO-V7V30JTZLZS
```

Figure 6-17. *The HOSTS file parameters*

Note NETBIOS is an API—it is not a protocol like TCP/IP. That's why it needs to be associated with a network protocol.

Configuring the Pull Subscription

The next step in the process is to configure the pull subscription. In Chapters 4 and 5, I showed you how to configure the pull subscription using the GUI and the T-SQL methods, but there is one more thing you need to do: you need to specify the location of the snapshot folder.

Note Chapter 4 discusses the configuration of snapshot replication using the GUI method, and Chapter 5 discusses the configuration using T-SQL.

With the GUI, you can specify the location of the snapshot folder for transferring files by FTP. Right-click on the pull subscription in the SSMS and select Properties from the menu. In the Properties section of the page, set the Snapshot location to "FTP folder" and the Snapshot folder to "Download from FTP folder," as shown in Figure 6-18. Then click OK.

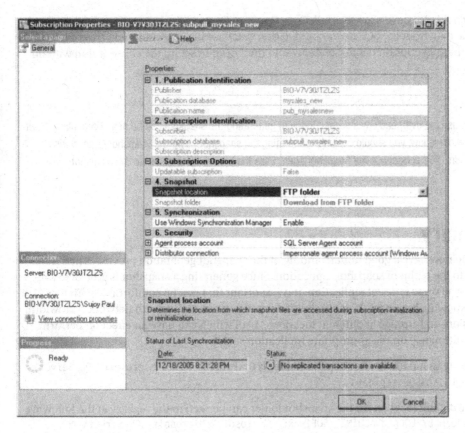

Figure 6-18. *Enabling the snapshot location on the FTP folder for the pull subscription*

If you are using T-SQL instead of the GUI, you must use the following stored procedures in the following sequence:

1. Execute `sp_addpullsubscription` on the subscription database on the Subscriber. Specify `@publisher` and `@publication`.

2. On the subscription database on the Subscriber server, use the `sp_addpullsubscription_agent` stored procedure. You need to specify `@publisher`, `@publisher_db`, `@publication`, and `@use_ftp='true'`. Then specify the Windows Authentication login for `@job_login` and `@job_password`.

3. On the publication database on the Publisher server, register the subscription using the `sp_addsubscription` stored procedure.

■ **Note** The configuration of pull subscriptions by T-SQL is discussed in Chapter 5. Table 5-6 lists the stored procedures and the parameters that you need for configuring pull subscriptions.

You could also have used the Bulk Copy Program (bcp) utility, as mentioned previously, to extract the data from the SQL Server publication database into a text file, and from there to the tables in the subscription database. You would then need to set up the subscription with no initialization.

■**Tip** Because the overhead costs associated with generating the snapshot can be high, particularly if network bandwidth is low, you should consider generating the snapshot using the Snapshot Agent during off-peak hours. This is because the Snapshot Agent uses the bcp utility to generate the snapshot.

Summary

You should now have a good understanding of the snapshot generation processes and how they fit into the realm of snapshot replication. Since generating a snapshot is crucial to synchronizing all three types of replication, it is important that you be comfortable with the process. Knowing how it works is also helpful when you are dealing with network bandwidth, compression, and storage at different locations, all of which can have an effect on performance and ultimately on the appropriate replication setup.

- The default path for the snapshot folder is C:\Program Files\Microsoft SQL Server\ MSSQL.1\MSSQL\repldata.

- The default location for the snapshot folder can be seen in the registry at the following place: HKEY_LOCAL_MACHINE\ SOFTWARE \Microsoft\ Microsoft SQL Server\ 90\ MSQL.1\Replication.

- Give write permissions to the Snapshot Agent, since it performs write operations as it makes a snapshot of the publication. Grant read permissions to the Distribution Agent, since it reads the files generated by the Snapshot Agent in the snapshot folder and transmits the messages to the Subscriber servers.

- Sparse files grow in increments of 64 KB.

- You can compress the snapshot files using the CAB format. If the file size exceeds 2 GB, however, you cannot use the CAB format.

- Use the sys.dm_tran_locks dynamic management view to monitor the locks held by the Snapshot Agent during the snapshot generation process. The sp_lock stored procedure has been deprecated.

- Snapshot replication makes use of sparse files to store data during snapshot generation.

- You can use the FTP method to store the snapshot. Subscriber servers will need read permissions on the folder where the snapshot is stored to download the snapshot.

- Pull subscriptions are used when the snapshot is generated by using FTP.

Now that you know how to configure the different database objects for snapshot replication using both the GUI and T-SQL methods, we will look at the internal workings of snapshot replication in the next chapter. I will show you the different steps executed by each of the agents involved in snapshot replication, the login information of the Publication Access List (PAL), and the system tables used by the distribution, publication, and subscription databases.

Quick Tips

- Compress the snapshot if the file size is less than 2 GB.

- Run the snapshot during off-hours.

- If the network traffic is high and the bandwidth low, consider alternative methods of generating the snapshot.

- When using the bcp utility, use the native format when transferring data between a SQL Server Publisher and a SQL Server Subscriber.

- If files are stored at both the default location and an alternative location, remember that files are copied first to the default location and then to the alternative location. This can have a considerable impact on performance.

- If using FTP to store a snapshot, assign a password to the Subscriber servers. Do not grant anonymous logins.

- You can open each of the schema files generated by the Snapshot Agent in a text editor and see the contents of the schema and index files.

CHAPTER 7

∎ ∎ ∎

Internals of Snapshot Replication

For replication to work seamlessly, the components must work together, from the Publisher server to the Subscriber server. Each has its own distinct part to play, and I will show you how they work under the hood. Once you know their internal workings, it is easier to interpret errors, optimize replication, and wherever possible, find alternative solutions to mitigate any problems. In this chapter, I will discuss in detail the internal workings of snapshot replication.

On completing this chapter, you will know much more about the following:

- The Publication Access List

- The steps taken by the Snapshot and Distribution Agents

- The internal workings of publications, push subscriptions, and pull subscriptions

On the Publisher Server

On the Publisher server, the components involved in replication are the publication, the publication database, and the Publication Access List, which contains a list of logins to grant access to the publication.

The Snapshot Agent needs to make a connection to the publication database before it can generate the snapshot that is transmitted to the Distributor server, and this needs to be done securely so that only users with the necessary permissions have access to the publications. To this end, the publication database maintains a list of the logins that can have access to the publication data. This is the Publication Access List.

The Publication Access List

SQL Server creates a Publication Access List (PAL) when you create a publication. The publication database contains a list of logins, hidden from the view. When an agent or user tries to connect to the publication database, SQL Server will first verify that the login is indeed stored for the publication before access is granted.

The login members in the PAL must be members of the sysadmin fixed server role, with the exception of the login that was used to create the publication in the first place. Members of the db_owner fixed database role on the publication database can also subscribe by default. They do not have to be added to the PAL.

Note You have already encountered the PAL in Chapter 4. In Figures 4-21 and 4-22, during the configuration of the Distribution Agent, the wizard informed us that the process account under which the Distribution Agent ran to connect to the Distributor server must be a member of the PAL.

To administer the logins within the PAL, right-click the publication object under the Object Explorer in the SQL Server Management Studio (SSMS), and select Properties. Then in the Publication Properties window, select the Publication Access List page, and you will see the login names and their associated types, as shown in Figure 7-1.

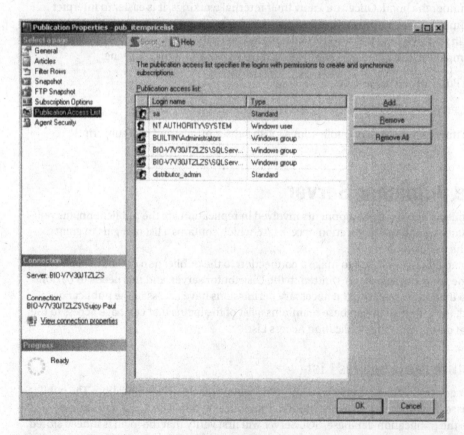

Figure 7-1. *The login names and types in the PAL*

You can remove members from the PAL by selecting the login and clicking the Remove button.

Caution Replication uses the `distributor_admin` login. Do not remove it from the PAL.

If you click on the Add button, it will show you a list of logins for that database, as shown in Figure 7-2, which shows the login I created in my name. You can then select the login and click OK to add the login to the PAL.

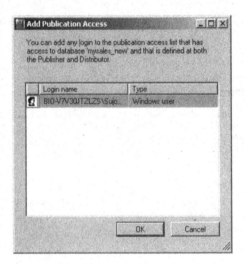

Figure 7-2. *Selecting a login to add to the PAL*

Note You can create a login using the Logins object under the Security object in the SSMS.

Consider the following when granting login access to the PAL:

- If the login uses only specific replication tasks, grant only permissions that are specific to that login's replication tasks in the PAL.

- If a remote Distributor server is used, the PAL must have login accounts for both the Publisher and the Distributor servers. The account must be defined as either a domain account or a local account on both servers. The passwords associated with the logins must be in synch.

- If the PAL contains the Windows account, and the domain makes use of the Active Directory, the account under which SQL Server is executed must have read permissions to the Active Directory.

In Figure 7-1 you can see the login names and their corresponding types. You can also execute the sp_help_publication_access stored procedure on the publication database on the Publisher server to see the same list of logins and groups that belong to the PAL. You need to be either a member of the sysadmin fixed server role or the db_owner fixed database role to execute this stored procedure. Listing 7-1 shows how you can execute the stored procedure on the publication whose PAL you wish to check.

Listing 7-1. *Executing* sp_help_publication_access *on a Publication*

```
/* Execute the stored procedure on the publication database
 that contains the publication */

Use mysales_new
Go


sp_help_publication_access 'pub_mysalesnew'
```

The output of this stored procedure is shown here:

```
loginname
  isntname    isntgroup
-----------------------------------------------------------------------
sa
 0          0
NT AUTHORITY\SYSTEM
 1          0
BUILTIN\Administrators
 1          1
BIO-V7V30JTZLZS\SQLServer2005SQLAgentUser$BIO-V7V30JTZLZS$MSSQLSERVER
 1          1
BIO-V7V30JTZLZS\SQLServer2005MSSQLUser$BIO-V7V30JTZLZS$MSSQLSERVER
 1          1
distributor_admin
 1          1
```

As you can see, running the stored procedure on the pub_mysalesnew publication shows the login names and whether they belong to a Windows user or group. The loginname column lists the logins that have permissions to access the publications. The isntname and isntgroup columns are of integer data type and return a value of 1 or 0. A value of 0 for both columns means that the login name is neither a Windows user nor does it belong to the Windows group. This is what you can see for the sa and distributor_admin logins, because both of them are SQL Server login names.

The `sp_help_publication_access` stored procedure first gets information about the Publisher server from the `sp_MSrepl_getdistributor_info` stored procedure. It checks to see whether the type of the Publisher is SQL Server or not, and then it sets the database context to that of the Distributor server. Next, it checks whether the logins have been dropped or not, and also the valid logins for the Distributor server. If the value of `@initial_list` is 1, it returns all the valid logins that existed on the Distributor server, including the current user. However, if the value of `@initial_list` is 0, it returns all the members that existed on the Distributor server when the publication was created who are members of the sysadmin fixed server role, and also PAL members who are not members of the sysadmin fixed server role. It retrieves this information from the `master.dbo.syslogins` table.

The parameters for `sp_help_publication_access` are as follows:

`@publication`: Specifies the name of the publication to access

`@return_granted`: Returns the login ID; the default value is 1

`@login`: Specifies the standard security login ID

`@initial_list`: Specifies whether all members with access to the publication should be returned or just those that had access before new members were added

You have already seen how to add a login to the PAL in Chapter 5, using the `sp_grant_publication_access` stored procedure in Listing 5-6. If you want to remove a login, you will have to execute the `sp_revoke_publication_access` stored procedure on the publication database on the Publisher server, as shown in Listing 7-2. In order to execute this stored procedure, you need to be either a member of the sysadmin fixed server role or the db_owner fixed database role.

Listing 7-2. *Removing a Login Name from the PAL*

```
/* Execute this on the publication database on the Publisher server */

sp_revoke_publication_access @publication='pub_mysalesnew',
@login=[BIO-V7V30JTZLZS\Sujoy Paul]
```

This stored procedure first does a security check using the `sys.sp_MSreplcheck_publish` stored procedure, and then it gets the name of the Publisher server using the `sp_MSrepl_getdistributorinfo` stored procedure. Next, it sets the database context to the Distributor server for those Publisher servers using SQL Server. It then checks that the publication exists and that the Publisher type is SQL Server, and then it drops the user for the PAL role. Finally, it revokes the connection of that login member using the `sys.sp_MSrevokeconnectreplication` stored procedure.

Now that you know what the PAL is and how it works, let's look at the inner workings of the publication database.

PAL ROLES

In order to enforce the PAL membership, replication creates a role. For snapshot and transactional replication, the role is `MSReplPAL_<publicationdatabaseID>_<publicationID>`. For merge replication, the role is `MSmerge_<publicationID>`. In the object explorer of the SSMS, if you open the Database Roles object under the Security object for the database mysales_new, you will see the role being added. In this case, the name of the role is `MSReplPAL_10_1`, as you can see here:

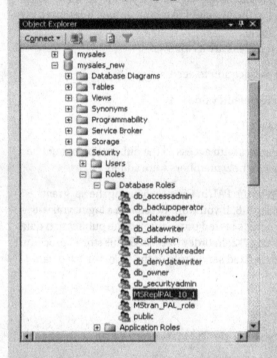

   This is added when you add the login to the PAL. The publication database ID in this case is 10, while the ID for the publication is 1.

The Publication

In order to understand the inner workings of the publication, let's look again at the steps you need to take to configure the publication for snapshot replication:

1. Enable the database for publication using the `sp_replicationdboption` stored procedure.

2. Add the publication using the `sp_addpublication` stored procedure.

3. Add logins to the PAL using the `sp_grant_publication_access` stored procedure.

4. Create articles and add them to the publication using the `sp_addarticle` stored procedure.

You have already seen the steps needed to add a login to the PAL, so the following three sections will discuss the other three steps.

Before we get into the details, though, we need to know whether the publication database is involved in replication. To find out, you simply execute the sp_dboption stored procedure on the publication database to find out if it is being published. Listing 7-3 shows how to ask the mysales_new database whether it is published or not.

Listing 7-3. *Finding Out Whether the Database Is Being Published or Not*

```
/* Execute this on the publication database on the Publisher server */

Use mysales_new
Go


Exec sp_dboption 'mysales_new'
```

The output is shown next. You can see that the database is being published.

```
The following options are set:
-----------------------------------
published
auto create statistics
auto update statistics
```

You need to be a member of the public role to view the options of the database, and everyone is a member of public by default. However, if you want to change the options, you need to be a member of the db_owner fixed database role.

Now that we have confirmed that this database is indeed being used for publication, let's look into each of the steps we took when we configured the publication. However, bear in mind that the configuration of the publication (whether using stored procedures or the GUI) actually enters values in the system tables that are set for replication. It is recommended that you back up the publication database soon after the configuration of a publication.

The seven system tables in the publication database for snapshot replication are shown in the E-R diagram in Figures 7-3 and 7-4. They are each described in Table 7-1. As we explore each of the steps involved in publication, you will learn about the functionality and actions of each of these tables.

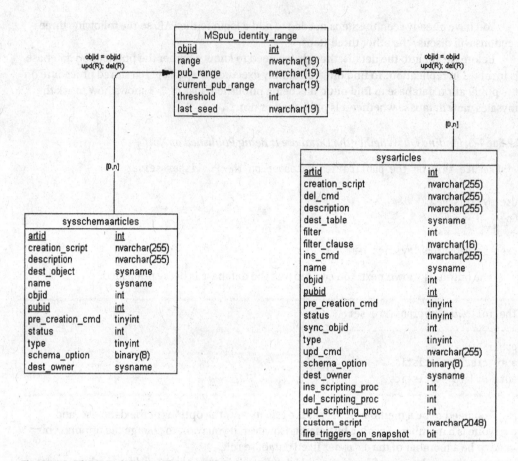

Figure 7-3. *The E-R diagram showing the* MSpub_identity_range, sysschemaarticles, *and* sysarticles *system tables used for snapshot replication in the publication database*

sysarticleupdates	
artid	int
pubid	int
sync_ins_proc	int
sync_upd_proc	int
sync_del_proc	int
autogen	bit
sync_upd_trig	int
conflict_tableid	int
ins_conflict_proc	int
identity_support	bit

syspublications	
description	nvarchar(255)
name	sysname
pubid	int
repl_freq	tinyint
status	tinyint
sync_method	tinyint
snapshot_jobid	binary(16)
independent_agent	bit
immediate_sync	bit
enabled_for_internet	bit
allow_push	bit
allow_pull	bit
allow_anonymous	bit
immediate_sync_ready	bit
allow_sync_tran	bit
autogen_sync_procs	bit
retention	int
allow_queued_tran	bit
snapshot_in_defaultfolder	bit
alt_snapshot_folder	nvarchar(255)
pre_snapshot_script	nvarchar(255)
post_snapshot_script	nvarchar(255)
compress_snapshot	bit
ftp_address	sysname
ftp_port	int
ftp_subdirectory	nvarchar(255)
ftp_login	sysname
ftp_password	nvarchar(524)
allow_dts	bit
allow_subscription_copy	bit
centralized_conflicts	bit
conflict_retention	int
conflict_policy	int
queue_type	int
ad_guidname	sysname
backward_comp_level	int
allow_initialize_from_backup	bit
min_autonosync_lsn	binary(10)
replicate_ddl	int
options	int

systranschemas	
tabid	int
startlsn	binary(10)
endlsn	binary(10)
typeid	int

syssubscriptions	
artid	int
srvid	smallint
dest_db	sysname
status	tinyint
sync_type	tinyint
login_name	sysname
subscription_type	int
distribution_jobid	binary(16)
timestamp	timestamp
update_mode	tinyint
loopback_detection	bit
queued_reinit	bit
nosync_type	tinyint

Figure 7-4. *The E-R diagram showing the* sysarticleupdates, syspublications, *and* systranschemas *system tables used for snapshot replication in the publication database*

Table 7-1. *System Tables Used for Snapshot Replication in a Publication Database*

Table	Description
MSpub_identity_range	Provides identity-range management support
Sysarticles	Contains a row for each article defined in the database
Sysarticleupdates	Contains a row for each article that supports immediate updating subscriptions
Syspublications	Contains a row for each publication for that database
Sysschemaarticles	Tracks schema-only articles
Syssubscriptions	Contains a row for each of the subscriptions in the database
Systranschemas	Tracks changes in the schema in the articles; this table is also stored in the subscription database

Enabling the Database for Replication

As you'll recall, the sp_replicationdboption stored procedure, which enables the database for replication, is executed on the publication database on the Publisher server. When you set the @value parameter to true as we did in Chapter 5 (Listing 5-4), with the @optname parameter set to publish, we essentially ensured that the publication database is enabled for all types of publication except for merge publication (publication that is used in merge replication; the @optname parameter is then set to merge publish). The @optname parameter determines whether the replication database option is enabled; it can be set to publish, merge publish, subscribe, or sync with backup. The @value parameter then determines whether the replication database option is enabled or disabled. This stored procedure creates the necessary security settings, the replication system tables, and the system stored procedures. It also adds the bit value in the category column in the sys.sysdatabases system view.

The sys.sysdatabases table contains a row for each database created for a server instance. Initially, when SQL Server is installed, there are entries for master, model, msdb, and tempdb databases. When databases are enabled for replication, the entries that are made in the category column are used by common replication maintenance jobs, such as Expired subscription clean up, to check for any existing publications. Then, depending on the presence of publications, it removes corresponding subscriptions. These bits also prevent users from accidentally dropping the database that is being used for replication.

The query in Listing 7-4 returns the databases that are being used for snapshot replication.

Listing 7-4. *Viewing Category Column in Bits on Replication*

```
/* Execute on any database */
Use mysales_new
Go

select name,dbid, category,filename from sys.sysdatabases
```

The output of this query is as follows:

name	dbid	category	filename
master	1	0	C:\Program Files\Microsoft SQL Server\MSSQL.1\MSSQL\DATA \master.mdf
tempdb	2	0	C:\Program Files\Microsoft SQL Server\MSSQL.1\MSSQL\DATA \tempdb.mdf
model	3	0	C:\Program Files\Microsoft SQL Server\MSSQL.1\MSSQL\DATA \model.mdf
msdb	4	0	C:\Program Files\Microsoft SQL Server\MSSQL.1\MSSQL\DATA \MSDBData.mdf
mysales_new	5	1	C:\Program Files\Microsoft SQL Server\MSSQL.1\MSSQL\Data \mysales_new.mdf

```
kiosk                    6    0     C:\Program Files\Microsoft SQL
                                    Server\MSSQL.1\MSSQL\Data
                                    \kiosk.mdf
ssisdb                   7    0     C:\Program Files\Microsoft SQL
                                    Server\MSSQL.1\MSSQL\Data
                                    \ssisdb.mdf
distribution71022        8    16    C:\Program Files\Microsoft SQL
                                    Server\MSSQL.1\MSSQL\Data
                                    \distribution71022.MDF
mysales                  9    0     C:\Program Files\Microsoft SQL
                                    Server\MSSQL.1\MSSQL\Data
                                    \mysales.mdf
subpull_mysales_new     10    0     C:\Program Files\Microsoft SQL
                                    Server\MSSQL.1\MSSQL\Data
                                    \subpull_mysales_new.mdf
subpush_mysales_new     11    0     C:\Program Files\Microsoft SQL
                                    Server\MSSQL.1\MSSQL\Data
                                    \subpush_mysales_new.mdf

(11 row(s) affected)
```

In this output, you can see the database name, the database ID, and the filenames. Note the category bit for the databases: databases that are not used for replication have a category bit of 0, while those that have been published for snapshot replication have a bit value of 1, as in the mysales_new database. Subscribing databases used for snapshot replication will have a category value of 2. The distribution database has a bit value of 16, as you can see in the output.

■**Note** Publications for transactional replication also have a bit value of 1 for the category column.

Adding the Publication

The purpose of the sp_addpublication stored procedure is to add the publication so that the Subscriber servers can subscribe to the publication. Whether you are using the script in Listing 5-4 to add the publication or the GUI method, the underlying principles remain the same.

■**Note** The sp_addpublication stored procedure is also used for transactional replication. This is described in Chapter 9.

When you execute sp_addpublication, it adds a row to the syspublications system table for every publication that you create. When you execute Listing 7-5, you will see that it retrieves the name of the publication for each publication defined in the database from the syspublications table.

Listing 7-5. *Finding the Names of the Publications That Have Been Added in the* syspublications *System Table*

```
/* Execute this on the publication database on the Publisher */

select name, repl_freq, status,
sync_method,
independent_agent,
immediate_sync,
allow_push,
allow_pull,
allow_anonymous,
retention,
snapshot_in_defaultfolder,
alt_snapshot_folder,
compress_snapshot,
replicate_ddl
from syspublications
```

The output of this script is as follows:

name	repl_freq	status	sync_method
independent_agent	immediate_sync	allow_push	allow_pull
allow_anonymous	retention	snapshot_in_defaultfolder	
alt_snapshot_folder	compress_snapshot	replicate_ddl	
pub_mysalesnew	1	1	0
1	1	1	1
1	0	1	
C:\files\unc		1	1
pub_itempricelist	1	1	0
1	1	1	1
1	0	1	
NULL		0	1

As you can see, the script retrieves the names of the publications: pub_mysalesnew and pub_itempricelist. The replication frequency (repl_freq) is set to 1 in both publications, which means they are not transaction based. Both the publications are active, as both of them have a value of 1 for status. The method of synchronization (sync_method) is 0 in both the publications. As you know, the bcp method is used to generate the snapshot, and a value of 0 for the synchronization method means that it is using the native format for bcp. You can only use this method if you are using SQL Server on both the Publisher and the Subscriber servers.

A value of 1 for the independent_agent indicates that the Distribution Agent is being used as a stand-alone program, and a value of 1 for the immediate_synch column means that the synchronization occurs every time the Snapshot Agent runs. You can see that both the publications support push (allow_push is 1), pull (allow_pull is 1) and anonymous (allow_anonymous is 1) subscriptions.

The retention period of 0 indicates that the publication is stored for an infinite period. The snapshot_in_defaultfolder setting is 1, which indicates that both publications will store the snapshot in the default folder. The location of the alternative snapshot folder (alt_snapshot_folder) is specified in the first publication, and the snapshot is compressed (compress_snapshot is 1) in the first publication but not in the second. Finally, the schema is replicated (replicate_ddl is 1) in both publications.

■**Caution** The distributor_admin login acts as the channel for transmitting the data held by the syspublications system table in the publication database to the MSpublications system table in the distribution database. Do not delete this login.

Adding the Articles

So what happens when you add articles to the publication? As you probably guessed, each of the articles for the publication gets added as a row in the sysarticles system table. The output of Listing 7-6 shows the articles that have been added in the sysarticles table when you add the articles in the publication.

Listing 7-6. *Finding the Articles Added in the* sysarticles *System Table When They Were Added to the Publication*

```
/* Execute this on the publication database */

select creation_script,
dest_table,
del_cmd,
ins_cmd,
upd_cmd,
name,
objid,
pubid,
type,
dest_owner
from sysarticles
```

The output is as follows:

creation_script	dest_table	del_cmd	ins_cmd
upd_cmd	name	objid	pubid
type	dest_owner		
NULL	AcccountsReceivable	SQL	SQL
SQL	AcccountsReceivable	437576597	1
1	myfinance		

NULL	AccountInvoice	SQL	SQL
SQL	AccountInvoice	501576825	1
1	myfinance		
NULL	BillTO	SQL	SQL
SQL	BillTO	2137058649	1
1	myorder		
NULL	CashReceipt	SQL	SQL
SQL	CashReceipt	469576711	1
1	myfinance		
NULL	Customer	SQL	SQL
SQL	Customer	69575286	1
1	myorder		
NULL	CustSales	SQL	SQL
SQL	CustSales	165575628	1
1	myorder		
NULL	Item	SQL	SQL
SQL	Item	261575970	1
1	myinventory		
NULL	OrderDetail	SQL	SQL
SQL	OrderDetail	21575115	1
1	myorder		
NULL	OrderHeader	SQL	SQL
SQL	OrderHeader	101575400	1
1	myorder		
NULL	PriceList	SQL	SQL
SQL	PriceList	373576369	1
1	myinventory		
NULL	PurchaseOrderDetail	SQL	SQL
SQL	PurchaseOrderDetail	341576255	1
1	myinventory		
NULL	PurchaseOrderHeader	SQL	SQL
SQL	PurchaseOrderHeader	309576141	1
1	myinventory		
NULL	SalesPerson	SQL	SQL
SQL	SalesPerson	37575172	1
1	myorder		
NULL	ShipTO	SQL	SQL
SQL	ShipTO	133575514	1
1	myorder		
NULL	Stock	SQL	SQL
SQL	Stock	2105058535	1
1	myorder		
NULL	StockItem	SQL	SQL
SQL	StockItem	229575856	1
1	myinventory		

NULL	Vendor	SQL	SQL
SQL	Vendor	405576483	1
1	myinventory		
NULL	Warehouse	SQL	SQL
SQL	Warehouse	197575742	1
1	myinventory		
NULL	ZONE	SQL	SQL
SQL	ZONE	2073058421	1
1	myorder		
NULL	Item	SQL	SQL
SQL	Item	261575970	2
1	myinventory		
NULL	PriceList	SQL	SQL
SQL	PriceList	373576369	2
1	myinventory		

In this output, you can see that the name of the destination table is contained in the schema, which is the destination owner. In our database, the myfinance schema is the owner of the AccountsReceivable table, as is shown in the preceding output. The type column indicates the kind of article—a value of 1 indicates that it is log-based. The pubid column contains the ID of the publication to which the article belongs, and the objid column lists the object ID of the published table. The del_cmd, ins_cmd, and upd_cmd columns are the commands used to replicate deletes, inserts, and updates, respectively. You can see that the commands are of type SQL.

■**Note** A *schema* is a database object that has been introduced in SQL Server 2005. It is a collection of database objects, such as tables, that have a single namespace and must be unique.

The Snapshot Agent

The previous chapters will have given you a good understanding of what the Snapshot Agent does. It is involved in the initial synchronization of the database objects and data, and it is primarily responsible for generating database objects and data from the publication database and storing them in the snapshot folder. So how does the Snapshot Agent work?

I mentioned earlier that agents are essentially SQL Server jobs, and the Snapshot Agent is no exception. It also executes a series of job steps. To see this, open the SQL Server Agent object in the Object Explorer in the SSMS. Then open the Jobs object, and select the Snapshot Agent object for the publication, as shown in Figure 7-5.

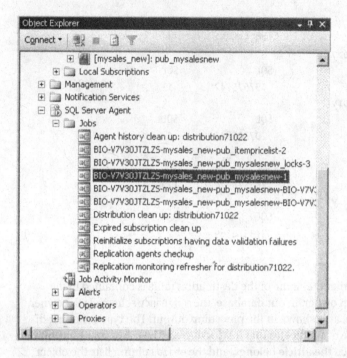

Figure 7-5. *Viewing agents listed as objects in the Jobs folder under the SQL Server Agent*

■**Note** Snapshot Agents are created for every publication you create. Snapshot Agents are listed as jobs under the Jobs folder in the SSMS. Their names follow this pattern:

`<Publisher>-<PublicationDatabase>-<Publication>-<integer>`

Now right-click on an agent, and select Properties in the menu. This will display the General page of the Job Properties window, as shown in Figure 7-6.

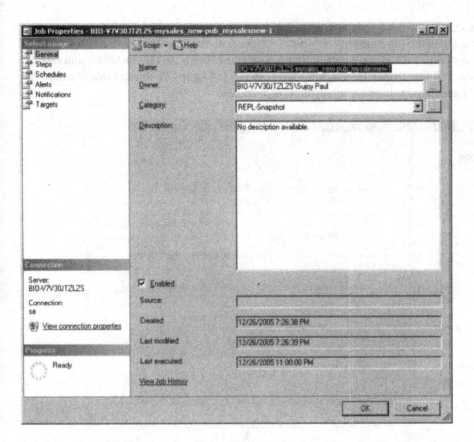

Figure 7-6. *Viewing the properties of the Snapshot Agent's connection to the Publisher*

Click on the ellipsis button beside the Category field, and you will see that there are three jobs listed under this snapshot, as shown in Figure 7-7.

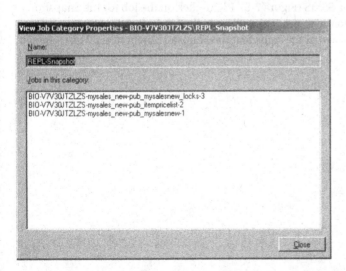

Figure 7-7. *Viewing the job category properties for the Snapshot Agent named* REPL-Snapshot

Close the dialog box to get back to the Job Properties window (Figure 7-6). Then click the Cancel button in the Job Properties window to get back to the SSMS (Figure 7-5). Now, right-click on any of the jobs for the Snapshot Agent under the Jobs object in the SSMS, and select View History. This will open the Log File Viewer shown in Figure 7-8. You can save the displayed information for future troubleshooting purposes.

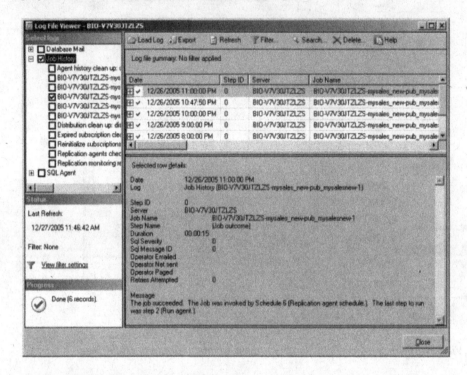

Figure 7-8. *Viewing the job history logs*

Click Close to get back to the SSMS (Figure 7-5). Right-click on the job for the Snapshot Agent, and select Properties from the menu. This will open the Job Properties window. Select the Steps page, and you will see a list of the steps that the Snapshot Agent takes. This is shown in Figure 7-9.

Figure 7-9. *Viewing the success and failure of the job steps performed by the Snapshot Agent*

By default, the agent takes three steps to execute the job:

1. Snapshot Agent startup message

2. Run agent

3. Detect nonlogged agent shutdown

You can change the sequence of these steps by moving them up or down in the list.

Now let's examine each of these steps. Select the first one and click the Edit button. This will take you to the Job Step Properties window shown in Figure 7-10.

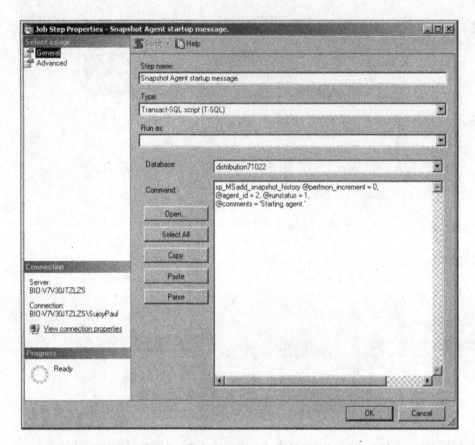

Figure 7-10. *Viewing the general settings for the Snapshot Agent's first job step—the startup message*

The agent uses the sp_MSadd_snapshot_history stored procedure to start the snapshot message, and executes it on the distribution database. As you can see in the figure, this is the script:

```
sp_MSadd_snapshot_history @perfmon_increment=0, @agent_id=2, @runstatus=1,
@comments='Starting agent'
```

The @perfmon_increment parameter updates the replication performance counters for a specific agent, @agent_id, associated with the id column in the MS_snapshotagents table. The performance counters that are updated on the successful execution of the agent are Snapshot: Delivered Cmds/Sec and Snapshot: Delivered Trans/Sec. The Snapshot: Delivered Cmds/Sec counter reports the average number of commands, and the Snapshot: Delivered Trans/Sec counter records the average number of transactions executed by the Snapshot Agent. Once the counters are added to the replication performance counter, the sp_MSadd_snapshot_history then adds the history of the data in the MSsnapshot_history table. You will find both the tables in the distribution database.

The @runstatus parameter records the status of the Snapshot Agent. The values of this parameter are shown in Table 7-2.

Table 7-2. *The Status Values of the* @runstatus *Parameter*

Value	Status
1	Start
2	Succeed
3	In progress
4	Idle
5	Retry
6	Failure

If the @runstatus parameter is idle, the idle record is inserted, or if the history of the row is idle, the row is updated in the MSsnapshot_history table.

Now select the Advanced page shown in Figure 7-11. The options on this page allow you to send the output of the job step to a table. This output is recorded in the sysjobstepslogs table in the msdb database. You can see the output in the table by clicking the View button, only after your job step has been executed once. You can see that on successful completion of the first step, the agent is set to go to the next step. However, for "On failure action," select "Quit the job reporting failure" from the drop-down box.

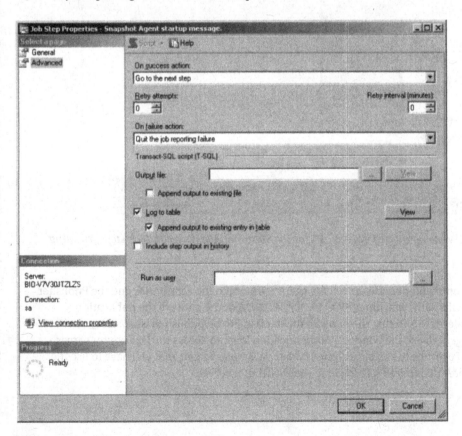

Figure 7-11. *Viewing the advanced settings for the Snapshot Agent's first job step—the startup message*

Tip If you log the job step in the table, you can view it using a text editor.

Click OK to return to the Job Properties window (Figure 7-9). Select the second job step and click Edit. This will open the window shown in Figure 7-12.

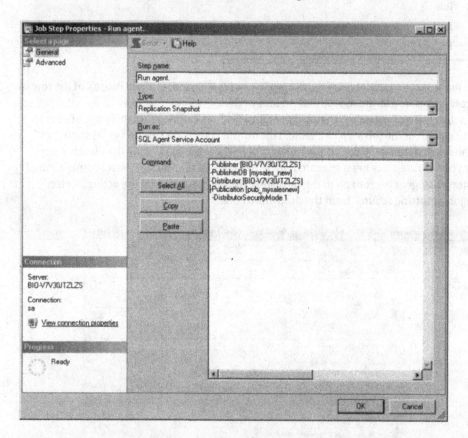

Figure 7-12. *Viewing the general settings for the Snapshot Agent's second job step—running the agent*

The command parameters tell the agent to run both the Distributor and the Publisher servers on the same machine (BIO-V7V30JTZLZS), that the name of the publication is pub_mysalesnew, and that the name of the database to be published is mysales_new. It also tells the agent to use the Windows Authentication login to access the Distributor server. (A value of 0 for the DistributorSecurityMode parameter means that you have to use the SQL Server Authentication to log in to the Distributor server.)

Next select the Advanced page, shown in Figure 7-13.

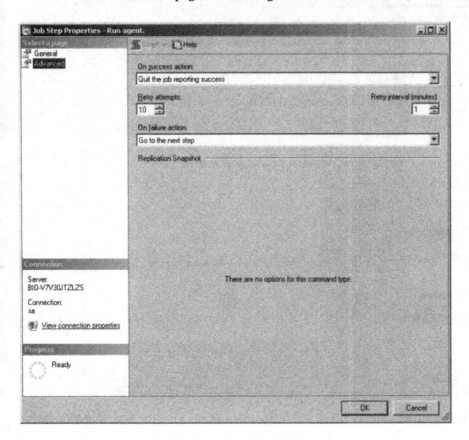

Figure 7-13. *Viewing the advanced settings for the Snapshot Agent's second job step—running the agent*

From the "On success action" drop-down box, select "Quit the job reporting success." Similarly, from the "On failure action" drop-down box, select "Go to step 3." If step 2 runs successfully, the entire job is successful and it quits. However, if it fails, it goes to step 3.

Now click OK. This will take you back to the Job Properties window (Figure 7-9). This time, select the third job step and click the Edit button. This will take you to the window shown in Figure 7-14.

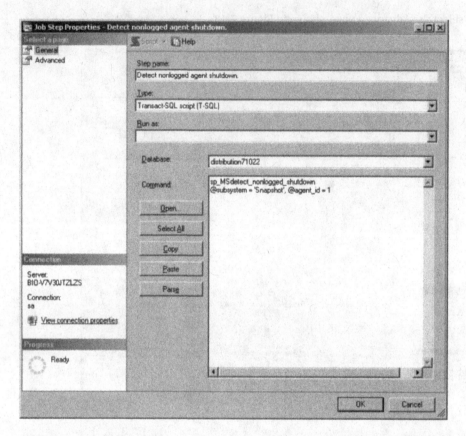

Figure 7-14. *Viewing the general settings for the Snapshot Agent's third job step—detecting errors*

This third step runs the following script to detect errors in either the Snapshot or Distribution Agents:

```
sp_MSdetect_nonlogged_shutdown @subsystem= 'Snapshot', @agent_id=2
```

The @subsystem parameter identifies the snapshot associated with the agent_id parameter, which is associated with the id column in the MSsnapshot_agents table. The sp_MSdetect_nonlogged_shutdown stored procedure then writes to the history of the job, and logs the messages in the SQL Server Agent's log and in the Replication Monitor.

Select the Advanced page, and you will see the window shown in Figure 7-15. Here you can view the output of the third step either by logging the messages to a text file or write the output of the job step to a table.

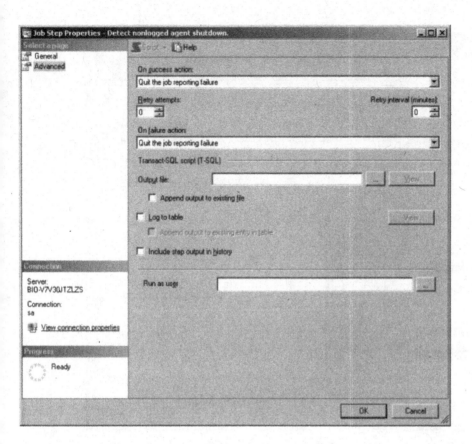

Figure 7-15. *Viewing the advanced settings for the Snapshot Agent's third job step—detecting errors*

You have now seen the three steps performed by the Snapshot Agent, but suppose you want to add or insert a step in the job. You can indeed add or move the steps depending on your business rules. Perhaps you want to add the name of the user who needs to view the pub_itempricelist publication at a remote site. You can simply add another step after the Snapshot Agent is run and before the agent logs the error messages.

For example, suppose we want to add a new user, apaul. In the Job Properties window (Figure 7-9), select step 3 and click the Insert button. Select the General tab and enter the following in the Command section.

```
CREATE USER [apaul]
FOR LOGIN [NT AUTHORITY\SYSTEM]
WITH DEFAULT_SCHEMA=[myinventory]
```

This is shown in Figure 7-16.

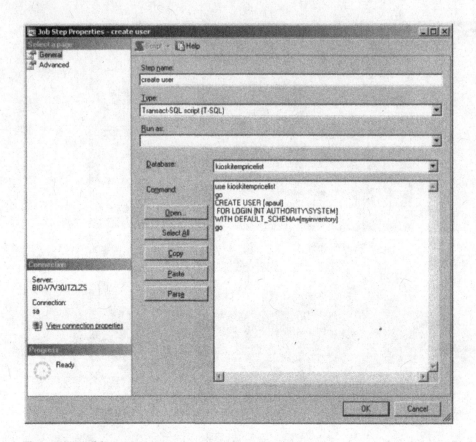

Figure 7-16. *Adding SQL scripts in the Command section*

By clicking the Parse button, you can check the SQL syntax. You can also run a SQL script by clicking the Open button and selecting the file. I have named the step "create user".

If you clicked the Parse button, click OK to get back to the Job Step Properties window (Figure 7-16). Now select the Advanced page of the Job Step Properties window. The configuration is shown in Figure 7-17. In the Output file text box, enter the directory and name of the file in which you want to view the logged steps of the execution of the text.

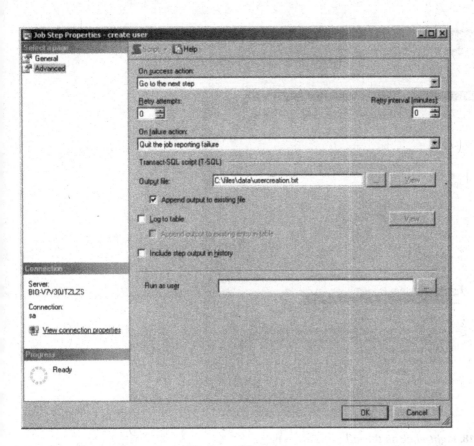

Figure 7-17. *Selecting the output file that will store the messages*

Click OK to get back to the Job Properties window (Figure 7-9). Click OK again to return to the SSMS. Now locate the agent you just finished configuring in the Object Explorer of the SSMS. It will be under the Jobs object, as shown in Figure 7-18.

Right-click on the job and select the Start Job option. You will see the window shown in Figure 7-19, which lists the four job steps. You can step through the job, or just go directly to any given step.

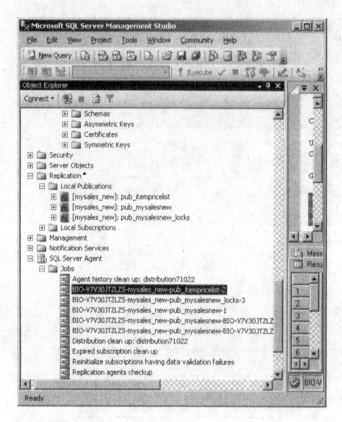

Figure 7-18. *Right-click on the job*

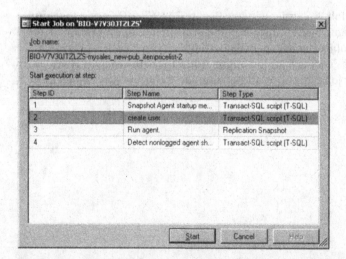

Figure 7-19. *Viewing the four job steps*

In this case, select step 2 and click the Start button. You can see that the step has been executed successfully in Figure 7-20.

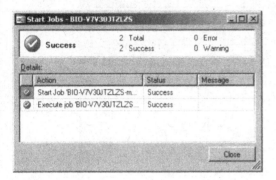

Figure 7-20. *The successful execution of job step 2*

In this section, I have shown you how the Snapshot Agent works, the steps it takes to generate the files, and the folder it stores them in. The Distribution Agent then picks up the messages and transmits them to the appropriate Subscriber servers. Let's look at how the Distribution Agent works.

The Distribution Agent

Once the snapshot of the publication is in the folder, the Distribution Agent takes up the responsibility of processing the messages and sending them to the necessary Subscriber servers.

As we did with the Snapshot Agent, let's look at the job steps for the execution of the Distribution Agent. Open the SQL Server Agent object in the Object Explorer in the SSMS. Then open the Jobs object, right-click on the Distribution Agent object (BIO-V7V30JTZLZS-mysales_new-pub_mysalesnew-BIO-V7V30JTZLZS-3 in this case), and select Properties. The agent's Job Properties window will open, as shown in Figure 7-21.

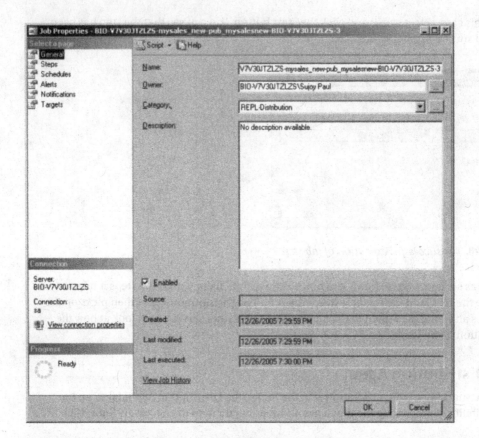

Figure 7-21. *Viewing the general properties of the Distribution Agent*

■**Tip** The name of the job for the Distribution Agent in the case of push subscriptions is `<Publisher>-`
`<Publicationdatabase>-<Publication>-<Subscriber>-<integer>`. For pull subscriptions, it is
`<Publisher>-<Publicationdatabase>-<Publication>-<Subscriber>-<subscriptiondatabase>-`
`<GUID>`.

Click the ellipsis button beside the Category field to view the list of jobs for the Distribution Agent. In the View Job Category Properties dialog box that opens, you can see the names of the subscriptions listed, as shown in Figure 7-22.

Click Close to return you to the Job Properties window (Figure 7-21). Select the Steps page, and you will notice that, just like the Snapshot Agent, the Distribution Agent consists of three steps by default. This is shown in Figure 7-23.

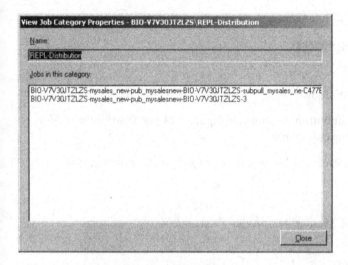

Figure 7-22. *Viewing the names of the subscriptions*

Figure 7-23. *Viewing the three default steps of the Distribution Agent*

The three steps in the Distribution Agent are as follows:

1. Distribution Agent startup message

2. Run agent

3. Detect nonlogged agent shutdown

Select step 1 and click the Edit button. As shown in Figure 7-24, the Distribution Agent startup message runs the following command:

```
sp_MSadd_distribution_history @perfmon_increment=0, @agent_id=6, @runstatus=1,
@comments='Starting agent'
```

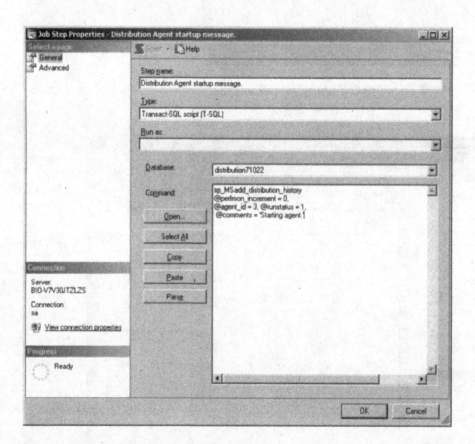

Figure 7-24. *Viewing the Distribution Agent's startup message step*

As in step 1 of the Snapshot Agent, the Distribution Agent updates the replication performance counters by using the @perfmon_increment parameter for a specific agent, @agent_id, which is associated with the id column in the MS_distributionagents table. The performance counters that are updated on the successful execution of the agent are Dist: Delivered Cmds/Sec, Dist: Delivered Latency/Sec, and Dist: Delivered Trans/Sec. The Dist: Delivered Latency/Sec counter reports the average time it took for the transactions to be delivered by the Distribution Agent. Once the counters are added to the replication performance counter, sp_MSadd_snapshot_history then adds the history of the data in the MSdistribution_history table. Both tables can be found in the distribution database.

If you select the Advanced page, shown in Figure 7-25, you will see that the settings for the Distribution Agent are the same as for the Snapshot Agent.

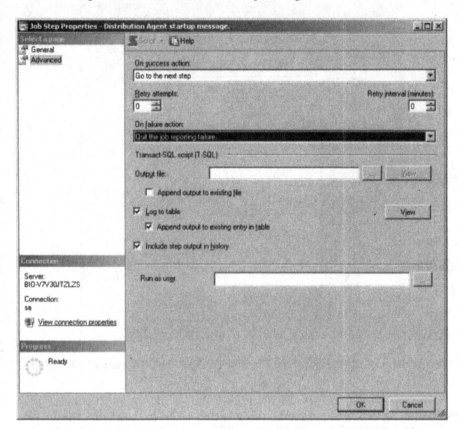

Figure 7-25. *Setting the actions taken on the success or failure of the Distribution Agent's first job step*

From the drop-down box for the "On failure action," select "Quit the job reporting failure." Note you can also save the messages by storing them in a table. Click the OK button twice to return to the Job Properties window (Figure 7-23).

Select step 2, and click the Edit button. As you can see in Figure 7-26, the following commands are issued in the Run agent step:

```
-Subscriber [BIO-V7V30JTZLZS]
-SubscriberDB [subpush_mysales_new]
-Publisher [BIO-V7V30JTZLZS]
-Distributor [BIO-V7V30JTZLZS]
-DistributorSecurityMode 1
-Publication [pub_mysalesnew]
-PublisherDB [mysales_new]
```

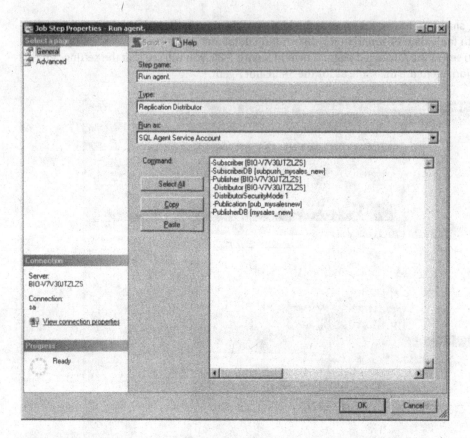

Figure 7-26. *Viewing the general settings for the Distribution Agent's second job step—running the agent*

The Distribution Agent looks for the subscription database, subpush_mysales_new, on the Subscriber server, BIO-V7V3OJTZLZS, to transfer the publication, pub_mysales_new, using the Windows Authenticated login. The Distribution Agent can continuously poll for new snapshots at polling intervals by adding the -Continuous option in the Run agent step.

■**Note** If the value of the DistributorSecurityMode is set to 0, that means it is using the SQL Server Authentication mode.

In Figure 7-26, you can see that the agent job step runs as the SQL Agent Service Account. This is the proxy account for the agent job step. A proxy account is one where the SQL Server Agent defines the security context under which the job step, Run agent, can be executed. The job step will run as a SQL Agent service continuously, until you manually stop the service.

Select the Advanced page and configure the settings as shown in Figure 7-27. In this case, if the job step is successful, the job step will quit, reporting success as shown. However, to specify what will happen if the job step is unsuccessful, select "Go to the next step" from the "On failure action" drop-down list. The job will go directly to step 3 if there is an error.

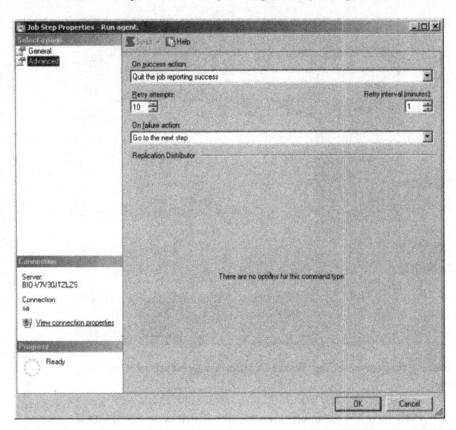

Figure 7-27. *Changing the advanced settings for the Distribution Agent's second job step—running the agent*

Click OK to return to the Job Properties window (Figure 7-23). Now choose step 3 and click Edit to open the window shown in Figure 7-28. You will see that the command issued is similar to the one issued for the Snapshot Agent:

```
sp_MSdetect_nonlogged_shutdown @subsystem = 'Distribution',
@agent_id = 6
```

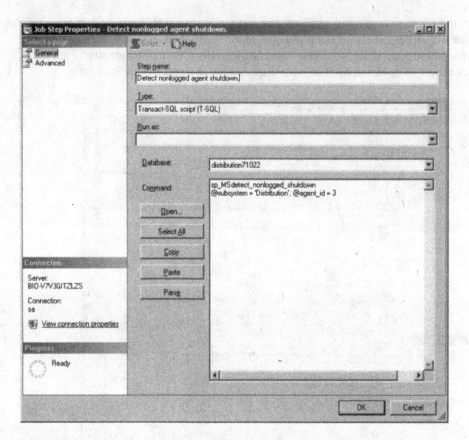

Figure 7-28. *Viewing the general settings for the Distribution Agent's third job step—detecting errors*

In this case, the @subsystem parameter identifies the Distribution Agent with the parameter agent_id, which is associated with the id column in the MSdistribution_agents table. As with the Snapshot Agent, the sp_Msdetect_nonlogged_shutdown stored procedure for the Distribution Agent then writes to the history of the job, and logs messages in the SQL Server Agent's log and in the Replication Monitor.

Finally, select the Advanced page and set the log to be written to a table, as shown in Figure 7-29.

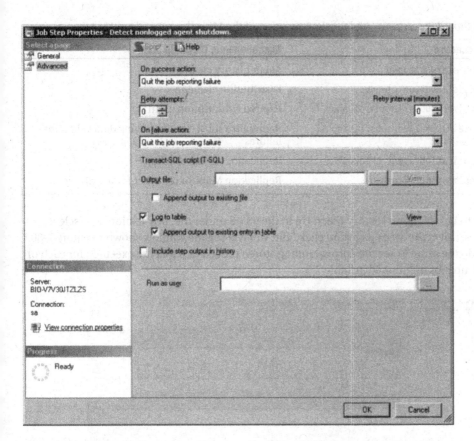

Figure 7-29. *Changing the advanced settings for the Distribution Agent's third job step—detecting errors*

The Miscellaneous Clean Up Jobs

As was mentioned in Chapter 2, creating the distribution database causes SQL Server to generate a set of miscellaneous clean up jobs. These were outlined in Table 2-1, but here I will identify the stored procedures that they execute and describe the internal workings of these clean up jobs.

Table 7-3 shows what stored procedure each clean up job is using.

Table 7-3. *Stored Procedures Used for the Execution of the Miscellaneous Clean Up Jobs*

Stored Procedure	Miscellaneous Clean Up Jobs
dbo.sp_MShistory_cleanup	Agent history clean up
dbo.sp_MSdistribution_cleanup	Distribution clean up
sys.sp_expired_subscription_cleanup	Expired subscription clean up
sys.sp_MSreinit_failed_subscriptions	Reinitialize subscriptions having data validation failures
sys.sp_replication_agent_checkup	Replication agents checkup
dbo.sp_replmonitorrefreshjob	Replication Monitor refresher for distribution

Right-click on Agent History Clean Up in the SSMS under the Jobs section, and select Properties. Select the Steps page and click Edit; you will see the window shown in Figure 7-30. You can do the same to see the corresponding stored procedures that are executed for each of the clean up jobs mentioned in Table 7-3.

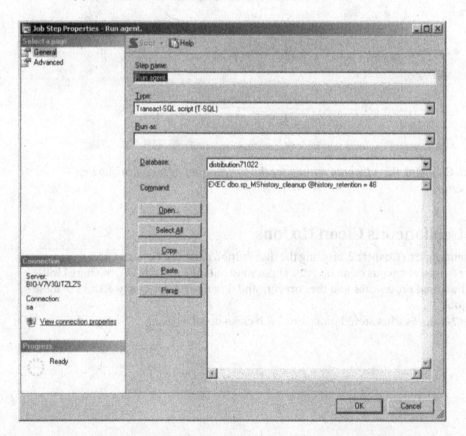

Figure 7-30. *Displaying the Run agent step of the Agent history clean up job*

As mentioned in Chapter 2, the clean up jobs are used for the routine maintenance and administration of replication. The following list describes how each of the clean up jobs work in snapshot replication.

- **Agent history clean up**: This job is used for all the different types of replication and is executed on the distribution database (in this server instance, the name of the distribution database is distribution71022) on the local Distributor server. It cleans up everything in the MSrepl_errors system table in the distribution database where the @history_retention exceeds 30 days plus 48 hours, which is specified in the command. It then deletes all but one row from the MSsnapshot_history table in the distribution database—the one row is left for monitoring purposes. It then takes out the rows from the MSdistribution_history system table. Finally, it finishes deleting the messages from the sysreplicationalerts system table.

- **Distribution clean up**: This job runs on the distribution database and removes the replicated transactions and commands, and then it updates the statistics periodically on the cleaned tables. It also deactivates those subscriptions that have not been synchronized within the maximum retention period. In my case the retention period is 72 hours.

■**Note** Agent history clean up, Replication agents checkup, and Distribution clean up run every 10 minutes by default.

- **Expired subscription clean up**: This job detects and removes subscriptions that have expired from both heterogeneous and SQL Server publications. It scans the sysdatabases system table and checks the category column for both the bit values of 1 and 4 to retrieve all the SQL Server publications, and then removes the expired subscriptions using the sys.sp_MSdrop_expired_subscription stored procedure.

- **Reinitialize subscriptions having data validation failures**: This job checks for validation failures by scanning for each of the publications in the sysreplicationalerts system table in the msdb database. It scans the alert_error_code column for a value of 20574, which indicates that there is a validation failure. Having found a validation failure, it then reinitializes the subscription for snapshot and transactional replication using the sp_reinitsubscription stored procedure.

- **Replication agents checkup**: This job finds out which agents are not logging correctly and writes to the Windows event log.

- **Replication Monitor refresher for distribution**: This job monitors the cached queries used by the Replication Monitor. It does so by scouring MSreplication_monitordata and then refreshes the queries.

On the Distributor Server

The implementation of snapshot replication that I have described in Chapters 4–6 uses the Publisher-Subscriber model, in which data is transmitted from the central Publisher to the different Subscriber servers using the distribution database. The distribution database resides on the Distributor server.

The Distribution Database

The distribution database is the key to understanding the workings of the different types of replication, and to troubleshooting when necessary. The E-R diagrams of the system tables in the distribution database used for snapshot replication are shown in Figures 7-31 through 7-35. I will explain most of these tables; I have included all of them because they're a useful reference.

MSsubscriber_info	
publisher	sysname
subscriber	sysname
type	tinyint
login	sysname
password	nvarchar(524)
description	nvarchar(510)
security_mode	int

MSarticles	
publisher_id	smallint
publisher_db	sysname
publication_id	int
article	sysname
article_id	int
destination_object	sysname
source_owner	sysname
source_object	sysname
description	nvarchar(255)
destination_owner	sysname

MSsync_states	
publisher_id	smallint
publisher_db	sysname
publication_id	int

MSpublication_access	
publication_id	int
login	sysname
sid	varbinary(85)

MSrepl_errors	
id	int
time	datetime
error_type_id	int
source_type_id	int
source_name	nvarchar(100)
error_code	sysname
error_text	ntext
xact_seqno	varbinary(16)
command_id	int
session_id	int

MSpublicationthresholds	
publication_id	int
metric_id	int
value	sql_variant
shouldalert	bit
isenabled	bit

MSpublisher_databases	
publisher_id	smallint
publisher_db	sysname
id	int
publisher_engine_edition	int

Figure 7-31. *The E-R diagram showing the* MSsubscriber_info, MSsync_states, MSrepl_errors, MSarticles, MSpublication_access, MSpublicationthresholds, *and* MSpublisher_databases *system tables used for snapshot replication in the distribution database*

MSrepl_commands	
publisher_database_id	int
xact_seqno	varbinary(16)
type	int
article_id	int
originator_id	int
command_id	int
partial_command	bit
command	varbinary(1024)
hashkey	int
originator_lsn	varbinary(16)

MSrepl_originators	
id	int
publisher_database_id	int
srvname	sysname
dbname	sysname
publication_id	int
dbversion	int

MSrepl_version	
major_version	int
minor_version	int
revision	int
db_existed	bit

MSrepl_identity_range	
publisher	sysname
publisher_db	sysname
tablename	sysname
identity_support	int
next_seed	bigint
pub_range	bigint
range	bigint
max_identity	bigint
threshold	int
current_max	bigint

MSsubscriptions	
publisher_database_id	int
publisher_id	smallint
publisher_db	sysname
publication_id	int
article_id	int
subscriber_id	smallint
subscriber_db	sysname
subscription_type	int
sync_type	tinyint
status	tinyint
subscription_seqno	varbinary(16)
snapshot_seqno_flag	bit
independent_agent	bit
subscription_time	datetime
loopback_detection	bit
agent_id	int
update_mode	tinyint
publisher_seqno	varbinary(16)
ss_cplt_seqno	varbinary(16)

MSpublications	
publisher_id	smallint
publisher_db	sysname
publication	sysname
publication_id	int
publication_type	int
thirdparty_flag	bit
independent_agent	bit
immediate_sync	bit
allow_push	bit
allow_pull	bit
allow_anonymous	bit
description	nvarchar(255)
vendor_name	nvarchar(100)
retention	int
sync_method	int
allow_subscription_copy	bit
thirdparty_options	int
allow_queued_tran	bit
options	int
retention_period_unit	tinyint

Figure 7-32. *The E-R diagram showing the* MSrepl_commands, MSrepl_originators, MSrepl_version, MSrepl_identity_range, MSpublications, *and* MSsubscriptions *system tables used for snapshot replication in the distribution database*

MSdistribution_agents	
id	int
name	nvarchar(100)
publisher_database_id	int
publisher_id	smallint
publisher_db	sysname
publication	sysname
subscriber_id	smallint
subscriber_db	sysname
subscription_type	int
local_job	bit
job_id	binary(16)
subscription_guid	binary(16)
profile_id	int
anonymous_subid	bigint
subscriber_name	sysname
virtual_agent_id	int
anonymous_agent_id	int
creation_date	datetime
queue_id	sysname
queue_status	int
offload_enabled	bit
offload_server	sysname
dts_package_name	sysname
dts_package_location	int
dts_package_password	nvarchar(524)
sid	varbinary(85)
queue_server	sysname
subscriber_security_mode	smallint
subscriber_login	sysname
subscriber_password	nvarchar(524)
reset_partial_snapshot_progress	bit
job_step_uid	bigint
subscriptionstreams	tinyint

Figure 7-33. *The E-R diagram showing the* MSdistribution_agents *system table used for snapshot replication in the distribution database*

MSreplication_monitordata	
lastrefresh	datetime
computetime	int
publication_id	int
publisher	sysname
publisher_srvid	int
publisher_db	sysname
publication	sysname
publication_type	int
agent_type	int
agent_id	int
agent_name	sysname
job_id	bigint
status	int
isagentrunningnow	bit
warning	int
last_distsync	datetime
agentstoptime	datetime
distdb	sysname
retention	int
time_stamp	datetime
worst_latency	int
best_latency	int
avg_latency	int
cur_latency	int
worst_runspeedPerf	int
best_runspeedPerf	int
average_runspeedPerf	int
mergePerformance	int
mergelatestsessionrunduration	int
mergelatestsessionrunspeed	float(53)
mergelatestsessionconnectiontype	int
retention_period_unit	tinyint

MSsnapshot_history	
agent_id	int
runstatus	int
start_time	datetime
time	datetime
duration	int
comments	nvarchar(255)
delivered_transactions	int
delivered_commands	int
delivery_rate	float(53)
error_id	int
timestamp	timestamp

Figure 7-34. *The E-R diagram showing the* MSreplication_monitordata *and* MSsnapshot_history *system tables used for snapshot replication in the distribution database*

MSdistribution_history	
agent_id	int
runstatus	int
start_time	datetime
time	datetime
duration	int
comments	nvarchar(4000)
xact_seqno	varbinary(16)
current_delivery_rate	float(53)
current_delivery_latency	int
delivered_transactions	int
delivered_commands	int
average_commands	int
delivery_rate	float(53)
delivery_latency	int
total_delivered_commands	int
error_id	int
updateable_row	bit
timestamp	timestamp

MSsnapshot_agents	
id	int
name	nvarchar(100)
publisher_id	smallint
publisher_db	sysname
publication	sysname
publication_type	int
local_job	bit
job_id	binary(16)
profile_id	int
dynamic_filter_login	sysname
dynamic_filter_hostname	sysname
publisher_security_mode	int
publisher_login	sysname
publisher_password	nvarchar(524)
job_step_uid	bigint

Figure 7-35. *The E-R diagram showing the* MSsnapshot_agents *and* MSdistribution_history *system tables used for snapshot replication in the distribution database*

Earlier in the chapter, I mentioned that creating a publication causes a row to be added in the syspublications system table in the publication database. The distributor_admin link is then used to transmit the rows to the MSpublications table in the distribution database.

Let's start by taking a look at the MSpublications system table. This table contains information for each publication. Listing 7-7 shows you the names of the publications and the associated types of subscriptions that are stored in the distribution database.

Listing 7-7. *Getting Information About the Publications*

```
/* Execute this on the distribution database */

select
publication_type,
publisher_db,
publication,
```

```
thirdparty_flag,
independent_agent,
immediate_sync,
allow_push,
allow_pull,
allow_anonymous,
retention,
sync_method,
vendor_name
from MSpublications
order by
publication_type
```

The output of this script is as follows:

| publication_type | publisher_db | publication | independent_agent |
| immediate_sync | allow_push | allow_pull | allow_anonymous |
retention	sync_method	vendor_name	
1	mysales_new	pub_mysalesnew	0
1	1	1	1
0	0	Microsoft SQL Server	
1	mysales_new	pub_itempricelist	0
1	1	1	1
0	0	Microsoft SQL Server	
1	mysales_new	pub_mysalesnew_locks	0
1	1	1	1
0	0	Microsoft SQL Server	

In this case, publication_type identifies the kind of publication that is being used. A value of 1 indicates that the publication is of snapshot type. The name of the publication database and the publication are defined by the columns publisher_db and publication, respectively.

You can see that in all the publications, the synchronization method uses the native format for the bulk copy program (sync_method is 0). This is also what we saw when we tried to retrieve the rows in the syspublications table in the publication database (Listing 7-5).

You can also see that the vendor for the publication database is SQL Server and that all the publications support push (allow_push), pull (allow_pull), and anonymous (allow_anonymous) subscriptions.

Now that we know the names of the publications, we can look up the articles in the publication in the MSarticles system table. Listing 7-8 shows you how to get this information for the publication database using the myinventory schema.

Listing 7-8. *Getting Information on the Articles in a Publication*

```
/* Execute this on distribution database */

select
publisher_db ,
publication_id ,
article ,
destination_object ,
source_owner ,
source_object
from MSarticles
where source_owner like 'myinventory'
```

The output of this script is as follows:

```
publisher_db  publication_id    article        destination_object
 source_owner  source_object
-----------------------------------------------------------------------
mysales_new       1             Item           Item
 myinventory      Item
mysales_new       1             PriceList      PriceList
 myinventory      PriceList
...
(16 row(s) affected)
```

The destination_object column contains the name of the table that is being sent to the Subscriber server, and the source_object holds the name of the table in the publication database.

Recall from the earlier "The Snapshot Agent" section that when the Snapshot Agent starts, it looks for the agent ID, which is associated with the id column in the MSsnapshot_agents table, in order to update the performance counters before the sp_MSadd_snapshot_history stored procedure adds the history of the data in the MSsnapshot_history system table. Listings 7-9 and 7-10 show you how to retrieve the data stored by the Snapshot Agents and the history of the snapshot data from the distribution database.

Listing 7-9. *Getting the Data Stored by the Snapshot Agent*

```
/* Execute this on the distribution database */
use distribution
go

select
id,
name,
publisher_db,
```

```
publication,
publication_type,
job_id,
publisher_security_mode,
publisher_login,
job_step_uid
from MSsnapshot_agents
```

The output of the script in Listing 7-9 is as follows:

```
id                      name
 publisher_db            publication
 publication_type        job_id
 publisher_security_mode       publisher_login
 job_step_uid
---------------------------------------------------------------
2                       BIO-V7V30JTZLZS-mysales_new-pub_itempricelist-2
 mysales_new            pub_itempricelist
 1                      0x8D800FD5CF5B354889B571BF77B813B4
 1                      ---
EOC8E478-121E-48E4-8597-06AF1C9687CE
1                       BIO-V7V30JTZLZS-mysales_new-pub_mysalesnew-1
 mysales_new            pub_mysalesnew
 1                        0xE62B8BEB58B43E4D8138E3ABBA2900EB
 1                        ---
77335488-9A01-444D-9EC3-1D59A65A1D48
 3                      BIO-V7V30JTZLZS-mysales_new-pub_mysalesnew_locks-3
 mysales_new            pub_mysalesnew_locks
 1                      0xEA4C1B8D44C6AF4298D9425C763516A5
 0                      sa
 E85D60DC-6FB5-4E48-846B-4C9EDF1F5C54
```

This output lists the name of the Snapshot Agent (name), the name of the publication database (publisher_db), the name of the publication (publication), and the type of publication (publication_type is 1, which means snapshot). The job_id is the job identification number. The publisher_security_mode column identifies the mode used by the agent to connect to the Publisher; a value of 1 indicates that the agent is using Windows Authentication. The login value of the Publisher is represented by publisher_login. The job_step_uid column contains the unique ID of the SQL Server Agent job step when Snapshot Agent is started.

Listing 7-10 shows how to get the history of the snapshot data. We want to know that the commands have been delivered successfully, so we want to know the running status of the agent, the start time for the execution of the job, the time when the message was logged, and the duration of the session. It's good to have the comments included too, so you will know what exactly is happening.

Listing 7-10. *Getting the History of the Snapshot*

```
/* Execute this on the distribution database */
use distribution
go

select
agent_id,
runstatus,
start_time,
time,
duration,
comments,
delivered_transactions,
delivered_commands,
delivery_rate,
error_id
from MSsnapshot_history where delivered_commands <>0
```

The output of this script is as follows:

```
agent_id   runstatus   start_time                      time
duration        comments
delivered_transactions                   delivery_rate      error_id
-----------------------------------------------------------------------------
1          3           2005-12-26 19:27:06.137          2005-12-26 19:27:11.270
1              [2%] Bulk copied snapshot data for article 'Customer' (25 rows)
0                                        25                 0
1          3           2005-12-26 19:27:06.137          2005-12-26 19:27:11.610
1              [3%] Bulk copied snapshot data for article 'Item' (25 rows).
0                                        25                 0
1          3           2005-12-26 19:27:06.137          2005-12-26 19:27:11.800
1              [5%] Bulk copied snapshot data for article 'OrderHeader' (25 rows)
0                                        25                 0
1          3           2005-12-26 19:27:06.137          2005-12-26 19:27:12.060
1              [6%] Bulk copied snapshot data for article 'OrderDetail' (48 rows)
0                                        48                 0
...
(62 row(s) affected)
```

In this output, the delivery_rate column indicates the average number of commands delivered per second. The error_id is the ID of the error in the MSrepl_errors system table. Should there be a failure in the Distribution Agent (or the Merge Agent in merge replication), the error messages will be logged in the MSrepl_errors system table. There were no errors for the result set of 62 rows in this example. The runstatus of 3 means that the job is still in progress. The different values of the runstatus were mentioned previously in Table 7-2.

The duration of execution is 1 second, while the delivery_rate for the Customer, Item, and OrderHeader is 25 seconds. In the case of OrderDetail, it is 48 seconds for delivering 48 rows.

Now let's look into the MSdistribution_history system table to see if there is a history of the data associated with the Distribution Agent on the local Distributor server. Listing 7-11 shows how to look up this history.

Listing 7-11. *Getting the History Associated with the Distribution Agent*

```
/* Execute this on the distribution database */
use distribution
go

select
agent_id,
runstatus,
start_time,
time,
duration,
comments,
delivered_transactions,
delivery_rate,
error_id
from MSdistribution_history where
delivered_commands <>0 and runstatus<>3
```

The output of this query is as follows:

```
agent_id    runstatus    start_time               time
duration    comments
delivered_transactions           delivery_rate            error_id
----------- -----------  ------------------------ ------------------------

3           2            2005-12-26 19:30:07.360  2005-12-26 19:30:17.497
10          Applied the snapshot to the Subscriber.
1                                196.51                  0
3           4            2005-12-26 19:31:15.760  2005-12-27 01:00:32.800
19757       No replicated transactions are available.
5                                6404.166875             0
4           2            2005-12-26 19:31:34.927  2005-12-26 19:31:49.280
15          Applied the snapshot to the Subscriber
1                                287.7                   0

(3 row(s) affected)
```

With this history data associated with the Distribution Agent, we can find out the history of the data for the Distribution Agent, except when the agent is in progress. A runstatus of 3 means that the agent is in progress. By setting the runstatus column to not equal 3, you will be able to read the history of the records and find out whether the snapshot has been applied or whether any replicated transactions are available, as shown in the preceding output. We also can view the comments in the MSdistribution_history table, and the error_id associated with the agent_id. You can see from the preceding output that where the agent has been successful, it mentions that it applied the snapshot to the Subscriber server. However, when it has been idle, there were no transactions to be replicated.

Tip To find out what the errors were, look at the comments column in the MSrepl_errors system table. It will provide you with information on the command or transaction that is causing the problem.

If we were to remove the where clause from the query in Listing 7-11, it would return more rows, and you would be able to see the application of different snapshot files generated by the Snapshot Agent in the comments column or whether the Distribution Agent has delivered the snapshot.

Now let's look at the information that is stored for the subscriptions. You will find this in the MSsubscriptions system table, which contains one row for each article that is published in the subscription. This table is stored on the distribution database in the local Distributor server. Listing 7-12 shows how to retrieve this information.

Listing 7-12. *Retrieving Information About the Subscriptions*

```
/* Execute this on the distribution database */
use distribution
go

select
publisher_db,
publication_id,
article_id,
subscription_type,
subscriber_db,
status,
independent_agent
from MSsubscriptions where subscriber_db like 'sub%'
```

The output of this query is as follows:

publisher_db subscriber_db	publication_id status	article_id	subscription_type independent_agent
mysales_new	1	1	0
subpush_mysales_new	1		1
mysales_new	1	2	0

```
subpush_mysales_new        1                       1
mysales_new                       1        3               0
subpush_mysales_new        1                       1
mysales_new                       1        4               0
subpush_mysales_new        1                       1
...
(40 row(s) affected)
```

This query lists the name of the publication database (publisher_db), the corresponding ID of the publication (publication_id), the ID of the article (article_id), and the type of subscription (subscription_type). A value of 0 specifies a push subscription. The name of the subscription database is in the subscriber_db column; a status of 1 means that the subscription has already been received by the Subscriber server. The independent_agent column indicates whether there is a stand-alone Distribution Agent running for the publication.

Now let's find out the names of the Publisher and Subscriber servers that are being used for push subscriptions. You can do this by using the MSsubscriber_info system table as shown in Listing 7-13.

Listing 7-13. *Determining the Publisher and Subscriber Servers for Push Subscriptions*

```
/* Execute this on the distribution database */
use distribution
go

select
publisher,
subscriber,
type,
security_mode
from MSsubscriber_info
```

The output of this script is as follows:

```
publisher          subscriber            type   security_mode
-------------------------------------------------------------------
BIO-V7V30JTZLZS    BIO-V7V30JTZLZS         0      1
```

The script retrieves the names of the Publisher and Subscriber servers that are involved in the push subscription. We also find out that this is a SQL Server Subscriber, since the type is 0—a value of 1 indicates an ODBC data source. The security_mode of 1 specifies that Windows Authentication is being used.

The functions of the other tables are described in Table 7-4. You can find more details in the BOL.

Table 7-4. *Functions of System Tables in the Distribution Database Used for Snapshot Replication*

Name	Function
MSdistribution_agents	Contains one row for each Distribution Agent running on the local Distributor server
MSpublicationthresholds	Contains one row for each threshold monitored; used to track the performance metrics of replication for a publication
MSpublisher_databases	Contains one row for each Publisher–publication database pair serviced by the local Distribution server
MSrepl_identity_range	Provides identity range management
MSrepl_commands	Contains rows of commands that have been replicated
MSrepl_version	Contains a row for the current installation of the replication system
MSsync_states	Tracks those publications that are still using the concurrent snapshot mode
MSrepl_originitors	Contains a row for each transaction updated from the Subscriber
MSreplication_monitordata	Contains one row for each monitored subscription; this is used by the Replication Monitor to monitor the cached data

The MSDB Database

Now that I have shown you the tables that store snapshot replication information in the distribution database, we will look at the workings of the msdb system database. You already know that this database is used for the jobs carried out by SQL Server. Since agents are nothing but a series of jobs carried out for replication, you will find that most of the tables store information regarding the agents, their profiles, and their parameters.

Figures 7-36 through 7-38 show the E-R diagrams for the system tables in the msdb database involved in replication.

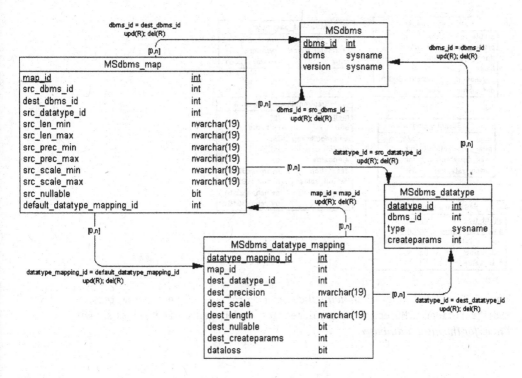

Figure 7-36. *The E-R diagram showing the* MSdbms, MSdbms_map, MSdbms_datatype, *and* MSdbms_datatype_mapping *system tables for the msdb database*

MSagent_profiles	
profile_id	int
profile_name	sysname
agent_type	int
type	int
description	nvarchar(3000)
def_profile	bit

MSagent_parameters	
profile_id	int
parameter_name	sysname
value	nvarchar(255)

MSdistributiondbs	
name	sysname
min_distretention	int
max_distretention	int
history_retention	int

MSreplmonthresholdmetrics	
metric_id	int
title	sysname
warningbitstatus	int
alertmessageid	int
alertnameid	int
description	nvarchar(3000)
default_value	nvarchar(8016)
min_value	nvarchar(8016)
max_value	nvarchar(8016)

MSagentparameterlist	
agent_type	tinyint
parameter_name	sysname
default_value	nvarchar(4000)
min_value	int
max_value	int

Figure 7-37. *The E-R diagram showing the* MSagent_profiles, MSagent_parameters, MSdistributiondbs, MSreplmonthresholdmetrics, *and* MSagentparameterlist *system tables for the msdb database*

sysreplicationalerts	
alert_id	int
status	int
agent_type	int
agent_id	int
error_id	int
alert_error_code	int
time	datetime
publisher	sysname
publisher_db	sysname
publication	sysname
publication_type	int
subscriber	sysname
subscriber_db	sysname
article	sysname
destination_object	sysname
source_object	sysname
alert_error_text	nvarchar(16)

MSdistpublishers	
name	sysname
distribution_db	sysname
working_directory	nvarchar(255)
security_mode	int
login	sysname
password	nvarchar(524)
active	bit
trusted	bit
thirdparty_flag	bit
publisher_type	sysname

MSdistributor	
property	sysname
value	nvarchar(3000)

Figure 7-38. *The E-R diagram showing the* MSdistributor, MSdistpublishers, *and* sysreplicationalerts *system tables for the msdb database*

In Chapter 4, I showed you the different profiles for the Snapshot and Distribution Agents. Those profiles are stored in the MSagent_profiles system tables of the msdb database. Listing 2-6 in Chapter 2 shows you how can retrieve the details for the different agent profiles.

We can also look up the different parameters for the agents. This information is stored in the MSagentparameterlist table. The script in Listing 7-14 retrieves the different parameters for the agents.

Listing 7-14. *Viewing Agent Profile Parameters*

```
/* Execute this on the msdb database */
use msdb
go

select agent_type,
parameter_name,
default_value,
min_value,
max_value
from MSagentparameterlist
where agent_type=1
```

The output of this script is as follows:

agent_type	parameter_name	min_value	max_value
1	70Subscribers	0	1
1	BcpBatchSize	100000	NULL
1	HistoryVerboseLevel	2	3
1	LoginTimeout	15	NULL
1	MaxBcpThreads	1	NULL
1	MaxNetworkOptimization	1	1
1	Output	NULL	NULL
1	OutputVerboseLevel	1	2
1	PacketSize	8192	32767
1	PublisherFailoverPartner	NULL	NULL
1	QueryTimeout	1800	NULL
1	StartQueueTimeout	0	300
1	UsePerArticleContentsView	0	1

```
(13 row(s) affected)
```

This output displays all the parameters for the Snapshot Agent's default profile. The value of 1 in the agent_type column means that it is a Snapshot Agent.

The default profile for the Snapshot Agent is generated by the system. We can create a user-defined profile by changing the values of the parameters and asking the Snapshot Agent to use the newly created profile instead of the default profile. You can, for example, create a user-defined profile that will help to optimize the delivery of the snapshot. Let's go back to view the profile of the Snapshot Agent using the SSMS and take another look at the list of parameters. I will then show you how to change the profile.

Open the SSMS, right-click the Local Publications object under Replication, and select Distributor Properties. Select the General page in the Distributor Properties window, click the Profile Defaults button at the lower right of the screen, and the Agent Profiles window will open. You will see a list of agents that are present. Select Snapshot Agents, and click the New button. It will ask you to create a New Agent Profile, as shown in Figure 7-39. Click OK.

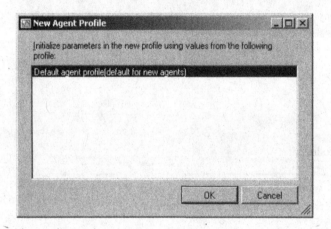

Figure 7-39. *Initializing the parameters for a new Snapshot Agent profile from the default profile*

The Properties window shown in Figure 7-40 will be displayed. Uncheck the "Show only parameters used in this profile" check box to display all the parameters for the profile. Select -MaxBcpThreads, click the row under the Value column, and set the value to 2, as in the figure. This value sets the bcp utility to run in parallel; a value of 2 will help the bcp utility run faster using parallel processing. Finally, give the profile a name, and click OK.

■**Caution** Do not increase MaxBcpThreads to a much higher level because it will have an impact on overall system performance.

This will take you back to the Agent Profiles window shown in Figure 7-41.

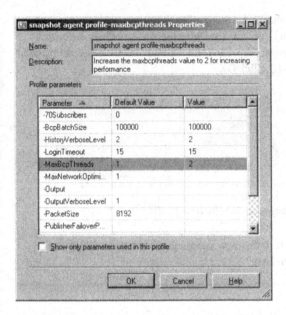

Figure 7-40. *Setting the value for the* MaxBcpThreads *parameter to* 2

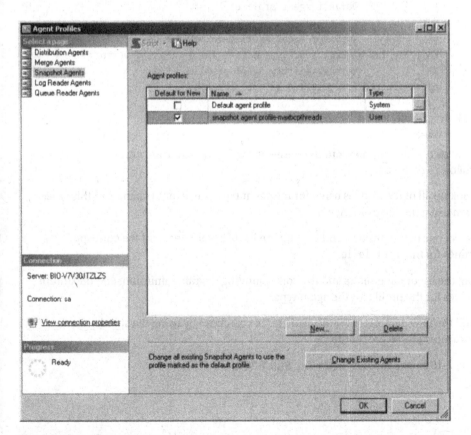

Figure 7-41. *Selecting the new agent profile*

Check the box in the Default for New column for the profile that you created (snapshot agent profile-maxbcpthreads), and the check box for the Default agent profile is automatically unchecked. The new profile is a User Type. Now click the Change Existing Agents button. You will see the message shown in Figure 7-42. Click OK.

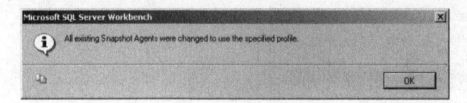

Figure 7-42. *Existing Snapshot Agents are changed to use the new profile*

Now if you run Listing 2-6, you will see that the new profile has been included in the MSagent_profiles table. The output is shown here:

```
agent_type   profile_id   profile_name
   type        description
-----------  -----------  -----------------------------------------------
1            1            Default agent profile
  0          NULL
1            17           snapshot agent profile-maxbcpthreads
  1          Increase the maxbcpthreads value to 2 for increasing performance
2            3            Verbose history agent profile.
  0          Agent profile for detailed history logging.
...
(17 row(s) affected)
```

You can also add a parameter to the profile using T-SQL. There are four steps that you need to follow to do this:

1. Look up all of the profiles listed for the agent type you want to change. In this case, I am using the Snapshot Agent.

2. Select one of the profiles, and look up the list of parameters and the corresponding values for that profile_id.

3. Get the list of parameters and the corresponding default, minimum, and maximum values for the profile for the agent type.

4. Add the new parameter for the profile_id you chose by using the sp_add_agent_parameter stored procedure.

Listing 7-15 shows you how to do this with T-SQL.

Listing 7-15. *Adding a New Parameter to the Snapshot Agent Profile*

```
/* Execute this on the msdb database */
use msdb
go
/*1.  List all the profiles for the Snapshot Agent */

exec sp_help_agent_profile @agent_type=1

/* 2. Select the profile_id from step 1. Find out the parameters
and the corresponding values that are being used */
/* profile_id=17 has a profile_name of Snapshot Agent profile-maxbcpthreads */

exec sp_help_agent_parameter @profile_id=17

/*3. Find out the available parameters and the corresponding
default, the minimum and the maximum values * /

select agent_type,
parameter_name,
default_value,
min_value,
max_value
from MSagentparameterlist
where agent_type=1

/*4. Now add the parameter MaxNetworkOptimization and set it to a value of 1*/

exec sp_add_agent_parameter @profile_id=17,
@parameter_name='MaxNetworkOptimization',
@parameter_value='1'
```

■**Note** The value of the @profile_id parameter might be different on your installation.

By now you should have a good fundamental knowledge of the internal workings of the publication database, the distribution database, and the msdb database. We will now look at how the different types of subscriptions work, and how they interact with the other components. The next section discusses the internal workings of subscriptions.

On the Subscriber Server

The Subscriber server receives transactions from the publication database on the Publisher server via the Distributor server. The Snapshot Agent delivers the snapshot, which is then used by the Distribution Agent to deliver the messages to the appropriate subscriptions.

We have discussed two kinds of subscriptions so far: push and pull subscriptions. You saw in Chapter 4 how to use the Windows Synchronization Manager (WSM) to pull subscriptions from the publications residing on the Publisher server. But before you could synchronize the subscription with the publication, you needed to configure the subscription properly—the subscription needs to be displayed in the WSM before you can start synchronizing. The subscription will not start pulling messages from the publication even if it is configured using the GUI.

■**Caution** Do not make changes to the registry unless you are sure that it will not affect your system adversely. Make a backup of the registry and try your changes on a test machine first.

The WSM uses the keys in the registry to display the list of subscriptions for the SQL Server. Specifically, it looks into the HKEY_LOCAL_MACHINE\SOFTWARE\Microsoft\Windows\ CurrentVersion\Syncmgr\Handlers key. As you can see in Figure 7-43, each subfolder under the Handlers section in the Registry Editor represents a clsid (also known as classid).

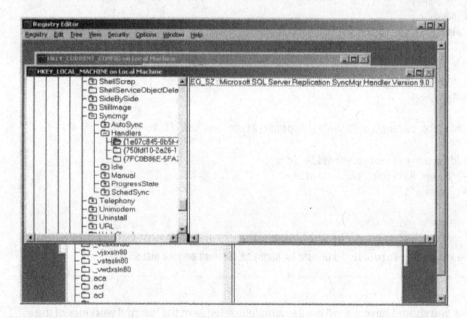

Figure 7-43. *Viewing the* HKEY_LOCAL_FOLDER *handlers*

■**Note** Microsoft has an explanation of the WSM for SQL Server 2000 and SQL Server 7.0 at the following site: http://support.microsoft.com/?id=292442.

WSM looks for the `replsync.dll` file in the registry when synchronization is started. The `replsync.dll` file is the value for this key and is used by the WSM as the SQL Server replication handler, as you can see in Figure 7-43.

Tip You will find this file in `C:\Program Files\Microsoft SQL Server\90\COM`.

You will find `replsync.dll` in `HKEY_CLASSES_ROOT\CLSID\Number\InprocServer32` in the registry, as shown in Figure 7-44.

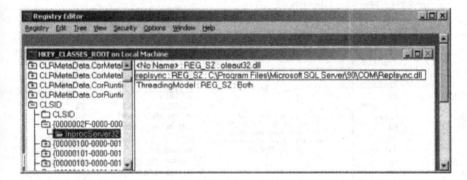

Figure 7-44. *Viewing the* `replsync.dll` *file in* `InprocServer32` *used by the WSM*

The subscriptions also have registry settings in the following location in the registry: `HKEY_LOCAL_MACHINE\SOFTWARE\Microsoft\Microsoft SQL Server\90\Replication\ Subscriptions`. Figure 7-45 shows the settings for the `subpull_mysales_new` pull subscription that is used by the WSM.

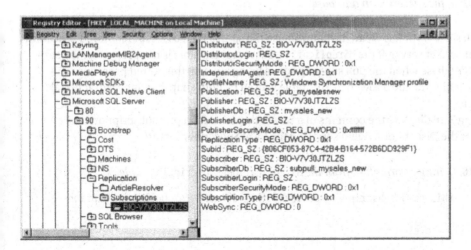

Figure 7-45. *Displaying the settings of the pull subscription used by WSM*

Now when you start the synchronization of the pull subscription by clicking the Synchronize button in the WSM, the progress of the synchronization is controlled by the `HKEY_LOCAL_MACHINE\SOFTWARE\Microsoft\Microsoft SQL Server\90\Tools\SQLEW\Replication` registry setting.

We've looked into the system requirements for the workings of the pull subscription, so let's now look into the system tables in the subscription database that we use for snapshot replication. The E-R diagram for these system tables is shown in Figure 7-46.

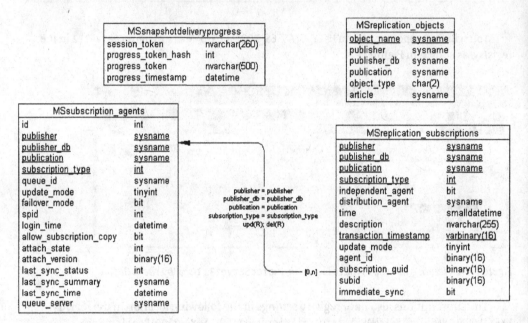

Figure 7-46. *The E-R diagram showing the* MSsnapshotdelivery, MSreplication_objects, MSsubscription_agents, *and* MSreplication_subscriptions *system tables used for snapshot replication in the subscription database*

A pull subscription is created when you use the `sp_addpullsubscription` stored procedure on the Subscriber server. If the `MSreplication_subscription` table is not present on the subscription database when the pull subscription is being created, this stored procedure will create the table and add a row to it. This table is used by both snapshot and transactional replication.

Listing 7-16 displays the contents of a row in this table for a pull subscription that I created for the Distribution Agent servicing the local Subscriber server.

Listing 7-16. *Getting Information from the* MSreplication_subscription *Table*

```
/* Execute this on a subscription database that is used for pull subscriptions */

Use subpull_mysales_new
Go
```

```
select publisher,
publisher_db,
publication,
independent_agent,
subscription_type,
distribution_agent,
time
from MSreplication_subscriptions
```

The output of this script is as follows:

```
publisher                          publisher_db        publication
independent_agent                  subscription_type
distribution_agent
time
-------------------------------------------------------------------------
BIO-V7V30JTZLZS                 mysales_new        pub_mysalesnew
1                                                  1
BIO-V7V30JTZLZS-mysales_new-pub_mysalesnew-BIO-V7V30JTZLZS-
subpull_mysales_ne-C477EB67-71BF-43B2-910D-1606CF512A08
2005-12-26 19:32:00

(1 row(s) affected)
```

This output displays the name of the Publisher server, the publication database, and the publication that is being used for pull subscription. The independent_agent column also indicates whether the Distribution Agent is used as a stand-alone agent. And as you know by now, a value of 1 for the subscription_type means that this is a pull subscription. The time column indicates the last time the Distribution Agent ran.

If you now want to find the status of the push subscriptions, you can run the sp_MSenumsubscriptions stored procedure on the subscription database whose status you want to look up. The output for the execution is shown here:

```
publisher              publisher_db      publication        replication_type
 subscription_type     last_updated                         subscriber_db
 update_mode           last_sync_status
 last_sync_summary                       last_sync_time
-------------------------------------------------------------------------
BIO-V7V30JTZLZS             mysales_new        pub_mysalesnew     0
0                      2005-12-27 08:01:00.000     subpush_mysales_new
0                           1
Synchronization in progress                 2005-12-27 06:09:52.797
```

Here you can see that subpush_mysales_new is the subscriber database, pub_mysalesnew is the publisher database, that the synchronization is still in progress, and when the subscription database was last synchronized.

Summary

You should now have a good understanding of the internals of snapshot replication. You should know that the publication database contains logins in the PAL, and you should be familiar with the job steps taken by both the Snapshot and the Distribution Agents. You should also be aware of the different system tables that store metadata in the publication, the distribution, the subscription, and the msdb databases.

- The publication database maintains a list of the logins that have access to it. It is called the Publication Access List (PAL).

- The PAL is created when the publication is created.

- When any agent or user tries to connect to the publication database, SQL Server will first verify that the logins are indeed stored in the publication before it grants any access.

- The publication database contains seven system tables that are used for snapshot replication: MSpub_identity_range, sysarticles, sysarticleupdates, syspublications, sysschemaarticles, syssubscriptions, systranschemas.

- The distributor_admin login acts as a tunnel that transfers the data held by the syspublications system table in the publication database to the MSpublications system table in the distribution database.

- The Snapshot Agent takes three steps to execute its job: Snapshot Agent startup message, Run agent, and Detect nonlogged agent shutdown.

- The Distribution Agent also takes three steps to execute its job: Distribution Agent startup message, Run agent, and Detect nonlogged agent shutdown.

- The system tables in the msdb database hold information on the agents, the profiles of the agents, and the parameters of the agent profiles.

- To display the list of subscriptions for SQL Server in the WSM, the WSM looks into the HKEY_LOCAL_MACHINE\SOFTWARE\Microsoft\Windows\CurrentVersion\Syncmgr\Handlers registry keys.

- The subscriptions have registry settings in HKEY_LOCAL_MACHINE\SOFTWARE\Microsoft\Microsoft SQL Server\90\Replication\Subscriptions.

In the next chapter, we will look at how to configure publications and subscriptions for transactional replication using the GUI method.

Quick Tips

- You can create a login using the Logins object under the Security object in the SSMS.

- The jobs for the Snapshot Agent have names in the form `<Publisher>-➥`
`<PublicationDatabase>-<Publication>-<integer>`.

- You can log the job steps for the Snapshot and the Distribution Agents in the table and also view it in a text editor.

- The name of the job for the Distribution Agent in push subscriptions has the form `<Publisher>-<PublicationDatabase>-<Publication>-<Subscriber>-<integer>`.

- The name of the job for the Distribution Agent in pull subscriptions has the form `<Publisher>-<Publicationdatabase>-<Publication>-<Subscriber>-➥`
`<subscriptiondatabase>-<GUID>`.

- By default, the Agent history cleanup, Replication agents checkup, and Distribution cleanup jobs run every 10 minutes.

- To find out about any errors while replicating, use the `MSrepl_errors` system table. Information on the command that is causing the problem will be shown.

CHAPTER 8

■ ■ ■

Configuring Transactional Replication Using the GUI

By now you should have a good grasp of the fundamentals and configuration of snapshot replication, and you know that one important consideration in snapshot replication is the high latency involved, *latency* being the time it takes to transfer data from the publication database to the subscription database. Unlike snapshot replication, transactional replication has low latency—the data is propagated to the subscriptions in real time.

Although transactional replication makes use of Snapshot Agent for the initial synchronization, subsequent changes in the data are made in small increments. Transactional replication makes use of the transaction log to transmit the messages. Table 8-1 lists the different SQL Server products that support transactional replication.

Table 8-1. *SQL Server Products That Support Transactional Replication*

SQL Server Products	Yes/No (Y/N)
SQL Server Workgroup Edition	Y (can publish to up to 5 Subscribers)
SQL Server Enterprise Edition	Y
SQL Server Standard Edition	Y
SQL Server Express Edition	Y (Subscriber only)

In this chapter, I will show you how to configure transactional replication using the GUI method, first setting up a publication and then the different kinds of subscriptions. The use of T-SQL in setting up transactional replication is discussed in Chapter 9.

■**Note** Before you proceed with this chapter, you should install the database script from Source Code/ Downloads at http://www.apress.com. The E-R diagram for the database is shown in Appendix A, and the SQL code for the database is given in Appendix B.

On completing this chapter, you will know how to use the GUI to do the following:

- Configure a standard publication

- Configure transactional publication with updatable subscriptions

- Configure the immediate and queued updating subscriptions

- Change the mode between immediate updating subscriptions and queued updating subscriptions

- Configure peer-to-peer transactional replication

Configuring Publications

Configuring publications in transactional replication is different from doing so for snapshot replication. In snapshot replication, there was only one type of publication. Transactional replication, however, is mostly carried out in a server-to-server environment, and the data is available in real time, so it is possible to use this method to keep a hot backup on another server.

By default, the Publisher transfers the data to the Subscribers for read-only purposes. This is known as standard publication. There are also two other methods of publication: transactional publication with updatable subscriptions, and transactional publication in a peer-to-peer topology. Table 8-2 briefly outlines the three types.

Table 8-2. *Different Types of Publication for Transactional Replication*

Types	Description
Standard publication	This default publication type is used mainly for Subscribers that have read-only permissions.
Transactional publication with updatable subscriptions	One Publisher server services multiple Subscriber servers, and updates can also be made on the Subscribers. Data is transmitted using the 2PC protocol, and conflicts are resolved.
Transactional publication in a peer-to-peer topology	Each site acts as both the Publisher and the Subscriber. Data availability is maintained all the time, so one site can be used as a hot backup for another. Each row can only be changed at one site.

I will introduce you to standard publication first and then demonstrate the other two types.

Configuring Standard Transactional Publications

Suppose for our business purposes we need to read only the inventory, order, and financial information. To do that, we will set up a standard transactional publication.

Open the SQL Server Management Studio (SSMS). Under the Replication folder in the Object Explorer, you'll find the Local Publications Object. Right-click on the Local Publications object and select New Publication. The New Publication Wizard will start up. Click Next, and it will ask for the name of the Distributor server, as shown in Figure 8-1.

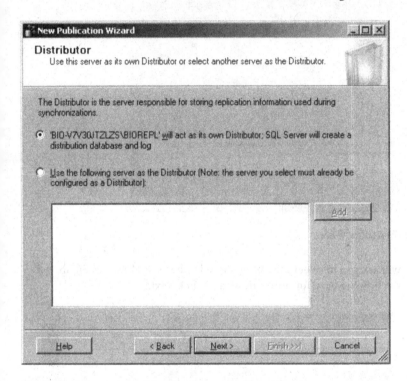

Figure 8-1. *Selecting the Distributor server*

You can either select the default Distributor, as shown in Figure 8-1, or click the Add button to choose another Distributor. Then click Next.

In the window shown in Figure 8-2, you can select the Snapshot folder. A UNC share is used so that the publication can be used for both push and pull subscriptions. For pull sub-scriptions, where the Distribution Agent resides on the Subscriber server, you have to use the UNC share. If you use the default path for the snapshot folder, the wizard will tell you that the folder cannot be used for pull subscriptions and you will have to use a push subscription. Having set the path, click Next.

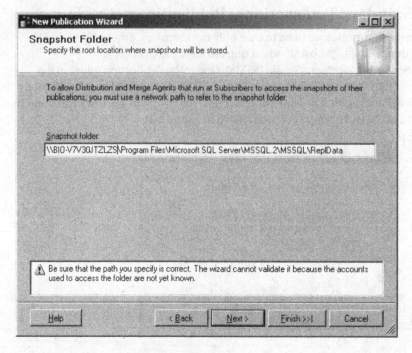

Figure 8-2. *Selecting the Snapshot folder*

The next window will ask you to select the publication database, as shown in Figure 8-3. Choose the database that is being used for publication, and click Next.

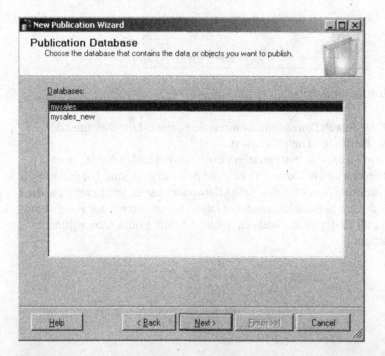

Figure 8-3. *Selecting the publication database*

The wizard now asks you what kind of publication you want to use for transactional replication, as shown in Figure 8-4. Select the standard transactional publication, which is the default. Then click Next.

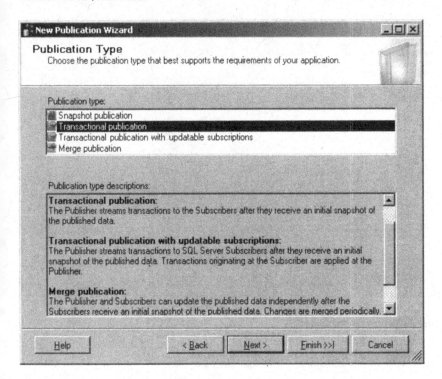

Figure 8-4. *Selecting the publication type*

Now you can select the tables and other database objects, such as views and stored procedures, that you want to publish as articles, as shown in Figure 8-5. For now, select only the tables. Click the plus sign next to a table to see its objects, and click in the check box to select a table.

In Figure 8-5, you can see a circle with a line through it on the icon for the OrderDetail table. This means that the table is not allowed to be published. If you select the table, the reason will be displayed at the bottom of the window. As you can see in Figure 8-6, for a table to be published it must contain a primary key, and the OrderDetail table does not have one.

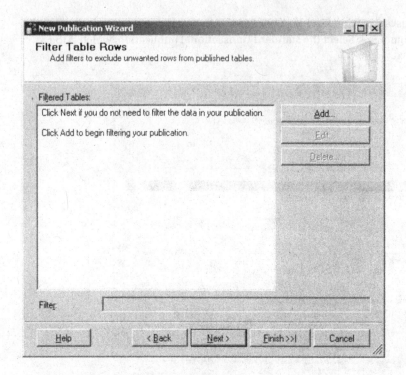

Figure 8-5. *Selecting objects to be published*

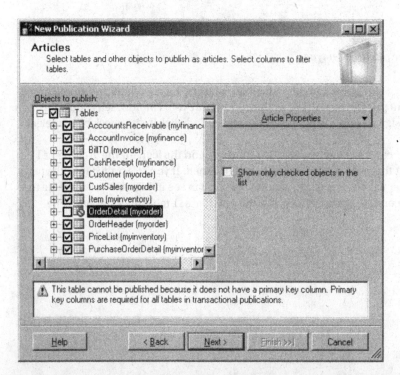

Figure 8-6. *Displaying the reason the table cannot be published*

Note Primary keys should be as narrow as possible for optimization purposes. If you want to include the table for transactional replication, simply add a primary key on the table. The OrderDetail table for the myorder schema was deliberately designed not to have a primary key to illustrate this point.

Now, highlight the Item table, click the Article Properties button, and select Set Properties of Highlighted Table from the drop-down list. This will open the Article Properties window shown in Figure 8-7.

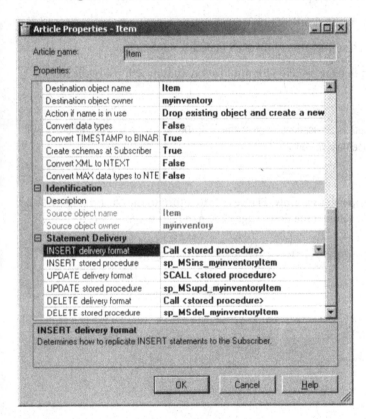

Figure 8-7. *Setting the Item article's properties*

Scroll down to the bottom of the Properties pane, and you will see the Statement Delivery section, which lists the methods of transmitting data changes to the Subscriber server in transactional replication. By clicking on the drop-down list for the delivery format, you can select the kind of propagation method you want from the different methods:

- Specify that you do not want to replicate the DML statements; in this case, the DML statements will not be replicated to the Subscriber server.

- Call a custom stored procedure; in this case you can write a custom stored procedure to replicate the DML operations.

- Call a stored procedure; this is the default. Transactional replication will generate the stored procedures for the necessary DML operations.

- Use insert, update, or delete statements to perform the DML operations; this method can be used with non-SQL Server Subscriber servers.

In this case, I chose to call stored procedures for the insert and delete statements, while the SCALL method was used for the update delivery format. Transactional replication creates the following stored procedures by default when the table article is created:

- sp_MSins_<tablename>: A stored procedure used in insert statements

- sp_MSupd_<tablename>: A stored procedure used in update statements

- sp_MSdel_<tablename>: A stored procedure used in delete statements

This is done for all tables that are selected for publication in transactional replication.

Note Tables that cannot be used as publications, such as the OrderDetail table shown previously, will not be displayed in the Article Properties window.

Click OK in the Article Properties window (Figure 8-7) to return to the wizard (Figure 8-5), and click Next. You will see the Filter Table Rows page shown in Figure 8-8.

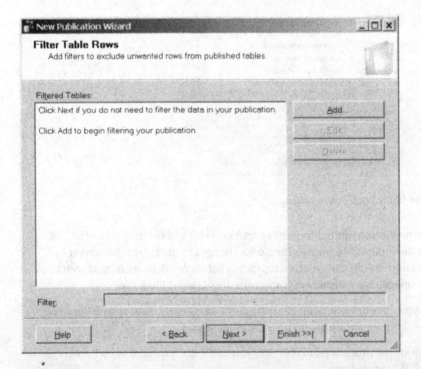

Figure 8-8. *Filtering table rows from published tables*

We are not going to filter the table now, so click Next again. This will take to the Snapshot Agent page shown in Figure 8-9.

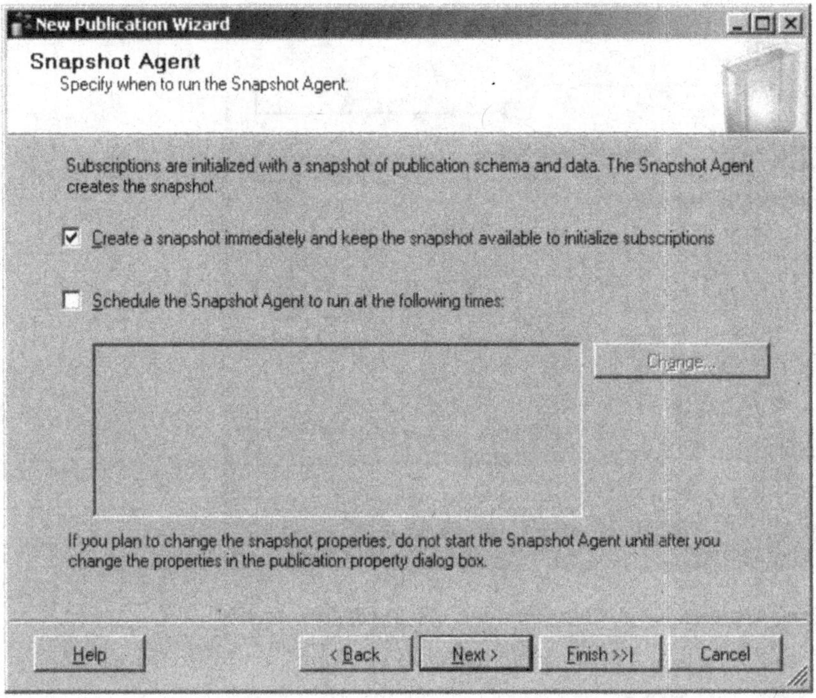

Figure 8-9. *Scheduling the Snapshot Agent*

Uncheck the "Schedule the Snapshot Agent to run at the following times" box. Since we are using transactional replication and are not going to change the properties of the publication, we do not need to use this feature. We just want to use the Snapshot Agent now to generate the initial snapshot. Click Next.

You will now see the Agent Security page shown in Figure 8-10, in which you can configure security for both the Snapshot and Log Reader Agents.

Click the Security Settings button for the Snapshot Agent, and you'll see the Snapshot Agent Security window, as shown in Figure 8-11. Select the security settings under which the Snapshot Agent will run.

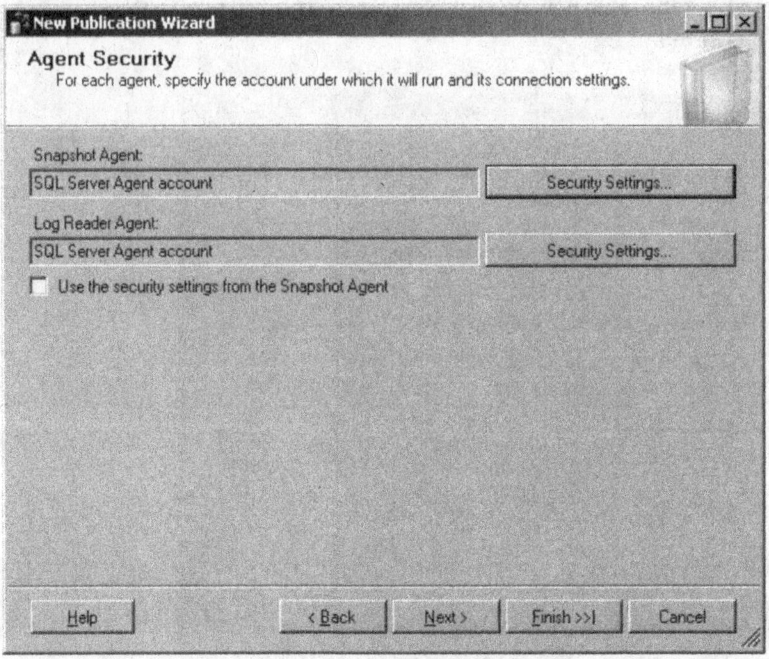

Figure 8-10. *Specifying accounts for the Snapshot and the Log Reader Agents*

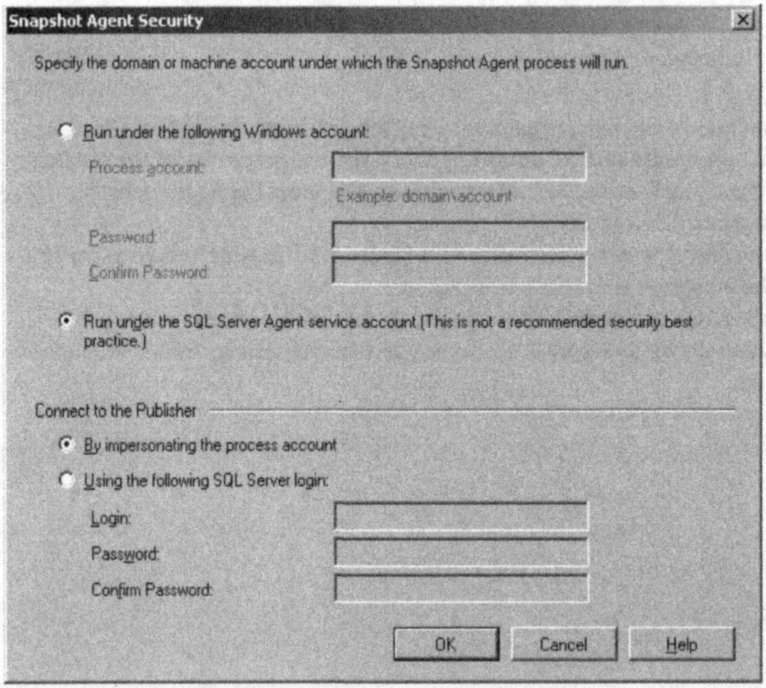

Figure 8-11. *Setting the Snapshot Agent process to run under the SQL Server Agent service*

Normally you should select the domain account for the Snapshot Agent, but in this case, since I am the only person using the machine, I chose the SQL Server Agent service account. In order to connect to the Publisher server, I chose to impersonate the process account (Windows account). Click OK to return to the Agent Security page (Figure 8-10), and repeat the process for the Log Reader Agent.

■**Caution** Use the domain account on the client machine for the SQL Server Agent, and not the Local Service Account.

Click Next in the Agent Security page, and you'll see the Wizard Actions page shown in Figure 8-12. Check both boxes to create the publication and generate a script file. Click Next to continue.

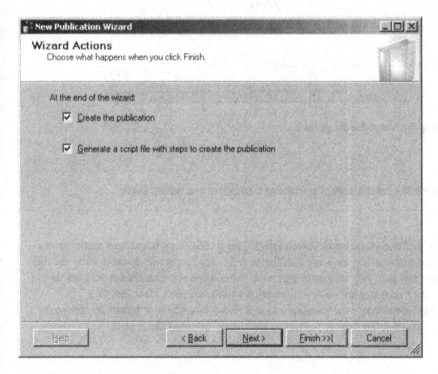

Figure 8-12. *Setting the wizard to create the publication*

Now the wizard will ask you to specify a location for the script file, as shown in Figure 8-13. Set the location and whether you want it to be appended to or to overwrite any existing file, and then click Next.

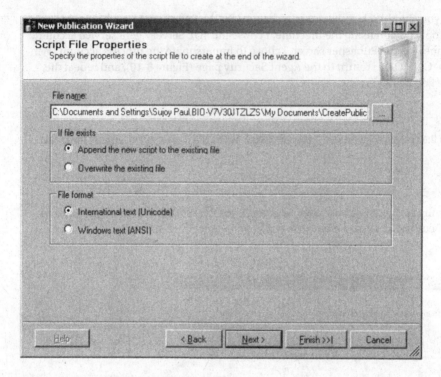

Figure 8-13. *Setting the script file properties*

■**Tip** It is a good practice to keep a script for creating publications and subscriptions.

The final page of the wizard asks you to specify the publication name and summarizes the settings for the publication, as shown in Figure 8-14. You can scroll down to view the full summary of the settings. If you are not happy with the results, you can always go back to the previous pages and make any necessary changes. If you're satisfied, click Finish.

The wizard will now create the publication and show its success or failure as shown in Figure 8-15. You can click the Report button to view, save, or email the report.

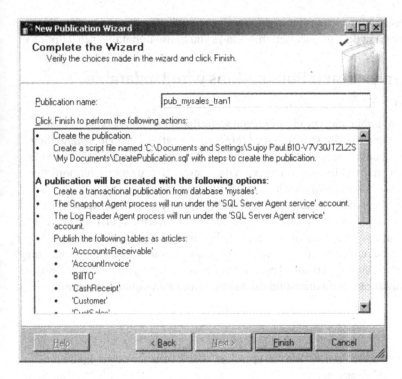

Figure 8-14. *Completing the wizard*

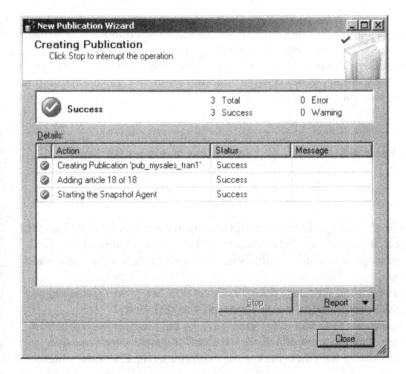

Figure 8-15. *The successful completion of the process*

Now that you have seen how to configure the standard publication for transactional repli-cation, let's look at how to set up a publication that allows you to use updatable subscriptions.

Configuring Transactional Publications with Updatable Subscriptions

You can use the standard publication mode when you want the Subscriber servers to have read-only privileges. However, suppose warehouses at remote locations need to update their inventory and send the changes back to the central Publisher server. How would you provide the Subscriber servers with the ability to update the data changes? It is in such situations that you need to use updatable subscriptions with transactional publication.

Updatable subscriptions with transactional publication allow you to make updates on any of the Subscriber servers and send them to the Publisher server, which can then act as a republishing Publisher and send the updates to other Subscriber servers. The topology is hierarchical in nature. Different Subscriber servers can update the same row at the same time, and conflicts will be resolved automatically. There are two kinds of updatable subscriptions with transactional publication: immediate updating subscriptions and queued updating subscriptions.

■**Caution** Once you have enabled the publication for updatable subscriptions, you cannot disable it. You have to drop the publication to stop it.

Both immediate updating subscriptions and queued updating subscriptions are enabled when you use transactional replication with updatable subscriptions, and it is possible to switch between the two modes. This is because when the update is made on one Subscriber server, it is transmitted using the 2PC protocol to the Publisher server first, and the committed data is then replicated to the other Subscriber servers.

■**Note** Transactional publication with updatable subscriptions can only be used with SQL Server Subscribers.

To configure a publication for updatable subscriptions, open the SSMS, right-click on the Local Publications object, and select New Publication to start up the New Publication Wizard. Click Next in the first wizard page, and in the Publication Database window, select the mysales database. Then click Next.

You'll now see the Publication Type page shown in Figure 8-16. Select the "Transactional publication with updatable subscriptions" publication type, and click Next.

This will display the Articles page shown in Figure 8-17. For this example, we will publish the StockItem, Item, Stock, and Warehouse tables, since the staff at remote warehouse sites need to update these articles and send them back to the Publisher server. Check the tables shown in Figure 8-17.

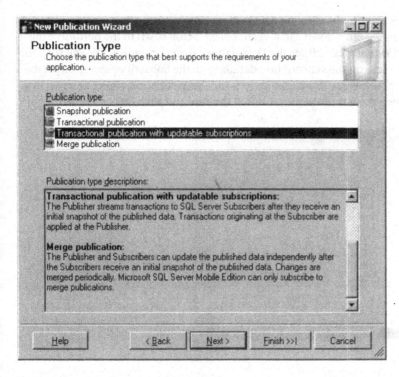

Figure 8-16. *Selecting the publication type*

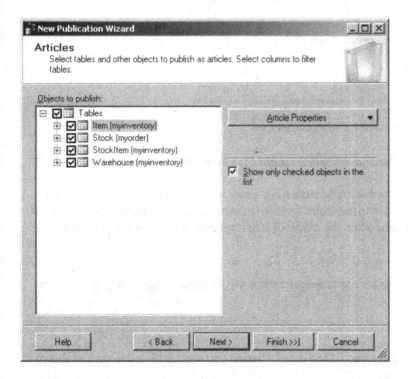

Figure 8-17. *Selecting the articles to be published*

Now select the StockItem table, click the Article Properties button, select Set Properties of Highlighted Article from the drop-down list, and click Next. Scroll down to the bottom of the Article Properties window, and you will see the Destination Object properties. We will keep the name of the object the same on the subscription database on the Subscriber server, so set the "Action if name is in use" setting as shown in Figure 8-18. The destination object owner is the schema of the table. Keep the rest of the properties as they are and click OK.

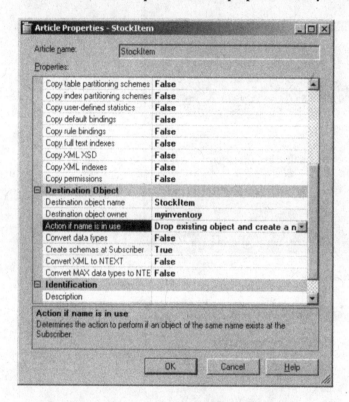

Figure 8-18. *Setting the destination object properties*

You should now be back at the Articles page of the New Publication Wizard (Figure 8-17). Click the Next button.

At this stage, the wizard will tell you that it is going to add a uniqueidentifier column called MSrepl_tran_version to the tables involved in this transactional publication, as shown in Figure 8-19. This is done when the snapshot is first generated. Click Next to continue.

■**Caution** Before setting up any updatable subscriptions with transactional publication, ensure that you have sufficient space.

In the next wizard page, you will be asked whether you want to filter the rows, as shown in Figure 8-20.

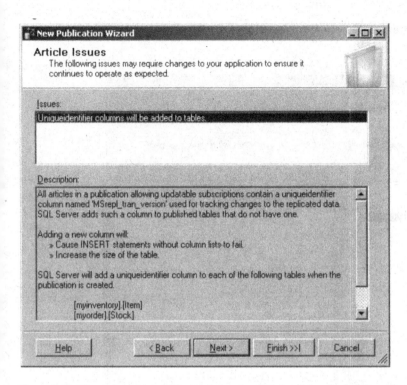

Figure 8-19. *The* uniqueidentifier *column is added only to the published tables*

Figure 8-20. *Choosing to filter table rows*

Click the Add button to filter out rows. You will see the Add Filter window shown in Figure 8-21.

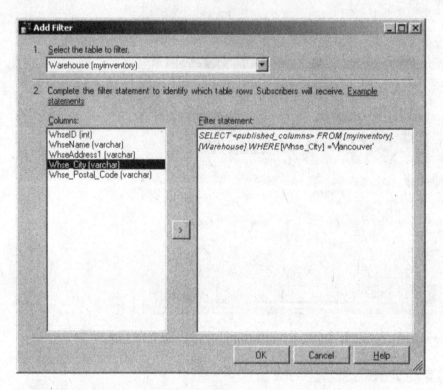

Figure 8-21. *Adding a filter to prevent specific rows from being replicated*

Since the subscriptions are being sent to Vancouver, there is no need for the Subscribers to update the city. Select Warehouse from the drop-down list in step 1, and in step 2, double-click on the Whse_city column in the left pane to display the filter statement. Add the value Vancouver for the column [Whse_city] to the filter statement as shown in Figure 8-21. Click OK when you're done.

■**Note** You can only enter the value of the column in the filter statement. You cannot modify the filter statement.

You will now see the Filter Table Rows page of the wizard, as shown in Figure 8-22. You can see that the filter value shows up at the bottom of the window, and you can add, edit, or delete the filter by clicking on the appropriate buttons. Click Next.

The next wizard page, shown in Figure 8-23, is where you schedule the Snapshot Agent if you wish to, or create a snapshot immediately for the initial synchronization. Click Next.

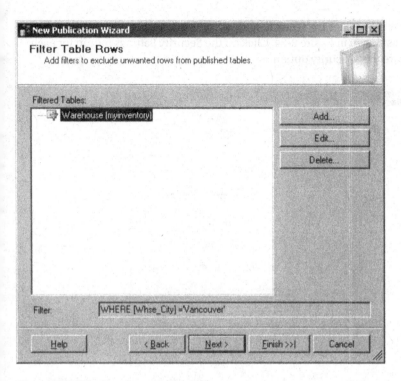

Figure 8-22. *Viewing the completed filter*

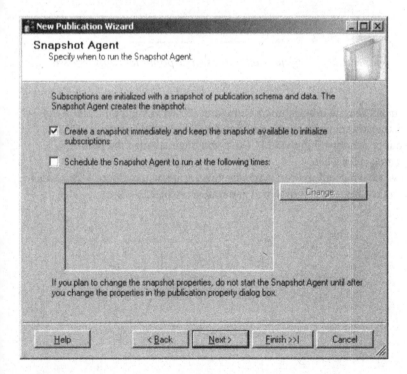

Figure 8-23. *Scheduling the Snapshot Agent to run immediately*

The wizard will now ask you for the security settings for the Snapshot, Log Reader, and Queue Reader Agents, as shown in Figure 8-24. Click on the Security Settings button for each of the agents to configure their security options.

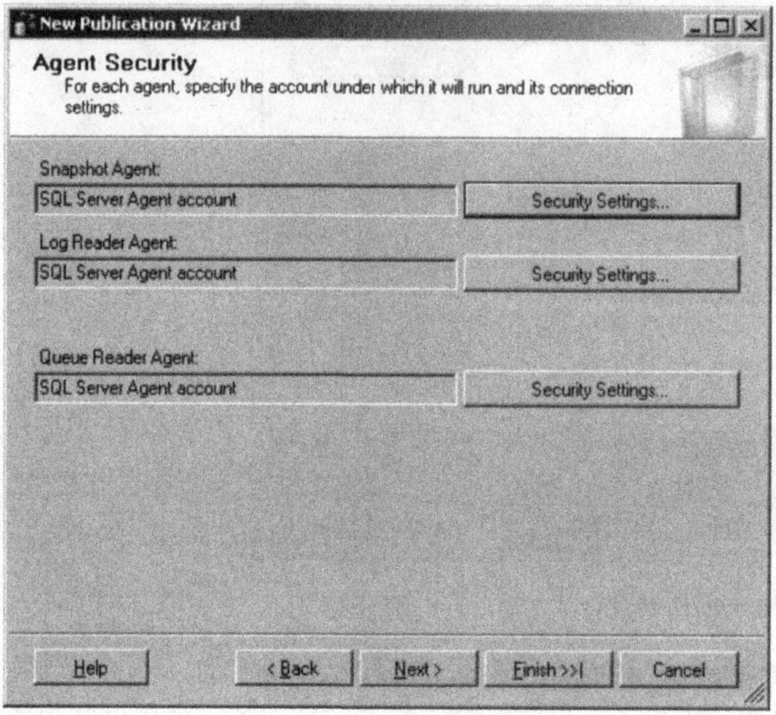

Figure 8-24. *Setting the agent security settings for updatable subscriptions for transactional publication*

For each agent, you will see a window similar to the one shown in Figure 8-25. Use the SQL Server Agent service account on the client machine for this example, and click OK to return to the Agent Security window (Figure 8-24). Once you have selected the security settings for the three agents, click Next.

The wizard will now ask what actions you want it to take, as shown in Figure 8-26. Check the box to create the publication, and optionally to generate a script. Click Next.

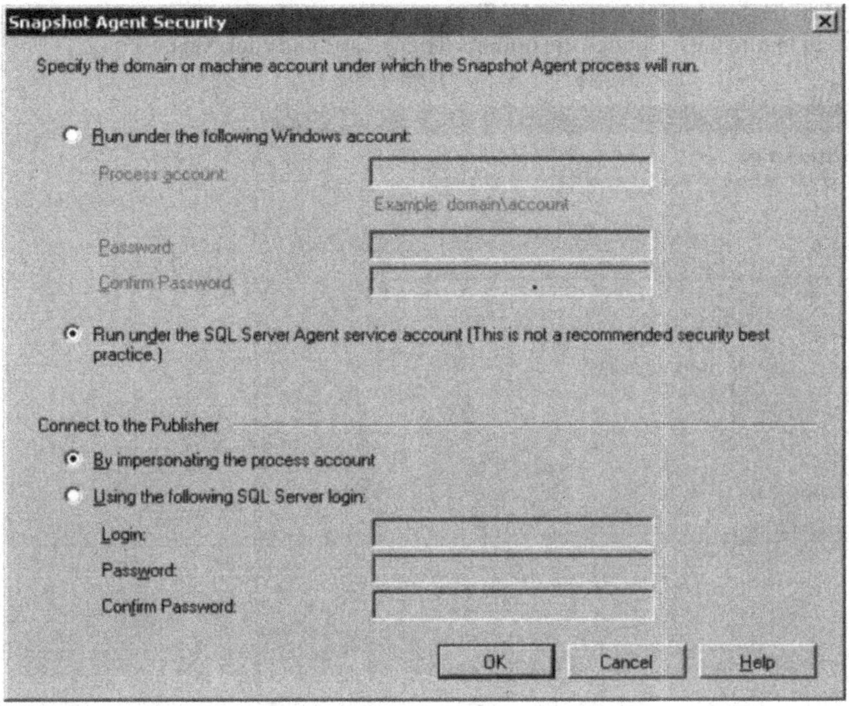

Figure 8-25. *Setting up Snapshot Agent security*

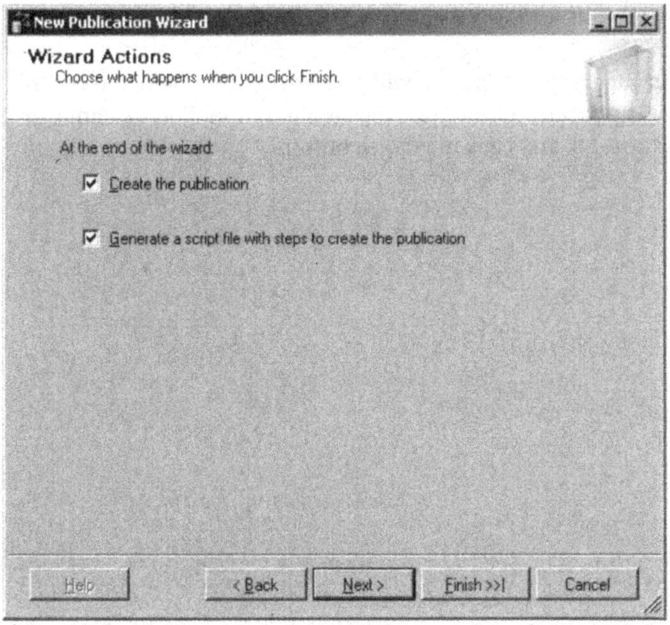

Figure 8-26. *Choosing the wizard's actions*

If you checked the box to generate a script file, you will see the Script File Properties wizard page shown in Figure 8-27. Change the options if necessary, and click Next.

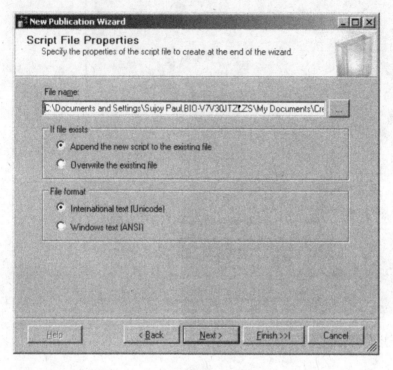

Figure 8-27. *Specifying a filename for the publication script*

Whether or not you chose to generate a script, you will now see the Complete the Wizard page. As before, this final page of the wizard summarizes the configuration. Enter a name for the publication, as shown in Figure 8-28, and click the Finish button.

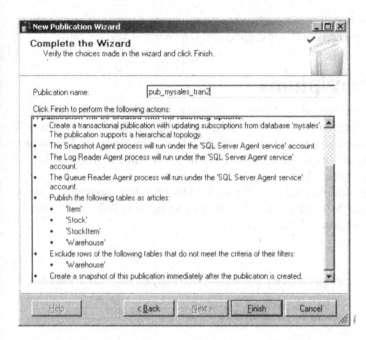

Figure 8-28. *Reviewing your configuration choices for the publication*

The wizard will now generate the publication and the articles, as shown in Figure 8-29.

Figure 8-29. *Successfully creating the publication*

Now that we have created two different publication types, we are ready to set up the subscriptions. The process of configuring both subscriptions is shown in the next section.

Configuring Subscriptions

Both push and pull subscriptions can be used in transactional replication. Push subscriptions are created on the Publisher server, and the Distribution Agent on the Distributor server delivers the transactions. In contrast, both pull and anonymous subscriptions reside on the Subscriber server and call for the delivery of transactions on demand only. As a result, the workload for the Publisher and the Distributor servers is less for pull subscriptions.

The configuration of push and pull subscriptions for standard publications using transactional replication is the same as the configuration for snapshot replication. Refer to Chapter 4 for the details of setting up push and pull subscriptions.

■**Note** Chapter 4 explains how to configure push and pull subscriptions using the GUI method. The T-SQL method is explained in Chapter 5.

Configuring Updatable Subscriptions for Transactional Publication

We created a publication for updatable subscription in the "Configuring Transactional Publications with Updatable Subscriptions" section earlier in this chapter. I also showed you the configuration for the security settings of the Log Reader, Snapshot, and Queue Reader Agents. Now we will configure a subscription.

■**Note** You must have the MS DTC installed on your machine if you want to allow publication to use updatable subscriptions. Chapter 9 shows you how to check whether MS DTC is running or not.

Open the SSMS. Right-click on the publication that has been set for "transactional publication with updatable subscription," and choose New Subscriptions from the menu. The New Subscription Wizard will start up; click Next on the Welcome page.

You will now see the wizard page shown in Figure 8-30. Click Next.

■**Note** If you start the wizard by right-clicking on the publication, the wizard will automatically choose the right publication, as shown in Figure 8-30.

In the Distribution Agent Location page of the wizard, choose the radio button for pull subscriptions, as shown in Figure 8-31, and click Next.

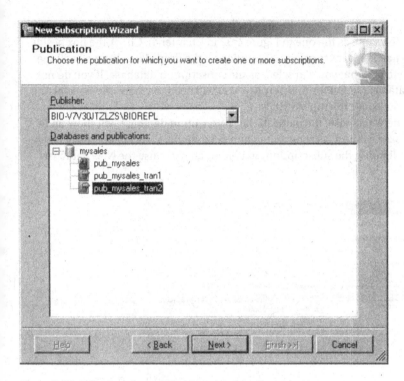

Figure 8-30. *Selecting the publication to subscribe to*

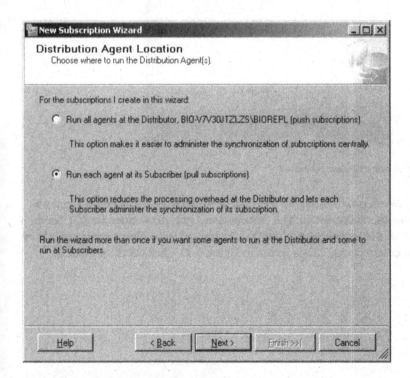

Figure 8-31. *Selecting a pull subscription*

The wizard will now ask you to select the Subscriber server and the subscription database (the wizard window is the same as the one in Figure 4-32 in Chapter 4). Check the box beside the Subscriber server that you want to select. If you click on the drop-down list, you will see the list of available databases that you can select as the subscription database. If you do not have a subscription database set up for this purpose, you will need to create one by selecting the New database option from the drop-down list.

After creating the new database, the name of the subscription database will show up in the Subscription Database column, as shown in Figure 8-32. In this case, I had already created a database prior to configuring the subscription, so I did not have to use the New database option. Click Next.

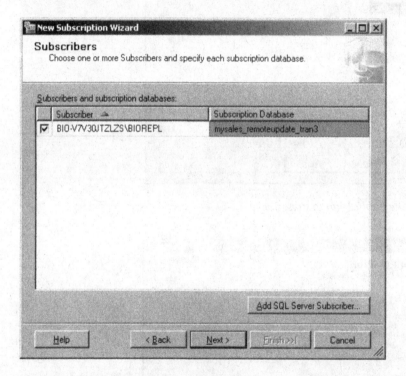

Figure 8-32. *Selecting the subscription database*

The wizard will now ask you to configure the security settings the Distribution Agent will use when synchronizing this subscription. The Distribution Agent runs under the SQL Server Agent service account, and its connection to the Distributor and Subscriber servers is made by impersonating the process account. This is shown in Figure 8-33. Click OK to continue.

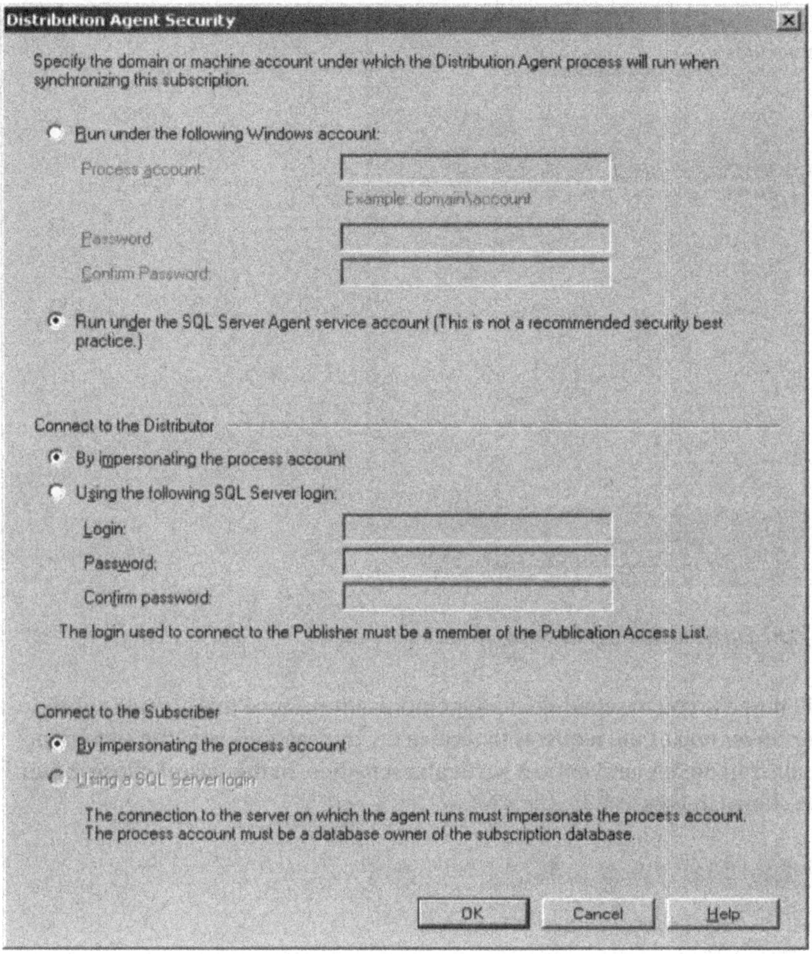

Figure 8-33. *Configuring the Distribution Agent security settings*

■Note The login that is used to connect to the Publisher server must be a member of the Publication Access List (PAL).

You will see the process accounts that the Distribution Agent uses to connect to the Distributor and Subscriber servers, as shown in Figure 8-34. Click Next.

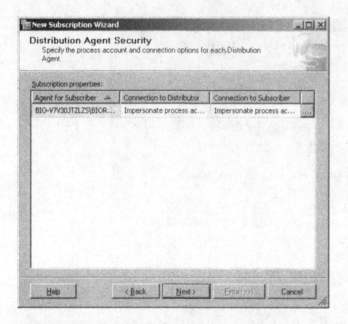

Figure 8-34. *Viewing the Distribution Agent security settings*

The wizard will now ask you to schedule the synchronization. Since this is a pull subscription, the Subscriber server makes the requests to receive the transactions, and the synchronization agent is usually run on demand or on a particular schedule. In this case, I chose to run on demand only, as shown in Figure 8-35. Click Next.

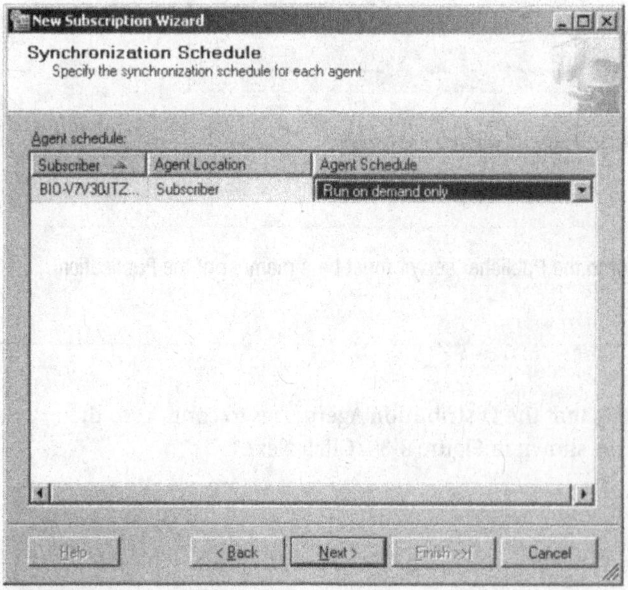

Figure 8-35. *Running the agent on demand only*

In the next wizard page, shown in Figure 8-36, you must check the box for the Replicate option, otherwise the data changes made at the Subscriber server will not be sent to the Publisher server. Then make sure that "Simultaneously commit changes" is selected in the Commit at Publisher column. This is the default selection for publications created with updating subscriptions. Click Next to continue.

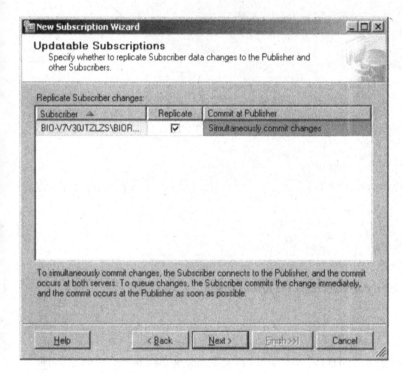

Figure 8-36. *Specifying when changes are committed*

■**Note** For queued updating subscriptions, follow the steps described for immediate updating subscriptions so far, but select "Queue changes and commit when possible" in the Updatable Subscriptions page of the wizard (Figure 8-36). The remaining parts of the configuration are same as those for immediate updating subscriptions.

The wizard will now lead you to the login parameters for the linked server, as shown in Figure 8-37. (If you have not configured a linked server, the SQL Server replication process will create one for you.) You need to specify the login used by the Subscriber server to connect to the Publisher server when the Subscriber is simultaneously committing changes to replicated data. The login must be included in the PAL for this publication. Click Next to continue.

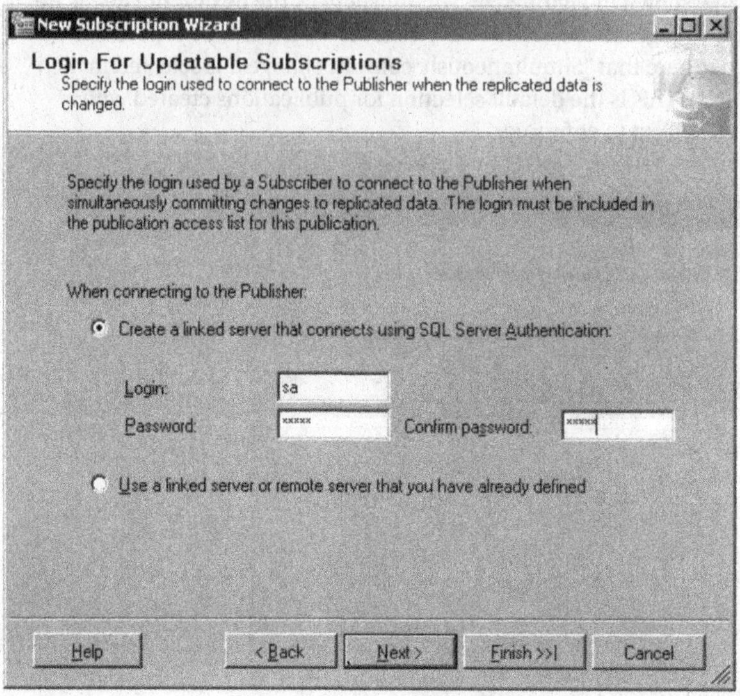

Figure 8-37. *Setting the login parameters for the linked server*

■**Note** The account used by the login to the linked server must already be there on the Publisher server.

The wizard will now ask you whether you want to initialize the subscriptions or not, as shown in Figure 8-38. Check the box in the Initialize column, and select Immediately in the Initialize When column. Click Next.

In the next wizard page, you can specify the wizard actions: the wizard can create the subscription and generate a script file for creating subscriptions, which you can use for future diagnostic purposes or run on other Subscriber servers that are using updatable subscriptions for transactional publication. This is shown in Figure 8-39. Make your selections and click Next.

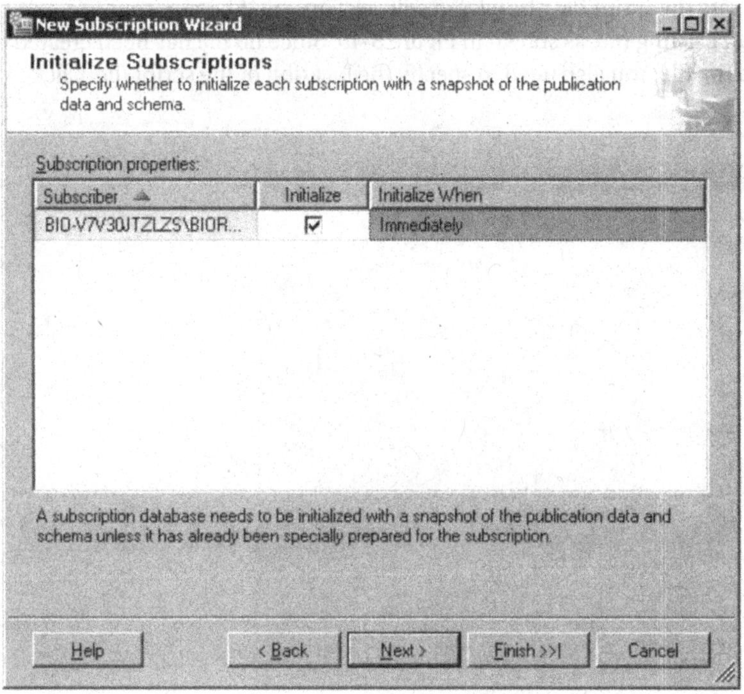

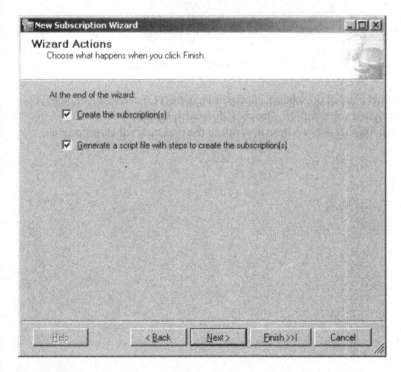

Figure 8-38. *Initializing the subscription immediately*

Figure 8-39. *Creating the subscription and generating a script file*

If you chose to generate the script file, the wizard will ask you whether you want to append to or overwrite an existing file, as shown in Figure 8-40. Since no file has been created as yet, I chose to append the file. You also need to specify the location of the script file. Click Next.

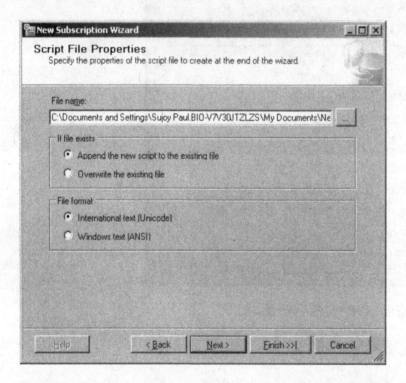

Figure 8-40. *The location of the script file for the creation of the subscription*

You are now at the final page of the wizard, shown in Figure 8-41. Review the choices you made to generate the updating subscription, and click the Finish button.

The wizard reports on its success or failure in creating the updating subscriptions, as shown in Figure 8-42.

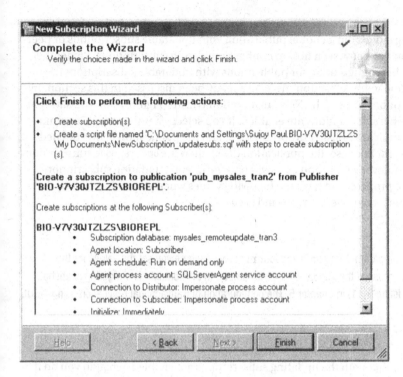

Figure 8-41. *Reviewing your configuration choices for the updating subscription*

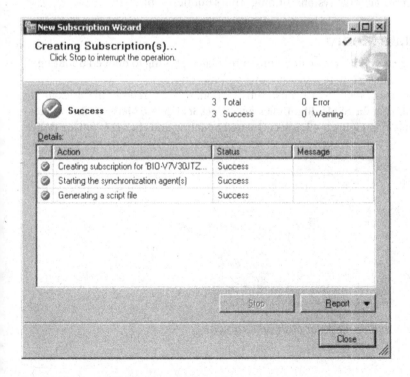

Figure 8-42. *Successfully creating the updating subscription*

As I mentioned at the beginning of the chapter, you can update subscriptions in transactional replication using either transactional publication with updatable subscriptions or peer-to-peer replication. You have now seen how to configure updating subscriptions. Remember that you can only use this configuration for publications with updatable subscriptions.

The two types of updatable subscriptions have already been discussed in this section. In the Updatable Subscriptions page of the New Subscription Wizard (Figure 8-36), you saw that both modes for updatable subscriptions are enabled. If you select "Simultaneously commit changes" from the Commit at Publisher drop-down list, and the publication allows queued updating subscriptions (in this case, the publication does), then the update_mode subscription property will be set to failover so that you can switch to the queued updating subscription mode. The update_mode property can have the following values when you add a subscription: read-only, failover, sync tran, queued tran, and queued failover.

■Note The @update_mode parameter of sp_addsubscription is where you set the values for the update_mode property. I discussed the @update_mode parameter in the context of configuring snapshot replication using T-SQL (Listing 5-11) in Chapter 5. The configuration of transactional replication using T-SQL is discussed in Chapter 9.

Now that you know that both the updating subscriptions are enabled, what do you do if you have to switch from one mode to another. Say, for example, there is a network failure and you need to keep the transactional system running. That's our next topic.

Switching Update Modes

In this section, I will show you how to switch from immediate updating to queued updating, or vice versa, for a push subscription, and then for a pull subscription.

For push subscriptions, first select the push subscription, mysales_remote3 in this example, from Local Subscriptions in the SSMS. Right-click and select Set Update Method. This will display the dialog box shown in Figure 8-43. Select Queued updating and click OK. You are done!

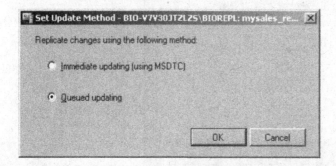

Figure 8-43. *Selecting the update mode for push subscriptions*

For pull subscriptions, right-click on the pull subscription that is enabled for updatable subscriptions, mysales_remotequeue_tran4 in this case, and select Properties. In order to change from queued updating to immediate updating, under the Subscription options change the "Subscriber update method" to "Immediately replicate changes," as shown in Figure 8-44.

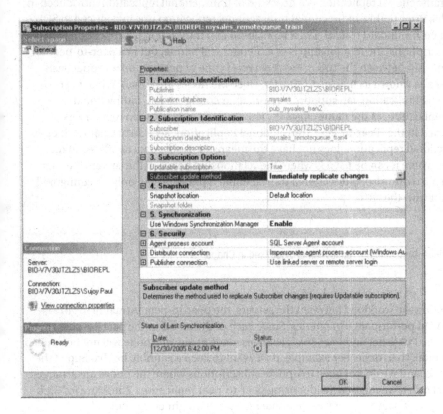

Figure 8-44. *Changing the queued updating subscription to immediately replicate changes*

Note If you need to change from immediate updating to queued updating for a pull subscription, change the "Subscriber update method" from "Immediately replicate changes" to "Queue changes."

You have now seen the different methods of configuring the publication and subscriptions for transactional publication. I have also shown you how to switch from one mode of updating a subscription to another.

In all these scenarios, the Snapshot Agent generates the snapshot during the initial synchronization.

Note Alternate methods of generating snapshots are discussed in Chapter 6.

Configuring Peer-to-Peer Transactional Replication

Peer-to-peer transactional replication is a new kind of transactional replication introduced in SQL Server 2005. Prior to this, bidirectional transactional replication was introduced in SQL Server 2000. In both standard transactional replication and transactional publication with updatable subscriptions, the relationship is of a hierarchical nature, but in a peer-to-peer format, the relationship between the two or more servers is one of partners on an equal basis (the topology is also known as master-to-master, since the nodes are equal). While peer-to-peer transactional replication can support *n*-nary server configuration, bidirectional transactional replication, as the name suggests, is supported only between two servers.

As mentioned in the "Peer-to-Peer Transactional Replication" section of Chapter 3, peer-to-peer transactional replication does not have the means to handle data conflicts, so the likely scenarios where it can be used is where the relationship between the servers is either read/read or read/write. Also, bidirectional transactional replication can only be configured using T-SQL, not with the GUI.

Note Bidirectional transactional replication is discussed in Chapter 9.

By distributing the workload between the servers, the peer-to-peer format helps in improving the read performance of queries. Since each of the nodes in the peer-to-peer topology act as both the Publisher and the Server, changes made at any one node will not be applied at other nodes more than once. For example, if we want to keep a running hot backup of the mysales database, and we do not need to update subscriptions where the nodes are arranged in a hierarchical order, we might consider using peer-to-peer replication. Therefore for high availability, the use of peer-to-peer transactional replication might be considered.

In this section, I will show you how to configure peer-to-peer transactional replication.

Setting Up the Publication

As a first step, you need to create a publication on the first node with the New Publication Wizard. The name of the server for the first node is BIOREPL. When creating the publication, you should choose transactional replication. Follow the wizard until you come to the Articles page of the wizard (shown previously in Figure 8-5). Select the Articles that you want to publish, and click the Article Properties button. You'll see the Article Properties window shown in Figure 8-45.

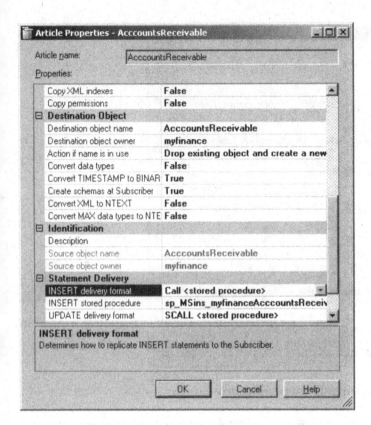

Figure 8-45. *Setting the properties for the articles*

You should go through each of the articles, ensuring that you do not change the settings for the "Destination object name" and "Destination object owner." Also ensure the INSERT, UPDATE, and DELETE delivery format options are set to INSERT, UPDATE, and DELETE stored procedures.

■**Note** You cannot filter any articles in a peer-to-peer framework, since the nodes are all equal.

When you come to the Snapshot Agent page of the wizard, choose the option to create a snapshot immediately, as shown in Figure 8-46.

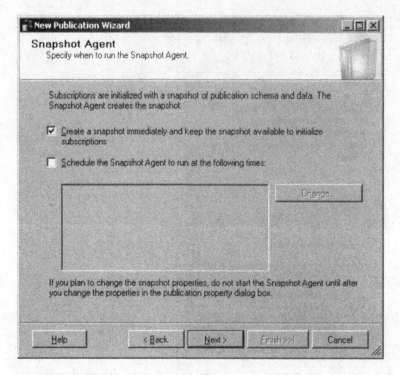

Figure 8-46. *Setting the Snapshot Agent to run immediately*

Then simply follow the instructions in the rest of the wizard, and when you come to the final page, enter a name for the publication. The same name will be used on the other servers.

Enabling the Publication for Peer-to-Peer Replication

You need to enable the publication for peer-to-peer replication. This is done by right-clicking on the publication, and selecting Properties. In the Publication Properties window, select the Subscription Options page, and in the "Updatable subscriptions" section set "Allow peer-to-peer subscriptions" to True from the drop-down list. Once the "Allow peer-to-peer subscriptions" option has been set to True and you have clicked OK, you cannot reset it to False; the properties under "Updatable subscriptions" section will be disabled, as shown in Figure 8-47.

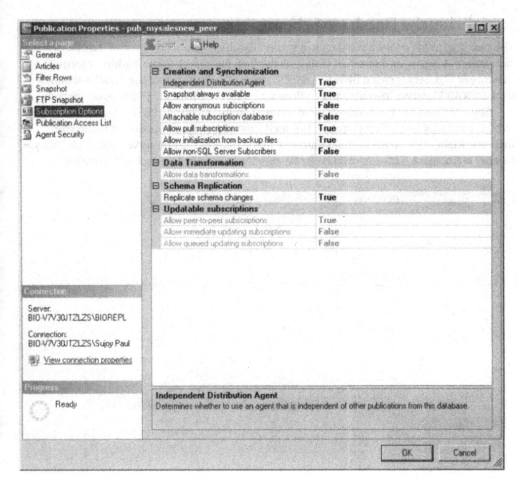

Figure 8-47. *Setting up the peer-to-peer subscriptions*

■**Note** You cannot use immediate updating and queued updating subscriptions when setting up peer-to-peer transactional replication.

Peer-to-peer transactional replication also requires that the `allow_initialize_from_backup` parameter is set to True. This will automatically be set to the default value of True when you enable the publication for peer-to-peer subscriptions as shown in Figure 8-47. It also sets the "Allow anonymous subscriptions" option to False, as required for peer-to-peer replication.

Initializing the Database Schema

The next step in the process is to create a second database on a second server that has the same name, schema, and same set of data as the first. For this example, I added a second instance of SQL Server called BIOREPL_PEER, made a backup copy of the mysales database on the BIOREPL server instance, and I will restore it on the BIOREPL_PEER server instance.

Since the name of the database to be restored on the BIOREPL_PEER instance also needs to be the same as on the first instance, I created a database called mysales on this server instance. Right-click on the mysales database in the BIOREPL_PEER server and select Tasks ➤ Restore ➤ Database. This will display the Restore Database window shown in Figure 8-48.

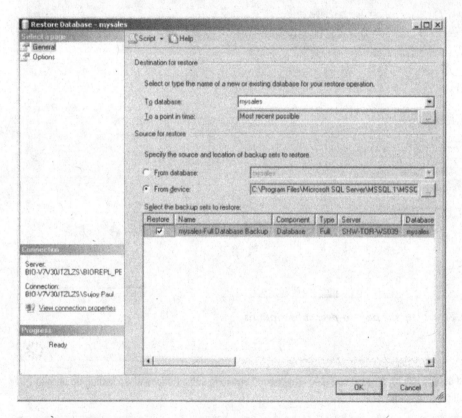

Figure 8-48. *Restoring the mysales database on the second server instance*

Select the Options page, as shown in Figure 8-49. Ensure that you do not check the "Preserve the replication settings" check box. In my case, I checked the box for "Overwrite the existing database," since I created this database originally on this server instance. Then click OK to restore the database.

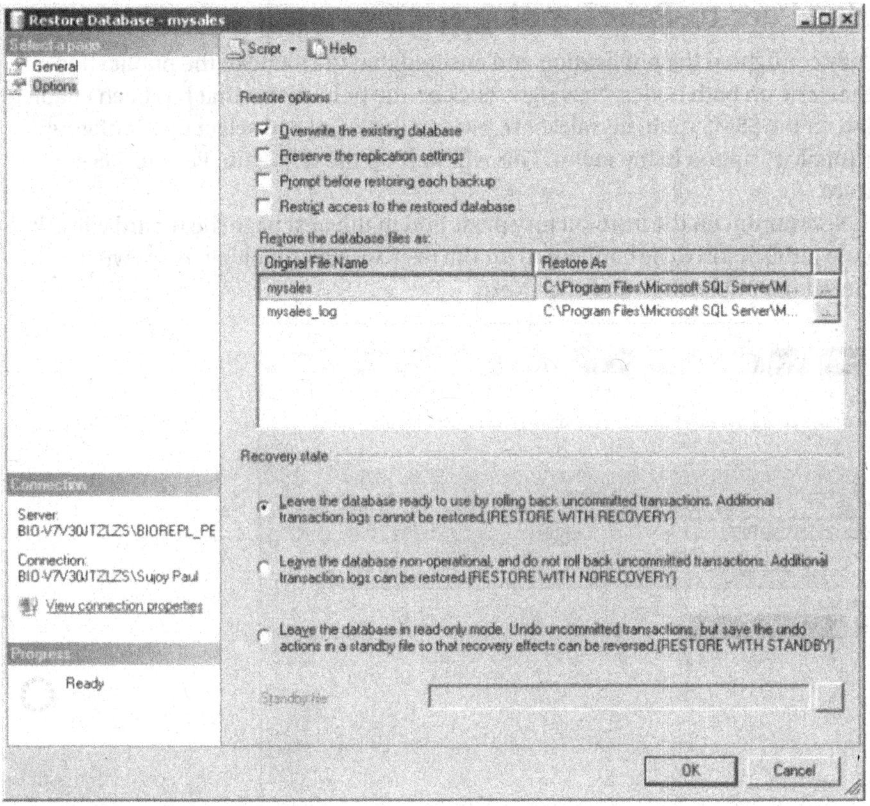

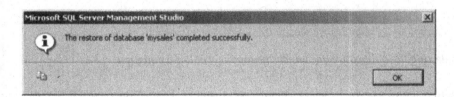

Figure 8-49. *Restoring the database*

Figure 8-50 shows the successful restoration of the database.

Figure 8-50. *The successful restoration of the mysales database on BIOREPL_PEER*

Tip You could alternatively use SSIS to copy the schema and data.

Now that we have set up the publication, enabled it for peer-to-peer replication, and initialized the database schema and the data, the next step is to configure the peer-to-peer topology.

Configuring Peer-to-Peer Topology

We have already configured the publication and ensured that the name of the publication database is the same on both nodes. Now right-click on the publication that has been enabled for publication on the SSMS (pub_mysalesnew_peer, in this case) and select the Configure Peer-to-Peer Topology option in the menu. This will start up the Configure Peer-to-Peer Topology Wizard.

Click the Next button on the introductory page, and in the next page the wizard will ask you to select the publication to be configured for the peer-to-peer topology, as shown in Figure 8-51. Select the publication and click Next.

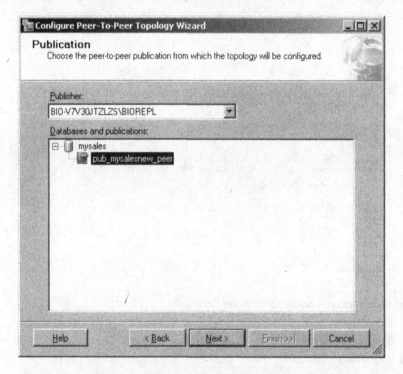

Figure 8-51. *Selecting the publication for which the topology will be configured*

The wizard will now ask you to select a peer server instance. I added the new SQL Server instance (BIOREPL_PEER) by clicking the Add SQL Server button on the Peers page of the Configure Peer-to-Peer Topology Wizard. This will open the Connect to Server dialog box, which will ask you to make a connection to the server instance, as shown in Figure 8-52.

After you connect to the server instance, it shows up in the Peers page of the wizard, as shown in Figure 8-53.

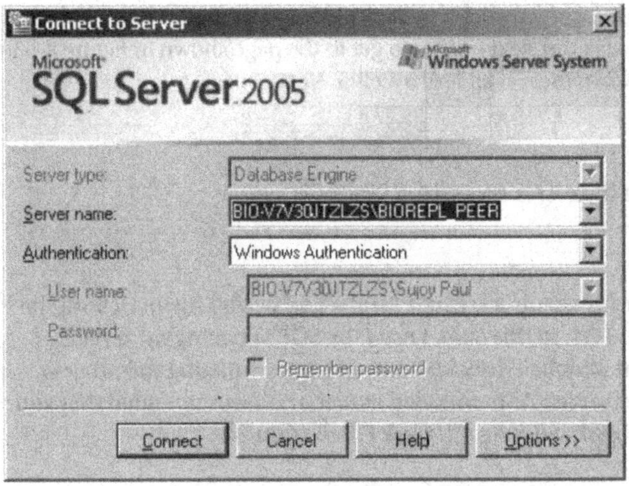

Figure 8-52. *Connecting to the BIOREPL_PEER server instance*

Figure 8-53. *Selecting peer server instances and their corresponding databases*

On selecting the BIOREPL_PEER server instance, the wizard warns us that the Distributor server for this instance has not been configured. So you have to go back and configure the Distributor server for this server instance.

After you configure the Distributor server, click the Back button to go to the Publication wizard page (Figure 8-51), and then click the Next button to get to the page shown in Figure 8-53, which should now accept the server instance. If all is okay, click Next.

Note The configuration of the Distributor server is discussed in Chapter 2.

The wizard will now ask you for the security settings for the Log Reader Agent in both the server instances, as shown in Figure 8-54. In this case, I used the SQL Server Agent service account to run the Log Reader Agent and the Windows account (impersonating the process account) to connect to the Publisher server. As mentioned earlier, it is recommended that you use the domain account to run the Log Reader Agent. Click OK to continue.

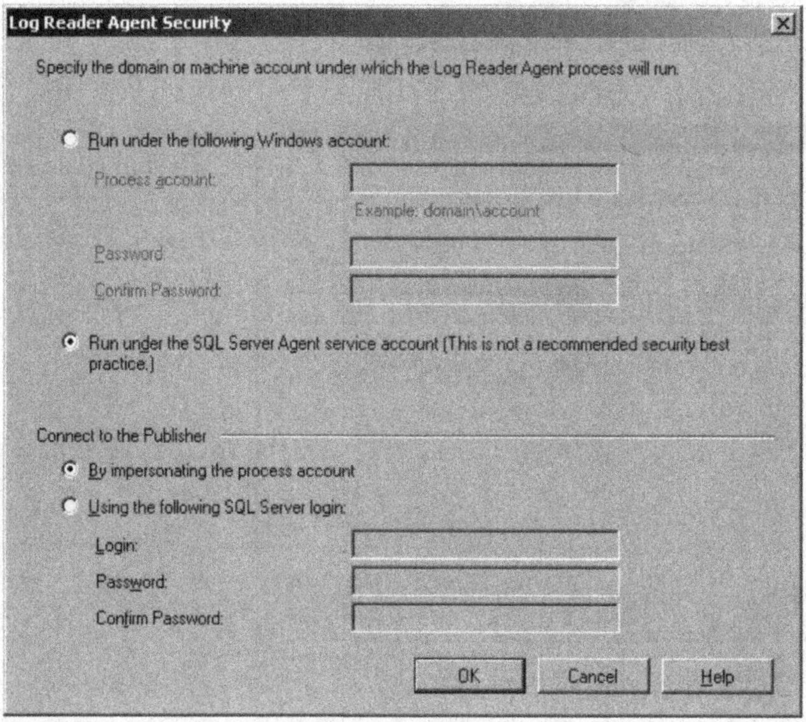

Figure 8-54. *Setting the Log Reader Agent accounts*

The next wizard is shown in Figure 8-55. As you can see, I am using the first peer's security settings for the other peer in this example. I recommend that you use different security settings. Click Next.

The wizard will now ask you for the security settings of the Distribution Agent. As with the Log Reader Agent, I am also running the Distribution Agent under the SQL Server Agent service account and connecting to the Distributor and Subscriber servers by impersonating the process account, as shown in Figure 8-56. Click OK to continue.

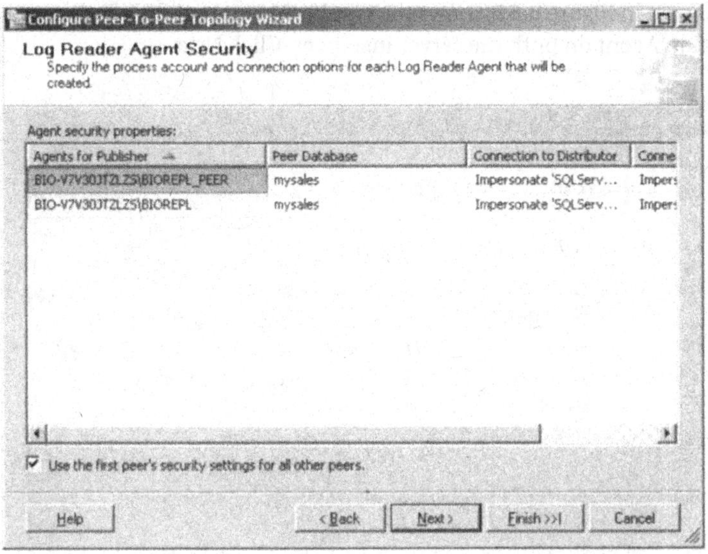

Figure 8-55. *Configuring the Log Reader Agent security settings*

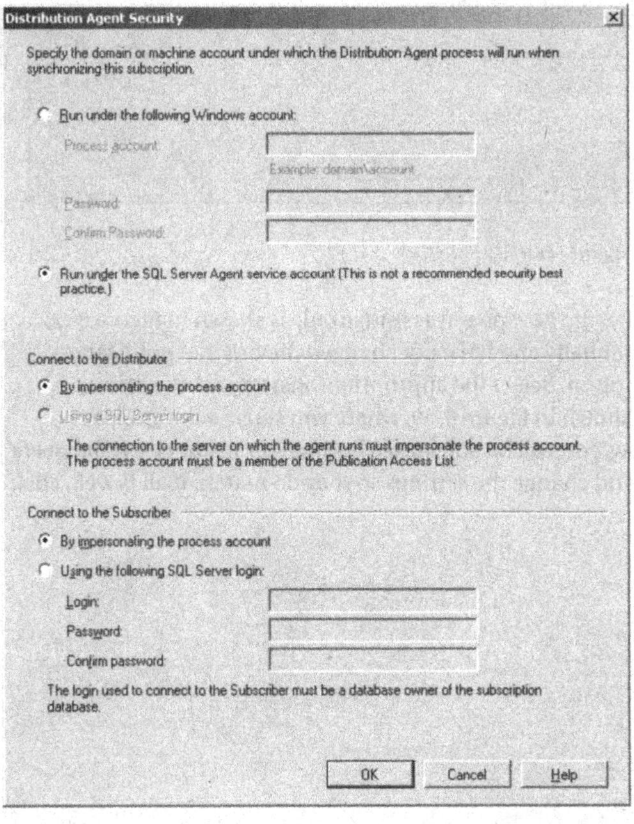

Figure 8-56. *Configuring the Distribution Agent accounts*

The next wizard page, shown in Figure 8-57, shows the results. Again, I set the same security settings for the Distribution Agent on both the server instances. Click Next.

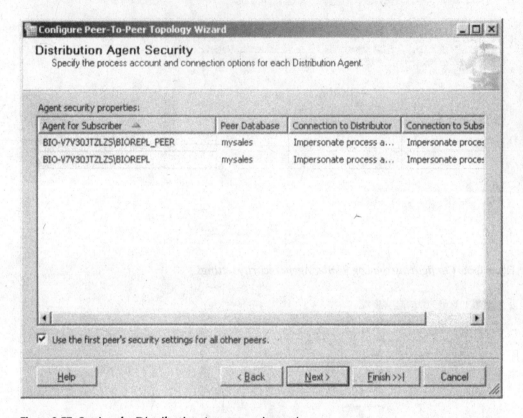

Figure 8-57. *Setting the Distribution Agent security settings*

Next, the wizard will ask you how the new peer was initialized, as shown in Figure 8-58. Since I created the peer database manually and have not changed the original publication database, I selected the first radio button. Select the appropriate answer and click Next.

The final page of the wizard is shown in Figure 8-59, where you can see the choices I made. If you scroll down the window, you will be able to see both server instances. If the peers do not match, you should go back and change the settings so they do match. If all is well, click the Finish button.

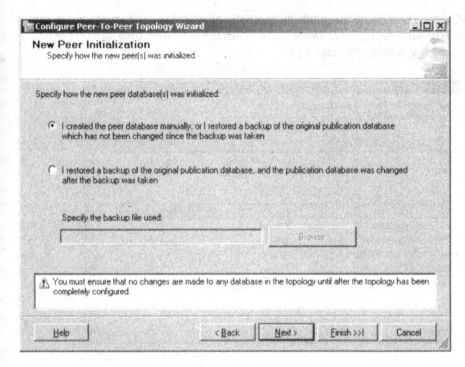

Figure 8-58. *Specifying how the new peer was initialized*

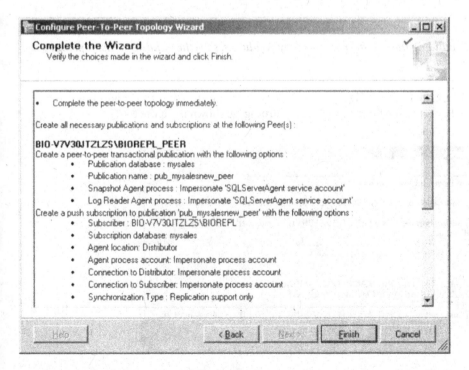

Figure 8-59. *Reviewing the peer-to-peer topology*

The wizard will now create the publication and the subscriptions on both the peers. It then proceeds to build the topology. However, as shown in Figure 8-60, only three out of four actions succeeded in building the topology.

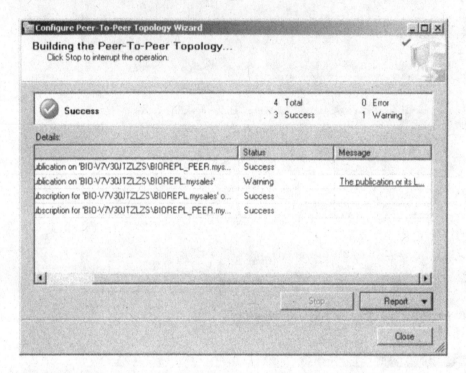

Figure 8-60. *Building the peer-to-peer topology. As always, save the building of the topology in a file.*

As you can see from the Figure 8-60, there is a warning. Click on the Report button and select View Report to see the reason for the warning, as shown in Figure 8-61.

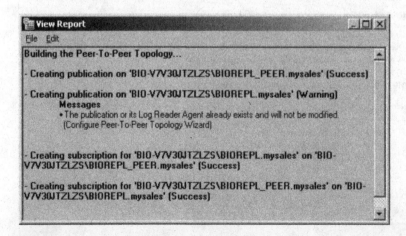

Figure 8-61. *Viewing the report*

The warning is that the Log Reader Agent already exists. It is an informational message only and does not require you to take any action. As usual, though, it is a good practice to save the report for future reference or troubleshooting.

Summary

In this chapter, I have shown you how to use the GUI method to configure the different types of publication used in transactional replication, namely standard publication, publication with updatable subscriptions, and peer-to-peer publication. I have also shown you how to use immediate updating and queued updating subscriptions for transactional publication.

You should also have a good understanding of how to change the mode of the updatable subscriptions and the consequences of doing so. You should also be aware of the concepts behind peer-to-peer replication, the likely situations in which will be used, and the steps that you need to take to configure it.

- There are three different types of publication in transactional replication that can be configured using the GUI: standard publication, publication with updatable subscriptions, and peer-to-peer publication.

- The initial synchronization of a publication to the Subscriber is done by the Snapshot Agent. Alternative methods of generating the snapshot can be used in transactional replication.

- Transactional replication uses the transaction log to transmit the changes.

- The Log Reader Agent reads the changes in the transaction log and transmits them; the Distribution Agent then picks them up and sends them to the Subscriber servers.

- Tables that do not contain a primary key cannot be used in transactional replication.

- The Log Reader Agent is used for standard publication.

- Both the Log Reader and the Queue Reader Agents are used for queued updating subscriptions.

- Updates made on the subscription database are transferred to the Publisher using the 2PC protocol.

- The MS DTC must be configured in order to use immediate updating subscriptions and queued updating subscriptions.

- It is possible to switch between the two modes of subscriptions.

- The relationship between the servers in a peer-to-peer configuration is equal.

- The name of the database should be the same on both servers.

In the next chapter, you will gain a better understanding of how transactional replication can be configured using the T-SQL method. Comparing the two methods will give you a strong grasp of transactional replication.

Quick Tips

- You cannot use immediate updating and queued updating subscriptions for peer-to-peer transactional replication.

- You cannot use vertical and horizontal filtering when setting up updatable subscriptions and queued updates.

- The Distribution Agent usually runs continuously for transactional replication.

- You cannot configure bidirectional transactional replication using the GUI. You have to configure it using the T-SQL method

CHAPTER 9

■ ■ ■

Configuring Transactional Replication Using T-SQL

In Chapter 8, I showed you how to configure publications and subscriptions for transactional replication using the GUI method. You have seen that transactional replication uses the transaction log to transmit the data changes after the publication and the subscription have been initially synchronized. You also learned that the latency of transactional replication is smaller than for snapshot replication.

In standard transactional replication, both push and pull subscriptions use the Snapshot, Distribution, and Log Reader Agents. For queued updating subscriptions, the Queue Reader Agent is also used. Remember that the MS DTC is used for both immediate and queued updating subscriptions.

In this chapter, I will show you how to use T-SQL to set up the different types of publication, updatable subscriptions, the peer-to-peer topology, and bidirectional transactional replication. The inner workings of transactional replication are discussed in Chapter 10.

On completing this chapter, you will know how to use the T-SQL method to do the following:

- Configure standard publication

- Configure transactional publication with immediate and queued updates

- Configure immediate and queued updating subscriptions

- Change modes between immediate and queued updating

- Configure peer-to-peer transactional replication

- Use the SQLCMD utility

- Configure bidirectional transactional replication

Tip If you have yet to download the database from Apress.com, you should do so now. The E-R diagram for the database can be found in Appendix A. The SQL code for the database can be found in Appendix B.

Configuring Publication

The steps for configuring transactional replication are generally the same as for configuring snapshot replication:

1. Create a Distributor server.

2. Create a distribution database.

3. Create a Publisher server.

4. Create one or more publications.

5. Add the articles to the publication.

6. Create a Subscriber server.

7. Create one or more subscriptions.

I showed you how to create a Distributor server, distribution database, and Publisher server in Chapter 2, using both the GUI and T-SQL methods.

For peer-to-peer transactional replication, I recommend that you create a separate Distributor server and distribution database for each server instance, rather than having all server instances being serviced by one Distributor server and distribution database. This way, if the central Distributor server on the network fails, you can still access the alternative Distributor server.

Transactional replication has three different types of publication, and the configuration of each type is different. Even the initial synchronization of the publication in transactional replication is different from synchronization in snapshot replication, as you will see in the next section, where we look at concurrent snapshot processing. While the configuration of push and pull subscriptions for standard publication in transactional replication is similar to snapshot replication, immediate updating and queued updating subscriptions need to be configured differently.

In the next section, I will show you how to configure the standard transactional publication.

DROPPING SUBSCRIPTIONS AND PUBLICATIONS

You can drop any pull and push subscriptions that you configured in Chapter 8.

To drop a pull subscription, first execute the sp_droppullsubscription stored procedure on the subscription database on the Subscriber server, and then execute sp_dropsubscription on the publication database on the Publisher server. You can also make use of the script in Listing 5-1 (in Chapter 5) to drop a pull subscription for transactional replication.

To drop a push subscription, you should first execute the sp_dropsubscription stored procedure on the publication database, and then use sp_subscription_cleanup on the subscription database to remove the replication metadata. You can use the code in Listing 5-2 (in Chapter 5) to drop a push subscription for transactional replication.

If you need to drop a publication, use the sp_droppublication stored procedure as discussed in Listing 5-3 (in Chapter 5).

Configuring Standard Transactional Publication

The steps taken to bind the publication database to the Publisher server for standard transactional publication are similar to those for the configuration of publication in snapshot replication, with some caveats. These are the steps for configuring standard transactional publication:

1. Enable the database for replication using the sp_replicationdboption stored procedure.

2. Determine whether the Log Reader Agent exists using the sp_helplogreader_agent stored procedure. If it exists, go on to step 3. If not, execute the sp_addlogreader_agent stored procedure to create a Log Reader Agent.

3. Create the publication using the sp_addpublication stored procedure.

4. Adding articles to the publication using the sp_addarticle stored procedure.

5. Create an agent for the publication using the sp_addpublication_snapshot stored procedure.

6. Start the Snapshot Agent to generate the initial snapshot using the sp_startpublication_snapshot stored procedure.

Enabling Publication for Transactional Replication

As with publication for snapshot replication (discussed in Chapter 5), we first need to enable the publication for transactional replication using the sp_replicationdboption stored procedure on the publication database, mysales_copy. Once the pub_mysales_copy_myinventory publication is enabled, we need to check whether the Log Reader Agent exists or not. If it does, we can add the publication.

The code in Listing 9-1 performs steps 1 and 3 from the preceding list for configuring standard publication for transactional replication (I set up the Log Reader Agent already).

Listing 9-1. *Enabling and Creating the Standard Publication for Transactional Replication*

```
/*Execute this on the publication database, mysales_copy */

use [mysales_copy]
exec sp_replicationdboption
@dbname = 'mysales_copy',
@optname = 'publish',
@value = 'true'
Go


/* Add the transactional publication */
/* The @synch_method is set to concurrent for
transactional replication */
```

```
use [mysales_copy]
exec sp_addpublication @publication = 'pub_mysales_copy_myinventory',
@description = 'Transactional publication of database ''mysales_copy'' from
Publisher ''BIO-V7V3OJTZLZS\BIOREPL_PEER''.',

@sync_method = 'concurrent',
@retention = 0, @allow_push = 'true', @allow_pull = 'true',
@allow_anonymous = 'true', @snapshot_in_defaultfolder = 'true',

@compress_snapshot = 'false',
@allow_subscription_copy = 'false', @add_to_active_directory = 'false',
@repl_freq = 'continuous', @status = 'active',

@independent_agent = 'true', @immediate_sync = 'true',
@allow_sync_tran = 'false', @autogen_sync_procs = 'false',
@allow_queued_tran = 'false',
@replicate_ddl = 1,

@allow_initialize_from_backup = 'false',
@enabled_for_p2p = 'false',
@enabled_for_het_sub = 'false'
go
```

The @value parameter for sp_replicationdboption has been set to true for the
mysales_copy publication database. The @optname parameter has been set to publish;
Table 9-1 shows the possible values for the @optname parameter.

Table 9-1. *Values for the* @optname *Parameter in the* sp_replicationdboption *Stored Procedure*

Value	Description
Merge publish	Specifies the database will be enabled or disabled for merge publication
publish	Specifies the database will be enabled or disabled for other types of publication
subscribe	Specifies the database is a subscription database
sync with backup	Enables the database for coordinated backup

■**Note** You use the sync with backup value for the @optname parameter to enable the database for
backup. This is discussed in Chapter 15.

The next step of the script adds the publication without setting up the Log Reader Agent.
This is because I already set up the Log Reader Agent prior to setting up this publication—you
can use the sp_helplogreader_agent stored procedure to find out whether the agent exists, as
shown in Listing 9-2.

Listing 9-2. *Finding Out Whether the Log Reader Agent Exists or Not*

```
/*Execute this on the publication database */

Use mysales_copy
Go


sp_helplogreader_agent
```

The output of this script looks like this:

id	name
publisher_security_mode	publisher_login
publisher_password	job_id
job_login	
job_password	
--	
2	BIO-V7V30JTZLZS\BIOREPL_PEER-mysales_copy-2
1	
*********	81BE4098-802E-4C3C-BDDE-40B4F974A5F6
NULL	
*********	

■**Tip** Specify the name of the Publisher server for the @publisher parameter for the sp_helplogreader_agent stored procedure only for non-SQL Server Publishers. If you do this for SQL Server Publishers, you will get an error message. The syntax for sp_helplogreader_agent is sp_helplogreader_agent @publisher.

The name column in the output contains the name of the Log Reader Agent, and the id column displays the ID of the agent. You can see that the Log Reader Agent is using Windows Authentication, as the value for the publisher_security_mode column is set to 1.

If you do not have a Log Reader Agent set up use the sp_addlogreader_agent stored procedure to add one. You would execute the following on the publication database in the Publisher server to set up the Log Reader Agent:

```
sp_addlogreader_agent @job_login, @job_password, @publisher_security_mode
```

The @job_login and @job_password parameters are the login and password for the Windows account under which the agent will run. The default value for @publisher_security_mode is 1, which is the Windows authentication used to connect to the Publisher server. In order to execute either of these stored procedures, you need to be a member of the sysadmin fixed server role or the db_owner fixed database role.

The next thing the script in Listing 9-1 does is add the publication with the sp_addpublication stored procedure. This is executed on the Publisher server. The procedure for adding a standard publication for transactional replication is similar to that for the addition of a publication in snapshot replication. I have put those parameters that have different values for transactional replication in bold; you can compare them with the values in Listing 5-4 in Chapter 5.

Notice the sync_method parameter is set to concurrent; this setting does not lock the tables during the generation of the snapshot, but it still uses the native bulk copy program (bcp) to generate the snapshot. This is unique for transactional replication.

The repl_freq parameter has been set to continuous, whereas in snapshot replication it was set to snapshot. Since transactional replication requires all committed transactions to be log-based, you must set it to continuous so that the Publisher can send the output continuously.

Tip For non-SQL Server Publishers, like Oracle, the repl_freq parameter should be set to continuous_c.

Both the immediate_sync and independent_agent parameters have been set to true. When the @independent_agent is set to true, a stand-alone Distribution Agent serves the publication. A value of false would mean the publication uses a shared Distribution Agent.

A value of true for the @immediate_sync parameter means that the snapshot will be created each time the Snapshot Agent runs and will be available to the subscriptions. The independent_agent parameter must be set to true when the immediate_sync parameter is set to true; if you set it to false, the snapshot will be created only if there is a new subscription.

The @replicate_ddl parameter is set to 1, which means that the articles or the schema definition can be altered and then transmitted to the Subscriber servers. I will show you how to change article definitions and replicate the changes at the end of this chapter.

The @enabled_for_p2p parameter has been set to false, since this publication is not going to be used for peer-to-peer replication.

Adding Articles to the Publication

After you have created the publication, the next step in the process is to add articles to the publication.

The articles that I have added in this example are StockItem, Customer, Item, Stock, Warehouse, and the usp_item_duplicates stored procedure, which removes any duplicate values from the Item table. Only the Warehouse table is horizontally filtered. Listing 9-3 shows you how to add and filter the tables.

Tip When creating your own stored procedures, follow a naming convention. It is better to name user-defined stored procedure as usp_<procedure name>. If you name a stored procedure as sp_<procedure name>, it will be stored in the master system database.

Listing 9-3. *Adding Articles, Including the* usp_item_duplicates *Stored Procedure*

```
/* Execute sp_addarticle for the StockItem article */

use [mysales_copy]
exec sp_addarticle @publication = 'pub_mysales_copy_myinventory',
@article = 'StockItem', @source_owner = 'myinventory',
@source_object = 'StockItem', @type = 'logbased',
@description = null,
@creation_script = null, @pre_creation_cmd = 'drop',
@schema_option = 0x000000000803509F,

@identityrangemanagementoption = 'manual',
@destination_table = 'StockItem', @destination_owner = 'myinventory',
@vertical_partition = 'false',

@ins_cmd = 'CALL sp_MSins_myinventoryStockItem',
@del_cmd = 'CALL sp_MSdel_myinventoryStockItem',
@upd_cmd = 'SCALL sp_MSupd_myinventoryStockItem'
GO

/* Execute sp_addarticle for the Customer article */

use [mysales_copy]
exec sp_addarticle @publication = 'pub_mysales_copy_myinventory',
@article = 'Customer', @source_owner = 'myorder',
@source_object = 'Customer', @type = 'logbased',

@description = null, @creation_script = null,
@pre_creation_cmd = 'drop', @schema_option = 0x000000000803509F,
@identityrangemanagementoption = 'manual',

@destination_table = 'Customer', @destination_owner = 'myorder',
@vertical_partition = 'false',

@ins_cmd = 'CALL sp_MSins_myorderCustomer',
@del_cmd = 'CALL sp_MSdel_myorderCustomer',
@upd_cmd = 'SCALL sp_MSupd_myorderCustomer'
GO

/* Execute sp_addarticle for the Stock article */

use [mysales_copy]
exec sp_addarticle @publication = 'pub_mysales_copy_myinventory',
@article = 'Stock', @source_owner = 'myorder',
@source_object = 'Stock', @type = 'logbased',
```

```
@description = null, @creation_script = null,
@pre_creation_cmd = 'drop', @schema_option = 0x000000000803509F,
@identityrangemanagementoption = 'manual',

@destination_table = 'Stock', @destination_owner = 'myorder',
@vertical_partition = 'false',

@ins_cmd = 'CALL sp_MSins_myorderStock',
@del_cmd = 'CALL sp_MSdel_myorderStock',
@upd_cmd = 'SCALL sp_MSupd_myorderStock'
GO

/* Execute sp_addarticle for the Item article */

use [mysales_copy]
exec sp_addarticle @publication = 'pub_mysales_copy_myinventory',
@article = 'Item', @source_owner = 'myinventory',
@source_object = 'Item', @type = 'logbased',

@description = null, @creation_script = null,
@pre_creation_cmd = 'drop', @schema_option = 0x000000000803509F,
@identityrangemanagementoption = 'manual',

@destination_table = 'Item', @destination_owner = 'myinventory',
@vertical_partition = 'false',

@ins_cmd = 'CALL sp_MSins_myinventoryItem',
@del_cmd = 'CALL sp_MSdel_myinventoryItem',
@upd_cmd = 'SCALL sp_MSupd_myinventoryItem'
GO

/* Execute sp_addarticle for the Warehouse article */

use [mysales_copy]
exec sp_addarticle @publication = 'pub_mysales_copy_myinventory',
@article = 'Warehouse', @source_owner = 'myinventory',
@source_object = 'Warehouse', @type = 'logbased',

@description = null, @creation_script = null,
@pre_creation_cmd = 'drop', @schema_option = 0x000000000803509F,
@identityrangemanagementoption = 'manual',

@destination_table = 'Warehouse',
@destination_owner = 'myinventory', @vertical_partition = 'false',
```

```
@ins_cmd =  'CALL sp_MSins_myinventoryWarehouse',
@del_cmd =  'CALL sp_MSdel_myinventoryWarehouse',
@upd_cmd =  'SCALL sp_MSupd_myinventoryWarehouse',
@filter_clause =  '[Whse_City] =''Vancouver'''

/*  Add the article filter */

exec sp_articlefilter @publication =  'pub_mysales_copy_myinventory',
@article =  'Warehouse', @filter_name =  'FLTR_Warehouse_1__63',

@filter_clause =  '[Whse_City] =''Vancouver''',
@force_invalidate_snapshot = 1,
@force_reinit_subscription = 1

/*  Add the article synchronization object */

exec sp_articleview @publication =  'pub_mysales_copy_myinventory',
@article =  'Warehouse', @view_name =  'SY C_Warehouse_1__63',
@filter_clause =  '[Whse_City] =''Vancouver''',
@force_invalidate_snapshot = 1, @force_reinit_subscription = 1
GO

/* Add the stored procedure */

use [mysales_copy]
go

/* Check the source owner and the destination owner of the
stored procedure before executing the following code.*/

exec sp_addarticle @publication =  'pub_mysales_copy_myinventory',
@article =  'usp_item_duplicates',
@source_owner =  'dbo', @source_object =  'usp_item_duplicates',

 @type =  'proc schema only',
@description = null, @creation_script = null,
@pre_creation_cmd =  'drop',
@schema_option = 0x0000000008000001,
@destination_table =  'usp_item_duplicates',
@destination_owner =  'dbo'
GO
```

This script adds the articles, StockItem, Customer, Item, Stock, and Warehouse to the publication and issues insert, delete, and update commands that should be propagated to the Subscribers using the sp_addarticle stored procedure. Most of the parameters for the stored procedure are similar to those in Listing 5-7 for snapshot replication, except for the ones displayed in bold. The @ins_cmd, @del_cmd, and @upd_cmd parameters for the Customer table have been set to CALL sp_MSins_myorderCustomer, CALL sp_MSdel_myorderCustomer, and SCALL sp_MSupd_myorderCustomer, respectively. These three parameters guide the changes of data in transactional replication.

Note If you do not want the changes to be propagated, set the insert, delete, and update parameters to none.

The stored procedures for the inserts (sp_MSins_myorderCustomer), updates (sp_MSupd_myorderCustomer), and deletes (sp_MSdel_myorderCustomer) are the default stored procedures used for transactional replication. The CALL syntax can be used for all three DML operations. The CALL syntax for the sp_MSins_<tablename> stored procedure passes the inserted values for all the columns to the Subscriber servers. The CALL syntax for the delete statement passes all the delete values for the primary key columns.

Although the @upd_cmd parameter uses SCALL, you can use the CALL syntax instead. The stored procedure for update statements using the CALL syntax first passes the updated values for all the columns in the articles, followed by the original values for the primary key columns, and it doesn't check whether the columns have indeed changed. This is not the case with the SCALL syntax, which passes the values for those columns that have been updated, followed by the original primary key columns, and then by a bitmask parameter to indicate the changed columns.

Note You can only use the SCALL syntax with update statements.

After all the articles are created and added, the horizontal filtering can be added. Since all the promotion has already been done in Vancouver, we want to find out how the items and the corresponding stocks are doing for other cities. You perform horizontal filtering by executing the sp_articlefilter stored procedure. I use a static filter in this example, since the subset of all the rows will be received by all the Subscribers. A static filter returns a single subset of data for the publication. This stored procedure is executed on the Publisher server on the publication database.

Note Dynamic filtering is carried out in merge replication. It is discussed in Chapters 11 and 13.

When you filter articles, you have to assign a name for the publication and the article you are going to filter, and a name for the filter. The `@filter_clause` parameter is essentially the WHERE clause without the need to specify one; a static filter is exemplified by the use of the WHERE clause in the SQL statement. In fact, you are prevented from specifying a WHERE clause. Since this parameter causes the snapshot to be invalidated, I have assigned a value of 1 to the `@force_invalidate_snapshot` parameter, which makes the current snapshot obsolete and causes a new snapshot to be generated. The default value of 0 specifies that the changes to the article do not make the snapshot invalid so that a new snapshot is not needed.

The `@force_reinit_subscription` parameter is set to 1, which forces existing subscriptions to reinitialize. Again, the default value is 0, which means that reinitialization is not necessary. If the reinitialization attempts to proceed while the default value is 0, it will generate an error message.

The `sp_articleview` stored procedure then needs to be run with the same parameters as `sp_articlefilter`; it creates a view that holds the information for the published article when a table is filtered either horizontally, as in this case, or vertically. This view is then used by the destination table as the filtered source of the schema and the data. To run either of these stored procedures, you need to be either a member of the `sysadmin` fixed server role or the `db_owner` fixed database role.

Tip If you want to do vertical filtering, you first need to add the article. Then execute the `sp_articlecolumn` stored procedure, specifying the names of the columns you want to add in the `@column` parameter and setting the `@operation` parameter to add. Finally, execute the `sp_articleview` stored procedure.

The script also added the `usp_items_duplicates` user-defined stored procedure as one of the articles that will be published. Notice the `@type` parameter, which has been set to proc schema only. This means that only the schema will be replicated. This is not supported by non-SQL Server Publisher servers.

If you now open the SSMS, select the publication database, and open the Programmability object, you will see the list of stored procedures generated by the execution of these stored procedures. This is shown in Figure 9-1. You can right-click any of these stored procedures and view the code by selecting Modify from the menu.

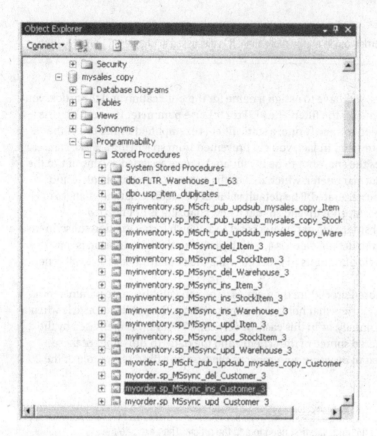

Figure 9-1. *User-defined stored procedures created by replication*

Creating the Snapshot Agent and Generating the Snapshot

The next step is to create the Snapshot Agent and then generate the new snapshot for the newly created publication. The Snapshot Agent is created on the publication database on the Publisher server, as shown in Listing 9-4.

Listing 9-4. *Creating the Snapshot Agent*

```
/* Execute the stored procedure on the current publication database */

exec sp_addpublication_snapshot
@publication = 'pub_mysales_copy_myinventory',
@frequency_type = 1,
@frequency_interval = 0,

@frequency_relative_interval = 0,
@frequency_recurrence_factor = 0,
@frequency_subday = 0,
```

```
@frequency_subday_interval = 0,
@active_start_time_of_day = 0,
@active_end_time_of_day = 235959,

@active_start_date = 0,
@active_end_date = 0,
@job_login = null,

@job_password = null,
@publisher_security_mode = 1
```

In this script, the @frequency_type parameter has been set to 1, which means that the Snapshot Agent will only run once; compare this to Listing 5-5 in Chapter 5, where the Snapshot Agent was scheduled to run weekly. The parameter in bold is used when running the Snapshot Agent for transactional replication, where you just need to execute the Snapshot Agent once for the initial delivery of the snapshot, as compared to the setting used when running the Snapshot Agent for snapshot replication. In this case, the Snapshot Agent uses Windows Authentication (@publisher_security_mode=1) to connect to the Publisher server.

Finally, we are ready to run the snapshot for the publication. We do so by executing the sp_startpublication_snapshot stored procedure from the publication database on the Publisher server, as shown in Listing 9-5. You need to be a member of the sysadmin fixed server role or the db_owner fixed database role to execute the stored procedure.

Listing 9-5. *Starting the Snapshot Agent Job*

```
/* Execute this on the publication database */
Use mysales_copy
Go

Exec sp_startpublication_snapshot 'pub_mysales_copy_myinventory'
Go
```

■**Note** If you have not created any subscription databases for any of the publication types for transactional replication, you need to create one.

Configuring a Push Subscription for Standard Publication

Now that you have set up a standard publication for transactional replication, I will show you how to set up a push subscription for a standard publication. You will find that it is similar to setting up a push subscription for snapshot replication (discussed in Chapter 5).

Listing 9-6 shows how to set up a push subscription.

Listing 9-6. *Setting Up a Push Subscription for Standard Transactional Replication*

```
/* Execute this on the publication database */
use mysales_copy
go

exec sp_addsubscription @publication =
'pub_mysales_copy_myinventory',
@subscriber =  'BIO-V7V3OJTZLZS\BIOREPL_PEER',
@destination_db =  'mysalescopy_stpub_remotepush',

@subscription_type =  'Push',
@sync_type =  'automatic',
@article =  'all',
@update_mode =  'read only',
@subscriber_type = 0

exec sp_addpushsubscription_agent @publication =
'pub_mysales_copy_myinventory',
@subscriber =  'BIO-V7V3OJTZLZS\BIOREPL_PEER',

@subscriber_db =  'mysalescopy_stpub_remotepush',
@job_login = null,
@job_password = null,
@subscriber_security_mode = 1,
@frequency_type = 64,

@frequency_interval = 0,
@frequency_relative_interval = 0,
@frequency_recurrence_factor = 0,
@frequency_subday = 0,
@frequency_subday_interval = 0,
@active_start_time_of_day = 0,

@active_end_time_of_day = 235959,
@active_start_date = 20060111,
@active_end_date = 99991231,

@enabled_for_syncmgr =  'False',
@dts_package_location = 'Distributor'
go
```

The parameters specified in this code are similar to those used for push subscriptions for snapshot replication. You can refer to Chapter 5 for explanations of these parameters.

Configuring a Pull Subscription for Standard Publication

The configuration of pull subscriptions for a standard publication for transactional replication is similar to their configuration for snapshot replication. The steps you need to take are shown in Listing 9-7.

Note Push and pull subscriptions for snapshot replication are discussed in Chapter 5.

Listing 9-7. *Setting Up a Pull Subscription for Standard Publication for Transactional Replication*

```
/*1. Execute this on the Publisher server on the publication
database */

use mysales_copy
go

exec sp_addsubscription @publication =
 'pub_mysales_copy_myinventory',
@subscriber =  'BIO-V7V3OJTZLZS\BIOREPL_PEER',
@destination_db =  'mysalescopyinven_stdpub_remotepull',

@sync_type =  'Automatic',
@subscription_type =  'pull',
@update_mode =  'read only'
Go

/* 2. Execute this on the subscription database on the Subscriber server */

use mysalescopyinven_stdpub_remotepull
go

exec sp_addpullsubscription @publisher =
'BIO-V7V3OJTZLZS\BIOREPL_PEER', @publication =
'pub_mysales_copy_myinventory',
@publisher_db =  'mysales_copy',

@independent_agent =  'True',
@subscription_type =  'pull',

@description =  '',
@update_mode =  'read only',
@immediate_sync = 1
```

```
exec sp_addpullsubscription_agent @publisher =
'BIO-V7V30JTZLZS\BIOREPL_PEER',
@publisher_db = 'mysales_copy',
@publication = 'pub_mysales_copy_myinventory',

@distributor = 'BIO-V7V30JTZLZS\BIOREPL_PEER',
@distributor_security_mode = 1,
@distributor_login = '',
@distributor_password = null,

@enabled_for_syncmgr = 'False',
@frequency_type = 64,
@frequency_interval = 0,
@frequency_relative_interval = 0,
@frequency_recurrence_factor = 0,

@frequency_subday = 0,
@frequency_subday_interval = 0,
@active_start_time_of_day = 0,
@active_end_time_of_day = 235959,
@active_start_date = 20060113,

@active_end_date = 99991231,
@alt_snapshot_folder = '',
@working_directory = '',
@job_login = null,
@job_password = null,
@publication_type = 0
GO
```

Now that I have shown you how to configure push and pull subscriptions for a standard publication, I will discuss the other types of publication and their subscriptions.

Configuring Transactional Publication with Updatable Subscriptions

Now that you know how to set up a standard publication using both the GUI and T-SQL methods, let's explore the case where you might have to set up publications with the privilege of updating the subscriptions. In Chapter 8, I showed you how to set up a publication and subscriptions for this purpose using the GUI, and now we'll do the same with T-SQL.

Since publications allow immediate subscriptions, we will use the 2PC protocol, which places a lock on all the components involved in the replication process. This means the latency, the time taken to transfer any updates from the Subscriber server to the Publisher server, is minimal compared with queued updating, where the updates are placed in the queue. However, you need to ensure that both the Publisher server and the corresponding Subscriber servers are running all the time. You also need to ensure that the MS DTC is running.

MS DISTRIBUTED TRANSACTION COORDINATOR

Before I show you how to set up the publication, you should check that the MS DTC is running as a service. To find out, open the command window and enter the following at the prompt:

```
net start
```

Now press Enter. You will see a list of services that are running on the system:

You can see that MS DTC (Distributed Transaction Coordinator) is running as a service. To look up the properties of the DTC services, open Component Services from the Control Panel, right-click on Services, Distributed Transaction Coordinator, and select Properties from the menu.

In SQL Server, you can check whether MS DTC is running by opening the Management object in the Object Explorer:

Once you know that the MS DTC is running, you can set up a publication for updatable subscriptions. The steps are the same as for the configuration of a standard publication, and they're shown in Listing 9-8. The parameters that need to be added for updatable subscriptions are displayed in bold.

Listing 9-8. *Configuring the Transactional Publication*

```
/*1. Enable the replication database */

use master

exec sp_replicationdboption @dbname = 'mysales_copy',
@optname = 'publish',
@value = 'true'

GO

/* 2. Add the transactional publication for immediate
update subscriptions */

use [mysales_copy]
go

exec sp_addpublication @publication = 'pub_updsub_mysales_copy',
@description = 'Transactional publication with updatable
subscriptions of database ''mysales_copy'' from Publisher
''BIO-V7V3OJTZLZS\BIOREPL_PEER''.',

@sync_method = 'concurrent',
@retention = 0,

@allow_push = 'true',
@allow_pull = 'true',
@snapshot_in_defaultfolder = 'true',

@allow_subscription_copy = 'false',
@add_to_active_directory = 'false',
@repl_freq = 'continuous',

@status = 'active',
@independent_agent = 'true',
@immediate_sync = 'true',

@allow_sync_tran = 'true',
@autogen_sync_procs = 'true',
@allow_queued_tran = 'true',
```

```
@conflict_policy = 'pub wins',
@centralized_conflicts = 'true',
@conflict_retention = 14,

@queue_type = 'sql',
@replicate_ddl = 1,
@allow_initialize_from_backup = 'false',

@enabled_for_p2p = 'false',
@enabled_for_het_sub = 'false'
GO

/* 3. Execute the stored procedure on the current publication database to
create the Snapshot Agent */

use [mysales_copy]
go

exec sp_addpublication_snapshot @publication =
'pub_updsub_mysales_copy', @frequency_type = 1,
@frequency_interval = 0,

@frequency_relative_interval = 0,
@frequency_recurrence_factor = 0,
@frequency_subday = 0,

@frequency_subday_interval = 0,
@active_start_time_of_day = 0,
@active_end_time_of_day = 235959,

@active_start_date = 0, @active_end_date = 0,
@job_login = null, @job_password = null,
@publisher_security_mode = 1

/* 4. Add the articles */

use [mysales_copy]
go
/* Execute sp_addarticle for the Customer article */

exec sp_addarticle @publication = 'pub_updsub_mysales_copy',
@article = 'Customer', @source_owner = 'myorder',
@source_object = 'Customer', @type = 'logbased',

@description = null, @creation_script = null,
@pre_creation_cmd = 'drop',
@schema_option = 0x0000000008035CDF,
```

```
@identityrangemanagementoption = 'manual',
@destination_table = 'Customer',
@destination_owner = 'myorder', @status = 16,

 @vertical_partition = 'false'
GO

/* Execute sp_addarticle for the Item article */

exec sp_addarticle @publication = 'pub_updsub_mysales_copy',
@article = 'Item', @source_owner = 'myinventory',
@source_object = 'Item', @type = 'logbased',

@description = null, @creation_script = null,
@pre_creation_cmd = 'drop',
@schema_option = 0x0000000008035CDF,

@identityrangemanagementoption = 'manual',
@destination_table = 'Item',
@destination_owner = 'myinventory', @status = 16,

@vertical_partition = 'false'
GO

/* Execute sp_addarticle for the StockItem article */

exec sp_addarticle @publication = 'pub_updsub_mysales_copy',
@article = 'StockItem', @source_owner = 'myinventory',
@source_object = 'StockItem', @type = 'logbased',

@description = null, @creation_script = null,
@pre_creation_cmd = 'drop',
@schema_option = 0x0000000008035CDF,
@identityrangemanagementoption = 'manual',

@destination_table = 'StockItem',
@destination_owner = 'myinventory',
@status = 16,
@vertical_partition = 'false'
GO

/* Execute sp_addarticle for the Warehouse article */

exec sp_addarticle @publication = 'pub_updsub_mysales_copy',
@article = 'Warehouse',
@source_owner = 'myinventory',
@source_object = 'Warehouse',
@type = 'logbased',
```

```
@description = '', @creation_script = null,
@pre_creation_cmd = 'drop',
@schema_option = 0x0000000008035CDF,
@identityrangemanagementoption = 'manual',

@destination_table = 'Warehouse',
@destination_owner = 'myinventory',
@status = 16,
@vertical_partition = 'false'
GO

/* Execute sp_addarticle for the usp_item_duplicates article */

exec sp_addarticle @publication = 'pub_updsub_mysales_copy',
@article = 'usp_item_duplicates',
@source_owner = 'dbo',
@source_object = 'usp_item_duplicates',

@type = 'proc schema only',
@description = null,
@creation_script = null,
@pre_creation_cmd = 'drop',
@schema_option = 0x0000000008000001,

@destination_table = 'usp_item_duplicates',
@destination_owner = 'dbo'
GO
```

As with standard publication, the first step of the script enables the database for replication.

In the second step, the publication is added using the sp_addpublication stored procedure. The retention period (@retention) has a default value of 336 hours; the value of 0 specified in the script is interpreted as infinite, which means that if the subscription is inactive, it is never removed.

Since you can use both push and pull subscriptions with updatable subscriptions, both the @allow_push and @allow_pull parameters are set to true. The @repl_freq parameter has been set to a default value of continuous, as the transactions are log-based for this type of replication.

I discussed the @independent_agent and @immediate_sync parameters in the "Enabling Replication and Creating the Publication" section of the chapter, and that explanation applies here.

The setting of the @allow_sync_tran parameter determines whether the publication is set up for immediate subscriptions—a setting of true means that it has. The @autogent_sync_procs parameter, when set to true, indicates that the synchronization of stored procedures for updatable subscriptions is generated on the Publisher server. The @allow_queued_tran parameter has been set to true, which means that it is set for queued updating. The @conflict_policy parameter is used for queued updating to specify the conflict policy followed. Thus, this publication has been configured for both immediate and queued updating subscriptions. Table 9-2 describes the values for the conflict policy settings.

Table 9-2. *Values of the Conflict Policy for the Queued Updating Option*

Value	Description
Pub wins	Publisher wins the conflict
Sub wins	Subscriber wins the conflict
Sub reinit	Reinitialize the subscription if there is a conflict
NULL	If the publication is a transactional replication, pub wins becomes the default

A value of true for the @centralized_conflicts parameter means that the conflict policy is stored on the Publisher server; it is retained for a period of 14 days (@conflict_retention) and SQL Server is used to store the transactions (@queue_type). The updated subscriptions do not allow any filtering, because the @vertical_filtering parameter has been set to false.

Having set up the publication, we will now set up the pull subscription for updatable subscriptions.

Configuring a Pull Subscription for Immediate Updating

In Chapter 8, I showed you how to configure immediate updating pull subscriptions using the GUI method. In this section, I will show you how to use T-SQL stored procedures to create a pull subscription. The steps that you need to take are as follows:

1. Verify that the publication supports immediate updating subscriptions.

2. Verify that the publication supports pull subscriptions.

3. Add the pull subscription on the Subscriber server.

4. Add a scheduled agent job to synchronize the pull subscription on the Subscriber server.

5. Configure the security information used by the synchronization triggers.

6. Add the subscription on the Publisher server.

Verifying that the Publication Supports Immediate Updating Subscriptions

For this example, I will be setting up the pull subscription for the pub_updsub_mysales_copy publication. So the first task is to see whether the publication has been enabled to support immediate updating subscriptions. You do this by executing the sp_helppublication stored procedure and checking that the allow_sync_tran option is set to 1 (we already know that it was set to true in the script in Listing 9-8).

Listing 9-9 shows how the stored procedure is executed.

Listing 9-9. *Verifying Whether the Publication Supports Immediate Updating Subscriptions*

```
/* Execute this on the publication database */

Use mysales_new
Go

sp_helppublication
```

The output of this script is shown next. For brevity, I will only show only those columns that are relevant.

Pubid	name	allow_push	allow_pull	allow_sync_tran
1	pub_mysales_copy_myinventory	1	1	0
4	pub_updatesub_mysalescopy	1	1	1
3	pub_updsub_mysales_copy	1	1	1

> **Note** For queued updates the `allow_queued_tran` column should be set to 1 to ensure that the publication supports queued updating subscriptions.

You can see that there are two publications, including pub_updsub_mysales_copy, which have been set up for immediate subscriptions. If the `allow_sync_tran` value is 0, you will have to enable the publication for immediate updating subscriptions—that process was shown in Listing 9-6.

Verifying that the Publication Supports Pull Subscriptions

The next step in the process is to check whether the publication supports pull subscriptions. We have already verified that the publication supports both push and pull subscriptions with the `sp_helppublication` stored procedure in Listing 9-9. The output shows their corresponding columns are set to 1.

Adding the Pull Subscription on the Subscriber

Now that we know the publication is enabled for immediate updating and that it also supports both pull and push subscriptions, the next step is to add the pull subscription on the Subscriber server.

As you know from Chapter 5, you create a pull subscription using the `sp_addpullsubscription` stored procedure. Listing 9-10 shows how this is done.

Listing 9-10. *Creating the Pull Subscription*

```
/* Execute this on the subscription database on the Subscriber that is going to be
used for pull subscription */

use mysalescopy_upd_remotepull
go

exec sp_addpullsubscription
@publisher='BIO-V7V30JTZLZS\BIOREPL_PEER',
@publication =  'pub_updsub_mysales_copy',
@publisher_db =  'mysales_copy', @independent_agent = 'True',

@subscription_type =  'pull',
@update_mode =  'failover',
@immediate_sync = 1
go
```

This code adds the pull subscription on the subscription database on the Subscriber server. In order to enable the subscription for immediate updates, we have to set the @update_mode parameter to synctran, but I have set it to failover mode. This means that it can not only be used for immediate updating subscriptions but also for queued updating subscriptions. When using this option, you also need to ensure that the publication is enabled for queued updating. The @immediate_sync parameter is set to 1; this should be the same as was specified when creating the publication using sp_addpublication on the Publisher server.

Adding the Pull Subscription Agent

Next, we need to schedule the agent to synchronize the pull subscription. You do this by executing the sp_addpullsubscription_agent on the subscription database on the Subscriber server, as shown in Listing 9-11.

Listing 9-11. *Adding the Scheduled Agent to Synchronize the Pull Subscription*

```
/* Execute this on the subscription database on the Subscriber server */

Use mysales_copy
Go

exec sp_addpullsubscription_agent
@publisher =  'BIO-V7V30JTZLZS\BIOREPL_PEER',
@publisher_db =  'mysales_copy', @publication =  'pub_updsub_mysales_copy',

@distributor =  'BIO-V7V30JTZLZS\BIOREPL_PEER',
@distributor_security_mode = 1, @distributor_login =  '',
@distributor_password = null,
```

```
@enabled_for_syncmgr = 'False',
@frequency_type = 64,
@frequency_interval = 0,

@frequency_relative_interval = 0,
@frequency_recurrence_factor = 0,
@frequency_subday = 0,

@frequency_subday_interval = 0,
@active_start_time_of_day = 0,
@active_end_time_of_day = 235959,

@active_start_date = 20060108,
@active_end_date = 99991231,
@alt_snapshot_folder = '', @working_directory = '',

@job_login = null, @job_password = null,
@publication_type = 0
GO
```

The script specifies the name of the publication, publication database, and Publisher server from which the subscriptions will be pulling the data. It also sets the security mode used to connect to the Distributor server when synchronizing—it is using Windows Authentication to connect to the Distributor server.

The @enabled_for_syncmgr parameter has been set to False, which means that the Windows Synchronization Manager will not be used to pull the subscriptions. The @frequency_type parameter is used to schedule the Distribution Agent job for this subscription. The value of 64 means that the Distribution Agent is running continuously.

The @publication_type parameter has been set to 0, which indicates that the type of replication for the publication is transactional. A value of 0 would mean snapshot replication, while a value of 2 would mean merge replication.

Configuring Security for the Synchronization Triggers

The sp_link_publication stored procedure sets the configuration and security of the Subscriber server's synchronization triggers when connecting to the Publisher server. This stored procedure enables the triggers on the Subscriber servers to allow updates to the Publisher server.

Note I already have an existing linked server, so I have used sp_link_publication. If you do not have a linked server, you will have to create one. Use sp_addlinkedserver 'name of the server', 'SQLServer' to create a SQL Server linked server.

The stored procedure is executed on the subscription database on the Subscriber server, as shown in Listing 9-12.

Listing 9-12. *Configuring the Subscriber Server Triggers for Immediate Updating Subscriptions*

```
/* Execute this on the subscription database on the Subscriber server */

use mysalescopy_upd_remotepull
go

exec sp_link_publication @publisher =
'BIO-V7V3OJTZLZS\BIOREPL_PEER',
@publication = 'pub_updsub_mysales_copy',
@publisher_db = 'mysales_copy',
@security_mode = 0,
@login = 'sa',
@password = null
go
```

This script specifies the name of the Publisher server, the publication, and the publication database to which the update subscriptions will be sent. The @security_mode parameter has been set to 0 so that it can use SQL Server Authentication when making updates on the publication server. When using SQL Server Authentication, you need to have a valid login and password.

Adding the Subscription on the Publisher Server

This is the final step of the process. As in snapshot replication for pull subscriptions, you need to enable the subscription on the Publisher server. Do so by executing the sp_addsubscription stored procedure on the Publisher server, as shown in Listing 9-13.

Listing 9-13. *Adding the Subscription on the Publisher Server*

```
/* Execute this on the publication database on the Publisher server */

use [mysales_copy]
go

exec sp_addsubscription @publication = 'pub_updsub_mysales_copy',
@subscriber = 'BIO-V7V3OJTZLZS\BIOREPL_PEER',
@destination_db = 'mysalescopy_upd_remotepull',

@sync_type = 'Automatic',
@subscription_type = 'pull',
@update_mode = 'failover'
GO
```

This script adds the name of the publication and the name of the Subscriber server. The @destination_db parameter specifies the name of the subscription database. You can see that the subscription type is pull, which is what you need to specify here. You also need to specify the @update_mode parameter—the value here should match with what you specified in Listing 9-10.

Now that you know how to configure pull subscriptions for immediate updating, I will show you how to configure push subscriptions for publication with immediate updating.

Configuring a Push Subscription for Immediate Updating

The steps that you need to take for push subscriptions for immediate updating are similar to those for pull subscriptions, except for the execution of some stored procedures:

1. Verify that the publication supports immediate updating subscriptions.

2. Verify that the publication supports push subscriptions.

3. Add the push subscription on the Publisher server.

4. Add the push subscription agent on the Publisher server.

5. Configure the security information used by the synchronization triggers.

We have already verified that the publication supports immediate updating subscriptions and push subscriptions in Listing 9-9. Listing 9-14 shows the remaining steps.

Listing 9-14. *Adding the Push Subscription and Agent, and Configuring the Triggers' Security Settings*

```
/* Execute this code on the publication database on the Publisher */

use mysales_copy
go

/* Add the push subscription on the Publisher */

exec sp_addsubscription @publication = 'pub_updsub_mysales_copy',
@subscriber =      'BIO-V7V3OJTZLZS\BIOREPL_PEER',
@destination_db =      'mysalescopy_upd_remotepush',

@subscription_type = 'Push',
@sync_type =     'automatic',
@article =     'all',

@update_mode = 'failover',
@subscriber_type = 0
go


/* Add the push subscription agent on the Publisher server */
```

```
exec sp_addpushsubscription_agent
@publication =    'pub_updsub_mysales_copy',
@subscriber =    'BIO-V7V3OJTZLZS\BIOREPL_PEER',
@subscriber_db =    'mysalescopy_upd_remotepush',

@job_login = null, @job_password = null,
@subscriber_security_mode = 1,
@frequency_type = 64,

@frequency_interval = 0,
@frequency_relative_interval = 0,
@frequency_recurrence_factor = 0,

@frequency_subday = 0,
@frequency_subday_interval = 0,
@active_start_time_of_day = 0,
@active_end_time_of_day = 235959,

@active_start_date = 20060108,
@active_end_date = 99991231,
@enabled_for_syncmgr = 'False'
go

/* Configure the security information using sp_link_publication on the
Subscriber server*/

use mysalescopy_upd_remotepush
go

exec sp_link_publication
@publisher =    'BIO-V7V3OJTZLZS\BIOREPL_PEER',
@publisher_db =    'mysales_copy',
@publication =    'pub_updsub_mysales_copy',

@distributor =    'BIO-V7V3OJTZLZS\BIOREPL_PEER',

@security_mode = 0,
@login =    'spaul',
@password = null
go
```

Except for the sp_link_publication stored procedure, all the other steps are executed on the Publisher server.

In this section I discussed the configuration of transactional publications with updatable subscriptions. In the next section, I will show you how to configure queued updating subscriptions.

Configuring a Push Subscription for Queued Updating

We have already configured the publication for queued updates while setting it up for updatable subscriptions (see the "Configuring Transactional Publication with Updatable Subscriptions" section of the chapter). The steps that you now need to take to create a queued updating push subscription are as follows:

1. Verify that the publication supports queued updating subscriptions.

2. Verify that the publication supports push subscriptions.

3. Add the push subscription on the Publisher server.

4. Add the push subscription agent on the Publisher server.

The publication is verified by executing the sp_helppublication stored procedure. Ensure that the value of the allow_queued_tran column is 1 and that the allow_push column is also set to 1.

Steps 3 and 4—configuring the push subscription for queued updating—are performed by the script in Listing 9-15.

Listing 9-15. *Configuration of the Push Subscription for Queued Updating*

```
/* Add the push subscription on the Publisher server */

use mysales_copy
go

exec sp_addsubscription @publication =    'pub_updsub_mysales_copy',
@subscriber =    'BIO-V7V3OJTZLZS\BIOREPL_PEER',
@destination_db =    'mysalescopy_qud_remotepush',

@subscription_type =    'Push',
@sync_type =    'automatic',
@article = 'all',

@update_mode = 'queued failover',
@subscriber_type = 0

/* Add the push subscription agent on the Publisher */

exec sp_addpushsubscription_agent @publication =
'pub_updsub_mysales_copy',
@subscriber =    'BIO-V7V3OJTZLZS\BIOREPL_PEER',
@subscriber_db =    'mysalescopy_qud_remotepush',

@job_login = null, @job_password = null,
@subscriber_security_mode = 1,
@frequency_type = 64,
```

```
@frequency_interval = 0,
@frequency_relative_interval = 0,
@frequency_recurrence_factor = 0,

@frequency_subday = 0, @frequency_subday_interval = 0,
@active_start_time_of_day = 0,
@active_end_time_of_day = 235959,

@active_start_date = 20060108,
@active_end_date = 99991231
@enabled_for_syncmgr =    'False'
go

/* Add the sp_link_publication since the subscription has the
@update_mode parameter
Set to 'queued failover' */

/* Execute this on the subscription database on the Subscriber server */

use mysalescopy_qud_remotepush
go

exec sp_link_publication @publisher =
'BIO-V7V30JTZLZS\BIOREPL_PEER',
@publisher_db = 'mysales_copy',
@publication ='pub_updsub_mysales_copy',

@distributor = 'BIO-V7V30JTZLZS\BIOREPL_PEER',
@security_mode = 0, @login =     'sa',
@password = null
go
```

The @update_mode parameter in the preceding script has been set to queued failover in the sp_addsubscription stored procedure. This enables support for queued updating, with immediate updating as a failover option. Because I have set the parameter to this value, I have to execute the sp_link_publication stored procedure to configure the security settings of the triggers.

Now that you know how to set up the push subscription for queued updating, it's time to learn how to configure pull subscriptions.

Configuring a Pull Subscription for Queued Updating

The steps in configuring the pull subscription for queued updating are as follows:

1. Verify that the publication supports queued updating subscriptions.

2. Verify that the publication supports pull subscriptions.

3. Add the pull subscription on the Subscriber server.

4. Add the pull subscription agent on the Subscriber server.

5. Add the subscription on the Publisher server.

As discussed in the previous section, you first need to verify that the publication supports both queued updating subscriptions and pull subscriptions using the sp_helppublication stored procedure. Once you know the publication supports those two features, you are ready to set up the remainder of the process. Listing 9-16 shows how to configure the pull subscription for queued updating.

Listing 9-16. *Configuring a Pull Subscription for Queued Updating*

```
/* 1. Execute this on the subscription database on the Subscriber server */

use mysalescopy_qud_remotepull
go

exec sp_addpullsubscription @publisher =
'BIO-V7V30JTZLZS\BIOREPL_PEER',
 @publication ='pub_updsub_mysales_copy',
@publisher_db = 'mysales_copy',

@independent_agent ='True',
@subscription_type ='pull',
@update_mode = 'queued failover',

@immediate_sync = 1

/* 2. Configure the security settings since the subscription has @update_mode
parameter set to 'queued failover' */
/* Execute this on the Subscriber server */

exec sp_link_publication @publisher = 'BIO-V7V30JTZLZS\BIOREPL_PEER',
@publication = 'pub_updsub_mysales_copy',
@publisher_db ='mysales_copy',

@security_mode = 0,
@login ='sa',
@password = null

exec sp_addpullsubscription_agent @publisher =
'BIO-V7V30JTZLZS\BIOREPL_PEER',
@publisher_db = 'mysales_copy',
@publication = 'pub_updsub_mysales_copy',

@distributor = 'BIO-V7V30JTZLZS\BIOREPL_PEER',
@distributor_security_mode = 1,
@distributor_login = '',
```

```
@distributor_password = null,
@enabled_for_syncmgr = 'False',
@frequency_type = 64,

@frequency_interval = 0,
@frequency_relative_interval = 0,
@frequency_recurrence_factor = 0,

@frequency_subday = 0,
@frequency_subday_interval = 0,
@active_start_time_of_day = 0,

@active_end_time_of_day = 235959,
@active_start_date = 20060108,
@active_end_date = 99991231,

@alt_snapshot_folder = '',
@working_directory =     '',
@job_login = null,

@job_password = null,
@publication_type = 0
Go


/* Add the subscription on the Publisher server */

use mysales_copy
go

exec sp_addsubscription @publication =
'pub_updsub_mysales_copy',
@subscriber =     'BIO-V7V30JTZLZS\BIOREPL_PEER',
@destination_db =     'mysalescopy_qud_remotepull',

@sync_type = 'Automatic',
@subscription_type = 'pull',
@update_mode = 'queued failover'
GO
```

As for pull subscriptions, the @update_mode parameter has been set to queued failover in the sp_addsubscription stored procedure. This means we have to execute the sp_link_publication stored procedure to configure the security settings of the triggers. I have already explained what the remaining portion of pull subscription does and how it works (see the "Configuring a Pull Subscription with Immediate Updating" section earlier in this chapter).

Switching Between Immediate and Queued Updating Subscriptions

In Chapter 8, I showed you how to switch between the immediate and queued updating modes using the SSMS. In this section, I will show you how to programmatically change between the two modes, provided you have used the failover option.

In all the listings for immediate and queued updating, I have used the failover option so that I can switch between the modes. If there are any changes in the downtime of the server, I can quickly change to the other mode. This flexibility comes with a caveat, particularly when you want to switch from queued updating to immediate updating: both the Subscriber and the Publisher servers have to stay connected, and any pending messages in the queue have to be sent to the Publisher server by the Queue Reader Agent.

To switch between the two modes, follow these two steps:

1. Verify that the subscription supports failover option by using sp_helpsubscription for push subscriptions or sp_helppullsubscription for pull subscriptions (see Listing 9-17). You need to check that the update_mode column has been set either to 4 (queued updating) or 3 (immediate updating).

2. Execute sp_setreplfailovermode on the subscription database (see Listing 9-18). For the @failover_mode parameter, specify immediate if the connection is restored, or queued if there is a temporary loss in connection.

Note You need to have the sysadmin fixed server role permission or to be a member of the db_owner fixed database role in order to execute the stored procedures mentioned in the preceding steps.

Listing 9-17 shows the execution of Step 1 for push subscription.

Listing 9-17. *Verifying the Subscription Supports the Failover Option*

```
/* Execute this on the publication database for the push subscription */
Use mysales_copy
Go


sp_helpsubscription 'pub_updsub_mysales_copy'
go
```

Note For pull subscriptions, use the sp_helppullsubscription stored procedure on the subscription database on the Subscriber server instead.

The output of this script, run through SSMS, is shown in Figure 9-2.

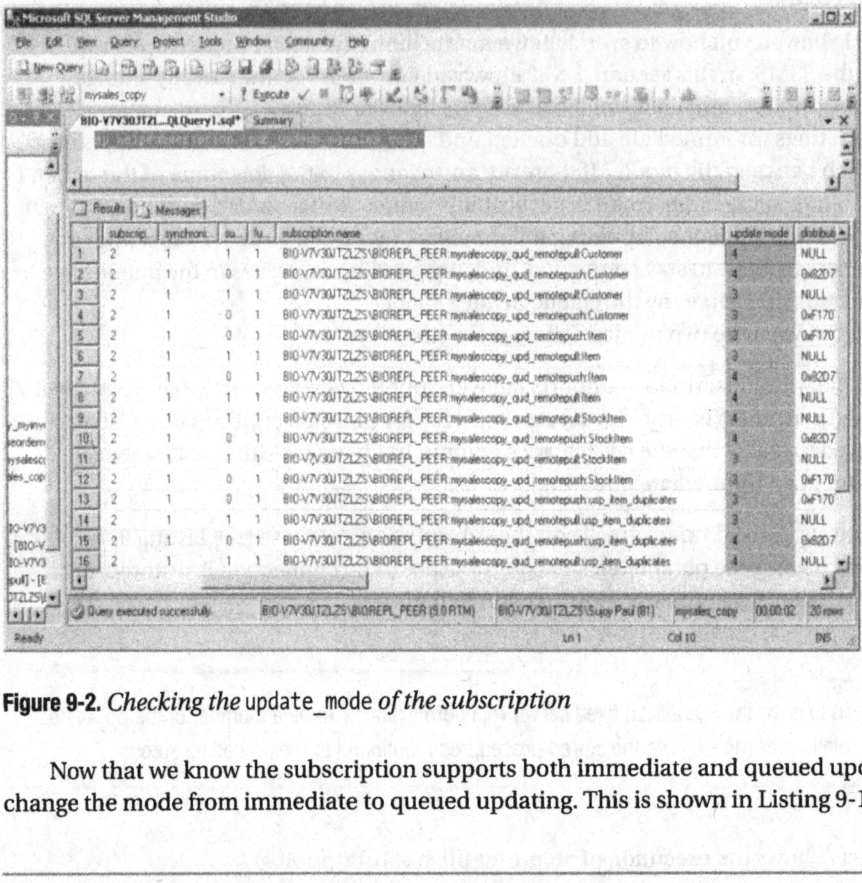

Figure 9-2. *Checking the* update_mode *of the subscription*

Now that we know the subscription supports both immediate and queued updating, let's change the mode from immediate to queued updating. This is shown in Listing 9-18.

■**Caution** Ensure that the subscription is set up for failover mode.

Listing 9-18. *Changing the Mode of the Updatable Subscription*

```
/* Execute this on the subscription database on the Subscriber server */

sp_setreplfailovermode 'BIOREPL_PEER','mysales_copy',
'pub_updsub_mysales_copy','queued'
```

■**Note** You need to have the Distribution Agent running while the script in Listing 9-18 is executed.

I have now shown you how to set up standard publication and immediate updating. In the next section, I will explain how to set up peer-to-peer transactional replication, introduced in SQL Server 2005.

Configuring Peer-to-Peer Transactional Replication

In Chapter 8, I showed you how to configure peer-to-peer replication, and one possible instance when you might want to use it. However, there are other considerations that you must take into account when you set up the peer-to-peer replication system, including its impact on performance.

In this section, I will show you how to set it up using T-SQL and then quiesce the replication topology. There are several steps that you need to take to set it up.

1. On node A, add the publication using sp_addpublication.

2. Add the articles to the publication using sp_addarticle.

3. Add the subscription on node A using sp_addsubscription.

4. Add the push subscription agent on node A using sp_addpushsubscription_agent.

5. On node B, add the publication using sp_addpublication.

6. Add the articles to the publication on node B using sp_addarticle.

7. Add the subscription on node B using sp_addsubscription.

8. Add the push subscription agent on node B using sp_addpushsubscription_agent.

So what I will do is to mention them and then write the code for each step. I will highlight the parameters that you need to use for each of the stored procedures.

Adding the Publication on Node A

The first step is adding the publication using the sp_addpublication stored procedure. Listing 9-19 adds the publication to the BIOREPL server:

Listing 9-19. *Adding the Publication on Node A, BIOREPL Server*

```
/*Execute this on the BIOREPL server */

use purchaseorder_repl
go

select DATABASEPROPERTYEX ('purchaseorder_repl', 'IsSyncWithBackup')
go
/* If the preceding select statement returns 0, execute
 sp_replicationdboption. If it returns a value of 1,
the database is enabled for publication.*/

sp_replicationdboption @dbname='purchaseorder_repl',
@optname='publish',
@value='true'
go
```

```
sp_addpublication @publication='pub_purchaseorder_repl',
@restricted='false',
@sync_method='native',

@repl_freq='continuous',
@allow_push='true',

@allow_pull='true',

@immediate_sync='true',
@allow_sync_tran='false',

@autogen_sync_procs='false',
@retention=60,
@independent_agent='true',

@enabled_for_p2p='true',
@status='active',
@allow_initialize_from_backup='true'
go
```

In this example, the @enabled_for_p2p and @allow_initialize_from_backup parameters must be set to true; @enabled_for_p2p is false by default. When it is set to true, you cannot use immediate and queued updating subscriptions when configuring peer-to-peer replication. Also, the @independent_agent parameter must be set to true and the @status parameter should be set to active.

Adding the Articles to the Publication on Node A

Listing 9-20 shows how to add the articles to the publication.

Listing 9-20. *Adding the Articles to the Publication on Node A*

```
/*Execute this on the publication database */
use purchaseorder_repl
go

sp_addarticle @publication='pub_purchaseorder_repl',
@article='vendor',
@source_owner='dbo',

@source_object='vendor',
@destination_table='[BIO-V7V30JTZLZS\BIOREPL_PEER].[purchaseorder_peer].[vendor]',

@type='logbased',
@creation_script='null',
@schema_option='null',
```

```
@status=16,
@ins_cmd='CALL sp_ins_vendor',
@del_cmd='XCALL sp_del_vendor',

@upd_cmd='XCALL sp_upd_vendor',
@sync_object='null'
Go
```

In this case, the @source_object parameter contains the name of the table that needs to match the table on node B, the second server. The @destination_table parameter specifies the name of the table on node B, which is the BIOPEER server in my case.

Adding the Subscription on Node A

Listing 9-21 shows how to add the subscription on node A.

Listing 9-21. *Adding the Subscription on Node A*

```
/* Execute this on the subscription database on node A, BIOREPL server */

exec sp_addsubscription @publication='pub_purchaseorder_repl',
@subscriber ='BIO-V7V30JTZLZS\BIOREPL_PEER',
@destination_db ='purchaseorder_peer',

@subscription_type = 'Push',
@sync_type = 'replication support only',
@article = 'all',

@subscriber_type = 0
Go
```

The name of the publication should be the one that was specified in the first step (Listing 9-19). The Subscriber server is node B, which is BIOREPL_PEER in this example. The @sync_type parameter is set to replication support only.

Adding the Push Subscription Agent on Node A

Listing 9-22 shows how to add the push subscription agent.

Listing 9-22. *Adding the Push Subscription Agent on Node A*

```
/* Execute this on node A, BIOREPL server, on the publication database */

exec sp_addpushsubscription_agent
@publication='pub_purchaseorder_repl',
 @subscriber =  'BIO-V7V30JTZLZS\BIOREPL_PEER',
@subscriber_db =  'purchaseorder_peer',
```

```
@job_login = null,
@job_password = null,
@subscriber_security_mode = 1,

@frequency_type = 64,
@frequency_interval = 0,
@frequency_relative_interval = 0,

@frequency_recurrence_factor = 0,
@frequency_subday = 0,
@frequency_subday_interval = 0,

@active_start_time_of_day = 0,
@active_end_time_of_day = 235959,
@active_start_date = 20060111,

@active_end_date = 99991231,
@enabled_for_syncmgr = 'False',
@dts_package_location = 'Distributor'
```

The sp_addpushsubscription_agent stored procedure adds a scheduled agent job on the publication database on node A for synchronizing a push subscription. The name of the Subscriber server is that of node B, BIOREPL_PEER, and it is specified by the @subscriber parameter. The name of the subscription database is specified by the @subscriber_db parameter. The other parameters are similar to the specifications mentioned while discussing sp_addpullsusbscription_agent (Listing 9-16).

Adding the Publication on Node B

Listing 9-23 shows how to add the publication on node B.

Listing 9-23. *Adding the Publication on Node B*

```
/*Execute this on node B, BIOREPL_PEER server */
/*Execute on the publication database */

use purchaseorder_peer
go
/* If the preceding select statement returns 0, execute
 sp_replicationdboption. If it returns a value of 1,
the database is enabled for publication. Go straight to
addition of the publication*/

sp_replicationdboption @dbname='purchaseorder_peer',
@optname='publish',
@value='true'
go
```

```
/*Addition of the publication*/
sp_addpublication @publication='pub_purchaseorder_peer',
@restricted='false',
@sync_method='native',
@repl_freq='continuous',

@status='active',
@allow_push='true',
@allow_pull='true',

@immediate_sync='false',
@allow_sync_tran='false',
@autogen_sync_procs='false',

@retention=60,
@independent_agent='true',
@enabled_for_p2p='true',

@status='active',
@allow_initialize_from_backup='true'
go
```

The publication is added on node B using sp_addpublication on the publication database, purchaseorder_peer. Before the publication is added, however, you need to check whether the publication is enabled for replication, as shown in Listing 9-19. Once the publication is enabled, the publication is added. The rest of the parameters are the same as in Listing 9-19.

Adding the Articles to the Publication on Node B

Listing 9-24 shows how to add the articles to the publication on node B.

Listing 9-24. *Adding the Articles to the Publication on Node B, BIOREPL_PEER*

```
/* Add this article to the publication */
/*Execute this on the publication database */
use purchaseorder_peer
go

exec sp_addarticle @publication='pub_purchaseorder_peer',
@article='vendor',
@source_owner='dbo',

@source_object='vendor',
@destination_table='[BIO-V7V3OJTZLZS\REPL].[purchaseorder_peer].[vendor]',
@type='logbased',
```

```
@creation_script='null',
@schema_option='null',
@status=16,

@ins_cmd='CALL sp_ins_vendor',
@del_cmd='XCALL sp_del_vendor',
@upd_cmd='XCALL sp_upd_vendor',

@sync_object=null
Go
```

Articles are added using the sp_addarticle stored procedure on the publication database in node B, just like they were for node A.

Adding the Subscription on Node B

Listing 9-25 shows how to add the subscription on node B.

Listing 9-25. *Adding the Subscription on Node B, BIOREPL_PEER*

```
/* Execute this on the subscription database on the BIOREPL_PEER server */

exec sp_addsubscription @publication='pub_purchaseorder_peer',
@subscriber ='BIO-V7V30JTZLZS\BIOREPL',
@destination_db ='purchaseorder_peer',

@subscription_type = 'Push',
@sync_type = 'replication support only',
@article = 'all',

@subscriber_type = 0
Go
```

Again, the subscription is added using sp_addsubscription on node B, BIPOREPL_PEER. This is similar to the addition of the subscription on node A, BIOREPL.

Adding the Push Subscription Agent on Node B

Listing 9-26 shows how to add the push subscription agent on node B.

Listing 9-26. *Add the Push Subscription Agent on Node B, BIOREPL_PEER*

```
/*Execute this on the publication database on node B*/
exec sp_addpushsubscription_agent
@publication='pub_purchaseorder_repl',
@subscriber =  'BIO-V7V30JTZLZS\BIOREPL',
@subscriber_db =  'purchaseorder_peer',
```

```
@job_login = null,
@job_password = null,
@subscriber_security_mode = 1,

@frequency_type = 64,
@frequency_interval = 0,
@frequency_relative_interval = 0,

@frequency_recurrence_factor = 0,
@frequency_subday = 0,
@frequency_subday_interval = 0,

 @active_start_time_of_day = 0,
@active_end_time_of_day = 235959,
@active_start_date = 20060111, @active_end_date = 99991231,

@enabled_for_syncmgr =  'False',
@dts_package_location = 'Distributor'
```

Checking the Configuration for Peer-to-Peer Replication

You should ensure that the Log Reader Agent is running on both the nodes by executing the sp_helplogreader_agent stored procedure as follows:

```
sp_helplogreader_agent @publisher
```

You need to specify the name of the Publisher server for the @publisher parameter.

If there are no Log Reader Agents configured, you need to add a Log Reader Agent by executing the sp_addlogreader_agent stored procedure on the publication database. This is shown in Listing 9-27.

Listing 9-27. *Adding the Log Reader Agent on Both the Nodes*

```
/* Execute this on the BIOREPL(A) node */

sp_addlogreader_agent @joblogin='spaul',
@jobpassword='****',
@publisher_security_mode=1,

@publisher_login='spaul'
@publisher_password='password',
go

/* Execute this on the BIOREPL_PEER(B) node */

sp_addlogreader_agent @joblogin='spaul',
@jobpassword='****',
@publisher_security_mode=1,
```

```
@publisher_login='spaul'
@publisher_password='password',
Go
```

Now that we have set up the topology, we need to check whether the other node has received all the changes. You do this by first inserting data on one of the nodes, and then ensuring that the data has indeed been received on the other node. Listing 9-28 shows how you can do it.

Listing 9-28. *Ensuring That All the Peer-to-Peer Nodes Have Received the Data*

```
/*1. Execute this on the purchaseorder_repl publication database on
the BIOREPL server */
/* insert the row first on the publication database */

insert into vendor values
(2,'Fern's Gardens','24 Wayne Blvd.','Toronto','M5H 2KL',
'1-800-123-4567')
go


/* 2. Execute this on the BIOREPL_PEER server node*/
/* Execute this on the publication database on this node */

/* Declare the table variable*/
declare @peertopeertable_received table
(id int,
publication sysname,
sent_date datetime,
description varchar(255));

/*Read the data from the MSpeer_request table */

insert into @peertopeertable_received
(id, publication, sent_date, description)select id,publication,sent_date,
description from MSpeer_request

/* Retrieve the data */

select * from @peertopeertable_received
go
```

In this case, we want to get the ID, the name of the publication, and the date the message was sent from the MSpeer_request table, and to store that information in the @peertopeertable_received table variable. The output of the listing is shown here:

Id	publication	sent_date		description
1	pub_purchaseorderrepl_peer	2006-01-11	22:49:31.767	NULL
2	pub_purchaseorderrepl_peer	2006-01-11	22:50:22.700	NULL
3	pub_purchaseorderrepl_peer	2006-01-11	22:51:30.920	NULL
4	pub_purchaseorderrepl_peer	2006-01-13	19:39:19.220	NULL

Now that we know the ID of the publication, we can use it to find the peer response by executing the sp_helppeerresponses stored procedure. This ID is equivalent to the request_id parameter in the sp_helppeerresponses stored procedure. Listing 9-29 shows the execution of the stored procedure.

Listing 9-29. *Ensuring BIOREPL_PEER Receives the Responses in the Result Set*

```
/* Execute this on the publication database on the node that is being checked */

Sp_helppeerresponses '4'
Go
```

Here is the output:

Request_id	peer	publication	received_date
4	BIO-V7V30JTZLZS\BIOREPL	purchaseorder_repl	2006-01-13 19:39:37.940

■**Tip** In order to quiesce peer-to-peer replication, you need to stop any kind of activity on the publication and then execute the code in Listings 9-24 and 9-25. Alternatively, you can quiesce peer-to-peer replication by using sp_requestpeerresponse on the publication database (instead of executing Listing 9-24), and then executing the code in Listing 9-25.

Configuring Bidirectional Transactional Replication

Now that you know how to set up peer-to-peer replication, it is appropriate to point out that SQL Server 2005 also supports *bidirectional transactional replication*, a similar topology for exchanging transactions between two servers in which a server that publishes data to a second server also subscribes to the same published data from the second server. However, bidirectional transactional replication helps to improve performance because it supports "no sync" initialization, as you will see in this section.

In the previous sections on transactional replication, you saw that the Snapshot Agent is used for the initial synchronization. The overhead cost of generating a snapshot that contains the schema and the associated data, triggers, and index files has already been discussed in the context of snapshot replication. On top of that, the Distribution Agent needs to transfer these files to the Subscriber server. So, if there is a way to circumvent the generation of the snapshot and still configure replication, it will be a lot faster.

Bidirectional transactional replication offers this alternative. There are no change-tracking triggers or extra columns added to tables to monitor changes and yet it offers the added advantage of having two databases on two different servers in a consistent stage, since the latency in transactional replication is small. While the advantages of bidirectional transactional replication are clear, they can be offset by the complexity of configuring conflict resolutions. There is no GUI that you can use to configure bidirectional transactional replication, nor are there any rich features that you can use to set up conflict resolution policies. Essentially, you have to design the conflict resolution manually. In this section, I will show you how to configure bidirectional transactional replication for the nonpartitioned method on the same server using two different databases.

Before we set up bidirectional transactional replication, however, you should ensure that you have configured the Distributor and the Publisher servers on the same machine. Then you need to enable both databases for replication using the sp_replicationdboption stored procedure as shown in Listing 9-30. Set the @optname parameter to publish and the @value parameter to true.

Listing 9-30. *Adding the Publication in mysales*

```
/*Execute this on the master database */

use master
go


---Enable the databases for transactional publishing.

EXEC sp_replicationdboption @publication='mysales',
@optname='publish',
@value=true;
EXEC sp_replicationdboption @publication='mysales2',
@optname='publish',
@value= true;
GO
```

The next step in the configuration process is to add the publication and the articles for the mysales database, and the Log Reader Agent. This is shown in Listing 9-31.

Listing 9-31. *Adding the Publication, Articles, and Log Reader Agent for the mysales Database*

```
/*Execute this on the mysales database */

DECLARE @publication AS sysname;
DECLARE @article1 AS sysname;
DECLARE @article2 AS sysname;
DECLARE @login AS sysname;
DECLARE @password AS varchar(512);
SET @publication = 'bidirectional_mysalespub';
SET @article1 = 'Item1';
SET @article2 = 'Item2';
SET @login = 'sa';
SET @password = 'sujoy';

--- Add the publication -----
use mysales
go

EXEC sp_addpublication @publication = @publication,
@restricted = 'false',
@sync_method = 'native',
@repl_freq = 'continuous',
@description = 'publ1',
@status = 'active',
@allow_push = 'true',
@allow_pull = 'true',
@allow_anonymous = 'false',
@enabled_for_internet = 'false',
@independent_agent = 'false',
@immediate_sync = 'false',
@allow_sync_tran = 'false',
@autogen_sync_procs = 'false',
@retention = 60;


--- Add the articles ---

EXEC sp_addarticle @publication = @publication,
@article = @article1,
@source_owner = 'myinventory',
@source_object = @article1,
@destination_table = @article2,
@type = 'logbased',
@creation_script = null,
@description = null,
@pre_creation_cmd = 'drop',
@schema_option = 0x00000000000000F1,
```

```
@status = 16,
@vertical_partition = 'false',
@ins_cmd = 'CALL  sp_MSins_myinventoryItem ',
@del_cmd = 'XCALL sp_MSdel_myinventoryItem',
@upd_cmd = 'XCALL sp_MSupd_myinventoryItem',
@filter = null,
@sync_object = null;
GO


--- Add the Log Reader Agent

EXEC sp_addlogreader_agent
@job_login = @login,
@job_password = @password,
@publisher_security_mode = 1;
go
```

As you can see in the listing, you need to add the publication using the sp_addpublication stored procedure. Once you have done so, you can add the articles to the publication using the sp_addarticle stored procedure with the following parameters:

- @publication: The name of the publication, which should correspond to what was specified in the sp_addpublication stored procedure

- @article: The name of the article

- @source_object: The name of the published table

- @destination_table: The name of the corresponding table on the subscription database

- @ins_cmd: The name of the insert stored procedure

- @del_cmd: The name of the delete stored procedure

- @upd_cmd: The name of the update stored procedure

Note that in Listing 9-31 I used the XCALL syntax for the delete and update stored procedures—this keeps a record of the previous and the current values. You can use any of the formats for calling the stored procedures.

Finally the script adds the Log Reader Agent using the sp_addlogreader_agent stored procedure.

You now need to do the same on the second database, as shown in Listing 9-32.

Listing 9-32. *Adding the Publication, Articles, and Log Reader Agent for the mysales2 Database*

```
/*Execute this on the mysales2 database */

DECLARE @publication AS sysname;
DECLARE @article1 AS sysname;
DECLARE @article2 AS sysname;
DECLARE @login AS sysname;
```

```
DECLARE @password AS nvarchar(512);
SET @publication = 'bidirectional_mysalespub2';
SET @article1 = 'Item';
SET @article2 = 'Item2';
SET @login = 'sa';
SET @password = 'sujoy';


--- Add the publication -----

EXEC sp_addpublication @publication = @publication,
@restricted = 'false',
@sync_method = 'native',
@repl_freq = 'continuous',
@description = 'pub2',
@status = 'active',
@allow_push = 'true',
@allow_pull = 'true',
@allow_anonymous = 'false',
@enabled_for_internet = 'false',
@independent_agent = 'false',
@immediate_sync = 'false',
@allow_sync_tran = 'false',
@autogen_sync_procs = 'false',
@retention = 60;


--- Add the articles ---

EXEC sp_addarticle @publication = @publication,
@article = @article2,
@source_owner = 'myinventory',
@source_object = @article2,
@destination_table = @article1,
@type = 'logbased',
@creation_script = null,
@description = null,
@pre_creation_cmd = 'drop',
@schema_option = 0x00000000000000F1,
@status = 16,
@vertical_partition = N'false',
@ins_cmd = 'CALL  sp_MSins_myinventoryItem2 ',
@del_cmd = 'XCALL sp_MSdel_myinventoryItem2',
@upd_cmd = 'XCALL sp_MSupd_myinventoryItem2',
@filter = null,
@sync_object = null;
GO
```

```
--- Add the Log Reader Agent
EXEC sp_addlogreader_agent
@job_login = @login,
@job_password = @password,
@publisher_security_mode = 1;
go
```

Now that the publication, articles, and Log Reader Agent have been added on both databases, we need to add the corresponding subscriptions. We will do this using the SQLCMD utility, so that we can execute one script on both databases and just change the variables for the two databases. This is shown in Listing 9-33.

Listing 9-33. *Adding Subscriptions for Both Databases*

```
:setvar logintimeout 120
:setvar server "BIO-V7V30JTZLZS\BIOREPL"
:setvar user "sa"
:setvar pwd "sujoy"
:connect $(server) -l $(logintimeout) -U $(user) -P $(pwd)

--Add the transactional subscription in mysales and mysales2

USE $(db)    ----mysales and mysales2
GO

DECLARE @publication AS sysname;
DECLARE @subscriber AS sysname;
DECLARE @subscription_db AS sysname;

SET @publication = '$(pubname)';
SET @subscriber = @@SERVERNAME;
/* for mysales the subdbname should be mysales2 and vice versa */
SET @subscription_db = '$(subdbname)';

EXEC sp_addsubscription @publication = @publication,
@article = 'all',
@subscriber = @subscriber,
@destination_db = @subscription_db,
@sync_type = 'none',
@status = 'active',
@update_mode = '$(value)',  --set to read-only by default
@loopback_detection = '$(boolean)'; --- must be true for bidirectional

EXEC sp_addpushsubscription_agent
@publication = @publication,
@subscriber = @subscriber,
```

```
@subscriber_db = @subscription_db,
@job_login = $(user),
@job_password = $(pwd);
GO
```

The setvar command is used to define the variables for the SQLCMD script; a $ sign must precede a variable name. In this case, I have defined the server, the username, and the password needed to connect to the BIO-V7V30JTZLZS\BIOREPL server. The logintimeout variable specifies the duration of the session after which the login is disconnected, and here it has been specified as 120 seconds. The connect command is a SQLCMD command that is used to connect to the server with the user and the password specified. The name of the executable for the SQLCMD utility is sqlcmd.exe, and it is located in the following directory: C:\Program Files\Microsoft SQL Server\90\Tools\Binn.

The subscription is added in the script by using the sp_addsubscription. It is here that the no-sync initialization is set, by setting the @sync_type parameter to none. The @update_mode parameter must be set to read-only, and the @loopback_detection parameter must be set to true for bidirectional transactional replication. This ensures that when data changes are sent to the Subscriber server, they are not sent back to the Publisher server.

Save the code in Listing 9-33 in a file with a .sql extension, and then open the command prompt and type the following (all on one line):

```
C:\>sqlcmd -i c:\files\bidirectionalsubscript.sql -v db=mysales,
pubname=pub1,subdbname=mysales2,value=read-only,boolean=true
```

The -i switch includes the file called bidirectionalsubscript.sql. The -v switch is used to set the values for the variables, which in this case are for the publication database, mysales. You need to run the same SQLCMD commands again, but with the variable values set for the publication database, mysales2.

Next, you need to create the insert, delete, and update stored procedures to handle any conflicts. The insert stored procedure is shown in Listing 9-34. Listings 9-34, 9-35, and 9-36 have been adjusted for the myinventory.Item table based on the configuration of bidirectional transactional replication in BOL.

Listing 9-34. *Creating Insert Stored Procedures on Both Publication Databases, mysales and mysales2*

```
-- Insert procedure, [sp_MSins_myinventoryItem] and [sp_MSins_myinventoryItem1]

create procedure [dbo].$[name]
@c1 int,@c2 varchar(30),@c3 int,@c4 varchar(20),@c5 varchar(10),@c6 char(4)
as

insert into "myinventory"."Item"(
 "ItemID"
,"Description"
,"Vendor"
,"Category"
,"Color"
,"Unit"
```

```
)
values (
 @c1
,@c2
,@c3
,@c4
,@c5
,@c6
 )
```

The delete stored procedure is shown in Listing 9-35. Again, you need to create it on both publication databases.

Listing 9-35. *Creating Delete Stored Procedures on Both Publication Databases, mysales and mysales2*

```
create procedure [dbo].[sp_MSdel_myinventoryItem]
@pkc1 int
as
delete "myinventory"."Item"
where "ItemID" = @pkc1
go
```

The update stored procedure also needs to be added on both publication databases, as shown in Listing 9-36.

Listing 9-36. *Creating Update Stored Procedures on Both Publication Databases, mysales and mysales2*

```
create procedure [dbo].[sp_MSupd_myinventoryItem]
 --Primary key is @c1
@old_c1 int int,@old_c2 varchar(30),old_@c3 int,@old_c4
 varchar(20),@old_c5 varchar(10),@old_c6 char(4),
@c1 int int,@c2 varchar(30),@c3 int,@c4 varchar(20),@c5 varchar(10),@c6 char(4)
as
DECLARE  @curr_c1 int, @curr_c3 int,@curr_c2 varchar(30),
@curr_c2 varchar(20),@curr_c5 varchar(10),@curr_c2 char(4);

select @curr_c3=Vendor,@curr_c2=Description,
 @curr_c4=Category,@curr_c5=Color,@curr_c6=Unit
from myinventory.Item where ItemID=@c1;

--Add values for conflicts on int columns; don't add for primary key columns
```

```
IF @curr_c3 != @old_c3
SELECT @c3 = @curr_c3 +
(@c3 - @old_c3);

-- Concatenate values for conflicts on varchar columns

IF @curr_c2 != @old_c2
SELECT @c2 = rtrim(@curr_c2) +
'_' + rtrim(@c2);
IF @curr_c4 != @old_c4
SELECT @c4 = rtrim(@curr_c4) +
'_' + rtrim(@c4);
IF @curr_c5 != @old_c5
SELECT @c5 = rtrim(@curr_c5) +
'_' + rtrim(@c5);
IF @curr_c6 != @old_c6
SELECT @c6 = rtrim(@curr_c6) +
'_' + rtrim(@c6);

--Update item table

UPDATE myinventory.Item SET Vendor = @c3,
Description = @c2,
Category =@c4,
Color =@c5,
Unit =@c6
WHERE ItemId = @old_c1;
go
```

Transactional Replication Stored Procedures

Before closing the chapter, I will summarize the stored procedures that you can use for trans-actional replication as a reference.

Table 9-3 lists the stored procedures used for dropping subscriptions.

Table 9-3. *Stored Procedures for Dropping Subscriptions*

Type of Subscription	Stored Procedure	Parameters	Server
Pull	sp_droppullsubscription	@publication, @publisher_db, @publisher	Subscriber
	sp_dropsubscription	@publication, @subscriber, @article	Publisher
Push	sp_dropsubscription	@publication, @subscriber, @article	Publisher
	sp_subscription_cleanup		Subscriber

Table 9-4 lists the parameters for standard publication for transactional replication.

Table 9-4. *Stored Procedures for Standard Publication*

Stored Procedure	Parameters
sp_replicationdboption	@dbname, @optname, @value
sp_helplogreader_agent	
sp_addlogreader_agent	@job_login, @job_password, @publisher_security_mode, @publisher_login, @publisher_password, @publisher
sp_addpublication	@synch_method, @repl_freq, @independent_agent, @immediate_sync, @replicate_ddl, @enabled_for_p2p
sp_addpublication_snapshot	@publication, @frequency_type, @publisher_security_mode, @publisher_login, @publisher_password
sp_addarticle	@ins_cmd, @del_cmd, @upd_cmd, @publication, @article
sp_startpublication_snapshot	@publication

Table 9-5 lists the stored procedures and parameters for publication with updatable subscriptions.

Table 9-5. *Stored Procedures for Configuring Publication with Updatable Subscriptions*

Stored Procedure	Parameters
sp_replicationdboption	@dbname, @optname, @value
sp_addpublication	@publication, @allow_push, @allow_pull, @repl_freq, @independent_agent = 'true', @immediate_sync = 'true', @allow_sync_tran = 'true', @autogen_sync_procs = 'true', @allow_queued_tran = 'true', @conflict_policy = 'pub wins', @centralized_conflicts = 'true', @conflict_retention = 14, @queue_type = 'sql'
sp_addpublication_snapshot	@publication, @frequency_type, @frequency_interval, @job_login, @job_password. For SQL Server Authentication, set @publisher_security_mode=0 and specify @publisher_login and @publisher_password.
sp_addarticle	@publication, @article, @type
sp_startpublication_snapshot	@publication

Table 9-6 shows the stored procedures and parameters used for pull subscriptions for publication with updatable subscriptions.

Table 9-6. *Stored Procedures for Configuring Pull Subscriptions for Publication with Updatable Subscriptions*

Stored Procedure	Parameters
sp_helppublication	@publication
sp_addpullsubscription	@publisher, @publication, @update_mode = 'failover', @immediate_sync = 1
sp_addpullsubscription_agent	@publisher, @publication, @publisher_db, @job_login, @job_password, @enabled_for_syncmgr, @publication_type
sp_link_publication	@publisher, @publication, @publisher_db, @security_mode, @login, @password
sp_addsubscription	@publication, @subscriber, @destination_type, @subscriber_type=pull, @destination_db, @update_mode

Table 9-7 shows the stored procedures and parameters used for push subscriptions for updatable publication.

Table 9-7. *Stored Procedures for Configuring Push Subscriptions for Publication with Updatable Subscription*

Stored Procedure	Parameters
sp_helppublication	@publication
sp_addsubscription	@publication, @subscriber, @subscriber_type, @subscriber_type=push, @update_mode
sp_addpushsubscription_agent	@subscriber_security_mode, @subscriber_db, @publication, @enabled_for_syncmgr
sp_link_publication	@publisher, @publication, @publisher_db, @security_mode, @login, @password

Table 9-8 shows the stored procedures used to switch between the two modes of updatable subscriptions.

Table 9-8. *Stored Procedures for Switching Between Immediate and Queued Updating*

Stored Procedure	Parameters
sp_helpsubscription	@publication
sp_helppullsubsription	@publication
sp_setreplfailovermode	@publisher, @publication_db, @publication, @failover_mode

Summary

In this chapter, you learned to drop both pull and push subscriptions for transactional replication. I then showed you how to configure the standard publication, the publication with immediate and queued updating, peer-to-peer replication, and nonpartitioned bidirectional transactional replication. I also demonstrated the use of the SQLCMD utility. I also showed you how to configure push and pull subscriptions for each of the publication types used in transactional replication.

You should now have a strong grasp on the configuration of transactional replication using both the GUI and the T-SQL methods.

- Drop a pull subscription using the sp_droppullsubscription stored procedure. Drop a push subscription using sp_dropsubscription.

- Enable the database to be set up for replication using the sp_replicationdboption stored procedure.

- Determine the existence of the Log Reader Agent using the sp_helplogreader_agent stored procedure.

- Create the publication using the sp_addpublication stored procedure.

- Create articles for the publication using the sp_addarticle stored procedure.

- Create an agent for the publication using the sp_addpublication_snapshot stored procedure.

- Start the snapshot using the sp_startpublication_snapshot stored procedure.

- Switch between the immediate updating and queued updating by first checking that the failover option is enabled.

- Use the sp_helpsubscription stored procedure to get a list of push subscriptions and the sp_helppullsubscription stored procedure to get a list of pull subscriptions. The sp_helpsubscription stored procedure is executed on the publication database on the Publisher server, and sp_helppullsubscription is executed on the subscription database on the Subscriber server.

- The MS DTC should be running when you are using updatable subscriptions, since the 2PC protocol is used for both immediate and the queued updating.

- In order to set up peer-to-peer replication, you need to add the Log Reader Agent using the sp_addlogreader_agent stored procedure, add the publication using sp_addpublication, add the article using sp_addarticle, add the subscription using sp_addsubscription, and add the subscription agent using sp_addpushsubscription_agent. You then need to do the same things on the other nodes.

- In order to set up bidirectional transactional replication, ensure that the @loopback_detection parameter for the sp_addsubscription stored procedure is set to true.

- Bidirectional transactional replication uses no-sync initialization.

- Bidirectional transactional replication provides better performance than peer-to-peer replication.

In the following chapter, you will learn about the internals of transactional replication. You will see how the concurrent snapshot processing works, what different system tables are used, and what changes occur under the hood for queued and immediate updating subscriptions.

Quick Tips

- You can ensure that the MS DTC is running by either seeing the green arrow in the SSMS under the Management object in the Object Explorer or by executing the net start command from the command prompt.

- When switching modes, use the queued updating option when the connection fails, and move back to immediate updating after the connection is restored.

- The repl_freq parameter will be set to continuous_c for non-SQL Server Publishers.

- For vertical filtering, first add the article. Then, execute the sp_articlecolumn stored procedure specifying the columns in the @column parameter and setting the @operation parameter to add. Finally, execute sp_articleview.

CHAPTER 10

■ ■ ■

Internals of Transactional Replication

In Chapters 8 and 9, I showed you how to configure transactional replication using both the GUI and T-SQL methods. Before you start reading this chapter, you should know how to set up the different components of transactional replication and the workings of snapshot replication.

As with snapshot replication, it is essential that you understand how the different components work in synch to make transactional replication function smoothly. In this chapter, I will first discuss how each of the job steps are executed by the different agents. Then I will show how each of the agents work behind the scenes in conjunction with transactional publication with updatable subscriptions, standard transactional publication, and peer-to-peer replication.

On completing this chapter, you will understand how the following processes work on the inside:

- Concurrent snapshot processing

- Information processing from the transactional log

- Transactional replication with queued updating subscription

- Transactional replication with immediate updating subscription

- Peer-to-peer transactional replication

- Standard transactional publication

Concurrent Snapshot Processing

You already know that generating a snapshot is the first step in setting up the different types of replication in SQL Server. Unfortunately, snapshot generation can be a time-consuming process, depending on the size of the tables and how much network bandwidth is available. Additionally, the Snapshot Agent places shared locks on all the publishing tables as snapshots are generated, as was mentioned in Chapter 6, and no changes or updates can be made while the locks are in place.

Note Snapshot generation is covered in Chapter 6.

In Listing 9-1 (in Chapter 9), the sp_addpublication stored procedure had the @sync_method parameter set to concurrent. This value tells the native bulk copy utility not to lock the tables during snapshot generation, but this feature is available only with transactional replication. So how different is the concurrent snapshot process from the processes used in other types of replication?

Note When you set up transactional publication using the GUI, concurrent snapshot processing is automatically used by default.

Concurrent snapshot processing allows users to make changes while a snapshot is being generated. The Snapshot Agent places a lock on the publication tables at the start of the synchronization process, and an entry is made in the publication database's transaction log. Until that time, the lock is held in place, but as soon as the entry is made in the log, the lock is released and you can start making data modifications again. Once the snapshot is completed, a second entry is made in the transaction log to mark the completion of the process. Any changes associated with the tables during the process are captured, and the Log Reader Agent forwards these transactions to the distribution database.

The Distribution Agent then forwards the snapshot to the Subscriber server, and the transactions that took place during snapshot generation are also forwarded to the appropriate Subscriber servers. The Distribution Agent places locks on the tables on the Subscriber servers to ensure that the correct subscribing servers are receiving the transactions before the agent releases the lock on the subscription database.

Concurrent snapshot processing involves a series of INSERT and DELETE statements for bulk copying the tables as one single transactional unit, which keeps the database in a consistent state. Consequently, any triggers or constraints that are designed to meet the business requirements of the Subscriber server will be melded into the single transaction and may lead to an inconsistent set of data during the generation process. As such, any columns that contain constraints with the IDENTITY property should be set to NOT FOR REPLICATION on the subscription database. It is not necessary to set the triggers and foreign key constraints on the subscription database to NOT FOR REPLICATION because they are disabled during concurrent snapshot processing. They are reenabled after the process.

Caution Do not make any changes on columns that are part of the clustering index during the concurrent snapshot process; otherwise it will fail.

The Transaction Log

A transaction log file is created every time a database is created. Data and log information are always kept in two separate files—the log files keep information about all the transactions that are logged in the database. Transaction log files are not only used during the recovery of the database, but also by the Log Reader Agent, which uses the log to send the messages to the distribution database during transactional replication.

Note Both the data and the transaction log file, by default, are located at `C:\Program Files\Microsoft SQL Server\MSSQL.1\MSSQL\Data`. The logical and the physical portions of the transaction log are discussed in Chapter 18.

The important question is whether we can read the transaction log file, and the answer is that it depends on what kind of information you are looking for. You can bulk copy the data using the bcp utility, but this does not provide any meaningful information concerning replication—all you can see is the data and not the internal processes.

However, there is an undocumented DBCC (Database Console Command) command that can show some information. Its use is shown in Listing 10-1.

Caution Use undocumented commands with caution. Back up the database and try it on a test machine first.

Listing 10-1. *Executing the DBCC Command*

```
/* Execute this on the database whose information you want. */

/* First turn the trace on using dbcc traceon.*/

DBCC traceon(3604)

/* Now declare the variable. */
declare @dbid int;

/* Select the db id and place the value in the variable. */
set @dbid=(select db_id('purchaseorder_repl'));

/* Then call the dbcc log command. */

dbcc log(@dbid,2)
/* Now turn the traceoff using dbcc traceoff.*/

DBCC traceoff(3604)
```

This script first turns the trace on to get a detailed output of the results. It then declares a variable that will store the database ID using the db_id() function, and then it passes the value of the variable to the DBCC log statement.

Tip When you turn the trace on, you can either set it at the server level or at the session level. If you set it at the server level, you are setting it globally, and the trace becomes visible to every connection on the server. If you set it for the session, it is visible only to the connection. To set the trace option globally, use DBCC traceon(number,-1).

The syntax for the DBCC log statement is as follows:

```
DBCC log ({dbid|dbname},[,type={0|1|2|3|4}])
```

In this statement, dbid or dbname is the ID of the database or the name of the database type, and the type can be one of the following:

- 0: Minimum information (the Current LSN, Operation, Context, and Transaction ID columns)

- 1: Information from type 0, plus the Tag Bits, Log Record Fixed Length, Log Record Length, Previous LSN, Flag Bits, and Description columns

- 2: Information from type 1, plus the AllocUnitId, AllocUnitName, PageID, Slot ID, Previous Page LSN, Number of Locks, and Lock Information columns

- 3: Full information on every operation

- 4: Full information on every operation, plus the Log Record column

Figure 10-1 shows the output of the DBCC command in Listing 10-1. As you can see, the total number of rows returned by the DBCC log command is 1150.

Now let's look at another command that allows us to better control the rows we receive. The syntax for this command is as follows:

```
::fn_dblog(@startlsn,@endlsn)
```

Here, @startlsn is the starting log sequence number (LSN) and @endlsn is the end LSN. If both parameters are set to NULL, it means that you want the information from the first LSN to the last LSN. In essence, you are retrieving all the information.

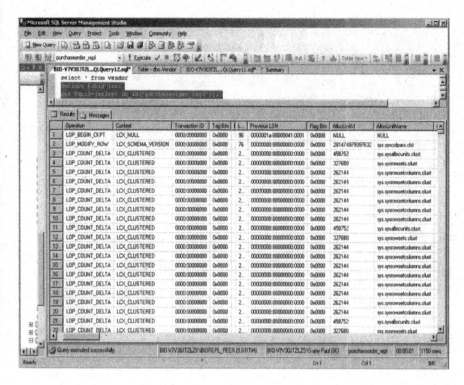

Figure 10-1. *The output of the* DBCC log *command for the purchaseorder_repl database*

Listing 10-2 shows how you can return all information.

Listing 10-2. *Returning All Information Using the* fn_dblog *Command*

```
/* Execute this on the publication database, purchaseorder_repl,
on the Publisher server, BIOREPL_PEER. */
/* You can use other databases as well, here I am using the purchaseorder_repl
database */

Use purchaseorder_repl
Go

select * from fn_dblog(null,null)
```

Figures 10-2 and 10-3 show the output from the script in Listing 10-2.

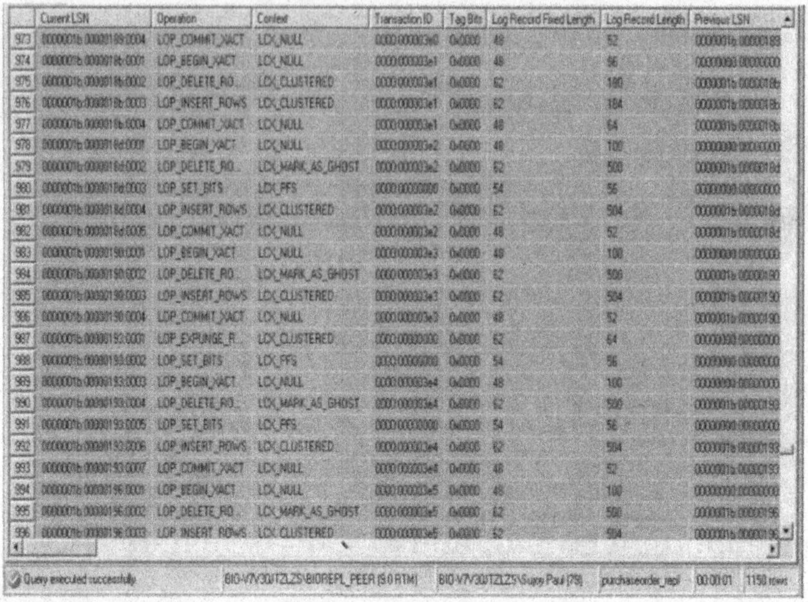

Figure 10-2. *The first part of the output of the* fn_dblog *command*

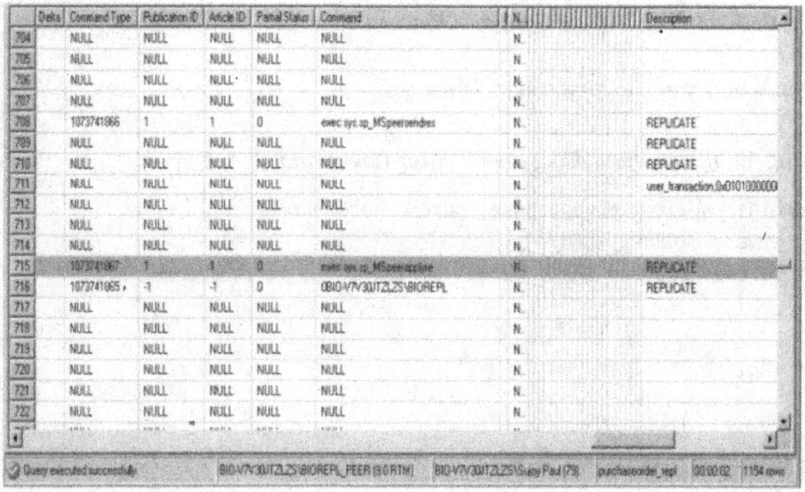

Figure 10-3. *The second part of the output of the* fn_dblog *command; the Command column shows you what commands were executed*

Take a look at row 974 in Figure 10-2. The Operation column states LOP_BEGIN_XACT, which means it is at the beginning of a transaction. On row 976, you can see that the operation carried out an insert (LOP_INSERT_ROWS).

Now let's take a look at Listing 10-3 to see how the commands are executed on the objects and the total number of rows inserted for each of the objects inserted.

Listing 10-3. *Retrieving All the Inserted Rows in the Publication Database, purchaseorder_repl*

```
/*Execute this on the publication database, purchaseorder_repl,
on the Publisher server, BIOREPL_PEER. */

select [AllocUnitId],
[AllocUnitName],
count([Current LSN])as TotalLSN,
command,description
from fn_dblog(null, null)
where Operation ='LOP_INSERT_ROWS'
group by  [AllocUnitId],[AllocUnitName],[command],[description]
go
```

In this case, the script retrieves the name of the object (AllocUnitName), the corresponding ID, the total number of rows (count([Current LSN])) affected by the insert operation (LOP_INSERT_ROWS), and the description. Figure 10-4 shows the output of this script.

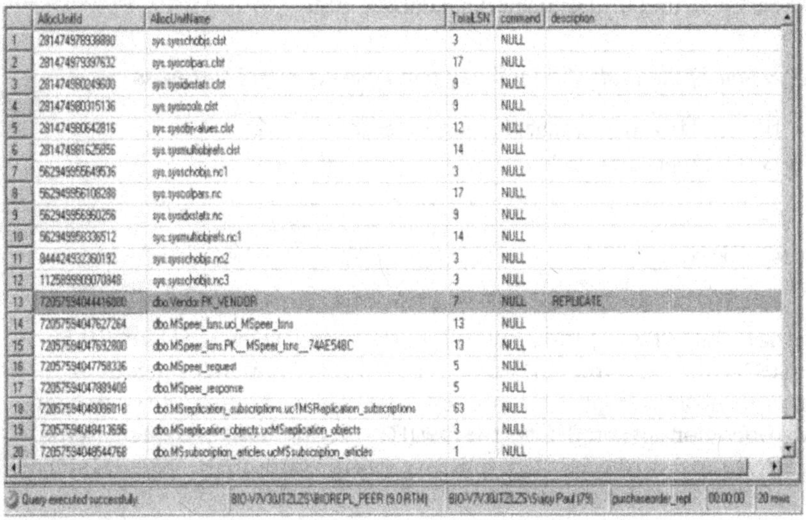

	AllocUnitId	AllocUnitName	TotalLSN	command	description
1	281474979339890	sys.sysschobjs.clst	3	NULL	
2	281474979397632	sys.syscolpars.clst	17	NULL	
3	281474980249600	sys.sysidxstats.clst	9	NULL	
4	281474980315136	sys.sysiscols.clst	9	NULL	
5	281474980642816	sys.sysobjvalues.clst	12	NULL	
6	281474981625856	sys.sysmultiobjrefs.clst	14	NULL	
7	562949955649536	sys.sysschobjs.nc1	3	NULL	
8	562949956108288	sys.syscolpars.nc	17	NULL	
9	562949956960256	sys.sysidxstats.nc	9	NULL	
10	562949958306512	sys.sysmultiobjrefs.nc1	14	NULL	
11	844424932360192	sys.sysschobjs.nc2	3	NULL	
12	1125899909070848	sys.sysschobjs.nc3	3	NULL	
13	72057594044416000	dbo.Vendor.PK_VENDOR	7	NULL	REPLICATE
14	72057594047627264	dbo.MSpeer_lsns.uci_MSpeer_lsns	13	NULL	
15	72057594047692800	dbo.MSpeer_lsns.PK__MSpeer_lsns__74AE548C	13	NULL	
16	72057594047758336	dbo.MSpeer_request	5	NULL	
17	72057594047803408	dbo.MSpeer_response	5	NULL	
18	72057594048006016	dbo.MSreplication_subscriptions.uc1MSReplication_subscriptions	63	NULL	
19	72057594048413696	dbo.MSreplication_objects.ucMSreplication_objects	3	NULL	
20	72057594048544768	dbo.MSsubscription_articles.ucMSsubscription_articles	1	NULL	

Query executed successfully. | BIO-V7V3UT2LZ5\BIOREPL_PEER (9.0 RTM) | BIO-V7V3UT2LZ5\Sujoy Paul (79) | purchaseorder_repl | 00:00:00 | 20 rows

Figure 10-4. *Output of the script in Listing 10-3, showing the total number of rows inserted for the purchaseorder_repl database*

From the output in Figure 10-4, you can see that the total number of rows being sent for replication (in row 13) is seven. On row 16, you can see that five rows are inserted into the MSpeer_request system table. This table is used to track the status requests for a publication in peer-to-peer transactional replication.

Now, if you execute the following query on the publication database, purchaseorder_repl,

```
Select * from MSpeer_request
```

you will see that the number of rows in the result set is the same as shown in Figure 10-4:

Id	publication	sent_date	description
1	pub_purchaseorderrepl_peer	2006-01-11 22:49:31.767	NULL
2	pub_purchaseorderrepl_peer	2006-01-11 22:50:22.700	NULL
3	pub_purchaseorderrepl_peer	2006-01-11 22:51:30.920	NULL
4	pub_purchaseorderrepl_peer	2006-01-13 19:39:19.220	NULL
5	pub_purchaseorderrepl_peer	2006-01-13 20:45:07.770	NULL

■**Note** The purchaseorder_repl database has been configured for peer-to-peer replication. Chapters 8 and 9 explain how to configure peer-to-peer replication using the GUI and T-SQL methods, respectively.

Next, we will update a row in the publication database. Then we will see how the update statement works inside the transaction log.

Listing 10-4 shows how to update a value in the database table.

Listing 10-4. *Updating a Row of the Table Vendor in the purchaseorder_repl Database*

```
/* Update a row in the publication database, purchaseorder_repl,
in the Publisher server, BIOREPL_PEER.*/

update vendor
set whse_postal_code='30033'
where vendorid=105
```

After executing the script in Listing 10-4, you will see the output shown in Figure 10-5. You can see that the LOP_BEGIN_XACT (row 407) and LOP_COMMIT_XACT (row 410) operations mark the beginning and end of the implicit transaction that surrounds the update statement. In between those two operations, it first deletes the row (LOP_DELETE_ROWS) and then inserts (LOP_INSERT_ROWS) the value (rows 408 and 409). It then enters the value in the MSreplication_ subscription table.

■**Note** Sometimes you will see the LOP_MODIFY_ROW operation. This means a single row has been modified.

If you checkpoint the database and then execute the script in Listing 10-4, the number of rows returned will be fewer than before you started the checkpoint. This is because the transaction is written to disk. You can check the Checkpoint Begin and Checkpoint End columns to determine where the checkpoints start and end.

	Cur..	Operation	C..	Transaction ID	Tag Bits	L..	L..	Pr..	AllocUnitId	AllocUnitName
398	00..	LOP_COMMIT_XACT	L..	0000:00000516	0x0000	48	E	0..	NULL	NULL
399	00..	LOP_BEGIN_XACT	L..	0000:00000517	0x0000	48	1	0..	NULL	NULL
400	00..	LOP_DELETE_ROWS	L..	0000:00000517	0x0000	62	E	0..	72057594048086016	dbo.MSreplication_subscriptions.uc1MSReplication_subscri..
401	00..	LOP_INSERT_ROWS	L..	0000:00000517	0x0000	62	E	0..	72057594048086016	dbo.MSreplication_subscriptions.uc1MSReplication_subscri..
402	00..	LOP_COMMIT_XACT	L..	0000:00000517	0x0000	48	E	0..	NULL	NULL
403	00..	LOP_BEGIN_XACT	L..	0000:00000518	0x0000	48	1	9..	NULL	NULL
404	00..	LOP_DELETE_ROWS	L..	0000:00000518	0x0000	62	E	0..	72057594048086016	dbo.MSreplication_subscriptions.uc1MSReplication_subscri..
405	00..	LOP_INSERT_ROWS	L..	0000:00000518	0x0000	62	E	0..	72057594048086016	dbo.MSreplication_subscriptions.uc1MSReplication_subscri..
406	00..	LOP_COMMIT_XACT	L..	0000:00000518	0x0000	48	E	0..	NULL	NULL
407	00..	LOP_BEGIN_XACT	L..	0000:00000519	0x0000	48	E	0..	NULL	NULL
408	00..	LOP_DELETE_ROWS	L..	0000:00000519	0x0000	62	1	0..	72057594044416000	dbo.Vendor.PK_VENDOR
409	00..	LOP_INSERT_ROWS	L..	0000:00000519	0x0000	62	E	0..	72057594044416000	dbo.Vendor.PK_VENDOR
410	00..	LOP_COMMIT_XACT	L..	0000:00000519	0x0000	48	E	0..	NULL	NULL
411	00..	LOP_BEGIN_XACT	L..	0000:0000051a	0x0000	48	1	0..	NULL	NULL
412	00..	LOP_DELETE_ROWS	L..	0000:0000051a	0x0000	62	E	0..	72057594048086016	dbo.MSreplication_subscriptions.uc1MSReplication_subscri..
413	00..	LOP_INSERT_ROWS	L..	0000:0000051a	0x0000	62	E	0..	72057594048086016	dbo.MSreplication_subscriptions.uc1MSReplication_subscri..
414	00..	LOP_COMMIT_XACT	L..	0000:0000051a	0x0000	48	E	0..	NULL	NULL
415	00..	LOP_BEGIN_XACT	L..	0000:0000051b	0x0000	48	1	0..	NULL	NULL
416	00..	LOP_DELETE_ROWS	L..	0000:0000051b	0x0000	62	E	0..	72057594048086016	dbo.MSreplication_subscriptions.uc1MSReplication_subscri..
417	00..	LOP_INSERT_ROWS	L..	0000:0000051b	0x0000	62	E	0..	72057594048086016	dbo.MSreplication_subscriptions.uc1MSReplication_subscri..
418	00..	LOP_COMMIT_XACT	L..	0000:0000051b	0x0000	48	E	0..	NULL	NULL
419	00..	LOP_BEGIN_XACT	L..	0000:0000051c	0x0000	48	1	0..	NULL	NULL
420	00..	LOP_DELETE_ROWS	L..	0000:0000051c	0x0000	62	E	0..	72057594048086016	dbo.MSreplication_subscriptions.uc1MSReplication_subscri..
421	00..	LOP_INSERT_ROWS	L..	0000:0000051c	0x0000	62	E	0..	72057594048086016	dbo.MSreplication_subscriptions.uc1MSReplication_subscri..
422	00..	LOP_COMMIT_XACT	L..	0000:0000051c	0x0000	48	E	0..	NULL	NULL

Figure 10-5. *The output of the* fn_dblog *command after executing the script in Listing 10-4*

The Log Reader Agent

The Log Reader Agent is responsible for tracking the transaction log on the publication database for any changes marked for replication. It then pushes them to the distribution database, where the Distribution Agent then picks up the messages. As such, the Log Reader Agent is scheduled to run continuously. The transaction log is cleared by SQL Server only after all the messages have been delivered to the distribution database.

Like the Snapshot and Distribution Agents, the Log Reader Agent also runs as a job and is listed under the SQL Server Jobs section in the SSMS. To look at it, open the Jobs object in the Object Explorer of the SSMS, right-click on the Log Reader Agent, and select Properties. You will see the General page of the Job Properties window, shown in Figure 10-6.

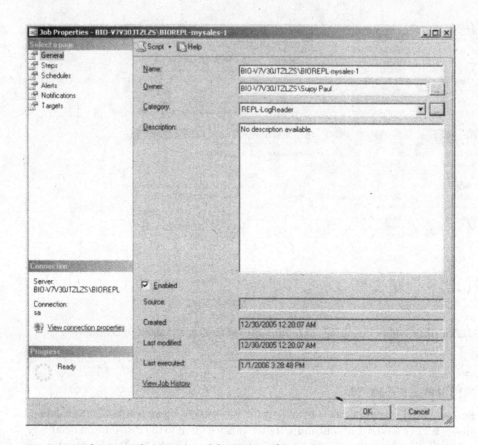

Figure 10-6. *The general properties of the Log Reader Agent*

■**Tip** The naming convention for the Log Reader Agent in the Job section of the SSMS is
`<Publisher>-<PublicationDatabase>-<integer>`.

If you now click the ellipsis button beside the Category field, you will see the list of jobs
for this Log Reader Agent, as shown in Figure 10-7. In this example, I have four jobs listed.
SQL Server allows you to have a Log Reader Agent for each publication database that is
marked for transactional replication. Click the Close button to return to the Job Properties
window (Figure 10-6).

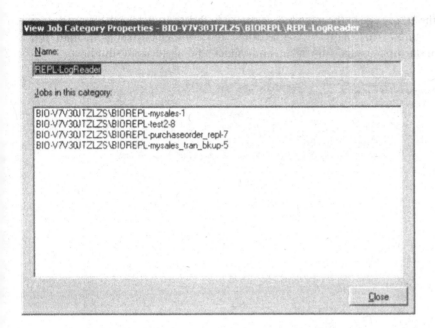

Figure 10-7. *Viewing the jobs scheduled to run for this Log Reader Agent*

If you now click the ellipsis button beside the Owner field, you will find the names along with the login types listed. If the names are not there, you can click the Browse button to select the name and match it with the corresponding login type that you want to associate with the agent. This is shown in Figure 10-8. Select an owner if you want to do so, and click OK twice to get back to the Job Properties window (Figure 10-6).

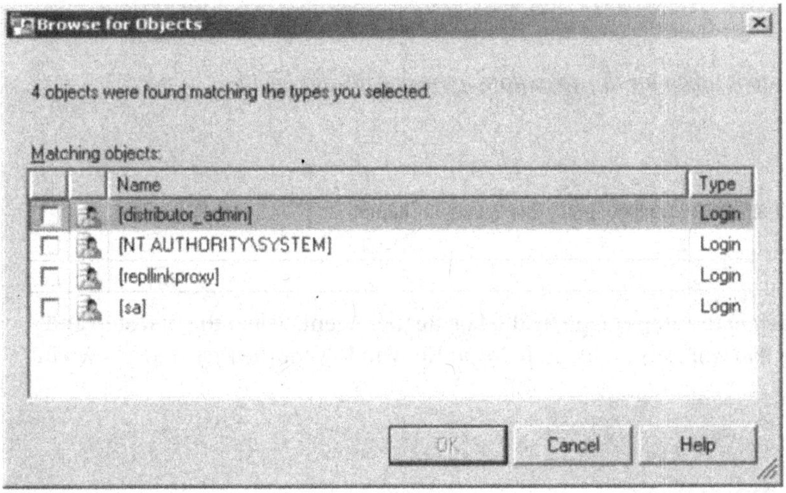

Figure 10-8. *Selecting a login name under whose account the Log Reader Agent will run*

Now select the Steps page in the left pane, as shown in Figure 10-9. Like the Snapshot Agent (shown in Figure 7-9 in Chapter 7), it takes three steps for the Log Reader Agent to run: Log Reader Agent startup message, Run agent, and Detect nonlogged agent shutdown.

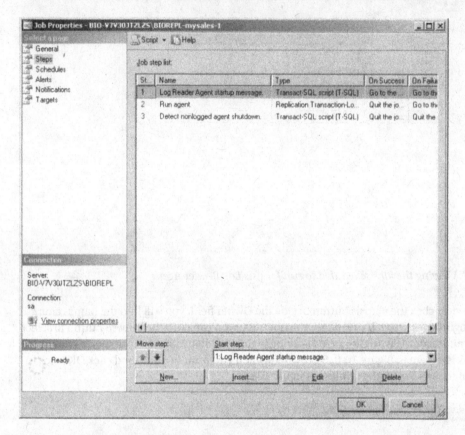

Figure 10-9. *The three steps taken for the execution of the Log Reader Agent*

■**Note** The internals of snapshot replication are discussed in Chapter 7.

Let's examine each of the steps taken by the Log Reader Agent. Select the first step and click the Edit button. You will see the Job Step Properties window for the first step, shown in Figure 10-10.

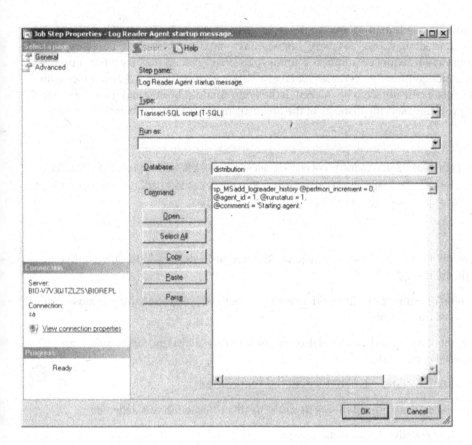

Figure 10-10. *Viewing the general settings for the Log Reader Agent's first job step—the startup message*

The Log Reader Agent uses the sp_MSadd_logreader_history stored procedure to start the log reader message and, like the Snapshot Agent, executes it on the distribution database. As you can see in Figure 10-10, it executes the following script behind the scenes:

```
sp_MSadd_logreader_history @perfmon_increment=0,
@agent_id=1, @runstatus=1,
@comments='Starting agent'
```

___

■**Note** You can execute this script only on the distribution database, and you have to be a member of the db_owner fixed database role.

___

The stored procedure first looks for the start_time, last_delivered_commands, last_delivered_transactions, last_delivery_latency, last_delivery_time, last_delivery_rate and last transaction sequence number columns in the MSlogreader_history table. It updates the performance counter for Logreader:Delivery Latency using the DBCC Addinstance command, which adds the object to be tracked in the Performance Monitor and then the script for the stored procedure sets the instance of the object using the DBCC Setinstance command.

■**Caution** Both these DBCC commands are undocumented, so use them with caution. The syntax for DBCC Addinstance is DBCC Addinstance(@object, @instance) and for DBCC Setinstance it is DBCC setinstance(objectname, countername,instancename, value).

If there are no start up messages logged, the stored procedure uses the current time to calculate the following:

- Number of transactions (latest-delivered transactions = delivered transactions – last-delivered transactions)

- Number of commands (latest-delivered commands = delivered commands – last-delivered commands)

- The duration of the agent to run in the current session

- The total delivery time of the agent since the first transaction was delivered

- The average delivery rate of the session

- The average delivery latency of the session

The stored procedure then calculates the average number of commands issued per transaction (delivered commands / delivered transactions) and sets the transaction sequence number (xact_seqno) to the last value of the transaction sequence number. The stored procedure, based on the value of the @perfmon_increment parameter, then increments the replication performance counters for a specific agent, @agent_id, associated with the id column in the MS_logreaderagents table using the DBCC incrementinstance command. The performance counters that are updated on the successful execution of the agent are Logreader: Delivered Trans/Sec and Logreader: Delivered Cmds/Sec. The Logreader: Delivered Cmds/Sec counter reports the average number of commands, while the Logreader: Delivered Trans/Sec counter reports the average number of transactions executed by the Log Reader Agent.

■**Note** DBCC Incrementinstance has the same syntax as DBCC Setinstance, and it is also an undocumented command.

Once the counters are updated, the stored procedure then adds the history of the data to the MSlogreader_history table. The @run_status parameter records the status of the Log Reader Agent. You will find the table in the distribution database.

Note The values for the @run_status parameter are described in Table 7-2 in Chapter 7.

Now select the Advanced page in the Job Step Properties window, shown in Figure 10-11. This is where you specify the steps the Log Reader Agent performs on the success or failure of the first step. As you can see, if the first step is successful, the agent can go to the next step, but if it is not, I have set the agent to "Quit the job reporting failure." If you want the Log Reader Agent to perform some other function if it fails, you can select the following from the drop-down list: Go to the next step, Quit the job reporting success, Go to step:[2]Run agent, or Go to step: [3]Detect nonlogged agent shutdown. As with the Snapshot Agent, you can log the information to a table and also store the output in a file.

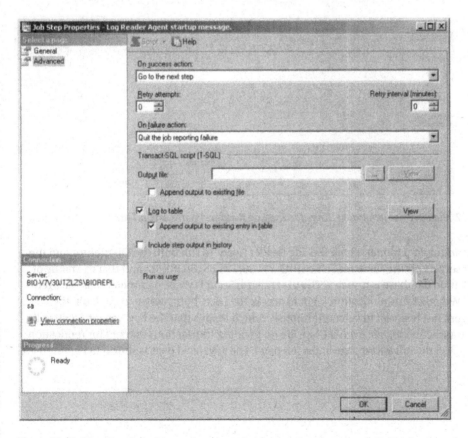

Figure 10-11. *Viewing the advanced settings for the Log Reader Agent's first job step—the startup message*

Click OK to return to the Job Properties window (Figure 10-9). Select the second job step and click the Edit button. This will open the Job Step Properties window for the second step, as shown in Figure 10-12.

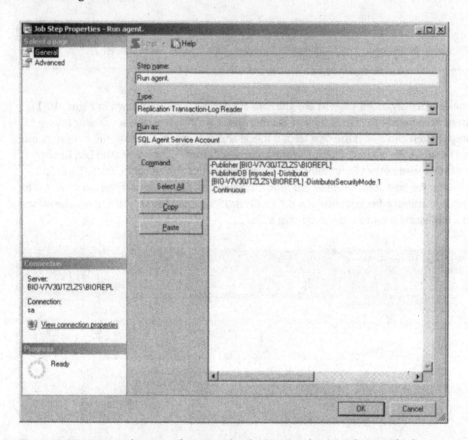

Figure 10-12. *Viewing the general settings for the Log Reader Agent's second job step—run agent*

The command parameters tell the Log Reader Agent to run both the Distributor and the Publisher servers on the same machine (BIO-V7V30JTZLZS\BIOREPL) and that the name of the publication database is mysales. The DistributorSecurityMode parameter tells the agent to use the Windows Authentication login to access the Distributor server. By default, the Log Reader Agent has been set to run continuously, which means that the Log Reader Agent will track the transaction log file even if there are no pending transactions marked for replication.

Now select the Advanced page in the left pane. The advanced page is shown in Figure 10-13.

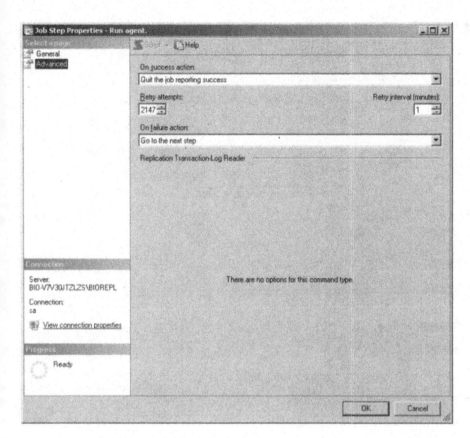

Figure 10-13. *Viewing the advanced settings for the Log Reader Agent's second job step—*
run agent

In the "On success action" drop-down list, select "Quit the job reporting success." Notice
the number of attempts the Log Reader Agent takes before it goes to step 3. In this case, it
makes 2,147 attempts. If the execution is successful before the Log Reader Agent reaches the
maximum number of attempts, it proceeds to the next step. However, if it fails, the agent is
flagged for retry after an interval of 1 minute.

Select "Go to the next step" from the "On failure action" drop-down list. If the second step
runs successfully, then it quits. However, if the second step fails, then it goes to the third step.

Click OK to get back to the Job Properties window (Figure 10-9). Select the third step and
click the Edit button. This will take you to the Job Step Properties window for the third step,
shown in Figure 10-14.

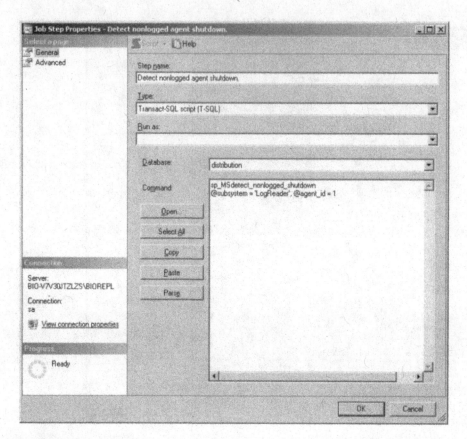

Figure 10-14. *Viewing the general settings for the Log Reader Agent's third job step—detect non-logged agent shutdown*

To detect Log Reader Agent errors and their causes, this step runs the following script:

```
sp_MSdetect_nonlogged_shutdown
@subsystem='LogReader', @agent_id=1
```

The stored procedure first retrieves the runstatus value from the MSlogreader_history table. If the runstatus is of type Succeed, Retry, or Failure, the @subsystem parameter identifies the log reader associated with the agent_id parameter (the id column in the MSlogreader_agents table is associated with the agent_id parameter). Finally, the stored procedure writes the history of the job and logs the messages in the SQL Server Agent's log and in the Replication Monitor.

Now select the Advanced page shown in Figure 10-15. As you can see, I have checked the boxes for "Log to table" and "Include step output in history" so that I can use the records for auditing. The agent will only log the step output if there are errors.

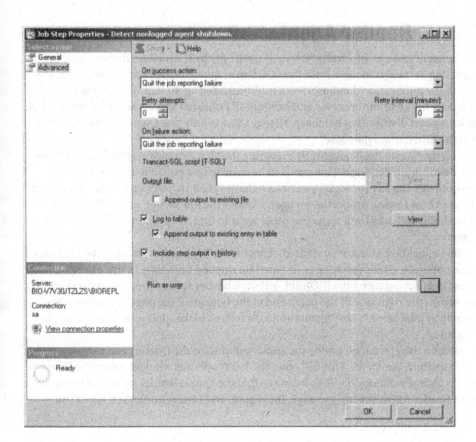

Figure 10-15. *Viewing the advanced settings for the Log Reader Agent's third job step—detect nonlogged agent shutdown*

Only members of the sysadmin fixed server role can issue operating-system level commands in the job steps.

Tip To find out the list of job steps for the agents that are configured to write the job step output in a table, execute select * from sysjobstepslogs from the msdb database.

The Queue Reader Agent

The Queue Reader Agent, as you know by now, is used only by transactional replication for queued updating. It takes messages from the SQL Server queue on the Subscriber server and sends them to the publication database. It is a multithreaded agent that runs on the distribution database on the Distributor server and services all Publisher servers and their publication databases for a given distribution database. Hence, there is only one Queue Reader Agent to be set up in the distribution database.

You set up the Queue Reader Agent by executing the sp_addqreader_agent stored procedure on the distribution database. This needs to be done before you add the publication. In order to execute this stored procedure, you need to have sysadmin fixed server role permission.

You've seen how to view properties for agents under the Job section of the SQL Agents folder in the SSMS, and now I will show you other ways to find the properties of the Queue Reader Agent.

Open the Replication Monitor by right-clicking on the Replication folder in the SSMS and selecting the publication that you have configured for queued updating. In this example, it is pub_mysales_queuedupdate on the BIOREPL_PEER Publisher server. Then select the Warnings and Agents tab on the right side of the pane, and at the bottom of the page you will see the agents running as jobs listed in the "Agents and jobs related to this publication" section, along with their status.

Right-click on the green icon beside the status column for the Queue Reader Agent, and select Properties from the menu. This will open the Job Properties window. Select the Steps page, which is shown in Figure 10-16. You can see that the Queue Reader Agent job has three steps: Queue Reader Agent startup message, Run agent, and Detect nonlogged agent shutdown.

Note The name of the Queue Reader Agent is listed as <DistributedServername>-<integer> under Jobs in the SSMS.

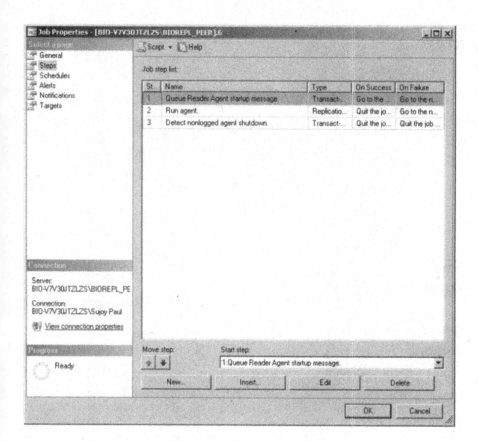

Figure 10-16. *Viewing the steps of the Queue Reader Agent job*

Note The user in the previous figure has 'sa' permissions.

The first job is already highlighted, so click the Edit button. This will open the Job Step Properties window shown in Figure 10-17.

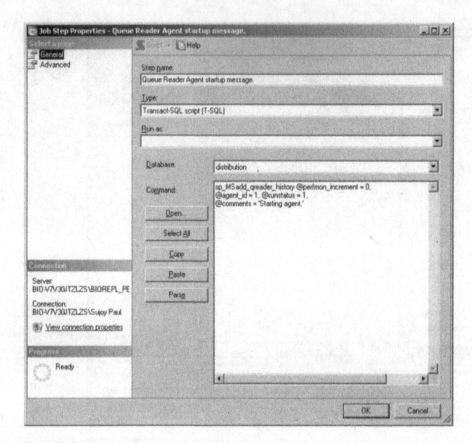

Figure 10-17. *Viewing the general settings for the Queue Reader Agent's first job step—the startup message*

The Queue Reader Agent executes the sp_MSadd_qreader_history stored procedure on the distribution database. As you can see in Figure 10-17, it executes the following script behind the scenes:

```
sp_Msadd_qreader_history @perfmon_increment=0,
@agent_id=1, @runstatus=1,
@comments='Starting agent'
```

The stored procedure updates the performance counter parameter, and if the Queue Reader Agent has already started, it uses the DBCC incrementinstance command to add performance counters for the Queue Reader Agent.

Note DBCC incrementinstance is an undocumented command; use it with caution. The syntax is dbcc incrementinstance(objectname, countername, instancename, value). If you want to find a list of all the DBCC commands, issue the DBCC traceon(2520) command and then use DBCC help('?').

The stored procedure then retrieves the start time from the MSqreader_history table if the agent has not started to run. It also finds out how long it takes for the agent to run, calculates the time for each of the commands to be processed, and updates the performance counters. The performance counters that are updated on the successful execution of the agent are QueueReader: Delivered Trans/Sec and QueueReader: Delivered Cmds/Sec. The QueueReader: Delivered Cmds/Sec counter reports the average number of commands, while the QueueReader: Delivered Trans/Sec counter reports the average number of transactions executed by the Queue Reader Agent. Once the counters are updated, the stored procedure then updates the history of the data in the MSqreader_history table, should the user want to log the errors. You will find the table in the distribution database.

Note The performance counters for the Logreader and QueueReader performance objects are discussed in Chapter 18, which covers the optimization of transactional replication.

Now select the Advanced page in the Job Step Properties window, as shown in Figure 10-18. As you can see, I have checked the boxes for "Log to table" and "Include step output in history."

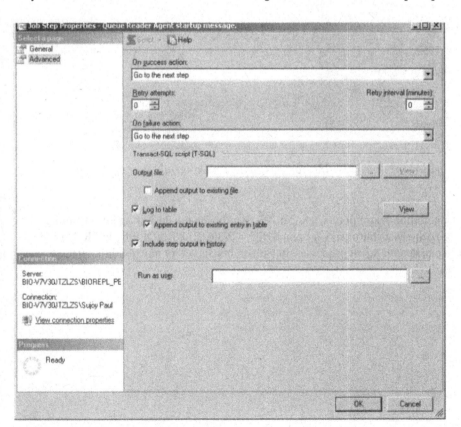

Figure 10-18. *Viewing the advanced settings for the Queue Reader Agent's first job step—the startup message*

Click OK to return to the Job Properties window (Figure 10-16). Select the second step and click the Edit button to open the window shown in Figure 10-19.

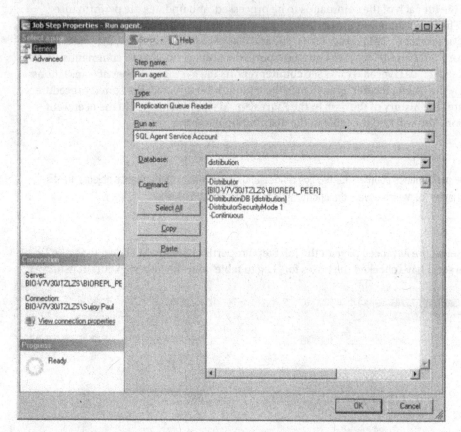

Figure 10-19. *Viewing the general settings for the Queue Reader Agent's second job step—run agent*

From the command parameters, you can see that the Queue Reader Agent is running continuously on the Distributor server named BIO-V7V30JTZLZS\BIOREPL_PEER. This means the Queue Reader Agent processes the Subscriber server for any pending queued subscriptions.

Now select the Advanced page in the left pane, as shown in Figure 10-20. These settings are similar to the ones we set for the Log Reader Agent (in the previous "The Log Reader Agent" section), except that different names are specified for the Distributor server and the distribution database in this case.

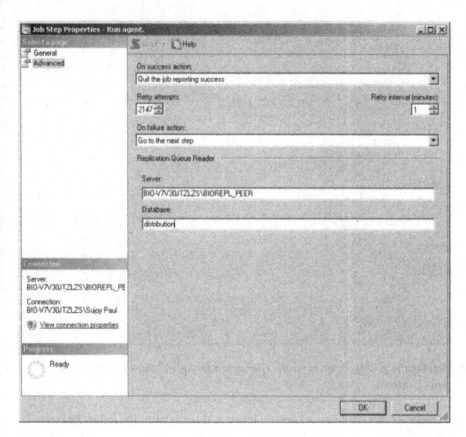

Figure 10-20. *Viewing the advanced settings for the Queue Reader Agent's second job step—run agent*

Click OK to return to the Job Properties window (Figure 10-16). Select the third job step and again click the Edit button. You will see the Job Step Properties window shown in Figure 10-21.

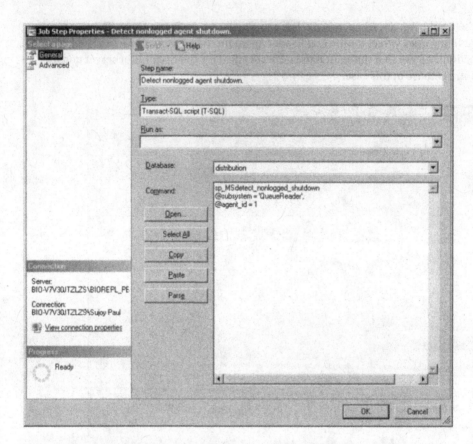

Figure 10-21. *Viewing the general settings for the Queue Reader Agent's third job step—detect nonlogged agent shutdown*

To detect Queue Reader Agent errors and their cause, this step runs the following script:

```
sp_MSdetect_nonlogged_shutdown
@subsystem='QueueReader',
@agent_id=1
```

The stored procedure first retrieves the runstatus value from the MSqreader_history table. If the runstatus is not of type Succeed, Retry, or Failure, the @subsystem parameter identifies the queue reader associated with the parameter agent_id (the id column in the MSqreader_agents table is associated with the agent_id parameter). Finally, the stored procedure writes the history of the job and logs the messages in the SQL Server Agent's log and in the Replication Monitor.

Now select the Advanced page, as shown in Figure 10-22. This is similar to the final step of the Log Reader Agent—the output is appended to the table, and the step output is included in the history.

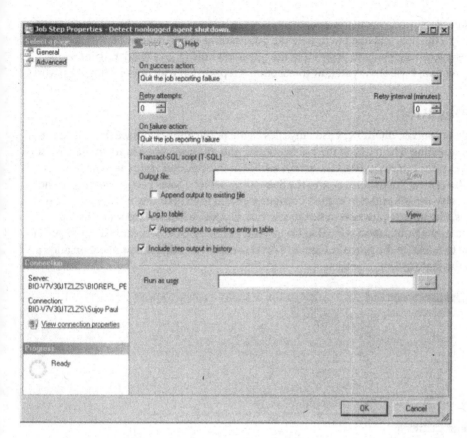

Figure 10-22. *Viewing the advanced settings for the Queue Reader Agent's third job step—detect nonlogged agent shutdown*

Now that I have described the different steps taken in the execution of both the Log Reader and Queue Reader Agents, we will look into how each of these agents function in conjunction with components of transactional replication to make the whole process work. We'll look at transactional replication with queued updating next.

Transactional Replication with Queued Updating

Subscriptions using queued updating can send transactions back to the central Publisher server, which then transmits them to other Subscriber servers using the 2PC protocol. Since data can be changed at both the publishing and subscribing servers, there are potential data conflicts that need to be resolved if data integrity is to be maintained. However, the benefit of making data changes at both the Publisher and Subscriber servers, albeit with a certain degree of latency and without maintaining a direct connection, can be advantageous in certain business scenarios.

For example, suppose a customer contact name or address changes; the sales representative working in the field will need to update the information. Using her remote connection, she updates the transaction and places it in the queue that the Queue Reader Agent reads.

In this section, I will show you how transactional replication with queued updating works.

The Publication

In the Publisher server, BIOREPL, I used mysales as the publication database that is to be used for queued updating. The name of the publication is pub_mysales_queueupd. In our case scenario, the Customer table is used as the article such that information about any customer is sent from the central Publisher server to the Subscriber servers. Sales people working in the field can receive the information at their convenience and then send any updates from their remote sites. The updates are sent to the queue that the Queue Reader Agent processes.

As soon as the publication is created for queued updating, SQL Server makes changes in the schema to facilitate the process. Figure 10-23 shows how creating the publication adds a column in the table used as an article.

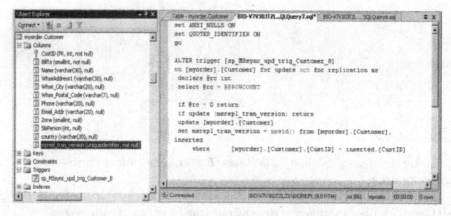

Figure 10-23. *Creating a column,* msrepl_tran_version, *in the table,* Customer, *that is used as an article*

In fact, for every table that is used as an article for a publication with queued updating, SQL Server adds a column, msrepl_tran_version, of uniqueidentifier data type. This column is used for change tracking and detecting any conflicts during the synchronization process.

Note If you configure the publication using the GUI, SQL Server will tell you that it is going to add the uniqueidentifier column.

Besides adding a column, SQL Server adds an update trigger called sp_MSsync_upd_trig_ Customer on the same table. You can see the code for the trigger in Figure 10-23. Notice that the trigger specifies NOT FOR REPLICATION. This means that the original identity values on the rows are maintained; when a new row is added, the identity value is incremented. Say, for example, an update is made on the customer information. This trigger will be fired and the msrepl_tran_version column will be updated with the new GUID. The queue holding the transaction will contain both the old and the new GUIDs.

When the Publisher server receives the new transaction, the GUID of the transaction is compared to that in the publication database. If the old GUID of the transaction matches with the one in the publication database, the publication is updated and the row is updated to the GUID of the Subscriber server so that both GUIDs match. If, however, the GUID of the trans-action is not in harmony with the publication in the Publisher server, a conflict is detected and both the GUIDs will be present in the publication database. This indicates that there are two different versions of the row. One row contains the transaction with the GUID from the Subscriber server, and the other is the one that already existed in the publication.

SQL Server also adds another table, called conflict_pub_mysales_queueupd_Customer, which is a conflict table. The system columns added are specific to queued updates:

- msrepl_tran_version

- origin_datasource

- conflict_type

- reason_code

- reason_text

- pubid

- tranid

- insertdate

- qcfttabrowid

These columns are shown in Figure 10-24.

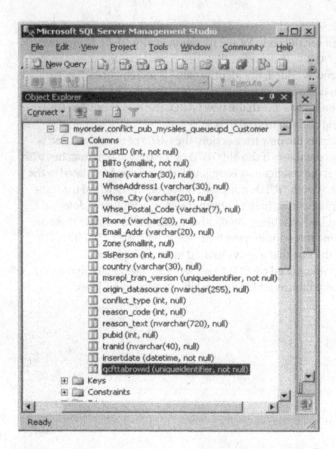

Figure 10-24. *Viewing new columns added by SQL Server to the conflict table,*
`conflict_pub_mysales_queueupd_Customer`

Transactional replication for queued updating subscription also adds insert, delete, and update stored procedures to the publication database, named `sp_MSsync_ins_<tablename>`, `sp_MSsync_del_<tablename>`, and `sp_MSsync_upd_<tablename>`, respectively. A stored procedure (`sp_MSscft_pub_mysales_queueupd_Customer`) to log the conflict information is also added in the publication database in the Publisher server and sent to the Subscriber server. This stored procedure will be executed if a conflict is detected by the Queue Reader Agent.

Initially if you insert, delete, or update a transaction on the publication database, the Log Reader Agent picks up the messages marked for replication and sends them to the distribution database, where they are held in the `MSrepl_commands` system table.

To see how the transactional publication with queued updating subscription works, I have inserted rows used for queued updating in the `Customer` table of the mysales publication database, as shown in Figure 10-25.

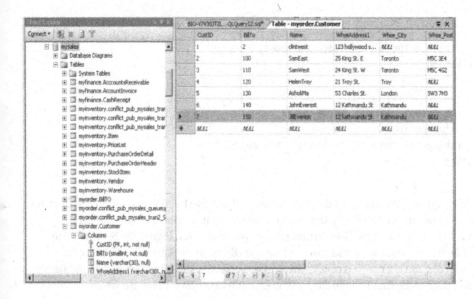

Figure 10-25. *Inserting values in the* Customer *table in the mysales database*

▪**Tip** To ensure that transactions marked for replication have already been sent to the Distributor server, and that no other transactions are waiting to be distributed in the publication database, you can use the sp_repltrans stored procedure.

After the rows are sent by the Log Reader Agent from the publication to the distribution database, the Distribution Agent picks up the insert commands from the MSrepl_commands table and executes the sp_MS_ins_Customer stored procedure on the subscribing database to insert the rows in the requisite table. The insert trigger does not get fired on the subscription database as the trigger is marked NOT FOR REPLICATION.

▪**Note** For the delete command, the Distribution Agent executes sp_MS_del_Customer on the subscribing database, and for the update command, it executes sp_MS_upd_Customer.

The system table, MSrepl_commands, contains rows of commands that have been replicated. If you were to retrieve the result set of the commands held in the MSrepl_commands table from the distribution database, as shown in Listing 10-5, you would not be able to see how the insert stored procedure was executed in the command column of the MSrepl_commands table. The command column is of data type varbinary, so it lists the commands executed in binary format.

Listing 10-5. *Retrieving Transactions Held in the* MSrepl_commands *Table*

```
/* Execute this on the distribution database. */
use distribution
go

select * from msrepl_commands where
publisher_database_id=
(select database_id from sys.databases where name
like 'mysales')
go
```

Thankfully, there is a way to read the commands that have been executed on the distribution database. The stored procedure that provides detailed information from the MSrepl_commands table in a human-readable format is sp_browsereplcmds. Figure 10-26 shows the output of this stored procedure. You can see that the Distribution Agent is executing the sp_MSins_myorderCustomer stored procedure and the inserted values are passed as parameters in the stored procedure that I put in the Customer table (as shown in Figure 10-25).

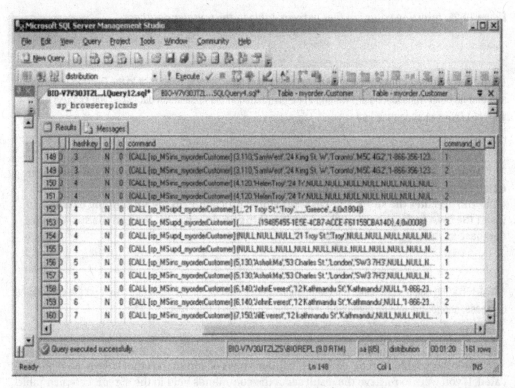

Figure 10-26. *Output of the* sp_browsereplcmds *stored procedure run on the distribution database*

Note Internally, the stored procedure adds the `myorder` schema name prior to the `Customer` table name.

In Figure 10-27, you can see that the transactions have been transmitted successfully on the subscription database, mysales_remote_queueupd.

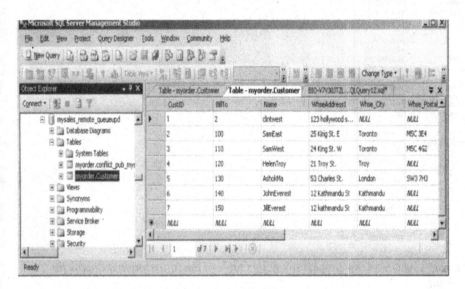

Figure 10-27. *Successful transmission of the insert values in the subscribing database*

Now that you know what system tables and columns have been added to the publication database, let's look into the changes made on the subscription database on the Subscriber server.

The Subscriptions

In the case of subscriptions with queued updating, replication allows you to make changes to the published data. As mentioned earlier, the GUID of the transaction sent by the subscribing server is matched with the GUID in the publication database. Consequently, creating a subscription for queued updating also results in adding the msrepl_tran_version column to each table in the subscription database that sends and receives changes. Figures 10-28 through 10-30 show the system tables in the subscription database for queued updating.

MSsubscription_properties	
publisher	sysname
publisher_db	sysname
publication	sysname
publication_type	int
publisher_login	sysname
publisher_password	varchar(524)
publisher_security_mode	int
distributor	sysname
distributor_login	sysname
distributor_password	varchar(524)
distributor_security_mode	int
ftp_address	sysname
ftp_port	int
ftp_login	sysname
ftp_password	varchar(524)
alt_snapshot_folder	varchar(255)
working_directory	varchar(255)
use_ftp	bit
dts_package_name	sysname
dts_package_password	varchar(524)
dts_package_location	int
enabled_for_syncmgr	bit
offload_agent	bit
offload_server	sysname
dynamic_snapshot_location	varchar(255)
use_web_sync	bit
internet_url	nvarchar(260)
internet_login	sysname
internet_password	varchar(524)
internet_security_mode	int
internet_timeout	int
hostname	sysname
publisherlink	sysname
publisherlinkuser	sysname
job_step_uid	varchar(16)

Figure 10-28. *The* MSsubscription_properties *system table in the subscription database for queued updating*

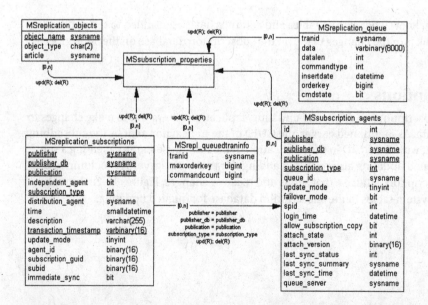

Figure 10-29. *The* MSreplication_object, MSreplication_queue, MSreplication_subscriptions, MSsubscription_agents, *and* MSrepl_queuedtraninfo *system tables in the subscription database for queued updating connected to the* MSsubscription_properties *table in Figure 10-28*

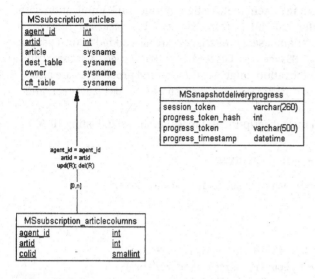

Figure 10-30. *The* MSsubscription_articles, MSsubscription_articlecolumns, *and* MSsnapshotdeliveryprogress *system tables in the subscription database for queued updating*

The functions of the system tables in queued updating subscriptions are shown in Table 10-1.

Table 10-1. *System Tables in the Subscription Database Involved in Queued Updating*

System Table	Function
MSreplication_queuedtraninfo	This table stores information about the queued commands that are using SQL-based queue updating
MSreplication_objects	Each row contains an object associated with replication
MSreplication_queue	This table stores the queued commands issued by all queued updating subscriptions using SQL-based queue updating
MSreplication_subscriptions	Each row contains information on replication for the Distribution Agent servicing the local subscription database
MSsnapshotdeliveryprogress	This table tracks files that have been successfully delivered to the Subscriber server after the snapshot has been applied
MSsubscription_agents	This table is used by the Distribution Agent and triggers of updatable subscriptions to track the subscription properties
MSsubscription_articlecolumns	This table contains the columns of the articles used for replication
MSsubscription_articles	This table contains information regarding the articles that are used in queued updating and immediate updating subscriptions
MSsubscription_properties	This table contains rows for the parameter information required to run replication agents on the Subscriber server

Besides the addition of the preceding system tables when transactional publication with queued updating subscription is configured, the `conflict_pub_mysales_queueupd_Customer` table is also added on the subscription database. Three triggers are also added to the `Customer` table in the subscription database: `trg_MSsync_ins_Customer`, `trg_MSsync_del_Customer`, and `trg_MSsync_upd_Customer`. As in the publication database, three stored procedures are also added in the subscription database: `sp_MSsync_ins_Customer`, `sp_MSsync_del_Customer`, and `sp_MSsync_upd_Customer`.

Now let's insert two new rows on the subscription database, as shown in Listing 10-6.

Listing 10-6. *Inserting Data in the Subscription Database*

```
/* Insert the records in the queued updating subscription database. */
Use mysales_remote_queueupd
go

Insert into myorder.Customer(CustID, BillTo, Name, WhseAddress1,
 Whse_City, Whse_postal_code, Phone, Country,msrepl_tran_version)
 values(8,160,'GauriMitra', '21 Laketown Ave.','Oakville',
'L6H 4A5','1-800-123-4567','Canada',newid())
Go
Insert into myorder.Customer(CustID, BillTo, Name, WhseAddress1,
 Whse_City, Whse_postal_code, Phone, Country,msrepl_tran_version)
 values(8,160,'GauriMitra', '21 Laketown Ave.','Oakville',
'L6H 4A5','1-800-123-4567','Canada',newid())
go
```

SQL Server fires the `trg_MSins_ins_Customer` trigger to capture the values that have been inserted and sent to the `MSreplication_queue` table. When making an insert, it records the after states of the insert action. So if the transaction is not committed, it will not be written to the table.

Once the transaction is committed, you can retrieve the data from the `MSreplication_queue` table in the subscription database, as shown in Figure 10-31.

The value of 1 in the `commandtype` column indicates that this is a user-defined transaction, and the date on which it was entered is indicated by the `insertdate` column. The value of 0 in the `cmdstate` column indicates that the data entered is complete; a value of 1 means it is partial. The `tranid` column is of `sysname` data type, while the `data` column is in `varbinary` format. The `orderkey` column reflects the order in which the transactions are entered in the subscription database.

Since the commands are being stored in `MSreplication_queue`, the next step in the delivery process is for the Queue Reader Agent to pick up the messages. We can check the number of commands picked up by the Queue Reader Agent from the message queue for a particular transaction (`tranid`) to find out how the Queue Reader Agent is functioning. This will allow us to locate where the commands are being held in the queued updating process. This is shown in Listing 10-7.

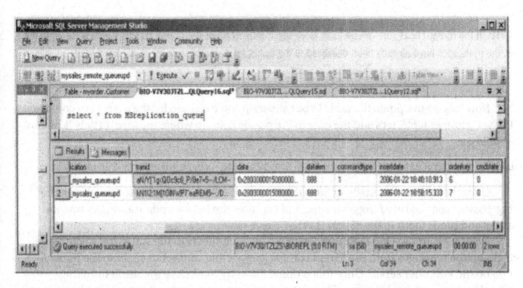

Figure 10-31. *Viewing the stored commands in the* MSreplication_queue *table*

Listing 10-7. *Retrieving the Number of Commands for a Transaction Waiting to Be Picked Up by the Queue Reader Agent*

```
/* Execute this on the subscription database.*/
Use mysales_remote_queueupd
Go

select a.commandcount,
b.publication
from MSrepl_queuedtraninfo a,
Msreplication_queue b
where a.tranid=b.tranid
go
```

The output is as follows:

Commandcount	publication
1	pub_mysales_queueupd
1	pub_mysales_queueupd

In this script, I selected the commandcount column from the MSrepl_queuedtraninfo table, and the name of the publication from the MSreplication_queue table for the same transaction ID (tranid). You can see that two inserts were issued and are waiting for the Queue Reader Agent.

■**Tip** If the MSreplication_queue table is empty, check whether the Queue Reader Agent is running. If it is, the messages have already been delivered to the publication database in the Publisher server.

Now let's try to update the table in our subscription database for the whse_city column. In the Customer table, let's add the data to the phone column where the whse_city is "London", as follows:

```
update myorder.Customer set Phone='44-071-123-4444' where whse_city='london'
```

Once the updates are made in the subscription database on the Subscriber server, the trg_MSsync_upd_Customer trigger is fired and captures the before update and after update states and sends them to the MSreplication_queue table.

Now let's start the Queue Reader Agent so that it connects to the subscription database, picks up the messages from the MSreplication_queue table, and sends them to the publication on the Publisher server. Once this is done, if you try to retrieve the result from the MSreplication_queue table, you will find that it is empty. The Queue Reader Agent has picked up the messages. If you check the publication database, you will see that the phone number has indeed been updated, as shown in Figure 10-32.

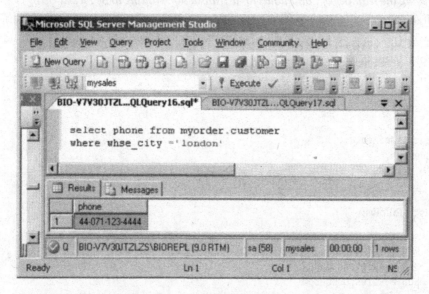

Figure 10-32. *Checking that the phone number has been updated in the publication database*

The Queue Reader Agent uses the sp_MSsync_upd_Customer stored procedure to update the data in the publication database on the Publisher server. It uses sp_MSsync_ins_Customer to insert the data. Likewise, for deleting data it uses sp_MSsync_del_Customer.

Conflict Detection and Resolution

Now that you have seen how messages in the queue are transferred from the Publisher to the Subscriber server and vice versa, let's see if any conflicts were encountered during the process. Right-click on the publication that you created for queued updating in the SSMS, and select View Conflicts from the menu. As you can see in Figure 10-33, I did not have any conflicts.

Figure 10-33. *No conflicts were encountered on the Publisher server for queued updating*

So how would you know what kind of conflict resolution has been set up? To find out, right-click on the publication in the SSMS and select Properties. Then select the Subscription Options page in the Publication Properties window, as shown in Figure 10-34. Under the "Updatable subscriptions" section, the Conflict resolution policy is set to "Keep the Publisher change." In this case, the Publisher wins if there is a conflict detected; this is the default.

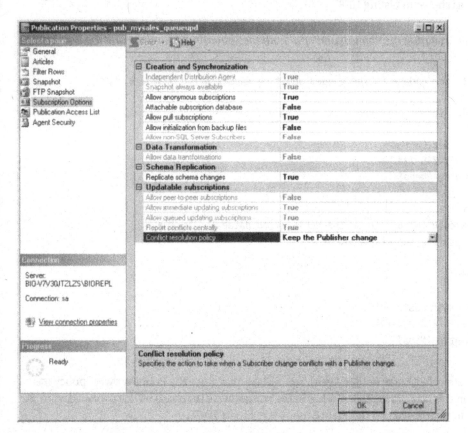

Figure 10-34. *Viewing the conflict resolution policy: Keep the Publisher change*

You cannot change the conflict-resolution policy while there is a subscription. If you try to do so, you will get an error message, as shown in Figure 10-35. You can change the policy only after the publication is created. The other options for conflict resolution are "Subscriber wins" and "Reinitialize the Subscription."

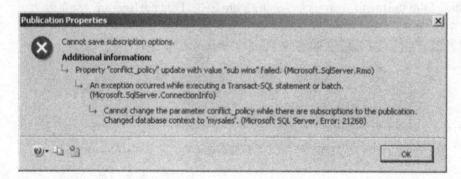

Figure 10-35. *Changing the conflict resolution policy while there is a subscription results in an error*

To demonstrate conflict resolution, let's try to update the phone number for the customer in Nepal, as shown in Listing 10-8.

Listing 10-8. *Updating the Phone Number in Both the Subscribing Database and the Publication Database*

```
/* Execute the update on the queued updating subscription database. */

Use mysales_remote_queueupd
go
update myorder.Customer
set Phone='1-866-234-5432'
where country='Nepal'
go

/* Now execute the update on the publication database for the
 queued updating subscription. */

use mysales
go
update myorder.Customer
set Phone='1-866-234-6789'
where country='Nepal'
go
```

Now start the Queue Reader Agent. You will see that since the Publisher wins policy has been set in this case, the updated value in the subscription database will be overwritten by the value set in the publication database as shown in Figure 10-36.

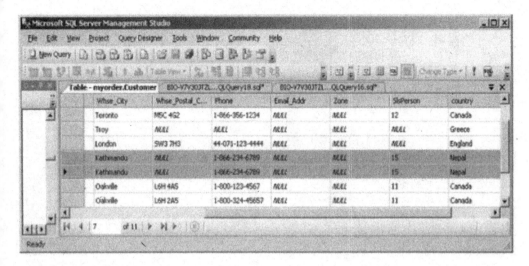

Figure 10-36. *The updated values in the subscription database are overwritten by the values set in the publication database*

The Queue Reader Agent executes the sp_MSsync_upd_Customer stored procedure, and SQL Server checks for any possible conflicts. Since we know there is a possible conflict, right-click on the publication in the SSMS and select View Conflicts from the menu. Figure 10-37 shows the Select Conflict Window that opens.

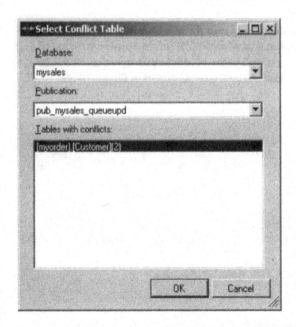

Figure 10-37. *Viewing the conflicted tables*

Click OK to open the Microsoft Replication Conflict Viewer, shown in Figure 10-38.

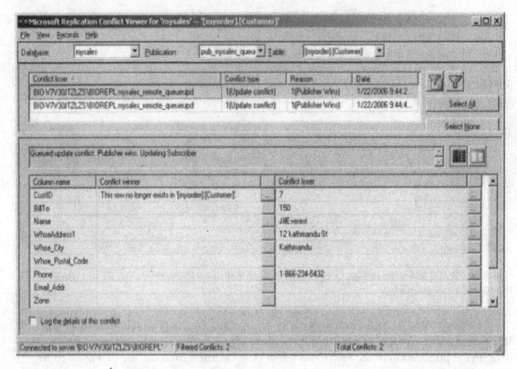

Figure 10-38. *The Conflict Viewer shows the conflict winner and loser*

SQL Server preserves the data for both the winner and the loser, and the Conflict Viewer shows you the loser, the winner, and the reason (Publisher Wins) for the resolution selected. It also shows you the loser data, which is also stored in the conflict table, `myorder.conflict_pub_mysales_queueupd_Customer` in the publication database, as shown in Figure 10-39.

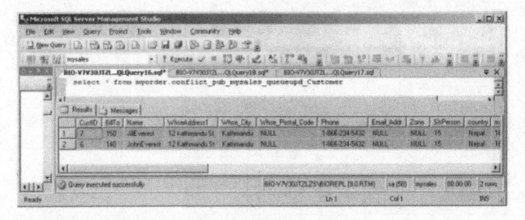

Figure 10-39. *Recording the losing data in the conflict table*

Now that you know the internals of queued updating for transactional replication, I will show you how the immediate updating for transactional replication works.

Transactional Replication with Immediate Updating

There is not much difference between the inner workings of queued and immediate updating subscriptions. In the case of immediate updating subscriptions, however, the connection needs to be maintained between the Publisher and Subscriber servers. Also, you don't need the Queue Reader Agent, since messages are not placed in the queue by the subscribing database. Unlike the standard publication, the subscriptions have the ability to update the data.

The Publication

Consider the case where the stock of items in the warehouse needs to be updated immediately at remote sites. This makes the central site more aware of what items exist in stock at different locations, so that all the remote sites are in sync. Any shortage of spare parts at one site can easily be alleviated, since updates are sent to the other subscribing servers.

For this example, the mysales publication database on the BIOREPL Publisher server will be used as the publication database for immediate updating. The name of the publication is pub_mysales_tran2, and the articles are shown in Figure 10-40.

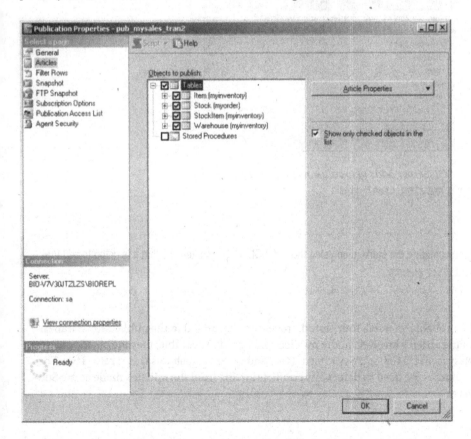

Figure 10-40. *The articles in the publication for immediate updating*

As with queued updating, immediate updating also makes schema changes. The msrepl_tran_version column is added to every table in the immediate updating subscription to track the GUID of the published tables. For this reason, you need to specify the column names whenever you are issuing an INSERT command.

In fact, for every table that is used as an article for a publication with queued updating, SQL Server adds the msrepl_tran_version column of data type uniqueidentifier. SQL Server also adds an update trigger called sp_MSsync_upd_trig_Item, set to NOT FOR REPLICATION, on each table. Finally, SQL Server adds a conflict table for each table used as an article. In this example, the name of the conflict table for the Item table is conflict_pub_mysales_tran2_Item. This is shown in Figure 10-41.

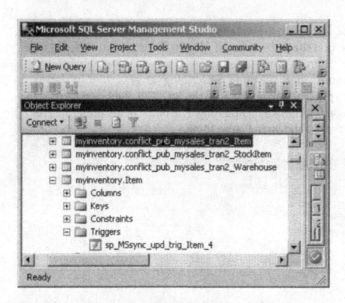

Figure 10-41. *SQL Server adds new columns to the conflict table,* conflict_pub_mysales_tran2_Item

---

■**Note** If you configure the publication using the GUI, SQL Server will tell you that it is going to add the uniqueidentifier column.

As you probably guessed, four stored procedures are added to the publication database for each of the articles involved in the publication. For the Item table, they are sp_MSsync_ins_Item, sp_MSsync_del_Item, sp_MSsync_upd_Item, and sp_MScft_pub_mysales_tran2_Item. These stored procedures are used to detect any conflicts arising from the updates made at the Subscriber server.

Changes made on the publication database on the Publisher server and marked for replication are picked up by the Log Reader Agent and forwarded to the distribution database, which acts as the store-and-forward queue. The Distribution Agent then forwards the transactions to the appropriate subscribing servers.

The Subscriptions

The system tables in the subscription database are the same as those for queued updating, shown in Figures 10-28 through 10-30. A column of uniqueidentifier data type is added to each of the tables used for immediate updating in the subscription database, which, as you know by now, is involved in tracking changes in the published data.

Besides the system tables involved in replication, the conflict_pub_mysales_tran2_Item table is also added on the subscription database. The other tables involved in the immediate updating subscription also have their own conflict tables.

Three triggers are added on the Customer table in the subscription database: trg_MSsync_ins_Item, trg_MSsync_del_Item, and trg_MSsync_upd_Item. As in the publication database, three stored procedures are also added: sp_MSsync_ins_Customer, sp_MSsync_del_Customer, and sp_MSsync_upd_Customer.

For each of the articles in immediate updating, SQL Server also adds insert, update, and delete stored procedures. For the Item table, the names of these stored procedures are sp_MSins_myinventoryItem, sp_MSupd_myinventoryItem, and sp_MSdel_myinventoryItem.

Note The MS DTC must be running for both immediate and queued updating to work.

Now let's insert new rows in the myinventory.Item table on the mysales_remote3 subscription database. The new rows are shown in Figure 10-42.

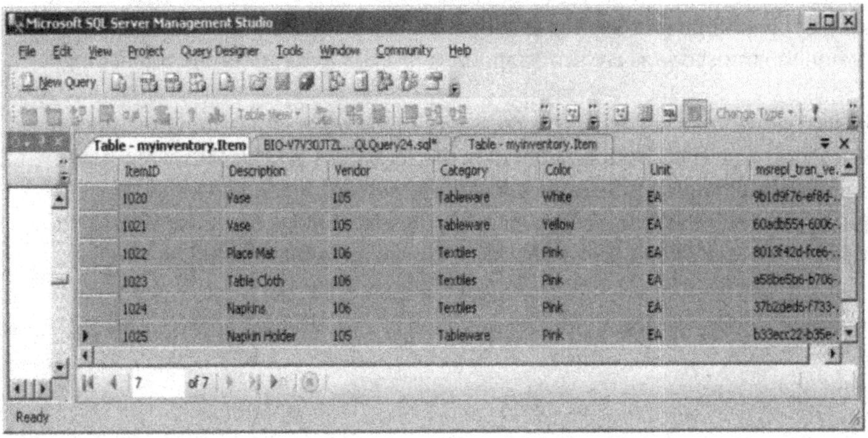

Figure 10-42. *Inserting new rows in the subscription database*

If you now check the mysales publication database, you will see that the rows have been updated, as shown in Figure 10-43.

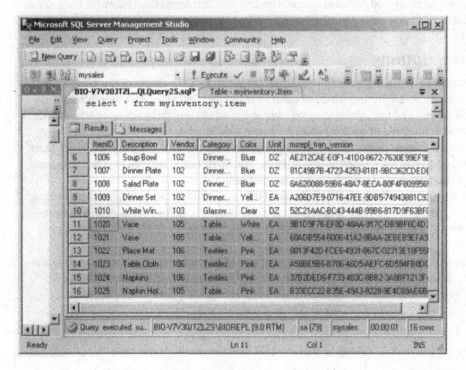

Figure 10-43. *Viewing updated rows in the* Item *table in the mysales publication database*

When the inserts were applied to the Item table in the subscription database, the trg_MSsync_ins_Item trigger is fired to capture the transactional change. This trigger then makes an RPC call to the Publisher server through the MS DTC. If there are no conflicts, the transactions are applied to the publication database. (It is worth noting that the 2PC protocol is used only when the transactions are sent from the subscribing server to the publishing server.)

The Publisher server then sends out the messages to the other subscribing servers via the Distributor server. The Distribution Agent uses the sp_MS_ins_myinventoryItem stored procedure to apply the changes to the other subscribing servers. If you now execute the sp_browsereplcmds stored procedure in Figure 10-44, the distribution database will run the sp_MS_ins_myinventoryItem stored procedure twice for each row that is being inserted.

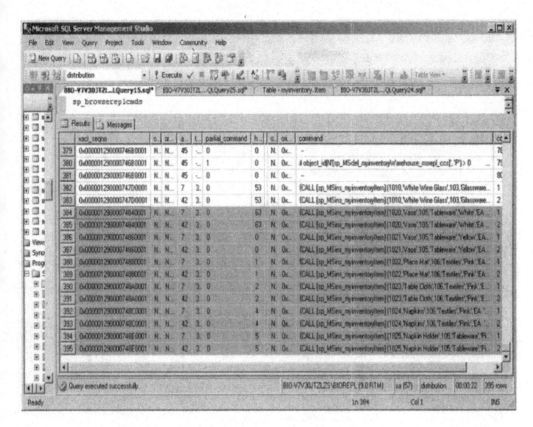

Figure 10-44. *Executing* `sp_browsereplcmds` *to see the stored procedures that are called from the subscribing database by the Distribution Agent*

To retrieve a list of articles and their corresponding destination tables in the publication database, you can query the `MSsubscription_articles` system table in the subscription database. You can also retrieve a list of stored procedures and the triggers associated with the immediate updating subscription by querying the `MSreplication_objects` system table. Both of these queries are shown in Figure 10-45.

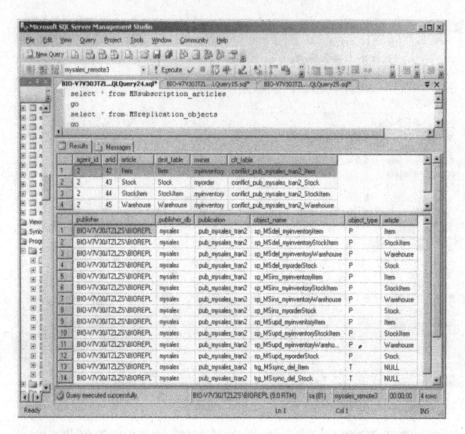

Figure 10-45. *Retrieving the names of the articles and their corresponding objects in an immediate updating subscription*

If conflicts are detected when the subscribing server sends out the changes to the publishing server, the transaction is rejected and rolled back on both the Publisher and Subscriber servers. The messages are then logged in the conflict table. As with queued updating, both the loser and winner rows are logged in the conflict table and can be viewed using the Conflict Viewer (shown in Figure 10-38). If you are using the "Subscriber wins" conflict policy, you cannot update the primary key column and should not use foreign key constraints either on the Publisher server or on the Subscriber server; see the BOL for more details.

Peer-to-Peer Replication

I showed you how to configure the peer-to-peer topology for transactional replication using the GUI and T-SQL methods in Chapters 8 and 9. In this section, I will discuss the internals of peer-to-peer replication.

■Note Chapter 8 discusses how to configure peer-to-peer replication using the GUI; Chapter 9 covers the T-SQL method.

Scalability, reliability, and availability are some of the benefits of using this configuration. However, conflicting situations can arise when simultaneous updates are made at two different nodes. While timestamping is one of the techniques used to alleviate this problem, this is a feature that is not available with peer-to-peer replication. In fact, conflict detection and resolution are not provided. This means that you have to ensure that updates made on rows at one node are synchronized to other nodes.

■Note To find out about the benefits and challenges of deploying peer-to-peer replication, see "Considerations for Deploying Peer-to-Peer Replication," by Melanie Kacerek, `http://www.quest-pipelines.com/ pipelines/dba/archives/PeertoPeer_Replication2.pdf`.

The system tables used in peer-to-peer replication are shown in Figures 10-46 through 10-48.

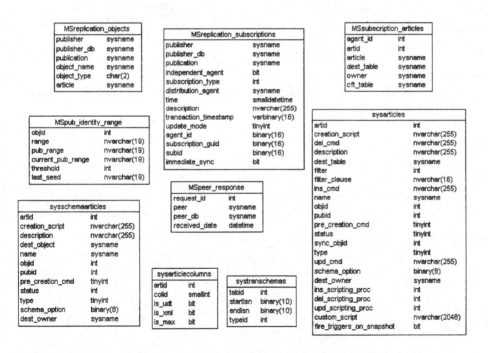

Figure 10-46. *The* MSreplication_objects, MSpub_identity_range, MSreplication_ subscriptions, MSsubscription_articles, sysarticlecolumns, MSpeer_response, systranschemas, sysschemaarticles, sysarticles *system tables used in peer-to-peer replication*

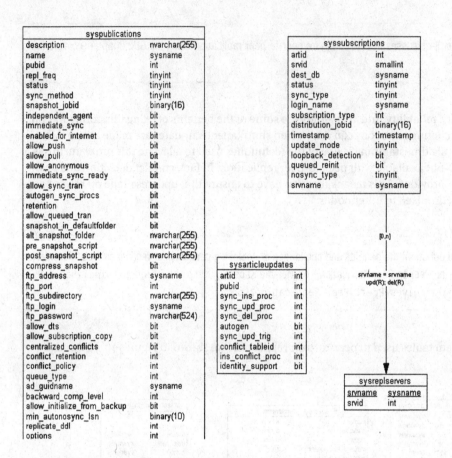

Figure 10-47. *The* syspublications, syssubscriptions, sysreplservers, *and* sysarticleupdates *system tables used in peer-to-peer replication*

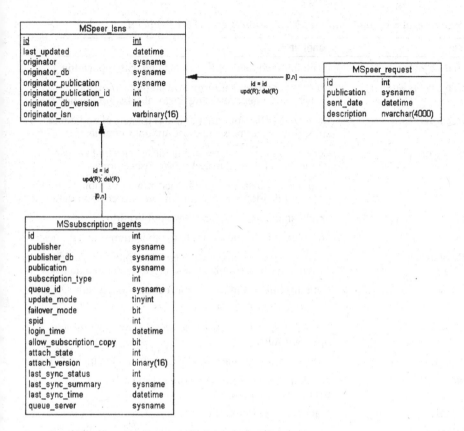

Figure 10-48. *The* MSpeer_lsns, MSpeer_request, *and* MSsubscription_agents *system tables in peer-to-peer replication*

The functions of the system tables involved in peer-to-peer replication are listed in Table 10-2.

Table 10-2. *System Tables in the Databases Involved in Peer-to-Peer Replication*

System Table	Function
MSreplication_objects	Contains each row's object associated with replication
MSreplication_subscriptions	Contains each row's information on replication for the Distribution Agent servicing the local subscription database
MSsubscription_agents	Used by the Distribution Agent and triggers of updatable subscriptions to track the subscription properties
MSsubscription_articles	Contains information regarding the articles that are used in queued and immediate updating subscriptions
MSpeer_lsns	Maps each transaction to a subscription; this table is stored in every publication database and in the subscription database
MSpeer_request	Tracks status requests for a given publication
MSpeer_response	Stores each node's response to a publication status request
MSpub_identity_range	Provides identity range management support; this table is stored in both the publication and subscription databases
sysarticlecolumns	Contains one row for each table column that is published
sysarticles	Contains a row for each article
sysarticleupdates	Contains a row for each article involved in immediate updating subscriptions
syspublications	Contains a row for each publication defined in the database
sysreplservers	Contains a row for the name of the server that is used for peer-to-peer replication
sysschemaarticles	Tracks schema-only articles
syssubscriptions	Contains a row for each subscription in the database; this table is stored in the publication database
systranschemas	Tracks schema changes in articles; this table is stored in both the publication and subscription databases

In the diagram for the system tables in peer-to-peer replication, there is a parent to child relationship between sysreplservers and syssubscriptions. The same relationship exists between MSpeer_lsns and MSpeer_request, and between MSpeer_lsns and MSsubscription_agents.

Besides the system tables in replication, peer-to-peer replication also adds the VID identity column of data type int in the Vendor table, which is used as an article in peer-to-peer replication. (The column name consists of the first initial of the table name plus ID.) Three stored procedures are also added in the database involved in the peer-to-peer replication. In this example for the BIOREPL server and the purchaseorder_repl database, the three procedures are sp_MSins_dboVendor, sp_MSdel_dboVendor, and sp_MSupd_dboVendor. Four database-level triggers are added on the purchaseorder_repl database: tr_MStran_alterschemaonly, tr_MStran_altertable, tr_MStran_altertrigger, and tr_MStran_alterview.

When you insert data in the Vendor table in the purchaseorder_repl database, the insert stored procedure is executed. As you can see in Figure 10-49, for each column in the table there is a corresponding parameter that is used to pass the insert value.

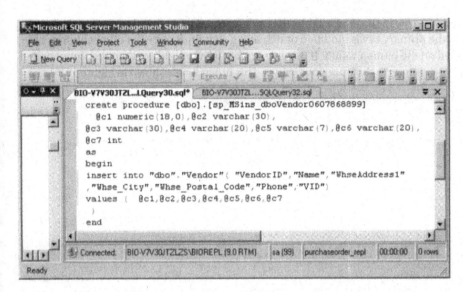

Figure 10-49. *The insert procedure executes when values are inserted in a peer-to-peer replication*

When the row is being deleted, the delete stored procedure is called; its purpose is to delete based on the primary key column of the Vendor table. If the @@rowcount global variable does not change (indicated by a @@rowcount variable value of 0), the row is not replicated to the other node, and an error message is sent, as shown in Figure 10-50.

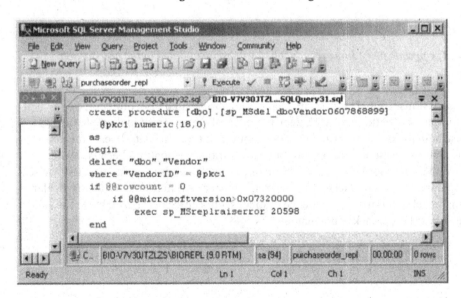

Figure 10-50. *The delete procedure executes when values are deleted*

If we update a row in the Vendor table, the update stored procedure is executed. It checks first whether the primary key is modified or not, and if so it finds out what other columns are updated based on the bitmap values. If the primary key is not modified, then the stored procedure resets the columns to their previous values. This procedure is shown in Figure 10-51.

```
create procedure [dbo].[sp_MSupd_dboVendor0607868899]
   @c1 numeric(18,0) = null,@c2 varchar(30) = null,
   @c3 varchar(30) = null,@c4 varchar(20) = null,
   @c5 varchar(7) = null,@c6 varchar(20) = null,@c7 int = null,@pkc1 numeric(18,0)
   ,@bitmap binary(1)
as
begin
if ( substring(@bitmap,1,1) & 1 = 1 )
begin
update "dbo"."Vendor" set
   "VendorID" = case substring(@bitmap,1,1) & 1 when 1 then @c1 else "VendorID" end
   ,"Name" = case substring(@bitmap,1,1) & 2 when 2 then @c2 else "Name" end
   ,"WhseAddress1" = case substring(@bitmap,1,1) & 4 when 4 then @c3 else "WhseAddress1" end
   ,"Whse_City" = case substring(@bitmap,1,1) & 8 when 8 then @c4 else "Whse_City" end
   ,"Whse_Postal_Code" = case substring(@bitmap,1,1) & 16 when 16 then @c5 else "Whse_Postal_Code" end
   ,"Phone" = case substring(@bitmap,1,1) & 32 when 32 then @c6 else "Phone" end
where "VendorID" = @pkc1
if @@rowcount = 0     if @@microsoftversion>0x07320000      exec sp_MSreplraiserror 20598
end
else
begin
update "dbo"."Vendor" set
   "Name" = case substring(@bitmap,1,1) & 2 when 2 then @c2 else "Name" end
   ,"WhseAddress1" = case substring(@bitmap,1,1) & 4 when 4 then @c3 else "WhseAddress1" end
   ,"Whse_City" = case substring(@bitmap,1,1) & 8 when 8 then @c4 else "Whse_City" end
   ,"Whse_Postal_Code" = case substring(@bitmap,1,1) & 16 when 16 then @c5 else "Whse_Postal_Code" end
   ,"Phone" = case substring(@bitmap,1,1) & 32 when 32 then @c6 else "Phone" end
where "VendorID" = @pkc1
if @@rowcount = 0     if @@microsoftversion>0x07320000      exec sp_MSreplraiserror 20598
end
end
```

Figure 10-51. *The update procedure executes when values are updated in the peer-to-peer replication*

In standard transactional replication, changes are propagated from one source to several destinations, but it is not the same with peer-to-peer replication. This topology also allows you to house both the publication and the subscription on the same database. In this topology, transactions can be sent from several sources to various destinations because all the peers receive all transactions that are sent from one node, otherwise they are rejected. These well-formed transactions are tracked by a marker (known as a watermark) for the particular publication; the marker is the last sequence number seen. The MSpeer_lsns table in the subscription database keeps track of the marker.

■**Note** For a detailed description of how the watermark is used to maintain transactional consistency in peer-to-peer replication, see "Well-Known Transactions in Data Replication," by Richard W. Tom, Kaushik Choudhury, and Qun Guo, http://www.freepatentsonline.com/20050165858.html.

I will now show how the messages are processed in one node before being sent to the other node. In order to do that, let's first insert two rows in the Vendor table in the purchase-order_repl database in the BIOREPL server instance, as shown in Figure 10-52.

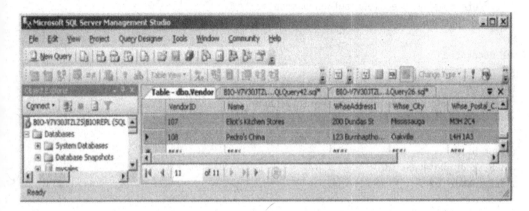

Figure 10-52. *Inserting values in the* Vendor *table in the BIOREPL node*

If we now look into the peer node, BIOREPL_PEER, we can see that the two rows have been added in the Vendor table, as shown in Figure 10-53.

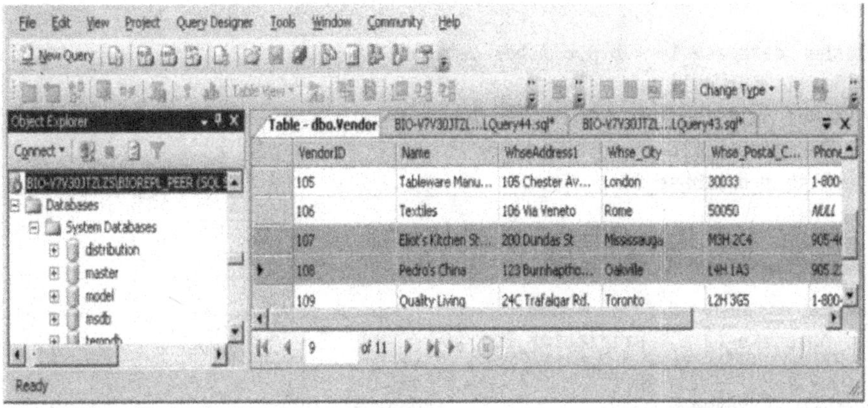

Figure 10-53. *Viewing the two rows that have been inserted in the* Vendor *table in the BIOREPL_PEER instance*

As I mentioned, a marker is used to tag commands in peer-to-peer replication. If you look into the distribution database, you will find that the originator_lsn column in the MSrepl_commands table and the publication_id and dbversion columns in the MSrepl_originators table contain values. If the publications were not enabled for peer-to-peer replication, these columns would be set to NULL to save storage. The originator_lsn column is the one that is used as the marker, and it is only used for peer-to-peer replication. We can view the commands that are tagged in peer-to-peer replication by executing the script shown in Listing 10-9.

Listing 10-9. *Viewing the Marker for Peer-to-Peer Replication*

```
/* Execute this on the distribution database. */
use distribution
go
set nocount on
go

/* Find the not null values for the originator_lsn,
 the publication_id, and the dbversion. */

select b.id,
a.publisher_database_id,
a.originator_lsn,

a.xact_seqno,b.publication_id,
b.srvname,

b.dbname,
b.dbversion
from MSrepl_commands a,MSrepl_originators b

where a.publisher_database_id = b.publisher_database_id and
a.originator_lsn is not null and
b.dbversion is not null and
b.publication_id is not null
order by a.publisher_database_id
go
```

The output for this script is as follows:

Id publisher_database_id	originator_lsn	
xact_seqno		
publication_id	srvname	dbname
dbversion		
3 7	0x00000356000001D00004	
0x0000064F00000097000D		
1	BIO-V7V3OJTZLZS\BIOREPL	purchaseorder_repl

```
278904166
3   7                          0x0000035700000280007
0x0000064F000000B00012
1                   BIO-V7V30JTZLZS\BIOREPL        purchaseorder_repl
278904166
4   7                          0x00000356000001D00004
0x0000064F00000097000D
1                   BIO-V7V30JTZLZS\BIOREPL_PEER  purchaseorder_repl
1838042866
4   7                          0x0000035700000280007
0x0000064F000000B00012
1                   BIO-V7V30JTZLZS\BIOREPL_PEER  purchaseorder_repl
1838042866
```

In the preceding output, you can see that the values for the Originator_lsn for the purchaseorder_repl database in both the servers is the same: 0x0000064F000000B00012. The commands held in the MSrepl_commands system table are used by the sp_MSget_repl_commands stored procedure based on the markers. In a peer-to-peer scenario, the commands are based on the log sequence number (LSN) for every publication included in the peer-to-peer topology. The markers used by sp_MSget_repl_commands are stored in the MScached_peer_lsns. Using the MScached_peer_lsns table, we can track the LSN in the log to see which commands will be delivered to the Subscriber server in a peer-to-peer topology. This is shown in Listing 10-10.

Listing 10-10. *Viewing the Marker Stored in the* MScached_peer_lsns *Table*

```
/* Execute on the distribution database. */
Use distribution
go

select agent_id,originator,originator_db,
originator_lsn, originator_db_version
from MScached_peer_lsns
go
```

The output is as follows:

```
Agent_id   originator                 originator_db
 originator_lsn            originator_db_version
46          BIO-V7V30JTZLZS\BIOREPL   purchaseorder_repl
 0x000004EE000001DE0004    278904166
```

The last transaction sequence number is made known to the subscribing server for each publication in the topology. Listing 10-11 shows how you can find the last transaction sequence number.

Listing 10-11. *Finding the Last Transaction Sequence Number*

```
/* Execute this on the distribution database. */
use distribution
go

/* Declare a variable to store the Publisher database id */

declare @publisherdbid int

/* Get the Publisher database id from the MSdistribution_agents
table. */

set @publisherdbid=
(select publisher_database_id
from msdistribution_agents

/* The name of the Publisher and the Subscriber database is
the same. */

where publisher_db=subscriber_db)

/* The maximum transaction sequence number is the
last sequence number. */

select max(xact_seqno) as lastseqno
from msrepl_commands
where publisher_database_id=@publisherdbid and command_id=1
go
```

This script first finds the publisher database ID from the MSdistribution_agents system table, and then gets the maximum transaction number from the MSrepl_commands system table for this publisher database ID. The maximum transaction number is the last sequence number. This is the output:

```
Lastseqno
0x0000064F000000B00012
```

You can see the last transaction sequence number (abbreviated in commands as lsns) in the previous output matches with the transaction sequence number displayed in bold in the output for Listing 10-9.

If you run the sp_browserreplcmds stored procedure on the distribution database, you will see that the transaction sequence number (xact_seqno) and the originator_lsn match with the output in Listing 10-9. The sp_MSins_dboVendor stored procedure is executed to transfer the inserted values. When you execute the sp_browserreplcmds stored procedure, you will see that the sp_MSins_dboVendor stored procedure is called under the Command column. This is shown in Figure 10-54.

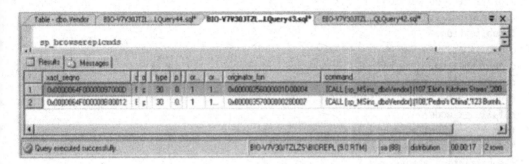

Figure 10-54. *Output of the* sp_browserreplcmds *stored procedure*

Now that we know that the messages are ready to be sent to the other peer, let's look at where the messages are being stored. The system tables of interest are MSpeer_lsns, MSpeer_request, and MSsubscription_agents.

The MSpeer_lsns table keeps a record of each transaction that is being sent to the subscription in peer-to-peer replication. The last transaction sequence number seen (lsns) in this table should match with the one in MScached_peer_lsns in the distribution database.

The MSpeer_request table tracks the status of the publication for the peer-to-peer node. This is shown in Listing 10-12.

Listing 10-12. *Tracking the Status of the Transactions for the Peer Node, BIOREPL_PEER*

```
/*Execute this on purchaseorder_repl on the BIOREPL_PEER node. */
use purchaseorder_repl
go

/* First check whether the stored procedure exists. */

IF OBJECT_ID ( 'usp_GetPeertoPeerList', 'P' ) IS NOT NULL
    DROP PROCEDURE usp_GetPeertoPeerList;
go
set nocount on
go
```

```
/*Create the stored procedure */

create procedure usp_GetPeertoPeerResponseList
as
select a.originator,
a.originator_db,
a.originator_db_version,
a.originator_lsn,
b.publication,
c.publisher,
c.publisher_db,
c.subscription_type,
c.update_mode,
c.failover_mode
from MSpeer_lsns as a,
MSpeer_request as b,
MSsubscription_agents as c
where a.id=b.id and a.id=c.id
order by originator_lsn
go
```

You need to use the exec `usp_GetPeertoPeerResponseList` stored procedure in order to see the output of the preceding script, shown here:

```
Originator                    originator_db        originator_db_version
 originator_lsn               publication
 publisher                    publisher_db
 subscription_type  update_mode  failover_mode
BIV7V30JTZLZS\BIOREPL_PEER   purchaseorder_repl   1838042866
 0x00                         pub_purchaseorderrepl_peer
 BIO-V7V30JTZLZS\BIOREPL     purchaseorder_repl
 0              0              0
```

Tip You can also execute the `sp_helppeerresponses` or `sp_helppeerrequests` stored procedure to get a return on all the responses or requests by a node involved in peer-to-peer replication.

Standard Transactional Publication

In the preceding sections, I discussed transactional replication with updating subscriptions and with peer-to-peer replication. In this section, I will discuss transactional replication with standard publication.

The Publication

The system tables in standard publication for transactional replication on the publication database are shown in Figures 10-55 through 10-57.

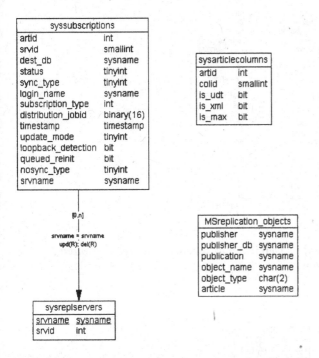

Figure 10-55. *The* syssubscriptions, sysarticlecolumns, sysreplservers, *and* MSreplication_ objects *system tables used in standard publication for transactional replication*

sysschemaarticles	
artid	int
creation_script	nvarchar(255)
description	nvarchar(255)
dest_object	sysname
name	sysname
objid	int
pubid	int
pre_creation_cmd	tinyint
status	int
type	tinyint
schema_option	binary(8)
dest_owner	sysname

syspublications	
description	nvarchar(255)
name	sysname
pubid	int
repl_freq	tinyint
status	tinyint
sync_method	tinyint
snapshot_jobid	binary(16)
independent_agent	bit
immediate_sync	bit
enabled_for_internet	bit
allow_push	bit
allow_pull	bit
allow_anonymous	bit
immediate_sync_ready	bit
allow_sync_tran	bit
autogen_sync_procs	bit
retention	int
allow_queued_tran	bit
snapshot_in_defaultfolder	bit
alt_snapshot_folder	nvarchar(255)
pre_snapshot_script	nvarchar(255)
post_snapshot_script	nvarchar(255)
compress_snapshot	bit
ftp_address	sysname
ftp_port	int
ftp_subdirectory	nvarchar(255)
ftp_login	sysname
ftp_password	nvarchar(524)
allow_dts	bit
allow_subscription_copy	bit
centralized_conflicts	bit
conflict_retention	int
conflict_policy	int
queue_type	int
ad_guidname	sysname
backward_comp_level	int
allow_initialize_from_backup	bit
min_autonosync_lsn	binary(10)
replicate_ddl	int
options	int

Figure 10-56. *The* sysschemaarticles *and* syspublications *system tables used in standard publication for transactional replication*

sysarticles	
artid	int
creation_script	nvarchar(255)
del_cmd	nvarchar(255)
description	nvarchar(255)
dest_table	sysname
filter	int
filter_clause	nvarchar(16)
ins_cmd	nvarchar(255)
name	sysname
objid	int
pubid	int
pre_creation_cmd	tinyint
status	tinyint
sync_objid	int
type	tinyint
upd_cmd	nvarchar(255)
schema_option	binary(8)
dest_owner	sysname
ins_scripting_proc	int
del_scripting_proc	int
upd_scripting_proc	int
custom_script	nvarchar(2048)
fire_triggers_on_snapshot	bit

systranschemas	
tabid	int
startlsn	binary(10)
endlsn	binary(10)
typeid	int

MSpub_identity_range	
objid	int
range	nvarchar(19)
pub_range	nvarchar(19)
current_pub_range	nvarchar(19)
threshold	int
last_seed	nvarchar(19)

Figure 10-57. *The* sysarticles, systranschemas, *and* MSpub_identity_range *system tables used in standard publication for transactional replication*

The syspublications system table stores the names of the publications, whether DDL changes can be replicated for transactional replication (a value of 1 for the replicate_ddl column means that DDL changes can be replicated); the syssubscriptions system table stores the names of the destination tables and the commands that are issued for inserts, deletes, and updates. The sysarticles system table records information on the articles that are being replicated.

Listing 10-13 shows how you can get the names of the subscription databases for the standard publication that allow push subscription.

Listing 10-13. *Getting the Names of Subscribing Databases for the Standard Publication*

```
/*Execute this on the mysales_copy publication database on the BIOREPL_PEER node*/
use mysales_copy
go

/* First check whether the stored procedure exists. */

IF OBJECT_ID ( 'usp_GetSubForStdPublication', 'P' ) IS NOT NULL
    DROP PROCEDURE usp_GetSubForStdPublication;
go
set nocount on
go

/*Create the stored procedure. */

create procedure usp_GetSubForStdPublication
as
select a.artid,b.dest_db,
b.subscription_type,b.timestamp,
b.srvname,c.pubid,
c.name,c.replicate_ddl
from syspublications c,
syssubscriptions b,
sysarticles a
where b.dest_db<>'virtual'and b.subscription_type=0
and a.artid=b.artid
and a.del_cmd <>'vcall%'and a.upd_cmd<>'vcall%' and
a.ins_cmd <>'vcall%'
and c.name='pub_mysales_copy_myinventory'
go
```

This script does not retrieve any updatable subscriptions. The CALL syntax used for executing stored procedures for updatable subscriptions is VCALL. In the preceding script, I have eliminated the retrieval of all updatable subscriptions by specifying that del_cmd, ins_cmd, and upd_cmd not use the VCALL command syntax. However, it does find out whether the pub_mysales_copy_myinventory publication supports schema changes (replicate_ddl) for push subscriptions (subscription_type).

Note Chapter 9 discusses the T-SQL parameters used in transactional replication.

If you execute the stored procedure created in Listing 10-13 on the publication database, mysales_copy, as follows, you can see the output in Figure 10-58.

```
Execute usp_GetSubForStdPublication
```

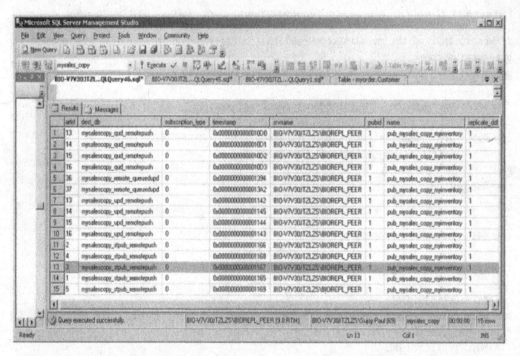

Figure 10-58. *Output of Listing 10-13*

DYNAMIC MANAGEMENT VIEWS

While discussing the internals of replication, be it snapshot or transactional, I have showed the workings of replication using the system tables. However, with SQL Server 2005, new features have been added, one of which is the dynamic management views (DMV). There are four DMV that are used for replication: sys.dm_repl_articles, sys.dm_repl_schemas, sys.dm_repl_traninfo, and sys.dm_repl_tranhash.

DMV provide information that can either be server-scoped or database-scoped and it can be used to monitor the performance of the system or diagnose possible errors. The views are found in all databases listed under the System Views object in the Object Explorer of the SSMS, and their names are all prefixed with the sys schema. There are twelve types of DMV. They are: Common Language Runtime, Database Mirroring, Database, Execution, Full-Text Search, I/O, Query Notifications, Replication, Service Broker, and SQL Operating System–Related Dynamic Management Views.

Now let's find out if any of the articles in the publication have been used for horizontal partitioning. Listing 10-14 shows you how.

Listing 10-14. *Articles in Horizontal Partitioning*

```
/* Execute this on the publication database. */
use mysales_copy
go

/* First check whether the stored procedure exists. */

IF OBJECT_ID ( 'usp_GetArticleUsedHorizontalPartition', 'P' ) IS NOT NULL
    DROP PROCEDURE usp_GetArticleUsedHorizontalPartition;
go
set nocount on
go

/*Create the stored procedure. */

create procedure usp_GetArticleUsedHorizontalPartition
as

select a.artid,
b.dest_db,
b.subscription_type,

b.timestamp,
b.srvname,c.pubid,
c.name,c.replicate_ddl

into dbo.syspubsubart
from syspublications c,
syssubscriptions b, sysarticles a

where b.dest_db<>'virtual'and b.subscription_type=0
and a.artid=b.artid
and a.del_cmd<>'vcall%'and a.upd_cmd<>'vcall%'
and a.ins_cmd<>'vcall%'
and c.name='pub_mysales_copy_myinventory'
go

/*Now select from the syspubsubart table */

select * from dbo.syspubsubart
go
```

```
/* Find the articles involved in horizontal partitioning */
select a.artid,
a.del_cmd,
a.ins_cmd,
a.upd_cmd,
a.dest_table,
a.filter_clause,
a.dest_owner,a.type,
b.dest_db,b.name
from sysarticles a, dbo.syspubsubart b
where a.artid=b.artid and
a.pubid=b.pubid and
a.filter<>0
go
```

Tip If you wanted to return all articles that are not filtered, set the `filter` column to 0.

This script is an extension of the code in Listing 10-13, and it creates a new table using the SELECT INTO statement and then retrieves the del_cmd, ins_cmd, and upd_cmd columns from the sysarticles table. To find out which articles have been involved in horizontal partitioning, we need to find out what the filter_clause contains. The output of this script is shown in Figure 10-59.

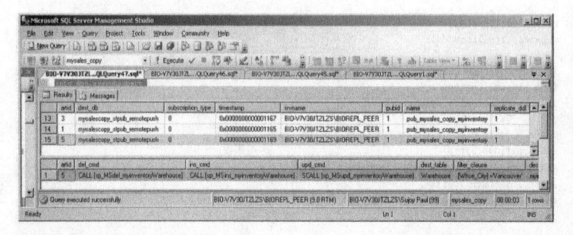

Figure 10-59. *Output of the script in Listing 10-14*

Notice in Figure 10-59 that stored procedures are used to transport insert, update, and delete commands. I have already shown you how they work while discussing peer-to-peer replication—refer to the "Peer-to-Peer Replication" section if you need to review.

As with the other transactional replication types discussed previously, I will show you how the trail of transactions is replicated as they move from the Publisher server to the Subscriber server. To this end, I inserted four rows into the myorder.Stock table in the mysales_copy database, which is being used as a publication database for the pub_mysales_copy_myinventory publication. I then checked to see that the data was replicated to the mysalescopy_std_remotepush subscription database. This is shown in Listing 10-15.

Listing 10-15. *Inserting Data into the* myorder.Stock *Table in the Publication Database*

```
/* Execute this on the mysales_copy publication database
 on the BIOREPL_PEER instance. */

Use mysales_copy
Go

/* Insert the values. */

insert into
myorder.Stock(StockId,Whse,QtyOnHand,QtyOnOrd,QtyAvail,ItemNum)
values(1026,31,25,5000,25,1026)
insert into
 myorder.Stock(StockId,Whse,QtyOnHand,QtyOnOrd,QtyAvail,ItemNum)
values(1027,31,1000,1700,100,1030)
insert into
 myorder.Stock(StockId,Whse,QtyOnHand,QtyOnOrd,QtyAvail,ItemNum)
values(1028,31,400,6000,150,1031)
insert into
myorder.Stock(StockId,Whse,QtyOnHand,QtyOnOrd,QtyAvail,ItemNum)
values(1029,21,1000,4000,3000,1032)

go

/*Now check to see that the data has been replicated
in the mysalescopy_std_remotepush subscription database */

use mysalescopy_std_remotepush
go

select stockid, Whse,QtyOnHand,QtyOnOrd,QtyAvail,ItemNum
from myorder.Stock
go
```

The Log Reader Agent picks up the transactions marked for replication from the transaction log, as shown in Figure 10-60.

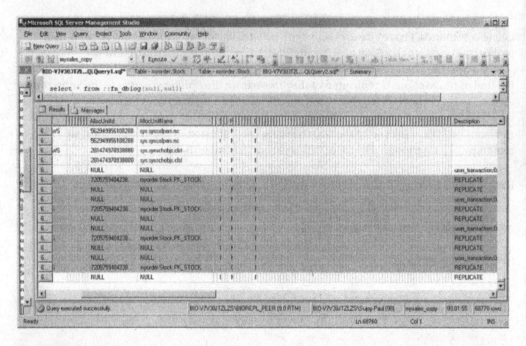

Figure 10-60. *The four values inserted in the* myorder.Stock *table are marked for replication in the transaction log*

The Log Reader Agent uses the sp_replcmds stored procedure to send in batches the transactions marked for replication from the publication database's transaction log to the distribution database.

■**Caution** Ensure that there is only one connection to the Publisher server when running the sp_replcmds stored procedure; otherwise stop the Log Reader Agent and restart it. Also, use this procedure for troubleshooting purposes only.

Once the transactions are committed in the distribution database, the Log Reader Agent uses the sp_repldone stored procedure to mark the completion of replication in the transaction log. The transactions are then ready to be purged.

Note Only committed transactions are forwarded to the distribution database.

Any transactions still waiting to be replicated are not purged. These transactions are written to both the MSrepl_commands and the MSrepl_transactions system tables in the distribution database. The insert operations are performed not as a set but singly.

Now suppose we want to update one of the rows that we inserted in Listing 10-15. Let's say we need to change the StockId column value from 1029 to 1030, and then we want to check whether the Log Reader Agent reads the updated transaction marked for replication and forwards it to the distribution database.

Once the column value is changed, we can run the DBCC Opentran command and check the output, as shown here:

```
Transaction information for database 'mysales_copy'.

Replicated Transaction Information:
        Oldest distributed LSN    : (165:341:3)
        Oldest non-distributed LSN : (165:348:1)
DBCC execution completed. If DBCC printed error messages,
 contact your system administrator.
```

You can see that the oldest non-distributed LSN is 165:348:1, while the oldest distributed LSN is 165:341:3. This means the replicated transaction is still waiting to be forwarded to the distribution database.

In this case, I checked to see if the Log Reader Agent was running in the first place, and it wasn't. I started the agent and then ran the DBCC Opentran command again, and the output is different, as you can see here:

```
Transaction information for database 'mysales_copy'.

Replicated Transaction Information:
        Oldest distributed LSN    : (165:348:7)
        Oldest non-distributed LSN : (0:0:0)
DBCC execution completed. If DBCC printed error
messages, contact your system administrator.
```

Now we can check the subscribing database to ensure that the data has been updated, as shown in Figure 10-61.

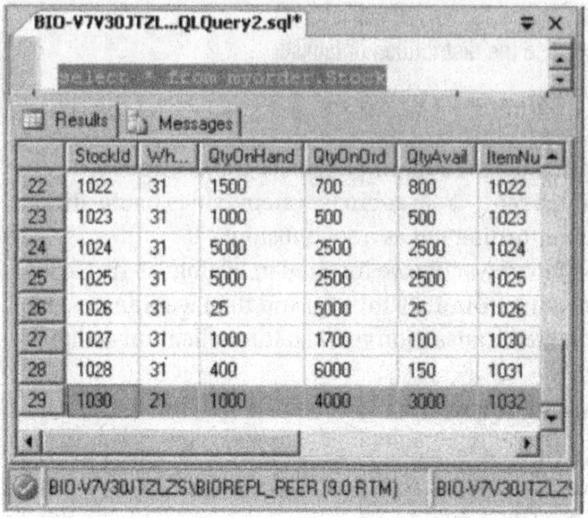

Figure 10-61. *Updated value on the subscription database*

If you now look into the log, you will see that the update is not a singleton. A *singleton update* is one where the update operation is conducted in a UPDATE statement. In fact, this one consists of a delete and an insert statement, as shown in Figure 10-62. This is called a *deferred update*.

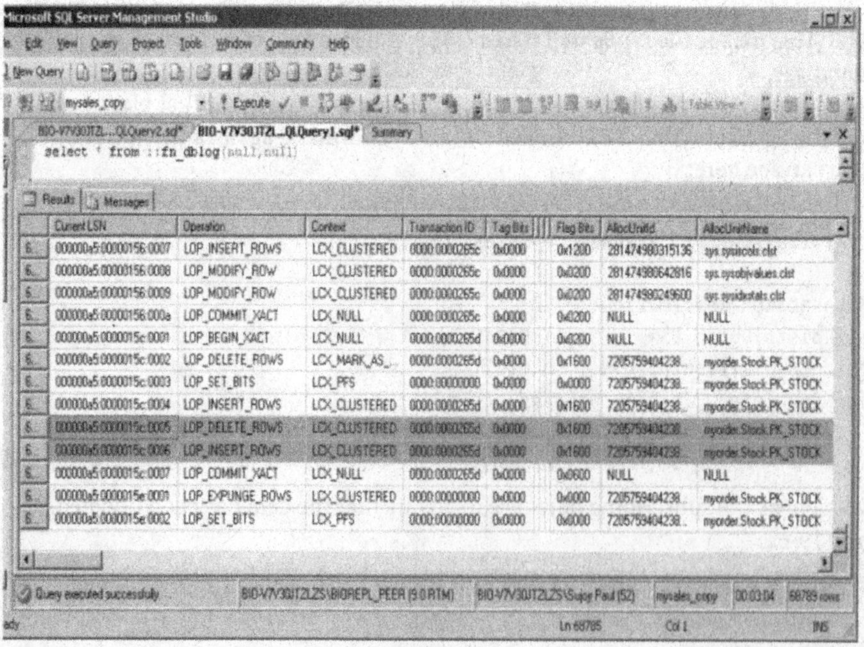

Figure 10-62. *Transaction log showing the deletion and the insertion of the updated row*

You can, however, make a deferred update into a singleton update by turning on the trace flag. This is accomplished by using the DBCC traceon (8207,-1) command on the publication database. Any new update made will then be replicated as a singleton update. So if you have a large set of updated data that needs to be replicated, you can use the singleton update to improve the performance.

However, if you are replicating multiple updates, they will still be replicated as DELETE or INSERT pairs. To set the trace flag on the server level, select the SQL Server Configuration Manager and stop the SQL Server service. Right-click on the SQL Server service in the Configuration Manager, and select Properties. Select the Advanced tab in the SQL Server Properties window and for the Startup Parameters option specify -T8207 at the end of the settings, as shown in Figure 10-63. Then restart the SQL Server service.

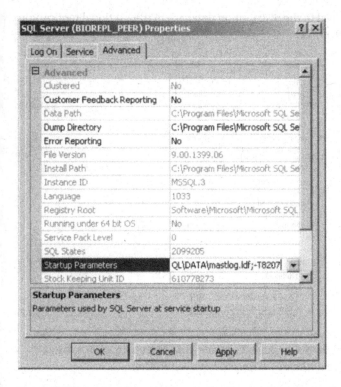

Figure 10-63. *Setting the trace flag on the Startup Parameters for the server*

■**Caution** Do not use this trace flag if you are using updating subscriptions, if a primary key can be updated on the subscription server, or if an update can be made on a unique constraint on the subscribing server. (Refer to http://support.microsoft.com/kb/q302341 for more information.)

The Distribution Database

The Log Reader Agent acts as the facilitator in forwarding and storing messages from the publication to the distribution database. This agent executes the dbo.sp_MSadd_replcommands stored procedure to read the records logged in the publication database's transaction log and insert them first in the MSrepl_transactions system table in the following columns: publisher_database_id, xact_id, xact_seqno, and entry_time. It then records the replicated commands in the MSrepl_commands system table after it checks for the publisher_database_id, srvname, and dbname columns in the MSrepl_originators system table.

The Distribution Agent then invokes the sys.sp_MSget_repl_commands stored procedure to pick up the messages from the MSrepl_commands table, and sends it to the appropriate subscribing servers.

The system views and tables used in the distribution database in transactional replication are shown in Figures 10-64 through 10-71.

sysextendedarticlesview	
artid	int
creation_script	nvarchar(255)
del_cmd	nvarchar(255)
description	nvarchar(255)
dest_table	sysname
filter	int
filter_clause	nvarchar(16)
ins_cmd	nvarchar(255)
name	sysname
objid	int
pubid	int
pre_creation_cmd	tinyint
status	int
sync_objid	int
type	tinyint
upd_cmd	nvarchar(255)
schema_option	binary(8)
dest_owner	sysname
ins_scripting_proc	int
del_scripting_proc	int
upd_scripting_proc	int
custom_script	nvarchar(2048)
fire_triggers_on_snapshot	int

syssubscriptions	
artid	int
srvid	smallint
dest_db	sysname
status	tinyint
sync_type	tinyint
login_name	sysname
subscription_type	int
distribution_jobid	binary(16)
timestamp	timestamp
update_mode	tinyint
loopback_detection	bit
queued_reinit	bit
nosync_type	tinyint
srvname	sysname

MSdistribution_status	
article_id	int
agent_id	int
UndelivCmdsInDistDB	int
DelivCmdsInDistDB	int

Figure 10-64. *The* sysextendedarticlesview, syssubscriptions, *and* MSdistribution_status *system views used in the distribution database in transactional replication*

sysarticlecolumns	
artid	int
colid	int
is_udt	int
is_xml	int
is_max	int

syspublications	
description	nvarchar(255)
name	sysname
pubid	int
repl_freq	tinyint
status	tinyint
sync_method	tinyint
snapshot_jobid	binary(16)
independent_agent	bit
immediate_sync	bit
enabled_for_internet	bit
allow_push	bit
allow_pull	bit
allow_anonymous	bit
immediate_sync_ready	bit
allow_sync_tran	bit
autogen_sync_procs	bit
retention	int
allow_queued_tran	bit
snapshot_in_defaultfolder	bit
alt_snapshot_folder	nvarchar(510)
pre_snapshot_script	nvarchar(510)
post_snapshot_script	nvarchar(510)
compress_snapshot	bit
ftp_address	sysname
ftp_port	int
ftp_subdirectory	nvarchar(510)
ftp_login	nvarchar(256)
ftp_password	nvarchar(1048)
allow_dts	bit
allow_subscription_copy	bit
centralized_conflicts	bit
conflict_retention	int
conflict_policy	int
queue_type	int
ad_guidname	sysname
backward_comp_level	int
allow_initialize_from_backup	bit
min_autonosync_lsn	binary(1)
replicate_ddl	int
options	int

sysarticles	
artid	int
creation_script	nvarchar(255)
del_cmd	nvarchar(255)
description	nvarchar(255)
dest_table	sysname
filter	int
filter_clause	nvarchar(16)
ins_cmd	nvarchar(255)
name	sysname
objid	int
pubid	smallint
pre_creation_cmd	tinyint
status	tinyint
sync_objid	int
type	tinyint
upd_cmd	nvarchar(255)
schema_option	binary(8)
dest_owner	sysname
ins_scripting_proc	int
del_scripting_proc	int
upd_scripting_proc	int
custom_script	nvarchar(2048)
fire_triggers_on_snapshot	bit

Figure 10-65. *The* sysarticles, sysarticlecolumns, *and* syspublications *system tables used in the distribution database in transactional replication*

MSpublication_access	
publication_id	int
login	sysname
sid	varbinary(85)

MSrepl_commands	
publisher_database_id	int
xact_seqno	varbinary(16)
type	int
article_id	int
originator_id	int
command_id	int
partial_command	bit
command	varbinary(1024)
hashkey	int
originator_lsn	varbinary(16)

MSpublications	
publisher_id	smallint
publisher_db	sysname
publication	sysname
publication_id	int
publication_type	int
thirdparty_flag	bit
independent_agent	bit
immediate_sync	bit
allow_push	bit
allow_pull	bit
allow_anonymous	bit
description	uniqueidentifier
vendor_name	uniqueidentifier
retention	int
sync_method	int
allow_subscription_copy	bit
thirdparty_options	int
allow_queued_tran	bit
options	int
retention_period_unit	tinyint

MSsnapshot_agents	
id	int
name	uniqueidentifier
publisher_id	smallint
publisher_db	sysname
publication	sysname
publication_type	int
local_job	bit
job_id	binary(16)
profile_id	int
dynamic_filter_login	sysname
dynamic_filter_hostname	sysname
publisher_security_mode	int
publisher_login	sysname
publisher_password	uniqueidentifier
job_step_uid	uniqueidentifier

Figure 10-66. *The* MSpublication_access, MSrepl_commands, MSpublications, *and* MSsnapshot_agents *system tables used in the distribution database for transactional replication*

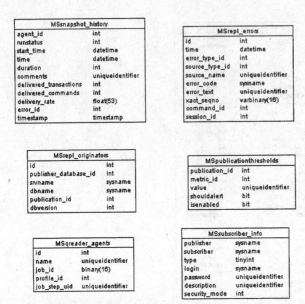

Figure 10-67. *The* MSsnapshot_history, MSrepl_errors, MSrepl_originators, MSpublicationthresholds, MSqreader_agents, *and* MSsubscriber_info *system tables used in the distribution database for transactional replication*

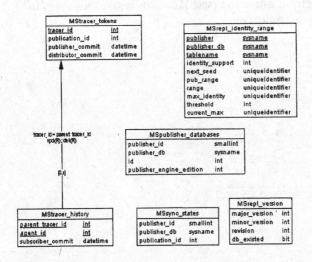

Figure 10-68. *The* MStracer_tokens, MSrepl_identity_range, MSpublisher_databases, MStracer_history, MSsync_states, *and* MSrepl_version *system tables used in the distribution database for transactional replication*

MSqreader_history	
agent_id	int
publication_id	int
runstatus	int
start_time	datetime
time	datetime
duration	int
comments	uniqueidentifier
transaction_id	uniqueidentifier
transaction_status	int
transactions_processed	int
commands_processed	int
delivery_rate	float(53)
transaction_rate	float(53)
subscriber	sysname
subscriberdb	sysname
error_id	int
timestamp	timestamp

MSrepl_transactions	
publisher_database_id	int
xact_id	varbinary(16)
xact_seqno	varbinary(16)
entry_time	datetime

sysschemaarticles	
artid	int
creation_script	uniqueidentifier
description	uniqueidentifier
dest_object	sysname
name	sysname
objid	int
pubid	int
pre_creation_cmd	tinyint
status	int
type	tinyint
schema_option	binary(8)
dest_owner	sysname

MSrepl_backup_lsns	
publisher_database_id	int
valid_xact_id	varbinary(16)
valid_xact_seqno	varbinary(16)
next_xact_id	varbinary(16)
next_xact_seqno	varbinary(16)

MSsubscriber_schedule	
publisher	sysname
subscriber	sysname
agent_type	smallint
frequency_type	int
frequency_interval	int
frequency_relative_interval	int
frequency_recurrence_factor	int
frequency_subday	int
frequency_subday_interval	int
active_start_time_of_day	int
active_end_time_of_day	int
active_start_date	int
active_end_date	int

MSsubscriptions	
publisher_database_id	int
publisher_id	smallint
publisher_db	sysname
publication_id	int
article_id	int
subscriber_id	smallint
subscriber_db	sysname
subscription_type	int
sync_type	tinyint
status	tinyint
subscription_seqno	varbinary(16)
snapshot_seqno_flag	bit
independent_agent	bit
subscription_time	datetime
loopback_detection	bit
agent_id	int
update_mode	tinyint
publisher_seqno	varbinary(16)
ss_cplt_seqno	varbinary(16)

Figure 10-69. *The* MSqreader_history, MSrepl_transactions, sysschemaarticles, MSrepl_backup_lsns, MSsubscriptions, *and* MSsubscriber_schedule *system tables used in the distribution database for transactional replication*

MSlogreader_history	
agent_id	int
runstatus	int
start_time	datetime
time	datetime
duration	int
comments	nvarchar(4000)
xact_seqno	varbinary(16)
delivery_time	int
delivered_transactions	int
delivered_commands	int
average_commands	int
delivery_rate	float(53)
delivery_latency	int
error_id	int
timestamp	timestamp

MSlogreader_agents	
id	int
name	nvarchar(100)
publisher_id	smallint
publisher_db	sysname
publication	sysname
local_job	bit
job_id	binary(16)
profile_id	int
publisher_security_mode	smallint
publisher_login	sysname
publisher_password	nvarchar(524)
job_step_uid	nvarchar(16)

MSreplication_monitordata	
lastrefresh	datetime
computetime	int
publication_id	int
publisher	sysname
publisher_srvid	int
publisher_db	sysname
publication	sysname
publication_type	int
agent_type	int
agent_id	int
agent_name	sysname
job_id	uniqueidentifier
status	int
isagentrunningnow	bit
warning	int
last_distsync	datetime
agentstoptime	datetime
distdb	sysname
retention	int
time_stamp	datetime
worst_latency	int
best_latency	int
avg_latency	int
cur_latency	int
worst_runspeedPerf	int
best_runspeedPerf	int
average_runspeedPerf	int
mergePerformance	int
mergelatestsessionrunduration	int
mergelatestsessionrunspeed	float(53)
mergelatestsessionconnectiontype	int
retention_period_unit	tinyint

MScached_peer_lsns	
agent_id	int
originator	sysname
originator_db	sysname
originator_publication_id	int
originator_db_version	int
originator_lsn	varbinary(16)

Figure 10-70. *The* MSlogreader_history, MSreplication_monitordata, MSlogreader_agents, *and* MScached_peer_lsns *system tables used in the distribution database for transactional replication*

MSdistribution_agents	
id	int
name	nvarchar(100)
publisher_database_id	int
publisher_id	smallint
publisher_db	sysname
publication	sysname
subscriber_id	smallint
subscriber_db	sysname
subscription_type	int
local_job	bit
job_id	binary(16)
subscription_guid	binary(16)
profile_id	int
anonymous_subid	nvarchar(16)
subscriber_name	sysname
virtual_agent_id	int
anonymous_agent_id	int
creation_date	datetime
queue_id	sysname
queue_status	int
offload_enabled	bit
offload_server	sysname
dts_package_name	sysname
dts_package_password	nvarchar(524)
dts_package_location	int
sid	varbinary(85)
queue_server	sysname
subscriber_security_mode	smallint
subscriber_login	sysname
subscriber_password	nvarchar(524)
reset_partial_snapshot_progress	bit
job_step_uid	nvarchar(16)
subscriptionstreams	tinyint
subscriber_type	tinyint
subscriber_provider	sysname
subscriber_datasrc	nvarchar(4000)
subscriber_location	nvarchar(4000)
subscriber_provider_string	nvarchar(4000)
subscriber_catalog	sysname

MSdistribution_history	
agent_id	int
runstatus	int
start_time	datetime
time	datetime
duration	int
comments	nvarchar
xact_seqno	varbinary(16)
current_delivery_rate	float(53)
current_delivery_latency	int
delivered_transactions	int
delivered_commands	int
average_commands	int
delivery_rate	float(53)
delivery_latency	int
total_delivered_commands	int
error_id	int
updateable_row	bit
timestamp	timestamp

MSarticles	
publisher_id	smallint
publisher_db	sysname
publication_id	int
article	sysname
article_id	int
destination_object	sysname
source_owner	sysname
source_object	sysname
description	nvarchar(255)
destination_owner	sysname

Figure 10-71. *The* MSdistribution_history, MSdistribution_agents, *and* MSarticles *system tables used in the distribution database for transactional replication*

Table 10-3 lists the functions of the system views in the distribution database, and Table 10-4 lists the functions of the system tables in the distribution database that are involved in transactional replication.

Note A syspublications system table is stored in the publication database, while a syspublications system view is stored in the distribution database. Similarly the syssubscriptions system table is stored in the publication database, while the syssubscriptions system view is stored in the distribution database.

Table 10-3. *Information Provided by the Functions to Each System View in the Distribution Database*

View Name	Information Type
sys.syspublications	Information about publication
sys.syssubscriptions	Information about subscriptions
sys.sysarticles	Information about articles
sys.sysarticlecolumns	Information about the columns in the articles
sys.sysextendedarticlesview	Information about published articles
sys.MSdistribution_status	Information on the status commands

Table 10-4. *The Functions of the System Tables in the Distribution Database*

System Table	Description
MSarticles	Contains a row for each replicated article
MScached_peer_lsns	Used in peer-to-peer replication; keeps track of the LSN in the transaction log for the commands that need to be sent to the Subscriber server
MSdistribution_agents	Stores a row for each Distribution Agent running on the local Distributor server
MSdistribution_history	Keeps a record of the history data for the Distribution Agent running on the local Distributor server
MSlogreader_agents	Keeps a record for each row of the Log Reader Agent running on the local Distributor server
MSlogreader_history	Keeps a record of the history of the Log Reader Agent running on the local Distributor server
MSpublication_access	Contains a row for each SQL Server login that has access to the publication of a Publisher server
MSpublications	Stores information for each publication that is replicated by any Publisher server
MSpublicationthresholds	Monitors the replication performance metrics with each row containing the threshold value
MSpublisher_databases	Contains a row for each database on the Publisher server that is serviced by the local Distributor server
MSqreader_agents	Keeps a record for each row of the Queue Reader Agent running on the local Distributor server
MSqreader_history	Keeps a record of the history of the Queue Reader Agent running on the local Distributor server

System Table	Description
MSrepl_backup_lsns	Stores the LSN of the "sync with backup" option for the distribution database
MSrepl_commands	Stores the replicated commands
MSrepl_errors	Contains information on the failures of Distribution and Merge Agents
MSrepl_identity_range	Contains information on the identity range management support
MSrepl_originators	Contains information on the origin of transactions for each updatable Subscriber server
MSrepl_transactions	Contains information for each replicated transaction
MSrepl_version	Contains information about the current version of the installation of replication
MSreplication_monitordata	Contains the cached data of the Replication Monitor with each row containing information on the subscription that is monitored
MSsnapshot_agents	Keeps a record for each row of the Snapshot Agent running on the local Distributor server
MSsnapshot_history	Keeps a record of the history of the Snapshot Agent running on the local Distributor server
MSsubscriber_info	Has been deprecated. Contains information for each Publisher/Subscriber pair that uses push subscription
MSsubscriber_schedule	Has been deprecated. Contains information on the default synchronization schedules for merge and transactional replication for each Publisher/Subscriber pair
MSsubscriptions	Contains information on each article that is in a subscription serviced by the local Distributor server
MSsync_states	Keeps track of those publications that are in concurrent snapshot mode
MStracer_history	Contains information on the tracer tokens received by the Subscriber server
MStracer_tokens	Contains information on the tracer tokens inserted in a publication
Sysschemaarticles	Keeps track of the schema-only articles for snapshot and transactional replication

The transactions are retained in both the MSrepl_commands and MSrepl_transactions tables for a period of up to 72 hours, by default, as shown in Figure 10-72. This means any transactions that have not been delivered to the subscriptions by that time will be cleaned up by the Distribution clean-up job, and the subscriptions will have to be reinitialized.

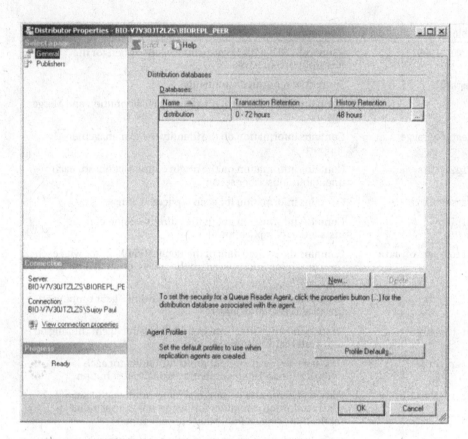

Figure 10-72. *Viewing the transaction and history retention periods*

The publication retention period is 336 hours, by default, and the subscriptions will be deactivated by the Expired subscription clean up job on the publishing server after that time. After the subscriptions are reactivated, the retention period will have to be recreated and reinitialized.

The history of the commands and the data is stored in the history tables for each of the agents, namely MSdistribution_history, MSlogreader_history, MSqreader_history (for publication with queued updates), and MSsnapshot_history. As you can see in Figure 10-72, they are stored for 48 hours by default.

Tip For long weekends and holidays, you might want to increase this period.

The MSrepl_commands table contains information regarding the location of the snapshot of the schema, and the bcp files, and other pre- or post-condition scripts. The MSrepl_transactions table contains commands that are waiting to be synchronized to the subscribing server.

The MSpublications system table contains one row for each publication that is replicated by the Publisher server. Listing 10-16 shows how rows are replicated.

Listing 10-16. *Replicating Rows from the Publication Database*

```
/* Execute this on the distribution database. */

Use distribution
Go


/* Select the id of the row, the push subscription values. */
/* Ensure that the sync_method is used for transactional replication */

select a.id,
b.allow_push,
b.publisher_db,

b.sync_method,
b.description
from MSpublications b,MSpublisher_databases a

where a.publisher_id=b.publisher_id
and b.publication_type=0
and b.publication ='pub_mysales_copy_myinventory'
order by a.id
go
```

The output of this listing is shown in Figure 10-73.

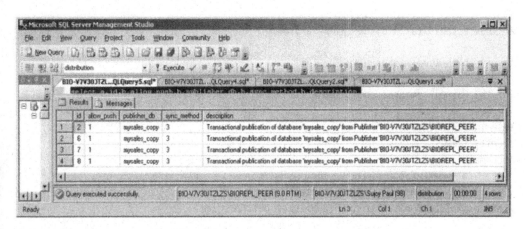

Figure 10-73. *The output of Listing 10-16*

You can see in the figure that mysales_copy is the database that is used for the pub_
mysales_copy_myinventory publication, and that the publication supports push subscription,
which is what I have configured for. The sync_method column returns a value of 3, which

means that concurrent snapshot processing is being used for the initial synchronization. The id column contains the identity of the row that is being replicated. In this case, four rows are being replicated for this publication. The description column validates the return of the sync_method column.

Next, let's see what transactions are being entered in the MSrepl_transactions and MSrepl_commands tables in the distribution database and that will be processed by the Distribution Agent. The script in Listing 10-17 retrieves the transaction sequence number and the date on which the entry was made in the distribution database. It also retrieves the last transaction sequence number.

Listing 10-17. *Retrieving the Transaction Sequence Number and the Date of Entry in the Distribution Database*

```
/*Execute this on the distribution database. */

Use distribution
Go

/* Create a table variable to hold the data. */

declare @transactionentry table
(xactseqno varbinary(16),
entrytime datetime,
command varbinary(1024)
)

/* Insert the data into the table variable. */

insert into @transactionentry
/* Select  transaction sequence numbers for the same publisher_database_id
For the MSrepl_commands and MSrepl_transactions system tables */

select b.xact_seqno,
b.entry_time,
a.command

from MSrepl_commands a, MSrepl_transactions b
where a.publisher_database_id=b.publisher_database_id

/* Now check the data. */
select * from @transactionentry

/*Now check the last transaction number. */

select max(xactseqno) as lastseqno from @transactionentry
go
```

The command column displays the command that was executed for the transaction in binary format. The output of the script is shown in Figure 10-74.

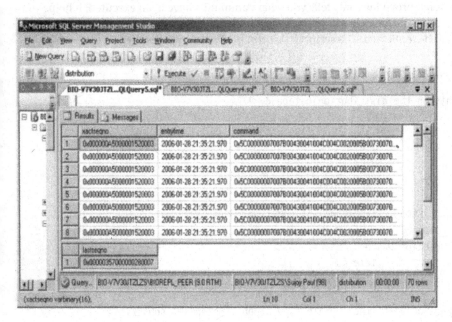

Figure 10-74. *Output of Listing 10-17*

Obviously, the output is in binary format and is not human-readable. However, by executing the sp_browsereplcmds stored procedure on the transaction sequence number, you will be able to see the commands that were issued for that transaction number. This is shown in Figure 10-75.

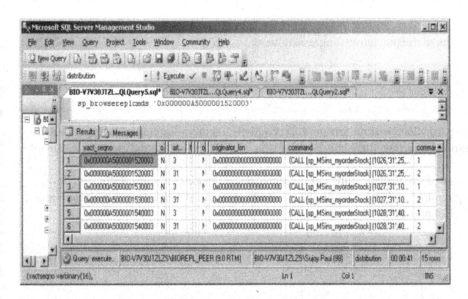

Figure 10-75. *The output of the* sp_browsereplcmds *stored procedure*

In Figure 10-75 you can see the commands that are executed from the start of the specified transaction sequence number.

But this stored procedure only tells you what commands have been executed; it helps you for troubleshooting purposes but does not tell you whether there are any undelivered transactions waiting to be replicated. The script in Listing 10-18 accomplishes this.

Listing 10-18. *Finding Out the Number of Undelivered Transactions*

```
/*Execute this on the distribution database. */

Use distribution
Go

/* Count the distinct number of transactions */

select  count(distinct xact_seqno) as undeliveredtransactions
from MSrepl_commands a
JOIN dbo.MSsubscriptions b
ON (a.article_id = b.article_id
AND a.publisher_database_id=b.publisher_database_id )

/* Want to know only for the 'mysalescopy_stpub_remotepush' subscribing
database and for push subscription.*/

where b.subscriber_db like 'mysalescopy_stpub_remotepush'

/* Now get the agent_id from the MSdistribution_agents table. */

and b.subscription_type=0 and b.agent_id=4
go
```

The output of the previous listing is as follows:

```
undeliveredtransactions
0
```

For the particular Distribution Agent ID of 4 there are no transactions waiting to be delivered. We earlier confirmed this to be the case, since the values we inserted earlier were already delivered.

If you want a list of all the publications and their corresponding subscriptions in transactional replication, you will have to use the MSsubscriptions and MSpublications system tables, as shown in Listing 10-19.

Listing 10-19. *Retrieving a List of Publications and Their Corresponding Subscriptions in Transactional Replication*

```
/* Execute this on the distribution database. */

Use distribution
Go

Select  * from MSsubscriptions a
Join MSpublications p
On (  a.publisher_id = p.publisher_id and
     a.publisher_db = p.publisher_db and
     a.publication_id = p.publication_id )
where
      (p.sync_method = 3 or p.sync_method = 4)
 and subscriber_db<>'virtual'
 go
```

Some of the output of this script is shown in Figure 10-76.

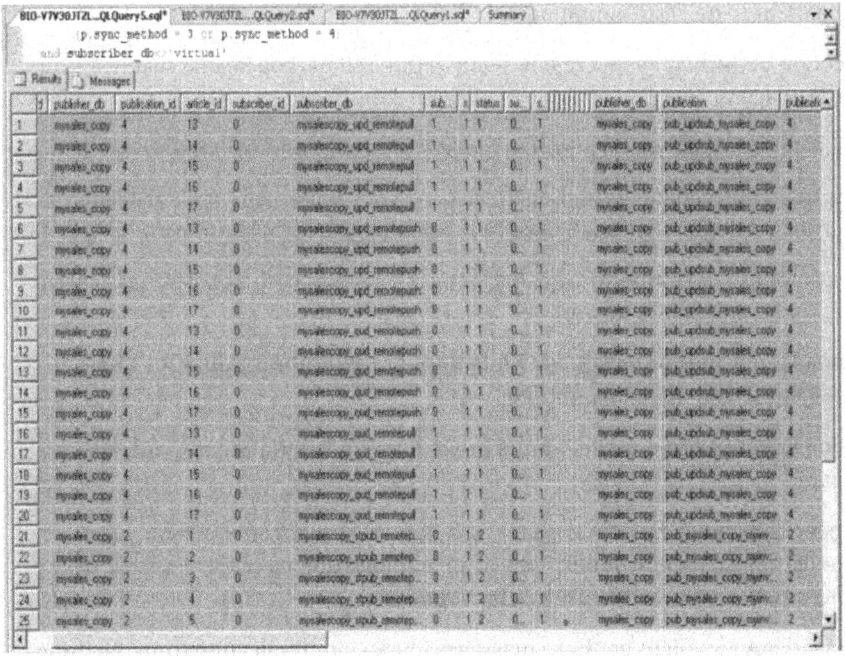

Figure 10-76. *Output of Listing 10-19; 34 rows were returned*

Summary

You should by now have a strong grasp on the fundamentals of configuring transactional replication using both the GUI and T-SQL methods. You should also have a good understanding of the internals of transactional replication. You should be aware of concurrent snapshot processing, the internals of the transaction log, and the different agents involved in processing transactions from the publishing server via the distributing server to the subscribing servers. You should also understand the basic functioning of queued and immediate updating subscriptions, conflict policies, peer-to-peer replication, and standard transactional replication.

- Transactional replication uses concurrent snapshot processing for the initial synchronization.

- Transactional replication does not place a shared lock on the tables during the synchronization process, unlike snapshot replication, so it is possible to perform uploads during the synchronization process.

- The transaction log can be read using either the DBCC log command or the ::fn_dbLog function statement.

- There are three agents involved in standard publication: the Snapshot Agent, the Log Reader Agent, and the Distribution Agent.

- The execution of the Log Reader Agent involves three steps: Log Reader Agent startup message, Run agent, and Detect nonlogged agent shutdown.

- The Queue Reader Agent is called when queued updating subscriptions are used.

- The execution of the Queue Reader Agent also involves three steps: Queue Reader Agent startup message, Run agent, and Detect nonlogged agent shutdown.

- Queued updating subscriptions make use of the 2PC protocol to transfer messages in the queue to the publishing server.

- You cannot change the conflict policy while there are still subscriptions for transactional replication with queued updating.

- Transactional replication executes stored procedures for insert, update, and delete statements.

- Peer-to-peer replication uses the MSpeer_lsns, MSpeer_request, and MSpeer_response system tables on each of the nodes. Peer-to-peer replication uses the MScached_peer_lsns table, which resides in the distribution database.

- The Log Reader Agent picks up those messages marked for replication from the transaction log and writes them to the MSrepl_transactions and MSrepl_commands system tables in the distribution database.

- Check the status of the messages in the distribution database by using the MSdistribution_status view.

- The dynamic management views (DMV) provide insider information at both the server level and the database level. They can be used for monitoring and troubleshooting.

- The four DMV used in replication are sys.dm_repl_articles, sys.dm_repl_schemas, sys.dm_repl_traninfo, and sys.dm_repl_tranhash.

In the next chapter, I will discuss how to set up merge replication using the GUI method. Configuration using the T-SQL method will be covered in Chapter 13, and the internals of merge replication will be covered in Chapter 14.

Quick Tips

- Updates are replicated as a pair of delete and insert statements. They are known as deferred updates.

- Deferred updates can be turned into singleton updates by setting the trace option to 8250.

- Increase the retention of both the transactions and the history during long weekends and holidays.

- Use the sp_browsereplcmds stored procedure to see, in text form, the commands that are executed in the distribution database.

- Use the dbcc opentran command to see whether there are still active transactions waiting to be replicated.

CHAPTER 11

■ ■ ■

Configuring Merge Replication Using the GUI

We have so far looked at snapshot and transactional replication using both the GUI and the T-SQL method, and you should know how to set up the different components of snapshot replication and have a good understanding of transactional replication. In this chapter, I will show you how to configure the different components of merge replication. We will set up the different kinds of publications first, and then the subscriptions that you can use for specific publications.

Table 11-1 lists the different SQL Server products that support merge replication.

Table 11-1. *SQL Server Products That Support Merge Replication*

SQL Server Product	Yes/No (Y/N)
SQL Server Workgroup Edition	Y (can publish to up to 25 Subscribers)
SQL Server Enterprise Edition	Y
SQL Server Standard Edition	Y
SQL Server Express Edition	Y (Subscriber only)

On completing this chapter, you will know how to use the GUI to do the following:

- Configure publications for download-only articles

- Configure publications for standard articles with parameterized filters

- Set up join filters

- Partition data with dynamic functions

- Create a pull subscription for client subscriptions

- Use Windows Synchronization Manager as an interactive resolver

- Create a push subscription for server subscriptions

Note If you have yet to install the database, you should do so. The E-R diagram for the database is shown in Appendix A, and the SQL code for the database is given in Appendix B.

Configuring Publication

In Chapter 8 I mentioned that snapshot replication has only one type of publication while transactional replication has three (see Table 8-2). For merge replication, a publication can be configured either to use standard articles or download-only articles. In this section, I will focus on the configuration of publication with download-only articles first, and then publication with standard articles. I will also demonstrate the configuration of parameterized filters. Join filters, as an extension of parameterized filters, will also be discussed in this section.

Configuring a Publication for Download-Only Articles

Consider the case where the central office should be the only office to make changes to the data for items, prices, and the names of the sales people. This data is then replicated to different offices. The central office is the central Publisher, and the different offices act as the Subscribers, where data changes are not allowed. In such a scenario, you would configure the publication with download-only articles.

Right-click on the Local Publications folder under the Replication object in the SSMS and select New Publication. This will start up the New Publication Wizard. Click Next in the Welcome page and you will see the Publication Database page shown in Figure 11-1. Choose the database that you want to use as the publication database—the one that contains the data or objects you want to publish. Then click Next.

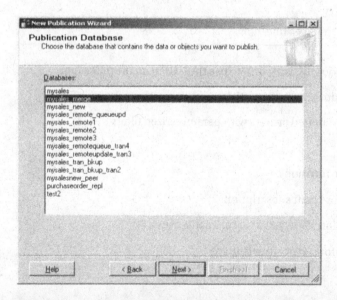

Figure 11-1. *Selecting the database for publication*

The next page will ask you to select the type of publication, as shown in Figure 11-2. Choose "Merge publication."

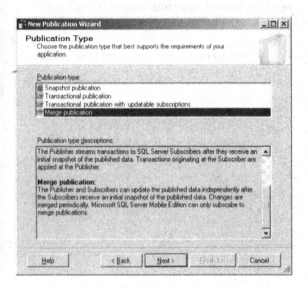

Figure 11-2. *Selecting the publication type*

You can see in Figure 11-2 that SQL Server gives you a brief explanation of what merge publication is. Click Next to continue.

In the next wizard page, you can select the subscriber types for the merge publication, as shown in Figure 11-3. For this example, choose SQL Server 2005 as the subscriber type.

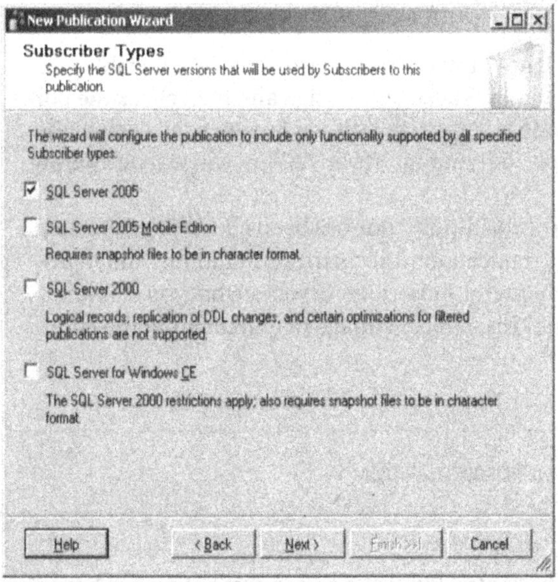

Figure 11-3. *Selecting the subscriber types*

Depending on the type of Subscriber server that you use, SQL Server will load the features for the publication. For example, if you select SQL Server 2005 as the Subscriber server, the publication compatibility level will be set such that the logical records feature is available. However, if you select SQL Server 2000, this feature will not be available. Click Next when you're done.

In the Articles wizard page, you can select the articles that are to be a part of the publication, as shown in Figure 11-4.

Figure 11-4. *Selecting the articles for the publication*

If you check the box beside Tables in Figure 11-4, the system will check all the tables. To avoid this, you need to expand the list of tables by clicking the + sign and then check the boxes for each of the tables that you want to include as an article. You can even expand each of the tables by clicking their + signs and select specific columns. If you do this, you will be filtering out columns.

Notice that the "Highlighted table is download-only" box has been checked for the Item table. This option is only available in merge replication with client subscriptions, and it prevents any tracking metadata from being sent to the Subscriber servers so that you cannot make any changes in the Subscriber servers. This reduces storage requirements at the Subscriber end and improves performance.

Note The optimization of merge replication is discussed in Chapter 19.

Since new items are usually added at the central Publisher server, this option has been checked for the Item table. If you have look-up tables that do not need to be updated at the subscribing end, consider making them download-only articles.

Note Server subscriptions can, however, make changes to the replicated data as stated in Figure 11-4.

We've looked at download-only articles, but there are two other kinds of articles that are used with merge replication: standard articles, and articles with parameterized row filters. Standard articles are the default, in which all the features of merge replication, like conflict resolvers, are available in both the Publisher and Subscriber servers, and you can update the data on either server. Articles with parameterized filters contain partitions of data that eliminate the possibility of any conflicts arising among multiple Subscriber servers and the Publisher server. Point-of-sales applications are an example of where merge replication with parameterized filters can be used.

Note Parameterized filters used to be known as *dynamic filters* prior to SQL Server 2005.

Once you have finished selecting the articles, click Next. This will display the Article Issues wizard page shown in Figure 11-5. In this page, the wizard lists issues that may require changes to your application to ensure it operates as expected.

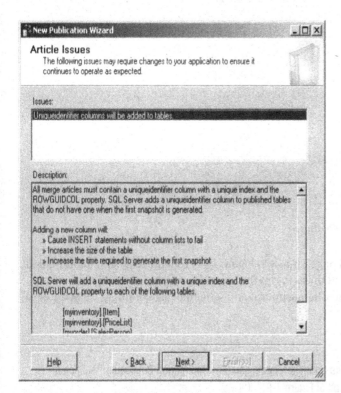

Figure 11-5. *A column with the* uniqueidentifier *data type is added to the tables*

In Figure 11-5, the issue is that, like transactional replication with updatable subscriptions, merge replication also requires the addition of a column with the `uniqueidentifier` data type. The column is added when the initial snapshot is created, unless you manually add it. So if you are performing INSERT operations in merge replication, you need to specify the column names of the tables; otherwise the INSERT operation will fail. Click Next to continue.

■**Note** Transactional replication is discussed in Chapters 8 through 10. The use of the GUI and T-SQL for configuration are discussed in Chapters 8 and 9, and Chapter 10 deals with the internals of transactional replication.

The next wizard page allows you to filter table rows, as shown in Figure 11-6. For this example, we will not add any filters, so click Next.

Figure 11-6. *Adding filters to the table rows*

In the Snapshot Agent wizard page, shown in Figure 11-7, I set the snapshot to be created immediately and I chose the default times to run the agent. If you want to change the schedule of the Snapshot Agent, click the Change button and schedule it accordingly. Click the Next button to continue.

■**Note** For the details of scheduling the Snapshot Agent, see the "Configuring Publication" section in Chapter 4, and specifically the discussion of Figure 4-9.

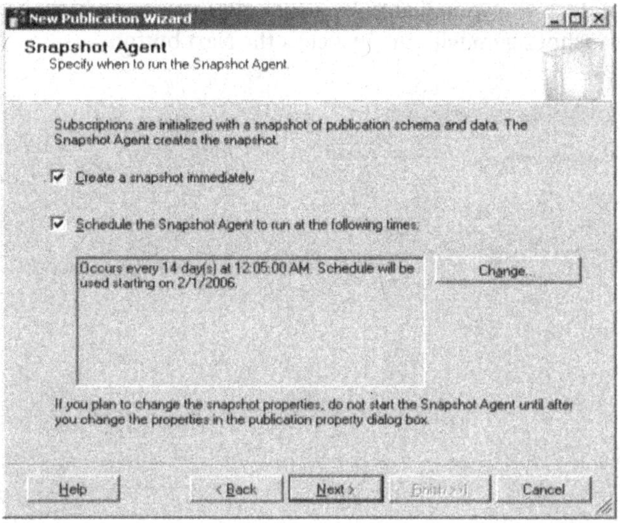

Figure 11-7. *Creating a snapshot and scheduling the agent*

The next wizard page lets you configure the snapshot security settings, as shown in Figure 11-8. While configuring publications for snapshot and transactional replication using the GUI, I used the SQL Server Agent service account to set the security settings of the Snapshot Agent. Here, I have chosen to run the Snapshot Agent under the Windows domain account. The SQL Server Agent service account has been disabled. Click OK to continue.

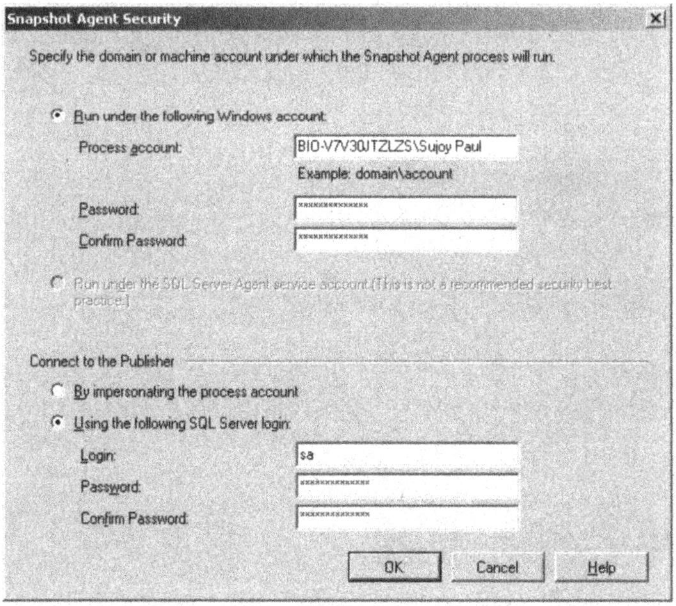

Figure 11-8. *Specifying the Snapshot Agent security settings for merge replication*

The Agent Security wizard page is next, shown in Figure 11-9. Since we have already specified the account under which the Snapshot Agent will run, just click the Next button.

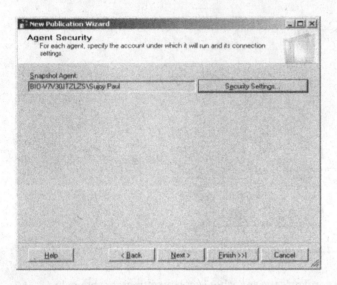

Figure 11-9. *Specifying the account under which the Snapshot Agent will run*

The next wizard page asks what actions you want to take to create the publication, as shown in Figure 11-10. Check the box to create the publication and click Next.

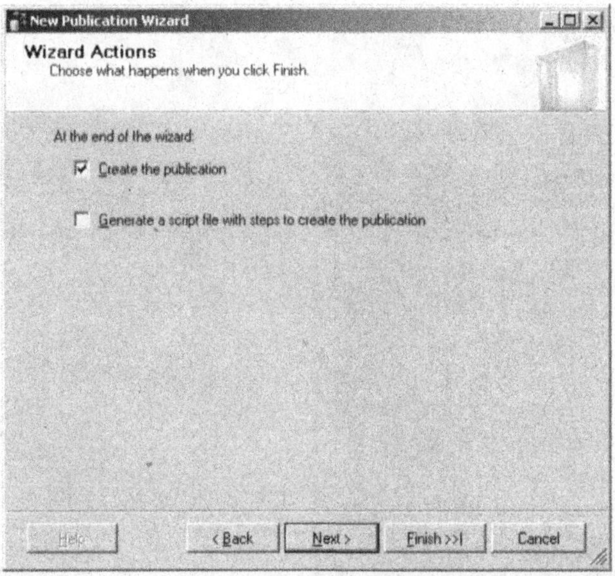

Figure 11-10. *Setting the wizard to create the publication*

Verify your choices and then click Finish to complete the wizard, as shown in Figure 11-11.

Figure 11-11. *Completing the publication wizard for download-only articles*

The engine will complete the process and then display the results, indicating whether the action for each step succeeded or failed. This is shown in Figure 11-12.

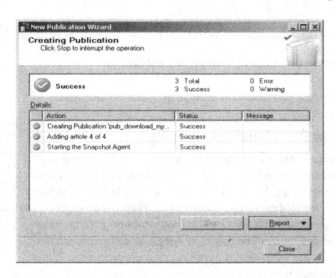

Figure 11-12. *Successful creation of the publication for all four articles*

Now, in the SSMS, right-click on the publication you have just created and select Properties. The Properties window for the publication will be displayed.

Select the Articles page in the Publication Properties window, and click the down arrow in the Article Properties button. If you select the Set Properties of All Table Articles option, you will see that the synchronizing direction is set to Bidirectional, which is the default. In this example, though, I have set the articles to be for download only for the Subscriber types, so I need to change the properties of the synchronization direction to "Download-only to Subscriber, prohibit Subscriber changes," as shown in Figure 11-13.

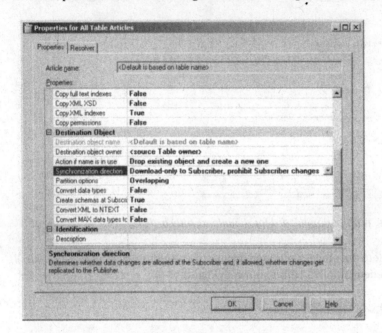

Figure 11-13. *Setting the properties of the articles for download-only publication*

Click the OK button twice so that the publication is ready to be synchronized again.

Configuring a Publication for Standard Articles

The previous section explained how to configure a publication for download articles only. Now let's look at how to configure a publication for standard articles. In this example, views and stored procedures will be included in articles. The views that are included in the articles are vw_CustomerInvoiceStatus, vw_ItemEnquiry, and vw_OrderStatus. These views enable us to find the invoice status of the customer, any items they want to inquire about, and the order status of any items, respectively. The usp_GetCustomerInvoicePaymentDue stored procedure uses the customer invoice view to find out which customers have to make payments. This is shown in the database script in Appendix B.

As in the previous section, start by right-clicking on the Local Publications folder in the SSMS and selecting New Publication. Click Next on the New Publication Wizard's welcome page, and on the next page select the database that you want to use for merge publication (as shown earlier in Figure 11-1). For this example, I have used another copy of the mysales_merge database, called mysales_mergevwusp. Click Next to continue.

Note The mysales_new, mysales, and mysales_merge databases have the same database schema. Different names have been used simply for demonstration purposes.

In the next page, select the publication type (as shown earlier in Figure 11-2) and click Next.

You will now see the Subscriber Types page of the wizard, which was shown earlier in Figure 11-3. However, if the database has already been set up for merge publication, the wizard page will look slightly different, as shown in Figure 11-14. Check the box for SQL Server 2005, and click Next.

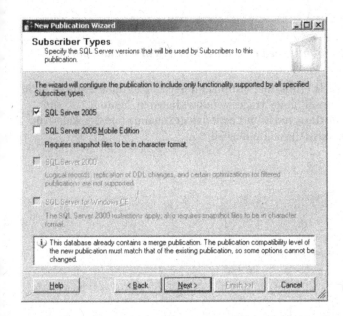

Figure 11-14. *Selecting the subscriber type for a database that has already been set up for merge replication*

The wizard will now ask you to select the articles. In this case we are using views and stored procedures as articles for publication. This is shown in Figure 11-15.

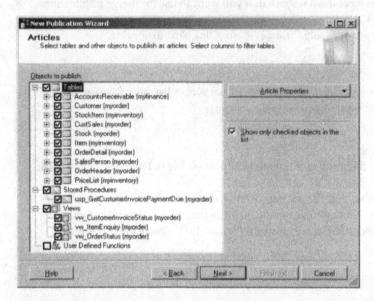

Figure 11-15. *Selecting the tables, views, and stored procedures involved in standard publication*

Click the down arrow in the Article Properties button, and select Set Properties of All Table Articles. This opens the Properties for All Table Articles window shown in Figure 11-16, and you can see that the synchronization direction is bidirectional and changes are tracked at the row level (changes can also be tracked at the column level).

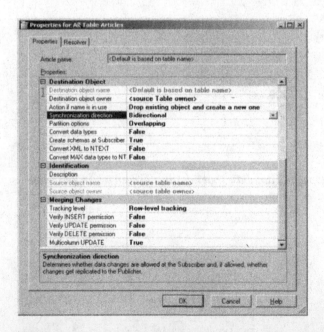

Figure 11-16. *Setting the properties for the table articles involved in standard publication*

You can see that the insert, delete, and update permissions for merge changes have been set to False. This is because the Merge Agent has access to the publication objects using the PAL, so it does not need these permissions.

Note The Publication Access List (PAL) was discussed in the context of the internals of snapshot replication. See the "The Publication Access List" section in Chapter 7.

Click on the Resolver tab and check the box to allow the Subscriber server to resolve conflicts interactively during on-demand synchronization only. This is shown in Figure 11-17. Click OK to return to the Articles page (Figure 11-15) and click Next to continue.

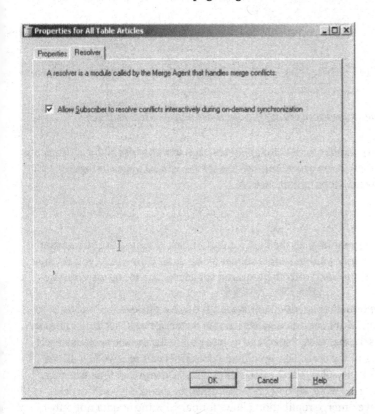

Figure 11-17. *Handling of merge conflicts using the resolver*

You will now see the Article Issues wizard page shown in Figure 11-18. It tells you that you should add the tables referenced by the views, and the objects referenced by the stored procedures. Since we have already done so, as shown in Figure 11-15, click Next.

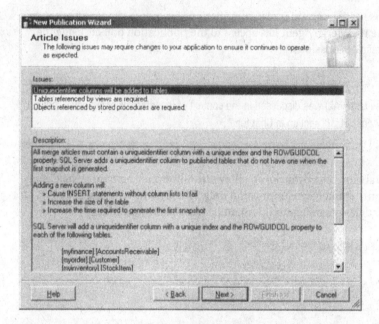

Figure 11-18. *Viewing the issues raised concerning the database objects used as articles*

You will see a wizard page similar to the one in Figure 11-6, and the rest of the settings are similar to the process described in the preceding section for the wizard pages in Figures 11-7 through 11-12. Simply follow the steps in that section.

Adding Filters

In both of the preceding configurations, all the data for the articles is sent to the Subscriber servers. But suppose that you only want to send a subset of the data. How would you do this? The answer is to use data filters to send only the required subset of data to the appropriate subscriptions.

While setting up transactional replication with updatable subscriptions in Chapter 8, in the "Configuring Transactional Publications with Updatable Subscriptions" section, I demonstrated the use of data filters. In that case, I specified a string value for the where clause used in the horizontal partitioning of the rows. The specified data subset was received by all the servers subscribing to the pub_mysales_tran2 publication. This is known as static filtering.

I mentioned column filtering while setting up publication for download-only articles earlier in this chapter. However, merge replication allows for partitioning of data not only by static and column filtering but also by two other methods: parameterized row and join filters.

Parameterized row filters are used to send different subsets of data to one or more subscriptions from the same publication. There are two kinds of parameterized row filters: nonoverlapping and overlapping. When each row in the published table belongs to only one partition, it is called a *nonoverlapping partition*. If the row belongs to two or more partitions, it is called an *overlapping partition*.

The data provided by the Subscriber servers is first sent to the Publisher, which then sends the data to other Subscriber servers. For example, in our pub_stdpub_mysalesmergevwusp publication with standard articles, we have the SalesPerson table as one of the articles. Sales personnel working in the field are assigned to customers in their specified zones. To ensure that the data is being received by the right sales person, we use the SUSER_SNAME() function, which returns the login associated with the SID (Security Identification Number) for the login name.

To set up parameterized filters, right-click on the pub_stdpub_mysalesmergevwusp publication in SSMS, and select Properties. In the Publication properties window, select the Filter Rows page, as shown in Figure 11-19.

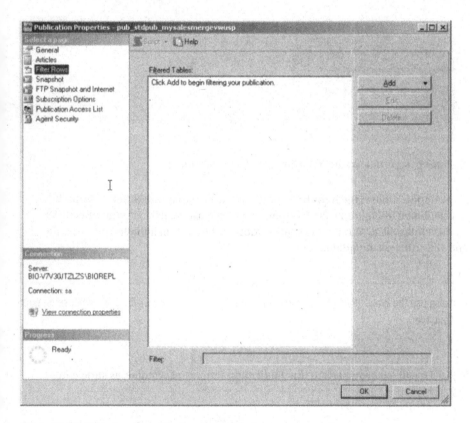

Figure 11-19. *Filtering the rows for the articles*

Click on the Add button, and select "Add filter property." The login name for each of the sales people is associated with the Name column of the SalesPerson table. The validity of the login for each of the sales people is checked when they log in by using the SUSER_SNAME() system function. The Merge Agent returns the login information dynamically when it connects to the Publisher server, and based on the information provided, the Publisher sends the required data set to the subscribing servers of the appropriate sales people. The filtering of the data based on the SUSER_SNAME() function is shown in Figure 11-20.

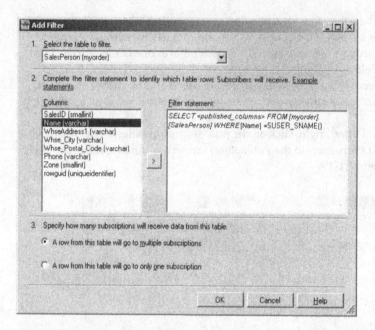

Figure 11-20. *Adding a parameterized filter for the* SalesPerson *table*

For this example, choose the "A row from this table will go to multiple subscriptions" radio button, as shown in Figure 11-20. (For performance reasons, it is better to select the "A row from this table will go to only one subscription" radio button, if that is the case; the Merge Agent will store less metadata.)

■**Tip** You can also use the HOST_NAME() function along with the SUSER_SNAME() function when setting up the parameterized filter.

Click OK. This will take you back to the Publication Properties window, as shown in Figure 11-21.

■**Note** The Data Partitions property is created only after the addition of the join filter.

Figure 11-21. *The publication properties with the filtered* SalesPerson *table*

If you click the Add button, you will see that the Add Join to Extend Selected Filter option is enabled. The join filter is an extension of the parameterized filter, which is why it is enabled only after a parameterized filter has been set. A join filter is much like joins in normal SQL—you set the join filter using the primary–foreign key relationship between the tables, although any business logic can be used as a join filter.

In our example, there is a many-to-many relationship between the SalesPerson and Customer tables. The physical model therefore contains the intermediate table, CustSales, so that the primary–foreign key relationship between the SalesPerson table and the Customer table is maintained. To ensure that each of the sales people has the right customer assigned, a join filter is issued. Click the Add button, and click the Add Join to Extend Selected Filter option.

You will now see the Add Join window in Figure 11-22. From the "Joined table" list box, select the [myorder].[CustSales] table, from the "Filtered table columns" list select the SalesID column, and from the "Joined table columns" list select the CustID column to make the join statement shown in the figure.

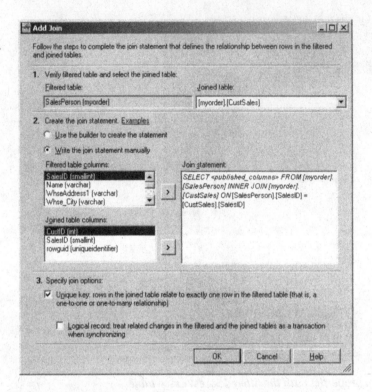

Figure 11-22. *Adding a join filter*

Check the "Unique key" box. The join filter uses a `join_unique_key` property to make use of the optimization process if the relationship between the parent and child tables is one-to-one or one-to-many. The `join_unique_key` property is used when the join condition has a unique column. Click OK to continue.

The Publication Properties window will now include the joined filter and the Find Table button, as shown in Figure 11-23.

Select the `CustSales` filtered table, as shown in Figure 11-23, click the Add button, and select the Add Join to Extend Selected Filter option again to establish the join filter between the `CustSales` and `Customer` tables. This will display the Add Join window shown previously in Figure 11-22. However, this time click the "Use the builder to create the statement" radio button.

Notice that when you add the columns to build the join filter in Figure 11-24, there is a preview section, which will show you the SQL statement used to build the filter. The operator column in the builder helps you establish the relationship between the tables.

Figure 11-23. *Adding the joined filter in the filtered rows section of the publication properties*

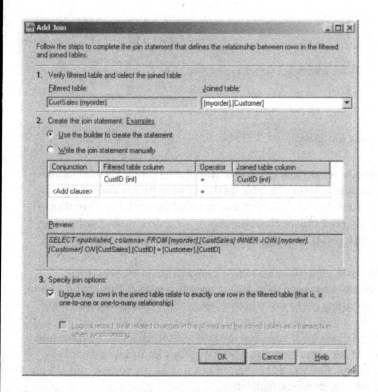

Figure 11-24. *Use the builder to build the join filter*

Once you have completed the join filter, click OK to return to the Publication Properties window. This is the same window as in Figure 11-23 but the Customer join filter has been added. Now select the Customer table and add the join with the OrderHeader table. Similarly add the OrderDetail table to the join filters to ensure that each sales person can only download their customer data. After you are finished, the filtered tables will have been added as shown in Figure 11-25.

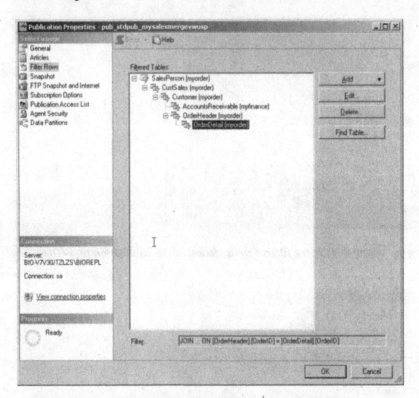

Figure 11-25. *All the filtered tables are added*

So far I have showed you how to add join filters to extend the functionality of parameterized row filtering. The relationship between the tables is that of primary key and foreign key in join filters, thereby allowing data in the tables that are included as articles to be replicated only if the data matches the join filter clause. However, this is not the only relationship that exists in a join filter. You can also group two tables if there is a logical relationship between them.

In Figure 11-25, you can see the join filter that exists between the OrderDetail and OrderHeader tables. We can group the related rows in the two tables so that they are processed as a logical unit. The logical grouping of the rows, in this case, will be used along with join filters.

To do this, select the OrderDetail table and click the Edit button. This will open the Add Join window shown in Figure 11-26. Check the "Logical record" box for this join. This means that all the related rows in a transaction will be processed as a unit by the engine, and not on a row-by-row basis as is the norm with merge replication.

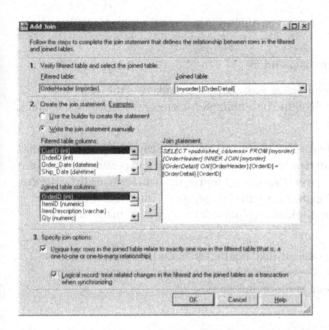

Figure 11-26. *Specifying logical record grouping for the* OrderHeader *and* OrderDetail *tables*

In our case, logical grouping will mean that all rows in the OrderHeader table that are related to a single OrderId value will be transmitted as one functional unit, and all rows in the OrderDetail table that are related to rows in the OrderHeader table will similarly be transmitted as one unit.

Tip You can specify logical grouping only on the parent table.

You might ask why I did not use a logical grouping between the SalesPerson, CustSales, and Customer tables. If you look into the E-R diagram for the database, you will find that the CustSales table has two parent tables: SalesPerson and Customer. Since the rows in CustSales are not associated with a single primary key row, you cannot use a logical relationship between the three tables.

The grouping of rows as one unit is one of the benefits of using logical records; the other benefit is being able to track and resolve conflicts simultaneously on multiple rows from multiple tables. Since logical conflict detection can only be set with the use of T-SQL, I will discuss that in the context of setting up merge replication using T-SQL (in Chapter 13).

Caution Using logical relationships has an impact on the performance of merge replication. The Merge Agent processes the changes for the entire logical record, instead of processing on a row-by-row basis as it normally does.

There are some considerations that must be fulfilled prior to setting up a logical grouping of rows:

- You must enable the precomputed partition.

- When a subscribing server synchronizes with the publishing server, the latter must determine the data set that each of the subscribing servers receives, based on the filters that are associated with them.

- When you use precomputed partitions, the membership of each of the partitions of the subscribing servers are evaluated prior to the synchronization and persistence of data so that when the subscribing server tries to synchronize, the data set is ready for download. This helps to optimize the process for the Merge Agent. Otherwise, the partition would have to be evaluated on the filtered columns for any changes made to the columns.

In order to enable the precomputed partition, right-click on the publication folder in the SSMS, and select Subscription Options. In the Publication Properties window, set the "Precompute partitions" option to True as shown in Figure 11-27.

Figure 11-27. *Setting the precomputed partitions option to* true

Now, ensure that the login names for the sales people are enlisted in the Publication Access List (PAL). Select the Publication Access List page in the Publication Properties window, as shown in Figure 11-28, and you can add the login names.

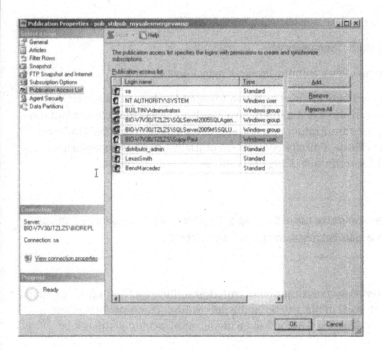

Figure 11-28. *Adding login names in the PAL*

Note The PAL is discussed in more detail in the "The Publication Access List" section of Chapter 7.

Next, you should ensure that you do not use nonoverlapping partitions on the filtered publication that is using logical relationships. In Figure 11-16, earlier in the chapter, all the articles had the Partition option set to Overlapping. It is, however, possible to set the option differently for each of the articles.

The very nature of merge replication permits autonomy, and making updates at both the Publisher and Subscriber servers only enhances the possibility of data conflicts. As such, detecting and resolving conflicts in merge replication is a primary requisite in planning for merge replication.

Note Setting up a conflict policy and using the Conflict Viewer is discussed in the "Conflict Detection and Resolution" section of Chapter 10.

If a conflict policy is set, the Merge Agent can detect the conflicts and, based on the conflict policy, resolve the disputes, accept the winning data, and transmit it to the other subscribing servers. You can view the winners and losers of the data conflicts using the Conflict Viewer.

The way a Merge Agent resolves a dispute depends on two factors:

- The type of subscription: client or server

- The type of conflict: row-level, column-level, or logical-level record

While the Conflict Viewer helps you to view the winning and losing records after the conflict has been resolved, you can also use the Interactive Resolver to view the conflicts prior to their resolution during the synchronization process. For this you have to use the Windows Synchronization Manager (WSM)—I discussed its use in pull subscriptions for snapshot replication in the "Starting Pull Subscriptions Using the WSM" section of Chapter 4.

Caution The Interactive Resolver makes use of the WSM. If the synchronization is performed outside WSM, the resolution will be done automatically, according to the conflict policy.

The Interactive Resolver is used in conjunction with the conflict resolver that is associated with the publication, or with each of the articles in the publication. There are four different kinds of conflict resolvers, as discussed in the "Merge Replication" section of Chapter 3:

- Default priority-based conflict resolver

- Business logic handler

- COM-based custom resolver supplied by Microsoft

- COM-based custom resolver

In our case, all the articles for this publication are set to use the default resolver except for the OrderHeader article.

With the default resolver, the conflict-resolution mechanism behaves differently according to the subscription type. If the subscription type is that of a subscribing server, as in our example, priority values are assigned to each of the subscribing servers, and the server node with the highest priority wins. If the subscription type is that of a client, as in the download-only publication, the first change written to the publishing server wins.

Let's set the OrderHeader article to use the COM-based resolver supplied by Microsoft. Select the Articles page in the Publication Properties window (Figure 11-28), select the OrderHeader table, click the down arrow on the Article Properties button, and select Set Properties of Highlighted Table Article. Select the Resolver tab and check the "Use a custom resolver (registered at the Distributor)" radio button as shown in Figure 11-29.

Select the Microsoft SQL Server DATETIME (Earlier Wins) Conflict Resolver, and enter the information needed by the resolver. In this case, the column should have a datetime data type. The OrderHeader table has the Order_Date and Ship_Date columns with a datetime data type. Choose the Ship_Date column, since the customer's delivery can be tracked based on the date it has been shipped.

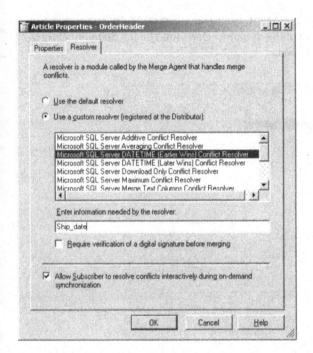

Figure 11-29. *Choosing the Microsoft-supplied COM-based custom resolver*

Since we want to use the Interactive Resolver, check the box that says "Allow Subscriber to resolve conflicts interactively during on-demand synchronization." Click the OK button to return to the Publication Properties window.

Now select the Data Partitions page, and click the Add button to add the values for the dynamic functions. The Add Data Partition window will open, as shown in Figure 11-30.

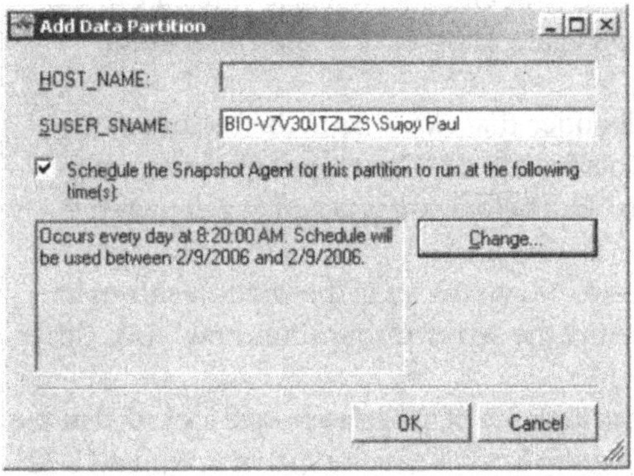

Figure 11-30. *Setting the value for the dynamic function* SUSER_SNAME()

Check the box to schedule the Snapshot Agent, as shown in Figure 11-30. Then, click the Change button to schedule the execution of the dynamic snapshot. The Job Schedule Properties window, shown in Figure 11-31, will open.

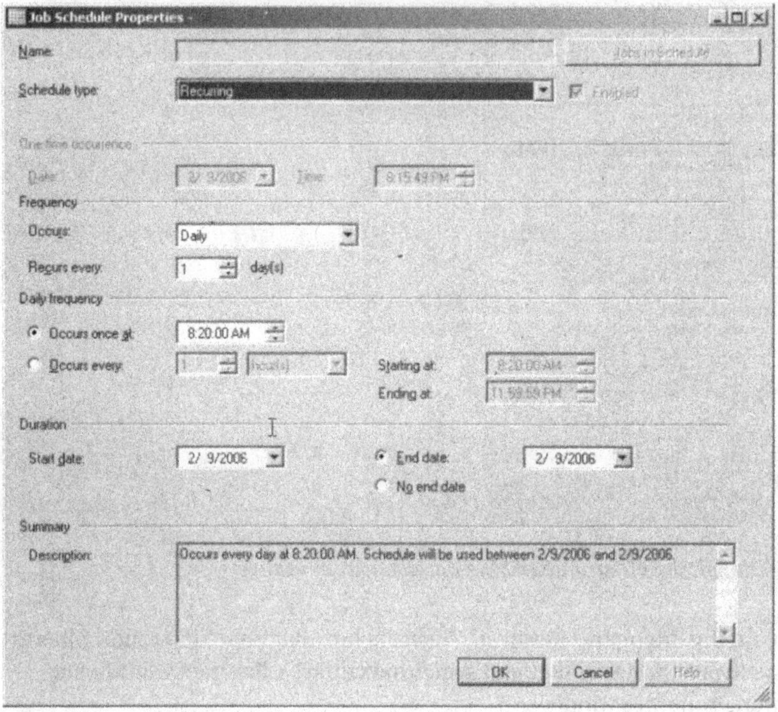

Figure 11-31. *Scheduling the dynamic snapshot*

Make sure the scheduling times are correct, and click OK. This will take you back to the Add Data Partition window (Figure 11-30); click OK again to get back to the Publication Properties window, as shown in Figure 11-32.

If you select the row, as in the figure, you will notice that two links at the bottom of the page are enabled: "Generate the selected snapshots now," and "Clean up the existing snapshots." Click the "Clean up the existing snapshots" link before you proceed to generate the dynamic snapshot.

If the time at which the snapshot is supposed to be run (as set in the window shown in Figure 11-31) has passed, you can click the "Generate the selected snapshots now" link. Otherwise click OK.

Note you have to generate dynamic snapshots for each of the sales people included in the SalesPerson table. In this example, the only sales person listed is the one shown in Figure 11-32.

Note If you do not have any existing snapshots, the "Current snapshot" column will show "none" in Figure 11-32.

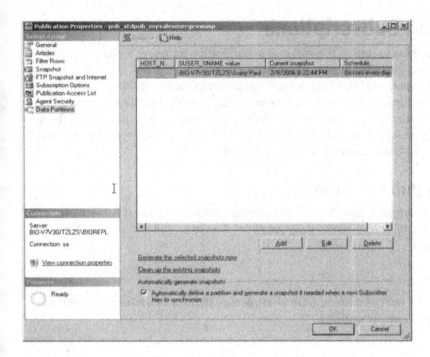

Figure 11-32. *Viewing the properties for the data partitions*

After the generation of the dynamic snapshot, in the SSMS, right-click on the publication and select the View Snapshot Agent Status option to see whether the articles have been generated. The View Snapshot Agent Status window will open, as shown in Figure 11-33.

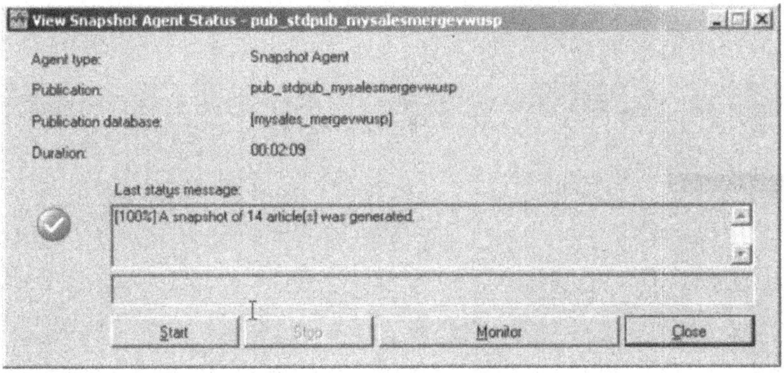

Figure 11-33. *Viewing the status of the Snapshot Agent*

You have now completed setting up the publication with parameterized filtering and generating the dynamic snapshot.

So far in this chapter, you have learned how to configure a publication for standard articles and articles for download only. You also learned how to add parameterized filters and extend them by adding join filters. In the next section, I will show you how to set up the different subscriptions for merge replication.

Configuring Subscriptions

Now that you know how to configure both kinds of publication for merge replication, I will explain how to set up the different subscriptions.

In merge replication, the Distribution Agent has no say in the distribution of the transactions. It is the Merge Agent that takes on this responsibility after the initial synchronization. The Merge Agent resides on the distributing server for push subscriptions, while it resides on the subscribing server for pull subscriptions. In either case, the distribution database acts as the store and forward queue, as in other types of replication.

Configuring Pull Subscriptions

To set up a pull subscription, right-click on the publication under the Local Publications folder in the SSMS, and select New Subscriptions from the menu. This will start the New Subscription Wizard.

■**Note** The color of the publication icon is yellow for merge replication. For transactional replication, it is blue, and it is purple for snapshot replication.

Click Next in the welcome page, and you will see the Publication page shown in Figure 11-34. Select the publication for pull subscription, and click Next.

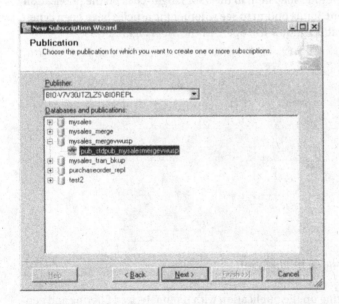

Figure 11-34. *Selecting the publication for pull subscription*

Next you will see the Merge Agent Location wizard page shown in Figure 11-35. It will ask you to select the kind of subscription you want. The Merge Agent runs on the subscribing server for pull subscriptions, so select the second option, and click Next.

■**Note** In this example, the pull subscription resides on the same server instance as the publication.

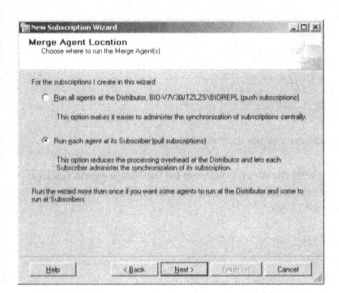

Figure 11-35. *Selecting a pull subscription*

The wizard will next ask you to select the Subscriber servers and the subscription databases, as shown in Figure 11-36. As you can see, I checked the boxes for the Subscriber and the subscription databases. Make your selections and click Next.

■**Note** If you do not have any subscription databases, you will have to create one. You can do so when you select the subscription database in Figure 11-36—it has an option to create a new database.

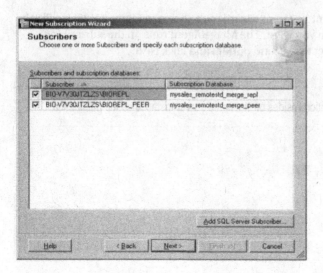

Figure 11-36. *Selecting the Subscriber servers and the subscription databases*

Now the wizard will ask you to specify the security settings for the Merge Agent. Click on the ellipsis button beside the Connection to Subscriber property; this will open the Merge Agent Security window shown in Figure 11-37.

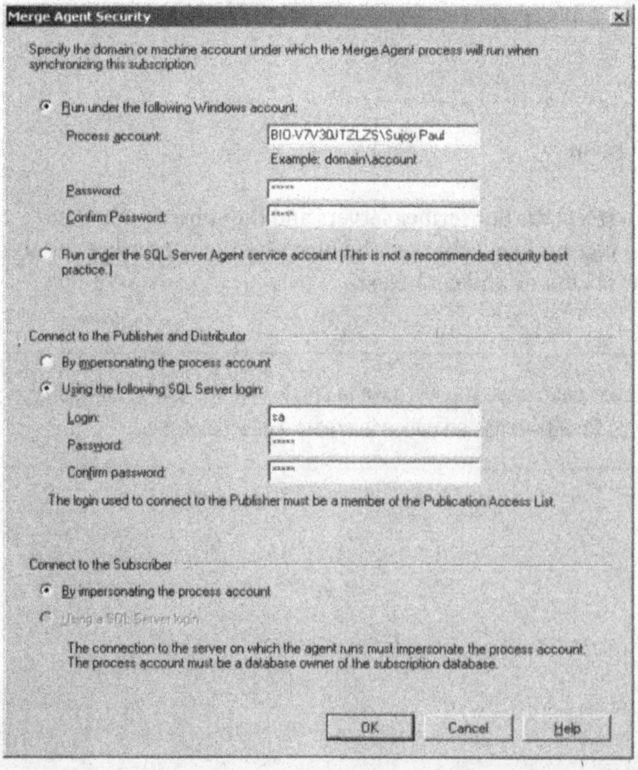

Figure 11-37. *Configuring the security settings for the Merge Agent*

The Merge Agent sits on the subscribing server in pull subscriptions, and it needs to impersonate the process account when it connects to the Subscriber server. It also needs to use the SQL Server login when it connects to the Publisher and Distributor servers. Enter these settings and click OK.

You will now see the Merge Agent Security wizard page shown in Figure 11-38. You need to specify the security settings for each of the Merge Agents running on each of the SQL Server Subscriber servers. Once you're done, click Next.

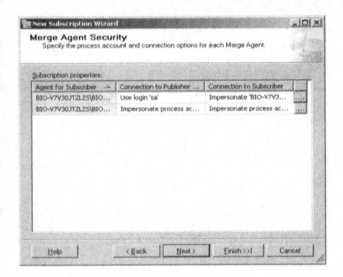

Figure 11-38. *Setting the process and connection options for each Merge Agent*

The wizard will now ask you to specify the synchronization schedule for the agent. In order to configure it as shown in Figure 11-39, click on the row in the Agent Schedule column, and then select "Define schedule" from the drop-down list.

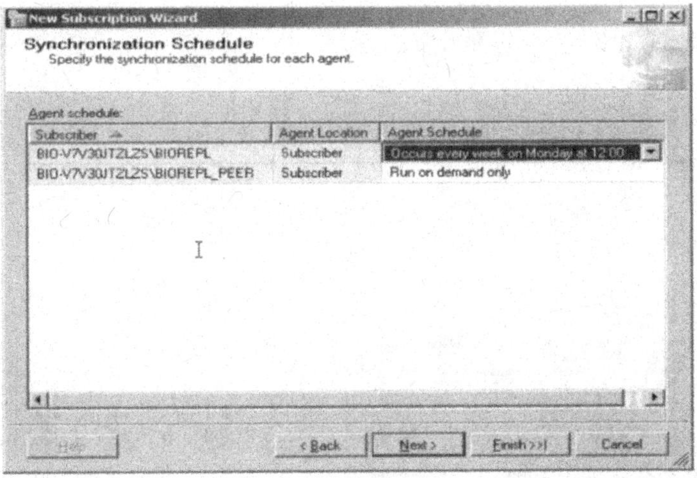

Figure 11-39. *Specifying the synchronization scheduling for the Merge Agent*

This will take you to the Job Schedule Properties window (shown earlier in Figure 11-31) where you can schedule the agent. Click OK to return to the Synchronization Schedule window (Figure 11-39).

Click Next, and the wizard will ask you whether you want to initialize the subscriptions, as shown in Figure 11-40. Make sure that the initialization is set to occur immediately, and click Next.

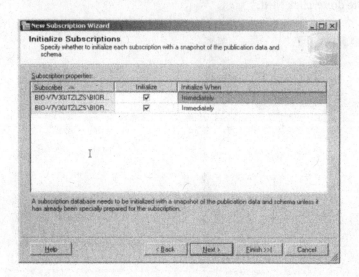

Figure 11-40. *Initializing the subscriptions*

The wizard will now ask you for the type of subscription and the priority that you want to set for resolving conflicts for a specific Subscriber server. This is shown in Figure 11-41. Since we are using the standard publication, select the Server subscription type. As you can see, I have assigned a priority setting of 75.00 for the subscribing servers in both instances. Click Next to continue.

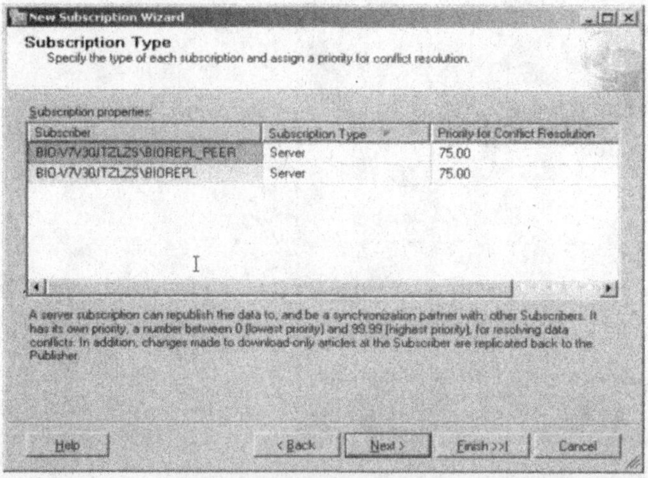

Figure 11-41. *Selecting subscription types and the priority settings for conflict resolution*

Note The priority settings can range from 0.00 to 99.99 for server subscriptions. The default value for client subscriptions is 0.

A client subscription is one that has the priority settings of the Publisher server, while a server subscription has a value that is set by the DBA or developer. Normally republishing Subscriber servers use server subscriptions, whereas read-only Subscriber servers use client subscriptions.

In this example, both server instances have the same value. You can, however, assign different priority values to the server subscriptions, and in that case, when the subscribing server with the higher priority value synchronizes with the Publisher server, the subscribing server with higher priority will take precedence over the one with the lower priority if there are any conflicts. In such a situation, if the Subscriber server with the lower priority loses out due to the conflict policy, any changes made in that server will be lost. To avoid this problem, I have set the same priority levels.

The wizard will now ask you to choose the actions you want to take to create the subscription, as in Figure 11-42. Make your choices and click Next.

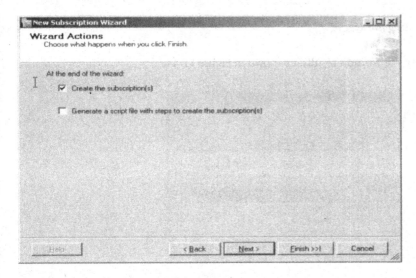

Figure 11-42. *Creating the subscription*

Now you'll see the final wizard page shown in Figure 11-43. Check the actions that you took to create the subscription, and if you're satisfied, click the Finish button.

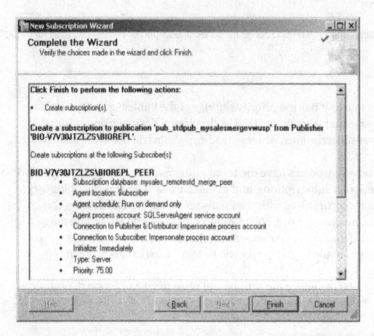

Figure 11-43. *Completing the wizard*

You will now see the wizard's results, as shown in Figure 11-44.

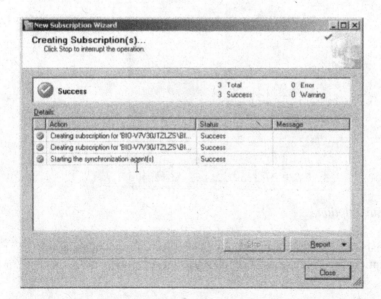

Figure 11-44. *Successfully creating the subscription*

Synchronizing with the Windows Synchronization Manager

We have just successfully set up a pull subscription, but we still have to synchronize with the
WSM in order for the pull subscription to make use of the Interactive Resolver.

To do so, right-click on the subscription that we just created from the Local Subscriptions folder in the SSMS, and choose Properties from the menu. This will open the Subscription Properties window shown in Figure 11-45. You need to enable the Use Windows Synchronization Manager and set "Resolve conflicts interactively" to True, as shown. Then click the OK button.

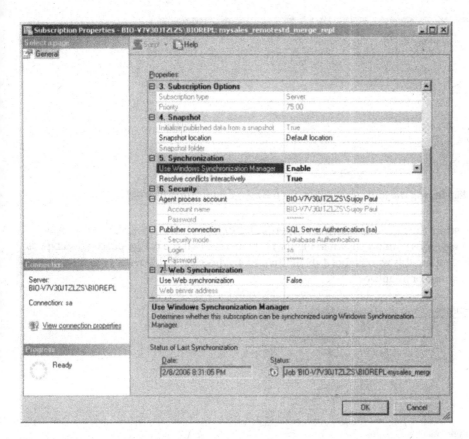

Figure 11-45. *Setting the pull subscription properties*

Note The use of WSM in pull subscriptions for snapshot replication is discussed in Chapter 4. Refer to the "Starting Pull Subscriptions Using the WSM" section of that chapter.

Now, as you did with the pull subscription to set up replication in Chapter 4, select Programs ➤ Accessories ➤ Synchronize from the Start menu. You will see the pull subscription for merge replication that we just configured, mysales_remotestd_merge_repl, listed, as shown in Figure 11-46.

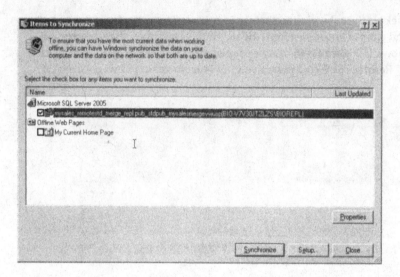

Figure 11-46. *Viewing the pull subscription for the merge replication in WSM*

If you select the item and click the Properties button, you will see the SQL Server Subscription Properties window shown in Figure 11-47. Notice that the merge publication type is specified; compare this with Figure 4-49 in Chapter 4, where the publication type is referred to as "Transactional or Snapshot."

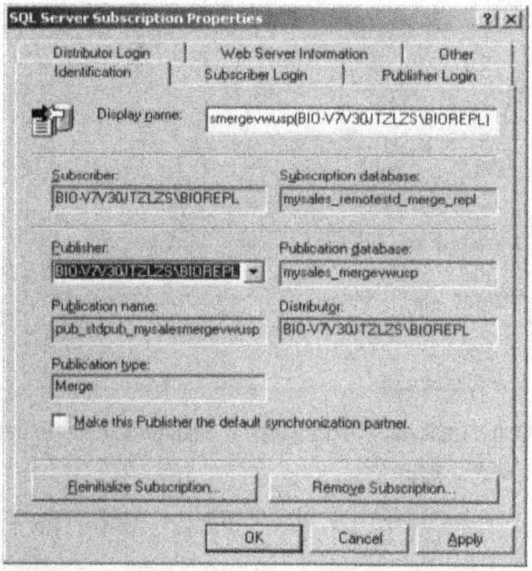

Figure 11-47. *Viewing the identification for the pull subscription*

Now let's look at the Web Server Information tab. This tab is not present in Figure 4-49 because you can use web synchronization with merge replication but not with transactional or snapshot replication. In our example, however, we are using logical records in the join filter, so we cannot use web synchronization for a subscription that uses this publication.

In the Publisher Login tab, the Windows Authentication for the current user is used for the login properties for the Subscriber, Publisher, and Distributor servers. You can see this in Figure 11-48. The current user for the Windows account is the login name (BIO-V7V30JTZLZS\ Sujoy Paul).

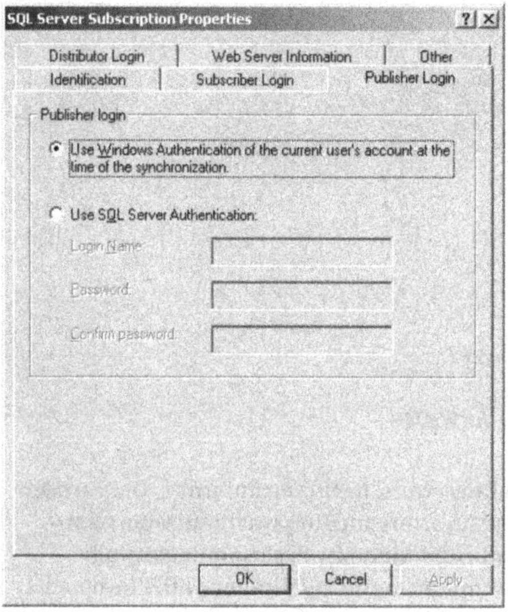

Figure 11-48. *Viewing the login properties for connecting to the Publisher server*

Now click the Other tab, shown in Figure 11-49. You will see that the Interactive Resolver is enabled in the "Conflict resolution mode" section. Click OK.

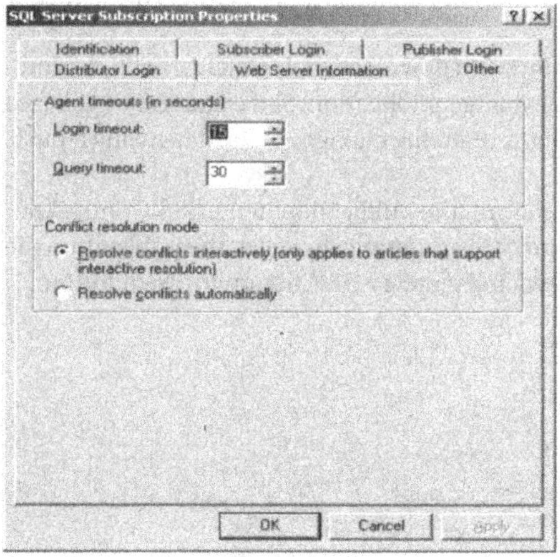

Figure 11-49. *Enabling the Interactive Resolver*

You will now see the Items to Synchronize window (Figure 11-46). Click the Synchronize button, and you will see the synchronization proceeding, as shown in Figure 11-50.

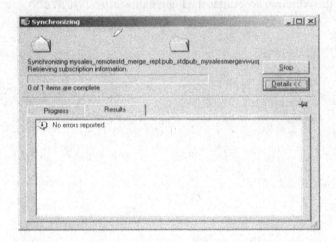

Figure 11-50. *Viewing errors in the Results tab of the WSM*

As it proceeds, click the Results tab to view any errors. If you get any errors, you can skip them in the Progress tab. In this case, there were no errors, and the synchronization completed its run. If the synchronization is successful, the window will close automatically.

Now let's look at how to set up a push subscription for the publication with download-only articles.

Configuring Push Subscriptions

As mentioned earlier, the Merge Agent resides on the Distributor server for push subscriptions. The Merge Agent processes the transactions, reconciles any conflicts, and transmits the messages to the required subscriptions. The distribution database merely stores the history of the messages.

Earlier in the chapter, I discussed publication with download-only articles, and I demonstrated by setting up the pub_download_mysalesmerge publication. Since data is not going to be updated at the subscribing end, we can push through the changes in the data using a push subscription.

To configure the push subscription, right-click on the publication in the SSMS and select New Subscriptions. The New Subscription Wizard will automatically select the publication for the subscription you want to create. This is shown in Figure 11-51. Click on the Next button.

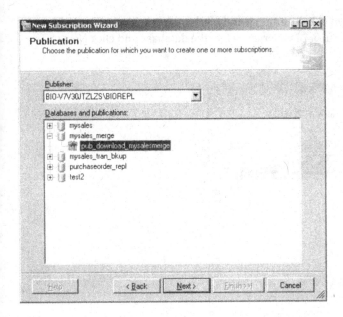

Figure 11-51. *Selecting the publication whose subscription you want to create*

The next wizard page lets you choose where to run the Merge Agent, as shown in Figure 11-52. Set the Merge Agent to run on the Distributor server, and click Next.

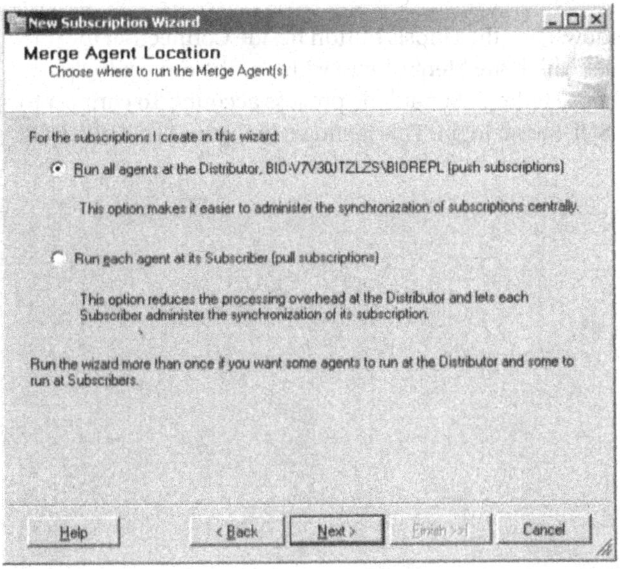

Figure 11-52. *Setting where the Merge Agent will run*

The next wizard page is shown in Figure 11-53, and it asks you to select the name of the subscription database on the Subscriber server. Select the database and click Next to continue.

Figure 11-53. *Selecting the subscription database for the Subscriber server, BIOREPL*

In the Merge Agent Security window, click the ellipsis button beside Connection to Subscriber to set up the account under which the Merge Agent will run. To connect to the Publisher and Distributor servers, choose to impersonate the process account. To connect to the Subscriber server, choose to use SQL Server login. This is shown in Figure 11-54. Click OK when you are done.

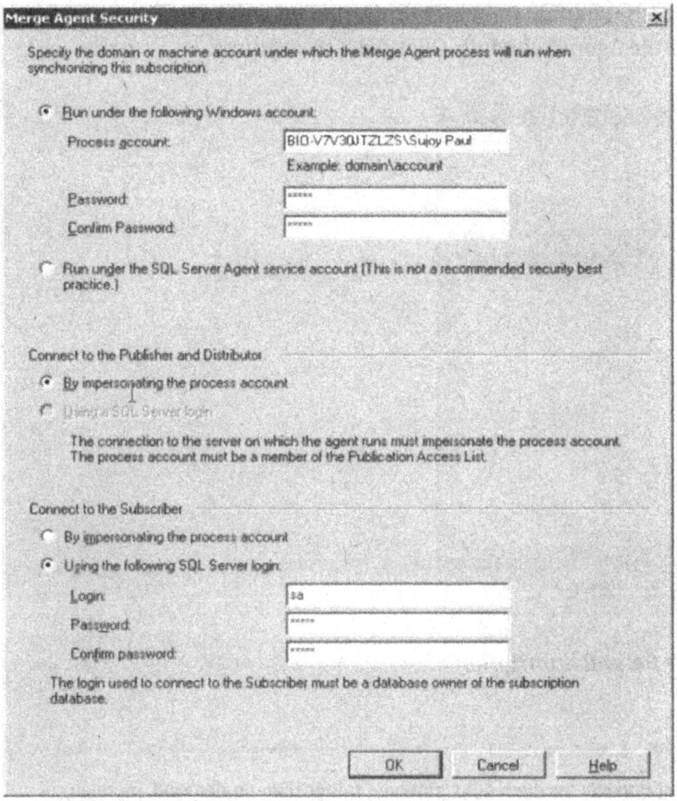

Figure 11-54. *Selecting the accounts under which the Merge Agent will run and make connections to the Publisher and Subscriber servers*

In the next wizard page, shown in Figure 11-55, you can specify the process account and connection options for each Merge Agent. When you are finished, click Next.

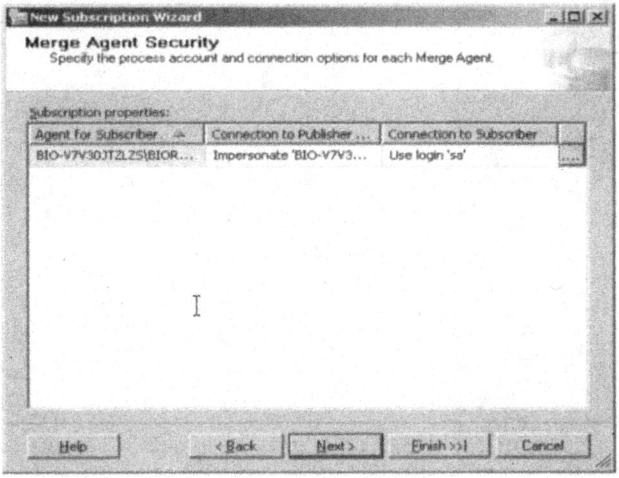

Figure 11-55. *Setting the subscription properties for the Merge Agent security account*

The wizard will now ask you to schedule the synchronization, as shown in Figure 11-56. Choose "Run continuously" for the Agent Schedule. Click Next to continue.

Figure 11-56. *Schedule the agents for synchronization*

■Tip Running the Merge Agent continuously for push subscriptions, rather than on demand, increases performance for replicated databases. Stopping and starting the agent involves more work for the engine.

Now the wizard will ask whether you want to initialize immediately, as shown in Figure 11-57. You do, so click Next.

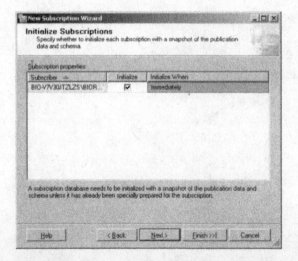

Figure 11-57. *Initializing the subscriptions immediately*

The wizard will ask you to select the type of subscription. The publication that I have selected is enabled for download only, so I have set the subscription type as Client, as you can see in Figure 11-58.

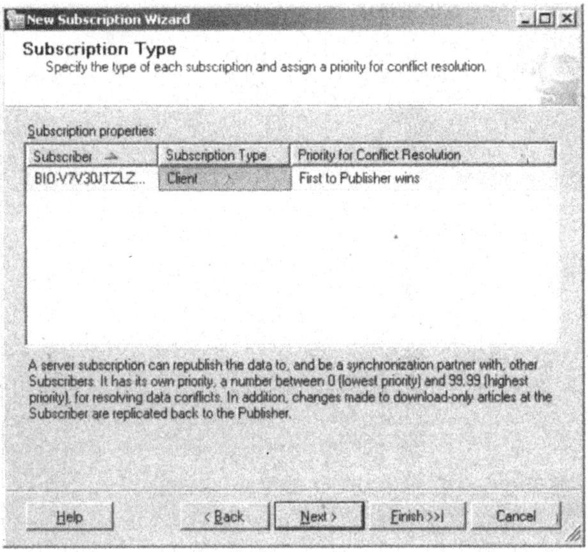

Figure 11-58. *Specifying a Client type subscription and the conflict resolution policy*

The conflict resolution policy is set to the first subscription that sends its message to the Publisher server. With this setting, the changed message from the Subscriber server, along with the metadata carrying the priority, is sent to the Publisher server during the synchronization, so that it does not lose out to messages sent subsequently by other subscriptions. Click Next.

You can now specify what the wizard will create, as shown in Figure 11-59. Click Next to continue.

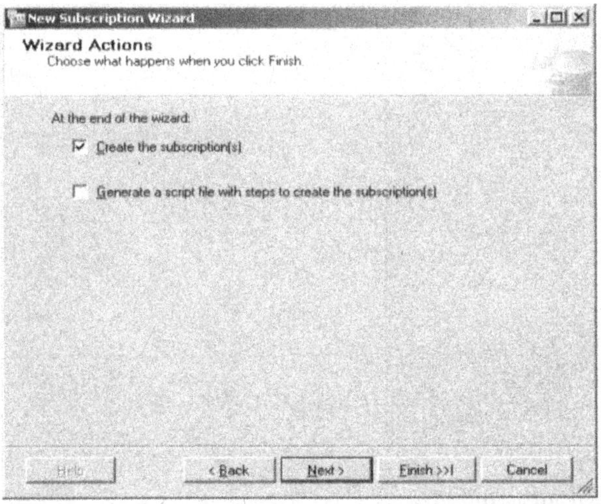

Figure 11-59. *Choosing to create the push subscription*

Finally, you can verify the choices you made, as shown in Figure 11-60. Click the Finish button to complete the wizard.

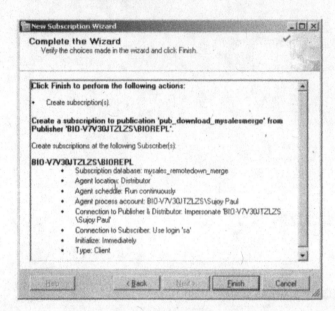

Figure 11-60. *Completing the subscription wizard for download-only publication*

The replication engine will generate the subscription and will show you whether the actions creating the subscriptions were a success or not. This is shown in Figure 11-61.

Figure 11-61. *Successfully creating the push subscription*

Summary

In this chapter, I discussed the different types of publication and the corresponding subscriptions that you can use. You should have a clear understanding of the differences between publications with download-only articles and the standard articles with parameterized filters. By now, you should also have a good idea of the differences between the Conflict Viewer and the Interactive Resolver that you can configure using the WSM. You should also be aware of the subscription types and the corresponding conflict policies that you can use.

- There are two different kinds of publications in merge replication. They are publication with download-only articles, and standard articles with parameterized filtering.

- The initial synchronization is done by the Snapshot Agent. The Distribution Agent is not used in merge replication.

- The Merge Agent transmits the messages to the subscribing servers and for republishing Subscriber servers back to the Publisher server.

- The Merge Agent resides on the Distribution server for push subscriptions and on the Subscription server for pull subscriptions.

- There are two types of subscriptions: client subscriptions and server subscriptions.

- Use client subscriptions for download-only articles, and server subscriptions for standard articles.

- Use publication with download-only articles for lookup tables.

- For publications with articles containing parameterized filters, use dynamic functions such as SUSER_SNAME(), SUSER_SID(), and HOST_NAME().

- The Conflict Viewer shows you the data for both the winner and the loser of the conflicts after the conflict has occurred. The Interactive Resolver enables you to manually resolve the conflicts during the process.

- You can use the Interactive Resolver with the WSM.

- You need to partition the data for each dynamic function that you used.

In the next chapter, I will show you how to synchronize over the web using merge replication. I have already showed you how to set up pull subscriptions for merge replication, and while pull subscription is the only form of subscription that you can use in web synchronization of merge replication, there are also certain conditions that you are required to meet.

Quick Tips

- Run the Merge Agent continuously for push subscriptions to optimize the performance, as more work needs to be done by the replication engine to stop and restart.

- Join filters are established based on the primary and foreign key relationship if you use the automatic join filter.

- Join filters use the `join_unique_key` property to make use of the optimization process.

CHAPTER 12

■ ■ ■

Web Synchronization with Merge Replication

In Chapter 11, I discussed the configuration of merge replication using the GUI method, including how you can set up a pull subscription using the WSM for publications containing dynamic functions. Sales people working in the field can use pull subscriptions with merge publication to download data via the Internet. In this context, I will discuss the synchronization of merge replication via the Internet. As background, you should have a basic understanding of the different components involved in merge replication and how to set it up before you proceed.

On completing this chapter, you will know how to do the following:

- Enable publication for web synchronization

- Configure SSL to facilitate communication between the IIS and the Subscriber servers

- Configure the server that is running IIS for web synchronization

- Assign permissions to the SQL Server Replication Listener

- Run the IIS in diagnostic mode to ensure the installation of a certificate for SSL and to test the IIS connection

- Configure a pull subscription for web synchronization

Web Synchronization Basics

With web synchronization, you can use the HTTPS protocol to replicate data to mobile users over the Internet or to remote databases across the corporate firewall. However, there are three main limitations:

- The remote databases have to be SQL Server databases

- The subscriptions being synchronized must be pull subscriptions

- Only merge replication (not snapshot or transactional replication) is supported

In addition to the replication components, you need a web server to use web synchronization. The web server is usually the Internet Information Services (IIS) server that comes with the Windows operating system. You can use either the IIS 5.0 or 6.0 version that comes with Windows XP and Windows 2003, respectively.

The use of different server components permits interesting replication topologies to be created for web synchronization. These are your options:

- Single server

- Two servers

- Multiple IIS servers and a SQL Server Publisher server

The single-server topology is the simplest one: IIS, the SQL Server Publisher server, and the Distributor server all reside on the same machine. The subscribing servers connect to the publishing server behind the corporate firewall via the IIS server. This topology is mainly used for intranet scenarios.

The two-servers topology involves the physical separation of the web server and the replication servers. In this case, you would configure the IIS server on one machine while placing the Publisher server and the Distributor server on another. Because the IIS server is behind the firewall, the subscribing servers will access the Publisher server via the IIS server.

The third topology involves the use of multiple IIS servers working with the SQL Server Publisher and Distributor servers. In such a scenario, you have multiple IIS servers to facilitate the demands of a large number of subscribing servers at the same time. To help in the load distribution, you can use multiple IIS servers that direct requests to the appropriate Publisher server.

Note You can always place the Distributor server on a remote location for either the multiple IIS or the two-servers topology.

Now that you know about the different topologies that you can use, we will look at how to set up web synchronization for subscribing servers using merge replication. There are three things to set up:

- A publication for web synchronization

- The IIS server that will synchronize the subscriptions

- Pull subscriptions that will use web synchronization

Configuring a Publication for Web Synchronization

Consider the case where a sales representative working in the field with a laptop needs to check the numbers and descriptions of items, which vendor has them in stock, and what the prices are. Using pull subscriptions, the sales representative can connect to the Publisher server configured for merge replication via the IIS and update the laptop's copies of the Item, Vendor, Stock, and PriceList tables. The Secured Sockets Layer (SSL) certificate is used on the HTTP protocol to connect to the Publisher server.

For this example, a publication called pub_mysales_mobile has been set up using the following tables as articles: Item, PriceList, PurchaseOrderDetail, PurchaseOrderHeader, Stock, StockItem, and Vendor. Once you have set up this publication for merge replication, you can configure it for web synchronization.

■**Note** Configuring merge replication using the GUI is discussed in Chapter 11. Note, however, that you cannot use logical groupings of records as discussed in Chapter 11 if you wish to use web synchronization.

To start the configuration, right-click on the publication and select Properties from the menu. In the Publication Properties window, select the FTP Snapshot and Internet page as shown in Figure 12-1.

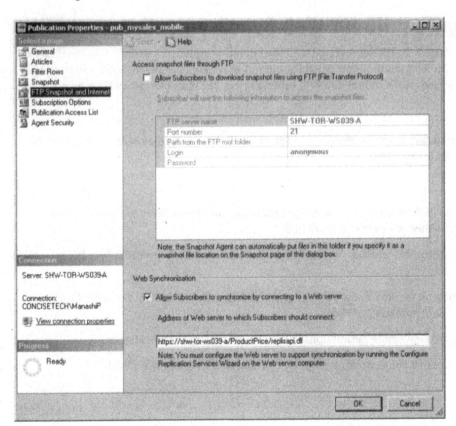

Figure 12-1. *Configuring a merge publication to allow web synchronization*

Check the box that says "Allow Subscribers to synchronize by connecting to a Web server." In the "Address of Web server to which Subscribers should connect" field, specify the address of the IIS server—this should be the URL associated with SSL, as shown in Figure 12-1. (The replisapi.dll part of the address specifies the Replication Listener that needs to have the right permissions—this is explained in the "Setting Permissions for the SQL Server Replication Listener" section of the chapter.) The name of the server in the URL must be the name specified when the SSL was created for the URL.

Note SQL Server uses the default port of 1433, so if you use any other port, you will have to specify the port number in the address of the web server. In this case, the address of the web server would be of this form: https://shw-tor-ws039-a:*portnumber*/ProductPrice/replisapi.dll.

Click OK to enable the publication for web synchronization. The next step is to set up SSL.

Configuring IIS for Web Synchronization

The setup process for IIS is integrated with the operating system. By default, it is installed as one of the Windows components when the operating system is installed, and it can run as an enterprise service while interacting with other services like Windows Active Directory.

Note I have assumed that the client components for SQL Server are already installed on your machine; if not, they need to be installed.

To set up pull subscriptions for merge publication to be synchronized over the Web, you need to follow these steps to configure IIS:

1. Configure SSL, which is required for communication between the Subscriber servers and IIS.

2. Configure the server that is running IIS for web synchronization using the Configure Web Synchronization Wizard.

3. Assign appropriate permissions to the SQL Server Replication Listener.

4. Ensure that SSL is working properly by running IIS in diagnostic mode.

Note It is possible to configure IIS for web synchronization manually, but the preferred method is to use the Configure Web Synchronization Wizard.

Configuring SSL for Web Synchronization

SQL Server uses SSL to facilitate communication between the subscribing servers and IIS. SSL ensures the authenticity, message integrity, and confidentiality of user subscriptions and encrypted network transmissions while users are connected through an Internet browser. In order to enable this form of security, you need to configure the SSL features of IIS.

Configuring SSL is accomplished by making use of certificates. A certificate, more precisely known as a *digital certificate*, ensures the genuineness of the holder's identity (the holder being the computer on which the application is running). These certificates are issued by trusted authorities, such as a certificate authority (CA), who act as guarantors to both the parties involved in the transfer of authenticated data.

What normally happens is that the party sending out the authenticated data sends a public key that has been certified by a CA that is accepted by the party receiving the data. This way, the authenticity, the message integrity, and the confidentiality are maintained.

Note Internet Explorer (IE) allows the user to reject the transfer even if it is from a sender with a trusted certificate.

There are two kinds of certificates: server and client certificates. You can only use server certificates for web synchronization of merge replication. Ensure that you have only one server certificate associated with the Internet URL that points to the machine where IIS is installed. The machine that has the web server will also contain the replication components. The subscriptions will select the first available certificate, which might not be the one you want.

So, the first thing you need to do is to get a certificate from a CA or other trusted third party. Do this by selecting Run ➤ inetmgr.exe from the Start menu. This will open the central administrative site of IIS. Expand the local computer node, right-click on Default Web Site, and select Properties. On the Directory Security tab, click the Server Certificate button in the Secure communications group box, and follow the wizard.

However, it is also possible to test the use of a certificate without actually going to the trouble of getting one from a CA. You can use the SelfSSL utility provided by Microsoft in the IIS 6.0 Resource Kit. SelfSSL lets you issue a personal certificate that you can use within a trusted domain for a small group of personnel. This certificate is fine for testing or diagnostic purposes, but it is not issued by any certified authority so it should not be used for a production environment.

The IIS Resource Kit can be downloaded from http://www.microsoft.com/downloads; search for IIS Resource Kit 6 IIS. You can only use this kit on the Windows 2003 and Windows XP operating systems.

Once you have downloaded the resource kit (IIS6ORKT.exe) you need to install it. Ensure that you are the administrator for IIS on the machine before you install, and then simply follow the InstallShield Wizard, selecting the defaults as shown in Figure 12-2.

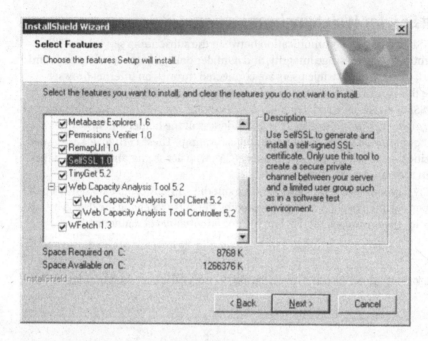

Figure 12-2. *Installing the IIS 6.0 Resource Kit*

I configured web synchronization for merge replication on Windows XP, service pack 2. I had IIS 5.1 already installed on my machine, so I only installed SelfSSL. Uncheck the boxes for the features that you do not want to install.

After the installation process is complete, select All Programs ➤ IIS Resources ➤ SelfSSL ➤ selfssl from the Start menu to open the DOS shell. On the DOS command line type **selfssl** as shown in Figure 12-3.

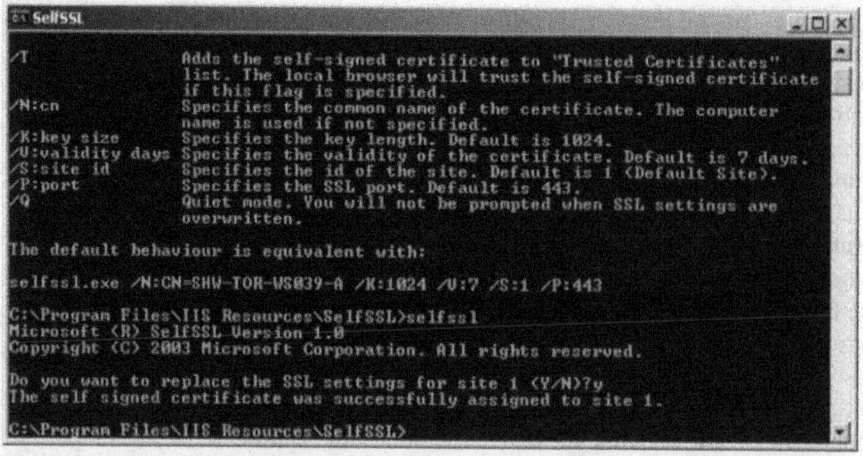

Figure 12-3. *Executing the SSL utility*

As you can see in Figure 12-3, the utility will ask whether you want to replace the SSL settings. Enter **y** to assign the signed certificate.

Note the default specifications. You can change the validity of the certificate from 7 days to an appropriate number by using the -V switch, assign a common name to the certificate using the -N switch, or ensure that the local browser treats this certificate as a trusted one by turning on the -T switch.

Now that we have assigned the certificate, we can test it on the local browser. Open Internet Explorer and type **https://<computername>**. This opens a Security Alert window. Click OK to display information regarding the security of the digital certificate that was assigned, as shown in Figure 12-4.

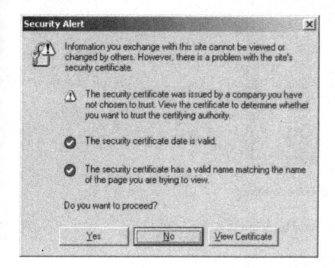

Figure 12-4. *Viewing the security information for a certificate*

If you click the View Certificate button, you will see the details of the certificate, as shown in Figure 12-5. You can see that the certificate is not trusted—we could have used the -T switch, as mentioned earlier, to make this a trusted certificate. Notice the name of the issuing authority and the dates for which the certificate is valid.

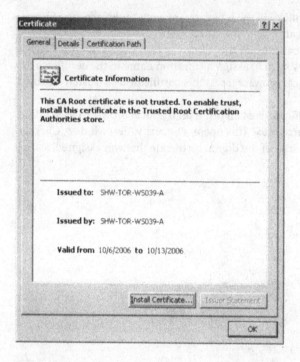

Figure 12-5. *Viewing the general details of the certificate*

Now click on the Details tab, as shown in Figure 12-6.

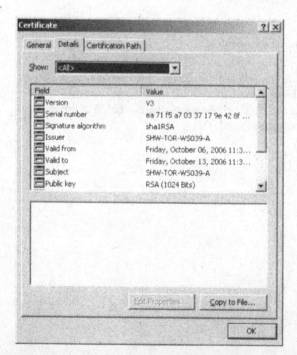

Figure 12-6. *Viewing the details of the certificate*

The Details tab shows that the certificate conforms to the X.509 standard for certificate syntax, and the format of the International Telecommunication Union, Telecommunication Standardization Sector (ITU-T), which contains the following:

- Version

- Serial number

- Signature algorithm

- Issuer

- Validity

- Subject

- Public key

- Enhanced key usage

- Thumbprint algorithm

- Thumbprint

If you select any of the fields, you will be able to see the details in the bottom pane.

Tip Select the public key to view the details in the bottom pane, and then make a copy of the key for safe storage by clicking the Copy to File button.

If you click on the Certification tab, you will see the path of the certification and the current status of the certificate, as shown in Figure 12-7.

Since we did not use the -T switch when we ran selfssl.exe from the DOS shell, we need to enable the trust. Click on the General tab again (Figure 12-5). As is explained in Figure 12-5, you enable trust by installing the certificate in the Trusted Root Certification Authorities store.

To do this, click on the Install Certificate button. This will start the Certificate Import Wizard. Click the Next button on the Welcome page, and you will see the Certificate Store page shown in Figure 12-8. I have allowed Windows to automatically select the certificate store.

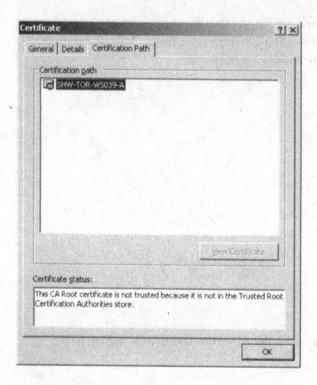

Figure 12-7. *Viewing the certification path of the certificate*

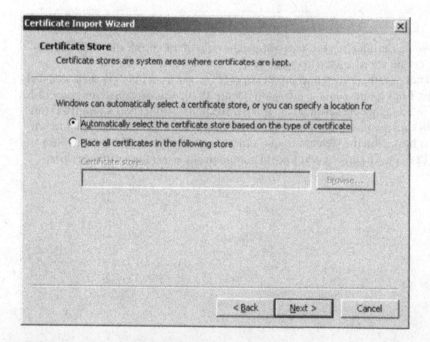

Figure 12-8. *Selecting a certificate store*

However, if you want to put all certificates in a particular store, choose the other option. After the Browse button is enabled, click it and select a physical location of the storage for the certificates, such as the Registry or the Local Computer, depending on the kind of certificate store that you want to use.

Regardless of where you store your certificates, you can click Next to continue to the page shown in Figure 12-9.

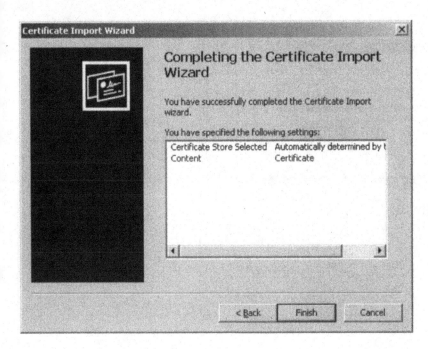

Figure 12-9. *Completing the Certificate Import Wizard*

Click on the Finish button, and a dialog box like the one in Figure 12-10 will be displayed.

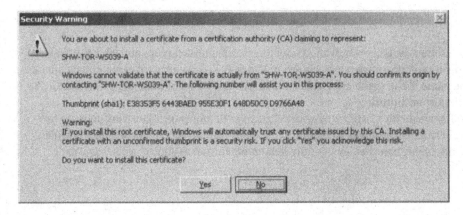

Figure 12-10. *Acknowledging the security warning for the certificate*

Click the Yes button, and the wizard will tell you that the import has been successful. Now if you open Internet Explorer, type **https://<computername>**, and click View Certificates, you will see that the certificate is trusted.

Now that the certificate has been installed, we can export it to the users on the Subscriber servers so that when they access the site they will have a secure line of communication. To do this, first open Internet Explorer. Select Tools ➤ Internet Options and click the Content tab, as in Figure 12-11.

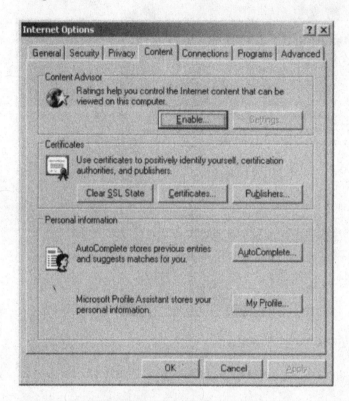

Figure 12-11. *Setting certificate options*

Now click the Certificates button to open the Certificates window, and click the Trusted Root Certification Authorities tab, as shown in Figure 12-12. If you scroll down the list box, you will see the name of the certificate you created in the Issued To column. Select the certificate and click the Export button.

You will now see the Certificate Export Wizard's Welcome page. Click Next to go to the Export File Format page, shown in Figure 12-13. Here you can see the file formats in which the certificate can be exported. Accept the default file format as shown, and click Next.

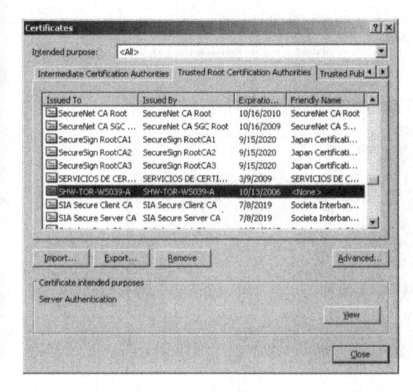

Figure 12-12. *Exporting the certificate from the Trusted Root Certification Authorities*

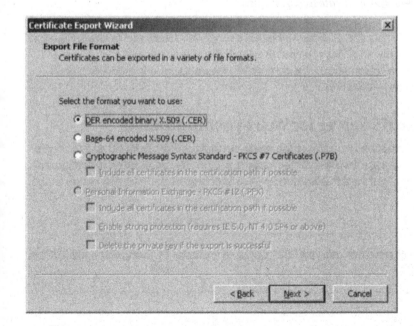

Figure 12-13. *Choosing a format type for exporting the file*

Now you can specify the name of the file; the file will have a .cer extension. Enter a name for the file, and click Next.

You will now see the final page of the Certificate Export Wizard, shown in Figure 12-14. Click the Finish button, and the wizard will inform you of its successful completion.

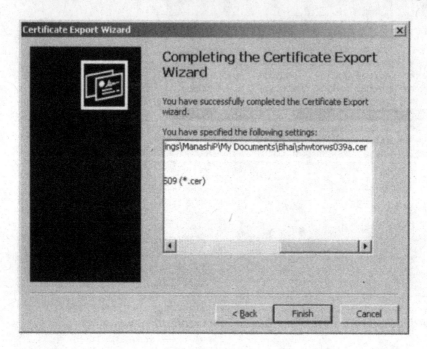

Figure 12-14. *Completing the Certificate Export Wizard*

Double-click on the .cer file, and you will be able to see the details and trustworthiness of the certificate. You can send this file to the publication Subscribers.

Now that we have set up the secured socket for IIS, the next step is to set up the server that runs IIS for web synchronization.

Configuring the IIS Server for Web Synchronization

For this configuration example, we will use the single-server topology: both IIS and the server components of replication are installed on the same machine. The publication is configured as explained in the "Configuring a Publication for Web Synchronization" section earlier in the chapter.

Note Configuring merge replication using the GUI is discussed in Chapter 11. Configuration with T-SQL is discussed in Chapter 13.

To configure the IIS server, open the SSMS and expand the Local Publications folder. Right-click on the publication, pub_mysales_mobile, and select Configure Web Synchronization. This will start the Configure Web Synchronization Wizard. Click Next in the Welcome page.

The wizard will now ask you for the type of Subscriber you are using, as shown in Figure 12-15—SQL Server or SQL Server Mobile Edition. Choose SQL Server and click Next.

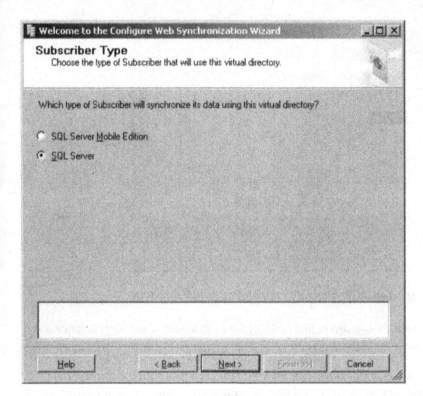

Figure 12-15. *Specifying the type of Subscriber that will use the virtual directory to synchronize the data*

The wizard will now ask you to select the web server and either create a virtual directory or configure an existing one. This is shown in Figure 12-16.

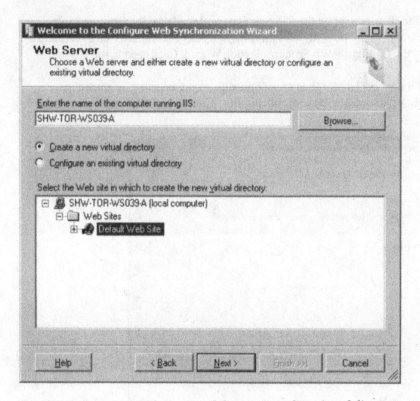

Figure 12-16. *Selecting a web server and the corresponding virtual directory*

You can either select a web server from a list of the existing web servers by clicking on the Browse button or select the Web site that the SQL Server replication engine picks up automatically.

Once you have selected the web server, click the "Create a new virtual directory" radio button. At the bottom of the pane, you will see the name of the computer running IIS. Expand the node and select Default Web Sites, as shown in Figure 12-16. Click Next to continue.

Now the wizard will ask you to enter an alias for the virtual directory, as shown in Figure 12-17. An alias is assigned to a virtual directory so that users, when using the web browser, can access the directory without knowing the exact physical location. This not only improves security but also makes it easier to move to another directory if necessary—you do not have to change the URL but merely reassign the mapping of the alias to the new directory.

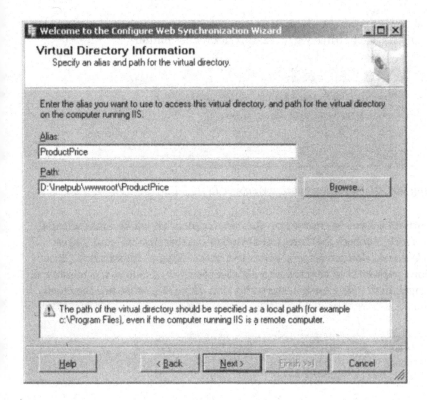

Figure 12-17. *Specifying an alias and the path for the virtual directory*

Specify the alias and the path for the virtual directory, and then click Next. The wizard will ask you whether it should create the new folder, since it does not exist, as shown in Figure 12-18. Click on the Yes button.

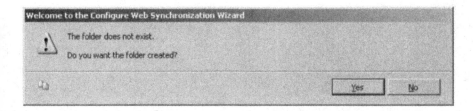

Figure 12-18. *Creating the new folder*

The wizard will now ask whether you want to copy the SQL Server Replication WebSync ISAPI DLL, `replisapi.dll`, as shown in Figure 12-19. Click the Yes button.

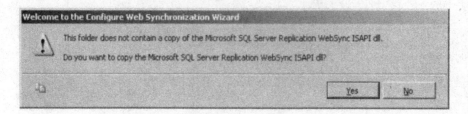

Figure 12-19. *Copying the SQL Server Replication WebSync ISAPI DLL*

Next, the wizard will ask you to choose how the client credentials will be authenticated, as shown in Figure 12-20. Uncheck the "Integrated Windows authentication" and "Digest authentication for Windows domain servers" boxes and check "Basic authentication." Basic authentication allows passwords to be transmitted in clear text, which means it is possible to intercept the messages. In this case, we are encrypting data using SSL, so we need to check Basic authentication.

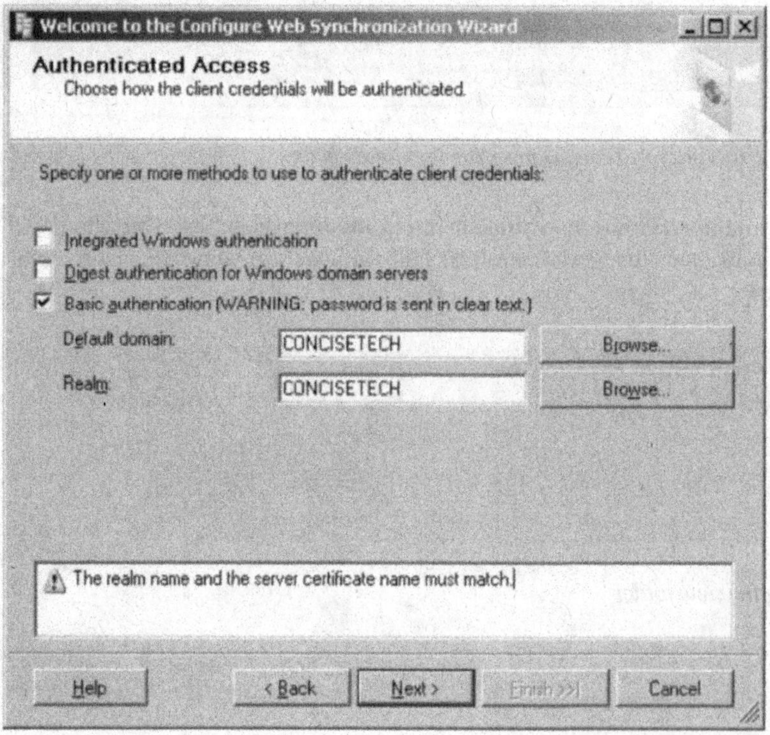

Figure 12-20. *Specifying authentication access details for the client*

Specify the default domain and the realm as shown in Figure 12-20, and click Next.

The wizard will now ask for those clients that will have access to the directory. Click the Add button, and you will see the Select Users or Groups window, as shown in Figure 12-21.

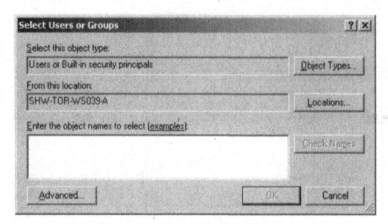

Figure 12-21. *The basic Select Users or Groups window*

Click the Advanced button, which will expand the window as shown in Figure 12-22. Click the Find Now button to find the location.

In Figure 12-22, although I am the only one with access to the machine I used the name of the user (highlighted). I also selected the Everyone user. (You will see both users shown in Figure 12-23.) Ensure that you give the right permissions to the users for accessing the directory, and click OK to return to the basic Select Users or Groups window (Figure 12-21).

Click OK again, and you will see the Directory Access wizard page, which will list the users you have given permissions to. This is shown in Figure 12-23.

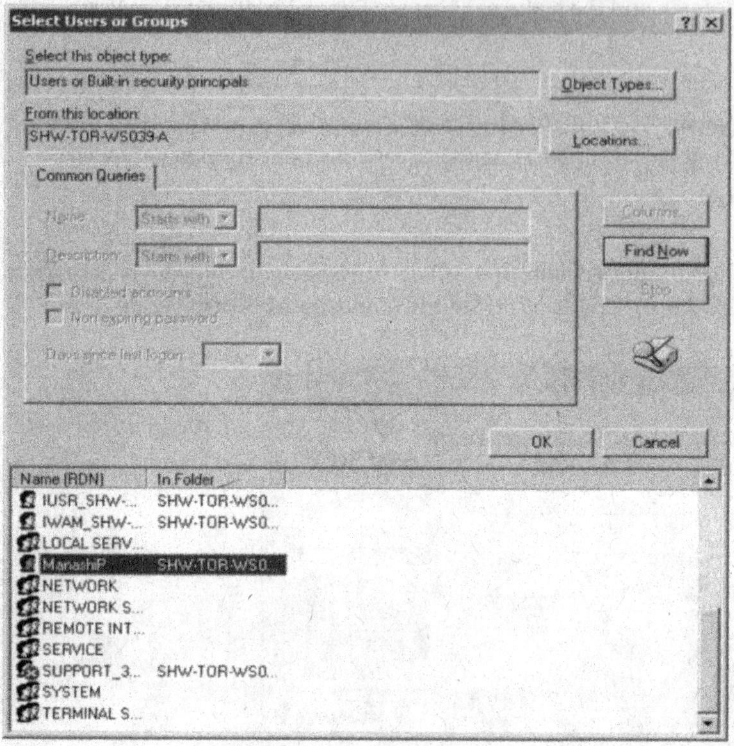

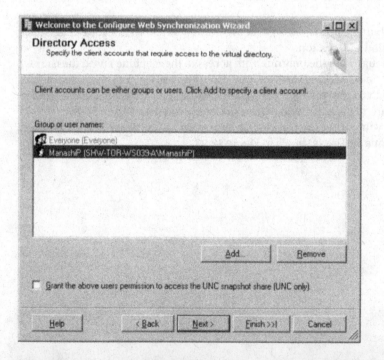

Figure 12-22. *Selecting user names in the advanced Select Users or Groups window*

Figure 12-23. *Viewing the names of clients who have directory access*

Tip If you are using the mobile edition, you should check the box for the UNC snapshot in Figure 12-23. This will open a Snapshot Share Access window where you specify the network path for the snapshot share.

Click the Next button to get to the final page of the wizard, as shown in Figure 12-24. Verify your choices and click the Finish button.

Figure 12-24. *Completing the wizard for web synchronization*

The wizard will now show the success or failure of the configuration, as in Figure 12-25.

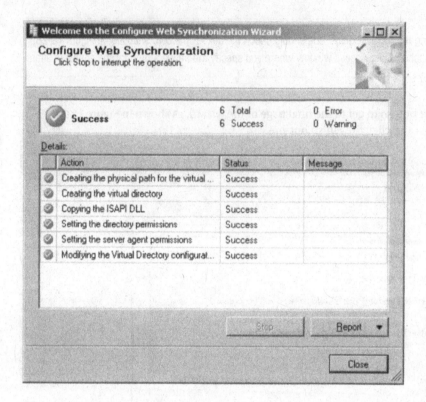

Figure 12-25. *The successful configuration of web synchronization*

Now that the IIS server has been configured for web synchronization, we need to give the right permissions to the Replication Listener.

Setting Permissions for the SQL Server Replication Listener

The SQL Server Replication Listener (replisapi.dll) handles the messages that need to be sent from the Publisher server to the Subscriber servers. When a subscribing server tries to access the web server, the IIS checks to see whether the subscriptions have the correct permissions to invoke the Replication Listener.

If you have not yet created any users to subscribe to the publication, you can do so by right-clicking My Computer and selecting Manage. Expand the Computer Management node, expand Local Users and Groups, right-click on the Users folder, and select New User.

After you have created users, the next step is to assign the permissions for the SQL Server Replication Listener (replisapi.dll). This file should have been already copied (Figure 12-19) to the D:\InetPub\wwwroot\ProductPrice\ProductPrice folder. Right-click on the folder containing the file for the replication listener, select Properties from the menu, and select Security.

On the Security tab, click the Add button; this will lead to a window similar to the one in Figure 12-21. Click the Advanced button, and then click the Find Now button. This will list the users as in Figure 12-22.

Select the user for that computer and click OK. Ensure that you have Read, Read & Execute, and List Folder Contents permissions. If you do not want any other users to have permissions, consider removing them for security reasons. Click OK.

Now that the subscribing users have been given the appropriate permissions, we should test to see that the Replication Listener is successfully invoked when the users connect to the web server running IIS.

Running IIS in Diagnostic Mode

The purpose of running IIS in diagnostic mode is to see whether the Replication Listener is invoked and the SSL certificate is correctly installed when users try to connect.

To turn on diagnostic mode, open Internet Explorer and select Tools ➤ Internet Options. In the Internet Options window, select the Connections tab and click the LAN Settings button. You will see the window shown in Figure 12-26.

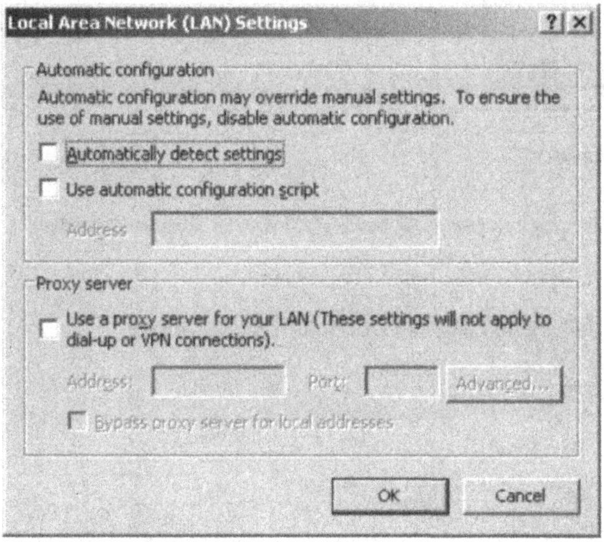

Figure 12-26. *Settings for the LAN*

Since a proxy server is not used on the LAN, uncheck the boxes for "Automatically detect settings" and "Use automatic configuration script." Click the OK button.

On the machine that the subscribing users will use to connect, open Internet Explorer and type the following:

```
https://shw-tor-ws039-a/ProductPrice/replisapi.dll?diag
```

Here the name of the server is shw-tor-ws039-a. The use of ?diag in the URL specifies diagnostic mode.

Note The version of Internet Explorer that I used in these examples is 6.0.2900.2180.

This URL will open the Security Alert window. Click OK, and you will see the Connect window shown in Figure 12-27. Specify the login information for the subscribing user and then click OK.

Figure 12-27. *Connecting the subscribing user*

Internet Explorer will now open the page containing the SQL Websync diagnostic information, as shown in Figure 12-28.

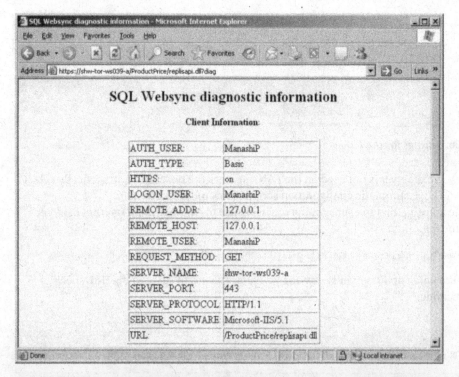

Figure 12-28. *Viewing the SQL Websync diagnostic information in Internet Explorer*

Scroll down to the bottom of the screen and ensure that the values in the Status column for the Class Initialization test are all SUCCESS, as in Figure 12-29.

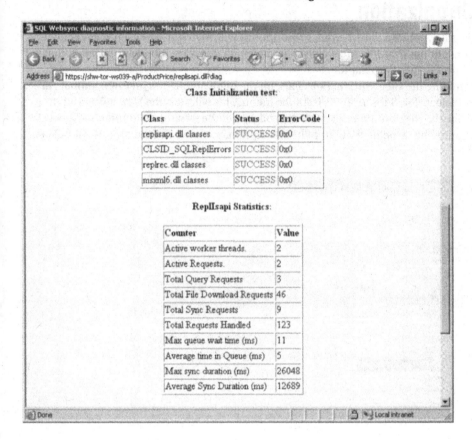

Figure 12-29. *Viewing the status of the SQL Websync tests*

Now close Internet Explorer and connect to the URL in diagnostic mode again (https://shw-tor-ws039-a/ProductPrice/replisapi.dll?diag). This time the Security Alert window should not appear. If it does, ensure that the security certificate is added to the certificate store as a trusted certificate. Otherwise the Merge Agent will fail when it tries to connect to the server that is running IIS.

So far we have configured the publication and enabled it to use web synchronization, and we have configured IIS for web synchronization. The final step of the process is to configure the subscriptions for web synchronization.

Configuring Subscriptions for Web Synchronization

As stated earlier, you can only use pull subscriptions with web synchronization and merge publication. For this example, we will use the same pub_mysales_mobile publication that we have used throughout this chapter.

To configure the subscription, right-click on the publication, pub_mysales_mobile, in SSMS, and select New Subscriptions from the menu. This will start the New Subscription Wizard. Click the Next button in the Welcome page, and the wizard will automatically select the publication that is being used for pull subscription, as shown in Figure 12-30. Click Next to continue.

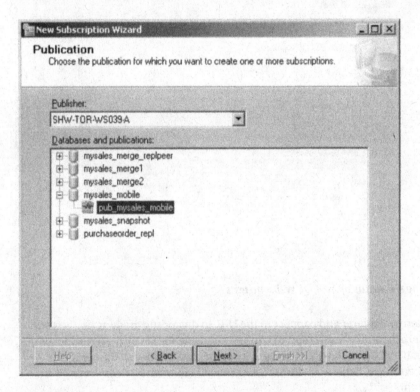

Figure 12-30. *Selecting the publication to be used for pull subscription*

Select the pull subscription option in the Merge Agent Location page, as shown in Figure 12-31. As you can see in the figure, the Merge Agent is located on the subscribing server, in contrast to push subscriptions, where the Merge Agent resides on the Distributor server. Click the Next button.

The next wizard page will ask you to associate the subscription database with the Subscriber server, as shown in Figure 12-32. From the drop-down box under the Subscription Database, select the database. Then click Next to continue.

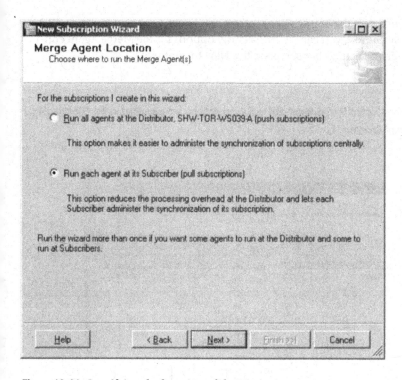

Figure 12-31. *Specifying the location of the Merge Agent*

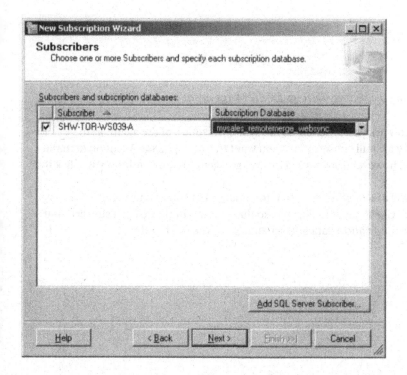

Figure 12-32. *Specifying the Subscriber server and the subscribing database*

Now you need to configure the Merge Agent security accounts, as shown in Figure 12-33. By clicking on the ellipsis button, you can set the security options for the Merge Agent connections to the Publisher and Subscriber servers. Click Next to continue.

Note The security settings for the Merge Agent and pull subscriptions are explained in the "Configuring Pull Subscriptions" section of Chapter 11.

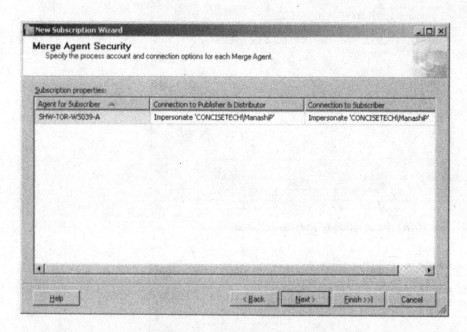

Figure 12-33. *Configuring the security settings for the Merge Agent*

The wizard will now ask you to schedule the synchronization of the agent, as in Figure 12-34. Normally for pull subscriptions you want to run the Merge Agent on demand only. For this example, however, I scheduled the Merge Agent to Run continuously. Click the Next button.

Now the wizard will ask whether you want to initialize the subscription and when, as shown in Figure 12-35. Check the Initialize box so that you can initialize each subscription with a snapshot of the publication data and schema. Click the Next button.

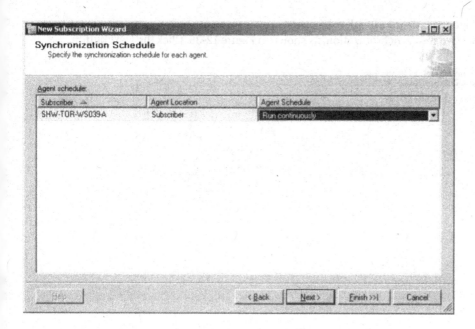

Figure 12-34. *Scheduling the Merge Agent*

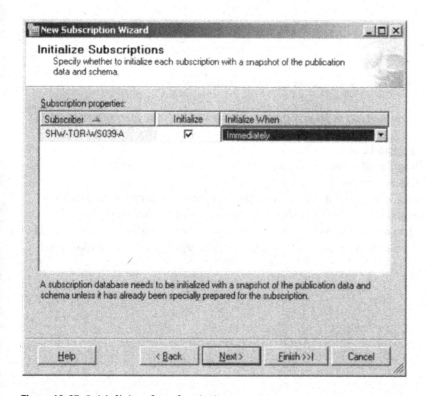

Figure 12-35. *Initializing the subscriptions*

This time the wizard will ask you whether you want to use web synchronization. Check the box for Use Web Synchronization, as shown in Figure 12-36. Click the Next button.

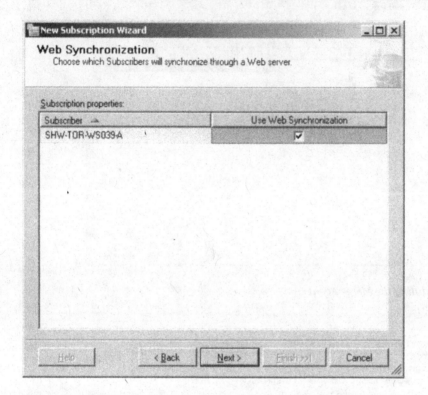

Figure 12-36. *Choosing web synchronization for the Subscriber server*

The wizard will now ask you to specify the Web server address that you need to connect to, as shown in Figure 12-37. This is the same URL that you specified in the Publication Properties window (Figure 12-1).

Specify the web server address, and then select the radio button for using Basic Authentication. Fill in the login information, and then click Next.

The wizard will ask what kind of subscription type you want to specify, as shown in Figure 12-38. Earlier in the chapter I mentioned that we wanted the sales representative to simply retrieve the data and not make any changes to it, so we want the subscription type to be the Client type. We do not want the subscribing servers to republish the data. Click Next to continue.

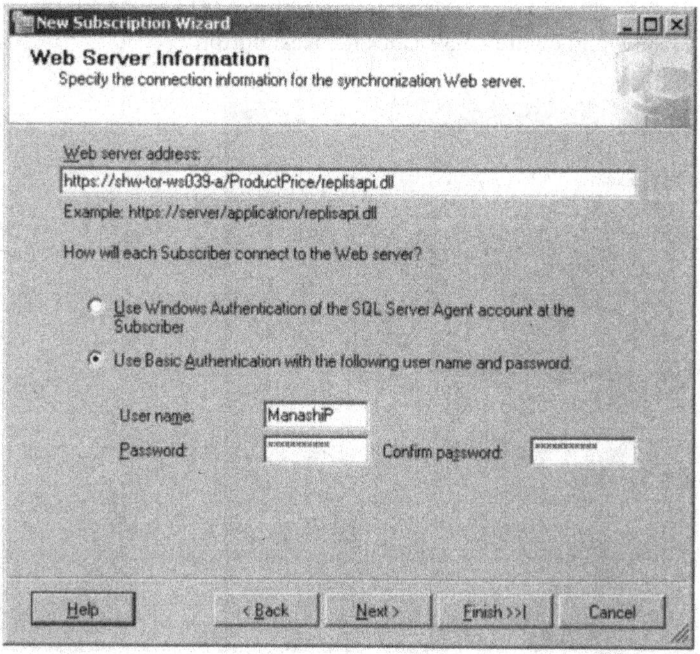

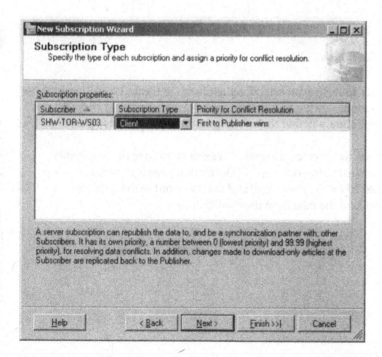

Figure 12-37. *Specifying connection information for synchronizing the web server*

Figure 12-38. *Setting the subscription type and the corresponding conflict policy*

In the next window, the wizard will ask you to create the subscription. Check the box for "Create the subscription(s)" as shown in Figure 12-39. Click the Next button.

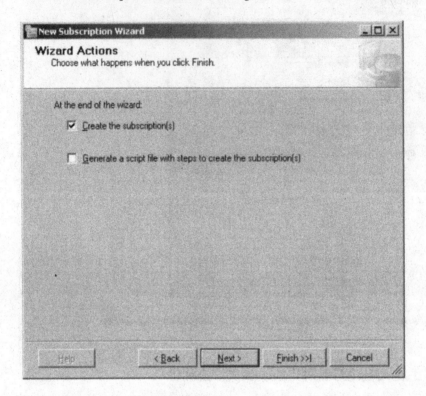

Figure 12-39. *Creating the subscription*

You now have the chance to verify your selections, as shown in Figure 12-40. If everything is correct, click the Finish button.

The final wizard page will show whether the subscription was successfully created, as shown as in Figure 12-41.

Now that the subscription has been configured, you need to log in to the Subscriber server with the URL you specified in the Web Server Information page of the wizard (Figure 12-37). You will be asked for the user name and the password so that you can use the Merge Agent to download the data from the Publisher server.

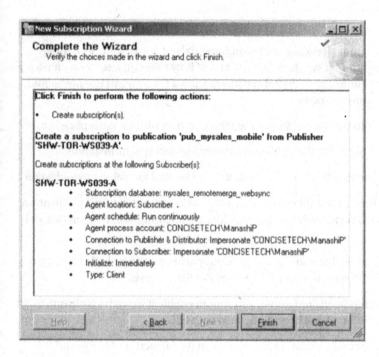

Figure 12-40. *Completing the wizard*

Figure 12-41. *Successful creation of the pull subscription*

Summary

You should now have a solid understanding of the fundamentals of publication with merge replication, of how to configure web synchronization, and of how to set up a server with IIS for web synchronization. If you cannot get a digital certificate from a CA, you can use the SelfSSL utility from Microsoft for testing purposes.

- You can only use pull subscriptions for web synchronization with merge replication.

- You can only use SQL Server as the Publisher when using web synchronization.

- A publication should not contain logical records if it is to be used for web synchronization.

- The three steps involved in setting up web synchronization are setting up a publication, setting up the IIS machine for web synchronization, and creating subscriptions for web synchronization.

- There are three topologies that you can use for web synchronization: single server, two servers, and multiple IIS servers with a SQL Server Publisher server.

- After the publication has been configured, you should enable it for web synchronization and specify the URL that has been associated with SSL.

- You can use SSL as the communication layer between the Subscriber servers and IIS.

- You can use the SelfSSL utility to create a personal digital certificate.

- SQL Server Replication Listener handles the messages between the Publisher server and the Subscriber server.

- The name of the SQL Server Replication Listener is replisapi.dll.

- Assign the right permissions to the SQL Server Replication Listener.

- Test the web synchronization configuration by running in diagnostic mode.

In the next chapter, I will show you how to use T-SQL to set up publication for both download-only and standard articles, and how to use join filters and data partitioning using dynamic functions. Finally, I will show you how to configure push and pull subscriptions for both client and server subscription types.

Quick Tips

- Use the -T switch when running the SelfSSL utility.

- The validity of a certificate created with SelfSSL is 7 days by default. You can change the validity by using the -V switch.

- SQL Server uses port number 1433 by default. If you use a different port number, you have to specify it in the URL.

- You can use SelfSSL only on Windows XP and Windows 2003.

- Use Basic Authentication instead of Windows Authentication to connect to a client.

CHAPTER 13

■ ■ ■

Configuring Merge Replication Using T-SQL

I explained how to set up merge replication using the GUI in Chapters 11 and 12. In this chapter, I will show you how to configure publications for both download-only and standard articles and how to configure subscriptions for those publications using T-SQL. I will also show you how to set up logical records and join filters, and how to use dynamic functions for data partitioning.

On completing this chapter, you will know how to use T-SQL to do the following:

- Configure publication for download-only articles

- Configure publication for standard articles with parameterized filters

- Set up join filters

- Partition data using dynamic functions

- Set up pull subscriptions for client subscriptions

- Set up push subscriptions for server subscriptions

- Set up identity range management

Note If you have yet to install the database, you should do so. The E-R diagram for the database is shown in Appendix A, and the SQL code for the database is given in Appendix B.

Configuring Publications

You must configure the Distributor server and the distribution database before you can set up the publishing server and the publication; this is true for snapshot, transactional, and merge replication. Chapters 5 and 9 discuss the steps for setting up snapshot and transactional replication using T-SQL.

Like transactional replication, merge replication makes use of the Snapshot Agent to generate the initial snapshot, although it is possible to manually synchronize the subscription without generating a snapshot (by first generating the publication, making a backup copy of the publication database, restoring the schema and the data on the subscription database, and then manually synchronizing the process). The autonomous nature of merge replication allows latency but also leads to new complexities, like conflict resolution. The changes made in merge replication, whether in the schema or data, are tracked by triggers, and any conflicts in changes on different servers are resolved using the conflict resolution policy. Merge replication can be used for client/server scenarios such as point-of-sale applications or sales force automation where you need to integrate data from multiple clients to the central server.

As mentioned in Chapter 11, you can use download-only articles if the subscriptions do not need to make any updates to the data. The subscriptions can view any changes made on the Publishing server at their discretion. Merge publication with standard articles, on the other hand, is used if you want to update data at the Subscriber servers. When you set up merge replication, standard articles are configured by default. Database objects, such as stored procedures and views, are always published as standard articles, regardless of the type of articles that you select.

The next section shows how merge publication with download-only articles can be configured using T-SQL.

DROPPING SUBSCRIPTIONS AND PUBLICATIONS

Before setting up transactional and snapshot replication using T-SQL, you need to drop the subscriptions and publications you created in Chapters 11 and 12.

You can drop a pull subscription created for merge replication by executing the `sp_dropmergepull` `subscription` stored procedure on the Subscriber server. The parameters for the stored procedure are `@publication`, `@publisher_db`, and `@publisher`. This stored procedure cleans up the metadata for the subscription database.

For push subscriptions, on the other hand, you first have to drop the subscription by executing the `sp_dropmergesubscription` stored procedure on the Publisher server, using the `@publication`, `@subscriber`, and `@subscriber_db` parameters. You then clean up the metadata on the subscription database by executing `sp_mergesubscription_cleanup` with the `@publication`, `@publisher`, and `@publisher_db` parameters on the Subscriber server.

Once you drop the subscriptions, you can then drop the publications. To drop a merge publication, execute `sp_dropmergepublication` with the `@publication` parameter. This stored procedure should be executed on the publication database on the Publisher server. You can then remove the replication objects using `sp_replicationdboption` using the `@dbname`, `@optname`, and `@value` parameters. Note that if the `@optname` parameter is `merge publish` and the `@value` parameter is set to `false`, the subscriptions for the merge publication will also be dropped.

Configuring Publication with Download-Only Articles

Download-only articles are used for subscriptions that do not have to issue any insert, delete, or update statements—they are used for read-only subscriptions. Changes are only made at the Publisher server on the publication database. As such, metadata changes are not made on the subscription database but only on the publication database. As was mentioned in Chapter 11, this can increase the performance of merge replication, since there is less storage required in subscription databases. You would normally use publication with download-only articles for client type subscriptions.

Here are the steps to configure publication with download-only articles:

1. Enable the database for replication using the sp_replicationdboption stored procedure.

2. Create the publication using the sp_addmergepublication stored procedure.

3. Create an agent for the publication using the sp_addpublication_snapshot stored procedure.

4. Grant publication access using the sp_grant_publication_access stored procedure.

5. Add articles for the publication using the sp_addmergearticle stored procedure.

6. Start the snapshot with the sp_startpublication_snapshot stored procedure.

Listing 13-1 shows you how to set up the replication and create the publication (steps 1 and 2 in the preceding list). In this example, the publication database is mysales_merge1.

Listing 13-1. *Setting Up the Database for Merge Replication and Creating a Publication*

```
/* Use the Publisher server to enable merge replication */

use master
go
sp_replicationdboption @dbname = 'mysales_merge1',
@optname = 'merge publish',
@value = 'true'
go

/* Create the merge publication on the mysales_merge1 database */

use [mysales_merge1]
go

/*Add the publication 'pub_download_mysalesmerge' */

sp_addmergepublication @publication = 'pub_downloadonly_mysalesmerge',
@sync_mode = 'native',
@retention = 14,
@allow_push = 'true',
@allow_pull = 'true',
```

```
@allow_anonymous = 'true',
@enabled_for_internet = 'false',
@snapshot_in_defaultfolder = 'true',
@allow_subscription_copy = 'false',
@dynamic_filters = 'false',
@conflict_retention = 14,
@keep_partition_changes = 'false',
@max_concurrent_merge = 0,
@max_concurrent_dynamic_snapshots = 0,
@use_partition_groups = 'false',
@publication_compatibility_level = '90RTM',
@replicate_ddl = 1,
@allow_subscriber_initiated_snapshot = 'false',
@allow_web_synchronization = 'false',
@allow_partition_realignment = 'true',
@retention_period_unit = 'days',
@conflict_logging = 'both',
@automatic_reinitialization_policy = 0
go
```

As with snapshot and transactional replication, this script enables the database for merge replication using the sp_replicationdboption stored procedure, where the @optname parameter has been set to merge publish. I outlined the different values for the @optname parameter in Table 9-1 in Chapter 9.

Having enabled the database for replication, the script creates the publication by executing the sp_addmergepublication stored procedure on the publication database on the Publisher server. Notice that since the Publisher server is a SQL Server Publisher, I have set the @sync_mode parameter to native type. This means that the initial synchronization of the subscriptions will be performed by the bulk copy program such that the output of all the tables is in native mode. (This is in contrast to the character-mode generation used for the SQL Server Mobile edition.)

I have not used any dynamic partitioning in this example, so the @dynamic_filters parameter has been set to false. I have not enabled the publication to use web synchronization or to use FTP for transferring the snapshot, so the @enabled_for_internet and @allow_web_synchronization parameters have been set to false. The snapshot is located in the default folder, as specified by the @snapshot_in_defaultfolder parameter.

I have set the @conflict_retention parameter to 14 days, which means that after 14 days, any conflict row that is present will be purged from the conflict table. The @conflict_logging parameter has been set to both, which means that the conflict records will be stored at both the Publisher and Subscriber servers. You can alternatively set the value for this parameter to publisher or subscriber. However, since the @publication_compatibility_level parameter has been set to true, the default value of both is set for @conflict_logging.

I set the @retention parameter to 14 days, which means that the subscription will have 14 days to synchronize; otherwise you will have to reinitialize the subscription by running the Snapshot Agent again. Both the @max_concurrent_merge and @max_concurrent_dynamic_snapshots parameters have been set to 0. The @max_concurrent_merge parameter allows any number of Merge Agent processes to run concurrently, and the @max_concurrent_dynamic_ snapshots parameter allows any number of concurrent Snapshot Agents to generate filtered data for snapshots of Subscriber partitions.

Note that I have set the @allow_partition_realignment parameter to true. This is the default value. Any changes in the partition of the data in the Publisher server are sent as deletes to the subscribing server.

The next step in the process is to create the Snapshot Agent for the publication using the sp_addpublication_snapshot stored procedure, and to grant access to the publication using the sp_grant_publication_access stored procedure. This is shown in Listing 13-2.

Listing 13-2. *Creating the Snapshot Agent and Access to the Publication*

```
/* Execute this on the publication database */

use [mysales_merge1]
go

/* Create the Snapshot Agent */

sp_addpublication_snapshot @publication = 'pub_downloadonly_mysalesmerge',
@frequency_type = 4,
@frequency_interval = 14,
@frequency_relative_interval = 1,
@frequency_recurrence_factor = 0,
@frequency_subday = 1,
@frequency_subday_interval = 5,
@active_start_time_of_day = 500,
@active_end_time_of_day = 235959,
@active_start_date = 0,
@active_end_date = 0,
@job_login = 'BIO-V7V30JTZLZS\Sujoy Paul',
@job_password = null,
@publisher_security_mode = 0,
@publisher_login = 'sa', @publisher_password = ''

/*Grant publication access */

exec sp_grant_publication_access @publication = 'pub_downloadonly_mysalesmerge',
@login = 'sa'
go
```

■ **Tip** The Snapshot Agent job is named as follows: <Publisher>-<Publicationdatabase>-➦ <publication>-<integer>.

The script in Listing 13-2 is discussed in the "Creating a Snapshot Agent" section of Chapter 5.

The next step of the process is adding the articles to the publication. The script in Listing 13-3 adds the Item, SalesPerson, Warehouse, and PriceList articles.

Listing 13-3. *Adding Download-Only Articles for Merge Publication*

```
/* Execute this on the publication database */

Use mysales_merge1
Go

/* Add the merge article, Item, to the publication */

sp_addmergearticle @publication = 'pub_downloadonly_mysalesmerge',
@article = 'Item',
@source_owner = 'myinventory',
@source_object = 'Item',
@type = 'table',
@pre_creation_cmd = 'drop',
@identityrangemanagementoption = 'none',
@destination_owner = 'myinventory',
@force_reinit_subscription = 1,
@column_tracking = 'false',
@subset_filterclause = '',
@vertical_partition = 'false',
@verify_resolver_signature = 0,
@allow_interactive_resolver = 'false',
@check_permissions = 0,
@subscriber_upload_options = 2,
@delete_tracking = 'true',
@compensate_for_errors = 'false',
@stream_blob_columns = 'false',
@partition_options = 0
Go

use [mysales_merge1]
go

/* Add the merge article, SalesPerson, to the publication */
sp_addmergearticle @publication = 'pub_downloadonly_mysalesmerge',
@article = 'SalesPerson',
@source_owner = 'myorder',
@source_object = 'SalesPerson',
@type = 'table',
@pre_creation_cmd = 'drop',
@identityrangemanagementoption = 'none',
```

```
@destination_owner = 'myorder',
@force_reinit_subscription = 1,
@column_tracking = 'false',
@subset_filterclause = '',
@vertical_partition = 'false',
@verify_resolver_signature = 0,
@allow_interactive_resolver = 'false',
@check_permissions = 0,
@subscriber_upload_options = 2,
@delete_tracking = 'true',
@compensate_for_errors = 'false',
@stream_blob_columns = 'false',
@partition_options = 0
Go

use [mysales_merge1]
go


/* Add the merge article, Warehouse, to the publication */

sp_addmergearticle @publication = 'pub_downloadonly_mysalesmerge',
@article = 'Warehouse',
@source_owner = 'myinventory',
@source_object = 'Warehouse',
@type = 'table',
@pre_creation_cmd = 'drop',
@identityrangemanagementoption = 'none',
@destination_owner = 'myinventory',
@force_reinit_subscription = 1,
@column_tracking = 'false',
@subset_filterclause = '',
@vertical_partition = 'false',
@verify_resolver_signature = 0,
@allow_interactive_resolver = 'false',
@check_permissions = 0,
@subscriber_upload_options = 2,
@delete_tracking = 'true',
@compensate_for_errors = 'false',
@stream_blob_columns = 'false',
@partition_options = 0
Go

use [mysales_merge1]
go


/* Add the merge article, PriceList, to the publication */
```

```
sp_addmergearticle @publication = 'pub_downloadonly_mysalesmerge',
@article = 'PriceList',
@source_owner = 'myinventory',
@source_object = 'PriceList',
@type = 'table',
@pre_creation_cmd = 'drop',
@identityrangemanagementoption = 'none',
@destination_owner = 'myinventory',
@force_reinit_subscription = 1,
@column_tracking = 'false',
@subset_filterclause = '',
@vertical_partition = 'false',
@verify_resolver_signature = 0,
@allow_interactive_resolver = 'false',
@check_permissions = 0,
@subscriber_upload_options = 2,
@delete_tracking = 'true',
@compensate_for_errors = 'false',
@stream_blob_columns = 'false',
@partition_options = 0
go
```

In this case, the sp_addmergearticle stored procedure is used to add new articles. The @pre_creation_cmd parameter has been set to drop, which means that if the table exists on the subscription database, it will be dropped and re-created. The other possible values are none and delete. If it is set to delete, a delete statement based on a where clause will be issued.

We are not using any identity range management right now, so I have set it to none. (Identity range management is discussed toward the end of the chapter.) The @force_reinit_subscription parameter has been set to 1, which means that any changes to the article will cause the reinitialization of the subscriptions. The default value is 0, so if articles are added to the publication, the subscription will not be reinitialized. Should the stored procedure detect any changes to the article and require the reinitialization of the subscriptions, however, the stored procedure will only report errors without taking any action.

The @column_tracking parameter has been set to false, which means that conflict detection will be done at the row level; if this table is used in other publications, we will have to use the same column-level tracking there. The @verify_resolver_signature parameter has been set to 0, which means that a digital signature is not required to verify whether a resolver is used. Since we are not going to use the Interactive Resolver with the WSM, I have set the @allow_interactive_resolver to false.

The @delete_tracking parameter has been set to true, which is the default value. This replicates the deleted values. If it were set to false, any rows deleted at either the subscription or the publication database would need to be manually deleted on the publication or the subscription database.

The @subscriber_upload_options parameter specifies whether the article is used for download only. If so, the value should either be 1 or 2: 1 indicates that changes are allowed on the subscription database but are not uploaded to the publication database, while 2 means that changes are not allowed on the subscription database.

Bear in mind that you need to be a member of the sysadmin fixed server role or db_owner fixed database role to execute the stored procedure.

Note If an article has been changed to download-only after the synchronization, you must reinitialize all the subscriptions.

Finally, we need to start the Snapshot Agent job. This is shown in Listing 13-4.

Listing 13-4. *Starting the Snapshot Agent Job*

```
/* Execute this stored procedure on the publication database */

Use [mysales_merge1]
Go


/* Start the Snapshot Agent job to generate the initial
snapshot for the publication */

Exec sp_startpublication_snapshot 'pub_downloadonly_mysalesmerge'
Go
```

Now that I have shown you how to set up the publication for download-only articles, I will show you how to configure the publication for standard articles.

Configuring Publication with Standard Articles

Although this section deals primarily with configuring standard articles for merge publication, I have also incorporated data partitioning and join filters. The articles contain the following tables, and the schema associated with the tables is shown in parentheses:

- AccountsReceivable (myfinance)

- Customer (myorder)

- CustSales (myorder)

- Item (myinventory)

- OrderDetail (myorder)

- OrderHeader (myorder)

- PriceList (myinventory)

- SalesPerson (myorder)

- Stock (myorder)

- StockItem (myinventory)

The publication also contains views (vw_CustomerInvoiceStatus, vw_ItemEnquiry, and vw_OrderStatus) and a stored procedure (usp_GetCustomerInvoicePaymentDue) as articles. The views will find the customer's invoice status, any items they want to enquire about, and the order status of any items respectively. The stored procedure locates customers whose payments are due.

I will first show you how to set up the merge publication, create the publication snapshot, and grant access to the publication. I will then demonstrate how to create the merge articles and join filters. I will also show you how to set up conflict resolution using Microsoft COM-based conflict resolvers.

Listing 13-5 shows how to set up the publication for standard articles.

Listing 13-5. *Setting Up the Publication for Standard Articles*

```
/* Enable the database for replication by executing this on the
master database.*/

use master
exec sp_replicationdboption @dbname = 'mysales_merge2',
@optname = 'merge publish',
@value = 'true'
go

/*Add the merge publication for standard articles using the default
agent schedule.*/
/* Execute this on the publication database. */

use [mysales_merge2]
go

sp_addmergepublication @publication = 'pub_stdpub_mysalesmerge2',
/* Need to add @publication_compatibility_level='90RTM'
when @conflict_logging is set to 'both' */

@publication_compatibility_level='90RTM',
@sync_mode = 'native',
@retention = 14,
@allow_push = 'true',
@allow_pull = 'true',
@allow_anonymous = 'true',
@snapshot_in_defaultfolder = 'true',
@allow_subscription_copy = 'false',
@dynamic_filters = 'true',
@conflict_retention = 14,
@keep_partition_changes = 'false',
@allow_synctoalternate = 'false',
@validate_subscriber_info = 'SUSER_SNAME()',
@max_concurrent_merge = 0,
@max_concurrent_dynamic_snapshots = 0,
```

```
@use_partition_groups = 'true',
@replicate_ddl = 1,
@allow_subscriber_initiated_snapshot = 'true',
@allow_web_synchronization = 'false',
@allow_partition_realignment = 'true',
@retention_period_unit = 'days',
@conflict_logging = 'both',
@automatic_reinitialization_policy = 0
GO

/* Now add the publication snapshot */

exec sp_addpublication_snapshot @publication
 = 'pub_stdpub_mysalesmerge2', @frequency_type = 4,
@frequency_interval = 14,
@frequency_relative_interval = 1,
@frequency_recurrence_factor = 0,
@frequency_subday = 1,
@frequency_subday_interval = 5,
@active_start_time_of_day = 500,
@active_end_time_of_day = 235959,
@active_start_date = 0,
@active_end_date = 0,
@job_login = null,
@job_password = null,
@publisher_security_mode = 0,
@publisher_login = 'sa',
@publisher_password = ''

/* Grant access to the publication. */

exec sp_grant_publication_access
@publication = 'pub_stdpub_mysalesmerge2',
@login = 'sa'
GO
exec sp_grant_publication_access
 @publication = 'pub_stdpub_mysalesmerge2',
@login = 'NT AUTHORITY\SYSTEM'
GO
exec sp_grant_publication_access
 @publication = 'pub_stdpub_mysalesmerge2',
@login = 'BUILTIN\Administrators'
GO
exec sp_grant_publication_access
@publication = 'pub_stdpub_mysalesmerge2',
@login = 'BIO-V7V30JTZLZS\SQLServer2005SQLAgentUser$BIO-V7V30JTZLZS$BIOREPL'
GO
```

```
exec sp_grant_publication_access
@publication = 'pub_stdpub_mysalesmerge2',
@login = 'BIO-V7V30JTZLZS\SQLServer2005MSSQLUser$BIO-V7V30JTZLZS$BIOREPL'
GO
exec sp_grant_publication_access
@publication = 'pub_stdpub_mysalesmerge2',
@login = 'BIO-V7V30JTZLZS\Sujoy Paul'
GO
exec sp_grant_publication_access
@publication = 'pub_stdpub_mysalesmerge2',
@login = 'distributor_admin'
GO
exec sp_grant_publication_access
@publication = 'pub_stdpub_mysalesmerge2',
@login = 'LexasSmith'
GO
exec sp_grant_publication_access
@publication = 'pub_stdpub_mysalesmerge2',
@login = 'BensMarcedez'
GO
```

As in Listing 13-1, I enabled the database for replication and then used the
sp_addmergepublication stored procedure to create the publication. However, there
are three major differences in the parameters in this case.

First, I set the @dynamic_filters parameter to true. This is because we want to use parameterized row filters. The SUSER_SNAME() system function has been used for the purpose of
dynamic data partitioning. The @validate_subscriber_info parameter lists the system functions used in the partition of Subscriber servers when parameterized filters are used. Second,
the @use_partition_groups parameter is set to true. This means that the publication uses precomputed partitions for optimizing the synchronization.

The @allow_subscriber_initiated_snapshot parameter is also set to true, which means
that the subscribing servers for this publication can initiate the snapshot process and generate a dynamic snapshot. In order to generate the initial snapshot, you will have to execute
sp_startpublication_snapshot after you set up the merge filters.

The next step is to add the articles to the publication using the sp_addmergearticle stored
procedure. This is shown in Listing 13-6.

Listing 13-6. *Adding Standard Articles to the Publication*

```
/* Execute this on the publication database. */
use [mysales_merge2]
go

/* Add the merge article, Customer, to the publication */

exec sp_addmergearticle @publication = 'pub_stdpub_mysalesmerge2',
@article = 'Customer',
@source_owner = 'myorder',
```

```
@source_object = 'Customer',
@type = 'table',
@creation_script = '',
@pre_creation_cmd = 'drop',
@identityrangemanagementoption = 'none',
@destination_owner = 'myorder',
@force_reinit_subscription = 1,
@column_tracking = 'false',
@subset_filterclause = '',
@vertical_partition ='false',
@verify_resolver_signature = 1,
@allow_interactive_resolver = 'true',
@check_permissions = 0,
@subscriber_upload_options = 0,
@delete_tracking = 'true',
@compensate_for_errors = 'false',
@stream_blob_columns = 'false',
@partition_options = 0
Go

use [mysales_merge2]
go

/* Add the merge article, Stock, to the publication */

exec sp_addmergearticle
@publication = 'pub_stdpub_mysalesmerge2',
@article = 'Stock',
@source_owner ='myorder',
@source_object = 'Stock',
@type = 'table',
@creation_script = '',
@pre_creation_cmd = 'drop',
@identityrangemanagementoption = 'none',
@destination_owner = 'myorder',
@force_reinit_subscription = 1,
@column_tracking = 'false',
@subset_filterclause = '',
@vertical_partition = 'false',
@verify_resolver_signature = 1,
@allow_interactive_resolver = 'true',
@check_permissions = 0,
@subscriber_upload_options = 0,
@delete_tracking = 'true',
@compensate_for_errors = 'false',
@stream_blob_columns = 'false',
@partition_options = 0
go
```

```
use [mysales_merge2]
go

/* Add the merge article, Item, to the publication */

exec sp_addmergearticle
@publication = 'pub_stdpub_mysalesmerge2',
@article = 'Item',
@source_owner = 'myinventory',
@source_object = 'Item',
@type = 'table',
@creation_script = '',
@pre_creation_cmd = 'drop',
@identityrangemanagementoption = 'none',
@destination_owner = 'myinventory',
@force_reinit_subscription = 1,
@column_tracking = 'false',
@subset_filterclause = '',
@vertical_partition ='false',
@verify_resolver_signature = 1,
@allow_interactive_resolver = 'true',
@check_permissions = 0,
@subscriber_upload_options = 0,
@delete_tracking = 'true',
@compensate_for_errors = 'false',
@stream_blob_columns = 'false',
@partition_options = 0
go

use [mysales_merge2]
go

/* Add the merge article, SalesPerson, to the publication */

exec sp_addmergearticle
@publication = 'pub_stdpub_mysalesmerge2',
@article = 'SalesPerson',
@source_owner = 'myorder',
@source_object = 'SalesPerson',
@type = 'table',
@creation_script = '',
@pre_creation_cmd = 'drop',
@identityrangemanagementoption = 'none',
@destination_owner = 'myorder',
@force_reinit_subscription = 1,
@column_tracking = 'false',
```

```
@subset_filterclause = 'cast([SalesID] as char(10))= SUSER_SNAME()',
@vertical_partition = 'false',
@verify_resolver_signature = 1,
@allow_interactive_resolver = 'true',
@check_permissions = 0,
@subscriber_upload_options = 0,
@delete_tracking = 'true',
@compensate_for_errors = 'false',
@stream_blob_columns = 'false',
@partition_options = 0
go

use [mysales_merge2]
go

/* Add the merge article, AccountsReceivable, to the publication */

exec sp_addmergearticle
@publication = 'pub_stdpub_mysalesmerge2',
@article = 'AccountsReceivable',
@source_owner = 'myfinance',
@source_object = 'AccountsReceivable',
@type = 'table',
@creation_script = '',
@pre_creation_cmd = 'drop',
@identityrangemanagementoption = 'none',
@destination_owner = 'myfinance',
@force_reinit_subscription = 1,
@column_tracking = 'false',
@subset_filterclause = '',
@vertical_partition = 'false',
@verify_resolver_signature = 1,
@allow_interactive_resolver = 'true',
@check_permissions = 0,
@subscriber_upload_options = 0,
@delete_tracking = 'true',
@compensate_for_errors = 'false',
@stream_blob_columns = 'false',
@partition_options = 0
Go

use [mysales_merge2]
go

/* Add the merge article, OrderHeader, to the publication */
```

```
exec sp_addmergearticle
@publication = 'pub_stdpub_mysalesmerge2',
@article = 'OrderHeader',
@source_owner ='myorder',
@source_object = 'OrderHeader',
@type = 'table',
@creation_script = '',
@pre_creation_cmd = 'drop',
@identityrangemanagementoption = 'none',
@destination_owner = 'myorder',
@force_reinit_subscription = 1,
@column_tracking = 'false',
/*@article_resolver = 'Microsoft SQL Server DATETIME (Earlier Wins)
Conflict Resolver',*/
@subset_filterclause = '',
/*@resolver_info = 'Ship_date',*/
@vertical_partition = 'false',
@verify_resolver_signature = 0,
@allow_interactive_resolver = 'true',
@check_permissions = 0,
@subscriber_upload_options = 0,
@delete_tracking = 'true',
@compensate_for_errors = 'false',
@stream_blob_columns = 'false',
@partition_options = 0
Go

use [mysales_merge2]
go

/* Add the merge article, PriceList, to the publication */

exec sp_addmergearticle
@publication = 'pub_stdpub_mysalesmerge2',
@article = 'PriceList',
@source_owner = 'myinventory',
@source_object = 'PriceList',
@type = 'table',
@creation_script = '',
@pre_creation_cmd = 'drop',
@identityrangemanagementoption = 'none',
@destination_owner = 'myinventory',
@force_reinit_subscription = 1,
@column_tracking = 'false',
@article_resolver = 'Microsoft SQL Server Maximum Conflict Resolver',
@subset_filterclause = '',
```

```
@resolver_info = 'Price',
@vertical_partition ='false',
@verify_resolver_signature = 1,
@allow_interactive_resolver = 'true',
@check_permissions = 0,
@subscriber_upload_options = 0,
@delete_tracking = 'true',
@compensate_for_errors = 'false',
@stream_blob_columns = 'false',
@partition_options = 0
Go

use [mysales_merge2]
go

/* Add the merge article, StockItem, to the publication */

exec sp_addmergearticle
@publication = 'pub_stdpub_mysalesmerge2',
@article = 'StockItem',
@source_owner = 'myinventory',
@source_object = 'StockItem',
@type = 'table',
@creation_script = '',
@pre_creation_cmd = 'drop',
@identityrangemanagementoption = 'none',
@destination_owner = 'myinventory',
@force_reinit_subscription = 1,
@column_tracking = 'false',
@subset_filterclause = '',
@vertical_partition ='false',
@verify_resolver_signature = 1,
@allow_interactive_resolver = 'true',
@check_permissions = 0,
@subscriber_upload_options = 0,
@delete_tracking = 'true',
@compensate_for_errors = 'false',
@stream_blob_columns = 'false',
@partition_options = 0
Go

use [mysales_merge2]
go

/* Add the merge article, CustSales, to the publication */
```

```
exec sp_addmergearticle
@publication = 'pub_stdpub_mysalesmerge2',
@article = 'CustSales',
@source_owner ='myorder',
@source_object = 'CustSales',
@type = 'table',
@creation_script = '',
@pre_creation_cmd = 'drop',
@identityrangemanagementoption = 'none',
@destination_owner = 'myorder',
@force_reinit_subscription = 1,
@column_tracking = 'false',
@subset_filterclause = '',
@vertical_partition ='false',
@verify_resolver_signature = 1,
@allow_interactive_resolver = 'true',
@check_permissions = 0,
@subscriber_upload_options = 0,
@delete_tracking = 'true',
@compensate_for_errors = 'false',
@stream_blob_columns = 'false',
@partition_options = 0
Go

use [mysales_merge2]
go

/* Add the merge article, OrderDetail, to the publication */

exec sp_addmergearticle
@publication = 'pub_stdpub_mysalesmerge2',
@article = 'OrderDetail',
@source_owner = 'myorder',
@source_object = 'OrderDetail',
@type = 'table',
@creation_script = '',
@pre_creation_cmd = 'drop',
@identityrangemanagementoption = 'none',
@destination_owner = 'myorder',
@force_reinit_subscription = 1,
@column_tracking = 'false',
@subset_filterclause = '',
@vertical_partition ='false',
@verify_resolver_signature = 1,
@allow_interactive_resolver = 'true',
@check_permissions = 0,
@subscriber_upload_options = 0,
```

```
@delete_tracking = 'true',
@compensate_for_errors = 'false',
@stream_blob_columns = 'false',
@partition_options = 0
Go


use [mysales_merge2]
go


/* Add the merge article, usp_GetCustomerInvoicePaymentDue, to the publication */

exec sp_addmergearticle
@publication = 'pub_stdpub_mysalesmerge2',
@article ='usp_GetCustomerInvoicePaymentDue',
@source_owner = 'myorder',
@source_object = 'usp_GetCustomerInvoicePaymentDue',
@type = 'proc schema only',
@pre_creation_cmd = 'drop',
@destination_owner = 'myorder',
@destination_object = 'usp_GetCustomerInvoicePaymentDue',
@force_reinit_subscription = 1
Go


use [mysales_merge2]
go


/* Add the merge article, vw_CustomerInvoiceStatus, to
the publication */

exec sp_addmergearticle
@publication = 'pub_stdpub_mysalesmerge2',
@article = 'vw_CustomerInvoiceStatus',
@source_owner = 'myorder',
@source_object = 'vw_CustomerInvoiceStatus',
@type = 'view schema only',
@pre_creation_cmd = 'drop',
@destination_owner = 'myorder',
@destination_object = 'vw_CustomerInvoiceStatus',
@force_reinit_subscription = 1
Go


use [mysales_merge2]
go


/* Add the merge article, vw_ItemEnquiry, to
the publication */
```

```
exec sp_addmergearticle
@publication = 'pub_stdpub_mysalesmerge2',
@article = 'vw_ItemEnquiry',
@source_owner= 'myorder',
@source_object = 'vw_ItemEnquiry',
@type = 'view schema only',
@pre_creation_cmd = 'drop',
@destination_owner = 'myorder',
@destination_object = 'vw_ItemEnquiry',
@force_reinit_subscription = 1
Go

use [mysales_merge2]
go

/* Add the merge article, vw_OrderStatus, to
the publication */

exec sp_addmergearticle
@publication = 'pub_stdpub_mysalesmerge2',
@article = 'vw_OrderStatus',
@source_owner = 'myorder',
@source_object = 'vw_OrderStatus',
@type = 'view schema only',
@pre_creation_cmd = 'drop',
@destination_owner = 'myorder',
@destination_object ='vw_OrderStatus',
@force_reinit_subscription = 1
go
```

For the Customer article, you can see that the @type parameter has been specified as table. This is the default value; the other possible values are shown in Table 13-1. Where tables have been included as articles, they have been assigned table type. For views, such as vw_ItemEnquiry, the parameter has been specified as view schema only, and for the usp_GetCustomerInvoicePaymentDue stored procedure, it has been specified as proc schema only.

Table 13-1. *Values for the* @type *Parameter for* sp_addmergearticle

Value	Description
Table	Table with schema and data
func schema only	Function with schema only
indexed view schema only	Indexed view with schema only
proc schema only	Stored procedure with schema only
synonym schema only	Synonym with schema only
view schema only	View with schema only

Since I want to detect conflicts at the row level, I have set the @column_tracking parameter to false.

Note If the same table is used in other merge publications, the @column_tracking parameter must have the same value.

Because we are going to use parameterized row filtering, I have set the @source_object parameter to the table that I included as the article. Also to allow parameterized row filtering, the @force_reinit_subscription and @partition_options parameters are set to 1 and 0 respectively. When @force_reinit_subscription is set to 1, it means that any changes in the article not only reinitializes the subscription but also gives permission to change. The @partition_options parameter is set to 0, which means that it supports overlapping partitions.

The other values for the parameter are shown in Table 13-2.

Table 13-2. *Values for the* @partition_options *Parameter for* sp_addmergearticle

Value	Description
0	Article filtering allows overlapping partition; occurs when the subset of data is not unique
1	Article filtering allows overlapping partition, but updates made at the Subscriber server do not alter the partition for the row
2	Article filtering produces nonoverlapping partitions, and multiple Subscriber servers can receive the same partition
3	Article filtering produces nonoverlapping partitions that are unique for each subscription

Because this example will use pull subscriptions and we will manually resolve conflicts using the Interactive Resolver, I have set the @allow_interactive_resolver parameter to true.

The @subset_filterclause parameter is used to dynamically determine the sales person at login time by using the SUSER_SNAME() dynamic function for the SalesPerson article. The @source_owner parameter holds the name of the schema that contains the table, while the @destination_owner is the owner of the object in the subscription database.

For the PriceList article, I have asked the Microsoft SQL Server Maximum Conflict Resolver to calculate the maximum of the column 'Price' should any conflicts arise. The @article_resolver parameter is assigned the value of the Microsoft SQL Server Maximum Conflict Resolver.

After adding the articles, the next step is to add the filters and start the Snapshot Agent, as shown in Listing 13-7.

Listing 13-7. *Adding the Parameterized and Join Filters and Starting the Snapshot Agent*

```
/*Add the merge article join filters on the publication database*/

use [mysales_merge2]
go


/*Add the join filter to the article AccountsReceivable */

exec sp_addmergefilter
@publication = 'pub_stdpub_mysalesmerge2',
@article = 'AccountsReceivable',
@filtername= 'AccountsReceivable_Customer',
@join_articlename = 'Customer',
@join_filterclause = '[Customer].[CustID] = [AccountsReceivable].[CustID]',
@join_unique_key = 1,
@filter_type = 1,
@force_invalidate_snapshot = 1,
@force_reinit_subscription = 1
Go

use [mysales_merge2]
go


/*Add the join filter to the article OrderHeader */

exec sp_addmergefilter
@publication = 'pub_stdpub_mysalesmerge2',
@article = 'OrderHeader',
@filtername ='OrderHeader_Customer',
@join_articlename = 'Customer',
@join_filterclause = '[Customer].[CustID] =[OrderHeader].[CustID]',
@join_unique_key = 1,
@filter_type = 1,
@force_invalidate_snapshot = 1,
@force_reinit_subscription = 1
Go

use [mysales_merge2]
go


/*Add the join filter to the article Customer */

exec sp_addmergefilter
@publication = 'pub_stdpub_mysalesmerge2',
@article = 'Customer',
@filtername ='Customer_CustSales',
@join_articlename = 'CustSales',
```

```
@join_filterclause = '[CustSales].[CustID] =[Customer].[CustID]',
@join_unique_key = 1,
@filter_type = 1,
@force_invalidate_snapshot = 1,
@force_reinit_subscription = 1
Go


use [mysales_merge2]
go


/*Add the join filter to the article OrderDetail */

exec sp_addmergefilter
@publication = 'pub_stdpub_mysalesmerge2',
@article = 'OrderDetail',
@filtername = 'OrderDetail_OrderHeader',
@join_articlename = 'OrderHeader',
@join_filterclause = '[OrderHeader].[OrderID] =[OrderDetail].[OrderID]',
@join_unique_key = 1,
@filter_type = 3,
@force_invalidate_snapshot = 1,
@force_reinit_subscription = 1
Go


use [mysales_merge2]
go


/*Add the join filter to the article CustSales */

exec sp_addmergefilter
@publication = 'pub_stdpub_mysalesmerge2',
@article = 'CustSales',
@filtername ='CustSales_SalesPerson',
@join_articlename = 'SalesPerson',
@join_filterclause = '[SalesPerson].[SalesID] =[CustSales].[SalesID]',
@join_unique_key = 1,
@filter_type = 1,
@force_invalidate_snapshot = 1,
@force_reinit_subscription = 1
Go


/* Start the Snapshot Agent on the Publisher server .*/

exec sp_startpublication_snapshot
@publication = 'pub_stdpub_mysalesmerge2'
go
```

In order to use a join filter, you have to use the sp_addmergefilter stored procedure. In this script, based on the partition that is created by joining two tables, I have added a new filter to the merge publication.

The @filtername parameter holds the name of the filter that you are assigning. The @join_articlename parameter contains the name of the parent table to which the current article, specified by the @article parameter, is going to be joined. For example, for the OrderHeader article, the parent table is Customer and the name of the filter is OrderHeader_Customer. They are joined by setting the @join_filterclause parameter to [Customer].[CustID] =[OrderHeader].[CustID].

The @join_unique_key parameter has been set to 1. The default value is 0, which means that the join is either a many-to-many or many-to-one join. However, in this case since there is a relationship between the primary key of the parent table (Customer) and the foreign key of the child table (OrderHeader), the value is set to 1, which means the join is either one-to-one or one-to-many.

Caution Ensure that the @join_unique_key parameter is set to 1 only if there is a unique constraint on the joining column in the parent table; otherwise there might be nonconvergence of data.

NON-CONVERGENCE

Nonconvergence of data essentially means that the data on the subscription database does not match the data on the publication database. This can happen if the data is partitioned when you are using parameterized filters but the data is out of context. This may happen due to constraint violations, the execution of scripts on the subscribing server but not on the publishing server, and the updating of data on the subscription database when it should be read-only.

In such circumstances, you can ensure that users cannot make any changes to read-only tables by creating a trigger for the table. For example, you can prevent sales people from inserting, deleting, or updating the Item table by writing a trigger as NOT FOR REPLICATION on the publication database. Then, when you add the publication using the sp_addmergepublication stored procedure, use the @pre_snapshot_script parameter to send it to the subscription databases as follows:

```
Create trigger readonly
On
Myinventory.Item
For insert, delete, update
NOT FOR REPLICATION
As
Print "You cannot insert, delete, update table Item"
Raiserror("Cannot perform any DML operations", 16,1)
Rollback
```

There are two ways of checking for nonconvergence. One way is to validate the subscription (I will cover this method while discussing the backup of replicated databases for merge replication in Chapter 16). The other method is to use the tablediff utility, which is discussed in Chapter 15.

Setting the @filter_type parameter to 1 means the filter is a join filter only. A value of 2 means it is a logical record relationship, while a value of 3 indicates that the filter is both a join filter and a logical record relationship.

The @force_invalidate_snapshot parameter has been set to 1, which means that any changes in the merge article might render the snapshot invalid and a new snapshot will be generated for existing subscriptions. A value of 0, which is the default, means the snapshot will not be invalidated, and if the procedure detects any changes it will only generate an error message.

Finally the snapshot is generated using the sp_startpublication_snapshot stored procedure.

There are two dynamic functions that can be used to generate dynamic snapshots in merge replication: SUSER_SNAME() and HOST_NAME(). In Listing 13-6, I showed you how you can use SUSER_SNAME() as the dynamic function for retrieving data based on the login information of the sales person. Data is partitioned according to the name of the sales person; when a sales person connects from a remote location and pulls the subscription, the publication database validates the login name based on the data provided by SUSER_SNAME() and sends the appropriate subscription to the sales person. Now I will show you how to use HOST_NAME() to generate the dynamic snapshot.

The HOST_NAME() dynamic function can similarly be used to find out which computer the sales person is pulling the subscription from. You can use this function with SUSER_SNAME() if you want to ensure that sales people get their subscriptions only when they use their assigned computers.

For our example, sales people will have the ability to insert invoice data for customers using the usp_InsertCustomerInvoice stored procedure. They will also be able to look up items of high value using the usp_GetItemAbovePremiumPrice stored procedure. The sales representatives will be subscribing to the Customer, Item, OrderHeader, OrderDetail, Stock, SalesPeople, AccountsReceivable, AccountsInvoice, PriceList, CustSales, and StockItem articles, so when they log in and try to download the subscription, the Merge Agent will check the computer name using the HOST_NAME() dynamic function and then send subscriptions accordingly. Listing 13-8 shows how you can set this up.

Listing 13-8. *Using the* HOST_NAME() *Dynamic Function to Set Up the Publication for Standard Articles*

```
/* Enable the database for replication on the master database */

use master
go
exec sp_replicationdboption @dbname = 'mysales_merge_replpeer',
@optname = 'merge publish',
@value = 'true'
go


/* Now add the merge publication on the mysales_merge_replpeer
   database on the BIOREPL_PEER instance */

use [mysales_merge_replpeer]
go
```

```
exec sp_addmergepublication
@publication = 'pub_mysales_mergereplpeer_hostname',
@sync_mode = 'native',
@retention = 14,
@allow_push = 'true',
@allow_pull = 'true',
@allow_anonymous = 'true',
@enabled_for_internet = 'false',
@snapshot_in_defaultfolder = 'true',
@dynamic_filters = 'true',
@conflict_retention = 14,
@keep_partition_changes = 'false',
@allow_synctoalternate = 'false',
@validate_subscriber_info = 'HOST_NAME()',
@max_concurrent_merge = 1,
@max_concurrent_dynamic_snapshots = 0,
@use_partition_groups = 'true',
@publication_compatibility_level = '90RTM',
@replicate_ddl = 1,
@allow_subscriber_initiated_snapshot = 'false',
@allow_web_synchronization = 'false',
@allow_partition_realignment = 'true',
@retention_period_unit = 'days',
@conflict_logging = 'both',
@automatic_reinitialization_policy = 0
go

/* Create the Snapshot Agent */

exec sp_addpublication_snapshot
@publication = 'pub_mysales_mergereplpeer_hostname',
@frequency_type = 4,
@frequency_interval = 14,
@frequency_relative_interval = 1,
@frequency_recurrence_factor = 0,
@frequency_subday = 1,
@frequency_subday_interval = 5,
@active_start_time_of_day = 500,
@active_end_time_of_day = 235959,
@active_start_date = 0,
@active_end_date = 0,
@job_login = null,
@job_password = null,
@publisher_security_mode = 1

/*Grant access to the publication */
```

```
exec sp_grant_publication_access
@publication = 'pub_mysales_mergereplpeer_hostname',
@login = 'sa'
go
sp_grant_publication_access
@publication = 'pub_mysales_mergereplpeer_hostname',
@login = 'distributor_admin'
go

/* Now add the merge articles */

use [mysales_merge_replpeer]
go
exec sp_addmergearticle
@publication = 'pub_mysales_mergereplpeer_hostname',
@article = 'Customer',
@source_owner = 'myorder',
@source_object = 'Customer',
@type = 'table',
@pre_creation_cmd = 'drop',
@identityrangemanagementoption = 'none',
@destination_owner = 'myorder',
@force_reinit_subscription = 1,
@column_tracking = 'false',
@subset_filterclause = '',
@vertical_partition = 'false',
@verify_resolver_signature = 1,
@allow_interactive_resolver = 'false',
@fast_multicol_updateproc = 'true',
@check_permissions = 0,
@subscriber_upload_options = 0,
@delete_tracking = 'true',
@compensate_for_errors = 'false',
@stream_blob_columns = 'false',
@partition_options = 0
Go

use [mysales_merge_replpeer]
go
/*Add the article, Item, to the publication */

exec sp_addmergearticle
@publication = 'pub_mysales_mergereplpeer_hostname',
@article = 'Item',
@source_owner = 'myinventory',
@source_object = 'Item',
@type = 'table',
```

```
@pre_creation_cmd = 'drop',
@identityrangemanagementoption = 'none',
@destination_owner = 'myinventory',
@force_reinit_subscription = 1,
@column_tracking = 'false',
@subset_filterclause = '',
@vertical_partition = 'false',
@verify_resolver_signature = 1,
@allow_interactive_resolver = 'false',
@fast_multicol_updateproc = 'true',
@check_permissions = 0,
@subscriber_upload_options = 0,
@delete_tracking = 'true',
@compensate_for_errors = 'false',
@stream_blob_columns = 'false',
@partition_options = 0
Go


use [mysales_merge_replpeer]
go


/*Add the article, OrderHeader, to the publication */

exec sp_addmergearticle
@publication = 'pub_mysales_mergereplpeer_hostname',
@article = 'OrderHeader',
@source_owner = 'myorder',
@source_object = 'OrderHeader',
@type = 'table',
@pre_creation_cmd = 'drop',
@identityrangemanagementoption = 'none',
@destination_owner = 'myorder',
@force_reinit_subscription = 1,
@column_tracking = 'false',
@subset_filterclause = '',
@vertical_partition = 'false',
@verify_resolver_signature = 1,
@allow_interactive_resolver = 'false',
@fast_multicol_updateproc = 'true',
@check_permissions = 0,
@subscriber_upload_options = 0,
@delete_tracking = 'true',
@compensate_for_errors = 'false',
@stream_blob_columns = 'false',
@partition_options = 0
Go
```

```
use [mysales_merge_replpeer]
go

/*Add the article, SalesPerson, to the publication */

exec sp_addmergearticle
@publication = 'pub_mysales_mergereplpeer_hostname',
@article = 'SalesPerson',
@source_owner = 'myorder',
@source_object = 'SalesPerson',
@type = 'table',
@pre_creation_cmd = 'drop',
@identityrangemanagementoption = 'none',
@destination_owner = 'myorder',
@force_reinit_subscription = 1,
@column_tracking = 'false',
@subset_filterclause = 'convert(char,[SalesID])HOST_NAME()',
@vertical_partition = 'false',
@verify_resolver_signature = 1,
@allow_interactive_resolver = 'false',
@fast_multicol_updateproc = 'true',
@check_permissions = 0x10,
@subscriber_upload_options = 0,
@delete_tracking = 'true',
@compensate_for_errors = 'false',
@stream_blob_columns = 'false',
@partition_options = 0
go

use [mysales_merge_replpeer]
go

/*Add the article, Stock, to the publication */

exec sp_addmergearticle
@publication = 'pub_mysales_mergereplpeer_hostname',
@article = 'Stock',
@source_owner = 'myorder',
@source_object = 'Stock',
@type = 'table',
@pre_creation_cmd = 'drop',
@identityrangemanagementoption = 'none',
@destination_owner = 'myorder',
@force_reinit_subscription = 1,
@column_tracking = 'false',
@subset_filterclause = '',
@vertical_partition = 'false',
```

```
@verify_resolver_signature = 1,
@allow_interactive_resolver = 'false',
@fast_multicol_updateproc = 'true',
@check_permissions = 0,
@subscriber_upload_options = 0,
@delete_tracking = 'true',
@compensate_for_errors = 'false',
@stream_blob_columns = 'false',
@partition_options = 0
Go

use [mysales_merge_replpeer]
go

/*Add the article, AccountsReceivable, to the publication */

exec sp_addmergearticle
@publication = 'pub_mysales_mergereplpeer_hostname',
@article = 'AccountsReceivable',
@source_owner = 'myfinance',
@source_object = 'AccountsReceivable',
@type = 'table',
@pre_creation_cmd = 'drop',
@identityrangemanagementoption = 'none',
@destination_owner = 'myfinance',
@force_reinit_subscription = 1,
@column_tracking = 'false',
@subset_filterclause = '',
@vertical_partition = 'false',
@verify_resolver_signature = 1,
@allow_interactive_resolver = 'false',
@fast_multicol_updateproc = 'true',
@check_permissions = 0,
@subscriber_upload_options = 0,
@delete_tracking = 'true',
@compensate_for_errors = 'false',
@stream_blob_columns = 'false',
@partition_options = 0
Go

use [mysales_merge_replpeer]
go

/*Add the article, OrderDetail, to the publication */
```

```
exec sp_addmergearticle
@publication = 'pub_mysales_mergereplpeer_hostname',
@article = 'OrderDetail',
@source_owner = 'myorder',
@source_object = 'OrderDetail',
@type = 'table',
@pre_creation_cmd = 'drop',
@identityrangemanagementoption = 'none',
@destination_owner = 'myorder',
@force_reinit_subscription = 1,
@column_tracking = 'false',
@subset_filterclause = '',
@vertical_partition = 'false',
@verify_resolver_signature = 1,
@allow_interactive_resolver = 'false',
@fast_multicol_updateproc = 'true',
@check_permissions = 0,
@subscriber_upload_options = 0,
@delete_tracking = 'true',
@compensate_for_errors = 'false',
@stream_blob_columns = 'false',
@partition_options = 0
Go

use [mysales_merge_replpeer]
go

/*Add the article, PriceList, to the publication */

exec sp_addmergearticle
@publication = 'pub_mysales_mergereplpeer_hostname',
@article = 'PriceList',
@source_owner = 'myinventory',
@source_object = 'PriceList',
@type = 'table',
@pre_creation_cmd = 'drop',
@identityrangemanagementoption = 'none',
@destination_owner = 'myinventory',
@force_reinit_subscription = 1,
@column_tracking = 'false',
@article_resolver = 'Microsoft SQL Server Averaging
Conflict Resolver', @subset_filterclause = '',
@resolver_info = 'Price',
@vertical_partition = 'false',
@verify_resolver_signature = 0,
@allow_interactive_resolver = 'false',
@fast_multicol_updateproc = 'true',
```

```
@check_permissions = 0,
@subscriber_upload_options = 0,
@delete_tracking = 'true',
@compensate_for_errors = 'false',
@stream_blob_columns = 'false',
@partition_options = 0
Go

use [mysales_merge_replpeer]
go

/*Add the article, AccountInvoice, to the publication */

exec sp_addmergearticle
@publication = 'pub_mysales_mergereplpeer_hostname',
@article = 'AccountInvoice',
@source_owner = 'myfinance',
@source_object = 'AccountInvoice',
@type = 'table',
@pre_creation_cmd = 'drop',
@identityrangemanagementoption = 'none',
@destination_owner = 'myfinance',
@force_reinit_subscription = 1,
@column_tracking = 'false',
@subset_filterclause = '',
@vertical_partition = 'false',
@verify_resolver_signature = 1,
@allow_interactive_resolver = 'false',
@fast_multicol_updateproc = 'true',
@check_permissions = 0,
@subscriber_upload_options = 0,
@delete_tracking = 'true',
@compensate_for_errors = 'false',
@stream_blob_columns = 'false',
@partition_options = 0
Go

use [mysales_merge_replpeer]
go

/*Add the article, CustSales, to the publication */

exec sp_addmergearticle
@publication = 'pub_mysales_mergereplpeer_hostname',
@article = 'CustSales',
@source_owner = 'myorder',
@source_object = 'CustSales',
```

```
@type = 'table',
@pre_creation_cmd = 'drop',
@identityrangemanagementoption = 'none',
@destination_owner = 'myorder',
@force_reinit_subscription = 1,
@column_tracking = 'false',
@subset_filterclause = '',
@vertical_partition = 'false',
@verify_resolver_signature = 1,
@allow_interactive_resolver = 'false',
@fast_multicol_updateproc = 'true',
@check_permissions = 0,
@subscriber_upload_options = 0,
@delete_tracking = 'true',
@compensate_for_errors = 'false',
@stream_blob_columns = 'false',
@partition_options = 0
Go

use [mysales_merge_replpeer]
go

/*Add the article, StockItem, to the publication */

exec sp_addmergearticle
@publication = 'pub_mysales_mergereplpeer_hostname',
@article = 'StockItem',
@source_owner = 'myinventory',
@source_object = 'StockItem',
@type = 'table',
@pre_creation_cmd = 'drop',
@identityrangemanagementoption = 'none',
@destination_owner = 'myinventory',
@force_reinit_subscription = 1,
@column_tracking = 'false',
@subset_filterclause = '',
@vertical_partition = 'false',
@verify_resolver_signature = 1,
@allow_interactive_resolver = 'false',
@fast_multicol_updateproc = 'true',
@check_permissions = 0,
@subscriber_upload_options = 0,
@delete_tracking = 'true',
@compensate_for_errors = 'false',
@stream_blob_columns = 'false',
@partition_options = 0
Go
```

```
use [mysales_merge_replpeer]
go

/*If the snapshot was already generated,
use @force_invalidate_snapshot=1*/

/*Add the article, usp_GetCustomerInvoicePaymentDue, to
the publication */

exec sp_addmergearticle
@publication = 'pub_mysales_mergereplpeer_hostname',
@article = 'usp_GetCustomerInvoicePaymentDue',
@source_owner = 'myorder',
@source_object = 'usp_GetCustomerInvoicePaymentDue',
@type = 'proc schema only',
@pre_creation_cmd = 'drop',
@destination_owner = 'myorder',
@destination_object = 'usp_GetCustomerInvoicePaymentDue',
@force_reinit_subscription = 1
Go


use [mysales_merge_replpeer]
go

/*Add the article, usp_GetItemAbovePremiumPrice, to
the publication */

exec sp_addmergearticle
@publication = 'pub_mysales_mergereplpeer_hostname',
@article = 'usp_GetItemAbovePremiumPrice',
@source_owner = 'myinventory',
@source_object = 'usp_GetItemAbovePremiumPrice',
@type = 'proc schema only',
@pre_creation_cmd = 'drop',
@destination_owner = 'myinventory',
@destination_object = 'usp_GetItemAbovePremiumPrice',
@force_reinit_subscription = 1
Go

use [mysales_merge_replpeer]
go
exec sp_addmergearticle

/*Add the article, usp_ InsertCustomerInvoice, to
the publication */
```

```
@publication = 'pub_mysales_mergereplpeer_hostname',
@article = 'usp_InsertCustomerInvoice',
@source_owner = 'myorder',
@source_object = 'usp_InsertCustomerInvoice',
@type = 'proc schema only',
@pre_creation_cmd = 'drop',
@destination_owner = 'myorder',
@destination_object = 'usp_InsertCustomerInvoice',
@force_reinit_subscription = 1
Go

use [mysales_merge_replpeer]

/*Add the article, vw_CustomerInvoiceStatus, to
the publication */

sp_addmergearticle
@publication = 'pub_mysales_mergereplpeer_hostname',
@article = 'vw_CustomerInvoiceStatus',
@source_owner = 'myorder',
@source_object = 'vw_CustomerInvoiceStatus',
@type = 'view schema only',
@pre_creation_cmd = 'drop',
@destination_owner = 'myorder',
@destination_object = 'vw_CustomerInvoiceStatus',
@force_reinit_subscription = 1
Go

use [mysales_merge_replpeer]
go

/*Add the article, vw_ItemEnquiry, to
the publication */

exec sp_addmergearticle
@publication = 'pub_mysales_mergereplpeer_hostname',
@article = 'vw_ItemEnquiry',
@source_owner = 'myorder',
@source_object = 'vw_ItemEnquiry',
@type = 'view schema only',
@pre_creation_cmd = 'drop',
@destination_owner = 'myorder',
@destination_object = 'vw_ItemEnquiry',
@force_reinit_subscription = 1
Go
```

```
use [mysales_merge_replpeer]
go

/*Add the article, vw_OrderStatus, to
the publication */

exec sp_addmergearticle
@publication = 'pub_mysales_mergereplpeer_hostname',
@article = 'vw_OrderStatus',
@source_owner = 'myorder',
@source_object = 'vw_OrderStatus',
@type = 'view schema only',
@pre_creation_cmd = 'drop',
@destination_owner = 'myorder',
@destination_object = 'vw_OrderStatus',
@force_reinit_subscription = 1
go

/* Now add the merge article join filters. */

use [mysales_merge_replpeer]
go

/* Add the join filter to AccountsReceivable */

exec sp_addmergefilter
@publication = 'pub_mysales_mergereplpeer_hostname',
@article = 'AccountsReceivable',
@filtername = 'AccountsReceivable_Customer',
@join_articlename = 'Customer',
@join_filterclause = '[Customer].[CustID] = [AccountsReceivable].[CustID]',
@join_unique_key = 1,
@filter_type = 1,
@force_invalidate_snapshot = 1,
@force_reinit_subscription = 1
Go

use [mysales_merge_replpeer]
go

/* Add the join filter to OrderHeader */

exec sp_addmergefilter
@publication = 'pub_mysales_mergereplpeer_hostname',
@article = 'OrderHeader',
@filtername = 'OrderHeader_Customer',
@join_articlename = 'Customer',
```

```
@join_filterclause = '[Customer].[CustID] = [OrderHeader].[CustID]',
@join_unique_key = 1,
@filter_type = 1,
@force_invalidate_snapshot = 1,
@force_reinit_subscription = 1
Go


use [mysales_merge_replpeer]
go


/* Add the join filter to Customer */


exec sp_addmergefilter
@publication = 'pub_mysales_mergereplpeer_hostname',
@article = 'Customer',
@filtername = 'Customer_CustSales',
@join_articlename = 'CustSales',
@join_filterclause = '[CustSales].[CustID] = [Customer].[CustID]',
@join_unique_key = 1,
@filter_type = 1,
@force_invalidate_snapshot = 1,
@force_reinit_subscription = 1
Go


use [mysales_merge_replpeer]
go


/* Add the join filter to OrderDetail */


exec sp_addmergefilter
@publication = 'pub_mysales_mergereplpeer_hostname',
@article = 'OrderDetail',
@filtername = 'OrderDetail_OrderHeader',
@join_articlename = 'OrderHeader',
@join_filterclause = '[OrderHeader].[OrderID] = [OrderDetail].[OrderID]',
@join_unique_key = 1,
@filter_type = 1,
@force_invalidate_snapshot = 1,
@force_reinit_subscription = 1
Go


use [mysales_merge_replpeer]
go


/* Add the join filter to CustSales */
```

```
exec sp_addmergefilter
@publication = 'pub_mysales_mergereplpeer_hostname',
@article = 'CustSales',
@filtername = 'CustSales_SalesPerson',
@join_articlename = 'SalesPerson',
@join_filterclause = '[SalesPerson].[SalesID] = [CustSales].[SalesID]',
@join_unique_key = 1,
@filter_type = 1,
@force_invalidate_snapshot = 1,
@force_reinit_subscription = 1
Go
/*Generate the publication snapshot */

exec sp_startpublication_snapshot
@publication = 'pub_mysales_mergereplpeer_hostname'
go
```

The same steps are used for configuring the publication in this script as in Listing 13-6. However, the sp_addmergepublication stored procedure has the @validate_subscriber_info parameter set to HOST_NAME(), where in Listing 13-6 it was set to SUSER_SNAME(). Also, here the @max_concurrent_merge parameter is set to a limit of 1 for the number of concurrent merge processes that can run at the same time—this is done to improve performance.

Another difference between the two is that in Listing 13-8, when adding the SalesPerson article to the publication using sp_addmergearticle, the subset_filterclause parameter sets the value of SalesId with this line: convert(char,[SalesID]) =HOST_NAME(). Since the HOST_NAME() function returns a value of char type, the convert function returns a data type of char, as the SalesID has a data type of int.

Note If you are using the GUI, you have to specify convert(char,[SalesID])=HOST_NAME() instead of the version in Listing 13-8. Otherwise, it will not be able to return the name of the computer, and you will get an error message.

I have also specified a value of 0x10 for the @check_permissions parameter. This means that any insert operations in the SalesPeople table will need to have the right permissions before data can be inserted. The PriceList article uses the Microsoft SQL Server Averaging Conflict Resolver to calculate the average list price on the Price column should there be any conflicts.

The @allow_subscriber_initiated_snapshot parameter has been set to false unlike in Listing 13-6. Listing 13-9 shows how DBAs can manually generate the dynamic snapshot for publications with parameterized filters by using the sp_adddynamicsnapshot_job stored procedure.

Before you execute the code in Listing 13-9, ensure that that the snapshot is ready. You can verify this by executing the following script on the publication database:

```
Select publisher, publisher_db, name, snapshot_ready
from sysmergepublications
where name='pub_mysales_mergereplpeer_hostname'
```

If the snapshot_ready column returns a value of 1, the snapshot is ready and you can execute the code in Listing 13-9. A value of 0 means the snapshot is not ready, and a value of 2 indicates that a new snapshot needs to be generated for the publication.

Tip You can specify the WAITFOR DELAY '00:00:10' T-SQL statement before finding out whether the snapshot is ready.

Listing 13-9. *Generating a Dynamic Snapshot for Publications with Parameterized Row Filters*

```
/*Execute this on the publication database. */

use [mysales_merge_replpeer]
go

/*Create a table variable. */

declare @dynamicsnapshot table
(id int,
    job_name sysname,
    job_id uniqueidentifier,
    dynamic_filter_login sysname NULL,
    dynamic_filter_hostname sysname NULL,
    dynamic_snapshot_location nvarchar(255),
    frequency_type int,
    frequency_interval int,
    frequency_subday_type int,
    frequency_subday_interval int,
    frequency_relative_interval int,
    frequency_recurrence_factor int,
    active_start_date int,
    active_end_date int,
    active_start_time int,
    active_end_time int
)

/* Declare variables and assign values to publication and HOSTNAME. */
```

```
declare @publication AS sysname;
declare @jobname AS sysname
declare @hostname AS sysname
set @publication = 'pub_mysales_mergereplpeer_hostname';
set @hostname = 'BIO-V7V30JTZLZS-SALES';

/* Add a data partition. */

sp_addmergepartition
@publication = @publication,
@host_name = @hostname;

/* Add the filtered data snapshot job. */

sp_adddynamicsnapshot_job
@publication = @publication,
@host_name = @hostname;

/* Insert into the table variable the data from the sp_helpdynamicsnapshot_job. */

insert into @dynamicsnapshot exec sp_helpdynamicsnapshot_job

/*Test to see that the values are successfully inserted. */

select * from @dynamicsnapshot

/* Find the name of the job for the dynamic snapshot, and then start the job.*/

select @jobname = (select distinct job_name from
@dynamicsnapshot where dynamic_filter_hostname = @hostname);

/* Start the job in the msdb database. */

exec msdb..sp_start_job @job_name = @jobname;
go
```

This script creates a table variable called @dynamicsnapshot that stores the data from the execution of sp_helpdynamicsnapshot_job for merge publication. Next, it assigns the values for @hostname and @publication and creates a data partition using the sp_addpartition stored procedure (you must have the sysadmin fixed server role or db_owner fixed database role in order to execute this stored procedure). Then, the script runs sp_adddynamicsnapshot_job to create the dynamic snapshot job, sp_helpdynamicsnapshot_job to determine the name of the job, and sp_start_job to start the job on the msdb database.

Note The initial snapshot must have already been generated before you can create a snapshot for each partition.

Unlike the SUSER_SNAME() dynamic function, it is possible to override the default value of HOST_NAME() with another value for a subscription. Since we are using parameterized filters, I will show you how to override the value when setting up the subscriptions.

In the next section, I will show you how to set up subscriptions for both kinds of publications and the use of client and server subscription types.

Configuring Subscriptions

Since publication with download-only articles is used for viewing only, and changes made at the Publisher server are transmitted to the subscription databases, we will use a push subscription. When we set up publication with standard articles, we will use a pull subscription.

While both push and pull subscriptions are used in all three types of replication, there are two additional types that can be used in merge replication for both push and pull subscriptions. They are *client* and *server* subscriptions.

Configuring Client-Type Push Subscriptions for Download-Only Articles

You will normally use client subscriptions in scenarios where you will not make any changes at the Subscriber server end. If you plan to make any changes on the Subscriber server, as in the case of republishing Subscriber servers, you will need to use a server subscription. Depending on the type of subscription you choose, you will also affect the conflict policy, as mentioned in Chapter 11 (see Figure 11-41 in the "Configuring Pull Subscriptions" section).

Note Chapter 11 explains how to set up merge replication using the GUI.

In this example, we want to know what items are available and what their prices are. The subscribing servers do not need to make any changes in the data, so we will be using push subscriptions. Listing 13-10 shows how to set up the subscription.

Listing 13-10. *Setting Up a Push Subscription for Merge Publication with Download-Only Articles*

```
/* Execute this on the publication database. */

Use mysales_merge1
Go

/* Create a temporary table to hold the values of merge
publication. */

create table #mergepublication (
id int,
name sysname,
description varchar(255),
status tinyint,
retention int,
syncmode tinyint,
allowpush int,
allowpull int,
allowanon int,
centralizedconflicts int,
priority float(8),
snapshotready tinyint,
publicationtype int,
pubid uniqueidentifier,
snapshotjobid binary(16),
enabledforinternet int,
dynamicfilter int,
hassubscription int,
snapshotdefaultfolder bit,
altsnapshotdefaultfolder nvarchar(255),
presnapshotscript nvarchar(255),
postsnapshotscript nvarchar(255),
compresssnapshot bit,
ftpaddress nvarchar(255),
ftpport int,
ftpsubdirectory nvarchar(255),
ftplogin sysname,
conflictretention int,
keeppartitionchanges int,
allowsubscriptioncopy  int,
allowsynctoalternate int,
validatesubscriberinfo nvarchar(500),
bkwdcomplevel int,
publishactivedir bit,
maxconcurrentmerge int,
maxconcurrentdynamicsnapshots int,
usepartitiongr int,
```

```
numarticles int,
replicateddl int,
pubnumber smallint,
allowsubintsnapshot bit,
allowwebsync bit,
websynchurl nvarchar(500),
allowpartrealign bit,
retentionperiodunit tinyint,
hasdownloadonlyarticles bit,
decentralizedconflicts int,
generationlevelthreshold int,
automaticreinitialpolicy bit)

/* Insert into the temp table the values of the merge publication. */

insert into #mergepublication exec sp_helpmergepublication;

/* Check to see that the insert worked. */

select * from #mergepublication;

/* Declare the variable. */

declare @allowpush int,

/*Assign the allowpush variable. */
set @allowpush=(select allowpush from #mergepublication)

/* If push subscription is not supported then use sp_changemergepublication
and set the value to true. */

if @allowpush <>1
begin
exec sp_changemergepublication
'pub_downloadonly_mysalesmerge','allow_push','true'
end
exec sp_addmergesubscription
@publication = 'pub_downloadonly_mysalesmerge',
@subscriber = BIO-V7V3OJTZLZS\BIOREPL',
@subscriber_db = 'mysales_remotedown_merge1',
@subscription_type = 'Push',
@sync_type = 'Automatic',
@subscriber_type = 'Local',
@subscription_priority = 0,
@use_interactive_resolver = 'False'

/* Add the merge push subscription agent on the
publication database. */
```

```
exec sp_addmergepushsubscription_agent
@publication = 'pub_downloadonly_mysalesmerge',
@subscriber ='BIO-V7V3OJTZLZS\BIOREPL',
@subscriber_db = 'mysales_remotedown_merge1',
@job_login = 'BIO-V7V3OJTZLZS\SujoyPaul',

/*Note you can only specify @job_password to null
if the @job_login is null. If the password is set
to null, the Merge Agent will be created and will
run under the SQL Server Agent Service account*/

@job_password = *****,
@subscriber_security_mode = 0,
@subscriber_login = 'sa',
@subscriber_password = null,
@publisher_security_mode = 1,
@frequency_type = 64,
@frequency_interval = 0,
@frequency_relative_interval = 0,
@frequency_recurrence_factor = 0,
@frequency_subday = 0,
@frequency_subday_interval = 0,
@active_start_time_of_day = 0,
@active_end_time_of_day = 235959,
@active_start_date = 0,
@active_end_date = 0

/* Finally drop the temp table. */

drop table #mergepublication
go
```

Tip You can also check whether the publication supports download-only articles by selecting the hasdownloadonlyarticles column. If the value is 1, the publication contains download-only articles.

This script first creates a temporary table named #mergepublication that will store the result of the sp_helpmergepublication stored procedure. Having inserted the result in the temporary table, it then checks to see if the publication supports push subscription (allowpush=1). If not, it uses sp_changemergepublication to set the allow push publication property to true. It then uses the sp_addmergesubscription stored procedure to create the push subscription.

You can see that the subscription has been specified as push. The @subscriber_type parameter has been set to local, which means that the subscription is of client type, and hence the @subscription_priority has been set to 0. If the subscription were of server type, you would have to specify a value between 0.00 and 100.00 for the priority. The @sync_type parameter has been set to automatic, which means that the schema and the initial data are transferred from the publishing database to the subscription database.

Next, the Merge Agent is added for the push subscription and is scheduled. The @subscriber_security_mode parameter has been set to 0, while the @publisher_security_mode parameter has been set to 1. This means that the SQL Server login credential is used to connect to the subscription database, and Windows Authentication is used to connect to the publication database.

Next, we'll look at how to set up a pull subscription for publication with standard articles.

Configuring Pull Subscriptions for Standard Articles

In Listings 13-5 through 13-7, I discussed the configuration of publication for standard articles with parameterized and join filters. Data is partitioned according to the name of the sales representative who needs to find out the information when they log in and pull the data from the central Publisher server. As such, a pull subscription is used.

The steps for configuring a pull subscription are as follows:

1. On the publication database on the Publisher server, register the subscription.

2. On the Subscriber server, create a pull subscription for the merge publication.

3. On the Subscriber server, add the pull subscription agent to synchronize the pull subscription.

In the following two sections, I will discuss how to set up a server-type pull subscription and then a client-type pull subscription.

Server-Type Subscriptions

In the case of pull subscriptions, you first need to register the subscription on the publication database using the sp_addmergesubscription stored procedure. The subscription database, mysales_remotestd_merge_peer, is registered on the other instance of the server, BIO-V7V30JTZLZS\BIOREPL_PEER. This is demonstrated in Listing 13-11.

Listing 13-11. *Registering the Subscription on the Publication Database*

```
/* Execute this on the publication database. */

use [mysales_merge2]
go


sp_addmergesubscription
@publication = 'pub_stdpub_mysalesmerge2',
@subscriber ='BIO-V7V30JTZLZS\BIOREPL_PEER',
@subscriber_db = 'mysales_remotestd_merge_peer',
@subscription_type = 'Pull',
@sync_type = 'Automatic',
@subscriber_type = 'Global',
@subscription_priority = 75,
@use_interactive_resolver = 'False'
Go
```

In this script, the type of subscription (pull) is specified by the @subscription_type parameter, and the synchronization type (@sync_type) is automatic. This means that the schema and the initial data for the publication tables will be transferred to the subscribing server; if it were set to none, the engine would assume that the subscribing server already has the schema and the data.

Unlike the push subscription set up in Listing 13-10, the @subscriber_type parameter here has been set to Global. This means that the subscribing server is visible to all other Subscriber servers, as well as to the Publisher server. The subscription priority for global subscriptions should be less than 100.0, and in this example I have specified it as 75.

The next steps in the process are to create the pull subscription on the subscription database and then add the pull subscription agent. The pull subscription is created with the sp_addmergepullsubscription stored procedure while the pull subscription agent is added using sp_addmergepullsubscription_agent. This is shown in Listing 13-12.

Listing 13-12. *Creating a Pull Subscription and Adding the Pull Subscription Agent*

```
/* Execute this on the subscription database. */

use [mysales_remotestd_merge_peer]
go

/* Create the pull subscription. */

sp_addmergepullsubscription
@publisher = 'BIO-V7V3OJTZLZS\BIOREPL',
@publication = 'pub_stdpub_mysalesmerge2',
@publisher_db = 'mysales_merge2',
@subscriber_type = 'Global',
@subscription_priority = 75,
@sync_type = 'Automatic'
Go


/* Add the pull subscription agent. */

sp_addmergepullsubscription_agent
@publisher = 'BIO-V7V3OJTZLZS\BIOREPL',
@publisher_db = 'mysales_merge2',
@publication = 'pub_stdpub_mysalesmerge2',
@distributor = 'BIO-V7V3OJTZLZS\BIOREPL',
@distributor_security_mode = 1,
@distributor_login = '',
@distributor_password = '',
@enabled_for_syncmgr = 'False',
@job_login = null,
@job_password = null,
@publisher_security_mode = 1,
@publisher_login = '',
@publisher_password = '',
```

```
@use_interactive_resolver = 'False',
@use_web_sync = 0
Go
```

The pull subscription is added on the subscription database using `sp_addmergepull➥` `subscription`. The parameter values entered for the stored procedure are the names of the Publisher server, the publication, and the publication database. The server-type subscription is specified by setting the `@subscriber_type` parameter to `Global`. The pull subscription agent is then added using `sp_addmergepullsubscription_agent`.

The WSM is not being used to pull the subscriptions, since the `@enabled_for_syncmgr` parameter has been set to `false`. The Interactive Resolver will not be used, since the `@use_interactive_resolver` parameter has been set to `false`. As such, conflicts will not be resolved manually. The `@use_web_sync` parameter has been set to 0, which means that web synchronization is enabled.

Note Web synchronization with merge replication is discussed in Chapter 12.

Client-Type Subscription

I have discussed how to set up pull subscriptions of the server type for publication with standard articles and using the `SUSER_SNAME()` dynamic function. Now let's look at the configuration of pull subscriptions where the value returned by the `HOST_NAME()` function is being overruled for the client type subscription. This is shown in Listing 13-13.

Listing 13-13. *Setting Up a Pull Subscription for Client Type Subscription*

```
/* Execute this on the publication database. */

use [mysales_merge_replpeer]
go

/* Enable the pull subscription on the publication database.*/

sp_addmergesubscription
@publication = 'pub_mysales_mergereplpeer_hostname',
@subscriber = 'BIO-V7V30JTZLZS\BIOREPL_PEER',
@subscriber_db = 'mysales_mergehost_sub',
@subscription_type = 'pull',
@subscriber_type = 'local',
@subscription_priority = 0,
@sync_type = 'Automatic'
go

/* Add the pull subscription on the subscription database. */
```

```
use [mysales_mergehost_sub]

sp_addmergepullsubscription
@publisher = 'BIO-V7V3OJTZLZS\BIOREPL_PEER',
@publication = 'pub_mysales_mergereplpeer_hostname',
@publisher_db = 'mysales_merge_replpeer',
@subscriber_type = 'Local',
@subscription_priority = 0,
@sync_type = 'Automatic'

/* Add the pull subscription agent on the Subscriber server. */

sp_addmergepullsubscription_agent
@publisher = 'BIO-V7V3OJTZLZS\BIOREPL_PEER',
@publisher_db = 'mysales_merge_replpeer',
@publication = 'pub_mysales_mergereplpeer_hostname',
@distributor = 'BIO-V7V3OJTZLZS\BIOREPL_PEER',
@distributor_security_mode = 1,
@distributor_login = '',
@distributor_password = null,
@enabled_for_syncmgr = 'False',
@job_login = null,
@job_password = null,
@publisher_security_mode = 1,
@publisher_login = null,
@publisher_password = null,
@use_interactive_resolver = 'False',
@dynamic_snapshot_location = null,
@use_web_sync = 0,
@hostname = 'BIO-V7V3OJTZLZS-SALES'
Go
```

In this script, you can see that the value returned by the HOST_NAME() function in the publication is overwritten by the @hostname parameter of the sp_addmergepullsubscription_agent stored procedure. To do so, you have to set the value of the host name for each of the subscribing servers; when the Merge Agent connects to the publishing server, it compares the value specified and then allows the sales person to pull the subscription.

Identity Range Management

So far, we have focused on replicating publications containing articles where the data type for the primary key columns did not contain the identity property. But what happens if you want to replicate articles containing columns with the identity property?

You can assign the identity property to only one column in a table, and normally it is the primary column. The identity property is associated with decimal, tinyint, smallint, int, bigint, and numeric data types, and it contains a seed, which is the initial value, and an increment by which successive identity numbers will be increased. Although you can assign both positive and negative numbers as values to the seed and the increment, the SQL Server engine defaults to 1 for both of them. However, the identity value is unique to the table, so you have to be careful when inserting the values for the identity column across the tables in the database. On top of that, if you are carrying out a large number of deletions, there will be gaps in the sequence of the identity values because those numbers will not be reclaimed after deletion. The problem can be acute if the column is involved in replication.

As you know by now, the autonomous nature of merge replication allows you to perform inserts and updates at both the Publisher and Subscriber servers. Consequently, if you are replicating the primary key containing the identity column from the Publisher server to the Subscriber server, it is essential that duplicate values in the primary key be avoided; otherwise inserts and updates will be rolled back. You have to assign different ranges of values for the identity column in each of the nodes to which data is being replicated to avoid primary key conflicts. For example, the primary key column for the Warehouse table has a data type of int, and if you alter the column to have the identity property, you have a range of values from –2,147,483,648 to 2,147,483,647 that you can assign to the Publisher and Subscriber servers. For an average number of Subscriber servers, the int data type should be able to handle the range of values without running the risk of being out of range, at which point any replicated data will be rolled back. Obviously, bigint, decimal, and numeric data types offer larger ranges, but you should keep the primary key column as narrow as possible for performance reasons.

For example, you can assign a range from 1 to 10,000 for the Publisher server at the central office, the Subscriber server at one location can have a range from 10,001 to 20,000, the Subscriber server at another location can have a range from 20,001 to 30,000, and so on. If an insert on the row containing the identity value of 5,000 is replicated from the Publisher to the Subscriber servers, there will be no primary key conflict and the row with the identity value of 5000 will be inserted on each of the Subscriber servers.

Replication does not increment the seed value for the identity key column; it merely inserts the row of the identity value of the Publisher server. This is achieved by using the NOT FOR REPLICATION (NFR) option on the identity column.

You can manage the identity ranges either automatically or manually. Suppose we want to use the identity range management option with the Warehouse table so that we do not have to assign primary key values for each of the warehouses. How do we set up merge replication using automatic range management?

Configuring Automatic Range Management

In this section, I will show you how to configure merge replication using automatic range management.

The first step is to change the WhseID column to support the identity property with NOT FOR REPLICATION (NFR) as shown in Listing 13-14.

Listing 13-14. *Assigning the* identity *Property to the* WhseID *Column*

```
Use mysales_pub_identity
Go
create table [myinventory].[Warehouse]
(
    WhseID          int     identity(1,1) not for replication not null,
    WhseName        varchar(20)           null    ,
```

```
    WhseAddress1         varchar(30)              null    ,
    Whse_City            varchar(20)              null    ,
    Whse_Postal_Code     varchar(7)               null    ,
    constraint PK_WAREHOUSE primary key (WhseID)
)
```

The next step is to set up merge publication and then add the articles to the merge publication. This is shown in Listing 13-15.

Listing 13-15. *Setting Up Merge Publication with Identity Range Management*

```
/* Enable the replication database */

use master
exec sp_replicationdboption @dbname =  'mysales_pub_identity',
@optname =  'merge publish',
@value =  'true'
GO


/* Adding the merge publication */

use [mysales_pub_identity]
exec sp_addmergepublication @publication =  'pub_mysales_identity',
@sync_mode =  'native',
@retention = 14,

@allow_push =  'true',
@allow_pull =  'true',
@allow_anonymous =  'true',

@enabled_for_internet =  'false',
@snapshot_in_defaultfolder =  'true',
@compress_snapshot =  'false',

@allow_subscription_copy =  'false',
@add_to_active_directory =  'false',
@dynamic_filters =  'false',

@conflict_retention = 14,
@keep_partition_changes =  'false',
@allow_synctoalternate =  'false',

@max_concurrent_merge = 0,
@max_concurrent_dynamic_snapshots = 0,
@use_partition_groups =  'false',
```

```
@publication_compatibility_level = '90RTM',
@replicate_ddl = 1,
@allow_subscriber_initiated_snapshot = 'false',

@allow_web_synchronization = 'false',
@allow_partition_realignment = 'true',
@retention_period_unit = 'days',

@conflict_logging = 'both',
@automatic_reinitialization_policy = 0
GO

/* Add the publication snapshot */
exec sp_addpublication_snapshot
@publication = 'pub_mysales_identity',
@frequency_type = 4,
@frequency_interval = 14,
@frequency_relative_interval = 1,
@frequency_recurrence_factor = 0,

@frequency_subday = 1,
@frequency_subday_interval = 5,
@active_start_time_of_day = 500,

@active_end_time_of_day = 235959,
@active_start_date = 0,
@active_end_date = 0,

@job_login = null,
@job_password = null,
@publisher_security_mode = 1

/* Grant publication access */
exec sp_grant_publication_access
@publication = 'pub_mysales_identity',
@login = 'sa'
GO

GO
exec sp_grant_publication_access
@publication = 'pub_mysales_identity',
@login = 'distributor_admin'
GO

/* Add the merge articles */
```

```
use [mysales_pub_identity]
go

exec sp_addmergearticle
@publication = 'pub_mysales_identity',
@article = 'Warehouse',
@source_owner = 'myinventory',

@source_object = 'Warehouse',
 @type = 'table',
@creation_script = '',

@pre_creation_cmd = 'drop',
@schema_option = 0x000000000C034FD1,

@identityrangemanagementoption = 'auto',
@pub_identity_range = 10000,
@identity_range = 1000,
@threshold = 80,

@destination_owner = 'myinventory',
@force_reinit_subscription = 1,
@column_tracking = 'false',

@subset_filterclause = '',
@vertical_partition = 'false',
@verify_resolver_signature = 1,

@allow_interactive_resolver = 'false',
@fast_multicol_updateproc = 'true',
@check_permissions = 0,

@subscriber_upload_options = 0,
@delete_tracking = 'true',
@compensate_for_errors = 'false',

@stream_blob_columns ='false',
@partition_options = 0
GO

use [mysales_pub_identity]
exec sp_changemergepublication 'pub_mysales_identity', 'status', 'active'
GO
```

The merge publication is created using the sp_addmergepublication stored procedure. The article for the identity range management is created using sp_addmergearticle, and the parameters of interest are @identityrangemanagement, @pub_identity_range, @identity_range, and @threshold. The @identityrangemanagement parameter has been set to auto because we want to use the automatic identity range management. The @pub_identity_range parameter is used to control the identity range size for Subscriber servers with server subscriptions, and it has been set to a value of 10000. The @identity_range parameter controls the identity range for both the Publisher and the Subscriber servers. The @threshold parameter has been set to 80. This parameter is expressed in percentage terms, and when the threshold value is exceeded, the Merge Agent will generate a new identity range.

Having configured the publication for identity range management, we can now set up the subscription. You need to create a subscription database, mysales_sub_identity, before you can execute Listing 13-16, which sets up a push subscription.

Listing 13-16. *Setting Up a Push Subscription*

```
use [mysales_pub_identity]
exec sp_addmergesubscription @publication = 'pub_mysales_identity',
@subscriber = 'BIO-V7V3OJTZLS\BIOREPL',
@subscriber_db = 'mysales_sub_identity',

@subscription_type = 'Push',
@sync_type = 'Automatic',
@subscriber_type = 'Global',

@subscription_priority = 75,
@description = null,
@use_interactive_resolver = 'False'

exec sp_addmergepushsubscription_agent
@publication = 'pub_mysales_identity',
@subscriber = 'BIO-V7V3OJTZLS\BIOREPL',

@subscriber_db = 'mysales_sub_identity',
@job_login = null,
@job_password = null,

@subscriber_security_mode = 1,
@publisher_security_mode = 1,
@frequency_type = 64,

@frequency_interval = 0,
@frequency_relative_interval = 0,
@frequency_recurrence_factor = 0,
@frequency_subday = 0,

@frequency_subday_interval = 0,
@active_start_time_of_day = 0,
@active_end_time_of_day = 235959,
```

```
@active_start_date = 20060822,
@active_end_date = 99991231,
@enabled_for_syncmgr = 'False'
GO
```

In this section, I focused on setting up merge replication with identity range management. You should be aware that although the use of the Identity property causes the automatic generation of unique sequential numbers that require minimal I/O processing, there can be significant gaps in the identity should the database server go down accidentally. While identity range management in merge replication allows replication to automatically manage these values, you should also be aware of the consequences of using automatic identity range management.

Merge Replication Stored Procedures

Before closing the chapter, I will summarize the stored procedures that are used for merge replication. Tables 13-3 through 13-8 list the stored procedures and their parameters.

Table 13-3. *Stored Procedures for Dropping Subscriptions*

Type of Subscription	Stored Procedure	Parameters	Server
Pull	sp_dropmergepullsubscription	@publication	Subscriber
		@publisher_db	
		@publisher	
Push	sp_dropmergesubscription	@publication	Publisher
		@subscriber	
		@subscriber_db	
	sp_mergesubscription_cleanup	@publication	Subscriber
		@publisher	
		@publisher_db	

Table 13-4. *Stored Procedures for Configuring Merge Publication with Download-Only Articles*

Stored Procedure	Parameters
sp_replicationdboption	@dbname, @optname, @value
sp_addmergepublication	@publication, @sync_mode, @allow_subscriber_initiated_snapshot, @max_concurrent_merge, @max_concurrent_dynamic_snapshots, @conflict_logging, @replicate_ddl, @automatic_reinitialization_policy, @allow_web_synchronization

Stored Procedure	Parameters
sp_addpublication_snapshot	@publication, @frequency_type, @publisher_security_mode, @publisher_login, @publisher_password
sp_grant_publication_access	@publication, @login, @password
sp_addmergearticle	@article, @source_owner, @source_object, @type, @pre_creation_cmd, @identityrangemanagementoption, @destination_owner, @force_reinit_subscription, @column_tracking, @subset_filterclause, @vertical_partition, @verify_resolver_signature, @allow_interactive_resolver, @check_permissions, @subscriber_upload_options, @delete_tracking, @compensate_for_errors, @partition_options
sp_startpublication_snapshot	@publication

Table 13-5. *Stored Procedures for Configuring Merge Publication with Standard Articles and Parameterized Filters*

Stored Procedure	Parameters
sp_replicationdboption	@dbname, @optname, @value
sp_addmergepublication	@publication, @sync_mode, @allow_subscriber_initiated_snapshot, @max_concurrent_merge, @max_concurrent_dynamic_snapshots, @conflict_logging, @replicate_ddl, @automatic_reinitialization_policy, @allow_web_synchronization, @allow_push, @allow_pull, @validate_subscriber_info, @use_partition_groups
sp_addpublication_snapshot	@publication, @frequency_type, @frequency_interval, @job_login, @job_password, @publisher_security_mode, @publisher_login, @publisher_password
sp_addmergearticle	@article, @source_owner, @source_object, @type, @pre_creation_cmd, @identityrangemanagementoption, @destination_owner, @force_reinit_subscription, @column_tracking, @subset_filterclause, @vertical_partition, @verify_resolver_signature, @allow_interactive_resolver, @check_permissions, @subscriber_upload_options, @delete_tracking, @compensate_for_errors, @partition_options, @article_resolver, @resolver_info
sp_addmergefilter	@publication, @article, @filtername, @join_articlename, @join_filterclause, @join_unique_key, @filter_type, @force_invalidate_snapshot, @force_reinit_subscription
sp_startpublication_snapshot	@publication

Table 13-6. *Stored Procedures for Generating the Dynamic Snapshots for Publications with Parameterized Row Filters*

Stored Procedure	Parameters
sp_addmergepartition	@publication, @host_name
sp_adddynamicsnapshot_job	@publication, @host_name
sp_helpdynamicsnapshot_job	@publication
sp_start_job	@jobname

Table 13-7. *Stored Procedures for Configuring Push Subscriptions*

Stored Procedure	Parameters
sp_helpmergepublication	@publication
sp_addmergesubscription	@publication, @subscriber, @subscriber_db, @subscription_type, @sync_type, @subscriber_type, @subscription_priority, @use_interactive_resolver
sp_addmergepushsubscription_agent	@publication, @subscriber, @subscriber_db, @job_login, @job_password, @subscriber_security_mode, @subscriber_login, @subscriber_password, @publisher_security_mode

Table 13-8. *Stored Procedures for Configuring Pull Subscriptions*

Stored Procedure	Parameters
sp_helpmergepublication	@publication
sp_addmergesubscription	@publication, @subscriber, @subscriber_db, @subscription_type, @sync_type, @subscriber_type, @subscription_priority, @use_interactive_resolver, @publisher, @publication
sp_addmergepullsubscription	@publisher, @publication, @publisher_db, @subscriber_type, @subscription_priority, @sync_type
sp_addmergepullsubscription_agent	@publisher, @publisher_db, @publication, @distributor, @distributor_security_mode, @distributor_login, @distributor_password, @enabled_for_syncmgr, @job_login, @job_password, @publisher_security_mode, @publisher_login, @publisher_password, @use_interactive_resolver, @dynamic_snapshot_location, @use_web_sync, @hostname

Summary

In this chapter, I showed you how to set up merge publication for download-only articles and for standard articles using parameterized filters. You should have a clear understanding of the differences between the two, and when to use the dynamic functions to partition the data. You should also know how to override the HOST_NAME() function when setting up subscriptions.

You should also be aware of the different Microsoft conflict resolvers that are available and how to set up of the default conflict resolver along with the Interactive Resolver.

Note The setting up of the Interactive Resolver using the WSM is discussed in Chapter 11.

I have also showed you how to set up push and pull subscriptions, and in what situations you might use them. We also looked at the use of client and server subscription types, which you can use for both push and pull subscriptions. Finally, I also discussed identity range management and showed you how to configure automatic identity range management for merge replication.

- You can drop a pull subscription using the sp_dropmergepullsubscription stored procedure, and drop a push subscription using sp_dropmergesubscription. Then clean up the metadata using sp_mergesubscription_cleanup for push subscriptions.

- There are two types of publication in merge replication: publication with download-only articles, and publication with standard articles.

- Enable the database for replication using the sp_replicationdboption stored procedure.

- Create a publication using sp_addmergepublication.

- Create articles for a publication using sp_addmergearticle.

- Create a parameterized filter for a standard article with sp_addmergefilter.

- Create an agent for a publication using sp_addpublication_snapshot.

- Start the Snapshot Agent for the initial generation of the snapshot using sp_startpublication_snapshot.

- You can either use the default conflict resolver or the Microsoft COM-based Conflict Resolver.

- In order to manually resolve conflicts, you have to use the Interactive Resolver with the WSM.

- Use the SUSER_SNAME() or the HOST_NAME() dynamic functions for parameterized row filters.

- The value for the HOST_NAME() function can be overridden in the subscription.

- Manually generate a dynamic snapshot using the sp_adddynamicsnapshot_job stored procedure.

- Create a merge partition using sp_addmergepartition.

- Determine the name of a job by using the sp_helpdynamicsnapshot_job stored procedure, and then add the job on the msdb database using sp_start_job.

- Both push and pull subscriptions have two types of subscriptions in merge replication: client subscriptions and server subscriptions.

- Server subscriptions are used for republishing servers, while client subscriptions are usually used for read-only subscriptions.

- Use the sp_addmergesubscription stored procedure to create a push subscription, and use sp_addmergepushsubscription_agent to start the merge push subscription.

- Use the sp_addmergesubscription stored procedure to enable a pull subscription on the publication database. Then use sp_addmergepullsubscription on the subscription database, and sp_addmergepullsubscription_agent to start the pull subscription.

- Identity range management can be automatic or manual.

- The parameters that should be taken into consideration when setting up identity range management for merge replication using sp_addarticle are @identityrangemanagement, @pub_identity_range, @identity_range, and @threshold.

- The conflict policy is set according to the type of subscription you use.

In the next chapter, I will discuss the internal workings of merge replication. I will show you the system tables that are used in both the publication and subscription databases and discuss the system stored procedures and database triggers that are used.

Quick Tips

- You must reinitialize all the subscriptions if an article has been changed to download-only after the initial synchronization.

- Column-level tracking must have the same value in each subscription for a table that is used in more than one merge publication.

- The initial snapshot must be generated before you can manually generate the snapshot for each partition.

■ ■ ■

The Internals of Merge Replication

By now you should have a good appreciation of the different types of replication and the possible topologies that can be used, depending on the business scenario. Before proceeding to look at the internals of merge replication, you should be comfortable setting up publication for both standard and download-only articles and know when each are used. You should also understand the use of parameterized and join filters. You should know when to override the HOST_NAME() dynamic function, and the consequences of doing so, and also how to plan for conflict resolution and implement it. These topics are all discussed in Chapters 11 through 13.

In this chapter, I will discuss the internals of merge replication. I will first focus on the steps taken by the Merge Agent, and then discuss subsystems and proxies to highlight how each of the replication agent's job steps works. I will also describe the initialization of the different merge replication types, and the enumeration process of the Merge Agent. Finally I will show you how conflict detection and resolution works in merge replication.

On completing this chapter, you will know how the following things work:

- Merge agent

- Subsystems and proxies

- SQLCMD utility

- Initialization of the merge publication with non-partitioning of data

- Initialization of the merge publication with parameterized filters

- Evaluation of partitions by the Merge Agent

- Enumeration process of the Merge Agent

- Conflict detection and resolution

The Merge Agent

In both snapshot and transactional replication, the Distribution Agent plays a pivotal role in transferring the data from the Publisher server to the Subscriber server. Although the Distribution Agent has no function in merge replication, the distribution database still plays an active role—it logs the agent history and tracks the changes made to articles by the Merge Agent during the synchronization.

Autonomy and latency are the two attractive features of merge replication. Once the initial synchronization is complete, the Merge Agent does the bulk of the work by transmitting the incremental changes from the Publisher server to the Subscriber server, or vice versa. In this section, we will delve into the inner workings of the Merge Agent.

To get started, open the SSMS, right-click on the Merge Agent job that you created, and select Properties. Select the General page as shown in Figure 14-1.

■**Tip** The Merge Agent job name follows the pattern *Publisher-publicationdatabase-publicationname-Subscriber-integer* for push subscriptions. In the case of pull subscriptions, it is *Publisher-publicationdatabase-publicationname-Subscriber-subscriptiondatabase-integer*.

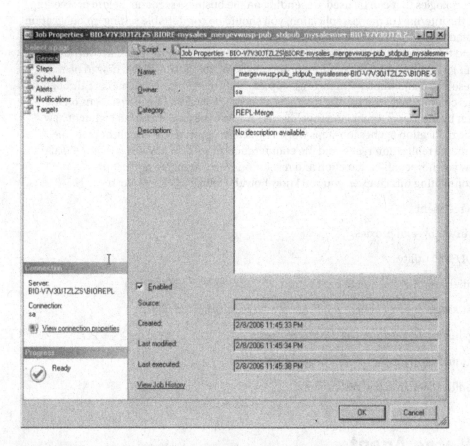

Figure 14-1. *Viewing the general job properties of the Merge Agent*

Note The View Job History link at the bottom of the Job Properties window (Figure 14-1) can also be accessed by right-clicking on the Merge Agent job in the SSMS and selecting View Job History from the menu.

Now click the ellipsis button beside the Category field, and you will see three jobs listed for the Merge Agent, as shown in Figure 14-2. Click Close to return to the Job Properties window (Figure 14-1).

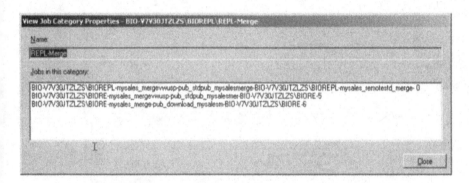

Figure 14-2. *Viewing the jobs for this Merge Agent*

Note In Chapter 13, I discussed the maximum number of concurrent merge processes. A value of 0 means that an infinite number of merge processes can run at any given time You can set the number of concurrent merge processes by using the @max_concurrent_merge parameter when calling sp_addmergepublication (see Listing 13-8 in Chapter 13).

To view the list of owners for the agent, click on the ellipsis button beside the Owner field. Click Close to return to the Job Properties window (Figure 14-1).

Now select the Steps page as shown in Figure 14-3 to view the steps taken by the Merge Agent. The three steps that the Merge Agent executes are like those of the other agents, but the inner workings are different for each of them.

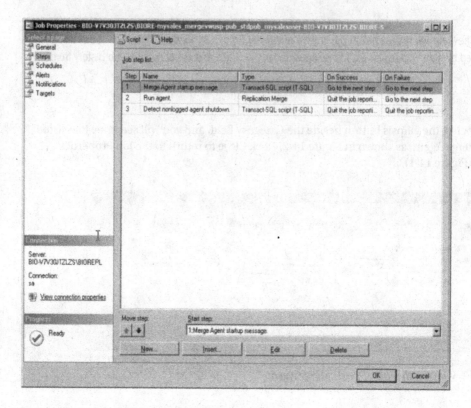

Figure 14-3. *Viewing the Merge Agent's three job steps*

The steps for the Merge Agent, as listed in Figure 14-3, are as follows:

- Merge Agent startup message

- Run Agent

- Detect nonlogged agent shutdown

Select step 1 as shown in Figure 14-3, and then click the Edit button. This will display the Job Step Properties window shown in Figure 14-4.

As you can see in the figure, when the Merge Agent is executed, the first step calls a stored procedure, as follows:

```
sp_MSadd_merge_history @perfmon_increment = 0,
@agent_id = 5, @runstatus = 1, @comments = 'Starting agent.'
```

Note You cannot disable this stored procedure, as it is used for tracking purposes.

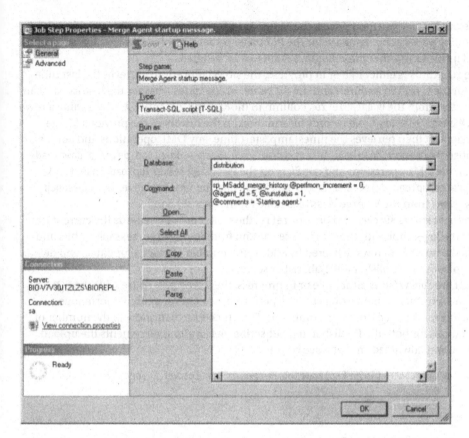

Figure 14-4. *Viewing the general settings for the Merge Agent's first job step—Merge Agent startup message*

This stored procedure is executed on the distribution database. It first accesses the MSmerge_sessions table, which records all the historical data of the previous sessions of the Merge Agent—whenever you start the Merge Agent, a new row is added to the table. By using this table, the agent determines the start time of the previous session of the Merge Agent, and then it uses the getdate() function to find the end of the session.

It uses this end time as the current time, and if the runstatus is set to start, it updates the performance counter using the following command:

```
dbcc incrementinstance ("SQL Replication Agents", "Running", "Merge", 1)
```

However, if the runstatus is succeed, retry, or failure, it uses the following command:

```
dbcc incrementinstance ("SQL Replication Agents", "Running", "Merge", -1)
```

■**Caution** DBCC incrementinstance is an undocumented DBCC command. You should try it on a test server before you use it on a production server. The syntax for the DBCC incrementinstance command is given in Chapter 10 (see the "The Queue Reader Agent" section).

The stored procedure then selects the Merge Agent specific to the publication, and the corresponding publication database for the Publisher server, from the MSmerge_agents system table, and it checks whether the runstatus is idle or in progress.

If the runstatus is either idle or in progress, the stored procedure retrieves the last time-stamp from the timestamp column and the bit value, which states whether the history row can be overwritten, from the updatable_row column in the MSmerge_history table by issuing a row lock. The MSmerge_history table records information on the history of the previous Merge Agent sessions. It then retrieves the timestamp, start time, any DML operations and conflicts on the Subscriber server (download_inserts, download_updates, download_deletes, download_conflicts), the DML operations and conflicts on the Publisher server (upload_inserts, upload_updates, upload_deletes, upload_conflicts), and the time to deliver the messages (delivery_time) from the MSmerge_sessions table for the past session.

If the runstatus is succeed, failure, or retry, the stored procedure finds the current time, associates the login time with the start_time column from the MSmerge_sessions table, and then finds the number of rows delivered by adding the number of inserts, updates, and deletes delivered to both the Publisher and Subscriber servers.

Next, if the runstatus is either idle or in progress, the stored procedure adds the SQL Replication Merge performance object to the performance counter in the Performance Monitor using the dbcc addinstance command. The procedure then adds up the number of DML operations for both the Publisher and Subscriber servers, and increments the upload changes/sec and download changes/sec counters.

```
dbcc incrementinstance ("SQL Replication Merge", "Downloaded Changes",
@agent_name, @changes)
```

or this one:

```
dbcc incrementinstance ("SQL Replication Merge", "Uploaded Changes",
 @agent_name, @changes)
```

The @changes parameter contains the total number of DML operations, while the @agent_name parameter holds the name of the Merge Agent. The stored procedure also adds up the number of conflicts on both the publication and subscription databases, and then increments the conflicts/sec counter by using the following command:

```
dbcc incrementinstance ("SQL Replication Merge", "Conflicts",
 @agent_name, @perfmon_conflict_count)
```

Next, select the Advanced page in the Job Step Properties window, as shown in Figure 14-5. As you can see, if the current step is successful, the agent goes to the next step; if it is not successful, the Merge Agent quits, reporting the failed action and logging it to the table.

Click OK to return to the Job Properties window (Figure 14-3). Select the second job step and click the Edit button. You will see the Job Step Properties window shown in Figure 14-6.

The parameters command in this step of the Merge Agent specify that the Publisher, Subscriber, and Distributor servers all run on the same machine (BIO-V7V30JTZLZS\BIOREPL). The name of the publication and subscription databases are mysales_mergevwusp and mysales_remotestd_mergepush. Remember that for push subscriptions, the Merge Agent runs on the Distributor server, and it uses Windows Authentication to connect to the Distributor server, as specified by setting DistributorSecurityMode to 1.

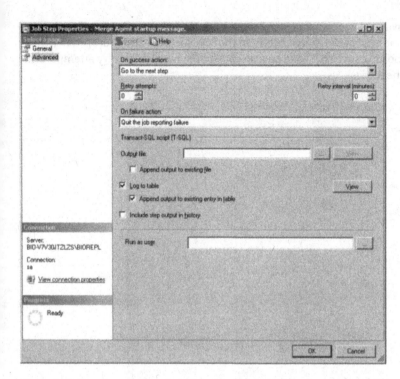

Figure 14-5. *Viewing the advanced settings for the Merge Agent's first job step—Merge Agent startup message*

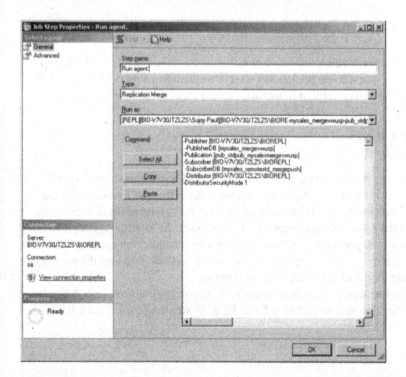

Figure 14-6. *Viewing the general settings for the Merge Agent's second job step—Run agent*

Now select the Advanced page as shown in Figure 14-7. Note that you can change the actions of the second job step of the Merge Agent. In the "On success action" drop-down list, select "Quit the job reporting success." You can also change the number of retry attempts and the interval between the retries.

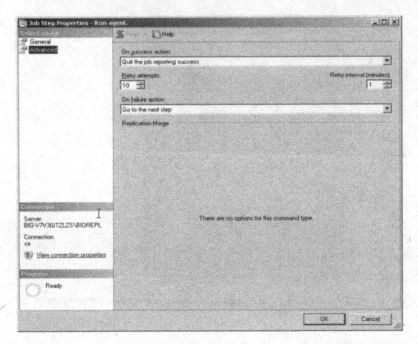

Figure 14-7. *Setting the advanced settings for the Merge Agent's second job step—Run agent*

Click OK to return to the Job Properties window (Figure 14-3). Select the third job step and click the Edit button. You will see the Job Step Properties window shown in Figure 14-8.

This step runs the following script to detect any errors in the Merge Agent job and their causes:

```
sp_Msdetect_nonlogged_shutdown
@subsystem='Merge', @agent_id=5
```

It first detects whether the agent was shut down without a logged reason, and then it retrieves the runstatus value from the MSmerge_sessions table in the distribution database. If the runstatus is Succeed, Retry, or Failure, the @subsystem parameter identifies the Merge Agent associated with the agent_id parameter (the id column in the MSmerge_agents table is associated with the agent_id parameter). Finally, like the other replication agents, it writes the history of the job using the sp_MSadd_merge_history stored procedure, and logs the messages in the SQL Server Agent's log and in the Replication Monitor.

Now select the Advanced page shown in Figure 14-9. As you can see, the agent quits the job regardless of whether this step succeeds or fails. If the job step is not successful, it logs the output of the step in the history table.

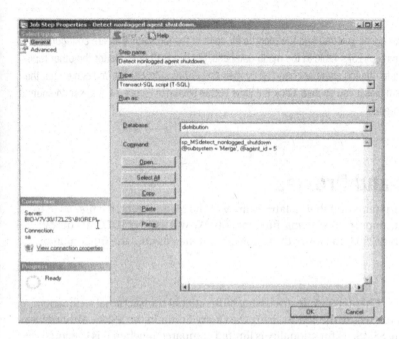

Figure 14-8. *Viewing the general settings for the Merge Agent's third job step—Detect nonlogged agent shutdown*

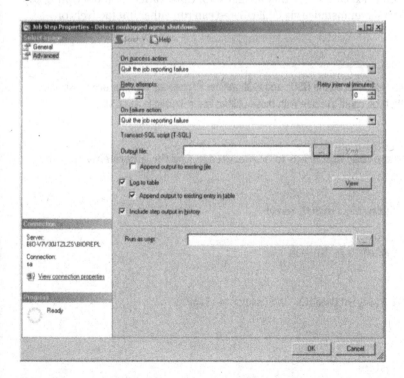

Figure 14-9. *Viewing the advanced settings for the Merge Agent's third job step—Detect nonlogged agent shutdown*

■**Note** For the Log Reader Agent, you can find the records for each of the job steps that are configured to write output in the `sysjobstepslogs` table in the msdb database, but this isn't possible for the other replication agents. The records for the job steps are handled by their respective subsystems. You can output the records to operating system files if you choose. Click the View button shown in Figure 14-9 to see the output in a text editor, such as Notepad.

Subsystems and Proxies

In order to explain subsystems and their relationship with the Merge Agent, we first need to look at the objects that support subsystems' functionality. We will use the SQLCMD utility (introduced in SQL Server 2005) to look at these objects and then discuss the functionality.

Using SQLCMD

I introduced SQLCMD in Chapter 9 while discussing bidirectional transactional replication, and I showed you how to execute the scripts using the Query Editor in the SSMS. Although you can use SQLCMD in the SSMS, its functionality is limited compared to when it is executed from the command prompt.

SQLCMD allows you to execute T-SQL that includes SQLCMD variables and scripting keywords. It connects to the server instance via OLE DB and can run either interactively or noninteractively.

■**Note** Although SQLCMD has replaced the OSQL and ISQL utilities in previous versions of SQL Server, many of the commands that you could execute with those utilities are still valid in SQLCMD.

Listing 14-1 shows the code that needs to be executed to find the subsystems present in SQL Server.

Listing 14-1. *Listing the Subsystems in SQL Server*

```
:setvar logintimeout 120
:setvar server "BIO-V7V30JTZLZS\BIOREPL"
:setvar user "sa"
:setvar pwd "sujoy"
:connect $(server) -l $(logintimeout) -U $(user) -P $(pwd)
USE msdb
go

sp_enum_sqlagent_subsystems
go
```

The setvar command is used to define the variables for the script. In this example, I have defined the server, the user name, and the password needed to connect to the BIO-V7V30JTZLZS\ BIOREPL server. The logintimeout variable specifies the time within which the user will have to log in, and it has been specified as 120 seconds. Otherwise the user will be disconnected.

The connect command is used to connect to the server with the user name and password specified. The $ sign must precede a variable name.

Note Only members of the sysadmin fixed server role or users with the SQLAgentOperatorRole fixed database role in the msdb database can execute the sp_enum_sqlagent_subsystems stored procedure.

Save the code in Listing 14-1 as a file with the .sql extension. You can use any text editor to create the file.

SETTING SQLCMD TO USE A TEXT EDITOR

In order to select a text editor in the SQLCMD utility, type the following command at the command prompt:

```
sqlcmd -SBIO-V7V30JTZLZS\BIOREPL -Usa -Psujoy
```

Once the connection to the server instance is established, type the following command:

```
set sqlcmdeditor=notepad
```

At the prompt on the next line, type 'ed'. This will open Notepad, and you can go ahead and use it. If you want to use another text editor instead of Notepad, you can specify it instead.

If your server doesn't allow remote connections, SQLCMD will fail to connect, and you will get an error message. To find out whether your server allows remote connections, open SQL Server 2005 Surface Area. The executable for SQL Server 2005 Surface Area Configuration is sqlsac.exe, and it is located in Program Files/Microsoft SQL Server/90/shared. It uses the Windows Management Instrumentation (WMI) to retrieve and modify the settings.

Select Surface Area Configuration for Services and Connections from the bottom of the window. This will open the window shown here:

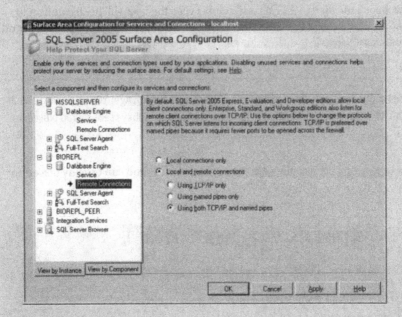

In the View by Instance pane, select the Remote Connection object for the server instance. Under "Local and remote connections," select "Using both TCP/IP and named pipes." Note that it is possible to export or import the settings from one instance, say BIOREPL, to another server. This can be done using the sac utility, found in the same location as sqlsac.exe. In order to export the agent settings of BIOREPL to another machine, you would use the following command:

```
sac out C:/files/agent.out -SBIO-V7V3OJTZLZS/BIOREPL -Usa -Psujoy -AG
```

Ensure that you have both TCP/IP and named pipes enabled. You will find them by opening the SQL Server Configuration Manager and then selecting SQL Server 2005 Network Configuration/Protocols for the server instance, BIOREPL. Then, under the Protocol name, check to see that the status for TCP/IP and named pipes are enabled. If they are not, set them. You may need to restart the machine and the services for the connection to the server using the SQLCMD utility for the changes to take effect.

Now open the command prompt, type the following, and then press Enter:

```
c:\>sqlcmd -i c:\files\enum_subsystems.sql -o c:\files\enum_subsystems_out.txt
```

The -i switch includes the file called enum_subsystems.sql, and the -o switch outputs the result set to the enum_subsystems_out.txt file. The result is shown in Figure 14-10.

■**Tip** To view the output in the command prompt itself, use the -e switch instead of the -o switch.

Figure 14-10. *Successfully connecting to the server using the SQLCMD utility*

If you open the output file, you will see results like the following:

```
Changed database context to 'msdb'.

subsystem                     description
subsystem_dll
agent_exe
start_entry_point             event_entry_point
stop_entry_point              max_worker_threads
 subsystem_id
------------------------------------- -----------------------------

TSQL                          Transact-SQL Subsystem
[Internal]
[Internal]
[Internal]                    [Internal]
[Internal]                    20
1

ActiveScripting               Active Scripting Subsystem
C:\Program Files\Microsoft SQL Server\MSSQL.1\MSSQL\binn\SQLATXSS90.DLL
NULL
ActiveScriptStart             ActiveScriptEvent
ActiveScriptStop              10
2

CmdExec                       Command-Line Subsystem
C:\Program Files\Microsoft SQL Server\MSSQL.1\MSSQL\binn\SQLCMDSS90.DLL
NULL
CmdExecStart                  CmdEvent
CmdExecStop                   10
3

Snapshot                      Replication Snapshot Subsystem
C:\Program Files\Microsoft SQL Server\MSSQL.1\MSSQL\binn\SQLREPSS90.DLL
C:\Program Files\Microsoft SQL Server\90\COM\SNAPSHOT.EXE
ReplStart                     ReplEvent
ReplStop                      100
4
```

```
LogReader                        Replication Transaction-Log Reader Subsystem
C:\Program Files\Microsoft SQL Server\MSSQL.1\MSSQL\binn\SQLREPSS90.DLL
C:\Program Files\Microsoft SQL Server\90\COM\logread.exe
ReplStart                        ReplEvent
ReplStop                         25
5


Distribution                     Replication Distribution Subsystem
C:\Program Files\Microsoft SQL Server\MSSQL.1\MSSQL\binn\SQLREPSS90.DLL
C:\Program Files\Microsoft SQL Server\90\COM\DISTRIB.EXE
ReplStart                        ReplEvent
ReplStop                         100
6


Merge                            Replication Merge Subsystem
C:\Program Files\Microsoft SQL Server\MSSQL.1\MSSQL\binn\SQLREPSS90.DLL
C:\Program Files\Microsoft SQL Server\90\COM\REPLMERG.EXE
ReplStart                        ReplEvent
ReplStop                         100
7


QueueReader                      Replication Transaction Queue Reader Subsystem
C:\Program Files\Microsoft SQL Server\MSSQL.1\MSSQL\binn\sqlrepss90.dll
C:\Program Files\Microsoft SQL Server\90\COM\qrdrsvc.exe
ReplStart                        ReplEvent
ReplStop                         100
8


ANALYSISQUERY                    Analysis query subsystem
C:\Program Files\Microsoft SQL Server\MSSQL.1\MSSQL\binn\SQLOLAPSS90.DLL
NULL
OlapStart                        OlapQueryEvent
OlapStop                         100
9


ANALYSISCOMMAND                  Analysis command subsystem
C:\Program Files\Microsoft SQL Server\MSSQL.1\MSSQL\binn\SQLOLAPSS90.DLL
NULL
OlapStart                        OlapCommandEvent
OlapStop                         100
10


SSIS                             SSIS package execution subsystem
C:\Program Files\Microsoft SQL Server\MSSQL.1\MSSQL\binn\SQLDTSSS90.DLL
C:\Program Files\Microsoft SQL Server\90\DTS\Binn\DTExec.exe
DtsStart                         DtsEvent
DtsStop                          100
11
```

This stored procedure lists the eleven names of the subsystems and corresponding executables, locations of the drivers, and the maximum number of worker threads.

The Roles of Subsystems and Proxies

A *subsystem* is a predefined set of functionality that is available to the SQL Server Agent proxy. A *proxy* can access any of the subsystems and, by providing security around its functionality, can decide which users can access the subsystem.

A SQL Server Agent proxy provides access to the security credentials of the Windows user in which context each of the job steps will run. Recall that there are three steps in the execution of the Merge Agent. So even if a proxy for a user is a member of the sysadmin fixed server role, it does not mean that the user will have full access to the subsystems. Hence the proxy needs to have prior access to the subsystem before the user can run the job step.

As you can see from the output in the previous section, except for Transact SQL (T-SQL) job steps, all job steps use proxies. Job steps that execute T-SQL do so under the security context of the owner of the job, and consequently do not need to use an SQL Server Agent proxy. As such, there is no SQL Server Agent subsystem for job steps that include T-SQL. The security context of the job steps containing T-SQL is set up by using the EXECUTE statement.

Caution Consider removing users from the SQL Server Agent who do not need access to the subsystems. Instead, create proxy accounts to limit access to the required subsystems.

In the previous output, you can see that the name of the merge subsystem (Replication Merge) driver is C:\Program Files\Microsoft SQL Server\MSSQL.1\MSSQL\binn\ SQLREPSS90.DLL and the executable is replmerge.exe. So what is a merge subsystem and how does it relate to the Merge Agent? The merge subsystem activates the Merge Agent.

Notice also that the maximum number of worker threads for the merge subsystem is 100. This is the number of threads that are active at any given time. SQL Server uses the native thread of the operating system to service the SQL Server processes, which means that it can simultaneously perform both server and database operations. This significantly aids in the optimizing process, since max_worker_threads pools the threads to service the SQL Server processes. So if you have several client connections to the SQL Server, dedicating a single thread to each of the connections will have an impact on SQL Server resources, and consequently on the performance of the engine. To alleviate this problem, you can change the max_worker_threads option.

Note If the number of client connections is fewer than the maximum number of worker threads, each thread will service a client connection. Otherwise, the worker threads will be pooled together. Once a thread has finished servicing a connection, it will move to service the next client connection.

Prior to SQL Server 2005, the setting for the subsystems, and hence max_worker_threads, was located in the registry: HKEY_LOCAL _MACHINE\SOFTWARE\Microsoft\MSSQLServer\MSSQL.x\ SQLServerAgent\Subsytems. Then you had to modify the value for max_worker_threads. However, the settings for max worker threads had their own implications. Depending on the default setting or the value that you specified in the registry, the agent would terminate the job step. This could be problematic for Log Reader Agents if the number of jobs exceeded the number specified by max_worker_threads, since they would be waiting in the queue.

In SQL Server 2005, the SQL Server Agent will check to see if the same type of job step is waiting to be executed after it exceeds the number of threads that you have specified. If the agent sees that there is another thread waiting, it will execute the step. Otherwise it will stop the thread.

■**Tip** The setting of max_worker_threads can be increased using the sp_configure stored procedure in the master database. You need to set show advanced options to 1 to determine the current setting of max_worker_threads, and then you can set the new value accordingly.

While discussing how the Merge Agent works, I explained how names are assigned to the Merge Agents. You know that agents are nothing but jobs behind the scenes, and that you have to specify security accounts for the agents in order for them to connect to the Publisher, Distributor, and Subscriber servers. In some instances, I specified that the agents impersonate the Windows account to connect to the Subscriber server, as in Figure 11-37 (in Chapter 11), when configuring pull subscriptions. Actually, though, each of the job steps for these agents runs under the security context of the proxy, whether it is being run in a continuous or a demand mode.

■**Note** Chapters 11 and 13 discuss the configuration of merge replication using the GUI and T-SQL, respectively.

As each of the job steps run in the security context of a proxy, the SQL Server Agent proxy provides access to resources outside the SQL Server system, such as user accounts of the Windows operating system. It does this by mapping the login account to a credential that stores information about the Windows account. A proxy for the corresponding credential is created using the sp_add_proxy stored procedure. The SQL Server Agent then checks which subsystem the proxy belongs to and gives access accordingly.

To view a list of credentials and proxies, open the SSMS and then the Object Explorer. Under the Security object, you will see the Credentials object, and within it a list of credentials, as shown in Figure 14-11. To see the proxies, open the SQL Server Agent object, and under the Proxies object you will see a list of subsystems to which the proxies belong. Open the Replication Merge subsystem, and you will see the list of proxies for this subsystem.

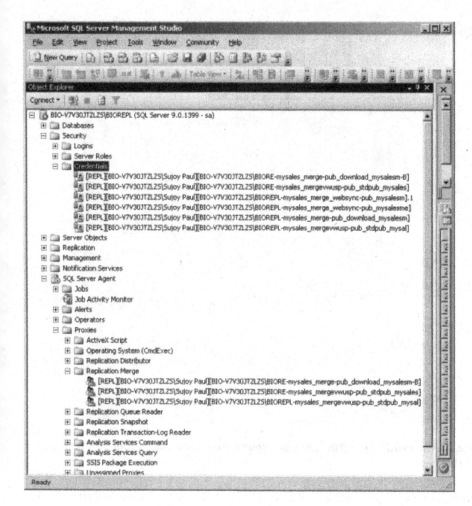

Figure 14-11. *Viewing the credentials and proxies for the server instance*
BIO-V7V30JTZLZS\BIOREPL

If you right-click on a credential name and select Properties from the menu, the
Credential Properties window will open, as shown in Figure 14-12.

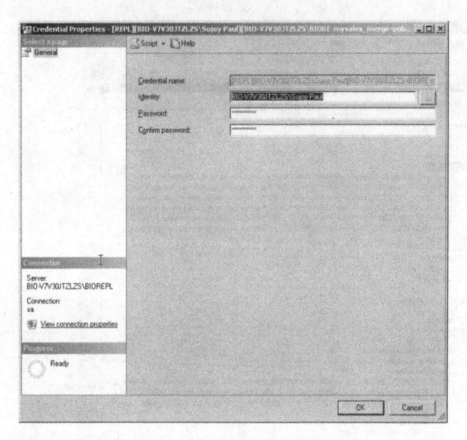

Figure 14-12. *The Credential Properties window shows the credential name and the identity of the credential*

If you click on the ellipsis button beside the Identity field, you will see a list of user accounts, as shown in Figure 14-13. By selecting the user from the user account, you can associate the identity with the credential name. Click OK to return to the Credential Properties window (Figure 14-12).

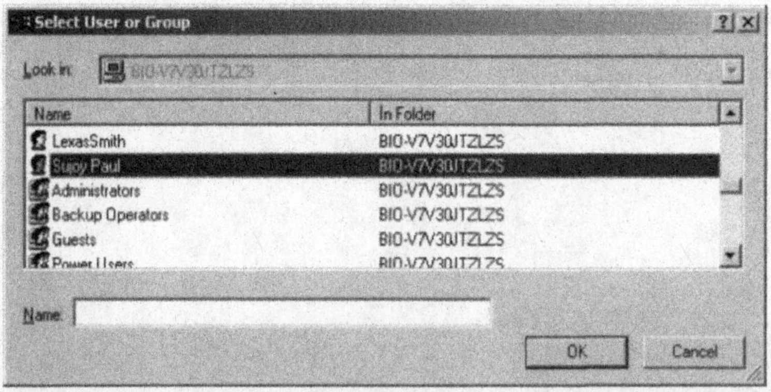

Figure 14-13. *Selecting a user account to be associated with a credential*

Note A credential can be associated with multiple user accounts, but a user account can be associated with only one credential.

You can see that the credential contains authentication information for the user. Since the identity is associated with the Windows account, the password is a secret. Click the OK button.

Note Credentials that have # sign preceding the credential name are system-generated credentials.

Now let's look at the proxies for the Replication Merge subsystem and the corresponding credential. Right-click on the proxy under the Replication Merge object in the Object Explorer, and select Properties. This will open the General page of the Properties window, as shown in Figure 14-14.

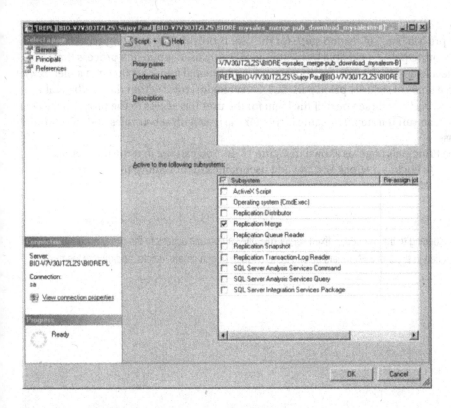

Figure 14-14. *Viewing the general properties of the proxy*

In Figure 14-4 you can see the name of the proxy and the credential with which it is associated. You can also see that the proxy belongs to the Replication Merge subsystem. Remember that you can associate a proxy with any number of subsystems.

Click on the ellipsis button beside the "Credential name" field. The wizard will ask you to select the credential name for this proxy. You can also browse the list of credentials, as shown in Figure 14-15. Click the Cancel button to return to the Properties window (Figure 14-14).

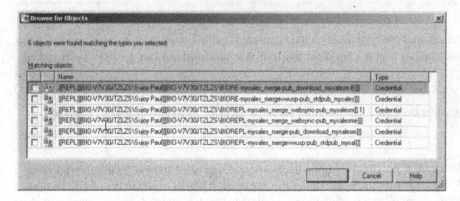

Figure 14-15. *Browsing the list of credentials that you can choose to associate with the proxy*

The user must have the right access to the proxy or the job steps will not be executed. Access to the proxy of each of the job steps for the user is provided by granting access to any of the security principals. A principal has a unique SID. Any user, group or a process that makes a request to access the SQL Server resource is a principal and is arranged in a hierarchy. There are three types of security principals: SQL Server logins, roles within the msdb database, and server roles. As you will see next, if the login for the user has access to the proxy, the user with the proxy can run the step. The same is true for the user with server roles and roles within msdb database.

Select the Principals page, as shown in Figure 14-16. You can see that the user names belong to the SQL Login principal. You can add user names to (or remove them from) any of the three principals.

■**Note** Users belonging to the `sysadmin` fixed server role have automatic access to the proxy account; they do not need to be added to the proxy. Members belonging to `sysadmin` can create, delete, and modify the proxy.

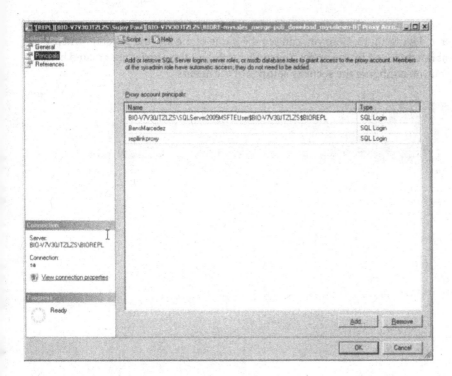

Figure 14-16. *Setting the proxy account principals*

Click on the OK button, and you will see the Add Principal window shown in Figure 14-17.

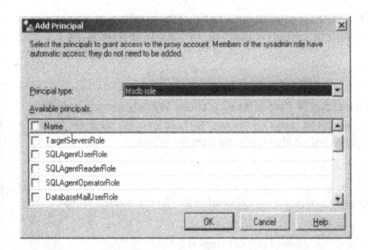

Figure 14-17. *The principals belonging to the msdb database role*

The users that belong to SQLAgentUserRole, SQLAgentReaderRole, and SQLAgentOperatorRole can create or execute the SQL Server Agent jobs. You can add the appropriate principals to the proxy by checking the appropriate check boxes.

Click Cancel to return to the Properties window (Figure 14-16). Now select the References page, as shown in Figure 14-18. Here you can see the name of the job, the job step, and the subsystem that is referenced by the proxy. The credentials and the proxies are created behind the scenes when you configure the security settings of the agents.

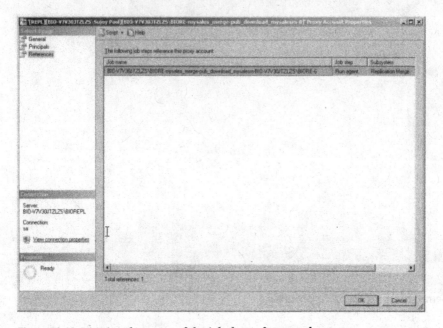

Figure 14-18. *Viewing the name of the job that references the proxy*

The script in Listing 14-2 shows how you can return a list of the proxies and the corresponding credentials for the Replication Merge subsystem. This is executed using the SQLCMD utility.

■**Note** You can execute the script in Listing 14-2 to find the list of proxies and corresponding credentials for other subsystems like the snapshot and log reader subsystems. You need to replace the SARG (Search Argument) of subsystem with snapshot instead of merge for the snapshot subsystem.

Listing 14-2. *Listing the Proxies and Corresponding Credentials for the Replication Merge Subsystem*

```
/*Set the SQLCMD variables and the connection settings first*/

:setvar logintimeout 120
:setvar server "BIO-V7V30JTZLZS\BIOREPL"
:setvar user "sa"
:setvar pwd "sujoy"
:connect $(server) -l $(logintimeout) -U $(user) -P $(pwd)
```

```
set nocount on

/* Need to run this on the msdb database */
use msdb
go

select a.subsystem_id,
a.subsystem,
a.description_id,
a.subsystem_dll,
a.agent_exe,
a.max_worker_threads,
c.flags,
d.proxy_id,
d.name as proxyname,
d.enabled,
d.description,
d.user_sid,
e.credential_id,
e.name as credentialname,
e.credential_identity,
e.create_date as credentialcreatedate,
e.modify_date as credentialmodifydate,
f.sid,
f.status,
f.createdate as logincreatedate,
f.name as loginname,
f.sysadmin,
f.isntuser

into #proxies

from syssubsystems a,
sysproxysubsystem b,
sysproxylogin c,
sysproxies d,
sys.credentials e,
sys.syslogins f

where a.subsystem_id=b.subsystem_id and
      b.proxy_id=c.proxy_id and
      c.proxy_id=d.proxy_id and
      d.credential_id=e.credential_id and
      c.sid=f.sid
```

```
/* Count to see that proxies exist */

declare @countmerge int
set @countmerge=
(select subsystem_id from #proxies
where subsystem like 'merge'
group by subsystem_id
having count(0)>1)

/* If the number of counts is 1 or more then find those proxies that belong to
 the merge subsystem */

if (@countmerge >0)
begin
select * from #proxies where subsystem like 'merge';
end

/*Finally drop the temp table #proxies */

drop table #proxies
go
```

This script first uses the SQLCMD variables and connection parameters as in Listing 14-1, since it will use the SQLCMD utility to export the output file. We can then load the file in the SSMS and view it in web form.

In this script, four system tables (syssubsystems, sysproxies, sysproxysubsystem, and sysproxylogin), a catalog view, and a compatibility view are used. The schema and the relationship, or rather the lack of it, are shown in Figure 14-19.

syssubsystems	
subsystem_id	int
subsystem	nvarchar(40)
description_id	int
subsystem_dll	nvarchar(255)
agent_exe	nvarchar(255)
start_entry_point	nvarchar(30)
event_entry_point	nvarchar(30)
stop_entry_point	nvarchar(30)
max_worker_threads	int

sysproxies	
proxy_id	int
name	sysname
credential_id	int
enabled	tinyint
description	uniqueidentifier
user_sid	varbinary(85)
credential_date_created	datetime

sysproxysubsystem	
subsystem_id	int
proxy_id	int

sysproxylogin	
proxy_id	int
sid	varbinary(85)
flags	int

Figure 14-19. *The schema for the four system tables used in Listing 14-2*

The script in Listing 14-2 inserts the values of subsystem_id, subsystem, description_id, subsystem_dll, agent_exe, and max_worker_threads from the syssubsystems table; flags from the sysproxylogin system table; proxy_id, name, enabled, description, and user_sid from the sysproxies system table into the #proxies temporary table. It then loads the credential_id, name, credential_identity, create_date, modify_date columns from the sys.credentials catalog view and the sid, status, createdate, name, sysadmin, and isntuser columns from the sys.logins compatibility view into the same temporary table. The subsystem_id, proxy_id, credential_id, and sid columns are joined using a where clause.

Once the data is inserted in the #proxies temporary table, the script uses the count function to determine whether any proxies for the merge subsystems exist. If they do, it retrieves all the data for the merge subsystem.

To run the script in Listing 14-2, use the SQLCMD utility as shown in Figure 14-20. As you can see, the output is directed to an output file with a .html extension (proxycredential.html). I'll show you how to view it in a moment.

Figure 14-20. *Executing the script in Listing 14-2 using the SQLCMD utility*

Here is the output of this script:

```
Changed database context to 'msdb'.

(22 rows affected)
subsystem_id subsystem description_id
subsystem_dll
agent_exe
max_worker_threads    flags         proxy_id
proxyname
enabled      description
user_sid
credential_id
credentialname
credential_identity
credentialcreatedate      credentialmodifydate
sid
status          logincreatedate          loginname
sysadmin       isntuser
------------ ---------------------------------------- -------------- -----------
7           Merge     14554
C:\Program Files\Microsoft SQL Server\MSSQL.1\MSSQL\binn\SQLREPSS90.DLL
```

```
C:\Program Files\Microsoft SQL Server\90\COM\REPLMERG.EXE
100              0              4
[REPL][BIO-V7V30JTZLZS\Sujoy Paul][BIO-V7V30JTZLZS\BIORE-
mysales_mergevwusp-pub_stdpub_mysales]
1        NULL
0x010500000000000051500000003FAD1462358A021ADBEB0C50E8030000
65540
[REPL][BIO-V7V30JTZLZS\Sujoy Paul][BIO-V7V30JTZLZS\BIORE-
mysales_mergevwusp-pub_stdpub_mysales]
BIO-V7V30JTZLZS\Sujoy Paul
2006-02-08 23:45:32.910 2006-02-08 23:45:32.910
 0x774916C8D662D94FBD31DA8A1D4B80E4
9    2006-02-09 14:09:18.397        BensMarcedez
0        0
```

```
7        Merge        14554
C:\Program Files\Microsoft SQL Server\MSSQL.1\MSSQL\binn\SQLREPSS90.DLL
C:\Program Files\Microsoft SQL Server\90\COM\REPLMERG.EXE
100              0              5
[REPL][BIO-V7V30JTZLZS\Sujoy Paul][BIO-V7V30JTZLZS\BIORE-
mysales_merge-pub_download_mysalesm-B]
1        NULL
0x010500000000000051500000003FAD1462358A021ADBEB0C50E8030000
65541
[REPL][BIO-V7V30JTZLZS\Sujoy Paul][BIO-V7V30JTZLZS\BIORE-
mysales_merge-pub_download_mysalesm-B]
BIO-V7V30JTZLZS\Sujoy Paul
2006-02-10 20:45:32.330            2006-02-10 20:45:32.330
0x010500000000000051500000003FAD1462358A021ADBEB0C501E040000
9    2005-12-29 23:57:16.607        BIO-
V7V30JTZLZS\SQLServer2005MSFTEUser$BIO-V7V30JTZLZS$BIOREPL
0        0
```

```
7        Merge        14554
C:\Program Files\Microsoft SQL Server\MSSQL.1\MSSQL\binn\SQLREPSS90.DLL
C:\Program Files\Microsoft SQL Server\90\COM\REPLMERG.EXE
100              0              5
REPL][BIO-V7V30JTZLZS\Sujoy Paul][BIO-V7V30JTZLZS\BIORE-mysales_merge-
pub_download_mysalesm-B]
1        NULL
0x010500000000000051500000003FAD1462358A021ADBEB0C50E8030000
65541
```

```
[REPL][BIO-V7V3OJTZLZS\Sujoy Paul][BIO-V7V3OJTZLZS\BIORE-
mysales_merge-pub_download_mysalesm-B]
BIO-V7V3OJTZLZS\Sujoy Paul
2006-02-10 20:45:32.330          2006-02-10 20:45:32.330
0x774916C8D662D94FBD31DA8A1D4B80E4
9    2006-02-09 14:09:18.397              BensMarcedez
0         0


7      Merge              14554
C:\Program Files\Microsoft SQL Server\MSSQL.1\MSSQL\binn\SQLREPSS90.DLL
C:\Program Files\Microsoft SQL Server\90\COM\REPLMERG.EXE
100              0         5
[REPL][BIO-V7V3OJTZLZS\Sujoy Paul][BIO-V7V3OJTZLZS\BIORE-
mysales_merge-pub_download_mysalesm-B]
NULL
0x0105000000000005150000003FAD1462358A021ADBEB0C50E8030000
65541
[REPL][BIO-V7V3OJTZLZS\Sujoy Paul][BIO-V7V3OJTZLZS\BIORE-
mysales_merge-pub_download_mysalesm-B]
BIO-V7V3OJTZLZS\Sujoy Paul
2006-02-10 20:45:32.330          2006-02-10 20:45:32.330
0x91967DA635AB8C4086E543C30D74F459
9      2005-12-30 18:34:04.183              repllinkproxy
0         0


(4 rows affected)
```

You can see from the preceding output that there were 22 rows inserted in the #proxies table, and that the merge subsystem has four proxies. You can see the subsystem ID for the merge subsystem, the driver for the subsystem, and the name of the executable for the agent. The maximum number of worker threads is shown to be 100, and the column flags in all cases have a value of 0, which means the proxy's login type is Windows Authentication (a value of 1 would mean it is using the SQL Server fixed server role, and a value of 2 would means it is using the msdb database role). You can also see the name of the corresponding proxy, and that all of them are enabled (a value of 0 means it is disabled). The name of the credential and the identity of the credential corresponding to the proxy are also shown. The login name of the user who is using the proxy is also listed.

While the output can be viewed in different file formats, the purpose of generating the output in HTML format is to make it web enabled. Open the SSMS, and select View ➤ Web Browser ➤ Home. Type the URL and specify the HTML file. For example, I have the IIS Server running and I have a separate folder to hold the file, so the URL in my case is http://localhost/replication_files/proxycredential1.html. You can see the output in Figure 14-21.

Figure 14-21. *The output of the script in Listing 14-2 in web format*

■**Note** Chapter 12 describes how to set up IIS.

In this chapter you have seen how the Merge Agent and the proxies and credentials with the Replication Merge subsystems work. In the following sections, we will look at the internal workings of publication for both the download-only and standard articles and then at how the subscriptions for the merge replication work behind the scenes.

Publication and Subscriptions

Chapters 11 through 13 explained how to configure publication for both download-only and standard articles, how to use parameterized filters for standard articles, and how to set up web synchronization for standard articles. In this section, I will discuss the inner workings of publication with download-only articles and then with standard articles, which can also be used for web synchronization.

Note The configuration of merge replication using GUI and T-SQL methods is detailed in Chapters 11 and 13; Chapter 12 describes how to set up merge replication with web synchronization.

Publication with Download-Only Articles

For download-only articles, metadata changes do not occur on the Subscriber server because updates are not made. You would use download-only articles where updates are made at the Publisher server, and they are sent to the Subscriber server for read-only purposes. If you are reading this book sequentially, you probably have already used the Item table to view a list of items that are available for the myinventory schema.

The Item table was included when the publication was set up for download-only articles during the configuration of merge replication using T-SQL in Chapter 13. As with transactional replication, a new column is added to the table when you set up the publication. The column, in this case, is called rowguid, and it is of data type uniqueidentifier, as you can see in Figure 14-22. You will find the same column in the other tables that are included as articles in the publication, namely PriceList, Warehouse, and SalesPerson. This column uniquely identifies every row involved in the publication.

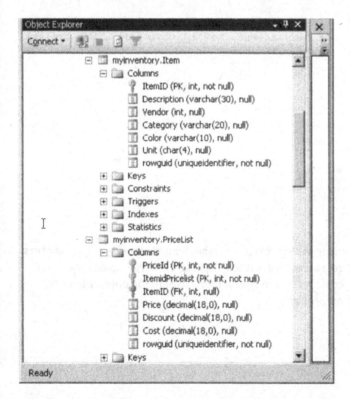

Figure 14-22. The rowguid column is included in the tables involved in publication with download-only articles

This column is created when the Snapshot Agent is run for the first time. Before the column is created in the published tables, system tables are introduced by the engine in the publication database and are built the first time you enable the database for merge replication using the sp_replicationdboption stored procedure. The entries for the publication are added to the system table when you execute sp_addmergepublication. The E-R diagrams for the system tables that are added to the publication database are shown in Figures 14-23 through 14-29.

MSdynamicsnapshotjobs	
id	int
name	sysname
pubid	uniqueidentifier
job_id	uniqueidentifier
agent_id	int
dynamic_filter_login	sysname
dynamic_filter_hostname	sysname
dynamic_snapshot_location	nvarchar(255)
partition_id	int
computed_dynsnap_location	bit

MSmerge_agent_parameters	
profile_name	sysname
parameter_name	sysname
value	nvarchar(255)

MSmerge_current_partition_mappings	
publication_number	smallint
tablenick	int
rowguid	uniqueidentifier
partition_id	int

MSdynamicsnapshotviews	
dynamic_snapshot_view_name	sysname

MSmerge_tombstone	
rowguid	uniqueidentifier
tablenick	int
type	tinyint
lineage	varbinary(311)
generation	bigint
logical_record_parent_rowguid	uniqueidentifier
logical_record_lineage	varbinary(311)

MSmerge_contents	
tablenick	int
rowguid	uniqueidentifier
generation	bigint
partchangegen	bigint
lineage	varbinary(311)
colv1	varbinary(2953)
marker	uniqueidentifier
logical_record_parent_rowguid	uniqueidentifier
logical_record_lineage	varbinary(311)

MSmerge_conflicts_info	
tablenick	int
rowguid	uniqueidentifier
origin_datasource	nvarchar(255)
conflict_type	int
reason_code	int
reason_text	nvarchar(720)
pubid	uniqueidentifier
MSrepl_create_time	datetime
origin_datasource_id	uniqueidentifier

Figure 14-23. *The E-R diagram showing the* MSdynamicsnapshotjobs, MSmerge_agent_parameters, MSdynamicsnapshotviews, MSmerge_current_partition_mappings, MSmerge_tombstone, MSmerge_contents, *and* MSmerge_conflicts_info *system tables used in the publication and subscription databases in merge replication*

MSmerge_articlehistory	
session_id	int
phase_id	int
article_name	sysname
start_time	datetime
duration	int
inserts	int
updates	int
deletes	int
conflicts	int
rows_retried	int
percent_complete	decimal(5,2)
estimated_changes	int
relative_cost	decimal(12,2)

MSmerge_genhistory	
guidsrc	uniqueidentifier
pubid	uniqueidentifier
generation	bigint
art_nick	int
nicknames	varbinary(1001)
coldate	datetime
genstatus	tinyint
changecount	int
subscriber_number	int

MSmerge_conflict_pub_download_mysalesmerge_Item	
ItemID	int
Description	varchar(30)
Vendor	int
Category	varchar(20)
Color	varchar(10)
Unit	char(4)
rowguid	uniqueidentifier
origin_datasource_id	uniqueidentifier

MSmerge_history	
session_id	int
agent_id	int
comments	ntext
error_id	int
timestamp	timestamp
updateable_row	bit
time	datetime

MSmerge_generation_partition_mappings	
publication_number	smallint
generation	bigint
partition_id	int
changecount	int

MSmerge_conflict_pub_download_mysalesmerge_PriceList	
PriceId	int
ItemidPricelist	int
ItemID	int
Price	decimal(18)
Discount	decimal(18)
Cost	decimal(18)
rowguid	uniqueidentifier
origin_datasource_id	uniqueidentifier

Figure 14-24. *The E-R diagram showing the* MSmerge_articlehistory, MSmerge_genhistory, MSmerge_history, MSmerge_conflict_pub_download_mysalesmerge_Item, MSmerge_generation_ partition_mappings, *and* MSmerge_conflict_pub_download_mysalesmerge_PriceList *system tables used in the publication and subscription databases in merge replication*

MSmerge_replinfo	
repid	uniqueidentifier
use_interactive_resolver	bit
validation_level	int
resync_gen	bigint
login_name	sysname
hostname	sysname
merge_jobid	binary(16)
sync_info	int

MSmerge_settingshistory	
eventtime	datetime
pubid	uniqueidentifier
artid	uniqueidentifier
eventtype	tinyint
propertyname	sysname
previousvalue	sysname
newvalue	sysname
eventtext	nvarchar(2000)

MSmerge_sessions	
subid	uniqueidentifier
session_id	int
agent_id	int
start_time	datetime
end_time	datetime
duration	int
delivery_time	int
upload_time	int
download_time	int
schema_change_time	int
prepare_snapshot_time	int
delivery_rate	decimal(12,2)
time_remaining	int
percent_complete	decimal(5,2)
upload_inserts	int
upload_updates	int
upload_deletes	int
upload_conflicts	int
upload_rows_retried	int
download_inserts	int
download_updates	int
download_deletes	int
download_conflicts	int
download_rows_retried	int
schema_changes	int
bulk_inserts	int
metadata_rows_cleanedup	int
runstatus	int
estimated_upload_changes	int
estimated_download_changes	int
connection_type	int
timestamp	timestamp
current_phase_id	int
spid	smallint
spid_login_time	datetime

MSmerge_errorlineage	
tablenick	int
rowguid	uniqueidentifier
lineage	varbinary(311)

MSmerge_supportability_settings	
pubid	uniqueidentifier
subid	uniqueidentifier
web_server	sysname
support_options	int
log_severity	int
log_modules	int
log_file_path	nvarchar(255)
log_file_name	sysname
log_file_size	int
no_of_log_files	int
upload_interval	int
delete_after_upload	int
custom_script	nvarchar(2048)
message_pattern	nvarchar(2000)
last_log_upload_time	datetime

MSrepl_errors	
id	int
time	datetime
error_type_id	int
source_type_id	int
error_code	sysname
error_text	ntext
xact_seqno	varbinary(16)
command_id	int
session_id	int

MSmerge_altsyncpartners	
subid	uniqueidentifier
alternate_subid	uniqueidentifier
description	nvarchar(255)

Figure 14-25. *The E-R diagram showing the* MSmerge_replinfo, MSmerge_settingshistory, MSmerge_sessions, MSmerge_errorlineage, MSmerge_supportability_settings, MSrepl_errors, *and* MSmerge_altsyncpartners *system tables used in the publication and subscription databases in merge replication*

MSmerge_identity_range	
subid	uniqueidentifier
artid	uniqueidentifier
range_begin	numeric(38)
range_end	numeric(38)
next_range_begin	numeric(38)
next_range_end	numeric(38)
is_pub_range	bit
max_used	numeric(38)

MSmerge_conflict_pub_download_mysalesmerge_SalesPerson	
SalesID	smallint
Name	varchar(30)
WhseAddress1	varchar(30)
Whse_City	varchar(20)
Whse_Postal_Code	varchar(7)
Phone	varchar(20)
Zone	smallint
rowguid	uniqueidentifier
origin_datasource_id	uniqueidentifier

MSmerge_log_files	
id	int
pubid	uniqueidentifier
subid	uniqueidentifier
web_server	sysname
file_name	nvarchar(2000)
upload_time	datetime
log_file_type	int
log_file	varbinary

MSmerge_conflict_pub_download_mysalesmerge_Warehouse	
WhseID	int
WhseName	varchar(20)
WhseAddress1	varchar(30)
Whse_City	varchar(20)
Whse_Postal_Code	varchar(7)
rowguid	uniqueidentifier
origin_datasource_id	uniqueidentifier

sysmergeschemachange	
pubid	uniqueidentifier
artid	uniqueidentifier
schemaversion	int
schemaguid	uniqueidentifier
schematype	int
schematext	nvarchar
schemastatus	tinyint
schemasubtype	int

MSmerge_past_partition_mappings	
publication_number	smallint
tablenick	int
rowguid	uniqueidentifier
partition_id	int
generation	uniqueidentifier
reason	tinyint

MSmerge_metadataaction_request	
tablenick	int
rowguid	uniqueidentifier
action	tinyint
generation	uniqueidentifier
changed	int

sysreplservers	
srvname	sysname
srvid	int

Figure 14-26. *The E-R diagram showing the* MSmerge_identity_range, MSmerge_conflict_pub_
download_mysalesmerge_SalesPerson, MSmerge_log_files, MSmerge_past_partition_mappings,
sysmergeschemachange, sysreplservers, *and* MSmerge_metadataaction_request *system tables
used in the publication and subscription databases in merge replication*

sysmergepartitioninfo	
artid	uniqueidentifier
pubid	uniqueidentifier
partition_view_id	int
repl_view_id	int
partition_deleted_view_rule	nvarchar
partition_inserted_view_rule	nvarchar
membership_eval_proc_name	sysname
column_list	nvarchar
column_list_blob	nvarchar
expand_proc	sysname
logical_record_parent_nickname	int
logical_record_view	int
logical_record_deleted_view_rule	nvarchar
logical_record_level_conflict_detection	bit
logical_record_level_conflict_resolution	bit
partition_options	tinyint

MSmerge_dynamic_snapshots	
partition_id	int
dynamic_snapshot_location	nvarchar(255)
last_updated	datetime
last_started	datetime

[0..n]

partition_id = partition_id
upd(R); del(R)

sysmergeschemaarticles	
name	sysname
type	tinyint
objid	int
artid	uniqueidentifier
description	nvarchar(255)
pre_creation_command	tinyint
pubid	uniqueidentifier
status	tinyint
creation_script	nvarchar(255)
schema_option	binary(8)
destination_object	sysname
destination_owner	sysname
processing_order	int

MSmerge_partition_groups	
partition_id	int
publication_number	smallint
maxgen_whenadded	bigint
using_partition_groups	bit
is_partition_active	bit

Figure 14-27. *The E-R diagram showing the* sysmergepartitioninfo, MSmerge_dynamic_ *snapshots,* sysmergeschemaarticles, *and* MSmerge_partition_groups *system tables used in the publication and subscription databases in merge replication*

sysmergearticles	
name	sysname
type	tinyint
objid	int
sync_objid	int
view_type	tinyint
artid	uniqueidentifier
description	nvarchar(255)
pre_creation_command	tinyint
pubid	uniqueidentifier
nickname	int
column_tracking	int
status	tinyint
conflict_table	sysname
creation_script	nvarchar(255)
conflict_script	nvarchar(255)
article_resolver	nvarchar(255)
ins_conflict_proc	sysname
insert_proc	sysname
update_proc	sysname
select_proc	sysname
metadata_select_proc	sysname
delete_proc	sysname
schema_option	binary(8)
destination_object	sysname
destination_owner	sysname
resolver_clsid	nvarchar(50)
subset_filterclause	nvarchar(1000)
missing_col_count	int
missing_cols	varbinary(128)
excluded_cols	varbinary(128)
excluded_col_count	int
columns	varbinary(128)
deleted_cols	varbinary(128)
resolver_info	nvarchar(255)
view_sel_proc	nvarchar(290)
gen_cur	bigint
vertical_partition	int
identity_support	int
before_image_objid	int
before_view_objid	int
verify_resolver_signature	int
allow_interactive_resolver	bit
fast_multicol_updateproc	bit
check_permissions	int
maxversion_at_cleanup	int
processing_order	int
upload_options	tinyint
published_in_tran_pub	bit
lightweight	bit
procname_postfix	nchar(32)
well_partitioned_lightweight	bit
before_upd_view_objid	int
delete_tracking	bit
compensate_for_errors	bit
pub_range	bigint
range	bigint
threshold	int
stream_blob_columns	bit
preserve_rowguidcol	bit

sysmergepublications	
publisher	sysname
publisher_db	sysname
name	sysname
description	nvarchar(255)
retention	int
publication_type	tinyint
pubid	uniqueidentifier
designmasterid	uniqueidentifier
parentid	uniqueidentifier
sync_mode	tinyint
allow_push	int
allow_pull	int
allow_anonymous	int
centralized_conflicts	int
status	tinyint
snapshot_ready	tinyint
enabled_for_internet	bit
dynamic_filters	bit
snapshot_in_defaultfolder	bit
alt_snapshot_folder	nvarchar(255)
pre_snapshot_script	nvarchar(255)
post_snapshot_script	nvarchar(255)
compress_snapshot	bit
ftp_address	sysname
ftp_port	int
ftp_subdirectory	nvarchar(255)
ftp_login	sysname
ftp_password	nvarchar(524)
conflict_retention	int
keep_before_values	int
allow_subscription_copy	bit
allow_synctoalternate	bit
validate_subscriber_info	nvarchar(500)
ad_guidname	sysname
backward_comp_level	int
max_concurrent_merge	int
max_concurrent_dynamic_snapshots	int
use_partition_groups	smallint
dynamic_filters_function_list	nvarchar(500)
partition_id_eval_proc	sysname
publication_number	smallint
replicate_ddl	int
allow_subscriber_initiated_snapshot	bit
distributor	sysname
snapshot_jobid	binary(16)
allow_web_synchronization	bit
web_synchronization_url	nvarchar(500)
allow_partition_realignment	bit
retention_period_unit	tinyint
decentralized_conflicts	int
generation_leveling_threshold	int
automatic_reinitialization_policy	bit

Figure 14-28. *The E-R diagram showing the* sysmergearticles *and* sysmergepublications *system tables used in the publication and subscription databases in merge replication*

sysmergesubscriptions	
subscriber_server	sysname
db_name	sysname
pubid	uniqueidentifier
datasource_type	int
subid	uniqueidentifier
replnickname	binary(6)
replicastate	uniqueidentifier
status	tinyint
subscriber_type	int
subscription_type	int
sync_type	tinyint
description	nvarchar(255)
priority	real
recgen	bigint
recguid	uniqueidentifier
sentgen	bigint
sentguid	uniqueidentifier
schemaversion	int
schemaguid	uniqueidentifier
last_validated	datetime
attempted_validate	datetime
last_sync_date	datetime
last_sync_status	int
last_sync_summary	sysname
metadatacleanuptime	datetime
partition_id	int
cleanedup_unsent_changes	bit
replica_version	int
supportability_mode	int
application_name	sysname
subscriber_number	int

sysmergesubsetfilters	
filtername	sysname
join_filterid	int
pubid	uniqueidentifier
artid	uniqueidentifier
art_nickname	int
join_articlename	sysname
join_nickname	int
join_unique_key	int
expand_proc	sysname
join_filterclause	nvarchar(1000)
filter_type	tinyint

Figure 14-29. *The E-R diagram showing the* sysmergesubscriptions *and* sysmergesubsetfilters *system tables used in the publication and subscription databases in merge replication*

The same schema can be found in databases for merge publication using push subscription.

Table 14-1 lists the system tables involved in the publication, the push subscriptions for merge replication, and the related functions.

Table 14-1. *System Tables Involved in Publication and Push Subscriptions for Merge Replication*

Table Name	Description
MSdynamicsnapshotjobs	Contains information on snapshot jobs for publication with parameterized filters.
MSdynamicsnapshotviews	Holds information on the temporary snapshot views created by the Snapshot Agent and used by the system for cleaning up views if the engine shuts down abnormally.
MSmerge_agent_parameters	Holds information about the profile name and the parameters of the Merge Agents.
MSmerge_altsyncpartners	Tracks the current synchronization partners for the Publisher server.
MSmerge_articlehistory	Holds information about changes made to each article during the synchronization session with one row for each article to which changes are made. This table is stored in the distribution database.

Table Name	Description
MSmerge_conflict_pub_download_mysales_merge_Item	Is an article specific conflict table that is used for logging conflicts. The name of the conflict table, Item, is appended to the publication name, which in turn is appended to MSmerge_conflict. The standard name of the table is MSmerge_conflict_*publicationname_articlename*.
MSmerge_conflict_pub_download_mysales_merge_PriceList	Same as the preceding table.
MSmerge_conflict_pub_download_mysales_merge_SalesPerson	Same as the preceding table.
MSmerge_conflict_pub_download_mysales_merge_Warehouse	Same as the preceding table.
MSmerge_conflicts_info	Records conflicts that occur while synchronizing a subscription to a merge publication. The data for the losing row is held in the MSmerge_conflict_*publicationname_articlename* table.
MSmerge_contents	Contains one row for each row modified in the publication since the last time it has been published. This table is stored in both the publication and subscription databases and is used by the Merge Agent to determine whether any changes have occurred.
MSmerge_current_partition_mappings	Stores a row for each partition ID a changed row belongs to.
MSmerge_dynamic_snapshots	Helps to track the location of the filtered data snapshot for each partition in publication with parameterized filters.
MSmerge_errorlineage	Stores rows for each deletion that has been carried out on the Subscriber server but not propagated to the Publisher server.
MSmerge_generation_partition_mappings	Tracks changes to partitions in a merge publication, and is also found in the subscription database.
MSmerge_genhistory	Contains a row for each generation that a Subscriber server is aware of within the retention period, so that common generations are not sent again to the subscribing servers. This table is found in both the publication and subscription databases.
MSmerge_history	Contains the history of all the descriptions and outcomes of the previous Merge Agent job sessions. This table is stored in the distribution database.
MSmerge_identity_range	Tracks numeric ranges assigned to identity columns for subscription to publications on which merge replication automatically manages the identity ranges.
MSmerge_log_files	Contains information about the type of log files for the publication.
MSmerge_metadataaction_request	Stores information for every compensating action taken by the merge process.

Continued

Table 14-1. *Continued*

Table Name	Description
MSmerge_partition_groups	Used for publication with parameterized filters. A column is added for every function used in the parameterized filter. If the SUSER_SNAME() function is used, a column called SUSER_SNAME_FN is added.
MSmerge_past_partition_mappings	Contains a row for each partition ID of a changed row that used to belong to but no longer belongs anymore.
MSmerge_replinfo	Tracks information about the sent and received generations. (Each collection of changes that is delivered either to a Publisher or a Subscriber server is called a generation.) This table is stored in both the publication and the subscription databases.
MSmerge_sessions	Contains history rows with the outcomes of the previous Merge Agent job sessions. This table is stored in the distribution database.
MSmerge_settingshistory	Contains information about when the initial property settings were made. It also maintains a history of the changes made to article and publication properties. This table is stored in both the publication and subscription databases.
MSmerge_supportablity_settings	Contains information about the name, path, type, and size of the log files.
MSmerge_tombstone	Contains information about the all the rows that are deleted and allows the transmission of the deletes to the subscribing server. This table is stored in both the publication and subscription databases.
MSrepl_errors	Contains information about the failure of Merge Agents. This table is stored in the distribution database.
sysmergearticles	Contains information for each merge article defined in the publication database.
sysmergepartitioninfo	Contains information on partitions for each article. This table is stored in the publication and subscription databases.
sysmergepublications	Contains information for each merge publication. This table is defined in both the publication and subscription databases.
sysmergeschemaarticles	Contains information about schema-only articles. This table is stored in both the publication and subscription databases.
sysmergeschemachange	Contains information about published articles generated by the Snapshot Agent. This table is stored in both the publication and subscription databases.
sysmergesubscriptions	Contains information for the subscribing server. This table is stored in both the publication and subscription databases.
sysmergesubsetfilters	Contains information about partitioned articles containing join filters. This table is found in both the publication and subscription databases.
sysreplservers	Contains information about the server involved in replication.

Besides the system tables, insert, update, and delete triggers are added on each of the tables that are included in the publication for merge replication, be it for download-only articles or standard articles. These triggers track the information changes for the articles involved in the merge publication.

The triggers are named according to their DML operations. For example, these are the names of the triggers for the Item table:

```
MSmerge_del_0595E710D1A24C13B46C39F1A8F580C9
MSmerge_ins_0595E710D1A24C13B46C39F1A8F580C9
MSmerge_upd_0595E710D1A24C13B46C39F1A8F580C9
```

The list of numbers at the end of the name is a globally unique identifier (GUID), which is retrieved from the artid column of the sysmergearticles table. The complete name of the trigger follows the pattern MSmerge_<DML>_GUID, and this is true of all the tables, such as PriceList, Warehouse, and SalesPerson, that were used as download articles.

Tip If you right-click on the trigger in the SSMS, select View Dependencies, and select Objects on Which <triggername> Depends, you will see that the trigger lists the user table and the sysmergearticles system table as dependencies.

The insert trigger, such as MSmerge_<ins>_GUID, first sets the transaction level to read committed. It finds out whether any rows are inserted for the article, and then it finds the highest generation for which the metadata has been cleaned by retrieving the maxversion_at_cleanup column from the sysmergearticles table for the table the trigger depends on. This is done by retrieving the value for the nickname column from the sysmergearticles table. The trigger then selects the latest generation from the view that is created for merge replication. The name of the view for the Item table is MSmerg_genvw_0595E710D1A24C13B46C39F1A8F580C9.

Note Four views with the name MSmerge_genvw_<GUID> are generated for each table used for publication with download-only articles. If you add another download-only article for publication, another view with the same name format will be generated. The columns for the views are guidsrc, pubid, generation, art_nick, nicknames, coldate, genstatus, changecount, and subscriber_number.

If the value for the latest generation is NULL, the trigger inserts values for the following columns in the view: guidsrc, genstatus, art_nick, nicknames, coldate, and changecount. If it is NOT NULL, the trigger updates the changecount column of the view by adding the value of the changecount column and the number of rows inserted for the article. If an error is encountered during either of these operations, the transaction is rolled back.

The trigger then finds the maximum version for the lineage column from the MSmerge_tsvw_0595E710D1A24C13B46C39F1A8F580C9 view. If it is NOT NULL, the trigger resets the lineage column to the higher version.

> **Note** Four views with the name `MSmerge_tsvw_<GUID>` are generated for each of the tables used for publication with download-only articles. The columns for the views are `rowguid`, `tablenick`, `type`, `lineage`, `generation`, `logical_record_parent_rowguid`, and `logical_record_lineage`.

Another column called `colv1` in the `MSmerge_ctsv_0595E710D1A24C13B46C39F1A8F580C9` view is also reset.

> **Note** Four views with names of the form `MSmerge_ctsv_<GUID>` are generated for each of the tables used for publication with download-only articles. The columns for the views are `tablenick`, `rowguid`, `generation`, `partchangegen`, `lineage`, `colv1`, `marker`, `logical_record_parent_rowguid`, and `logical_record_lineage`.

The `MSmerge_del_GUID` trigger finds out whether any rows have been deleted for the article. Like the insert trigger, it finds the highest generation for which the metadata has been cleaned, and it selects the latest generation from the view that is created for merge replication. The `changecount` column for the view is updated by adding the value of the `changecount` column and the number of rows deleted for the article. If the trigger finds any rows being deleted for the article, it inserts the following columns in the `MSmerge_tsvw_GUID` view: `rowguid`, `tablenick`, `type`, `lineage`, and `generation`. If any errors are generated, it deletes the rows from the `MSmerge_ctsv_GUID`.

The `MSmerge_upd_GUID` trigger first determines whether any rows for the article are updated and, like the previous triggers, retrieves the oldest version from the `sysmergearticlecolumns` system table stored in the publication database. Then it uses the intrinsic `column_update()` function to set the bits for updated columns. Next, it updates the `changecount` column, since the view is updated by adding the value of the `changecount` column and the number of rows updated for the article. The trigger then checks to see whether any partition, join filter in the partition, or column in the logical relationship has changed, and it updates the `MSmerge_ctsv_GUID` view.

Two views have been added: `sysmergepartitioninfoview` and `sysmergeextendedarticlesview`. The former provides partition information for table articles, and the latter provides information about the articles involved in the merge publication. Both views are found in the publication and subscription databases.

Besides the DML triggers for the four tables that are used as articles in the merge publication, replication also adds four DDL triggers that are database-scoped:

- `MSmerge_tr_alterschemaonly`
- `MSmerge_tr_altertable`
- `MSmerge_tr_altertrigger`
- `MSmerge_tr_alterview`

All these DDL triggers call the `sys.sp_MSmerge_ddldispatcher` stored procedure. The `MSmerge_tr_alterschemaonly` trigger is fired whenever a function or a stored procedure is altered. The `MSmerge_tr_altertable` trigger is fired whenever a table is altered; the `MSmerge_tr_altertrigger` and `MSmerge_tr_alterview` triggers are fired for trigger and view alterations.

DATABASE TRIGGERS

Database-scoped and server-scoped triggers are DDL triggers that have been introduced in SQL Server 2005. Unlike DML triggers, which are fired when DML operations take place, DDL triggers are fired when changes are made in the DDL, like CREATE, ALTER, and DROP. As such, they can be used to monitor the administration of the database or the server. However, as with DML triggers, transactions can be committed or rolled back after the completion of the transaction, and this can even include nested triggers.

DDL triggers are created using the create trigger statement just like DML triggers. However, there are certain things that you cannot do with DDL triggers. For example, you cannot use the INSTEAD OF triggers and the inserted and deleted tables like the DML triggers.

The EVENTDATA() function is used to capture the events that fire DDL triggers. It returns a data type of XML. It returns numerous events, but the following three items are included for all event types:

- Type of event

- Time when the event was fired

- The System Process ID (SPID) of the connection that fired the trigger

The following code executes a DDL trigger that will prevent the creation, alteration, and dropping of tables, views, and stored procedures on the mysales_merge database.

```
create trigger ddlmysales_merge
on database
for drop_table, drop_view, drop_procedure,
alter_table, alter_view, alter_procedure,
create_table, create_view, create_procedure
as
declare @eventdata xml

set @eventdata=eventdata()

select
@eventdata.value('(/EVENT_INSTANCE/EventType)[1]','varchar(100)')
as [EventType],
@eventdata.value('(/EVENT_INSTANCE/PostTime)[1]','varchar(100)') as [PostTime],
@eventdata.value('(/EVENT_INSTANCE/SPID)[1]','varchar(25)') as [SPID],
@eventdata.value('(/EVENT_INSTANCE/ServerName)[1]','varchar(30)')
as [Servername],
@eventdata.value('(/EVENT_INSTANCE/LoginName)[1]','varchar(30)') as [Loginname],
@eventdata.value('(/EVENT_INSTANCE/TSQLCommand/CommandText)[1]','varchar(2000)')
as [CommandText]

raiserror('Create, drop and alter statements for tables,
views and procedures not allowed',16,1)
rollback
go
```

You will find that the trigger is created in the Database Triggers object under the Programmability object of the mysales_merge database in the Object Explorer of the SSMS. If you try to create, alter, or drop a table you will get the following error message:

```
(1 row(s) affected)
Msg 50000, Level 16, State 1, Procedure ddlmysales_merge, Line 20
Create, drop and alter statements for tables,
views and procedures not allowed
Msg 3609, Level 16, State 2, Line 1
The transaction ended in the trigger. The batch has been aborted.
```

This code creates a trigger that is database-scoped by using the statement `create trigger` on the database. Then the `Eventdata()` function triggers the events for the SPID, the server name, the login name, the T-SQL command, the event type, and the time when the trigger event was executed. The `value` method is used to return the event data. If you execute this code,

```
Select * from sys.trigger_events
```

you will get the following result set:

	object_id	type	type_desc	is_first	is_last
1	978102525	22	ALTER_TABLE	0	0
2	994102582	42	ALTER_VIEW	0	0
3	1010102639	52	ALTER_PROCEDURE	0	0
4	1010102639	62	ALTER_FUNCTION	0	0
5	1026102696	72	ALTER_TRIGGER	0	0
6	1330103779	1	INSERT	0	0
7	1346103836	2	UPDATE	0	0
8	1362103893	3	DELETE	0	0
9	1426104121	1	INSERT	0	0
10	1442104178	2	UPDATE	0	0
11	1458104235	3	DELETE	0	0
12	1522104463	1	INSERT	0	0
13	1538104520	2	UPDATE	0	0
14	1554104577	3	DELETE	0	0
15	1618104805	1	INSERT	0	0
16	1634104862	2	UPDATE	0	0
17	1650104919	3	DELETE	0	0
18	1662628966	21	CREATE_TABLE	0	0
19	1662628966	22	ALTER_TABLE	0	0
20	1662628966	23	DROP_TABLE	0	0
21	1662628966	42	ALTER_VIEW	0	0
22	1662628966	43	DROP_VIEW	0	0
23	1662628966	52	ALTER_PROCEDURE	0	0
24	1662628966	53	DROP_PROCEDURE	0	0

BIO-V7V30JTZLZS\BIOREPL (9.0 RTM)   sa (54)   mysales_merge

Stored procedures are also created for handling DML operations for each of the published tables. The stored procedures are named following the patterns MSmerge_ins_sp_GUID, MSmerge_del_sp_GUID, and MSmerge_upd_sp_GUID. For the Item table, therefore, you could have the following stored procedures MSmerge_ins_sp_0595E710D1A24C13B46C39F1A8F580C9, MSmerge_del_sp_0595E710D1A24C13B46C39F1A8F580C9, and MSmerge_upd_sp_ 0595E710D1A24C13B46C39F1A8F580C9 (the last part of each name will vary).

Another set of insert stored procedures is also created with the name batch appended. So, again for the Item table, you would have an insert procedure called MSmerge_ins_sp_ 0595E710D1A24C13B46C39F1A8F580C9_batch.

A set of select stored procedures is also added: MSmerge_sel_sp_ 0595E710D1A24C13B46C39F1A8F580C9 and MSmerge_sel_sp_0595E710D1A24C13B46C39F1A8F580C9_ metadata.

So, when you insert data in the Item table, the insert stored procedure is executed. It checks the security by ensuring that the user is a member of the PAL and is a member of the db_owner database role, makes an entry in the MSmerge_contents system table, and commits the transaction.

Note The PAL is discussed in the "The Publication Access List" section of Chapter 7.

The rowguid in the MSmerge_contents table is the rowguid of the row that is inserted. The next time synchronization occurs, this row will be sent to the Subscriber server; once the synchronization is successfully completed, the row is then removed from the MSmerge_ metadataaction_request table. The code that does this is shown in Figure 14-30.

Figure 14-30. *The insert stored procedure is executed for merge publication*

If any rows are to be deleted from the Item table, the delete stored procedure is executed. It first checks whether any of the rows are waiting to be deleted. It then checks whether the rows have already been deleted, and whether they exist in the Item user table. If they exist, the stored procedure makes an entry in the MSmerge_tombstone system table for the rows that have been deleted. The rowguid of the MSmerge_tombstone table is the rowguid of the row that has been deleted, and the next time synchronization is executed, the Merge Agent sends a message to the subscribing server to delete the row. If the deleted row is referenced in MSmerge_contents because data has been either inserted or updated, it is removed from the MSmerge_contents table. If the rows were previously deleted, the metadatatype, generation, and lineage columns of the MSmerge_tombstone system table are still updated.

In the case of updating rows in the Item table, the update stored procedure is executed. Like the delete procedure, it ensures security by checking whether the user is a member of the PAL and is a member of the db_owner database role. It then updates the Item table and makes data changes in the MSmerge_contents table like when rows are inserted.

Conflict tables are also added in the publication database, and they have the name MSmerge_conflict_publicationname_articlename, as mentioned in Table 14-1. Each of the tables that is included as an article will have a corresponding conflict table containing the schema of the article. Two other columns are added to the conflict tables, rowguid and origin_datasource_id, both of which are of uniqueidentifier type.

The initial synchronization in merge publication with download-only articles is different than when a publication contains parameterized filters. In this case, the generation of the snapshot is similar to snapshot replication.

Note Dynamic snapshots for parameterized filters are discussed in Chapters 11 and 13. Snapshot generation, including the use of sparse files, FTP location, and UNC shares, is discussed in detail in Chapter 6.

The initial snapshot is generated with the following types of files being created for each article in the publication database:

- Schema files (.sch)

- Trigger files (.trg)

- Constraint and index files (.dri)

- Data files (.bcp)

- System files (.sys)

- Conflict table files (.cft)

The files are in the default location unless an alternate location has been specified.

Note When generating the initial snapshot using the Snapshot Agent, it is the bcp that copies the file behind the scenes, as discussed in Chapter 7. The bcp used in replication is a normal bcp, not a fast bcp, since indexes are present in the table and are also being generated.

Now let's look at the workings of parameterized filters for standard articles. You will find the same system tables being generated in the publication database as for publication with download-only articles.

Publication with Standard Articles and Parameterized Filters

The system tables generated for publication with standard articles are the same as for publication with download-only articles, so you can refer to the E-R diagram shown in Figures 14-23 through 14-29.

A publication can either have filters or no filters at all. If a publication has filters, they can either be static or dynamic. A static filter is one where all the subscribing servers receive the same subset of data. Dynamic filtering allows each of the subscribing servers to receive a different portion of the data from each of the table articles.

Dynamic filtering can be very useful if you have thousands of subscriptions requiring different partitions of data. The cost of maintaining publications for each of the subscriptions can be greatly reduced by using dynamic data partitions. You do this by using the @subset_filter parameter for the sp_addmergepublication stored procedure. For example, in Listing 13-8 (in Chapter 13) this parameter was set as follows:

```
@subset_filterclause = 'convert(char,[SalesID] )= HOST_NAME()'
```

Note Listing 13-8 in Chapter 13 shows you how to use the HOST_NAME() dynamic function in setting up merge publication for standard articles.

Initializing Subscriptions for Dynamic Partitioning of Data

Initializing a dynamic partition is actually a two-step process. In the first step, a schema snapshot generates the objects and the schema without the data. Then it initializes the subscription with the snapshot of the objects, the schema, and any relevant data for the particular subscription. If several subscriptions are supposed to receive the same partition of data, the snapshot is created only once, and all subscribers to the same partition are initialized from that snapshot. Snapshots can be generated either by allowing the Snapshot Agent to send a pregenerated snapshot, or by allowing the subscriptions to request snapshot generation using the Data Partitions properties in the SSMS, as shown in Chapter 11.

The initialization of subscriptions that subscribe to a merge publication with dynamic filtering is different compared to initialization with static or no filtering. In the discussion of initializing download articles (see the "Publication with Download-Only Articles" section earlier in this chapter) with no filtering, snapshots were created using the bcp utility. This method, as you know, copies the files created during the generation of the snapshot.

This is not the case with dynamic filtering, where a two-step process is used to do the initial synchronization, resulting in an impact on performance. To an extent, the performance of the initialization and subsequent synchronization is dependent on the values assigned to some parameters when you set up the publication for parameterized filters. The parameters of interest are @use_partition_options and @keep_partition_options for the sp_addmergepublication stored procedure.

In Listing 13-5 (in Chapter 13), I set the @use_partition_options parameter to true and the @keep_partition_options parameter to false. Both of these parameters have an effect on synchronization performance, although the @use_partition_options parameter is supposed to have a greater impact.

Note The @keep_partition_options parameter has been deprecated in SQL Server 2005.

The initialization, as mentioned earlier, is a two-step process. Once the schema and the objects are generated by the Snapshot Agent, it has no way of knowing how to send the partitioned data to the required subscriptions. That's when the sp_MSinitdynamicsubscriber stored procedure is used by the merge process to track the tables and fill them with data. Listing 14-3 shows you how to view the code for the system stored procedure that is used in the generation of the dynamic snapshot.

Listing 14-3. *Viewing the Code for the* sp_MSinitdynamicsubscriber *Stored Procedure*

```
/*Execute this on the publication database */

Use mysales_mergevwusp
go
sp_helptext 'sp_MSinitidynamicsubscriber'
go
```

The code for the stored procedure (which is the output of the script in Listing 14-3) is shown in Figure 14-31.

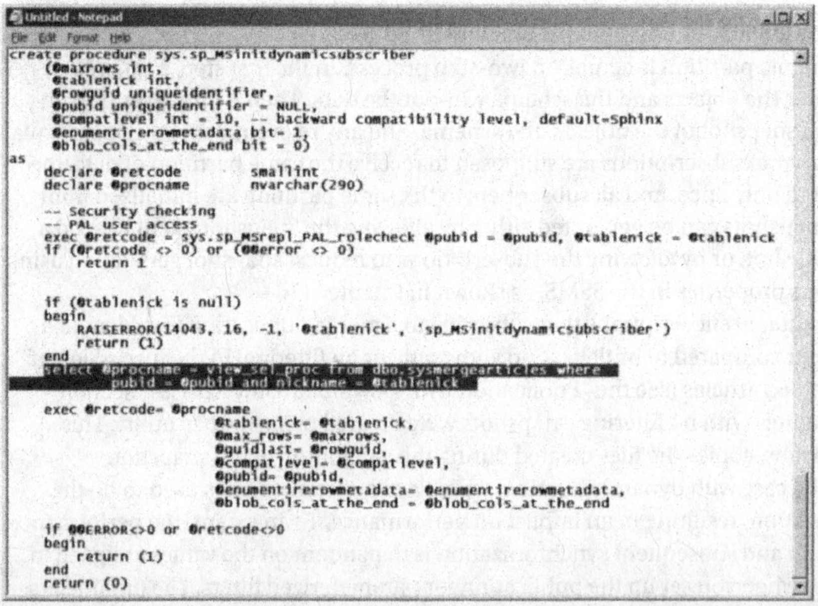

Figure 14-31. *Viewing the code for the* sp_MSinitdynamicsubscriber *stored procedure*

You can see that the stored procedure first checks whether the user has PAL access, and then it finds the `view_sel_proc` column from the `sysmergearticles` system table based on the nickname of the article. This column actually stores the name of the stored procedure used by the Merge Agent to initially populate the article for merge publication with dynamic partitioning.

To find out the names of the stored procedures used to initially populate each of the articles used with parameterized filters, and whether there are join filters associated with them, we can use the code in Listing 14-4.

Listing 14-4. *Checking the Stored Procedures in* `view_sel_proc` *for Associated Dynamic Filters*

```
/* Execute this on the publication database */

Use mysales_mergevwusp
Go

select a.filtername,
a.join_articlename,
a.join_unique_key,
a.expand_proc,
a.join_filterclause,
a.filter_type,
b.column_tracking,
b.status,
b.insert_proc,
b.update_proc,
b.select_proc,
b.metadata_select_proc,
b.resolver_info,
b.view_sel_proc
from sysmergesubsetfilters a,sysmergearticles b
where a.art_nickname=b.nickname
go
```

This script returns the name of the partition filter, the names of the articles involved in the join filter, whether there is a unique key associated with the join filter, and the types of filters being used, all from the `sysmergesubsetfilters` system table.

It also indicates whether column-level tracking is used to detect and resolve conflicts, which procedures are being used to insert, update, and select during synchronization, and the kind of conflict resolver being used. The names of the stored procedures used during the initial synchronization are also returned. All these values are retrieved from the `sysmergearticles` system table.

Both these tables have a one-to-one cardinality, and they are joined by the `nickname` column in `sysmergarticles` and the `art_nickname` column in `sysmergesubsetfilters`.

Here is the output of the code in Listing 14-4:

```
Filtername                    join_article_name    join_unique_key
expand_proc
Join_filter_clause
filter_type
column_tracking               status
Insert_proc
Update_proc
Select_proc
Metadata_select_proc
Resolver_info
View_select_proc
-----------------------------------------------------------------


AccountsReceivable_Customer   Customer                 1
MSmerge_expand_13
[Customer].[CustID] = [AccountsReceivable].[CustID]
1
0                             1
MSmerge_ins_sp_EA5CA67ECB9E43781A6BFA3A3EA14622
MSmerge_upd_sp_EA5CA67ECB9E43781A6BFA3A3EA14622
MSmerge_sel_sp_EA5CA67ECB9E43781A6BFA3A3EA14622
MSmerge_sel_sp_EA5CA67ECB9E43781A6BFA3A3EA14622_metadata
NULL
MSmerge_sel_EA5CA67ECB9E43781A6BFA3A3EA14622


Customer_CustSales            CustSales                1
MSmerge_expand_12
[CustSales].[CustID] = [Customer].[CustID]
1
0                             1
MSmerge_ins_sp_2757B341B56843FD1A6BFA3A3EA14622
MSmerge_upd_sp_2757B341B56843FD1A6BFA3A3EA14622
MSmerge_sel_sp_2757B341B56843FD1A6BFA3A3EA14622
MSmerge_sel_sp_2757B341B56843FD1A6BFA3A3EA14622_metadata
NULL
MSmerge_sel_2757B341B56843FD1A6BFA3A3EA14622


CustSales_SalesPerson         SalesPerson              1
MSmerge_expand_9
[SalesPerson].[SalesID] = [CustSales].[SalesID]
1
0                             1
MSmerge_ins_sp_2FECAB1A04FA41911A6BFA3A3EA14622
MSmerge_upd_sp_2FECAB1A04FA41911A6BFA3A3EA14622
MSmerge_sel_sp_2FECAB1A04FA41911A6BFA3A3EA14622
MSmerge_sel_sp_2FECAB1A04FA41911A6BFA3A3EA14622_metadata
NULL
```

```
MSmerge_sel_2FECAB1A04FA41911A6BFA3A3EA14622

OrderDetail_OrderHeader        OrderHeader        1
MSmerge_expand_15
[OrderHeader].[OrderID] = [OrderDetail].[OrderID]
3
0                              1
MSmerge_ins_sp_BABD7822A0EF45EB1A6BFA3A3EA14622
MSmerge_upd_sp_BABD7822A0EF45EB1A6BFA3A3EA14622
MSmerge_sel_sp_BABD7822A0EF45EB1A6BFA3A3EA14622
MSmerge_sel_sp_BABD7822A0EF45EB1A6BFA3A3EA14622_metadata
NULL
MSmerge_sel_BABD7822A0EF45EB1A6BFA3A3EA14622

OrderHeader_Customer           Customer           1
MSmerge_expand_14
[Customer].[CustID] = [OrderHeader].[CustID]
1
0                              1
MSmerge_ins_sp_2F6FED04290246C71A6BFA3A3EA14622
MSmerge_upd_sp_2F6FED04290246C71A6BFA3A3EA14622
MSmerge_sel_sp_2F6FED04290246C71A6BFA3A3EA14622
MSmerge_sel_sp_2F6FED04290246C71A6BFA3A3EA14622_metadata
Ship_date
MSmerge_sel_2F6FED04290246C71A6BFA3A3EA14622
```

In this output, you can see that all the filters are join filters (filter_type is 1) and that all the join filters are using a unique key (join_unique_key is 1). You can also see that column-level tracking is not used, because the value is 0. The expand_proc column lists the name of the stored procedure that is used by the Merge Agent to find the rows that need to be sent to the subscribing servers. The only filter that has the conflict resolver set is the OrderHeader_Customer join, which uses the Ship_date column. The procedures listed in the view_sel_proc column for each of the parameterized filters are used to query the partition view to retrieve the partition data. For the SalesPerson article, which was at the top of the hierarchy in the join filter, the name of the stored procedure is MSmerge_sel_2FECAB1A04FA41911A6BFA3A3EA14622.

Before we look at how the MSmerge_sel_2FECAB1A04FA41911A6BFA3A3EA14622 stored procedure works, let's see which objects it depends on. The code in Listing 14-5 lists these objects.

Listing 14-5. *The Objects on Which the* MSmerge_sel_2FECAB1A04FA41911A6BFA3A3EA14622 *Stored Procedure Depends*

```
/*Execute this on the publication database */
Use mysales_mergevwusp
Go
Sp_depends 'MSmerge_sel_2FECAB1A04FA41911A6BFA3A3EA14622'
go
```

The output of the code in Listing 14-5 is shown in Figure 14-32.

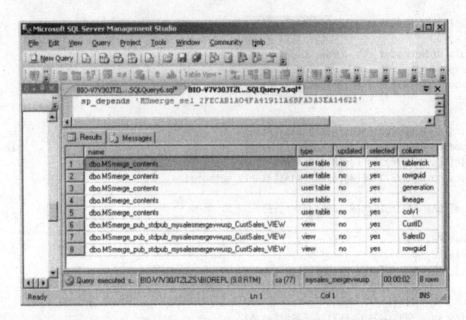

Figure 14-32. *The objects on which* MSmerge_sel_2FECAB1A04FA41911A6BFA3A3EA14622 *depends*

You can see that the stored procedure essentially depends on the MSmerge_contents table and the MSmerge_pub_stdpub_mysalesmergevwusp_CustSales_View view. In the table, the columns of interest are tablenick, rowguid, lineage, colv1, and generation; in the view, the columns are CustID, SalesID, and the rowguid columns.

Let's now look at the code for the stored procedure. The output for the partial code of the stored procedure that contains the select query generated by the SQL Server engine is as follows:

```
create procedure dbo.[MSmerge_sel_2FECAB1A04FA41911A6BFA3A3EA14622] (
    @tablenick int,
    @max_rows int = NULL,
    @guidlast uniqueidentifier = '00000000-0000-0000-0000-000000000000',
    @compatlevel int = 10,
    @pubid uniqueidentifier = NULL,
    @enumentirerowmetadata bit= 1,
    @blob_cols_at_the_end bit = 0
)
as
begin
    ---------------------

        if @blob_cols_at_the_end = 0
        begin
            select top (@max_rows)
                @tablenick,
                t.[rowguid],
```

```
                coalesce(c.generation,1),
                case
                        when 0=@enumentirerowmetadata then null
                        when @compatlevel >= 90 then coalesce(c.lineage, @lin)
                        else {fn LINEAGE_90_TO_80(coalesce(c.lineage, @lin))}
                end,
                case
                        when 0=@enumentirerowmetadata then null
                        when @compatlevel >= 90 or
@coltracked = 0 then coalesce(c.colv1, @cv)
                        else {fn COLV_90_TO_80(coalesce(c.colv1, @cv), @colv80)}
                end,
 t.*
                from [dbo].[MSmerge_pub_stdpub_mysalesmergevwusp_CustSales_VIEW] t
left outer join  dbo.MSmerge_contents c on
                        t.[rowguid] = c.rowguid  and
c.tablenick = @tablenick where t.[rowguid] > @guidlast
                        order by t.[rowguid]
        end
        else
        begin
            select top (@max_rows)
                @tablenick,
                t.[rowguid],
                coalesce(c.generation,1),
                case
                        when 0=@enumentirerowmetadata then null
                        when @compatlevel >= 90 then coalesce(c.lineage, @lin)
                        else {fn LINEAGE_90_TO_80(coalesce(c.lineage, @lin))}
                end,
                case
                        when 0=@enumentirerowmetadata then null
                        when @compatlevel >= 90 or
@coltracked = 0 then coalesce(c.colv1, @cv)
                        else {fn COLV_90_TO_80(coalesce(c.colv1, @cv), @colv80)}
                end,
 t.*
                from [dbo].[MSmerge_pub_stdpub_mysalesmergevwusp_CustSales_VIEW] t
 left outer join  dbo.MSmerge_contents c on
                        t.[rowguid] = c.rowguid  and
c.tablenick = @tablenick where t.[rowguid] > @guidlast
                        order by t.[rowguid]
        end

        return (1)
    end
```

```
        insert into #belong (tablenick, rowguid, flag, skipexpand, partchangegen)
            select ct.tablenick, ct.rowguid, 0, 0, ct.partchangegen
                from   #contents_subset ct,
[dbo].[MSmerge_pub_stdpub_mysalesmergevwusp_CustSales_VIEW] t
where ct.tablenick = @tablenick
                and ct.rowguid = t.[rowguid]
    if @@error <> 0
    begin
        raiserror('Error selecting from view' , 16, -1)
        return (1)
```

You can see that data is retrieved from the MSmerge_pub_stdpub_mysalesmergevwusp_ CustSales_VIEW view and is inserted in the #belong temporary table. If you look into the other stored procedures in the view_sel_proc column, you will find that the definitions of those stored procedures are similar.

The #belong temporary table is created by the execution of sp_MSsetupbelongs, which runs along with sp_MSinitdynamicsubscriber. The Merge Agent calls the sp_MSsetupbelongs stored procedure, to evaluate which subscription should receive the filtered rows.

This stored procedure first creates two temporary tables for each of the filtered articles: #belongs and #notbelongs. It then uses the value obtained from the dynamic function at the Subscriber server to query if any row in MSmerge_contents and MSmerge_tombstone belongs to the subscription in question. Metadata entries are made in the two temporary tables depending on whether the partitioned data belongs to the subscription. If not, there is no need to make any entries to either of the two temporary tables. However, if the data belongs to the subscription, metadata entries are made as follows:

- If the row in MSmerge_contents is an insert or an update that does not change the filtered column, an entry are made in the #belongs table.

- If the row in MSmerge_tombstone is a deletion or an update that causes the filtered column to change, an entry is made in the #notbelongs table.

If you try to find the objects that depend on the sp_MSsetupbelongs stored procedure using the sp_depends stored procedure, you will get the following output:

```
Object does not reference any object, and no objects reference it.
```

Besides the previously mentioned views that are generated, partitioning of the data causes additional views to be generated depending on the base tables involved in the partitioning. The views generated for the partitioning of the data are named as follows: MSmerge_ *publication_article*_Partition_view. The tables involved in the partition in our example are

SalesPerson, CustSales, Customer, AccountsReceivable, OrderHeader, and OrderDetail. The schema generated for the views is as follows:

```
/*1. Create a partition view for StockItem_PARTITION_VIEW */

create view  dbo.[MSmerge_pub_stdpub_mysalesmergevwusp_StockItem_PARTITION_VIEW]
as  select [StockItem].[rowguid], partition_id = -1 from
 [myinventory].[StockItem] [StockItem] where
({fn ISPALUSER('1A6BFA3A-3EA1-4622-9D55-F4088742AF4E')} =
1 or permissions
(405576483) & 0x1b <> 0)


/*2. Create a partition view for StockItem_VIEW */

create view dbo.[MSmerge_pub_stdpub_mysalesmergevwusp_StockItem_VIEW]
 as  select  * from [myinventory].[StockItem] where
({fn ISPALUSER('1A6BFA3A-3EA1-4622-9D55-F4088742AF4E')} = 1)


/*3. Create a partition view for CustSales_VIEW */

create view dbo.[MSmerge_pub_stdpub_mysalesmergevwusp_CustSales_VIEW]
 as select  [CustSales].*  from [myorder].[CustSales] [CustSales] ,
 [dbo].[MSmerge_pub_stdpub_mysalesmergevwusp_SalesPerson_VIEW]
 [SalesPerson] where  ( [SalesPerson].[SalesID] =
 [CustSales].[SalesID])   and
({fn ISPALUSER('1A6BFA3A-3EA1-4622-9D55-F4088742AF4E')} = 1)


/*4. Create a partition view for CustSales_PARTITION_VIEW */

create view dbo.[MSmerge_pub_stdpub_mysalesmergevwusp_CustSales_PARTITION_VIEW]
as select [CustSales].[CustID], [CustSales].[SalesID],
 [CustSales].[rowguid], [SalesPerson].partition_id from
 [myorder].[CustSales] [CustSales] ,
[dbo].[MSmerge_pub_stdpub_mysalesmergevwusp_SalesPerson_
PARTITION_VIEW] [SalesPerson] where
( ( [SalesPerson].[SalesID] = [CustSales].[SalesID]) ) and
({fn ISPALUSER('1A6BFA3A-3EA1-4622-9D55-F4088742AF4E')} = 1 or
 permissions(341576255) & 0x1b <> 0)


/*5. Create a partition view for Customer_VIEW */
```

```
create view dbo.[MSmerge_pub_stdpub_mysalesmergevwusp_Customer_VIEW]
 as select  [Customer].* from [myorder].[Customer] [Customer] ,
 [dbo].[MSmerge_pub_stdpub_mysalesmergevwusp_CustSales_VIEW]
[CustSales] where  ( [CustSales].[CustID] = [Customer].[CustID])  and
({fn ISPALUSER('1A6BFA3A-3EA1-4622-9D55-F4088742AF4E')} = 1)
```

/*6. Create a partition view for Customer_PARTITION_VIEW */

```
create view dbo.[MSmerge_pub_stdpub_mysalesmergevwusp_Customer_PARTITION_VIEW]
as select [Customer].[CustID], [Customer].[rowguid],
[CustSales].partition_id from [myorder].[Customer] [Customer] ,
[dbo].[MSmerge_pub_stdpub_mysalesmergevwusp_CustSales_PARTITION_VIEW]
[CustSales] where ( ( [CustSales].[CustID] = [Customer].[CustID]) )
and ({fn ISPALUSER('1A6BFA3A-3EA1-4622-9D55-F4088742AF4E')} = 1 or
permissions(245575913) & 0x1b <> 0)
```

/*7. Create a partition view for AccountsReceivable_VIEW */

```
create view dbo.[MSmerge_pub_stdpub_mysalesmergevwusp_AccountsReceivable_VIEW]
as select  [AccountsReceivable].*  from
[myfinance].[AccountsReceivable] [AccountsReceivable] ,
[dbo].[MSmerge_pub_stdpub_mysalesmergevwusp_Customer_VIEW] [Customer]
where  ( [Customer].[CustID] = [AccountsReceivable].[CustID])  and
({fn ISPALUSER('1A6BFA3A-3EA1-4622-9D55-F4088742AF4E')} = 1)
```

/*8. Create a partition view for AccountsReceivable_PARTITION_VIEW*/

```
create view dbo.[MSmerge_pub_stdpub_mysalesmergevwusp_AccountsReceivable_PARTITION
_VIEW]
as select [AccountsReceivable].[CustID],
[AccountsReceivable].[rowguid], [Customer].partition_id from
[myfinance].[AccountsReceivable] [AccountsReceivable] ,
[dbo].[MSmerge_pub_stdpub_mysalesmergevwusp_Customer_PARTITION_VIEW]
[Customer] where ( ( [Customer].[CustID] =
[AccountsReceivable].[CustID]) ) and ({fn ISPALUSER('1A6BFA3A-3EA1-
4622-9D55-F4088742AF4E')} = 1 or permissions(613577224) & 0x1b <> 0)
```

/*9. Create a partition view for OrderHeader_VIEW*/

```
create view
dbo.[MSmerge_pub_stdpub_mysalesmergevwusp_OrderHeader_VIEW]
as select  [OrderHeader].*  from [myorder].[OrderHeader] [OrderHeader]
, [dbo].[MSmerge_pub_stdpub_mysalesmergevwusp_Customer_VIEW]
[Customer] where  ( [Customer].[CustID] = [OrderHeader].[CustID])
 and ({fn ISPALUSER('1A6BFA3A-3EA1-4622-9D55-F4088742AF4E')} = 1)
```

/*10. Create a partition view for OrderHeader_PARTITION_VIEW*/

```
create view
dbo.[MSmerge_pub_stdpub_mysalesmergevwusp_OrderHeader_PARTITION_VIEW]
as select [OrderHeader].[CustID], [OrderHeader].[OrderID],
[OrderHeader].[rowguid], [Customer].partition_id from
[myorder].[OrderHeader] [OrderHeader] ,
[dbo].[MSmerge_pub_stdpub_mysalesmergevwusp_Customer_PARTITION_VIEW]
[Customer] where ( ( [Customer].[CustID] = [OrderHeader].[CustID]) )
and ({fn ISPALUSER('1A6BFA3A-3EA1-4622-9D55-F4088742AF4E')} = 1 or
permissions(277576027) & 0x1b <> 0)
```

/*11. Create a partition view for OrderDetail_VIEW*/

```
create view
dbo.[MSmerge_pub_stdpub_mysalesmergevwusp_OrderDetail_VIEW]
as select  [OrderDetail].*  from [myorder].[OrderDetail] [OrderDetail]
, [dbo].[MSmerge_pub_stdpub_mysalesmergevwusp_OrderHeader_VIEW]
[OrderHeader] where  ( [OrderHeader].[OrderID] =
[OrderDetail].[OrderID])  and ({fn ISPALUSER('1A6BFA3A-3EA1-4622-9D55-
F4088742AF4E')} = 1)
```

/*12. Create a partition view for OrderDetail_PARTITION_VIEW */

```
create view
dbo.[MSmerge_pub_stdpub_mysalesmergevwusp_OrderDetail_PARTITION_VIEW]
as select [OrderDetail].[OrderID], [OrderDetail].[rowguid],
[OrderHeader].partition_id from [myorder].[OrderDetail] [OrderDetail],
 [dbo].[MSmerge_pub_stdpub_mysalesmergevwusp_OrderHeader_PARTITION_VIEW]
[OrderHeader] where ( ( [OrderHeader].[OrderID] =
[OrderDetail].[OrderID]) ) and ({fn ISPALUSER('1A6BFA3A-3EA1-4622-
9D55-F4088742AF4E')} = 1 or permissions(197575742) & 0x1b <> 0)
```

Like publication with download-only articles, views and stored procedures are also generated. In our case, for the pub_stdpub_mysalesmergevwusp publication, which uses data partitioning, the tables used in the join filters are shown in Figure 14-33.

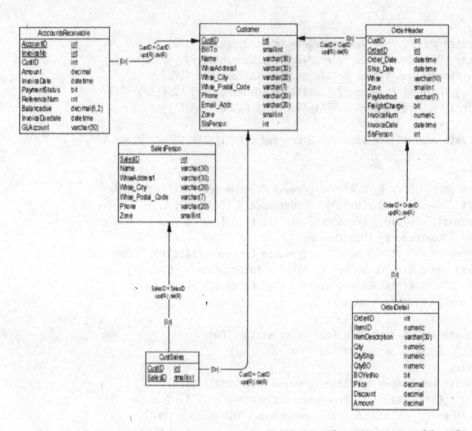

Figure 14-33. *E-R diagram for the tables used in join filters in the partitioning of data for the pub_stdpub_mysalesmergevwusp merge publication*

■**Note** Setting up merge filters using the GUI and T-SQL is described in Chapters 11 and 13.

The initialization of the publication causes the generation of the system tables, views, and triggers in the same way they were generated during the publication with download-only articles. Insert (MSmerge_ins_GUID), update (MSmerge_upd_GUID), and delete (MSmerge_del_GUID) triggers are generated to track changes in the articles. Tables like the MSmerge_contents table are used to store the records during insert and update operations so that they can be transmitted to the subscribing servers during the next synchronization. The MSmerge_tombstone table is used for storing deleted rows. The MSgeneration_history table contains a row for each generation, which is actually a collection of all the changes that are delivered from the publishing server to the subscribing server.

Note Generations are closed every time the Merge Agent runs.

Insert, update, and delete stored procedures are also generated; they are executed when you perform insert, update, and delete operations on the standard articles involved in the merge publication. These stored procedures were discussed in the context of the output for Listing 14-4.

Listing 14-6 shows code that returns the number of generations that have already been sent to the subscriptions, the number of changes for those generations, and the articles corresponding to the nickname.

Listing 14-6. *Determining the Total Number of Changes for a Generation That Is Already Closed*

```
/*Execute this on the publication database */
Use mysales_mergevwusp
Go

select a.generation,
count(*) as changecount,
b.nickname
from MSmerge_genhistory a,
MSmerge_contents c,
sysmergearticles b
where  c.generation = a.generation
and b.nickname=c.tablenick
and c.generation = a.generation
and  a.genstatus<>0
group by a.generation, b.nickname
go
```

This script finds the total number of changes that have occurred in a generation that has already been closed, and the corresponding articles indicated by the nickname of the article.

If you look at the sysmergearticles table shown in Figure 14-28, you will see that the nickname column has a int data type. The integer values correspond to the article definition of the merge publication and are assigned by the merge setup process. The value of nickname is assigned depending on the Declarative Referential Integrity constraints; if there is a foreign key constraint between a parent table and a child table, for example, nickname will have a smaller value for the parent table than for the child table. However, if there are no foreign key constraints, the value will be assigned to nickname depending on the order in which the article was added to the publication.

The Merge Agent uses the integer value of nickname to locate the article. The order in which the Merge Agent processes articles depends on how the @processing_order parameter was set when the articles were added using the sp_addmergearticle stored procedure. By default, the value of the @processing_order parameter is 0, which means that the processing order is unordered.

Note For more information on article processing order in merge replication, see the following web site: http://support.microsoft.com/default.aspx?scid=kb;[LN];307356.

If the genstatus column in the MSmerge_genhistory table has a value other than 0, it indicates that the generation is already closed. Normally, every time a change is made, the generation is 0 until the changes have been sent to the subscriptions. Once it has been sent, the value is increased.

The output of Listing 14-6 is as follows:

Generation	changecount	nickname
11	1	4026003
15	1	4026003

The script in Listing 14-7 shows which generation has been deleted after being sent to the MSmerge_tombstone table.

Listing 14-7. *Finding the Generation That Has Been Deleted*

```
/*Execute this on the publication database */

Use mysales_mergevwusp
Go
select a.generation,
count(*) as changecount,
b.nickname
from MSmerge_genhistory a,
MSmerge_tombstone t,
sysmergearticles b
where t.generation = a.generation
and b.nickname=t.tablenick
and a.genstatus<>0
group by a.generation, b.nickname
go
```

The output of the code in this listing is as follows:

Generation	changecount	nickname
13	4	4026003

The Merge Agent's Evaluation of Partitions

Data in merge publications is partitioned by setting up parameterized and join filters. How you send the subset of data, or partition, from the publishing server to the subscribing server depends on the values used in the system functions, such as the SUSER_SNAME() or HOST_NAME() functions.

This process of determining which partition of data needs to be sent to which subscribing server is called *partition evaluation*. Depending on the value of the @partition_options para-meter in the sp_addmergearticle stored procedure, a row in the published table will belong to one partition and be sent to one Subscriber server, or it will belong to one partition and be sent to more than one Subscriber server, or it will belong to more than one partition and be sent to more than one Subscriber server. In our example, @partition_options has been set to 0, which means that the row belongs to more than one partition and is being sent to more than one subscribing server.

Partition evaluation depends on whether the precomputed partition feature is enabled or not. By default, it is set to true and this is the case in our example. I will focus on the use of the precomputed partition feature for partition evaluation.

Note If the precomputed partition feature is not used, partition evaluation is done using the SetUpBelongs process, which calls the sp_MSsetupbelongs stored procedure.

In addition to the MSmerge_contents and MSmerge_tombstone system tables, there are other tables that are used for tracking data changes in filtered tables for publication with parameter-ized filters: MSmerge_partition_groups, MSmerge_current_partition_mappings, and MSmerge_past_partition_mappings.

When you create data partitions using sp_addmergepublication or use the GUI to create data partitions in the publication properties, a row is added to the MSmerge_partition_groups table for each precomputed partition. (Note that if the subscription for the Subscriber server requires a data partition and no such entry exists in MSmerge_partition_groups, a partition will be created automatically.) For every system function that is used to dynamically partition rows, a new column is added. So in the mysales_mergevwusp publication, when the SUSER_SNAME() system function was used on the SalesID column of the SalesPerson table, a column called SUSER_SNAME_FN was added to the table.

Note The use of data partitions for parameterized filters is discussed in Chapters 11 and 13.

The MSmerge_current_partition_mappings table contains a row that combines entries from the MSmerge_contents and MSmerge_partition_groups tables. So if you update a row in a table that belongs to two different partitions, a row is inserted in the MSmerge_contents table, and two rows are entered in the MSmerge_current_partition_mappings table.

The MSmerge_past_partition_mappings table contains a row for each row that no longer belongs to the partition. So if a row is deleted from a user table that is involved in data partitioning, one row is entered in the MSmerge_tombstone table and one or more rows are entered in the MSmerge_past_partition_mappings table. The value in the filtered column can also change such that the column is no longer used for partitioning; in this case, a row is entered in the MSmerge_contents table and in the MSmerge_past_partition_mappings table.

Table 14-2 describes the tables that are affected by DML operations in a publication with parameterized filters.

Table 14-2. *Tables Affected by DML Operations in a Publication with Parameterized Filters*

DML Operation	Table Description
Insert	An entry is made in the MSmerge_contents table, and a partition mapping is added on the MSmerge_current_partition_mappings table for each partition that the row belongs to.
Update	An entry is made in the MSmerge_contents table and in MSmerge_current_partition_mappings. If the row is being moved to another partition, an entry is made in the MSmerge_current_partition_mappings table, and another entry is made in MSmerge_past_partition_mappings.
Delete	An entry is made in the MSmerge_tombstone table, and one is removed from the MSmerge_current_partition_mappings table and entered in the MSmerge_past_partition_mappings table.

The initial synchronization for merge publication with parameterized filters using the Snapshot Agent is different from the process mentioned earlier. In this case, the initial files do not contain any data. The snapshot is generated according to the partition of the subscribing server. Data for parameterized filters is copied to the subscribing server in one of the following ways:

- If the location of the snapshot is provided at the command prompt during the execution of the Merge Agent, the snapshot is applied from that location.

- If the snapshot has already been generated, the location is retrieved from the MSmerge_dynamic_snapshots table, and the snapshot is applied.

- If the snapshot for the data partition has already been generated for another subscribing server, apply it to the Subscriber server or generate and apply the snapshot for the Subscriber server. In this case, it is assumed that the publication permits the subscribing server to generate snapshots.

- The Subscribing server is initialized using SELECT statements against the table.

In order to find out whether the snapshot has already been generated, determine the location of the dynamic snapshot, and identify the dynamic login name for the agent_id, you can use the code in Listing 14-8.

Listing 14-8. *Determining the Location of the Dynamic Snapshot and the Dynamic Login Name*

```
/* Execute this on the publication database used for parameterized filters */
Use mysales_mergevwusp
Go

select a.name,
a.pubid,
a.job_id,
a.agent_id,
a.dynamic_filter_login,
a.dynamic_snapshot_location,
b.partition_id,
b.last_started
from MSdynamicsnapshotjobs a
left outer join  MSmerge_dynamic_snapshots b on
a.partition_id=b.partition_id
go
```

This script selects the identification number for the publication, the job, the name of the agent, the login name, and the location of the snapshot from the MSdynamicsnapshotsjobs table. It uses a left outer join to retrieve all rows that have a job for the partition. The join is on the partition_id column with the MSmerge_dynamic_snapshots table. This is the output:

```
Name
Pubid
Job_id
Agent_id
Dynamic_filter_login
Dynamic_snapshot_location
Partition_id
Last_started

dyn_BIO-V7V30JTZLZS\BIOREPL-mysales_mergevwusp-
pub_stdpub_mysalesmergevwusp-17_sa__31
1A6BFA3A-3EA1-4622-9D55-F4088742AF4E
13713D9F-9642-4A29-B484-0992656AFEEE
sa
C:\Program Files\Microsoft SQL Server\MSSQL.1\MSSQL\ReplData\unc\BIO-
V7V30JTZLZS$BIOREPL_MYSALES_MERGEVWUSP_PUB_STDPUB_MYSALESMERGEVWUSP\sa
_9\
NULL     NULL
```

```
dyn_BIO-V7V3OJTZLZS\BIOREPL-mysales_mergevwusp-
pub_stdpub_mysalesmergevwusp-17_BIO-V7V3OJTZLZS\__27
1A6BFA3A-3EA1-4622-9D55-F4088742AF4E
C16134FC-26FB-4793-800A-A7F374CE4AF2
BIO-V7V3OJTZLZS\Sujoy Paul
C:\Program Files\Microsoft SQL Server\MSSQL.1\MSSQL\ReplData\unc\BIO-
V7V3OJTZLZS$BIOREPL_MYSALES_MERGEVWUSP_PUB_STDPUB_MYSALESMERGEVWUSP\BI
O-V7V3OJTZLZSBSu_8\
8    2006-03-26 17:06:17.770
```

Tip If you wanted the output to generate only rows in the MSmerge_dynamic_snapshots table (in Listing 14-8), you could use a right outer join instead of the left outer join.

Conflict tables are also created as they were for publication with download-only articles. The conflict tables are similarly named: MSmerge_conflict_<publicationname>_<article>.

The Merge Agent's Enumeration Process

After the publication has been initialized and the snapshot generated, the Merge Agent is run to transmit the data from the publishing server to the subscribing server. When the Merge Agent runs, it uses the triggers and the system tables to track and enumerate the changes and log the metadata in system tables, and it executes stored procedures to perform these tasks.

The following system tables are used for the enumeration of publication with download-only articles and publication with parameterized filters:

- MSmerge_genhistory: This table stores each generation in a row.

- Sysmergesubscriptions: This table stores information about subscriptions that are used for publication, including the generation. It is found in both the publication and subscription databases and stores information about the publication and the corresponding subscription.

- MSmerge_generation_partition_mappings: This table is used for publication with parameterized filters, and it stores a generation containing changes for the partition. The row in this table is a unique combination of rows in MSmerge_genhistory and MSmerge_partition_groups. This table is stored in both the publication and subscription databases.

The stored procedures that are used for enumeration are as follows:

- Sp_MSmakegeneration: This stored procedure is responsible for closing the generations at the beginning of the enumeration process. When this procedure is executed, it first closes all the open generations in MSmerge_genhistory for both the filtered and unfiltered tables. If a generation contains changes relevant to a partition, a row is inserted in the MSmerge_generation_partition_mappings table. Otherwise no row is inserted, and the Merge Agent does not enumerate the changes for the partition.

- Sp_MSenumchanges: This stored procedure enumerates the changes since the last synchronization. It determines the generation from which point the enumeration starts, based on the sentgen and recgen columns of the sysmergesubscriptions tables. If the values for sentgen and recgen are the same, changes are enumerated based on the next generation in MSmerge_genhistory. For unfiltered tables, the enumeration is done by joining the MSmerge_genhistory, MSmerge_contents, and MSmerge_tombstone tables to decide which changes must be sent. For filtered tables, MSmerge_generation_partition_mappings is joined to MSmerge_current_partition_mappings, MSmerge_contents, MSmerge_past_partition_mappings, and MSmerge_tombstone to decide which changes are relevant to the partition the subscribing server should receive.

- Sp_MSgetmetadata: This stored procedure is called to decide what kind of DML operation should be used if a change made at one node is applied to another node. It is at this point that conflict detection and resolution is performed.

Conflict Detection and Resolution

You should already have a clear understanding about how messages are sent from the Publisher server to the Subscriber server, and vice versa, in merge replication. However, this process can lead to problems, such as constraint violations or data conflicts during the transfer of data from one node to another. These conflicts can be resolved manually using the Interactive Resolver in the WSM or by letting the Conflict Resolver detect the conflicts and resolve them based on the subscription type you set. I explained in Chapters 11 and 13 how to use the Interactive Resolver and the automatic conflict detection and resolution techniques. The Interactive Resolver helps in resolving the conflicts manually, and you can use the Conflict Viewer to automatically resolve the conflicts.

CONFLICT RESOLVERS

The conflict resolvers are stored in the registry. Open the Registry Editor by selecting Run ➤ regedt32 from the Start menu, and go to HKEY_LOCAL_MACHINE/SOFTWARE/Microsoft/Microsoft SQL Server/90/Replication/ArticleResolver. There you will find the list of available conflict resolvers:

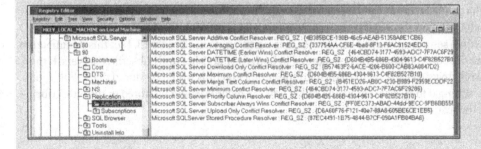

You can also use `sp_enumcustomresolvers` to find the list of custom resolvers that are registered on the distribution database. This stored procedure can be executed in the publication database. Use this code to find the list of the conflict resolvers registered:

```
/*execute this on the publication database */
Use merge_mysalesvwusp
Go
Exec sp_enumcustomresolvers
```

The output is as follows:

You can see that the `resolver_clsid` for each of the conflict resolvers matches what is specified in the registry. The `is_dotnet_assembly` column tells you whether it is a COM-based resolver (if the value is 0) or a business logic handler (if the value is 1). Note that only members of the `sysadmin` fixed server role and `db_owner` fixed database role can execute this procedure.

So how does the Merge Agent detect and resolve conflicts? The tables that are of primary interest in this process are `MSmerge_contents`, `MSmerge_genhistory`, and `MSmerge_tombstone`. In addition, conflict tables are created, with names in the following format: `MSmerge_conflict_publicationname_articlename`. These conflict tables have the same schema as the tables used as articles and an additional column called `origin_datasource_id`, which is of `uniqueidentifier` data type. The `MSmerge_conflicts_info` table is also used because it tracks conflicts when synchronizing subscriptions to the publication.

The conflict records can be created in both the publishing and the subscribing servers, depending on how the `@conflict_logging` parameter is set when `sp_addmergepublication` is used. While setting up the publication for data partitioning in Chapter 13, I set this parameter to both, so the conflict tables will be recorded in both the Publisher and Subscriber servers. If the `@conflict_logging` were set to `publisher`, the conflict records would be stored in the Publisher server; setting it to `subscriber` would mean that the records would be stored in the Subscriber server that caused the conflict.

■ **Note** Listing 13-5 in Chapter 13 shows you how to set data partitioning using T-SQL.

The foremost table that is used to detect conflicts is MSmerge_contents. When an insert or an update is performed, and the Merge Agent is fired, merge replication triggers are fired and entries are made in the MSmerge_contents table. The Merge Agent looks into the lineage column for row-level conflict metadata; for column-level conflicts the colv1 column is used.

The Merge Agent compares the metadata when it enumerates the changes in the data for each row in the publication and subscription databases. If it detects a conflict in the changed data, the conflict resolver for the article is fired by the Conflict Resolver to determine the conflict winner. The winning row is applied to the Publisher and Subscriber servers, while the losing row is sent to the conflict table.

Having resolved the conflict, the Merge Agent then enters the data in the tables according to the conflict types. If the conflict has arisen due to insert or update operations, it enters the losing rows in the MSmerge_conflict_*publicationname_articlename* tables, and the general information about the conflict is entered in the MSmerge_conflicts_info table. However, for delete conflicts, the losing rows are stored in the MSmerge_conflicts_info table—no rows are written in the MSmerge_conflict_*publicationname_articlename* table.

Note that the Merge Agent purges the rows from the conflict tables for each of the articles once the retention period is exceeded. This, by default, is 14 days. The retention period can be altered using the @conflict_retention parameter of the sp_addmergepublication stored procedure.

■ **Note** The @conflict_retention parameter is discussed in the "Configuring Publication with Download-Only Articles" section of Chapter 13.

The very nature of merge replication, with its ability to send messages in both directions between the Publisher and Subscriber servers can lead to conflicts when the same rows are sent from one node to another. Totally eliminating conflicts is not possible, but you can alleviate the problems by using the provided conflict resolvers or by designing one. To do this, though, you need to know what causes conflicts in the first place.

The behavior of conflict detection and resolution is dependent on the following:

- The kind of conflict tracking being used. This means whether you are using row-level, column-level, or logical-level tracking.

- The kinds of subscriptions used when setting up merge replication. This has got nothing to do with push or pull subscriptions but whether the subscription is client or server.

- The kind of conflict resolver that is used: the default conflict resolver, article-based resolvers like the Microsoft-supplied COM-based conflict resolver, or the business logic handler.

The first two points determine how the Merge Agent resolves a conflict on detecting it. In Chapter 11 I set the row-tracking level while setting up the publication with standard articles. However, the subscription policy was set when configuring the subscriptions, be they pull or push. If you set a priority value, you are setting a server subscription. In that case, the priority value is normally set between 0 and 99.99 (I used a value of 75.00 in Chapter 11). The highest value is 100.00, which is what the Publisher server has. The Subscriber server must have a value less than that of the Publisher server, even though the Subscriber server has the ability to republish data back to the Publisher server.

■**Note** The setting up of the subscription policy using the GUI and T-SQL is described in Chapters 11 and 13.

When you make changes in the Subscriber server, entries are made in the metadata. When the next synchronization is started, the metadata changes are carried with the changed data to the Publisher server and subsequently to other subscribing servers. This ensures that rows with the highest subscription policy do not lose out to the ones with a lower subscription policy.

If the Subscriber server does not republish the data, you obviously want to use the client subscription. The client-level subscription has the priority level of the publishing server. In a way, the Publisher server controls the whole process, because it determines the priority level. Unlike the server subscription, no rows are tracked, so when you make changes in the Subscriber server and start synchronizing, the Publisher server sets the priority level, and this is retained for subsequent synchronizations.

However, remember that the tracking of conflicts and the subscription policy work in tandem before SQL Server determines which rows gets precedence over which. In Chapter 11 we set the article to row-level tracking (see Figure 11-16). For row-level tracking, changes that are made to the same row at different nodes will be regarded as a conflict regardless of whether changes are made on the same column or not, as the conflict is detected when changes are made on the same row. So if the name and the phone number of a sales person (in the SalesPerson table) and a customer (in the Customer table) are updated at different nodes, using row-level tracking will help to detect the conflict. Since detection is done at the row level, any changes in either of the columns will be captured.

The flip side of using row-level conflict tracking is that it creates workload across the network. However, if we were to use column-level tracking, any changes to either of the two columns in the two tables would not be detected, and an error would have gone unnoticed. Although detection is done at the column level, it is worth pointing out that resolution for both column-level and row-level tracking is done at the row level.

■**Note** Wherever possible, use row-level instead of column-level tracking. Column-level tracking makes use of the colv1 table with entries of varbinary type and adds a significant overhead in the storage of the publication database. Row-level tracking can help optimize the synchronization process for merge replication.

Summary

In this chapter, I discussed the steps taken by the Merge Agent to download the messages from publications to subscriptions. I also described how the initial synchronization works for both publication with download-only articles and publication with parameterized filters.

You should know that publication with data partitioning is a two-step process, unlike the bulk copying procedure used by publication without parameterized filters. You should also know the views and partition views created by SQL Server to help the Merge Agent initially populate the tables on the subscription database.

I discussed the generation of triggers and stored procedures for change tracking in merge replication. By now you should also be familiar with the different types of conflict policies, the system tables used for conflict resolution, and the resolvers used to detect and resolve the conflicts and how they work.

I also discussed the enumeration process for merge replication, and the system tables involved: MSmerge_contents, MSmerge_genhistory, and MSmerge_tombstone. I also showed you how to use the new SQLCMD command utility, which has replaced the ISQL and OSQL utilities in previous versions of SQL Server.

- Merge replication uses the Snapshot Agent for the initial synchronization of data.

- Merge replication makes use of the Snapshot and the Merge Agents. The Distribution Agent has no part in merge replication.

- The snapshot process for nonpartitioned data involves the generation of the snapshot, schema, and the data, which are then transferred to the subscriptions using the bcp utility.

- The initial synchronization for publication with parameterized filters is a two-step process. The first step in the synchronization of publication with parameterized filters involves generating the schema and the objects. The second step involves populating data for the objects for the respective subscriptions; this step is performed by the Merge Agent by executing the sp_MSinitdynamicsubscriber and sp_MSsetupbelongs stored procedures.

- The execution of the Merge Agent involves three steps: Merge agent startup message, Run agent, and Detect nonlogged agent shutdown.

- You cannot change from row-level tracking to column-level tracking if you use the same article in another publication.

- Row-level tracking uses less storage overhead compared to column-level tracking, since column-level tracking uses the colv1 column to track the conflicts.

- The detection of column-level tracking is carried out at the column level, but the resolution for both row-level and column-level tracking is done at the row level.

- Row-level tracking has the ability to detect more conflicts.

- Merge replication executes stored procedures for insert, update, and delete statements.

- You can view the list of subagents in your system by using the sp_enum_sqlagent_subsystems stored procedure on the msdb database.

- Use the sp_enumcustomresolvers stored procedure to get a list of conflict resolvers provided by SQL Server.

- The @use_partition_options parameter is used by default for optimizing the performance of publication with parameterized filters.

- The precomputed partitions feature will not be set to true until the Snapshot Agent is run the first time. It will show as "Set automatically when snapshot is created" in the Subscription options for the publication properties.

- You can either resolve conflicts manually using the Interactive Resolver of the WSM or automatically by using the Conflict Viewer.

Now that you have a good understanding of snapshot, transactional, and merge replication, and the scenarios where you would use them, the next chapter will discuss how to back up and recover replicated databases.

Quick Tips

- The Merge Agent for push subscriptions is named *Publisher-publicationdatabase-publicationname-Subscriber-integer*. For pull subscriptions, it is *Publisher-publicationdatabase-publicationname-Subscriber-subscriptiondatabase-integer*.

- You can use any text editor for writing SQL queries by using the SQLCMD utility.

- You can import or export the settings of one server instance to another by using the sac utility. The name of the executable is sqlsac.exe.

- To find the list of dependencies for triggers or any other objects, use the sp_depends stored procedure.

- Generations are closed every time the Merge Agent runs.

Backup and Recovery of Snapshot and Transactional Replication

So far, I have primarily focused on the different types of replication that you can use with SQL Server. I will now show you how to administer replicated databases by first backing up and then restoring them. Before proceeding with this chapter, you should have a fundamental understanding of the Simple, Full, and Bulk Logged recovery models that SQL Server supports and how the transaction log works during the backup and restoration of the databases.

On completing this chapter, you will know how to do the following:

- Back up databases for snapshot replication

- Back up databases for transactional replication

- Use the tablediff utility to check for table differences

- Validate transactional replication

- Restore databases for snapshot replication

- Restore databases for transactional replication

- Use log shipping with the publication database for transactional replication

Snapshot Replication

Snapshot replication involves transferring the whole replica intermittently to the subscribing servers. Since low latency is an integral feature of snapshot replication, it is possible to resynchronize the subscriptions if the subscription and the publication databases are not in sync. However, the network bandwidth and overhead cost associated with transferring snapshots may preclude you from doing so, particularly at peak time on production databases. Having a backup of the required database can offset the costs associated with the downtime of production databases.

You need a backup strategy that meets the requirements for your situation. Suppose the mysales database used for snapshot replication is being replicated intermittently, since the discounts on items occur on a semiannual basis. If any schema changes, such as the addition of a column, occur on the publication database, they need to be reflected on the subscription databases. In that situation, we could back up the publication database whenever there is a schema change. How often and where you should back up the publication database depends on the frequency with which you perform insert, update, or delete operations or make schema changes.

It is worth pointing out at this stage that backups of replicated databases must be restored on the same server. Otherwise you will lose the replication settings and will have to re-create publications and subscriptions once the backup has been restored.

■**Note** Database snapshots and snapshot replication are not related to each other. A database snapshot is essentially a read-only, static view of the source database.

You should consider backing up the following databases for snapshot replication:

- Publication database on the Publisher server

- Distribution database on the Distributor server (or on the Publisher server if the distribution and the publication databases are on the same server)

- Subscription database on the Subscriber server

- Master and msdb databases on the Publisher, Distributor, and Subscriber servers

---

■**Note** The msdb database contains information about the agents, while the master database contains information concerning publications, subscriptions, and articles. The E-R diagrams of the databases involved in snapshot replication are shown in Chapter 7 and those for transactional replication are shown in Chapter 10.

If you are backing up the publication database, you should also consider backing up the distribution database at the same time. You should also ensure that no new publications or subscriptions are added while the backup is in progress.

You should back up the publication database any time you perform the following actions:

- Make schema changes on any of the publication tables

- Add a publication or a subscription

- Add new articles to an existing publication

- Drop a publication or an article

- Perform a publication-wide reinitialization of the subscriptions

Backing Up the Publication Database

To view the properties of the database, right-click on the database under the Object Explorer in the SSMS and select Properties from the menu. Select the Options page. You can see that the database that has been created for snapshot publication in the SSMS (the BIO-V7V30JTZLZS\ BIOREPL_PEER instance in this example), has a recovery model of Full. This is shown in Figure 15-1.

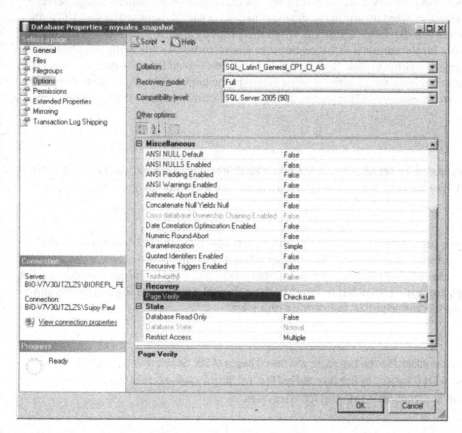

Figure 15-1. *Viewing the database properties for the publication database used in snapshot replication*

If you are familiar with the backup and recovery of SQL Server, you will know that the engine uses the database and all the logged information to restore the databases in the Full Recovery model. Since every operation is logged, including bulk and index creation, it is possible to recover the database to any point in time.

There are two other recovery models: Simple Recovery and Bulk Logged Recovery. The Simple Recovery model makes use of the full or differential restoration copies of the database. You can only recover to the point when the last backup was made, and any entries made after the last backup will be lost. The Bulk Logged Recovery model, like the Full Recovery model, uses both the database and the logs to restore the database. However, unlike the Full model it only logs the operation of bulk load and create index. It does not make entries for the whole transaction. The log is smaller and the performance is faster, but you cannot recover to a point in time.

Notice that in Figure 15-1, which shows the Options page of the Database Properties window, the Page Verify property for the Recovery option has been set to Checksum. You have two other options for this property: None or Torn_page_detection.

The Checksum property is an interesting feature that has been introduced in SQL Server 2005. It determines whether any of the database pages have been damaged by disk I/O path errors as a result of database corruption. When this property is set to Checksum, it calculates the checksum for the contents of the whole page, and records the value in the page header when the page is written to disk. Next time, when the page is read from the disk, the checksum is recomputed and compared with the value stored in the page header. If the value does not match, an error message of 824 is sent to the SQL Server error log and to the Windows event viewer.

Note Checksum is the default setting in SQL Server 2005; Torn_page_detection was the default in SQL Server 2000. They are mutually exclusive—you can only use one of them for any given database.

The Torn_page_detection setting reserves a particular bit of the 512-byte sector of the 8 KB page and stores the bit in the page header when it is written to disk. Later, when the page is read from the disk, a comparison is made between the bit stored in the page header and the actual page, and any mismatch is reported both on the SQL Server error log and the Windows event log as error message 824, indicating a torn page.

Note For more information on torn pages and the I/O basics of SQL Server, refer to the excellent article, "SQL Server 2000 I/O Basics," by Bob Dorr. You will find it at http://www.microsoft.com/technet/ prodtechnol/sql/2000/maintain/sqlIObasics.mspx.

If Page Verify is set to NONE, no value will be generated on the header page when database pages are written to disk. In fact, SQL Server will ignore the value if it is present in the page header.

Click the OK button in the Database Properties window, and you will be returned to the SSMS. Right-click on the database that has been used for snapshot publication, select Tasks, and then select Back Up from the menu. Select the General page of the Back Up Database window, as shown in Figure 15-2.

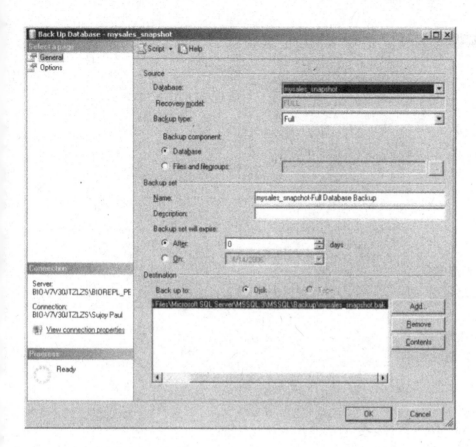

Figure 15-2. *Viewing the general backup settings for the mysales_snapshot database, which is used for snapshot publication*

In this figure, you can see the backup model used, which is Full (as was set in Figure 15-1), and the name of the backup file that is being written to the disk. In the "Backup set" section, give a name to the backup database. In the Destination section, you will see that the backup is saved to the disk. The location of the backup file is also shown. If you need to change the location of the file, click the Remove button and then click the Add button and specify a new location for the file.

Now select the Options page in the pane on the left side, and you will see the window shown in Figure 15-3. I chose the default for the "Back up to the existing media set" option by selecting "Append to the existing backup set." This procedure preserves existing backup sets and appends the new information to the backup set. Normally, I would select "Overwrite all existing backup sets" to overwrite all existing backup sets with the recent backup, but this is the first backup so there are no existing backups. I also checked "Verify backup when finished" to ensure that the backup set is complete and readable. The Checksum property (set with the "Perform checksum before writing to media" option) is also checked when backing up the database. This will cause a significant increase in the workload, while decreasing the throughput of the backup operation.

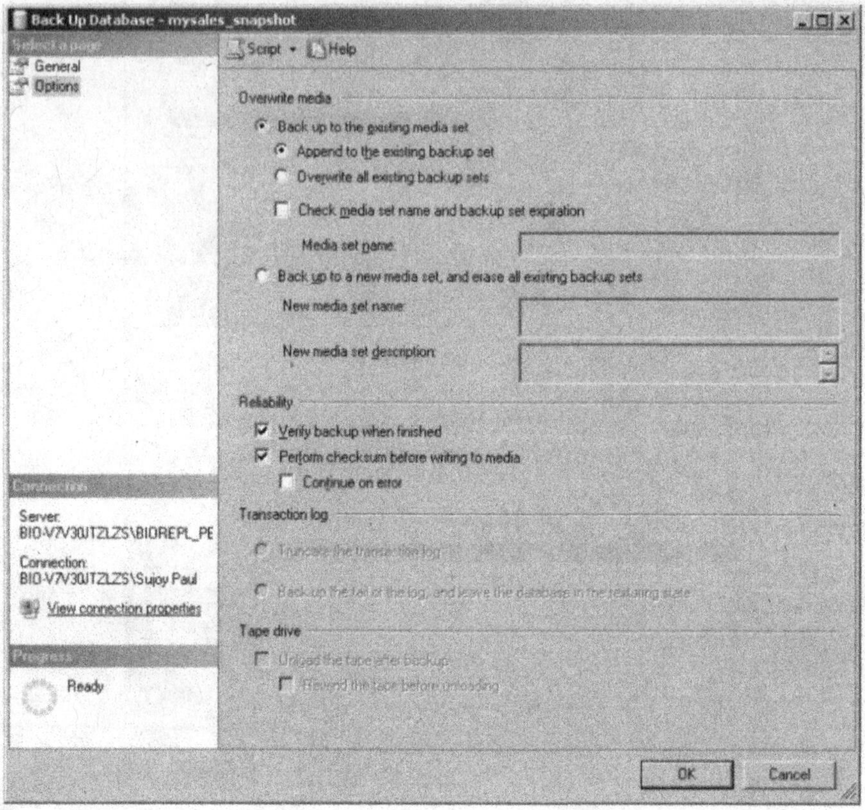

Figure 15-3. *Viewing the backup options for the mysales_snapshot database*

To see how SQL Server writes the backup script behind the scenes, click on the Script toolbar button at the top of the Back Up Database window (Figure 15-3). This will display the following output. By clicking on the down arrow in the Script button you can select Script Action to New Query Window, which displays the output in the Query Editor of the SSMS.

```
BACKUP DATABASE [mysales_snapshot]
TO  DISK =
N'C:\Program Files\Microsoft SQL
 Server\MSSQL.3\MSSQL\Backup\mysales_snapshot.bak'
WITH NOFORMAT,
INIT,
 NAME = N'mysales_snapshot-Full Database Backup',
SKIP,
 NOREWIND,
 NOUNLOAD,
 STATS = 10,
CHECKSUM
```

```
GO
declare @backupSetId as int
select @backupSetId = position from msdb..backupset where
 database_name=N'mysales_snapshot' and backup_set_id
=(select max(backup_set_id) from msdb..backupset where
 database_name=N'mysales_snapshot' )
if @backupSetId is null
begin
raiserror(N'Verify failed. Backup information for database
''mysales_snapshot'' not found.', 16, 1)
end
RESTORE VERIFYONLY
FROM  DISK =
N'C:\Program Files\Microsoft SQL
 Server\MSSQL.3\MSSQL\Backup\mysales_snapshot.bak'
WITH  FILE = @backupSetId,
 NOUNLOAD,
 NOREWIND
Go
```

You can see that SQL Server overwrites any existing data in the backup data file by using the INIT option.

You can also see that the Checksum parameter has been set for the backup of the database. When you specify this option, the backup T-SQL statement verifies the consistency of the data in the database with any checksum or any torn page indication in the database. If a page checksum exists, it will back up the page and verify the checksum status and the ID of the page. The pages are not modified by the database. They are simply backed up the way they are found in the database.

If the checksum verification is not consistent, the backup fails. This is because the STOP_ON_ERROR parameter for the backup statement instructs it to do so. This is the default behavior.

Note The RESTORE VERIFYONLY statement does not restore the database. It only verifies that the backup set is complete and readable, checks the status of the checksum, ensures that the header field of the database page contains the page ID, and checks that there is enough space where the backup copy is made.

We can modify the preceding script to make it more generic, so that we can use it to back up other databases, like the subscription database, using the SQLCMD utility. Listing 15-1 shows you how.

Listing 15-1. *Generic Backup Script for Use with Other Databases Involved in Snapshot Replication*

```
/* Execute this using the SQLCMD utility */

/* Declare the SQLCMD variables */

:setvar logintimeout 120
:setvar server "BIO-V7V30JTZLZS\BIOREPL"
:setvar user "sa"
:setvar pwd "sujoy"
:connect $(server) -l $(logintimeout) -U $(user) -P $(pwd)

/*Back up the database */

BACKUP DATABASE $(db) TO
DISK = '$(path)\$(db).bak'
WITH NOFORMAT, INIT,
NAME = '$(db)Database Backup',
SKIP,
NOREWIND,
NOUNLOAD,
STATS = 10,
CHECKSUM
Go

declare @backupSetId as int
select @backupSetId = position from msdb..backupset
where
database_name='$(db)' and backup_set_id=
(select max(backup_set_id) from msdb..backupset where database_name='$(db)' )

/* If backup does not exist, raise the error */

if @backupSetId is null
begin
raiserror('Verify failed. Backup information for database ''$(db)''
 not found.', 16, 1)
end

RESTORE VERIFYONLY
FROM  DISK = '$(path)\$(db).bak'
WITH  FILE = @backupSetId,
NOUNLOAD,
NOREWIND
go
```

Save the preceding code as an SQL script. Then open the command prompt from the Start menu, and execute the following:

```
SQLCMD -iC:\Backupdatabase.sql -vdb="mysales_copy" path="C:\files"
```

In this command, I specified the path for the backup copy of the database and the name of the database that I want to back up.

You can also back up using the Back Up Database window (Figure 15-3). Click the OK button, and you will see that the backup succeeded, as shown in Figure 15-4.

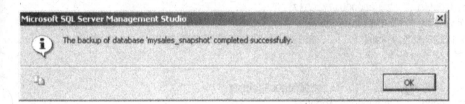

Figure 15-4. *Successful backup of the database*

The entry for the checksum is made in the backupset system table of the msdb database. If there is damage, it will be marked in the is_damaged column of the table. Listing 15-2 shows which databases in the server instance have the checksum option enabled, and whether there are any damages.

Listing 15-2. *Checking to Find Out Which Databases Have the Checksum Option Enabled*

```
/*Execute this on the msdb database */

Use msdb
Go

select backup_size,
database_name,
first_lsn,last_lsn,
checkpoint_lsn,
name,
user_name,
server_name,
is_damaged,
has_backup_checksums
from backupset
order by has_backup_checksums desc
go
```

In this script, the has_backup_checksums column tells us which database has the checksum enabled. A value of 1 means that it is enabled, while a value of 0 means it is disabled. If there is a torn page or the checksum status is not consistent, that information would be recorded in the is_damaged column. The first and the last LSN are also recorded. The output of the script in Listing 15-2 follows:

```
backup_size        database_name    first_lsn
last_lsn              checkpoint_lsn
name
user_name                          server_name
is_damaged     has_backup_checksums
-------------------------------------------------------------


1853952            mysales_snapshot    25000000017700037
25000000019500001    25000000017700037
mysales_snapshot-Full Database Backup
BIO-V7V30JTZLZS\Sujoy Paul        BIO-V7V30JTZLZS\BIOREPL_PEER
0                  1


2566656            mysales            25000000005500001
26000000032800001    26000000031000037
mysales-Full Database Backup
sa                                 SHW-TOR-WS039
0                  0


2553344            mysales            133000000085000140
133000000090700001    133000000085000140        •
mysales-Full Database Backup
BIO-V7V30JTZLZS\Sujoy Paul        BIO-V7V30JTZLZS\BIOREPL_PEER
0                  0
```

You can see that only mysales_snapshot is enabled for checksum, and that there is no damage.

Due to the overhead cost associated with using the checksum, not only will the performance of the backup operation be affected, but it will also have an impact on the system's CPU. To determine this effect on CPU usage, we can first find out if there are any tasks waiting to be completed. To do this, you can use the sys.dm_os_schedulers dynamic management view, which gives a glimpse of the internal workings of the server. The script in Listing 15-3 will indicate whether there are any tasks waiting to be completed.

Listing 15-3. *Finding Tasks Waiting to Be Run for the* CPU_id *Associated with the Scheduler*

```
/* Execute this on the database that is being used for backup
with checksum enabled */

Use mysales_snapshot
go

select
scheduler_id,
current_tasks_count,
runnable_tasks_count,
```

```
is_online,
cpu_id,
current_workers_count,
active_workers_count,
work_queue_count,
pending_disk_io_count
from
sys.dm_os_schedulers
order by scheduler_id
go
```

This script finds the ID of the scheduler with which the CPU (cpu_id) is associated. It also finds out whether there are any tasks waiting to be run on the scheduler (runnable_tasks_ count). The is_online column indicates whether there are any schedulers that are not in the affinity mask—a value of 0 would indicate that it is not in the affinity mask. The script also returns the number of workers associated with the scheduler (current_workers_count) and the number of workers associated with the task (active_workers_count).

The output of the script is shown in Figure 15-5. We can see that there are currently no tasks waiting to run for any of the schedulers and that all of them are associated with the CPU_id of 255. Note that there is only 1 regular query that is being run (scheduler_id less than 255) and that there are 13 worker threads associated with the current task (the value for current_workers_count is 31). If the current_workers_count is greater than the active_ workers_count, the work_queue_count should be 0 and this is indeed the case here.

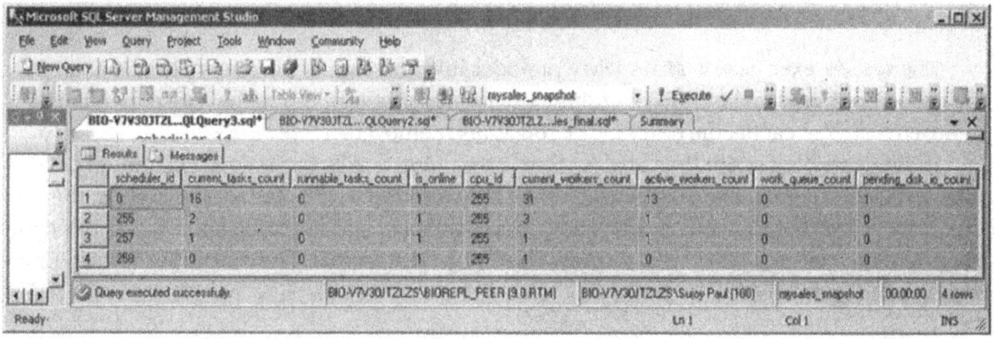

Figure 15-5. *The output for the script in Listing 15-3*

Next, we want to know which batch of SQL statements or procedures are consuming the most CPU time. To determine this, we need to use the dm.sys_exec_query_stats DMV (I mentioned the 12 different DMVs in Chapter 12). However, the sql_handle and plan_handle columns, which tell us which SQL statements belong to the same procedure or batch, are of type varbinary. In order to read the SQL statements in text format, we need to use the sys.dm_exec_sql_txt view. This is shown in Listing 15-4.

Listing 15-4. *Determining the Average CPU Time for the Batch of SQL Statements*

```
/* Execute this on the publication database*/
Use mysales_snapshot
go

select  top 20
(total_worker_time/execution_count) AS AvgCPUTime,
total_worker_time,
execution_count,
statement_start_offset,
statement_end_offset,
(select text from sys.dm_exec_sql_text(sql_handle)) AS querytext
from
sys.dm_exec_query_stats
order by AvgCPUTime desc
go
```

■**Note** You can include the `plan_handle` and `sql_handle` columns in the preceding listing. However, the data type for both columns is `varbinary`. In order to see them in text format, you need to use `sys.dm_exec_sql_text`.

The `sys.dm_exec_query_stats` DMV provides information on the query plans that are in the cache. Each row in the DMV contains a query plan that is in the cache. Once the plan is removed from the cache, the entry in the row is also removed.

In the preceding script the `total_worker_time` column tells us the total amount of CPU time, in microseconds, that was taken by the CPU since the query plan was compiled; the `execution_count` column tells us how many times the plan was executed since it was last compiled. The `dm_exec_sql_text` view displays the SQL in text format. The output for Listing 15-4 is shown in Figure 15-6.

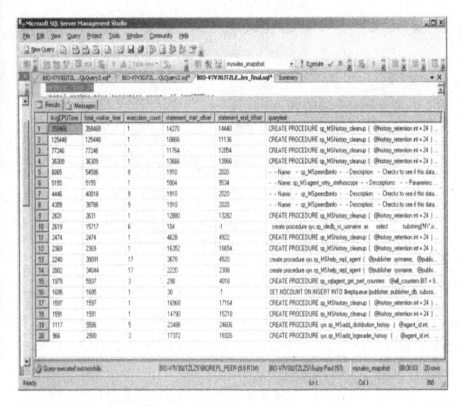

Figure 15-6. *The output for the script in Listing 15-4*

Restoring the Publication Database

After backing up the database, the next requirement in a backup strategy is to ensure that the database can be restored properly from the backup. You should try this in a test environment to see that it works correctly.

Right-click on the publication database used for snapshot replication, and select Tasks ➤ Restore ➤ Database. This will open the Restore Database window shown in Figure 15-7.

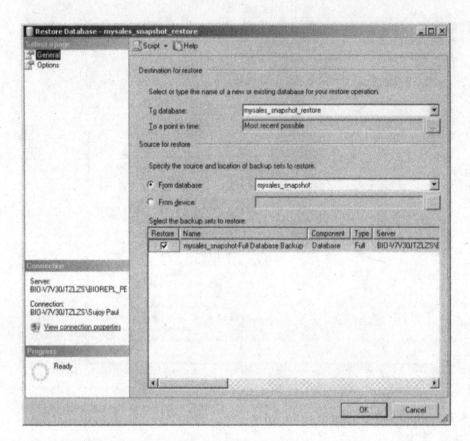

Figure 15-7. *Viewing the general restoration properties for the mysales_snapshot database*

If you scroll to the right in the lower-right pane of that window, you will be able to see the First LSN, Last LSN, and CheckPoint LSN columns, as shown in Figure 15-8. Notice that the values for these columns are the same as in the output of Listing 15-2. You can also see that I have set the mysales_snapshot database as the source for the restore.

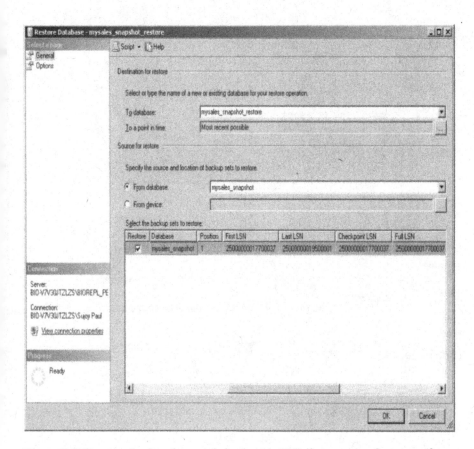

Figure 15-8. *Viewing the first, last, and checkpoint LSNs for restoring from mysales_snapshot*

Now select the Options page of the Restore Database window, as shown in Figure 15-9. Since this is the first time I am restoring the database, I do not need to overwrite any existing database. However, I want to preserve the replication settings and be prompted before the restoration, so I checked these boxes. The latter option is particularly useful if you have a tape drive and need to restore from a taped backup. Preserving the replication settings is equivalent to using the KEEP_REPLICATION option in the RESTORE DATABASE statement. The files will be restored as specified.

Note When you use the KEEP_REPLICATION option in the RESTORE DATABASE statement, you also need to select RESTORE WITH RECOVERY so that any uncommitted transactions are rolled back.

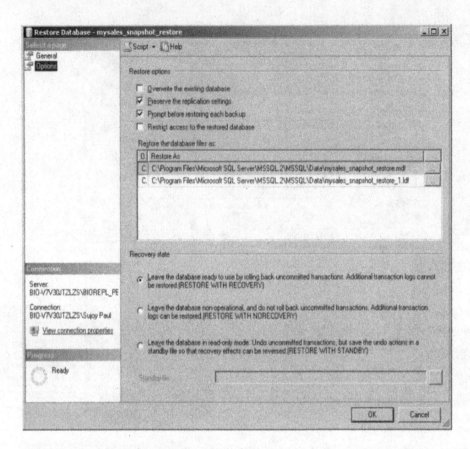

Figure 15-9. *Viewing the restoration options for the mysales_snapshot database*

Click the script button to see how SQL Server works behind the scene. The script is as follows:

```
RESTORE DATABASE [mysales_snapshot_restore]
FROM  DISK = 'C:\Program Files\Microsoft SQL
Server\MSSQL.3\MSSQL\Backup\mysales_snapshot.bak'
WITH  FILE = 1,
MOVE 'mysales_snapshot' TO
'C:\Program Files\Microsoft SQL
 Server\MSSQL.2\MSSQL\Data\mysales_snapshot_restore.mdf',
MOVE 'mysales_snapshot_log' TO
N'C:\Program Files\Microsoft SQL
 Server\MSSQL.2\MSSQL\Data\mysales_snapshot_restore_1.ldf',
KEEP_REPLICATION,
 NOUNLOAD,
 STATS = 10
GO
```

Note This restoration was carried out on the same server instance as the backup of the database.

I have modified the preceding restoration script to make it more generic as I did with the backup script. It is shown in Listing 15-5.

Listing 15-5. *Generic Restoration Script for Use with Other Databases Involved in Snapshot Replication*

```
/* Execute this using the SQLCMD utility */

/* Declare the SQLCMD variables */
:setvar logintimeout 120
:setvar server "BIO-V7V30JTZLZS\BIOREPL"
:setvar user "sa"
:setvar pwd "sujoy"
:connect $(server) -l $(logintimeout) -U $(user) -P $(pwd)

/*Restore the database */

RESTORE DATABASE $(db1) FROM
DISK = '$(path)\$(db).bak'
WITH  FILE = 1,
MOVE '$(db)' TO
'$(path1)\$(db1).mdf',
MOVE '$(log)' TO '$(path1)\$(log1).ldf',
KEEP_REPLICATION,
NOUNLOAD,
STATS = 10
GO
```

You can use the SQLCMD utility to execute the restoration script in Listing 15-5. Note that in the backup statement, I specified CHECKSUM verification, so the restore operation will verify the checksum by default. If the restore operation does not find the checksum in the backup script, the restore operation will fail. By default the restore operation will stop and fail if it encounters an error. You need to execute the following from the command prompt for Listing 15-5 to work:

```
SQLCMD -iC:\files\restoremysales.sql
-vdb1="mysales_snapshot_restore"
path="'C:\Program Files\Microsoft SQLServer\MSSQL.3\MSSQL\Backup"
db="mysales_snapshot"
path1="C:\Program Files\Microsoft SQLServer\MSSQL.2\MSSQL\Data"
log="mysales_snapshot_log"
log1="mysales_snapshot_restore_1"
```

Click the OK button in the Restore Database window (Figure 15-9), and if the restoration is successful, you will see the dialog box shown in Figure 15-10.

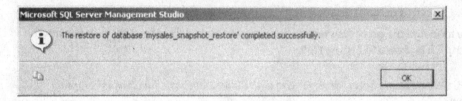

Figure 15-10. *The successful restoration of the publication database*

■**Tip** The `restorehistory` system table in the msdb database keeps a record of the restoration of databases.

We have looked at how to back up and restore the publication database; let's look at how to do the same for the other databases involved in snapshot replication.

Considerations for Other Databases

The distribution database contains information about the profiles of both the Snapshot and Distribution Agents. It also stores the historical data of the snapshot and maintains the identity range management through the use of the `MSrepl_identity_range` table. You should therefore backup the distribution database when you make the following changes:

- Create or modify the agent profiles

- Change the parameters for the agent profiles

- Change the scheduling of the agents, specifically for push subscriptions

- Add a new range of identities with automatic range identity management

Once the snapshot has been synchronized with the subscription database, you should back up the subscription database. You should also consider backing it up if you drop any subscriptions attached to the subscription database. You should also regularly back up those subscription databases that have pull subscriptions enabled.

Having backed up the publication, distribution, and subscription databases, you should then back up the msdb and master databases.

The msdb database contains all the information about the jobs, their history, and the profiles, and we all know by now that the replication agents are nothing but jobs under the hood. So you should consider backing up the msdb database at the appropriate server end when you make any of the following changes:

- Modify replication agent profiles

- Change the scheduling of the agents for push subscriptions

- Drop a subscription or publication

- Disable replication in general, or disable any of the publications

You should back up the master database when you back up the msdb database. You should also back up the master database when you do any of the following:

- Add or drop a publication

- Add or drop a subscription

- Add or drop a distribution database

- Disable replication in general, or disable a publication or a subscription database

You now know how to back up and restore the databases for snapshot replication. In the next section, I will discuss backup and recovery strategies for the different types of transactional replication.

Transactional Replication

I discussed the different types of transactional replication in Chapters 8 and 9: standard publication, publication with updatable subscriptions, the newly introduced peer-to-peer transactional replication, and bidirectional transactional replication.

▪Note Chapter 8 discusses how to configure transactional replication using the GUI, while Chapter 9 describes the T-SQL method.

In this section, I will first discuss the backup and recovery strategy for standard publication, followed by the strategy for publication with updatable subscriptions. Finally, I will show you how to implement the backup methodology for the peer-to-peer topology. The same databases should be backed up for transactional replication as for snapshot replication.

Validating Subscriptions

In order to eliminate any nonconvergence of data between the publishing and subscription databases, you should validate the data to ensure the databases are in sync. You should also consider validating the replicated data before you back up the publication database. I will show you how to validate replicated data for the standard publication; the method is the same for the other types of transactional replication.

Right-click on the publication in the SSMS and select Validate Subscriptions from the menu. The Validate Subscriptions window will open as shown in Figure 15-11. For this example, I chose to validate pub_mysales_copy_myinventory, which is a standard publication for transactional replication. Currently this publication has two subscriptions.

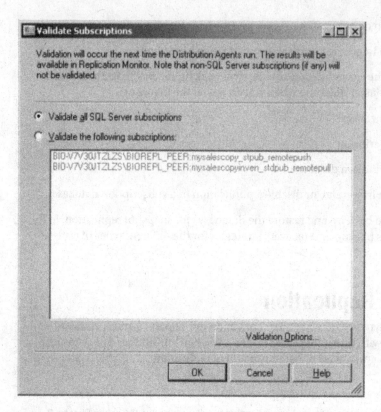

Figure 15-11. *Validating all the subscriptions for standard publication for transactional replication*

■**Caution** Although validation does not interrupt the replication process, you should ensure that no updating activity is carried out in the publication database or, in case of publication with updatable subscriptions, that no updates are made on the subscription databases.

To validate all the subscriptions for the publication, select the "Validate all SQL Server subscriptions" option. To validate only one subscription, select the "Validate the following subscriptions" option and select the required subscription. Then click the Validation Options button. This will open the Subscription Validation Options dialog box shown in Figure 15-12.

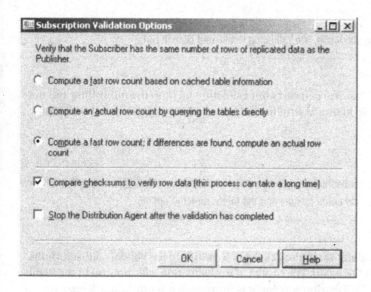

Figure 15-12. *Setting the validation options for the subscriptions*

For transactional replication, validation is done by the Distribution Agent; the Merge Agent performs the validation for merge replication. There are three types of validation that can be performed:

- **Rowcount validation:** The agent checks that the rowcount on the publishing database matches that on the subscription database. It does not validate that the content of the rows match with each other.

- **Rowcount and binary checksum:** The agent compares the rowcount on both the publishing and the subscribing databases, and then uses the checksum algorithm to validate the data. If the rowcount does not match, then it does not use the checksum algorithm.

- **Rowcount and checksum:** This validation type has been deprecated.

SQL Server, when using either the rowcount or the checksum validation type, compares each value for the columns on the publication table with that on the subscription table, except for columns that contain text, ntext, or image data types. While performing these calculations, the engine temporarily places a shared lock on the rows for those tables whose validation is being conducted. Once the validation is complete, it releases the lock.

However, when binary checksums are used, a 32-bit redundancy check (CRC) is implemented on a column-by-column basis and not on the physical row on the data page. This allows the computation to be done on any row, since it does not matter whether the columns of the table are in any physical order in the data page. Binary checksums consume a lot of processor resources, so validating large amounts of data should be done in off-peak hours.

Also, replication validates only the tables and does not validate objects such as stored procedures. While binary checksums can be used to validate any published table, checksums on their own cannot validate published tables containing column filters or logical table structures where there is a difference in column offsets.

Note For more information on validation, see Validating Replicated Data in BOL.

It is worth pointing out that you can carry out validation on both the publishing and the subscribing tables if they have identical structures. The column data types and the lengths should also be the same.

Tip If you are validating Oracle subscriptions, you can only use the rowcount validation type. You will have to select the "Compute an actual row count by querying the tables directly" option.

Once you have set the validation option, click OK to return to the Validate Subscriptions window (Figure 15-11). Click OK again. The results of the validation will show up in the Replication Monitor. Ensure that the Distribution Agent is running; if it is not, you will need to manually start it for the validation to take effect.

Once the validation is complete, you need to view the results to check whether it is working properly. Right-click on the publication in the SSMS and select Launch Replication Monitor. This will open up the Replication Monitor, as shown in Figure 15-13.

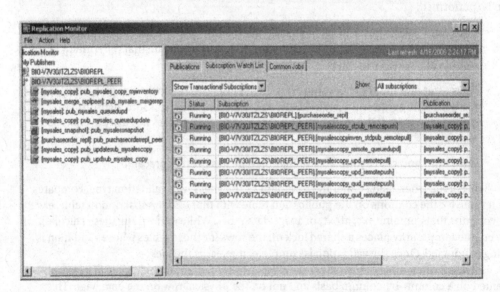

Figure 15-13. *Monitoring the subscriptions for the standard publication*

You can see the server instance and publications in the left pane. To view the validation results, select the Subscription Watch List tab, right-click on the subscription, and select View Details. This will open the window shown in Figure 15-14. Select the Distributor To Subscriber History tab to view the actions. You can see that the tables have been validated using the row-count and binary checksum validation.

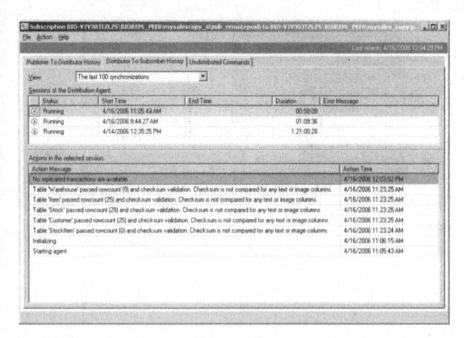

Figure 15-14. *Checking the subscription validation for standard publication*

■**Tip** If you execute SELECT * FROM MSDISTRIBUTION_HISTORY in the distribution database, you will also be able to see the status of the validation in the comments column.

Logging Validation Errors

Although the validation was successful, we did not have any contingency plan to capture errors should the validation fail. One way of resolving this problem is to create a replication alert that will log the failure of the validation and, if need be, reinitialize the subscriptions.

In the SSMS open SQL Server Agent, and then open Alerts. Right-click on "Replication: Subscriber has failed data validation" and enable it by selecting Enable from the menu. Similarly, select Properties from the menu. This will open the window shown in Figure 15-15.

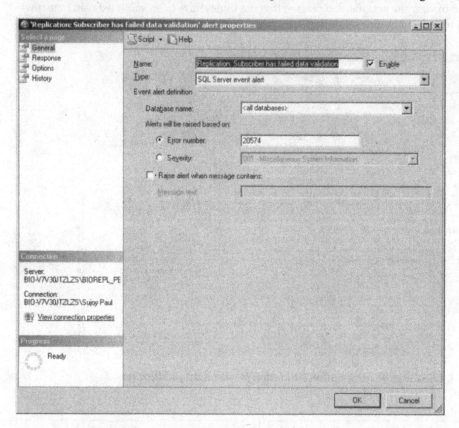

Figure 15-15. *Viewing the subscriber data-validation failure alert properties*

This alert has been set for all the databases in this server instance. In the event of a validation failure, it will register a 20574 error message that will be logged in the Application log of the Windows Event Viewer.

Select the Response page in the left pane, as shown in Figure 15-16.

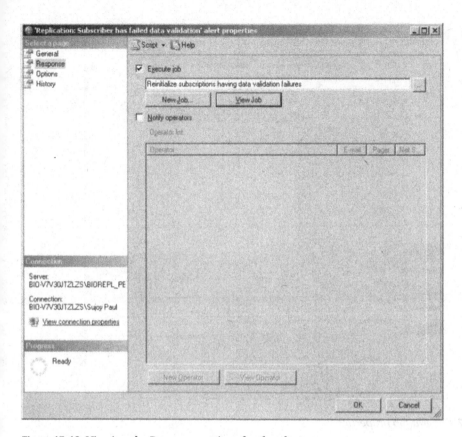

Figure 15-16. *Viewing the Response settings for the alert*

Now click on the View Job button to see the properties for the job, as shown in Figure 15-17.

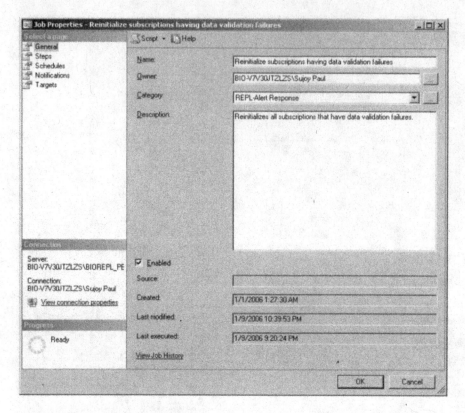

Figure 15-17. *General job properties*

In the Category field, select REPL-Alert Response from the drop-down list, and then click on the ellipsis button. This will open the View Job Category Properties window shown in Figure 15-18.

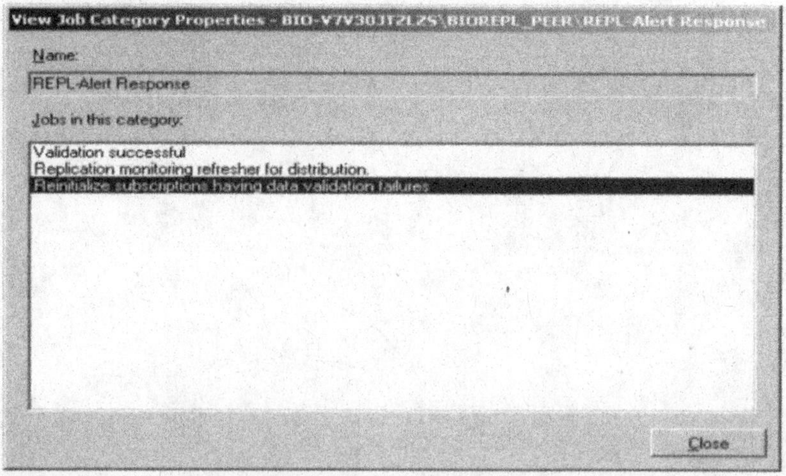

Figure 15-18. *Setting the job category properties for REPL-Alert Response*

Select "Reinitialize subscriptions having data validation failures," and then click the Close button. This will return you to the Job Properties window (Figure 15-17). Select the Steps page in the left pane, as shown in Figure 15-19.

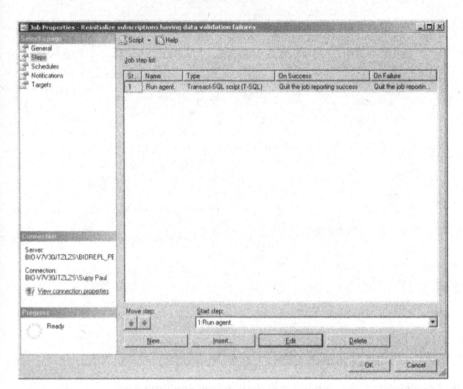

Figure 15-19. *Viewing the one job step*

If you click on the Edit button, you will see that the agent executes the following statement:

```
exec sys.sp_MSreinit_failed_subscriptions @failure_level = 1
```

The agent reinitializes all subscriptions should the validation fail (@failure_level=1).

Select the Notifications page in the left pane of the Job Properties window (Figure 15-19), and you will see that the error is written in the Windows Event Viewer, as mentioned earlier. This is shown in Figure 15-20.

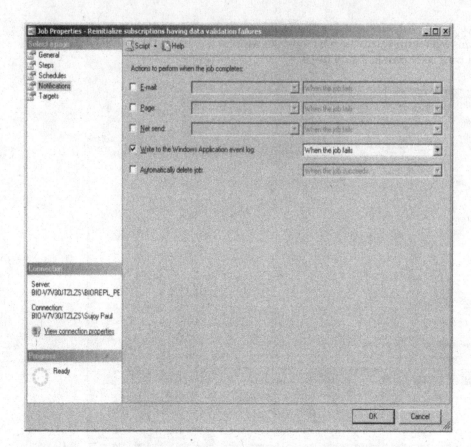

Figure 15-20. *The validation failure is notified in the Windows Application log*

Click the OK button to return to the window in Figure 15-15. Click OK again to set the alert.

The next time you run the validation of the publication, any error messages that occur will be logged on the Application log of the Event Viewer.

Standard Read-Only Transactional Replication

In standard read-only transactional replication, the subscriptions are read-only. Changes made at the Publisher server are transferred to the Subscriber server either in real time or with a certain time lag, depending on the business requirements. It is therefore imperative that you back up the publication database.

However, your backup and recovery strategy for standard read-only transactional replication should also include the restoration of the replicated databases. The process of restoring the publication database from backup depends on the replication options. However, the restoration for the master and msdb system databases from backup are the same for snapshot replication, standard read-only transactional replication with updating subscriptions, and peer-to-peer transactional replication.

In this section, I will discuss the backup and restoration of the publication database for standard read-only transactional replication. The server instance that I used for this example is connected using Windows Authentication.

Backing Up the Publication Database

To back up the publication database, we can use a modified version of the code in Listing 15-1 and then run the backup script using the SQLCMD utility. Listing 15-6 shows the modified script.

Listing 15-6. *Backup Script Running on a Windows-Authenticated SQL Server Instance*

```
/*Execute using SQLCMD utility on the BIO-V7V30JTZLZS\BIOREPL_PEER instance*/

/*Declare the variables to be used for Windows Authentication; the username and
password are not specified */
:setvar logintimeout 120
:setvar server "BIO-V7V30JTZLZS\BIOREPL_PEER"
:connect $(server) -l $(logintimeout)

/*Back up the database */

BACKUP DATABASE $(db) TO  DISK = N'$(path)\$(db).bak'
WITH NOFORMAT, INIT,
NAME = N'$(db)Database Backup',
SKIP,
NOREWIND,
NOUNLOAD,
STATS = 10,
CHECKSUM
GO

/* Locate the appropriate backup set and files */

declare @backupSetId as int
select @backupSetId = position from msdb..backupset where
 database_name='$(db)' and backup_set_id=
(select max(backup_set_id) from msdb..backupset where database_name='$(db)' )

/*Verify that the backup is available */

if @backupSetId is null
begin
raiserror
(N'Verify failed. Backup information for database ''$(db)'' not found.', 16, 1)
end
```

```
/*Restore the database */

RESTORE VERIFYONLY FROM  DISK = N'$(path)\$(db).bak'
WITH  FILE = @backupSetId,  NOUNLOAD,  NOREWIND
GO
```

We can run this script from the command prompt by executing the following:

```
SQLCMD -E -ic:\Backupdatabasepeer.sql -vdb="mysales_copy" path="C:\files"
```

The -E switch is used when connection to the server is made by using trusted Windows authentication. The output is shown in Figure 15-21.

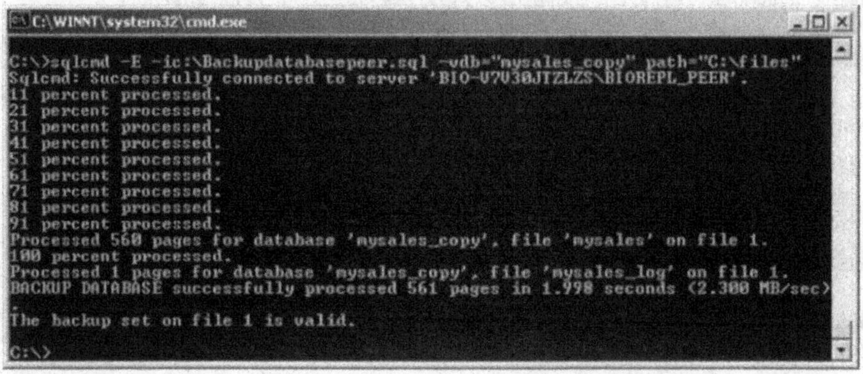

Figure 15-21. *Backing up a standard read-only transactional publication*

Restoring the Publication Database

Having backed up the database, we can use the wizard to restore the database as mysales
_copy_restore. Once the database is restored, we need to check that the restoration process for the current replication option, which involves checking for any undelivered commands for the subscription and nonconvergence of data is complete.

First we will check whether the database is enabled with the sync with backup option. Listing 15-7 shows you how to check for this option. If the value is 0, this option has not been enabled. A value of 1 would mean that it has been enabled.

Listing 15-7. *Check for the* sync with backup *Option*

```
/* Can be executed either on the publication or the distribution database*/
/*In this case, check it on the publication database */

Use mysales_copy_restore
Go


SELECT DATABASEPROPERTYEX
('mysales_copy_restore','IsSyncWithBackup')
Go
```

As you can see from the preceding listing, this option can be enabled either on the publication or distribution database. Enabling this option on either of the two has its pros and cons.

Setting it on the distribution database ensures that the transactions in the log do not get truncated in the publication database until they have been backed up in the distribution database. You can restore the distribution database from the last backup, and any undelivered transactions will be transmitted from the publishing database to the distribution database and replication remains unaffected by the process. Although it has no effect on latency, there will be a delay in the truncation of the log in the publication database until all the transactions have been backed up in the distribution database.

Setting this option in the publication database, as in this case, increases latency. This is because transactions will not be delivered to the distribution database until they have been backed up in the publication database. Consequently there is a time lag between when the transaction is committed in the publication database and when it is delivered to the distribution database.

Since this option was not set in the publication database, it is possible that the restored database does not contain transactions that have already been delivered to the distribution database and subsequently to the subscription database. If that were the case, you would have to ensure that all the subscriptions for the publication database are in sync with all the outstanding commands of the distribution database. Then you would need to manually apply any transactions that were not delivered in the restored database. To ensure that the subscription and distribution databases are in sync, run the Distribution Agent until the outstanding commands have been delivered to the subscription database.

In this example, the Distribution Agent runs continuously, so we need to check whether the outstanding commands have been delivered. To do this, open the Replication Monitor and select the publication as shown in Figure 15-22.

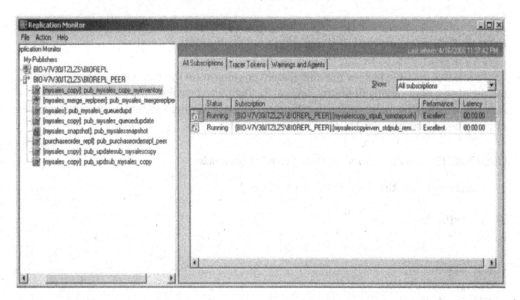

Figure 15-22. *Viewing a list of subscriptions for the standard publication,*
pub_mysales_copy_myinventory

Right-click on the green arrow in the right pane, select the subscription, select View Details, and select Undistributed Commands. You will see any undistributed commands, as shown in Figure 15-23. As you can see, the subscription database is not waiting for any undistributed commands from the distribution database, so they are in sync.

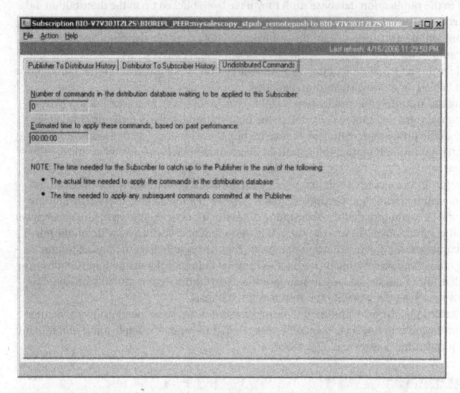

Figure 15-23. *Viewing undistributed commands in the subscription database*

While it is possible to view the undelivered commands in the Replication Monitor, the overhead cost of retrieving them this way can be high. It is possible, however, to retrieve the same information by querying the distribution database. Listing 15-8 shows how you can find out whether the commands have been delivered or not.

Listing 15-8. *Finding the Number of Undelivered Commands*

```
/* Execute this on the distribution database */

Use distribution
Go

select a.agent_id,
a.UndelivCmdsInDistDB,
a.DelivCmdsInDistDB,
b.name,
```

```
b.publisher_db,
b.publication
from MSdistribution_status a,MSdistribution_agents b
where a.agent_id=b.id and
b.publication='pub_mysales_copy_myinventory' and
b.name=
'BIO-V7V30JTZLZS\BIORE-mysales_copy-pub_mysales_copy_myin-BIO-V7V30JTZLZS\BIORE-17'
go
```

This script determines how many commands have been delivered and how many are still left undelivered for the publication and the Distribution Agent (b.name) servicing the publication. The two tables used are MSdistribution_status and MSdistribution_agents. This script needs to be executed on the distribution database. The output is as follows:

```
Agent_id     UndelivCmdsInDistDB      DelivCmdsInDistDB
Name
Publisher_db
Publication
-----------------------------------------------------------------------------


17           0                        10
BIO-V7V30JTZLZS\BIORE-mysales_copy-pub_mysales_copy_myin-BIO-V7V30JTZLZS\BIORE-17
mysales_copy
pub_mysales_copy_myinventory

17           0                        5
BIO-V7V30JTZLZS\BIORE-mysales_copy-pub_mysales_copy_myin-BIO-V7V30JTZLZS\BIORE-17
mysales_copy
pub_mysales_copy_myinventory

17           0                        5
BIO-V7V30JTZLZS\BIORE-mysales_copy-pub_mysales_copy_myin-BIO-V7V30JTZLZS\BIORE-17
mysales_copy
pub_mysales_copy_myinventory

17           0                        5
BIO-V7V30JTZLZS\BIORE-mysales_copy-pub_mysales_copy_myin-BIO-V7V30JTZLZS\BIORE-17
mysales_copy
pub_mysales_copy_myinventory

17           0                        5
BIO-V7V30JTZLZS\BIORE-mysales_copy-pub_mysales_copy_myin-BIO-V7V30JTZLZS\BIORE-17
mysales_copy
pub_mysales_copy_myinventory
```

You can see that there are no commands left to be delivered.

Although we have validated the data for replication, validation merely provides a success or failure result. It does not tell us whether there are any differences between the source and the destination tables. At this stage, you should check to see whether there are indeed any differences between the source and destination tables.

To do this, you have to use a utility tool introduced in SQL Server 2005, called tablediff. You will find the executable in this directory: C:\Program Files\Microsoft SQL Server\90\COM. Figure 15-24 shows a list of the parameters for the utility.

Figure 15-24. *The parameters of the tablediff utility*

Listing 15-9 shows how you can use tablediff to find out whether there is any nonconvergence between the publication database, mysales_copy, and the subscription database, mysalescopy_stpub_remotepush, for the Item table. You need to run the utility for each of the articles to ensure that there is no data nonconvergence. In this example, both databases are running on the same server instance, BIO-V7V30JTZLZS\BIOREPL_PEER. The parameters used for tablediff in this example are listed in Table 15-1.

Listing 15-9. *Checking for Nonconvergence Between the Publication and Subscription Databases*

```
/* Run from the command prompt */

tablediff -sourceserver BIO-V7V30JTZLZS\BIOREPL_PEER -sourcedatabase
 mysales_copy -sourcetable Item -sourceschema myinventory -
destinationserver BIO-V7V30JTZLZS\BIOREPL_PEER -destinationdatabase
 mysalescopy_stpub_remotepush -destinationtable Item -
destinationschema myinventory
-f C:\files\tabledifferencepeer.sql -o C:\files\tablediffoutput.txt
```

Table 15-1. *Parameter Settings for* tablediff *in Listing 15-9*

Parameter	Value
sourceserver	BIO-V7V30JTZLZS\BIOREPL_PEER
sourcedatabase	mysales_copy
sourcetable	Item
sourceschema	myinventory
destinationserver	BIO-V7V30JTZLZS\BIOREPL_PEER
destinationdatabase	mysalescopy_stpub_remotepush
destinationtable	Item
destinationschema	myinventory
f	C:\files\tabledifferencepeer.sql
o	C:\files\tablediffoutput.txt

The -f switch is used to generate a SQL file that will help to fix the data on the subscription server so that it matches that on the publishing server. If there is data convergence, the SQL file will not be generated, as you will see in this case. The -o switch is used to generate an output text file.

■**Note** In the preceding example, I used Windows Authentication to connect to the server instance. If you are using SQL Server Authentication, you can also use the -sourceuser and -sourcepassword options.

When you run the tablediff utility, it will list the parameters and their corresponding values on the command prompt, as shown in Figure 15-25.

Figure 15-25. *Executing the tablediff utility*

If you open the output file, you will see the result of the execution, as shown here:

```
Table [mysales_copy].[myinventory].[Item] on BIO-
V7V3OJTZLZS\BIOREPL_PEER and Table
[mysalescopy_stpub_remotepush].[myinventory].[Item] on BIO-
V7V3OJTZLZS\BIOREPL_PEER are identical.
The requested operation took 14.52088 seconds.
```

In this example there is no data nonconvergence, so the SQL file was not generated.

If you don't specify the -sourceschema and -destinationschema parameters, you will get an error message, as shown in Figure 15-26.

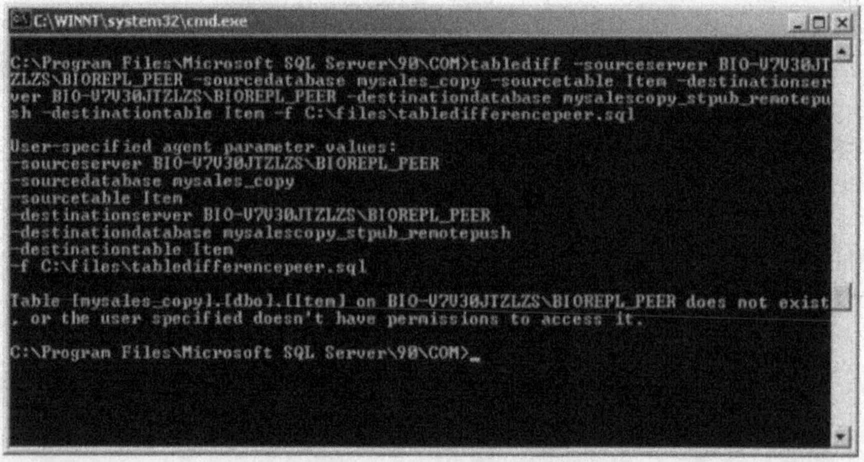

Figure 15-26. *Error message generated by not including the* -sourceschema *and* -destinationschema *parameters*

Once you have checked for data convergence for all of the articles, you need to check that the database is configured for all the publications and the subscriptions. To do this, open the SSMS and open the Local Publications folder. Right-click on the publication that is attached to the database you have restored, and select Properties. You should go through each of the publication properties and ensure that the right values are set. In my case, I did not set up the agent security settings on the mysales_copy_restore database in the restoration of the database. I configured it using the agent security setting option. Refresh the server instance so that the settings can take effect.

In order to view the restored publication database and the corresponding subscriptions, open the Local Publications object under Replication in the Object Explorer of the SSMS. You will see the restored publication database. In Figure 15-27, you can see the pub_mysales_copy_myinventory publication and the subscriptions associated with the mysales_copy_restore database.

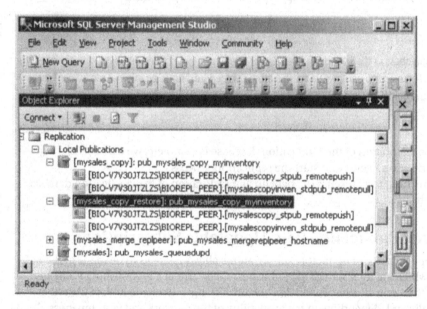

Figure 15-27. *Viewing the restored publication database and the corresponding subscriptions*

■**Tip** If you run the sp_repltrans stored procedure on the publication database, it will tell you whether there are any transactions marked for replication but waiting to be sent to the distribution database. In this example, I did not have any.

Now that the configuration is finally set, you can run the sp_replrestart stored procedure in the publication database to ensure that the replication data on both the publication and distribution database are in sync. The procedure matches the highest LSN of the distribution database with that of the publication database. On executing the procedure, you will get a message indicating whether it was successful or not, as shown in Figure 15-28.

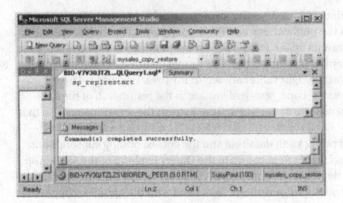

Figure 15-28. *Successful completion of the* sp_replrestart *stored procedure*

■**Caution** Only members of the sysadmin fixed server role or db_owner fixed database role can execute sp_replrestart. There are no parameters for this stored procedure. This is an internal replication stored procedure. Follow the guidelines in the BOL for the execution of this stored procedure.

Now that the restoration of the publication database is complete, we can start the Log Reader and Distribution Agents and start the replication process.

In the next section, I will discuss the backup and restoration of the publication database for updatable subscriptions.

Transactional Publication with Updatable Subscriptions

Transactional replication with updatable subscriptions allows changes to be made at the Subscriber servers, which are then sent to the Publisher server, and in a republishing Publisher, the changes are then sent to other Subscriber servers. Changes are made at the Subscriber server occasionally and, depending on the availability of the network and your business requirements, you can either configure a transactional publication with immediate or queued updating subscription.

In this section I will describe the backup and restoration of transactional publication with queued updating subscriptions. The publication database I used for this example is the mysales database on the BIO-V7V30JTZLZS\BIOREPL instance.

Backing Up the Publication Database

Before backing up the database, we need to check whether the sync with backup option is enabled on both the publication and the distribution databases. If not, this option needs to be enabled.

The sync with backup setting ensures that all transactions are backed up before being delivered to the distribution database. This means that you can use the last backup of the publication database to restore, since the distribution database will not have any transactions that the restored publication database will not have. This option has effects on both the latency and throughput, since transactions cannot be delivered to the distribution database until they have been backed up in the publication database.

You can also set this option on the distribution database. When you do so, the SQL Server engine ensures that the log is not truncated for the publication database until after all the transactions delivered to the distribution database are backed up. This means you can use the last restored distribution database; transactions from the publication database will be delivered to the distribution database without affecting the replication process. However, the downside of this is that the transaction log of the publication database will grow in size.

Listing 15-10 shows you how to enable this option.

Listing 15-10. *Enabling the* sync with backup *Option*

```
/* Use the sqlcmd utility to execute the script */

/*Declare the variables */
:setvar logintimeout 120
:setvar server "BIO-V7V30JTZLZS\BIOREPL"
:setvar user "sa"
:setvar pwd "sujoy"
:connect $(server) -l $(logintimeout) -U $(user) -P $(pwd)

/*Enable the sync with backup option */

Use $(db)
Go
if DATABASEPROPERTYEX
('$(db)','$(property)')=0
exec sp_replicationdboption '$(db)','sync with backup','true'
else
print "'$(db)' is already enabled for sync with backup"
Go
```

The DATABASEPROPERTYEX function returns the current settings of the specified database for the property specified. A value of 0 for the IsSynchWithBackup option indicates that this is not enabled. The sp_replicationdboption is then executed, setting the sync with backup option to true.

Using the SQLCMD utility, you can see that this option is already enabled for the publication database, as shown in Figure 15-29.

Figure 15-29. *The* sync with backup *option is enabled for the publication database*

The next step of the process is to back up the publication database. To do this, we can use a modified version of the backup script in Listing 15-6. This is shown in Listing 15-11.

Listing 15-11. *Backup Script for a Publication Database That Has the* sync with backup *Option Enabled*

```
/*Execute this with the SQLCMD utility */

/*Declare the variables */

:setvar logintimeout 120
:setvar server "BIO-V7V30JTZLZS\BIOREPL"
:setvar user "sa"
:setvar pwd "sujoy"
:connect $(server) -l $(logintimeout) -U $(user) -P $(pwd)

Use $(db)
Go

/*Check the property of the database and then run a DBCC Checkdb */

IF DATABASEPROPERTYEX
('$(db)','$(property)')='FULL'
and
DATABASEPROPERTYEX
('$(db)','$(property1)')='Online'
begin
dbcc checkdb('$(db)') with physical_only
end
go

/*Back up the database */
```

```
BACKUP DATABASE $(db)
TO  DISK = N'$(path)\$(db).bak' WITH NOFORMAT, INIT,
NAME =
N'$(db)Database Backup',
SKIP,
NOREWIND,
NOUNLOAD,
STATS = 10,
CHECKSUM
GO

declare @backupSetId as int
select @backupSetId = position from
msdb..backupset where database_name='$(db)' and
backup_set_id=(select max(backup_set_id) from msdb..backupset
where database_name='$(db)' )

/*Verify the backup information for the database */

if @backupSetId is null
begin
raiserror(N'Verify failed. Backup information for database ''$(db)''
not found.', 16, 1)
end

/*Restore the database */

RESTORE VERIFYONLY FROM
DISK = N'$(path)\$(db).bak'
WITH  FILE = @backupSetId,
NOUNLOAD,
NOREWIND
GO
```

This script first checks whether the recovery model for the database is Full and also whether the Status property is Online. If the database is set to Full and is Online, then it runs dbcc checkdb to check the validity of the database. Since Checksum is the default for the page verification of the recovery model, the script uses the physical_only option with dbcc checkdb. This option checks torn pages, checksum failures, and the physical integrity of the page and record headers, including the physical structure of the B-trees and the allocation of the database. It does not provide any informational messages when you set this option.

The script in Listing 15-11 is run from the command prompt using the SQLCMD utility:

```
C:\sqlcmd -SBIO-V7V30JTZLZS\BIOREPL -iC:\backupdatabase.sql -
vdb="mysales" property="Recovery" property1="Status" path="C:\files"
```

The output is shown in Figure 15-30.

```
C:\WINNT\system32\cmd.exe                                              _ □ x

C:\>sqlcmd -SBIO-U7U30JTZLZS\BIOREPL -iC:\backupdatabase.sql -vdb="mysales" prop
erty="Recovery" property1="Status" path="C:\files"
Sqlcmd: Successfully connected to server 'BIO-U7U30JTZLZS\BIOREPL'.
Changed database context to 'mysales'.
DBCC results for 'mysales'.
CHECKDB found 0 allocation errors and 0 consistency errors in database 'mysales'
.
DBCC execution completed. If DBCC printed error messages, contact your system ad
ministrator.
11 percent processed.
22 percent processed.
34 percent processed.
45 percent processed.
51 percent processed.
Processed 1192 pages for database 'mysales', file 'mysales' on file 1.
61 percent processed.
70 percent processed.
80 percent processed.
90 percent processed.
100 percent processed.
Processed 1050 pages for database 'mysales', file 'mysales_log' on file 1.
BACKUP DATABASE successfully processed 2242 pages in 4.153 seconds (4.422 MB/sec
).
The backup set on file 1 is valid.

C:\>
```

Figure 15-30. *Output from running the script in Listing 15-11*

■**Caution** The script in Listing 15-11 will back up the database even if there are errors found by dbcc checkdb.

As you can see in Figure 15-30, DBCC checkdb with physical_only did not show any informational messages, as it does when you use it without the physical_only option.

Restoring the Publication Database

First, restore the database as shown earlier in the "Snapshot Replication" section of the chapter. You should then verify that all the commands have been distributed to the subscription databases.

To do that, you can either modify Listing 15-8 by changing the name of the Distribution Agent and the publication, or you can view the number of undistributed commands using the Replication Monitor. In this example, there are no undistributed commands in the Replication Monitor for the pub_mysales_queueupd publication with queued updating subscription. This is shown in Figure 15-31.

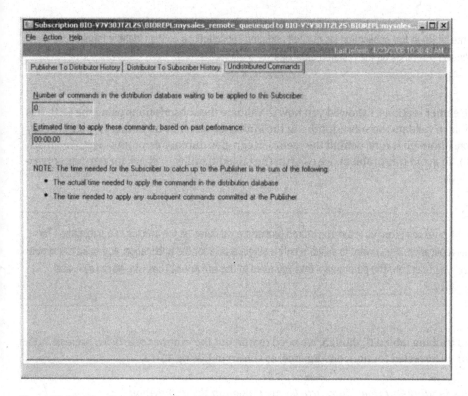

Figure 15-31. *Viewing the number of undistributed commands for a publication with a queued updating subscription*

Next, we need to delete any rows that exist in the MSreplication_queue system table. To do so, connect to the Subscriber server for the publication that is using queued updating subscription. This table stores all the queued commands issued by all queued updating subscriptions.

■**Note** You do not have to perform this step for publications with immediate updating subscriptions.

Listing 15-12 shows how to delete the rows from the table.

Listing 15-12. *Deleting Rows from* MSreplication_queue

```
/*Execute this on the subscription database that subscribes to
 queued subscriptions*/

use mysales_remote_queueupd
go
if ((select count(*) from MSreplication_queue) >0)
delete from MSreplication_queue
go
```

■**Note** If the tables in the publication for queued updating subscriptions contain identity ranges, you need to assign the same settings on the restored database.

In the earlier sections, I showed you how to validate the subscriptions using the GUI. It is also possible to validate the subscriptions at the Publisher server by executing sp_publication_ validation. Although it runs behind the scenes, it can give dubious error messages (see BOL for details). To avoid this problem, we can run the tablediff utility to check for any nonconvergence of data.

■**Tip** The sp_publication_validation stored procedure validates all the articles in a publication for transactional replication. If you want to validate only a single article for the publication, you need to execute sp_article_validation. The parameters that you need to use are @publication, @article, and @rowcount_only.

Before running tablediff, though, we need to find out the number of articles present in the publication to be tested for nonconvergence, as shown in Listing 15-13.

Listing 15-13. *Finding Out How Many Articles Are Present in the Publication*

```
/*Execute this on the publication database */

/*Declare the variables */

:setvar logintimeout 120
:setvar server "BIO-V7V30JTZLZS\BIOREPL"
:setvar user "sa"
:setvar password "sujoy"
:connect $(server) -l $(logintimeout) -U $(user) -P $(password)

use $(db)
go

select a.artid,
a.dest_table,
a.name as sourcetable,
a.dest_owner as destinationowner,
b.name as publicationname,
c.dest_db as subscriptiondatabase
from sysarticles a, syspublications b,
syssubscriptions c
where a.pubid=b.pubid and a.artid=c.artid
```

```
and c.dest_db='$(subname)'
and b.name='$(pubname)'
go
```

This script uses the sysarticles, syspublications, and the syssubscriptions system tables. The artid, dest_table, sourcetable, and dest_owner columns are retrieved from the sysarticles table, while the name of the publication and the corresponding subscriptions are taken from the syspublications and syssubscriptions tables, respectively. Using the SQLCMD utility, the script in Listing 15-13 can find the articles for any publication. The execution of the script with the SQLCMD utility is shown in Figure 15-32.

Figure 15-32. *Executing the script in Listing 15-13 with the SQLCMD utility*

The output for this script follows:

```
Changed database context to 'mysales'.
artid        dest_table
sourcetable
destinationowner
publicationname
subscriptiondatabase
-----------
100          Customer
Customer
myorder
pub_mysales_queueupd
mysales_remote_queueupd

(1 rows affected)
```

There is only one table that needs to be tested for nonconvergence with the tablediff utility: Customer. The table present in the publication database is identical with that in the subscription database.

The next step is to find out whether the restored database has an up-to-date configuration, and in this case it does.

Finally, we can run sp_replrestart to resynchronize the metadata with the Distributor server's metadata.

Peer-to-Peer Replication

As you know, peer-to-peer replication has been introduced in SQL Server 2005. While both standard and updatable subscriptions can be hierarchical, peer-to-peer transactional replication transmits messages between nodes that are at the same level. As such, you can make use of peer-to-peer replication in cases such as load balancing or hot backups.

■**Note** The configuration of peer-to-peer replication using the GUI and T-SQL is discussed in Chapters 8 and 9, respectively.

In Chapters 8 and 9, peer-to-peer replication was configured between two instances of the server, BIO-V7V30JTZLZS\BIOREPL_PEER and BIO-V7V30JTZLZS\BIOREPL. If either of them gets corrupted, we will have to restore the damaged publication database from the one that is working. Obviously, this involves a different implementation of the restoration process.

For this example, we will assume that the purchaseorder_repl database in BIO-V7V30JTZLZS\BIOREPL_PEER is not functioning and is not available. The first thing that we need to do is remove the subscription metadata from the distribution database of this server.

You can do this by executing sp_removedistpublisherdbreplication from the distribution database. This stored procedure drops the metadata for the subscriptions associated with the publication first, and making use of cursors, it then drops all the metadata for the articles that belong to the publication. Finally, it drops the metadata for the publication and for all the agents listed for that publication. This is shown in Listing 15-14.

Listing 15-14. *Dropping the Metadata from the Distribution Database*

```
/*Execute this on the distribution database on the node that failed */

Use distribution
Go

/*Specify the name of the publication database and the name of the publication */

sp_removedistpublisherdbreplication 'pub_purchaseorderrepl_peer',
'purchaseorder_repl'
Go
```

■**Note** You have to be a member of the sysadmin fixed server role or the db_owner fixed database role to run this stored procedure.

Having removed the metadata for the publication, the next step is to drop the subscription from the publication. In Listings 5-1 and 5-2 (in Chapter 5) I demonstrated how to drop pull and push subscriptions, respectively. Here, I will modify Listing 5-2 so that it can be used to drop push subscriptions for either snapshot or transactional replication using the SQLCMD utility.

For peer-to-peer replication, the subscription that is being dropped is a push subscription. The modified script is shown in Listing 15-15.

Listing 15-15. *Dropping a Subscription from the Publication for Peer-to-Peer Replication*

```
/*Execute this on the distribution database on the
publishing server that is working */

/*Declare the variables */

:setvar logintimeout 120
:setvar server "BIO-V7V30JTZLZS\BIOREPL"
:setvar user "sa"
:setvar password "sujoy"
:connect $(server) -l $(logintimeout) -U $(user) -P $(password)
:setvar subtype 0

/*For pull subscriptions, set the subtype variable to 1.*/

:setvar statusnum 2

use $(db)
go

/*Declare a table variable */

declare @subscription_push table
(publisher_id smallint,
publisher_db sysname,
subscriber_db sysname,
subscription_type int,
sync_type tinyint,
status tinyint);

/* Insert data into the table variable from the MSsubscriptions table in
the distribution database*/

insert into @subscription_push
select
publisher_id,
publisher_db,
subscriber_db,
subscription_type,
```

```
sync_type,
status from $(db)..MSsubscriptions
where subscription_type=$(subtype) and status=$(statusnum)

/* Check the data of the @subscription_push table variable */

select * from @subscription_push

/* Declare table variable that will store the Publisher and the Subscriber
information from the MSSubscriber_info table */

declare @subscriberinfo table
(publisher sysname,
subscriber sysname);

/* Insert the data into the @subscriberinfo table variable */

insert into @subscriberinfo
select publisher,subscriber from $(db)..MSsubscriber_info

/* Check the data for the @subscriberinfo table variable */
select * from @subscriberinfo

/* Finally on the Publisher server on the publication
database, remove the subscription for the Publisher*/

use $(pubdb)
go

exec sp_dropsubscription '$(pubname)','$(article)','$(subserver)'
go
```

You can use the SQLCMD utility to execute this script, as shown in Figure 15-33. For push subscriptions, the $(subtype) variable is set to 0.

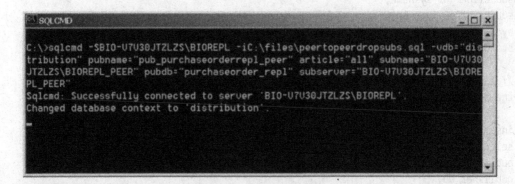

Figure 15-33. *Executing the script in Listing 15-15 with SQLCMD*

The next step in the process is to back up the purchaseorder_repl database on the BIO-V7V30JTZLZS\BIOREPL server and then restore it on the BIO-V7V30JTZLZS\ BIOREPL_PEER server. Ensure that the database is using the Full recovery model, as it has been in this chapter.

It is also important when you restore the database that the "Preserve the replication options" check box not be checked in the Options page of the Restore Database window under the "Restore options" group box, as shown in Figure 15-34. Otherwise you will have the publication settings for the BIO-V7V30JTZLZS\BIOREPL server instance transferred to BIO-V7V30JTZLZS\BIOREPL_PEER. I have also used the RESTORE WITH RECOVERY statement, by selecting the first option in the Recovery state section, in order to roll back uncommitted transactions.

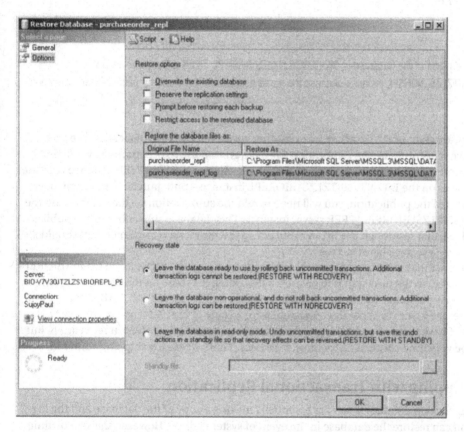

Figure 15-34. *Unchecking all the "Restore options" check boxes before restoring the database*

■**Note** The "Preserve the replication options" setting is equivalent to the KEEP_REPLICATION option.

The successful recovery of the purchaseorder_repl database from the BIO-V7V30JTZLZS\
BIOREPL server instance to BIO-V7V30JTZLZS\BIOREPL_PEER is shown in Figure 15-35.

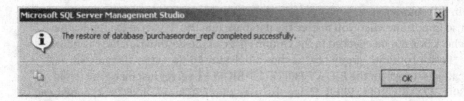

Figure 15-35. *The successful restoration of purchaseorder_repl in BIO-V7V30JTZLZS\
BIOREPL_PEER*

Note The name of the database in BIO-V7V30JTZLZS\BIOREPL_PEER is the same as in the
BIO-V7V30JTZLZS\BIOREPL instance because the name needs to be the same for peer-to-peer replication.

The restoration of the database from another server removes the replication properties,
so you have to reconfigure the publication from the ground up. In this example, you'll first
need to create a new publication on the BIO-V7V30JTZLZS\BIOREPL_PEER instance with the
same name as on the BIO-V7V30JTZLZS\BIOREPL instance—pub_purchaseorderrepl_peer.
Having created the publication, you will need to add the subscription on the database on the
BIO-V7V30JTZLZS\BIOREPL_PEER server instance. This database subscribes to the publication database that resides on the BIO-V7V30JTZLZS\BIOREPL server instance. You should also
set the @sync_type parameter to true.

Remember that we dropped the subscribing database on the BIO-V7V30JTZLZS\BIOREPL
server instance, so the next step is to create a subscribing database on the BIO-V7V30JTZLZS\
BIOREPL server instance for the publication database on BIO-V7V30JTZLZS\BIOREPL_PEER.
In this case, the @sync_type parameter should have a value of replication support only.

So far, I have focused on backing up and restoring databases involved in replication, but
this can be very time consuming for large databases. That's where log shipping comes in.

Log Shipping with Transactional Replication

When you back up databases, you are essentially making a copy of the database and the log
so that you can restore the database in the event of system failure. However, this can be time
consuming if you have a VLDB (very large database). Also, if your application is using transactional replication, the downtime might not be acceptable for your business. Log shipping
offers an alternative, and it can be used with transactional or merge replication.

While hardware clustering offers failover, the licensing may not be cost effective for all
organizations. Log shipping, as the name implies, allows a copy of the transaction log of the
primary database to be sent from the primary server to a secondary database on a secondary
server so that depending on the frequency with which the logs are backed up, both the databases are synchronized. Although the failover for log shipping is not automatic (you have to
manually fail over from the primary to the secondary server), the downtime might be within
acceptable limits.

Since all the DML operations made on the transaction log of the primary database are copied to the secondary database by log shipping, this method can be used with transactional replication. Log shipping involves backing up the primary database and the transaction log, copying the transactional log backup file to the secondary server, and restoring the log on the secondary database so that both the primary and the secondary databases are in sync. These operations all run as jobs—a backup job, copy job, and restore job.

The configuration of log shipping requires that you have a primary server and a secondary server. Optionally, you can also use a monitor server, which keeps a record of all the backups, the copies, and the restoration process, and gives you a status report that you can view in the SSMS. It also raises alerts should there be a failure in any of the operations. These operations are performed on the monitor server by the alert job. If the monitor server is not configured, the alert job is created on both the primary and secondary servers.

When log shipping is used with replication, consider the following points:

- The secondary server should be configured as a Publisher server in the Distributor server.

- If the primary server goes down, data will not be replicated to subscriptions.

- Since failover from the primary to the secondary server is not automatic, you have to manually revert to the secondary server.

- Ensure that you have enough disk space and memory on both servers, since the overhead costs are high.

- If the primary server is the Publisher server, and it goes down, and you manage to bring back the primary server, replication can continue.

- There is no guarantee that log shipping will recover any loss of data should there be any failure of the primary database.

Before you configure log shipping for a publication database used for transactional replication, you need to back up the publication database on the primary server. The backup recovery mode should either be Full or Bulk Logged; you cannot use the Simple recovery mode to enable log shipping.

You then need to restore the publication database on the secondary server. This will be your secondary database. The name of the secondary database should be the same as the primary database.

You should also back up the master and msdb databases on the primary server. If the Distributor server is located on the same server as the Publisher server, as in this example, back up the distribution database. You should also back up the master service key on the primary server.

■**Note** Although you can back up and restore the databases using SSMS, it is better to use T-SQL when complex backup and restore statements are required.

Once the backups and restores are done, you can configure log shipping. Open the SSMS and connect to the server that is going to be used as the primary server. Once you are connected to the primary server, open Databases in the Object Explorer and select the publication database, which is going to be used as the publication database. This will be your primary database. Ensure that the sync with backup option is set to on for the publication database. You can execute the script in Listing 15-10 for this purpose.

Next right-click on the database and select Tasks ➤ Ship Transaction Logs. This will open the Database Properties window, as shown in Figure 15-36. (This figure shows the complete configuration of the log settings. Initially everything will be disabled except for the "Enable this as a primary database in a log shipping configuration" setting.) Select the Transaction Log Shipping page and make sure the "Enable this as a primary database in a log shipping configuration" box is checked.

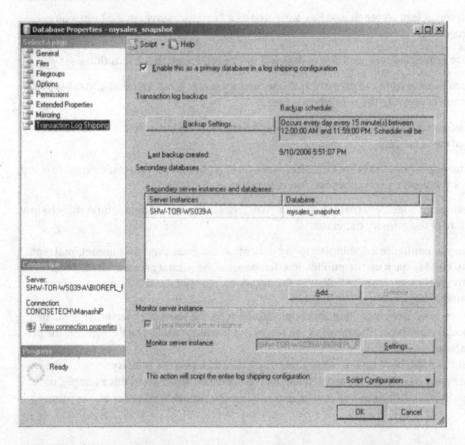

Figure 15-36. *Viewing the transaction log shipping settings for the database*

Click the Backup Settings button. This will open the Transaction Log Backup Settings window, as shown in Figure 15-37. Ensure that the primary database is located in the primary server and that the SQL Server Agent service account has read and write permissions on the folder.

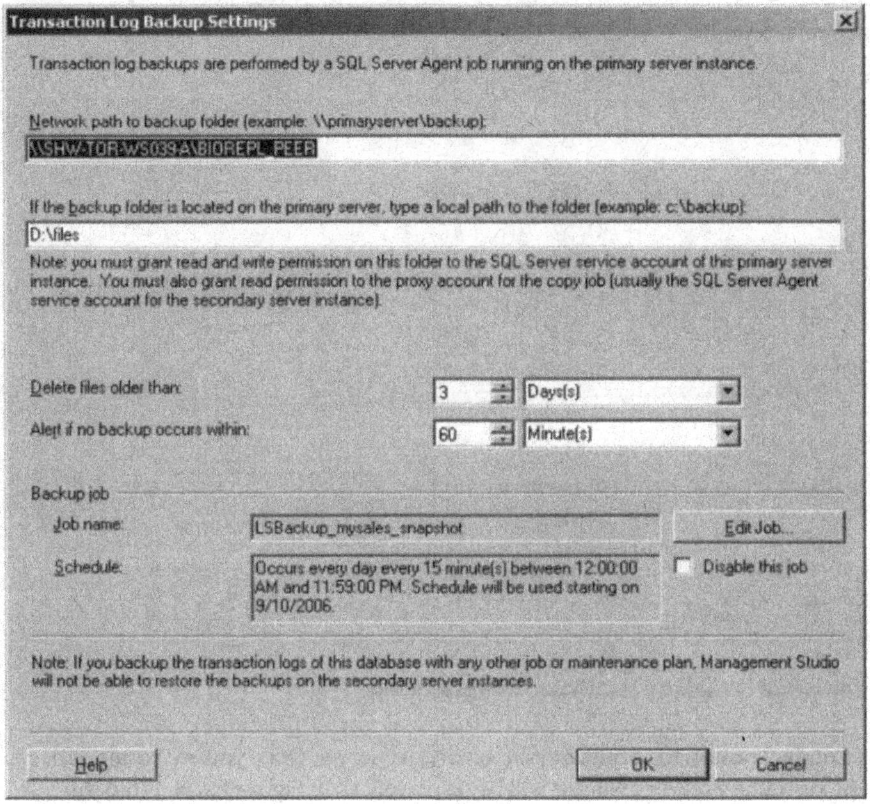

Figure 15-37. *Configuring the backup settings for the transaction logs*

Specify the network path as a UNC share for the backup, as shown in Figure 15-37. Also, specify a local path where the backup will be stored. Then specify a date after which the backup files will be deleted. In this example, I chose three days. You can also raise a threshold alert if the backup does not occur within a specific time frame (60 minutes, in this example). At the bottom of the window, the name and the schedule of the job are also displayed. If necessary, you can edit the name and the schedule by clicking the Edit Job button. Click OK to return to the Database Properties window (Figure 15-36).

In the Database Properties window, the Add button under the "Secondary server instances and databases" box is enabled. Click it to add the secondary server and corresponding database. The Secondary Database Settings window will open, as shown in Figure 15-38.

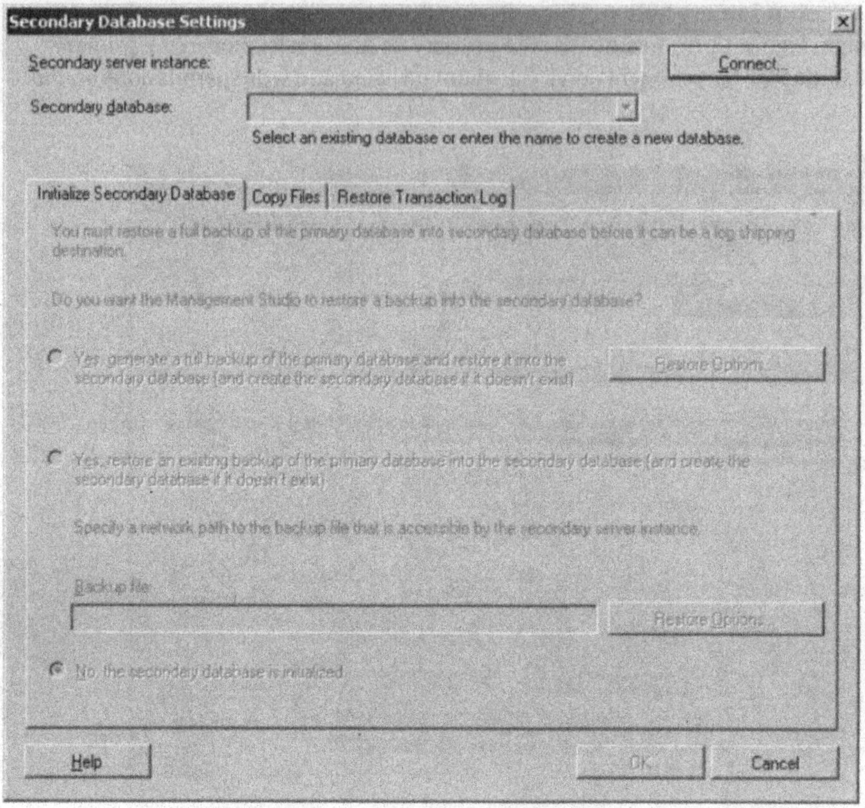

Figure 15-38. *The initial Secondary Database Settings window*

Click the Connect button to connect to the secondary server. Once you are connected, the name of the secondary server instance will be displayed, as in Figure 15-39. From the "Secondary database" drop-down list, select the database that you restored on the secondary server; this will be the secondary database for the publication database. Then click "No, the secondary database is initialized" radio button.

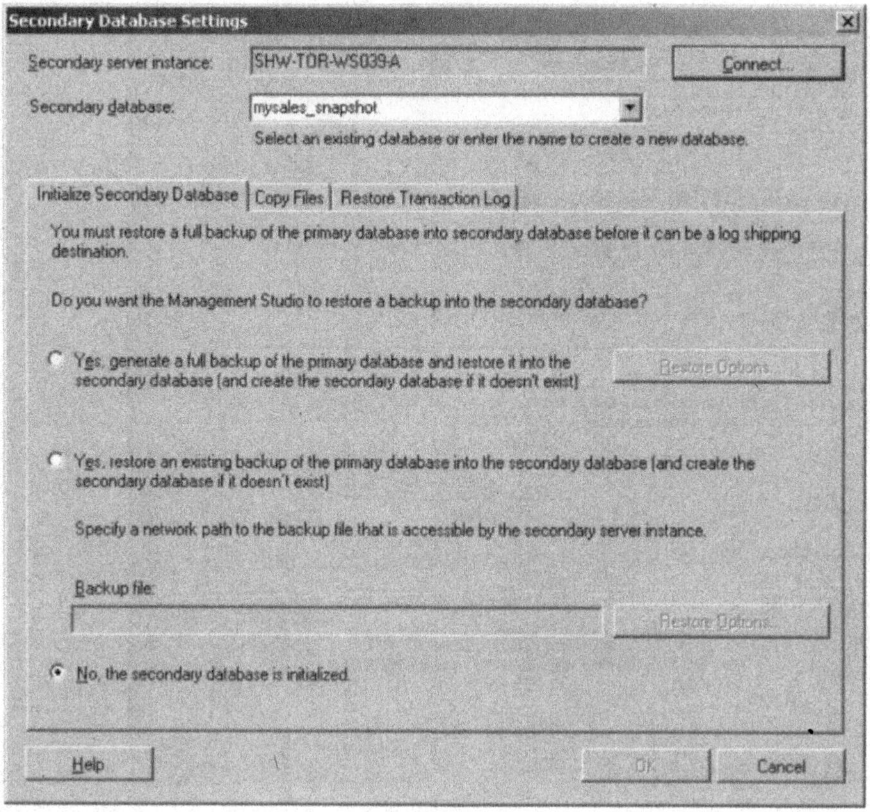

Figure 15-39. *The Initialize Secondary Database tab of the Secondary Database settings*

Next, select the Copy Files tab, as shown in Figure 15-40. Specify the destination folder to which the primary database will be copied in the secondary server. This folder location is relative to the secondary server, so you need to specify a local path. Then select the appropriate time after which the copied files should be deleted, and enter a job name for the copy job.

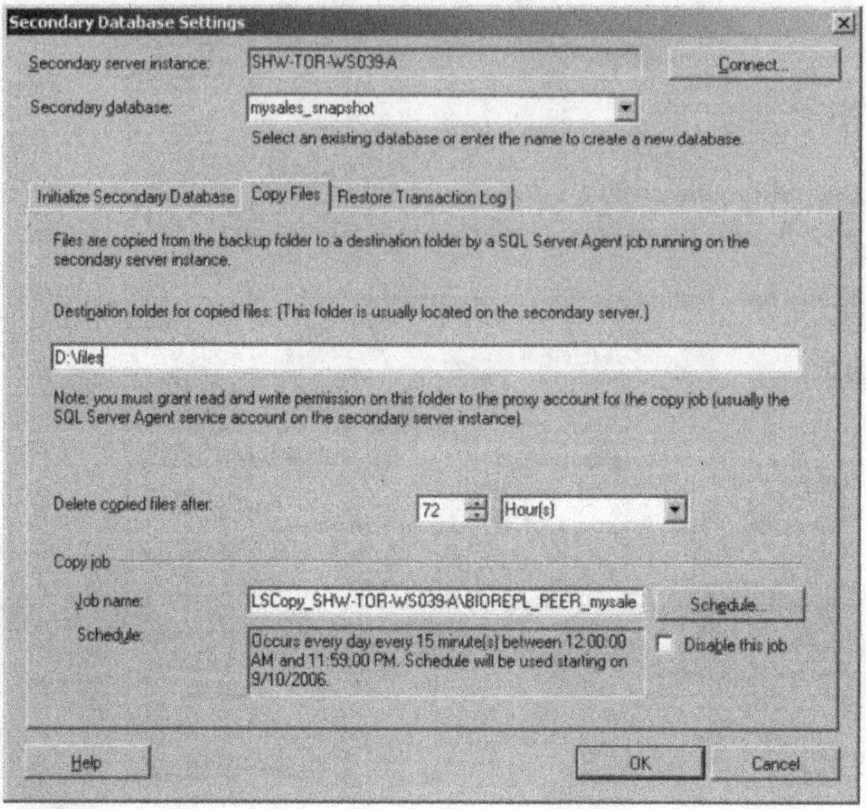

Figure 15-40. *Configuring the copy job that will copy files to the secondary database*

Now click the Restore Transaction Log tab, as shown in Figure 15-41. As you can see, I selected the "Standby mode" option for when the transaction log is restored on the secondary database. Since I do not want any users connected to the database, I checked the "Disconnect users in the database when restoring backups" box.

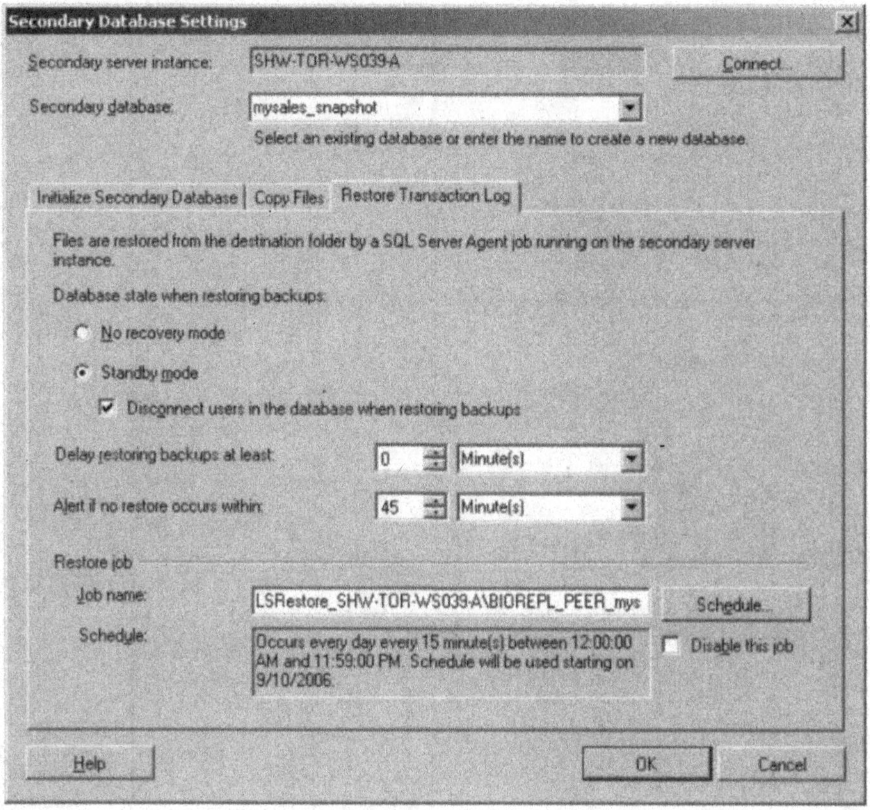

Figure 15-41. *Restore Transaction Log tab for Secondary Database Settings*

You can also select a time if you want to delay the restoring process. In this example, there is no delay in the restoration, but you might consider using it if you think there might be situations when accidental deletions of critical data might occur. If you delay the restoration, you might be able to retrieve the data from the secondary database.

As with the primary database, specify a threshold time for the restoration before an alert is raised. I selected 45 minutes from the drop-down list. Also, give the restore job a name.

Click OK to return to the Database Properties window (Figure 15-36). You will see the name of the secondary server and the secondary database listed.

Click the Settings button beside "Monitor Server instance" to set the server that will monitor the log shipping process. This will open the Log Shipping Monitor Settings window shown in Figure 15-42. Click the Connect button, and select the server that should be the monitor server. Once you configure the server, the Connect button and the name of the monitor server will be disabled (as in Figure 15-42).

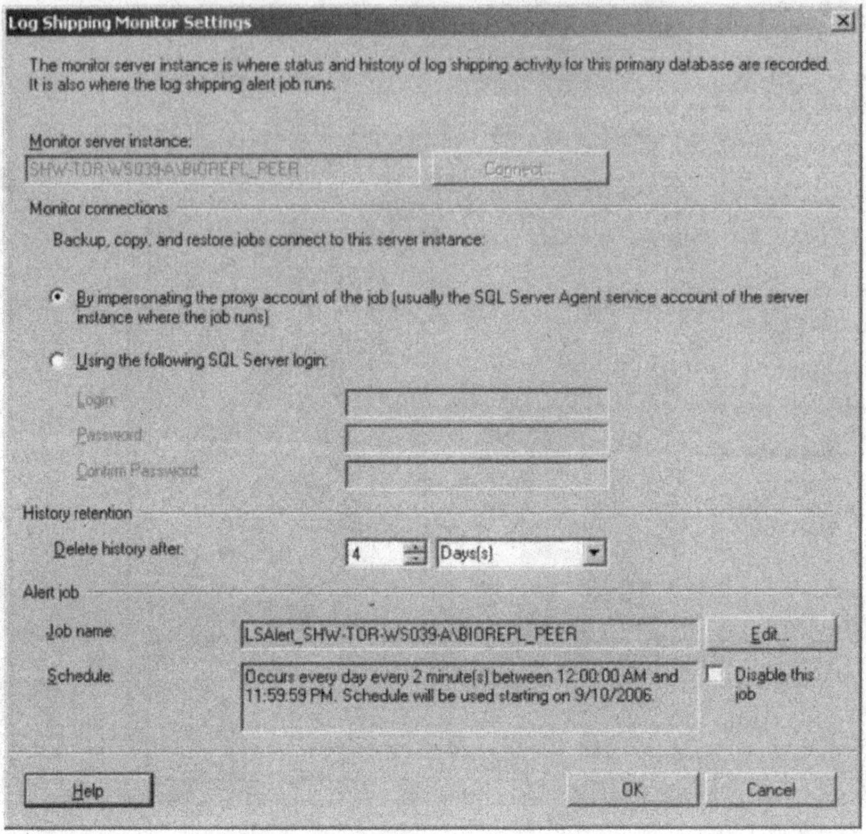

Figure 15-42. *Configuring the log shipping monitor*

Select the "By impersonating the proxy account of the job" radio button, and for history retention, choose the number of days after which the history records should be deleted. At the bottom of the window, the name of the alert job is given, and also the schedule. Click OK to return to the Database Properties window (Figure 15-36).

■**Tip** By clicking the Script Configuration button in the Database Properties window (Figure 15-36) you can save the script in a file and use it in other configurations for log shipping with transactional replication.

Click the OK button to see if the configuration is successful or not. If any of the steps in the configuration fails, the process will stop and roll back. The success of the process is shown in Figure 15-43.

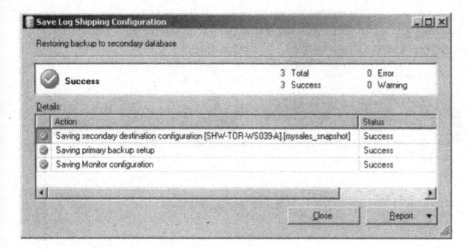

Figure 15-43. *Successfully configuring log shipping*

You can click the Report button and view the report, as shown in Figure 15-44. You should save this report for troubleshooting purposes.

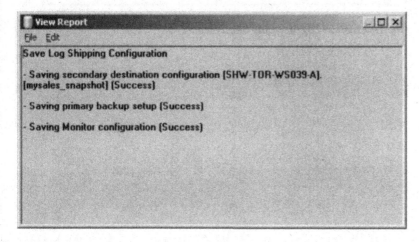

Figure 15-44. *Viewing the configuration report*

You can now check the status of transactional log shipping for the monitor, primary, or the secondary server. Just connect to any one of the servers using SSMS and select the server. On the Summary page, click Reports, and from the drop-down list select Transaction Log Shipping Status, as shown in Figures 15-45 and 15-46. In this example, the primary server is also the monitor server, so the status report for the monitor server lists the name of the primary and the secondary servers, and the report displays the status and the name of the primary server along with the primary database and the status of the backup job. It also displays the secondary server and the secondary database along with the copy and restore status of the most recent log backup.

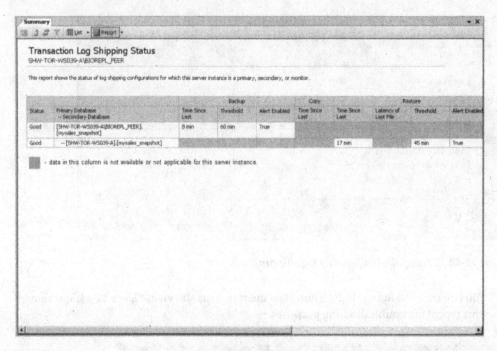

Figure 15-45. *Viewing the Transaction Log Shipping Status report*

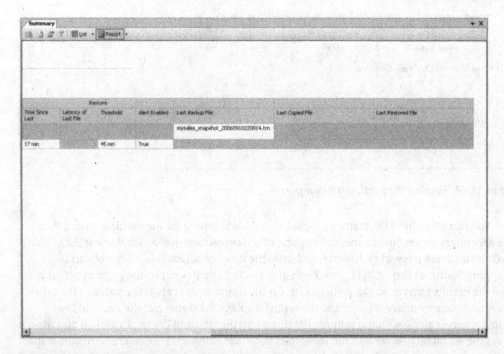

Figure 15-46. *The continuation of the Transaction Log Shipping Status report*

Note You cannot use the SSMS Maintenance Wizard to configure log shipping as in SQL Server 2000.

If the Publisher server fails now, you have to carry out a series of steps to fail over to the secondary server:

1. Restore the last transaction log on the secondary database.

2. Ensure that the replication settings are enabled by setting Keep_Replication on for the Restore Log With statement.

3. Restore the master, msdb, and distribution databases of the primary server onto the secondary server. Before you restore these databases, check to see that the latest replication configuration settings for the publication are there.

4. On the secondary server, rename the computer and the SQL Server instance to match the primary server.

5. On the secondary server, restore the master service key.

Summary

In this chapter, I discussed the various backup and restoration techniques for both snapshot and transactional replication, mainly for the publication database. I also introduced you to the concept of validating the subscriptions for transactional replication. The back up process for different publication models for transactional replication have been exemplified using the SQLCMD utility. Preventing nonconvergence of data was also discussed, using the new table-diff utility tool. I also described how you can restore the publication database in a peer-to-peer replication topology and how to configure log shipping for use with transactional replication.

- Back up the publication database on the Publisher server, the distribution database on the Distributor server (or the Publisher server, if the distribution and the publication databases are both on the same server), and the subscription database on the Subscriber server for both snapshot and transactional replication.

- Back up the master and msdb databases on the Publisher, Distributor, and Subscriber servers.

- Consider backing up the publication database when you make schema changes on any of the publication tables, such as adding a publication or a subscription, adding new articles to an existing publication, dropping a publication or an article, or reinitializing subscriptions.

- The databases should be in Full or Bulk Logged recovery model to back up the transaction log.

- Checksum is the default for the Page Verify property of the Full recovery model.

- Checksum has an impact on the CPU while backing up the database.

- The sys.dm_os_schedulers dynamic management view can be used to track the CPU for the server.

- By validating the subscription database, you can find out whether there are any undelivered commands for the database for transactional replication. You should validate the data at the subscription so that it matches the publication before and also after you backup the publication database.

- The undelivered commands can be viewed using the Replication Monitor.

- The sync with backup option can be enabled either on the publication or distribution database.

- You can find out whether the sync with backup option is enabled or not by using the DATABASEPROPERTYEX function. The IsSynchWithBackup property will return a value of 1 if it is enabled.

- The sp_replicationdboption stored procedure is used to enable the sync with backup option.

- The restoration of the database should enable KEEP_REPLICATION for both snapshot and transactional replication, but not for peer-to-peer replication.

- The sp_replrestart stored procedure ensures that the replicated data in the publication database for transactional replication with standard publication is in sync with the distributed database.

- Executing the DBCC CHECKDB command with the physical_only option checks for both torn page and checksum failures.

- For queued updating subscriptions, delete all the rows from MSreplication_queue table in the distribution database.

- You do not have to delete rows from MSreplication_queue for publication with immediate updating subscriptions.

- The sp_publication_validation stored procedure produces errors for publication with updatable subscriptions. As such, you need to run the tablediff utility to check for any nonconvergence of data.

- Failover for log shipping is not automatic. You have to manually failover from the primary server to the secondary server.

- Log shipping requires a primary server, a secondary server, and an optional monitor server.

In the next chapter, I will discuss the backup and restoration of databases involved in merge replication.

Quick Tips

- A database snapshot is a read-only, static view of the database. It is not related to snapshot replication.

- Checksum and torn page detection are mutually exclusive for the Page Verify property.

- Checksum is the default for the Page Verify property.

- The Restore Verify Only option does not restore the database but checks the checksum of the database and verifies that the backup of the database is complete.

- The restorehistory system table in the msdb database keeps a record of the restoration of all the databases.

CHAPTER 16

■■■

Backup and Recovery of Merge Replication

In Chapter 15, I discussed backing up and restoring databases for both snapshot and transactional replication. In this chapter, I will illustrate backup and restoration for merge replication. I briefly touched upon the different recovery models in Chapter 15, and here I'll assume that you understand the basics of backup and recovery procedures for SQL Server. If you need to brush up on the techniques, the BOL is a good place to start.

On completing this chapter, you will know how to do the following:

- Back up databases for merge replication

- Validate merge replication

- Restore databases for merge replication using no-sync initialization

- Restore subscribing databases

- Use log shipping with merge replication

Publication with Download-Only Articles

As you know, merge replication supports two kinds of publications: download-only and standard articles. Download-only articles are used for subscriptions where no updates are made on the Subscriber. In other words, download-only subscriptions are essentially read only; updates are carried out at the publishing end. In this section, I will discuss the backup and restoration of databases for merge publication with download-only articles.

Note I discussed the configuration of merge publication with download-only articles using the GUI and T-SQL in Chapters 11 and 13, respectively.

As with snapshot and transactional replication, you should consider backing up the following databases for merge replication:

- Publication database on the Publisher server

- Distribution database on the Distributor server (or on the Publisher server if the distribution and publication databases are both on the same server)

- Subscription database on the Subscriber server

- Master and msdb databases on the Publisher, Distributor, and Subscriber servers

Note that the distribution database does not have any significant part to play in merge replication, so it is less critical. You should, however, back up the master and the msdb databases on the Publisher and Subscriber servers at the same time you back up the publication and the subscription databases.

Backing Up the Publication Database

Before you back up the publication database used for merge replication, ensure that the database is set to Full Recovery model so that when you back up the database, the log is also backed up.

■Note The backup and restoration of the databases for snapshot and transactional replication using the GUI and the SQLCMD utility are discussed in Chapter 15.

Also, as mentioned in Chapter 15, the Page Verify property should be set to checksum. You can see this when you select the Recovery property on the Options page of the Database Properties for the database (see Figure 15-1 in Chapter 15).

■Note In Chapters 11 and 13, I discussed the configuration of merge replication. The backup method, as explained in this chapter, can also be used to manually set up subscriptions for merge replication.

For this example, I made a backup of the mysales_merge database, a publication database.

Restoring the Publication Database for Push Subscription

We will assume that the subscription database has become unavailable and restore the database. Then we will need to synchronize the publication with the subscription or reinitialize all the subscription. In this case, we will manually initialize the subscription from the restored database of publication.

First, though, the database needs to be restored properly. Do so, making sure to uncheck the "Preserve the replication settings" check box as shown in Figure 15-34 in Chapter 15. This keeps the publication settings of the published database from being copied to the subscription database.

We now need a snapshot of the publication so that the replication objects and metadata can be copied to the subscription database during the initial synchronization. If you do not have a snapshot of the publication, you need to generate one at this stage.

Caution Ensure that no data changes are made on the publication database between when you back up the publication database and restore it on the subscription database. This will ensure that once the subscription database has been synched with the publication database there are no outstanding commands left to be delivered.

Create a new subscription for merge replication using either the GUI or T-SQL. If you are using the GUI, right-click the publication in the SSMS and select New Subscription from the menu. Follow the wizard until you come to the Initialize Subscriptions page. Uncheck the Initialize box, and the Initialize When setting will be "Do not initialize," as shown in Figure 16-1.

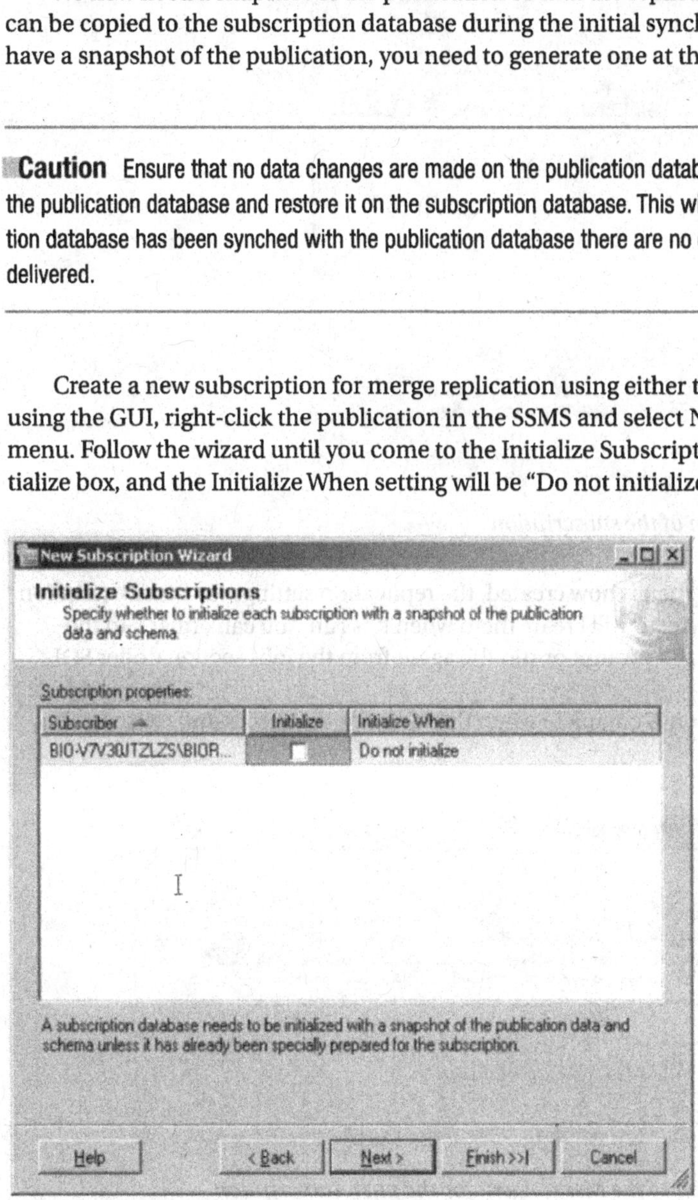

Figure 16-1. *Unchecking the Initialize box*

Once you have completed the wizard, the subscription will be created as shown in Figure 16-2.

Figure 16-2. *Successful creation of the subscription*

Even though the subscription is now created, the replication settings for the subscription are still not there. The Merge Agent will create them when it is run. You can either run the Merge Agent from the command prompt or run the agent from the Jobs section under SQL Server Agent in the SSMS.

The initial synchronization is complete when the Merge Agent successfully executes, as shown in Figure 16-3.

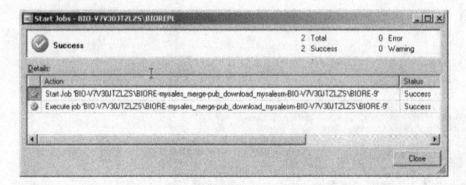

Figure 16-3. *Successful execution of the Merge Agent for the push subscription*

■**Note** I had to reboot the machine in order for the synchronization to take effect.

Before you start sending out new messages from the merge publication to the subscription, you should validate the subscription. You can either check all the subscriptions for the publication, or a specific subscription. Listing 16-1 shows how to execute sp_validatemergesubscription, which validates all the subscriptions for the publication (pub_download_mysalesmerge in this example).

Listing 16-1. *Validating All Subscriptions for a Merge Publication*

```
/*Execute this on the publication database */

:setvar logintimeout 120
:setvar server "BIO-V7V3OJTZLZS\BIOREPL"
:setvar user "sa"
:setvar pwd "sujoy"
:connect $(server) -l $(logintimeout) -U $(user) -P $(pwd)

/*Specification of the level --- rowcount and binary checksum */

:setvar level 3

/*Execute this on the publication database */

use $(db)
go

/*Need the publication name and the level */

sp_validatemergepublication '$(mergepublication)',$(level)
go
```

The script in Listing 16-1 is executed using the SQLCMD utility, as shown in Figure 16-4.

Figure 16-4. *Executing the script in Listing 16-1 using the SQLCMD utility*

■**Note** You can use Listing 16-1 to validate all subscriptions for merge publication with a level of 3.

In Listing 16-1, I used sp_validatemergepublication to validate all the subscriptions that belong to the publication. The value specified for the level denotes whether the procedure validates the subscriptions using rowcount only (level is 1), rowcount and checksum (level is 2), or rowcount and binary checksum (level is 3). The value 2 for level can only be used with earlier versions of SQL Server. For SQL Server 2000 and 2005, this value is set to 3.

You also need to check that the current database is marked for merge publication, or you will get an error message. This can be done by executing the script in Listing 16-2. The category column stores information on the different kinds of replication using bitmaps.

Listing 16-2. *Checking Whether the Database Is Set for Merge Publication*

```
/*Execute this on the publication database */
Use mysales_merge
Go


/*Find the name of the database and the category */
select name,category from sys.sysdatabases
/*category=4 means that it is set for merge publication*/
where category=4
go
```

The sp_validatemergepublication stored procedure sets the schematype column for the sysmergeschemachange table to 66 once the validation is complete for the publication. You can check for this value using the script in Listing 16-3.

Listing 16-3. *Checking the Validation of the Database*

```
/* execute this on the publication database */
Use mysales_merge
Go

select b.name as [publication name], a.schematype,
b.publisher,
b.publisher_db
from sysmergeschemachange a,
sysmergepublications b
where a.pubid=b.pubid and
a.schematype=66
go
```

This script selects the name of the publication, the publisher, and the publication database (publisher_db) from the syspublications table, it selects the schematype from the sysmergeschemachange table, and it joins the two tables with the publication ID (pubid). The output is as follows:

Publication name	schematype
publisher	
publisher_db	
pub_download_mysalesmerge	66
BIO-V7V3OJTZLZS\BIOREPL	
mysales_merge	
pub_download_mysalesmerge	66
BIO-V7V3OJTZLZS\BIOREPL	
mysales_merge	
pub_download_mysalesmerge	66
BIO-V7V3OJTZLZS\BIOREPL	
mysales_merge	
pub_download_mysalesmerge	66
BIO-V7V3OJTZLZS\BIOREPL	
mysales_merge	
pub_download_mysalesmerge	66
BIO-V7V3OJTZLZS\BIOREPL	
mysales_merge	
pub_download_mysalesmerge	66
BIO-V7V3OJTZLZS\BIOREPL	
mysales_merge	
pub_download_mysalesmerge	66
BIO-V7V3OJTZLZS\BIOREPL	
mysales_merge	

VALIDATING INDIVIDUAL SUBSCRIPTIONS

Although, in this section, I validated all the subscriptions for the publication, it is possible to validate individual subscriptions for merge publication. To do that, you can use the sp_validatemergesubscription stored procedure. This procedure is executed on the publication database on the Publisher server. The parameters that need to be included are publication, subscriber, subscriber_db, and level. As with sp_validatemergepublication, ensure that the database is set for merge publication.

Validating the publication database using either the GUI or the stored procedure only reveals whether the validation has been successful or not. The *subscription* is validated after the Merge Agent is run, so you need to run the Merge Agent for each of the subscriptions for that particular publication in order to view the results of the validation.

Restoring the Publication Database for Pull Subscription

Now I will show you how to restore the database for pull subscription. As for push subscription, we could restore the database from the backup and then initialize the subscription with the no-sync option. However, when we restored the database for push subscription, the subscribing database had the same tables as the publication database. In pull subscription, not all the tables are published articles for the subscription. It is therefore incumbent on the developer to remove the unnecessary tables from the subscribing database before the users start receiving the messages.

In this example, the subscribing database for the mysales_merge publication database had only four articles, namely Item, PriceList, Warehouse belonging to the myinventory schema, and SalesPerson belonging to the myorder schema. What I will do in this instance is first export the schema and the data, and then create the subscription with the no-sync initialization.

The first step is to create a database that will be used as the subscribing database for pull subscriptions. The name of the database is mysales_merge_exportpulldownload1. Then, in the SSMS, right-click on the publishing database and select Tasks ➤ Export Data. This will start the SQL Server Import and Export Wizard. Click Next in the welcome page. This will display the Choose a Data Source page shown in Figure 16-5.

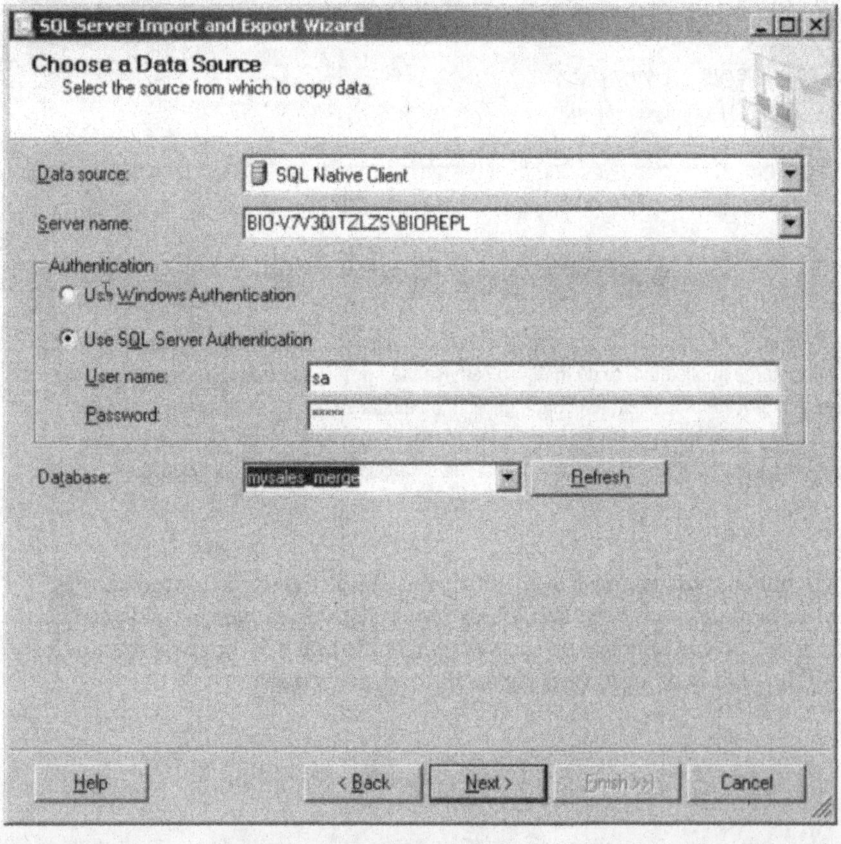

Figure 16-5. *Choosing the data source for the publishing database*

■**Note** In order to export the data as shown in Figure 16-5, you need to have SSIS installed.

From the "Data source" drop-down list, select SQL Native Client. This is a new kind of data access technology introduced in SQL Server 2005, and it combines the features of the SQL OLE DB driver and SQL ODBC driver into one native driver.

■**Note** The SQL Native Client is an application programming interface (API). For more information, see the BOL.

From the Database drop-down list, select the name of the publication database whose schema and data you want to copy. In the Authentication section, set the kind of authentication you want to use to access the database. Click Next to continue.

The next wizard page, shown in Figure 16-6, allows you to choose the export destination. Select the name of the Subscriber server, as shown in the figure. In this case, both the Publisher and the Subscriber servers reside on the same machine. Click the Next button.

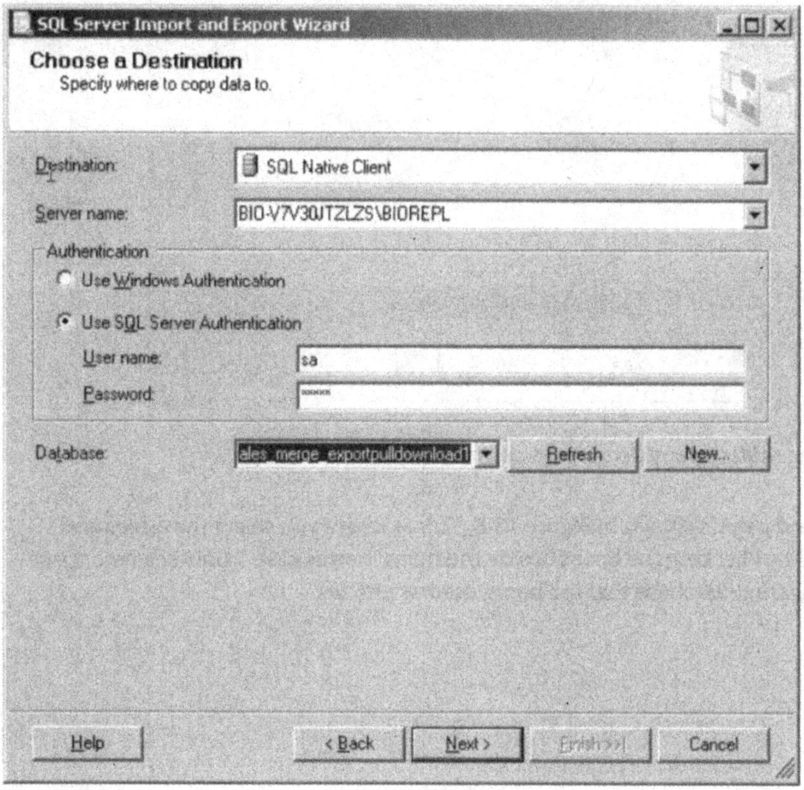

Figure 16-6. *Setting the destination for the subscription database*

Note By clicking on the New button, you can also create a new database at this stage, instead of doing so earlier. If you create the database here, it will automatically be selected in the Database field.

In the next wizard page, select the method that you want to use to copy, as shown in Figure 16-7, and then click Next.

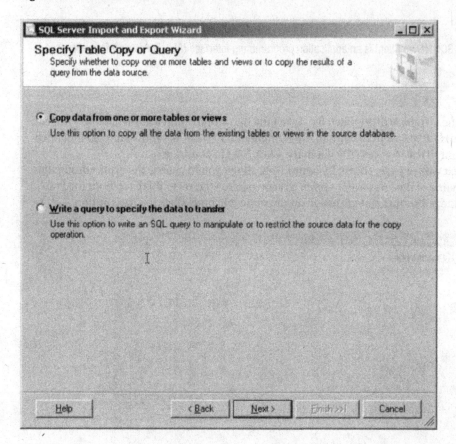

Figure 16-7. *Copying tables from the source to destination database*

The next wizard page is shown in Figure 16-8. This is where you select the tables and views to be copied by checking the boxes beside the items. In this case, I only selected those tables in the publication database that are being used as articles.

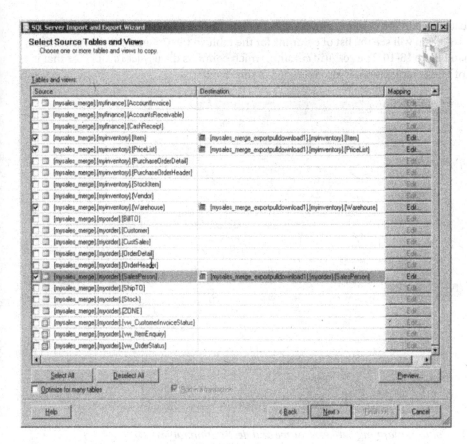

Figure 16-8. *Mapping between source and destination tables*

You can preview the dataset by selecting a table, as shown in Figure 16-8, and clicking the Preview button. Figure 16-9 shows the resulting Preview Data window. Click OK to return to the Select Source Tables and Views window (Figure 16-8).

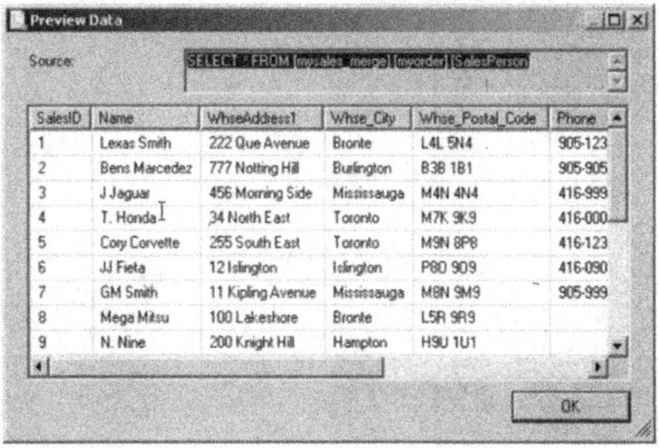

Figure 16-9. *Previewing data for the* SalesPerson *article*

You can also edit the columns. If you click the Edit button in the mapping column shown in Figure 16-8, you will see the list of columns for the table in the Column Mappings window, as shown in Figure 16-10. The rowguid column, which contains the uniqueidentifier that is required of merge replication, is also included in this display.

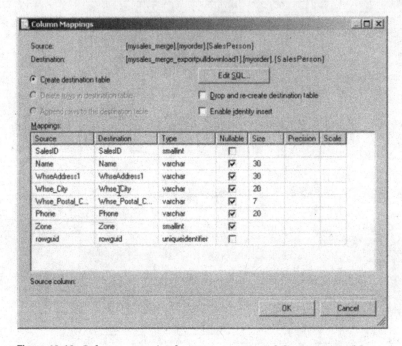

Figure 16-10. *Column mapping between source and destination tables*

Click the Edit SQL button at the top of the window, and you will see that you can edit the SQL statement that creates the destination table, as shown in Figure 16-11.

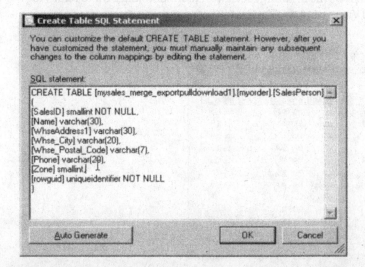

Figure 16-11. *Editing the destination table*

Since we do not need to change the data types or columns, click the Cancel button to return to the Column Mappings window (Figure 16-10), and click Cancel again to return to the Select Source Tables and Views window (Figure 16-8).

In Figure 16-8, notice that there is an "Optimize for many tables" check box near the bottom. This is designed to speed up the transfer. The transfer can also be done in one transaction if you check the "Run in a transaction" check box. (This box is only enabled when you check the "Optimize for many tables" check box.)

Click the Next button to continue to the Save and Execute Package page of the wizard, shown in Figure 16-12. You can execute the package immediately or save it for executing later. As you can see, I chose both so that in the event that I need it again, I only need to execute the package. The package is saved in the file system. Click the Next button to continue.

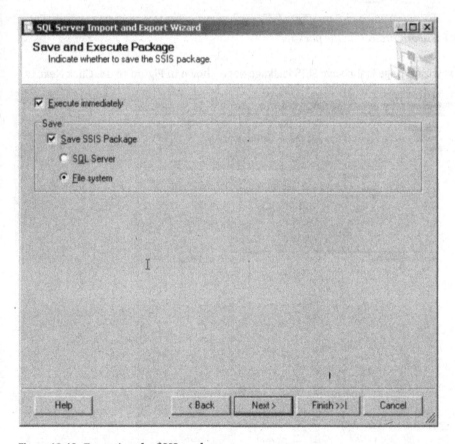

Figure 16-12. *Executing the SSIS package*

■**Tip** You can import a package saved in the file system into the SQL Server system.

You can password protect the package if you wish, as shown in Figure 16-13. Click the OK button.

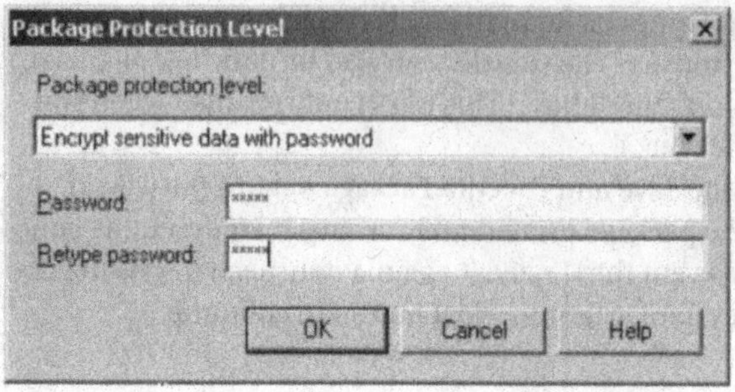

Figure 16-13. *Password protecting the package*

The next wizard page is the Save SSIS Package page, shown in Figure 16-14. Click Next.

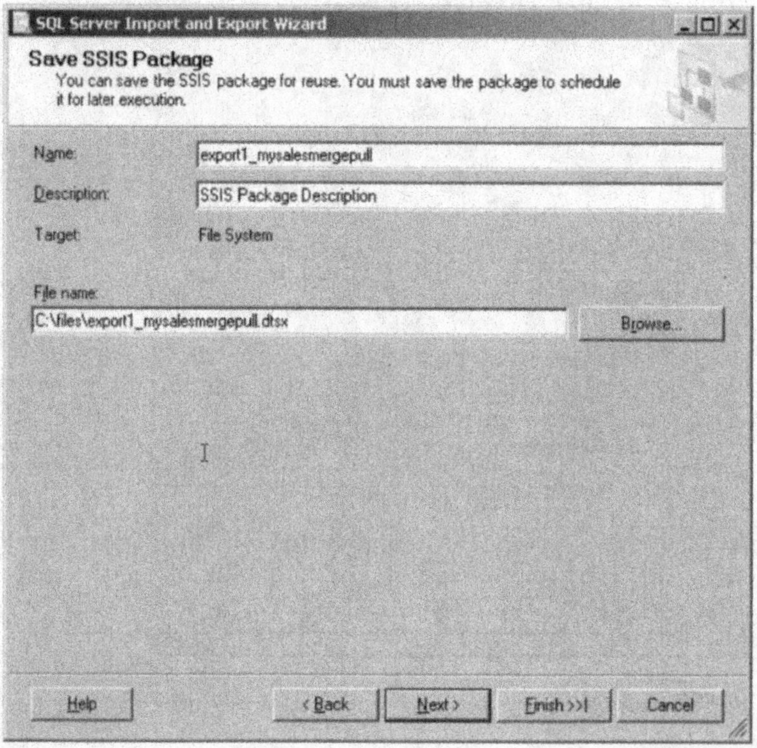

Figure 16-14. *Saving the package as a file*

The Complete the Wizard page shown in Figure 16-15 summarizes the export settings. Review the choices and click the Finish button.

Next, you will see the whether the export was a success or a failure, as shown in Figure 16-16.

Figure 16-15. *Reviewing the export choices*

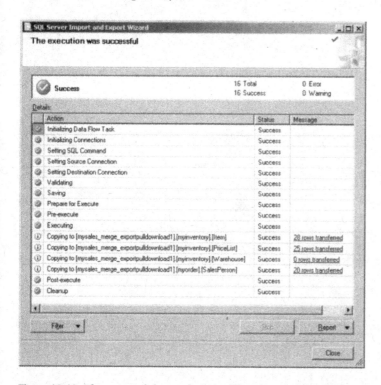

Figure 16-16. *The successful completion of the export of the publication tables to the subscription tables*

This is one way of ensuring that the correct number of rows for each of the tables have been transferred from the source to the destination database. For example, the Warehouse table has no rows transferred in Figure 16-16, so I went back to the source database to see whether there any rows for that table, and I found there were none. The transfer has been successful. Click the Close button.

VIEWING THE SSIS PACKAGE

In Figure 16-14, I saved the package as a file. In that figure, you can see that it is also possible to save it in SQL Server. The package, in that case, gets stored in the msdb database.

To get a better preview of the package, you can also view it using Integration Services. Open Integration Services, select File ➤ Open/File, and load the file specified in Figure 16-14. As shown next, you can click on the Control Flow tab, and you will see the flow of the package:

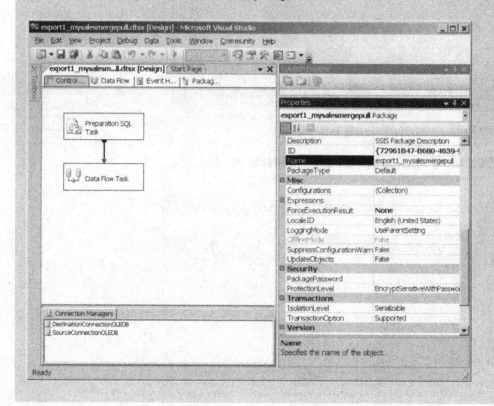

In the preceding image, you can see the properties of the package listed at the right; and in the middle, notice that the control flow consists of the Preparation SQL Task, a Precedent Constraint (indicated by the green arrow), and the Data Flow Task.

Double-click on the Preparation SQL Task to open the Execute SQL Task Editor window, shown here:

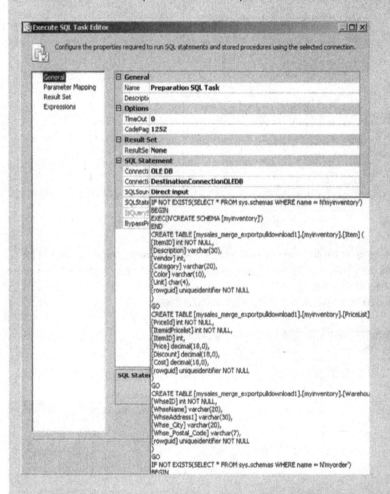

Select the General page in the left pane. Then move the mouse beside the SQLStatement property, and you will see the script that creates the tables on the destination database, mysales_merge_exportpulldown-load1. Click the Cancel button to get back to the Integration Services window.

The green arrow is an indicator of the workflow process. The next step, Data Flow Task, will be executed depending on the condition set in this stage. Double-click on the green arrow to view the Precedence Constraint Editor window:

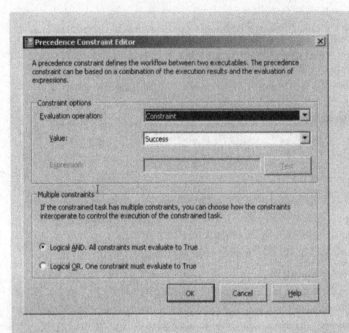

You can see that the value for the precedence constraint is Success; the green arrow is indicative of the value specified here. If we were to set it to Failure, the color would have been red. Click the Cancel button to return to the Integration Services window.

Double-click on the Data Flow Task, and you will see the following display:

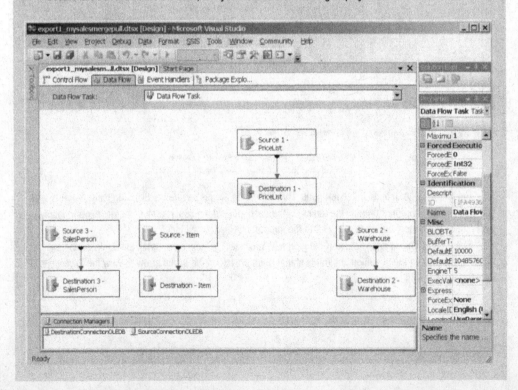

You can see the four source tables and the corresponding destination tables. If you double-click on any of the green arrows and select Metadata, you will be able to see the column names and corresponding data types, as shown here:

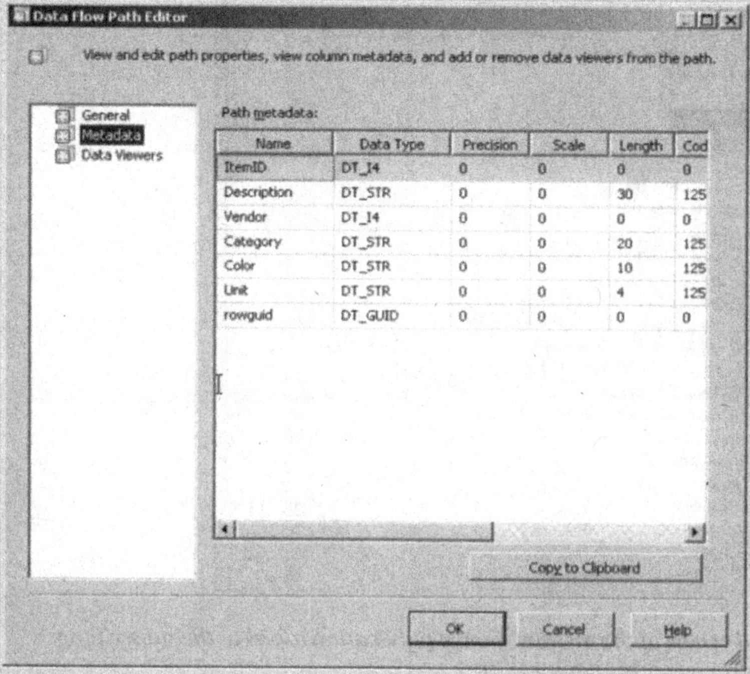

If you now open the SSMS and open the tree hierarchy for the database we just exported the schema and the data to, you will find that there are no system tables for merge replication. You can see this in Figure 16-17.

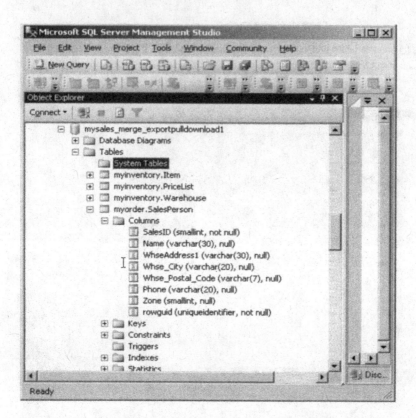

Figure 16-17. *Successful export of the mysales_merge publication tables to the subscribing database, mysales_merge_exportpulldownload1*

■**Tip** Before proceeding to the next step, ensure that you have the snapshot for the publication.

The next step is to create a subscription with the no-sync initialization, as we did earlier for the push subscription. Follow the New Subscription Wizard and, as in Figure 16-1, uncheck the Initialize box. The subscription type is Client, as shown in Figure 16-18.

The successful creation of the pull subscription should look like Figure 16-2. You can now view the system tables generated for merge replication, as shown in Figure 16-19.

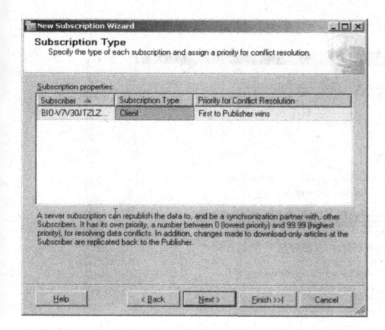

Figure 16-18. *Selecting the client subscription type for the pull subscription*

Figure 16-19. *Viewing the merge replication system tables generated by the no-sync initialization of pull subscription*

The newly created pull subscription is shown in Figure 16-20.

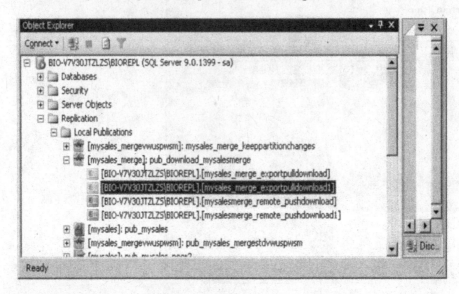

Figure 16-20. *The newly created pull subscription*

Let's now look at the script that generates the pull subscription with no-sync initialization. You will find that in order to initialize the pull subscription with T-SQL after the restoration of the database, the script employs the following steps:

1. Add the merge subscription on the publication database on the Publisher server using sp_addmergesubscription. The @sync_type parameter should be set to none.

2. Add the publication for the subscription on the subscription database on the Subscriber server using sp_addmergepullsubscription and setting @sync_type to none.

3. Add a new agent job to schedule the synchronization of the pull subscription using the sp_mergepullsubscriptionagent on the Subscriber server.

4. Run the Merge Agent for the subscription.

The script generated for steps 1–3 follows.

```
----------------BEGIN: Script to be run at Publisher
'BIO-V7V30JTZLZS\BIOREPL'---------------
--Step1
use [mysales_merge]
exec sp_addmergesubscription @publication = 'pub_download_mysalesmerge',
@subscriber = 'BIO-V7V30JTZLZS\BIOREPL',
@subscriber_db = 'mysales_merge_exportpulldownload',
@subscription_type = 'pull', @subscriber_type = 'local',
@subscription_priority = 0,
```

```
@sync_type = 'None'
GO
----------------END: Script to be run at Publisher
'BIO-V7V30JTZLZS\BIOREPL'----------------

----------------BEGIN: Script to be run at Subscriber
'BIO-V7V30JTZLZS\BIOREPL'
----------------Step 2
use [mysales_merge_exportpulldownload]
exec sp_addmergepullsubscription @publisher =
'BIO-V7V30JTZLZS\BIOREPL',
@publication = 'pub_download_mysalesmerge',
@publisher_db = 'mysales_merge',
@subscriber_type = 'Local',
@subscription_priority = 0, @description = '',
@sync_type = 'None'

--Step3
exec sp_addmergepullsubscription_agent @publisher =
'BIO-V7V30JTZLZS\BIOREPL', @publisher_db = 'mysales_merge',
@publication = 'pub_download_mysalesmerge',
@distributor = 'BIO-V7V30JTZLZS\BIOREPL',
@distributor_security_mode = 1,
@distributor_login = '',
@distributor_password = null,
@enabled_for_syncmgr = 'False',
@frequency_type = 64, @frequency_interval = 0, @frequency_relative_interval = 0,
 @frequency_recurrence_factor = 0, @frequency_subday = 0,
 @frequency_subday_interval = 0, @active_start_time_of_day = 0,
@active_end_time_of_day = 235959, @active_start_date = 20060510,
@active_end_date = 99991231, @alt_snapshot_folder = '',
@working_directory = '', @use_ftp = 'False', @job_login = null,
@job_password = null, @publisher_security_mode = 1,
@publisher_login = null, @publisher_password = null,
@use_interactive_resolver = 'False', @dynamic_snapshot_location = null,
@use_web_sync = 0
GO
----------------END: Script to be run at Subscriber
'BIO-V7V30JTZLZS\BIOREPL'----------------
```

In the preceding script, the publication is first notified of the merge subscription using the sp_addmergesubscription stored procedure. The parameters that are used are the name of the Subscriber server and the subscription database. Setting the @sync_type parameter to none is particularly important. If you look at the earlier configuration of the pull subscription for merge publication in Chapter 13, you will notice that @sync_type was set to Automatic.

Note Chapter 13 discusses the configuration of merge replication using T-SQL.

Since, this script uses the `local` subscriber type, the priority of the subscription has been set to 0. Also, note that the `@use_interactive_resolver` parameter is set to `False`.

The next step involves setting up the pull subscription for the merge publication. Using `sp_addmergepullsubscription`, the engine specifies the name of the publication, the Publisher server, and the publication database, and it sets the `@sync_type` parameter to none. The `sp_addmergepullsubscriptionagent` stored procedure is used to set the synchronization for the Merge Agent and, as such, the parameters for the names of the Publisher, Distributor, and Subscriber servers are included.

The final step in the process is to run the Merge Agent for the initial synchronization so that the objects and the metadata are copied to the subscriptions. You can run the Merge Agent from the command prompt as shown in Listing 16-4.

Listing 16-4. *Executing the Merge Agent*

```
/* Can be used as a batch file */
/*Step 1: Declare the variables first */

declare @cmd varchar(4000),
@publisher varchar(100),
@publicationDB varchar(100),
@publication varchar(100),
@subscriptionDB varchar(100),
@login varchar(3),
@password varchar(6)

/*Step 2: Assign values to the variables */

set @publisher='BIO-V7V30JTZLZS\BIOREPL'
set @publicationDB='mysales_merge'
set @publication='pub_download_mysalesmerge'
set @subscriptionDB=''mysalesmerge_remote_exportpulldownload1'
set @login='xxxx'
set @password='xxxx'

/Step 3: Assign the parameters to the Merge Agent and
store them in the @cmd variable */
/* The following command should be all on one line. It is displayed on multiple
lines here because of the limitations of the page. */

set @cmd='"C:\Program Files\Microsoft SQL Server\90\COM\REPLMERG.EXE"
-Publication @publication
-Publisher @publisher
-Subscriber  @publisher
```

```
-Distributor @publisher
-PublisherDB @publicationDB
-SubscriberDB @subscriptionDB
-PublisherSecurityMode 0
-PublisherLogin @login
-PublisherPassword @password
-OutputVerboseLevel 2
-SubscriberSecurityMode 0
-SubscriberLogin @login
-SubscriberPassword @password
-SubscriptionType 1
-DistributorSecurityMode 0
-DistributorLogin @login
-DistributorPassword @password
-Validate 3
-ParallelUploadDownload 0'

/*execute the @cmd variable with the xp_cmdshell*/
exec xp_cmdshell '@cmd'
go
```

This script first declares the variables (in step 1) so that values can be assigned to them (in step 2). In step 3, parameters and their values are assigned for the Merge Agent. The security modes for the Publisher, Distributor, and Subscriber servers have been set to use SQL Server Authentication (PublisherSecurityMode, DistributorSecurityMode, and SubscriberSecurityMode are set to 0). As such, you need to specify the logins and passwords for connecting to the servers. In this example, all of them reside on the same machine, so they all have the same login and password.

Note the Validate parameter. While discussing the restoration of the subscription database using push subscription, I mentioned that all subscriptions can be validated for a particular publication by executing the sp_validatemergepublication stored procedure. In this case, by specifying the Validate parameter, the script essentially asks the Merge Agent to validate the subscription. There are four possible values for the Validate parameter, and they are listed in Table 16-1.

Table 16-1. *Values for the Validate Parameter*

Values	Description
0	No validation.
1	Row-count validation only.
2	Row-count validation with checksum. This is valid only for SQL Server 7.0 Subscribers; for SQL Server 2005 and SQL Server 2000 Subscribers, the parameter is automatically set to 3.
3	Row-count with binary checksum validation.

Synchronizing Subscriptions with No-Sync Initialization Using T-SQL and SQLCMD

Now that I have shown you how to restore the databases for push and pull subscriptions using no-sync initialization, I will show you how to incorporate the T-SQL commands in the SQL-CMD utility for more flexibility. This way we can use a script to synchronize subscriptions with no-sync initialization for merge publication.

I will use a push subscription to exemplify the process. Listing 16-5 shows the process.

Listing 16-5. *Adding a Merge Subscription for Use with SQLCMD*

```
:setvar logintimeout 120
:setvar server "BIO-V7V30JTZLZS\BIOREPL"
:setvar user "sa"
:setvar pwd "sujoy"
:connect $(server) -l $(logintimeout) -U $(user) -P $(pwd)
/* Execute this on the Publisher server */

use $(pubdb)
go
exec sp_addmergesubscription @publication ='$(pubname)',
@subscriber='$(server)',
@subscriber_db='$(subdb)',
@subscription_type ='$(subtype)',
@sync_type ='$(synctype)',
@subscriber_type ='$(subscribertype)',
@subscription_priority=0,
@description = null,
@use_interactive_resolver='$(boolean)'
Go
```

The values for the parameters are marked as SQLCMD variables. In this case, the $synctype variable can either be none, as in the no-sync initialization, or Automatic, as was done in Chapter 13 while setting up the merge subscription. Although this is used to mark the subscription for the publication, you can also use it when configuring a pull subscription.

Save this listing as a file. Using the SQLCMD utility, you can use this file to set up a push or pull subscription.

The next step is to configure the push subscription agent that is executed on the publishing database. This is shown in Listing 16-6.

Listing 16-6. *Adding the Job for the Push Merge Subscription Agent*

```
/*Execute this on the publication database */
sp_addmergepushsubscription_agent @publication='$(pubname)',
@subscriber = '$(server)', @subscriber_db ='$(subdb)',
@subscriber_security_mode = 0,
@subscriber_login = '$(user)', @subscriber_password =
```

```
'$(pwd)', @publisher_security_mode = 1,
@enabled_for_syncmgr = '$(boolean)'
go
```

Note that when the @subscriber_security_mode parameter is set to 0, meaning that SQL
Server authentication is used, you have to specify the login and password for the connection.
The @publisher_security_mode parameter is set to use Windows Authentication (its value is 1).

Save this script as a file. I saved it as addmergepushsub.sql.

In the SQLCMD utility the :r variable can be used to call one or more files from within a
file. (If you call several files, they should be separated by commas.) The script in Listing 16-7
will use this variable to call the file for Listing 16-6 from Listing 16-5. First, though, we need to
check whether the file exists. The whole process is shown in Listing 16-7.

Listing 16-7. *Calling One File from Within Another File*

```
:setvar logintimeout 120
:setvar server "BIO-V7V3OJTZLZS\BIOREPL"
:setvar user "sa"
:setvar pwd "sujoy"
:connect $(server) -l $(logintimeout) -U $(user) -P $(pwd)

/* Execute this on the publisher server */

use $(pubdb)
go
exec sp_addmergesubscription @publication ='$(pubname)',
@subscriber='$(server)',
@subscriber_db='$(subdb)',
@subscription_type ='$(subtype)',
@sync_type ='$(synctype)',
@subscriber_type ='$(subscribertype)',
@subscription_priority=0,
@description = null,
@use_interactive_resolver='$(boolean)'
Go

WAITFOR DELAY '00:00:05'

declare @filelist table
( fileexist int,
filedir int,
parentdir int
)

insert @filelist
exec master..xp_fileexist 'C:\files\addmergepushsub.sql'
end
```

```
declare @fileexist int
set @fileexist=(select fileexist from @filelist)
if @fileexist=1
begin
:r C:\files\addmergepushsub.sql
end
else
:Exit
Go
```

As you can see, before the script calls the file using the :r variable, it checks whether the file exists. This is done by executing the code shown in Figure 16-21. The output is shown in the bottom half of the pane in Figure 16-21.

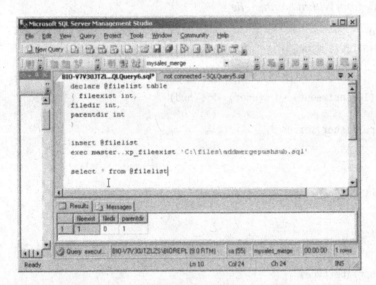

Figure 16-21. *Verifying the existence of a file*

The script uses the table variable to store the information retrieved by executing the xp_fileexist stored procedure. If the file exists, the fileexist column will return a value of 1.

In Listing 16-7, the file is called if the return value is 1; otherwise, the SQLCMD utility will exit, as specified by the :Exit variable.

Backing Up and Restoring Subscription Databases

In the previous section, I discussed the restoration of publication databases for download-only articles and the situation where the subscription database becomes unavailable and how to recover from the backup of a publication database. In this section, I will talk about the restoration of subscription databases from backups of those databases.

Before backing up the subscription database, you should synchronize it with the publication database. You should synchronize it again after the database is restored to ensure that the subscribing database is up to date with the changes in the Publisher server.

However, prior to restoring the subscription database from the backup, you should check the retention period of the publication. This can be done by executing the following stored procedure:

```
sp_helpmergepublication 'pub_download_mysalesmerge'
```

In this command, pub_download_mysalesmerge is the name of the publication. This will tell you about the retention period of the publication.

Tip You can also view the retention period of the publication by retrieving the retention column of the sysmergepublications table from the publication database.

In this example, the retention period is 14 days, which means that after 14 days, the metadata for the subscription will be removed and the subscription will be deactivated. After that, you have to reinitialize the subscription. Subscriptions that are not reinitialized will be dropped by the Expired subscription clean up job.

The Expired subscription clean up job is used for maintenance purposes, as was mentioned in Chapter 2. Open the SSMS, and you can see the job under the Jobs section. Right-click on it and select Steps from the menu. Select the Run Agent step and click the Edit button. You will see the Job Step Properties window shown in Figure 16-22.

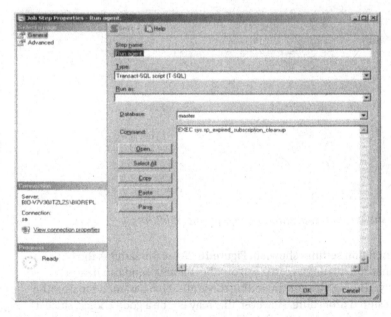

Figure 16-22. *Viewing the name of the stored procedure used in the execution of the Expired subscription cleanup job*

The stored procedure that is used to execute the Expired subscription clean up job is sp_expired_subscription_cleanup, and it is run from the context of the master database.

You need to enable this job in order for it to work. Otherwise the subscriptions will not be dropped even after the retention period has expired, and you will have to manually drop or reinitialize the subscription.

If you look at the schedule properties, you will see that this job runs daily on the Publisher server. However, you can reinitialize subscriptions within 27 days, since the stored procedure retains the metadata for double the retention period, which in this case would be 28 days. After that time, it will clean up the metadata for push subscriptions.

For pull subscriptions, however, you have to manually clean up the metadata. You can see the retention settings on the General page of the Publication Properties window, as shown in Figure 16-23.

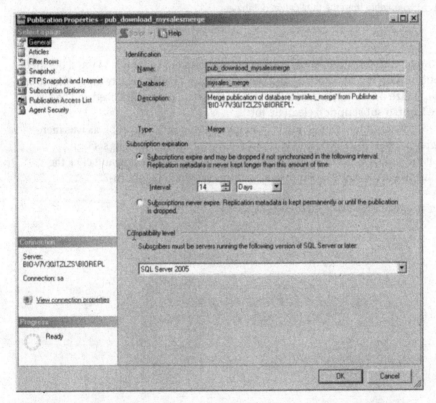

Figure 16-23. *Viewing the subscription expiration settings for the publication*

The subscription expiration settings shown in Figure 16-23 are the same as the retention period. Note that you do not have to clean out the metadata and can instead hold on to it permanently. This can be done by setting the @retention parameter to 0 for the sp_addmergepublication stored procedure. However, this may not be a good choice, since it will impede the performance of merge replication.

■**Note** The optimization of merge replication is discussed in Chapter 19.

The retention period has a grace period of 24 hours to accommodate different time zones. Also, if you have a republishing topology, ensure that the retention period for the republishing server is less than or equal to that of the master publishing server. Otherwise, it might lead to nonconvergence.

Finally, while you can change the retention period using the sp_changemergepublication stored procedure, you should reinitialize all the subscriptions for the publication in order to avoid any possible nonconvergence.

Note The distribution database is not important in merge replication. It mainly stores the errors, the history, and the records of the Merge Agent. If you need to back it up, you should do so when you back up the publication database.

You now know how to restore both the publication and the subscription databases for merge replication. It's time to look at validation.

Validating Subscriptions for Merge Replication

Before setting up validation, you need to enable the replication alerts for when the Subscriber server fails data validation and also for when the Subscriber server passes data validation. These alerts, as with transactional replication, generate error messages 20574 and 20575, respectively.

The replication alerts can be enabled using the SSMS, as shown in the previous chapter, they can also be configured using the sp_add_alert stored procedure, which is what I will do in this case. This is shown in Listing 16-8.

Listing 16-8. *Enabling the Replication Alerts and Sending Out the Notifications*

```
/*Execute this on the msdb database */
Use msdb
Go

/*Create a table variable to store the information from sp_help_alert */
declare @alertlist table
( id int,
name sysname,
event_source varchar(100),
event_category_id int,
event_id int,
message_id int,
severity int,
enabled tinyint,
delay_between_responses int,
last_occurrence_date int,
last_occurrence_time int,
```

```
        last_response_date int,
        last_response_time int,
        notification_message varchar(512),
        include_event_description tinyint,
        database_name sysname null,
        event_description_keyword varchar(100),
        occurrence_count int,
        count_reset_date int,
        count_reset_time int,
        job_id uniqueidentifier,
        job_name sysname null,
        has_notification int,
        flags int,
        performance_condition varchar(512),
        category_name sysname null,
        wmi_namespace sysname null,
        wmi_query varchar(512),
        type int
        )
        insert @alertlist exec
        sp_help_alert

        /*Declare a variable for the cursor */
        declare @alertname sysname

        /*Declare the cursor name updatealertnotification */

        declare updatealertnotification cursor for

        /* Do not want to enable any other replication alerts other than the ones that
        will be used for validation */

        /* There is a space between Replication: and S below. If you omit it,
        the engine will not return the right result set. */

        select name from @alertlist
        where enabled=0 and name like 'Replication: S%'

        /*Open the cursor */

        open updatealertnotification

        /*Fetch the first result and store it in the variable */

        fetch next from updatealertnotification
        into @alertname
```

```
/*Check to see if there are any rows to fetch */

while @@fetch_status=0
begin

/*Use sp_update_alert to enable the alerts used for validation
for the database 'mysales_merge' */

exec sp_update_alert @name=@alertname,@database_name='mysales_merge',@enabled=1,
@include_event_description_in=4;

/* The alerts are then notified using the sp_update_notification*/

exec sp_update_notification @alert_name=@alertname,
@operator_name='BIO-V7V30JTZLZS\Sujoy Paul',@notification_method=4

/* Then fetch the next record */

fetch next from updatealertnotification
into @alertname
end

/*Close and deallocate the cursor */

close updatealertnotification
deallocate updatealertnotification

/*Finally check whether the alerts have been enabled*/

select * from @alertlist
go
```

This script first declares a table variable that stores information retrieved from the execution of the sp_help_alert stored procedure. This stored procedure retrieves all the information about alerts that are defined in the server, and you can use a cursor to find only those alerts that are disabled, since not all replication alerts are used for validating subscriptions.

The sp_update_alert stored procedure is used to enable the replication alerts for the mysales_merge database. The @include_event_description_in parameter is set to 4, which specifies that it will send the SQL Server error to the Windows Event log and also to the operator using the net send command.

The alerts are then notified using the sp_update_notification stored procedure.

The script in Listing 16-8 is executed on the msdb database. The output is wide, so it is shown in two parts, in Figures 16-24 and 16-25.

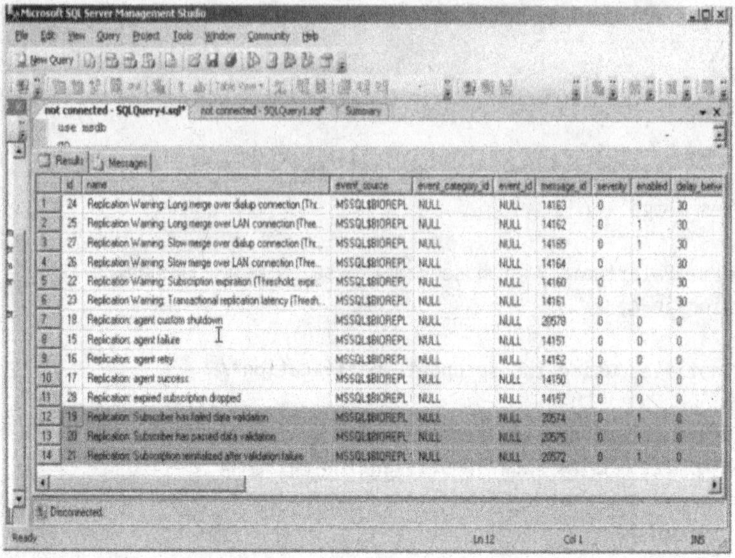

Figure 16-24. *The first part of the output from Listing 16-8, showing the enabling of replication alerts for validating subscriptions*

■**Note** The message_id column corresponds to the error numbers for the alerts. The error numbers 20,574 and 20,575 correspond to failed data validation and passed data validation, respectively.

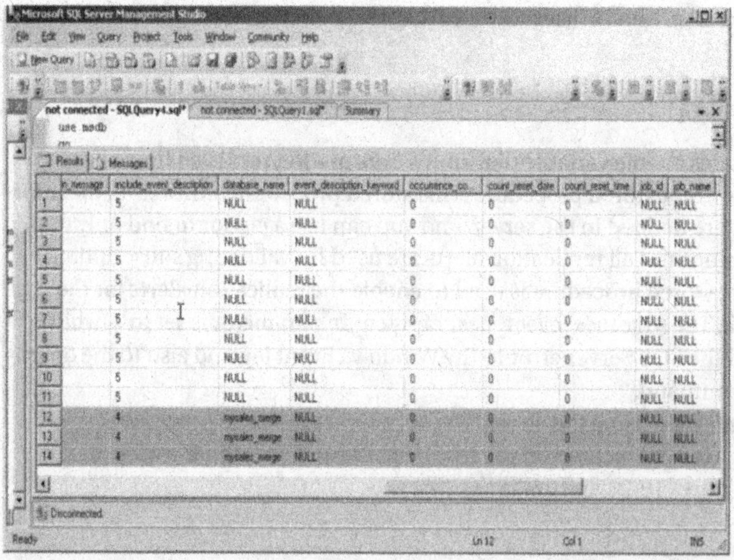

Figure 16-25. *The second part of the output from Listing 16-8, showing the enabling of replication alerts with the* database_name *column showing the name of the database, mysales_merge, for validating subscriptions*

Now that the alerts are enabled for replication, we can use the SSMS to validate the subscription for the pub_download_mysalesmerge merge publication with download-only articles. In the SSMS, open the publication, right-click on the subscription, and select Validate Subscription. (Alternatively, you can right-click on the publication and select Validate All Subscriptions.) This will open the Validate Subscription window shown in Figure 16-26.

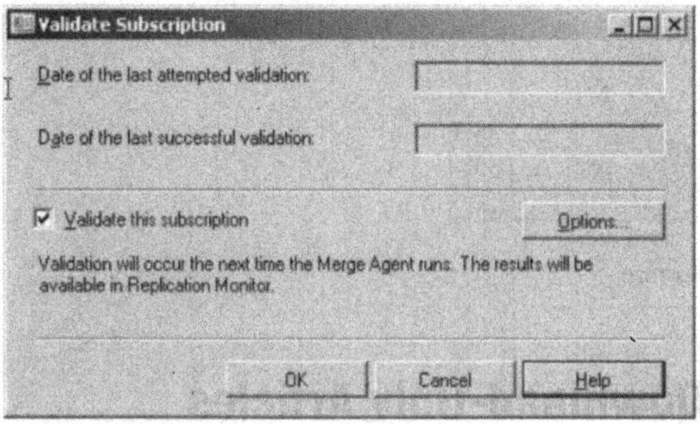

Figure 16-26. *Validating a single subscription*

Check the "Validate this subscription" box and then click the Options button. This will display the Subscription Validation Options window shown in Figure 16-27. You can see that the subscription validation option is set to "Verify the row counts only". Click the OK button to return to the Validate Subscription window (Figure 16-26). Click the OK button again to dismiss the Validate Subscription window. The validation will be performed the next time the Merge Agent is executed.

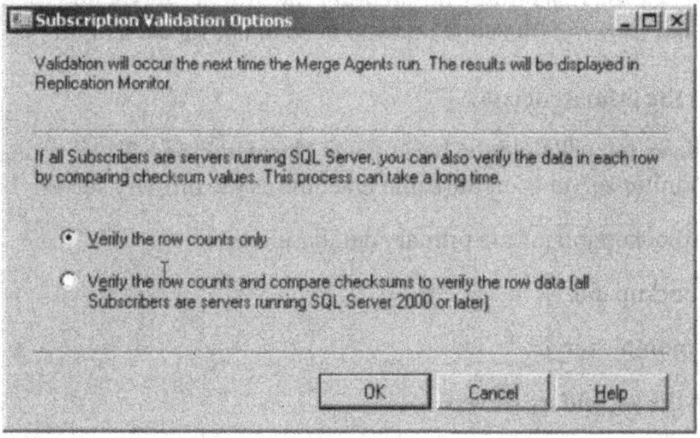

Figure 16-27. *Viewing the validation options for the subscription*

In the SSMS, under the Local Subscriptions object, right-click on the subscription for the pub_dowload_mysalesmerge publication and select View Synchronization Status. Start the Merge Agent if it is not running. You will be able to see any messages regarding validation. In my case, there were no messages, as shown in Figure 16-28.

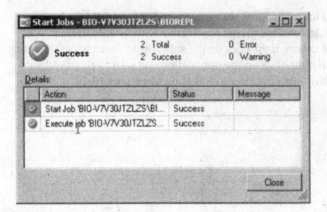

Figure 16-28. *Success of the synchronization*

Log Shipping with Download-Only Articles

In Chapter 15, I discussed how to set up log shipping for publication with transactional replication using the GUI (see the "Log Shipping with Transactional Replication" section). In this section, I will show you how to set up log shipping for merge publication with download-only articles using the SQLCMD utility and T-SQL.

As with log shipping for transactional replication, ensure that you have a backup copy of the primary database and that you have initialized the secondary database by restoring it with the primary database. Also, check to see that you have a UNC share, so that the log backups are available to the secondary server before you set up log shipping for merge replication.

The steps that you need to take to set up log shipping are pretty much the same in both the primary and secondary servers. I will first outline the steps for the primary server and then for the secondary server. I will then show you the code that you need to use for each of the configuration steps.

These are the steps taken in the primary server:

1. Set up the primary database that will hold the backup job. This database will also monitor log shipping if the monitor server is on the same machine as the primary server.

2. Create a schedule for the backup job for the primary database.

3. Set the schedule for the backup job.

4. Add the alert job for the monitor server.

These are the steps taken in the secondary server:

1. Set up the information on the primary server and the corresponding primary database on the secondary server.

2. Set up a schedule for the copy and restore jobs.

3. Add the secondary database on the secondary server.

Finally, we need to add the information of the secondary database on the primary server.

Configuring Log Shipping on the Primary Server

The configuration of the primary server is shown in Listing 16-9.

Listing 16-9. *Configuring Log Shipping on the Primary Server*

```
/* Run this script on the Primary server
The monitor server is also located on the Primary server */

:setvar logintimeout 120
:setvar server "BIO-V7V30JTZLZS\BIOREPL"
---:setvar user "sa"
---:setvar password "sujoy"
:connect $(server) -l $(logintimeout)
--- -U $(user) -P $(password)

/*Execute this from msdb database */

use msdb
go

DECLARE @LS_BackupJobId     AS uniqueidentifier
DECLARE @LS_PrimaryId       AS uniqueidentifier
DECLARE @SP_Add_RetCode     As int


EXEC @SP_Add_RetCode = master.dbo.sp_add_log_shipping_primary_database
    @database ='$(primarydb)                    -----'mysales_snapshot'
    ,@backup_directory ='$(backupfilepath)'     -----'D:\files'
    ,@backup_share ='$(sharename)'              -----
'\\SHW-TOR-WS039-A\BIOREPL_PEER'
    ,@backup_job_name ='$(backupjobname)'       -----'LSBackup_mysales_snapshot'
    ,@backup_retention_period = 4320
            ,
/* change the variable name if the monitor server is located
other than the primary server */

@monitor_server ='$(server)'        -----'SHW-TOR-WS039-A\BIOREPL_PEER'
    ,@monitor_server_security_mode = $(securitymode)
    ,@backup_threshold = 60
    ,@threshold_alert_enabled = 1
    ,@history_retention_period = 5760
    ,@backup_job_id = @LS_BackupJobId OUTPUT
    ,@primary_id = @LS_PrimaryId OUTPUT
    ,@overwrite = 1

IF (@@ERROR = 0 AND @SP_Add_RetCode = 0)
BEGIN
```

```
DECLARE @LS_BackUpScheduleUID    As uniqueidentifier
DECLARE @LS_BackUpScheduleID     AS int


EXEC msdb.dbo.sp_add_schedule
    @schedule_name ='($schedulename)'
  ---'LSBackupSchedule_SHW-TOR-WS039-A\BIOREPL_PEER1'
    ,@enabled = $(enabled)
    ,@freq_type = 4
    ,@freq_interval = 1
    ,@freq_subday_type = 4
    ,@freq_subday_interval = 15
    ,@freq_recurrence_factor = 0
    ,@active_start_date = 20060910
    ,@active_end_date = 99991231
    ,@active_start_time = 0
    ,@active_end_time = 235900
    ,@schedule_uid = @LS_BackUpScheduleUID OUTPUT
    ,@schedule_id = @LS_BackUpScheduleID OUTPUT

EXEC msdb.dbo.sp_attach_schedule
    @job_id = @LS_BackupJobId
    ,@schedule_id = @LS_BackUpScheduleID

/* EXEC msdb.dbo.sp_update_job
    @job_id = @LS_BackupJobId
    ,@enabled = 0 */
```

In this script, the SQLCMD utility variables are first declared and set to connect to the primary server.

Once the connection is established to the msdb, the sp_add_log_shipping_primary_ database stored procedure is executed to add the primary database to the primary server. This stored procedure first generates a primary ID and makes an entry in the primary database column of the log_shipping_primary_databases system table in the msdb database based on the parameters provided. It also creates a job ID for the backup job that is also added to the log_shipping_primary_databases system table. Since the parameter for the monitor server is used, the stored procedure will make an entry for the local monitor in the log_shipping_ monitor_primary system table. The SQLCMD utility variables that are passed are database, backup_share, backup_directory, backup_job_name, monitor_server, and monitor_security_ mode. The value for the monitor_security_mode parameter can be either 1 (Windows authentication) or 0 (SQL Server authentication).

The script then creates a schedule for the backup job in the primary server using the sp_add_schedule stored procedure. The SQLCMD variables that are passed are the name of the schedule for the job (schedule_name) and whether the job is enabled or not (enabled). The default value for enabled is 1, while a value of 0 means the job is disabled.

The script then attaches the schedule to the job.

Configuring Log Shipping on the Secondary Server

Having set up the configuration on the primary server, the next step is to set up the configuration on the secondary server. This is shown in Listing 16-10.

Listing 16-10. *Configuring Log Shipping on the Secondary Server*

```
/* Run this script on the Secondary server
The monitor server is also located on the Primary server */
:setvar logintimeout 120
:setvar server "BIO-V7V30JTZLZS\BIOREPL_PEER"
---:setvar user "sa"
---:setvar password "sujoy"
:connect $(server) -l $(logintimeout)
--- -U $(user) -P $(password)


use msdb
go


DECLARE @LS_Secondary__CopyJobId     AS uniqueidentifier
DECLARE @LS_Secondary__RestoreJobId    AS uniqueidentifier
DECLARE @LS_Secondary__SecondaryId    AS uniqueidentifier
DECLARE @LS_Add_RetCode     As int


EXEC @LS_Add_RetCode = master.dbo.sp_add_log_shipping_secondary_primary
    @primary_server = '$(primaryserver)    ---'SHW-TOR-WS039-A\BIOREPL_PEER'
    ,@primary_database = '$(primarydb)'    --- 'mysales_snapshot'
    ,@backup_source_directory = '$(sharename)'   ---same as specified in
primary'\\SHW-TOR-WS039-A\BIOREPL_PEER'
    ,@backup_destination_directory = '$(backupfilepath)  ----'D:\files'
    ,@copy_job_name = '$(copyjobname) ----
'LSCopy_SHW-TOR-WS039-A\BIOREPL_PEER_mysales_snapshot'
    ,@restore_job_name = '$(restorejobname)'
----'LSRestore_SHW-TOR-WS039-A\BIOREPL_PEER_mysales_snapshot'
    ,@file_retention_period = 4320
    ,@monitor_server = '$(primaryserver)  ---'SHW-TOR-WS039-A\BIOREPL_PEER'
    ,@monitor_server_security_mode =$(securitymode)        ----1
    ,@overwrite = 1
    ,@copy_job_id = @LS_Secondary__CopyJobId OUTPUT
    ,@restore_job_id = @LS_Secondary__RestoreJobId OUTPUT
    ,@secondary_id = @LS_Secondary__SecondaryId OUTPUT

IF (@@ERROR = 0 AND @LS_Add_RetCode = 0)
BEGIN
```

```
DECLARE @LS_SecondaryCopyJobScheduleUID      As uniqueidentifier
DECLARE @LS_SecondaryCopyJobScheduleID       AS int

/*create the copy schedule */
EXEC msdb.dbo.sp_add_schedule
    @schedule_name ='DefaultCopyJobSchedule'
    ,@enabled = 1
    ,@freq_type = 4
    ,@freq_interval = 1
    ,@freq_subday_type = 4
    ,@freq_subday_interval = 15
    ,@freq_recurrence_factor = 0
    ,@active_start_date = 20060910
    ,@active_end_date = 99991231
    ,@active_start_time = 0
    ,@active_end_time = 235900
    ,@schedule_uid = @LS_SecondaryCopyJobScheduleUID OUTPUT
    ,@schedule_id = @LS_SecondaryCopyJobScheduleID OUTPUT


/*attach the schedule to the job */

EXEC msdb.dbo.sp_attach_schedule
    @job_id = @LS_Secondary__CopyJobId
    ,@schedule_id = @LS_SecondaryCopyJobScheduleID

DECLARE @LS_SecondaryRestoreJobScheduleUID      As uniqueidentifier
DECLARE @LS_SecondaryRestoreJobScheduleID       AS int

/*create the restore schedule */
EXEC msdb.dbo.sp_add_schedule
    @schedule_name ='DefaultRestoreJobSchedule'
    ,@enabled = 1
    ,@freq_type = 4
    ,@freq_interval = 1
    ,@freq_subday_type = 4
    ,@freq_subday_interval = 15
    ,@freq_recurrence_factor = 0
    ,@active_start_date = 20060910
    ,@active_end_date = 99991231
    ,@active_start_time = 0
    ,@active_end_time = 235900
    ,@schedule_uid = @LS_SecondaryRestoreJobScheduleUID OUTPUT
    ,@schedule_id = @LS_SecondaryRestoreJobScheduleID OUTPUT


/* Attach the restore schedule to the job */
```

```
EXEC msdb.dbo.sp_attach_schedule
    @job_id = @LS_Secondary__RestoreJobId
    ,@schedule_id = @LS_SecondaryRestoreJobScheduleID


END



DECLARE @LS_Add_RetCode2    As int



IF (@@ERROR = 0 AND @LS_Add_RetCode = 0)
BEGIN

/*Add the secondary database to the secondary server */

EXEC @LS_Add_RetCode2 = master.dbo.sp_add_log_shipping_secondary_database
    @secondary_database = '$(secondarydb)'    --'mysales_snapshot'
    ,@primary_server = '$(primaryserver)'     ---'SHW-TOR-WS039-A\BIOREPL_PEER'
    ,@primary_database = '$(primarydb)'       ---'mysales_snapshot'
    ,@restore_delay = 0
    ,@restore_mode = 1
    ,@disconnect_users    = 1
    ,@restore_threshold = 45
    ,@threshold_alert_enabled = 1
    ,@history_retention_period    = 5760
    ,@overwrite = 1

END



/*IF (@@error = 0 AND @LS_Add_RetCode = 0)
BEGIN

EXEC msdb.dbo.sp_update_job        · '
    @job_id = @LS_Secondary__CopyJobId
    ,@enabled = 1

EXEC msdb.dbo.sp_update_job
    @job_id = @LS_Secondary__RestoreJobId
    ,@enabled = 1

END
*/
```

As for the primary server, this script uses the SQLCMD utility variables to connect to the secondary server.

Once the connection is established, the `sp_add_log_shipping_secondary_primary` stored procedure adds the names of the primary server, the monitor server, the copy job, the restore job, the share name for the source backup directory, and the file path name of the destination backup on the secondary server. It then creates the schedule for the copy and restore jobs, and attaches the schedules to the jobs.

Finally it adds the secondary database by executing the `sp_add_log_shipping_secondary_` `database` stored procedure.

Adding the Secondary Server Information to the Primary Server

Having configured both the primary and secondary servers and attached the primary and secondary databases, the final step is to add the secondary database information to the primary server. This is shown in Listing 16-11.

Listing 16-11. *Adding the Secondary Database Information to the Primary Server*

```
/* Run this script on the Primary server
The monitor server is also located on the Primary server */
:setvar logintimeout 120
:setvar server "BIO-V7V30JTZLZS\BIOREPL"
---:setvar user "sa"
---:setvar password "sujoy"
:connect $(server) -l $(logintimeout)
--- -U $(user) -P $(password)


use msdb
go


EXEC master.dbo.sp_add_log_shipping_primary_secondary
    @primary_database = '$(primarydb)'      ----N'mysales_snapshot'
    ,@secondary_server = '$(secondaryserver)'  ----N'SHW-TOR-WS039-A'
    ,@secondary_database = '$(secondarydb)'    ----N'mysales_snapshot'
    ,@overwrite = 1
go
```

The name of the secondary database is added to the primary server by executing the `sp_add_log_shipping_primary_secondary` stored procedure. The parameters passed are the names of the primary and secondary databases. The name of the secondary server on which the secondary database is located is also specified.

If the Publisher server now fails on the primary server, you need to follow the series of steps mentioned in the "Log Shipping with Transactional Replication" section in Chapter 15.

Summary

In this chapter, I discussed the restoration of the databases for publication with download-only articles for merge replication. I used the no-sync initialization to synchronize the subscriptions, both push and pull, with the publication database for merge replication.

By now you should have a good understanding of how to validate either all the subscriptions or an individual subscription using both the GUI and T-SQL. I also showed you how to use the SQLCMD utility to create a push subscription by restoring a backed up publication database.

You should also have a good understanding of retention periods and their use in the expired subscription clean up agent.

- Back up the publication database on the Publisher server and the subscription database on the Subscriber server.

- Back up the master and msdb databases on the Publisher and the Subscriber servers.

- The Distribution Agent does not play any significant part in the merge replication process.

- The databases for merge replication, as with transactional replication, should be in Full Recovery or Bulk Logged Recovery mode to back up the transaction log.

- Use sp_validatemergepublication to validate all the subscriptions for a particular merge publication.

- Individual subscriptions can be validated using sp_validatemergesubscription.

- The SQL Server Import and Export method can be used to copy the schema and data from the publication database to the subscription database.

- The SSIS package needs to be installed in order to use the SQL Server Import and Export method.

- Uncheck the Initialize box when creating a subscription using the GUI method for no-sync initialization.

- The SQL Native Client is a combination of the SQL OLE DB driver and the SQL ODBC driver.

- The SSIS package can be saved either as a file or in SQL Server.

- The SSIS package, if saved as a file, can be opened in SQL Server Integration Services.

- Within the SQLCMD utility, you can load several files using the :r variable. The file names must be separated by commas.

- Synchronize the subscription database with the publication database before backing up and after restoring the database so that it is up to date with the publication database.

- The retention period determines the time after which the subscription will be deactivated.

- The subscriptions for merge publication will have to be reinitialized after the expiry of the retention period.

- The retention period is 14 days by default, although the subscription metadata can be held permanently. It is better to have a time limit; otherwise it will have an effect on the performance of merge replication.

- The sp_expired_subscription_cleanup stored procedure is used to deactivate the subscription metadata. Push subscriptions are dropped by the Expired subscription clean up job. For pull subscriptions, this needs to be done manually.

- The retention period has a grace period of 24 hours to accommodate time differences.

- The replication alerts for validation can be enabled using sp_update_alert and can be notified using the sp_update_notification.

In the next chapter, I will discuss the performance and tuning of both snapshot and transactional replication, and how to optimize them. The subsequent chapter will describe the optimization of merge replication.

Quick Tips

- When you back up the publication database, ensure that no data changes are being made on the publication database when the backup is made or when it is restored.

- The sp_validatemergepublication stored procedure sets the schematype column for the sysmergeschemachange table to 66 once the validation is complete for the publication.

- The SQL Native Client is a new API.

- The success of the Precedent Constraint Editor is shown in green, while failure is marked in red.

- The error numbers 20574 and 20575 correspond to failed data validation and passed data validation, respectively.

- The retention period of the publication can be seen in the retention column of the sysmergepublications system table.

■ ■ ■

Optimizing Snapshot Replication

Having configured snapshot replication and learned how to administer it, we need to consider how snapshot replication functions for the topology selected for the business. In order for snapshot replication to function efficiently, it should be optimized by the DBA. You not only need to factor in the design of the publication database and hardware configurations, but you should also consider the parameter settings of the Snapshot and Distributor Agents, the kind of T-SQL statements executed, and whether there are any locks. Fortunately, there are tools that can help you identify potential bottlenecks in the system and how to alleviate any problems.

In this chapter, I will deal with the performance and tuning of snapshot replication. The next two chapters will discuss the optimization of transactional and merge replication.

On completion of this chapter, you will know all about the following:

- Using the System Monitor

- Using the SQL Server Profiler

- Correlating data between the System Monitor and the SQL Server Profiler

- Best practices for snapshot replication

Optimizing Performance

Monitoring the performance and tuning of a database is a key function in the administration of any backend system. Different components, such as server hardware, processors, and memory; network hardware and configuration; database design and configuration; and the transaction log, contribute to the optimal performance of SQL Server. Even whether the system is geared for OLTP or OLAP can have an impact on the database system.

Note SQL Server Analysis Server is used for OLAP. You cannot replicate any OLAP objects, such as dimensions and cubes.

Introducing replication into the configuration adds to the complexity of the optimization process. While the same key ingredients play an active part in the optimization of a replicated system, added factors like publication design, the number of articles in the publication, the existence of any filters, subscription options (such as push or pull, snapshot generation, and the parameter settings of replicated agents) can significantly affect how the system operates.

Once the replicated topology is in place, constant monitoring of the system is warranted for efficient functioning. An effective plan that will properly harness the system resources should be in place. Tweaking the system when the performance is impeded might be counter-productive and short-sighted. For example, a slow-performing query might be improved by changing the index structure of the column that is being accessed. This might in turn have repercussions on other queries that use the same column in the table. It therefore becomes crucial to monitor the overall health of the system, rather than focusing on individual components.

By monitoring the health of the replicated system, you are better able to determine all the parameters that enable the system to function properly. A baseline can be drawn against which you can measure whether the replicated topology is functioning at par or below. Components that drag the system below the acceptable level can then be fine-tuned.

Once you start consistently and regularly tracking performance measurements for the objects that directly impact the system, you can use statistical analysis tools, like linear regression, to forecast the behavior of the system. This is a more proactive approach to the optimization of the replicated system. Early detection of problems can lead to a speedier resolution. Any aberration in the system can be dealt with immediately instead of after the fact, when performance becomes poor.

■**Note** For an excellent description of SQL Server performance, consult *The Definitive Guide to SQL Server Performance Optimization*, by Don Jones (Realtimepublishers.com, 2003).

Before implementing replication on a production environment, you can draw up a performance baseline on a testing environment and use this benchmark on a production setup. You will then have a better idea of how the replication process is working and can mimic the test cases by incorporating on a production environment.

A distributed environment like replication has different performance considerations than a system that employs a client application that accesses a traditional database system. The efficacy of a replicated environment lies in latency, concurrency, throughput, the duration of the synchronization, and in its hardware resources. Latency is the amount of time that it takes for transactions to be transmitted, and it is the cornerstone that determines the type of replication you choose. Throughput determines the number of commands that can be sent from one node to another. Concurrency indicates the number of replication processes the system can handle. All three factors have to be taken into consideration when determining the health of a replicated system.

Performance measurements, as mentioned earlier, should be taken at regular intervals as follows:

- Take measurements soon after the implementation of the replication topology. Although there might not be any significant impact soon after the implementation, you will know the base level at which the system operates.

- Gather information at regular intervals both during peak hours and off-peak hours for query processing, replication agents and alerts, and snapshot generation.

- Measure the time it takes to back up and restore the replicated databases and system databases, such as the distribution and msdb databases.

- Take measurements as necessary to check the health of the system.

Note I discussed how to back up and restore the databases used in snapshot replication in Chapter 15.

Once you have gathered all the information over a period of time on the performance, you can set a baseline and use it to determine how the system is performing. If the system functions below the acceptable level, you can take remedial measures, like fine-tuning the queries or increasing the memory of the system.

The autonomous nature of replicated systems, coupled with different hardware resources, can sometimes make it difficult to pinpoint the exact nature of a problem. If a server that was earlier able to handle 50 connections suddenly cannot handle even 5 connections, you know there is a problem with the hardware, and you may consider increasing the hardware resources. Tools like the operating system's System Monitor, SQL Server's SQL Server Profiler, the Database Engine Tuning Advisor, the Replication Monitor, and the Activity Monitor in the SSMS can all help trace problems, gather information, and monitor the processes that affect the optimization of the system.

Using the System Monitor

The Windows System Monitor is a server-wide tool. It comes with the Windows operating system and can be used to monitor and measure the performance of the SQL Server objects and SQL Server's use of the system-wide resources. By monitoring disk activity, memory usage, and the activity of the processors, along with SQL Server's performance objects like locks, agents, and replication objects, you can log the activity of the replication system and chart it graphically. Each of these objects can have one or more counters that you can use to monitor performance.

When you use the System Monitor, you are taking in real-time data. So if you log the messages for a period of time, you will have an image of how the system is functioning and therefore an idea of the overall health of the system. However, the flip side of using only this tool is that you cannot measure performance at a granular level.

The name of the executable for the System Monitor is perfmon. Be careful not to run the System Monitor from the machine on which the database server is installed, since it consumes a lot of resources. It is better to run it from a client machine.

■**Note** After Windows NT 4.0, the Performance Monitor was renamed as the System Monitor.

You can start the System Monitor by selecting Run from the Start menu, typing **perfmon**, and clicking the OK button. In the Performance window, select System Monitor under the Console Root as shown in Figure 17-1. This figure shows the Performance window after I have chosen some performance objects and the corresponding counters.

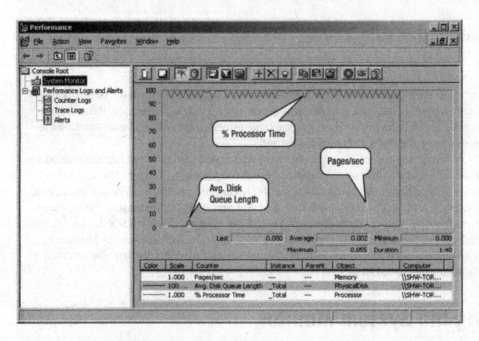

Figure 17-1. *The System Monitor*

■**Tip** You can freeze the display in the System Monitor by clicking on the icon with the red circle with the X in it. Clicking on it again will restart monitoring.

PERFORMANCE COUNTERS

While the list of performance counters can be found in the System Monitor tool, it is also possible to list the names of the performance objects and their corresponding counters by using the `sys.dm_os_performance_counters` dynamic management view. To find the performance objects for replication, you can execute the following script:

```
Use master
go
select * from sys.dm_os_performance_counters
where object_name like 'SQLServer:Replication%'
```

This is the output:

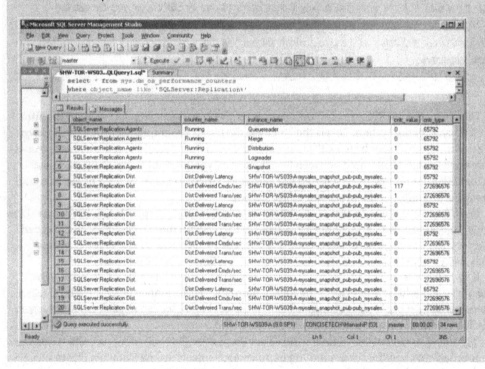

In Figure 17-1, you can see the graphical display of each of the counters selected for the performance objects. For the Memory object, the counter that has been selected is Pages/Sec. There are several counters for the Memory object, but I chose this counter because I want to see the number of pages retrieved from the disk due to hard page faults, or written to disk to free up space. The counter is graphed in yellow, and there are some peaks and valleys. This is indicative of low paging, which is what you want. A high value would indicate excessive paging, which can happen if there is a lot of page swapping going on. That would mean that SQL Server was using the virtual memory of the operating system and swapping data from physical memory to virtual memory; this should be avoided. If you think there is excessive paging, monitor the Memory: Page Faults/sec counter to ensure that excessive paging is not causing the disk activity.

Remember that SQL Server can dynamically allocate memory to the physical memory of the operating system. If SQL Server does not need as much memory for a particular action, it will release the memory to the operating system. However, if you have configured memory manually, it is possible for page swapping to occur.

The next counter that is being monitored is Avg.Disk Queue Length for the PhysicalDisk performance object. It measures the activity of the disk, telling you the response time for disk I/O operations. It gives you an indication of whether there are any bottlenecks for SQL Server because it tells you how many system requests are waiting to access the disk. Normally this counter should not be higher than 1.5 or 2 per physical disk. If you want to see how busy the server is with read/write operations, use the %DiskTime counter.

Tip If you want to know what disk activity is specifically caused by SQL Server, you can use the SQL Server:Buffer Manager performance object. The counters that you want to check are the Page reads/sec and Page writes/sec, which tell you how many pages are read from and written to disk, respectively.

I also selected the %Processor Time counter for the Processor object in order to monitor the CPU usage of the system. This is the line near the top of the graph. This counter monitors the amount of time taken by the CPU to execute a thread that is not idle. If the counter consistently shows usage of anything between 80–90 percent, you probably need to upgrade the CPU or add other processors. I selected the _Total instance because I wanted to measure the average performance of the processor in my system.

If you have multiple processors installed, you can use the System: %Total Processor Time counter to find the average of all the processors in the system. Another counter that you can use to find any bottlenecks in the system is the System: Processor Queue Length counter, which tells you how many threads are in the queue waiting for processor time.

If you do not have any counters listed, as shown in Figure 17-1, right-click in the right pane and select Add Counters from the menu. From the "Performance object" list box, select Memory, and from the "Select counters from" list select Pages/sec. Then click the Add button, and click the Close button. This is shown in Figure 17-2.

Right-click on any of the counters and select Properties. This will show you which counters you have selected and the corresponding performance objects. In the Data tab, if you select any of the counters in the System Monitor Properties window, you can see the color-coding and the line style for that counter, as shown in Figure 17-3.

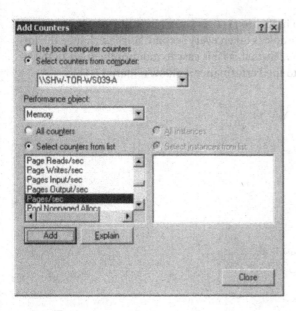

Figure 17-2. *Selecting a counter from the* Memory *performance object*

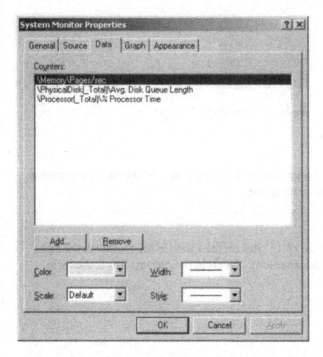

Figure 17-3. *Viewing counter properties in the System Monitor*

Now select the General tab, as shown in Figure 17-4. As you can see, the display is set to be displayed in graphical format, and a sample is taken every second. You can change the format if you wish; I prefer to use the graphical format, as it is easy to monitor the trace in the System Monitor. Click Cancel to go back to the Performance window (Figure 17-1).

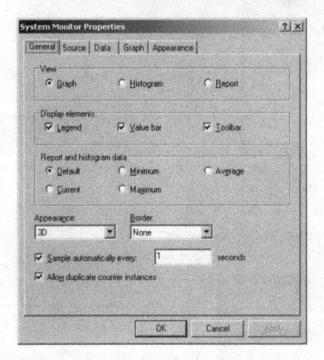

Figure 17-4. *Viewing display options for the System Monitor*

Note You can save the counter data in a report format. This way you can see how each of the counters was performing, and if necessary reuse the counters later.

In the Performance window (Figure 17-1), click on the + icon in the toolbar in the right pane to see the list of counters and corresponding objects in the system. This is shown in Figure 17-5.

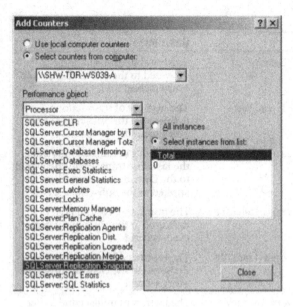

Figure 17-5. *Viewing some of the counters for SQL Server, including the performance objects for replication*

In the Add Counters window, you can see the performance objects that give an indication of how replication is working:

- SQLServer: Replication Agents

- SQLServer: Replication Dist

- SQLServer: Replication Logreader

- SQLServer: Replication Merge

- SQLServer: Replication Snapshot

Table 17-1 outlines what each of the performance objects for replication does.

Table 17-1. *The Performance Objects for Replication*

Performance Object	Counter	Description
Replication Agents	Running	The number of agents currently running
Snapshot	Snapshot:Delivered Cmds/sec	The number of commands delivered to the Distributor server every second
Snapshot	Snapshot:Delivered Trans/sec	The number of transactions delivered to the Distributor server every second

Continued

Table 17-1. *Continued*

Performance Object	Counter	Description
Replication Dist	Dist:Delivered Cmd/sec	The number of commands delivered to the Subscriber server every second
Replication Dist	Dist:Delivered Trans/sec	The number of transactions delivered to the Subscriber server every second
Replication Dist	Dist:Delivery Latency	The latency in milliseconds since the last time transactions delivered to the Distributor server were applied to the Subscriber server
Replication Logreader	Logreader:Delivered Cmds/sec	The number of commands delivered to the Distributor server every second
Replication Logreader	Logreader:Delivered Trans/sec	The number of transactions delivered to the Distributor server every second
Replication Logreader	Logreader:Delivery Latency	The latency in milliseconds since the last time transactions applied at the Publisher server were delivered to the Distributor server
Replication Merge	Merge:Conflicts/sec	The number of conflicts occurring during the merge process every second
Replication Merge	Merge:Downloaded Changes/sec	The number of rows replicated from the Publisher server to the Subscriber server
Replication Merge	Merge:Uploaded Changes/sec	The number of rows replicated from the Subscriber server to the Publisher server

For snapshot replication, you mainly need the SQLServer:Replication Snapshot and SQLServer: Replication Dist objects, although if you are running other types of replication on the same system, you might want to use the Replication Agents performance object to find out how many agents are running.

■**Note** The optimization of transactional and merge replication is shown in Chapters 18 and 19, respectively.

You can choose the SQLServer:Replication Snapshot performance object from the Add Counters window (Figure 17-5), but I want to show you how to set up the objects for snapshot replication in such a way that we can capture the baseline data. In the Performance window (Figure 17-1), therefore, right-click Counter Logs and select Add Counters. Give a name to the baseline in the Add Counters window, as shown in Figure 17-6.

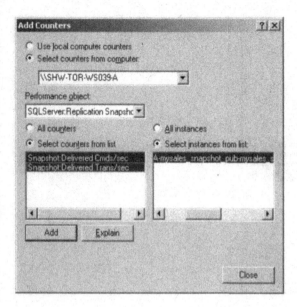

Figure 17-6. *Selecting counters for the* SQLServer:Replication Snapshot *performance object*

The name of the Snapshot Agent is shown in the "Select instances from list" list automatically. To add both counters, select the counters and click the Add button. If you cannot remember exactly what each of the counters does, select the one that you want to know about, and click the Explain button. An explanation of the counter will be displayed, as shown in Figure 17-7.

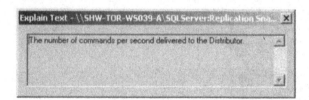

Figure 17-7. *Viewing an explanation of the* Snapshot:Delivered Cmds/sec *counter*

Next, let's see how the Distribution Agent is performing for the push subscription created for the mysales_snapshot_pub publication. Since latency is more important in transactional replication than in snapshot replication, I chose the Dist: Delivered Cmds/sec and Dist: Delivered Trans/sec counters. This is shown in Figure 17-8.

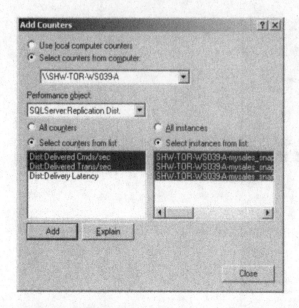

Figure 17-8. *Adding counters for the* `SQLServer:Replication Dist` *performance object*

In Chapter 6, I mentioned that locks are held by the Snapshot Agent on the database and the objects for the publication at the time of synchronization. We can get information on all the locks held by the SQL Server engine and all the locks on the database and database objects.

To do this, I selected the `_Total` and `Database` instances for the `SQLServer:Locks` performance object. The counters that are of interest here are `Average Wait Time`, `Lock Timeouts/sec`, and `Number of Deadlocks/sec`. This is shown in Figure 17-9.

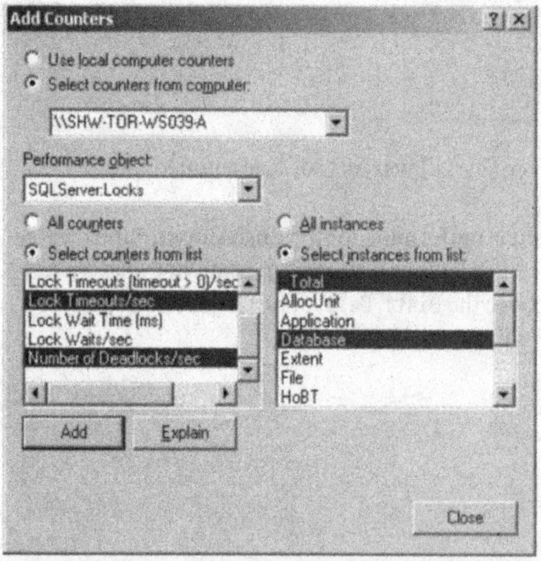

Figure 17-9. *Adding performance counters for the* `SQLServer:Locks` *object*

■**Note** If you scroll up the counter list in Figure 17-9, you will be able to see the Average Wait Time counter.

The Average Wait Time counter gives us an indication of the average time it took to obtain the lock, while the Lock Timeouts/sec counter tells us the number of attempts that were made without establishing the lock. The Number of Deadlocks/sec counter tells us the number of locks that resulted in a deadlock every second. ›

Next, we can check the effect of bulk copying the publication database. To do this, I chose the SQLServer:Databases performance object, as shown in Figure 17-10. The Bulk Copy Rows/sec counter gives us an indication of the number of rows that are copied per second, while the Bulk Copy Throughput/sec counter tells us how much data has been bulk copied every second.

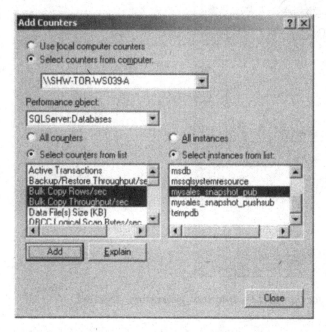

Figure 17-10. *Adding performance counters for the* SQLServer:Databases *object*

After entering all the counters for the objects, you can start the monitoring. However, if you were to close the System Monitor now and reopen it, you would find that all the settings were lost. To capture the baseline data for all these counters, right-click on the Counter Logs item under Performance Logs and Alerts in the Performance window (Figure 17-1) and select New Log Settings from the menu. It will ask you to assign a name for the baseline setting, as shown in Figure 17-11. Enter a name and click OK.

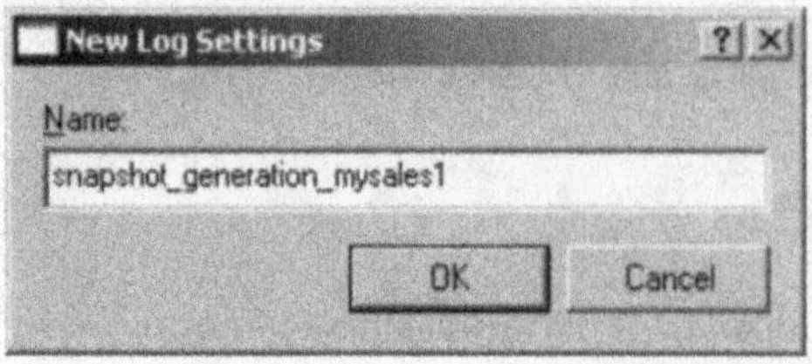

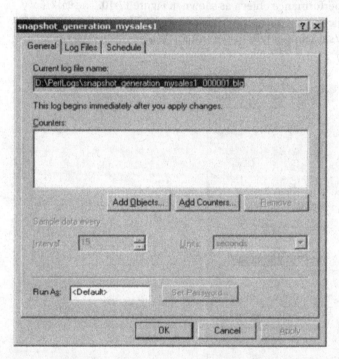

Figure 17-11. *Entering a name for the baseline dataset*

You will now see the window shown in Figure 17-12.

Figure 17-12. *The name of the log file for the baseline, snapshot_generation_mysales1*

If you click the Add Objects button, you will see the list of all the performance objects, but you cannot see the individual counters for particular performance objects. It will select all the counters for the object, as you can see in Figure 17-13. Click the Close button to return to the window in Figure 17-12.

■**Caution** If you double-click on any of the objects listed in Figure 17-13, the objects will be added.

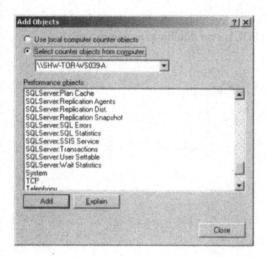

Figure 17-13. *Adding performance objects*

Click the Add Counters button. This will open a window in which you can add the counters. The window will be similar to the one in Figure 17-6 or those in Figure 17-8, 17-9, or 17-10 depending on the performance objects selected.

After the counters have been added, you will see that the empty Counters pane in Figure 17-12 is filled up, as shown in Figure 17-14. When monitoring the performance to collect the baseline data, I usually set the System Monitor to sample the data every 15 minutes, as shown in the figure.

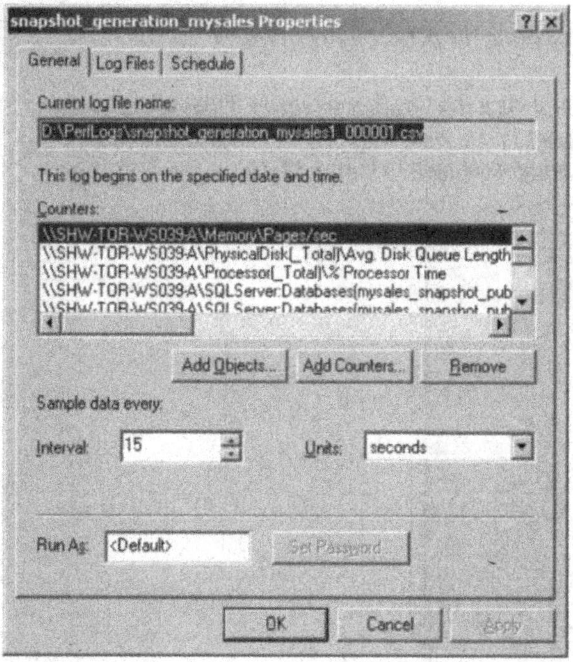

Figure 17-14. *Viewing the counters added to the snapshot_generation_mysales1 counter log*

You can also see that the log file has a `.csv` extension. Select the Log Files tab to choose the file type for the log. You can even save it in a SQL Server database, as you can see in Figure 17-15.

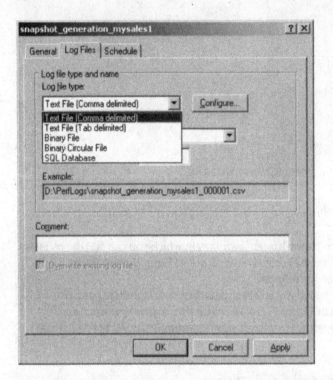

Figure 17-15. *Choosing the log files type for storing the performance counters*

For this example, select the text file and click the Configure button. This will open the Configure Log Files window shown in Figure 17-16. Note that you can set the size of the log file if you wish. Click OK to return to the window shown in Figure 17-15.

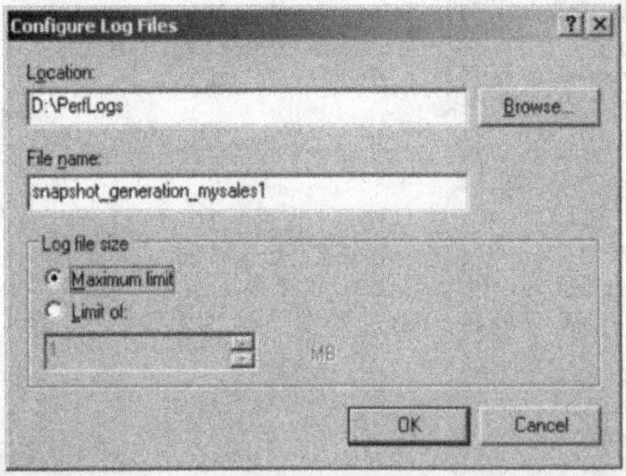

Figure 17-16. *Configuring the log file*

Now select the Schedule tab, as shown in Figure 17-17. In this example, the start time of the log has been specified and the logging will stop after one day. If the log file closes, such as if it exceeds the size specified, it will start a new log. The log filenames end with a four-digit number that has leading zeros and that increments by 1 every time a new log file is created.

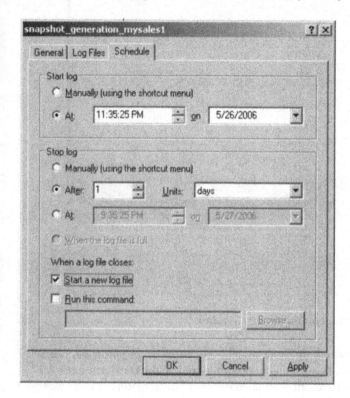

Figure 17-17. *Scheduling the counter log*

Select Counter Logs in the System Monitor, and you will see the counter log that has just been created on the right side. Select it and then execute it.

While the log is being executed, open the Activity Monitor located under the Management object in the SSMS. Click the View Filter Settings link in the left pane under Status of Activity Monitor. This will open the Filter Settings window shown in Figure 17-18, where we can monitor the resources of SQL Server.

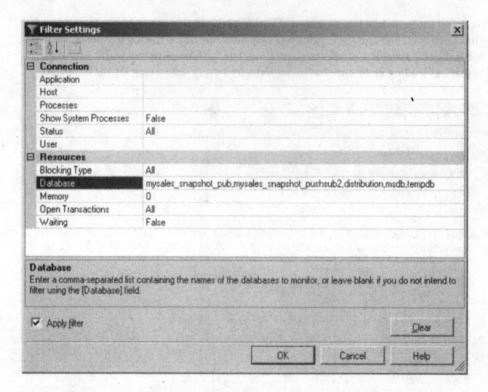

Figure 17-18. *Viewing the filter settings for the Activity Monitor*

The Blocking Type property determines the blocking condition of the processes. I have chosen all processes, to see which are blocking or being blocked. In the Database section, I have selected the publication and subscription databases for snapshot replication, as well as the distribution, msdb, and tempdb databases.

The Memory property is set to 0, which means that I do not want the filter to monitor the memory. For this process, the filter monitors the number of pages that are allocated to the procedure cache for the processes allocated.

The Open Transactions setting is All, which means none of the open transactions are filtered. The Waiting property has been set to False.

You should also ensure that there are no locks when the snapshot is generated for the publication database in snapshot replication. One way to do this is, before the database is configured for snapshot publication, to refresh the Activity Monitor to see any of the locks held while the database is at a steady mode. This is shown in Figure 17-19.

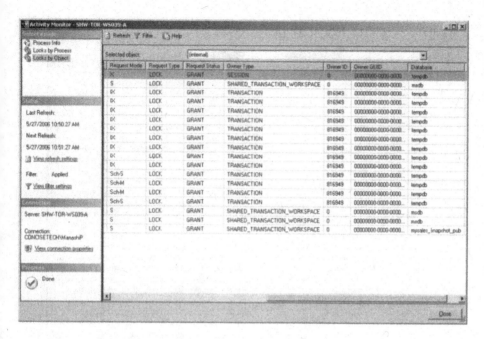

Figure 17-19. *Monitoring activity when the database is idle*

Now you can start configuring the snapshot publication using the GUI while the System Monitor is still running.

■**Note** The configuration of snapshot publication and subscriptions is described in Chapters 4 and 5.

While the publication is being configured, you can open the Activity Monitor and see the locks held by the databases, as shown in Figure 17-20. The Request Mode column shows the types of locks being held. You can see that there are shared locks held by the mysales_snapshot_pub publication database and the distribution database.

The next step is to set up the push subscription configuration, but first take a look at the Activity Monitor again. Now you will not find any shared locks held on either the publication or the distribution database. You can see this in Figure 17-21.

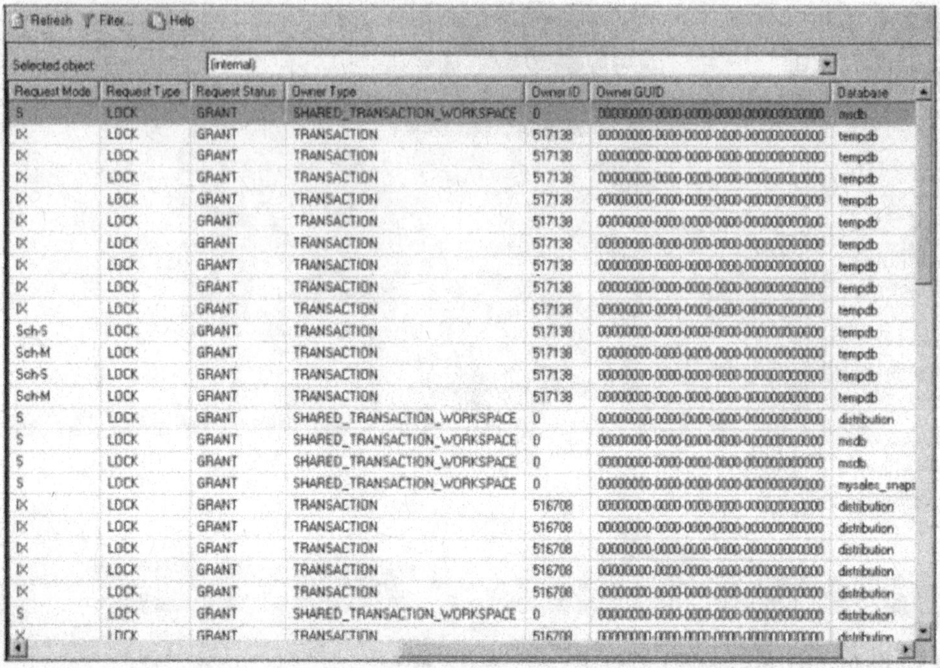

Figure 17-20. *Viewing locks held by the mysales_snapshot_pub and distribution databases in the Activity Monitor while the publication is being configured*

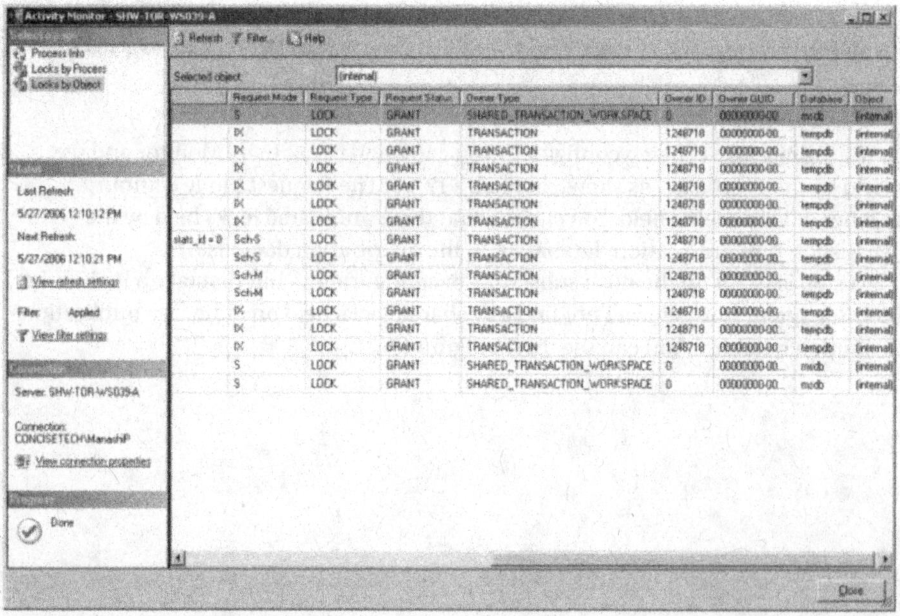

Figure 17-21. *No locks are held on the mysales_snapshot_pub publication or the distribution database*

Soon after you select the publication for snapshot replication, a shared lock is held on the publication database, as you can see in Figure 17-22.

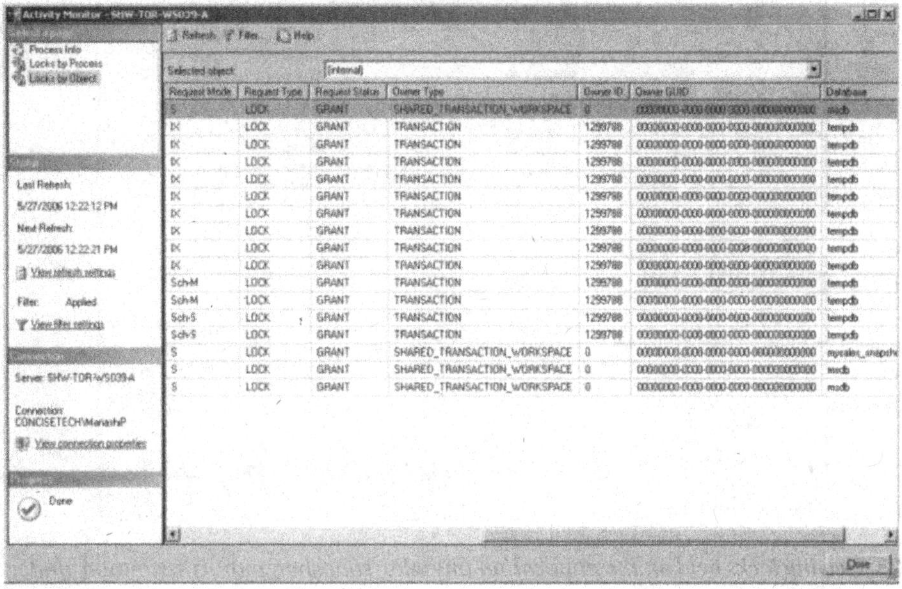

Figure 17-22. *Viewing a shared lock held on the publication database, mysales_snapshot_pub*

After you finish configuring the push subscription, take a look at the Activity Monitor again, as shown in Figure 17-23. You will find that database objects on the publication, msdb, distribution databases initially hold shared locks (the Request Mode value is S). In my case, the process ID for the objects locked on the distribution database is 61; the process ID might be different on your machine.

The shared lock is held on the mysales_snapshot_pushsub1 subscription database and the distribution database. The process ID for the objects locked on the distribution database is 61, in my case. Finally, an exclusive lock is held by an application on the distribution database, as shown in Figure 17-23.

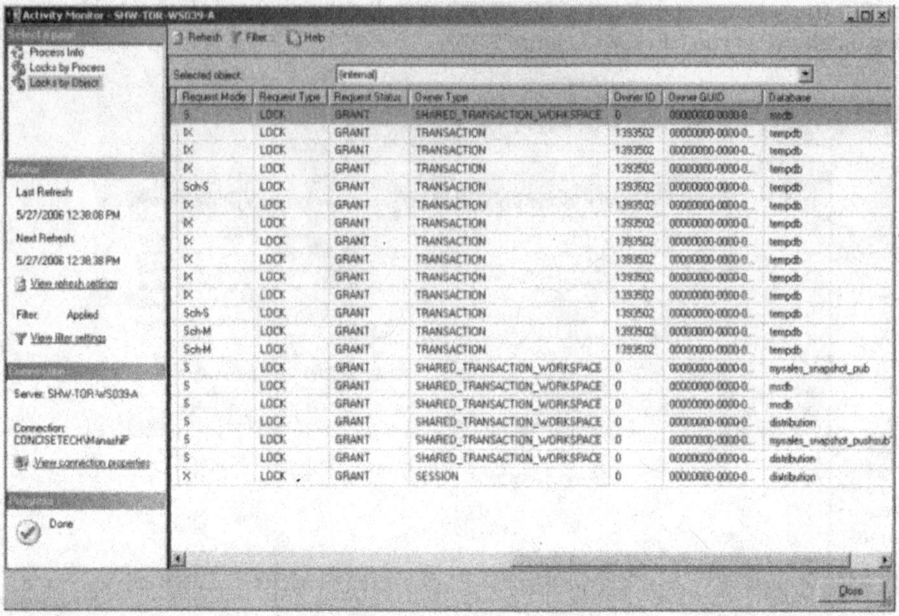

Figure 17-23. *Viewing locks held on the publication (mysales_snapshot_pub), distribution, and subscription (mysales_snapshot_pushsub) databases*

You can list the locks held by the different databases according to the SPID (Server Process Identifier) by using the sys.dm_trans_locks dynamic management view, as shown in Listing 17-1.

Listing 17-1. *Listing Locks Held by the Different Databases*

```
/*Execute this on the publication database */

use mysales_snapshot_pub
go

SELECT a.resource_type,
a.resource_associated_entity_id,
a.request_status,
a.request_mode,
a.request_session_id as spid,
a.request_owner_type as [OwnerType],
a.resource_description,
b.dbid,
b.name
FROM sys.dm_tran_locks a,
sys.sysdatabases b
WHERE a.resource_database_id >=1
Go
```

This script uses the `sys.dm_tran_locks` dynamic management view to find the `resource_ type`, which can specify a database or another object, like an application, page, key, extent, or file. The `request_session_id` in the script is the `spid` of the object. There are eight databases on this server, which you can find by executing the `select * from sys.sysdatabases` query. The `resource_database_id` column is used to scope out the database.

In the output of this script, shown in Figure 17-24, the `resource_status` column reveals the current status of the request, and the `request_mode` shows the kind of locks held by the particular object. I also included the `dbid` and name of the databases in the output.

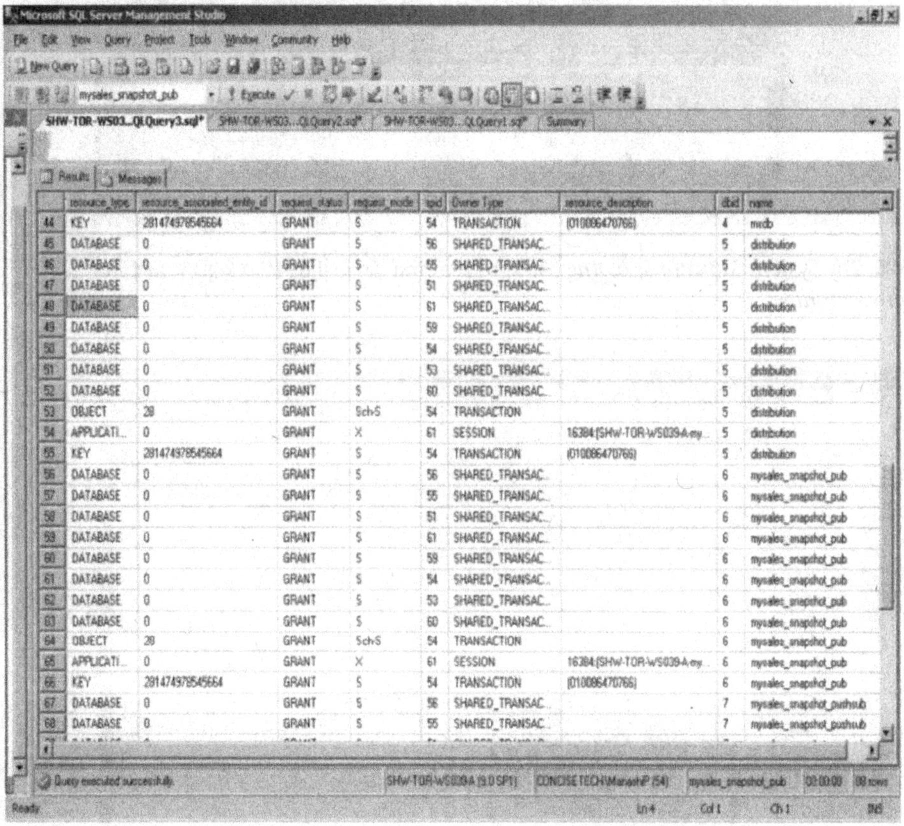

Figure 17-24. *The output of the script in Listing 17-1*

If we now go back to the Performance window of the System Monitor (Figure 17-1), add snapshot and distribution counters, and execute the counters again, we will get results like those shown in Figure 17-25. In this figure, the first big spike is in the `Snapshot:Delivered Cmds/sec` counter, and the second includes the `Snapshot:Delivered Trans/sec` counter.

We have already measured the baseline by collecting the data for the snapshot_ generation_mysales1 counter log. The file generated was then opened in Excel and a chart made as shown in Figure 17-26.

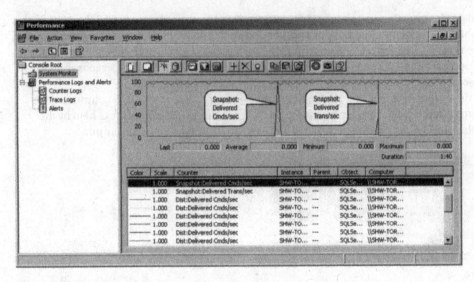

Figure 17-25. *The System Monitor showing the* Replication Snapshot *and* Replication Dist *performance counters*

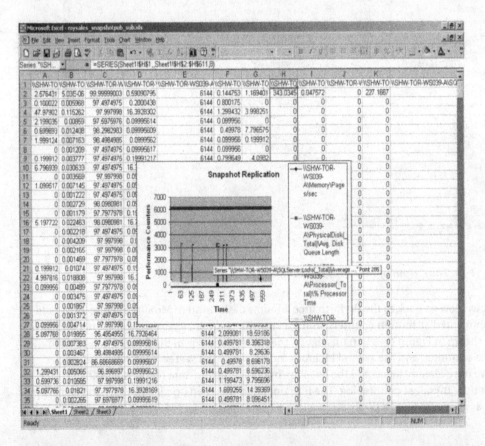

Figure 17-26. *Viewing the output of the counter log in Excel*

You can create a chart of the log data by selecting Chart type of Line and the correspon-ding Chart subtype of "Line with markers displayed at each data value" from the Chart Wizard in Excel and then following the instructions. Clicking a line will display the column containing the data. In Figure 17-26, you can see vertical lines.

Let's look at the first four lines of output data in detail. These are in Figure 17-27.

\SHW-TOR-WS039-A \Memory \Pages/sec	\SHW-TOR-WS039-A \Physical Disk (_Total) \Avg. Disk Queue Length	\SHW-TOR-WS039-A \Processor (_Total) \% Processor Time	\SHW-TOR-WS039-A \SQLServer: Databases (distribution) \Transactio ns/sec	\SHW-TOR-WS039-A \SQLServer:Databas es (mysales_snapshot_ pushsub1) \Data File (s) Size (KB)	\SHW-TOR-WS039-A \SQLServ er:Databa ses(msdb) \Transacti ons/sec	\SHW-TOR-WS039-A \SQLServ er:Databa ses (tempdb) \Transacti ons/sec	\SHW-TOR-WS039-A \SQLServ er:Locks (_Total) \Average Wait Time (ms)	\SHW-TOR-WS039-A \SQLServ er:Locks (_Total) \Lock Timeouts/ sec	\SHW-TOR-WS039-A \SQLServer: Locks (_Total) \Number of Deadlocks/s ec	\SHW-TOR-WS039-A \SQLServ er:Locks (_Databas e) \Average Wait Time (ms)	\SHW-TOR-WS039-A \SQLServer:Locks (Database) \Lock Timeouts/sec
2.576431	5.03E-06	99.99999003	0.58090795	6144	0.144753	1.169401	343.0345	0.047572	0	227.1667	1.67E-05
0.100022	0.006968	97.4974975	0.2000438	6144	0.800175	0	0	0	0	0	0
47.97902	0.115262	97.997998	16.3928302	6144	1.299432	3.998251	0	0	0	0	0
2.199035	0.00859	97.5975976	0.09995614	6144	0.099956	0	0	0	0	0	0

Figure 17-27. *Viewing the first four lines of output from the performance counters*

The first three columns in Figure 17-27 display the counter data for the Memory, Physical Disk, and Process performance objects. For the SQLServer:Databases(distribution)\ Transactions/sec performance counter (in the fourth column), you can see that the number of transactions started for the distribution database is highest in the third line, with a value of 16.3928302. Correspondingly, higher paging (Memory:Pages/sec) is registered, with a value of 47.97902. This pattern can be seen throughout the data set. The highest number of transactions registered every second for the distribution database is 29.4870652, and the corresponding value for pages/sec is 1343.29.

The subscription database did not grow in size. It remained at 6144 KB throughout the collection period. You can verify the size of the database by opening the Windows Explorer and searching for the primary data file (an .mdf file) of the subscription database. In my case, it is located in D:\Program Files\Microsoft SQL Server\MSSQL.1\MSSQL\Data.

Notice the SQLServer:Locks(_Total)\Number of Deadlocks/sec counter in Figure 17-27. It registered a value of 0, which indicates there were no locks held during the operation. If there was a number other than 0, it would mean a deadlock had been registered and we would have encountered problems. The Locks(_Total)\Average Wait Time counter shows that there was an average wait time of 343.0345 milliseconds for a lock request only once.

Although I registered the Replication Snapshot and Replication Dist counters, none of the data shows up in the log file, even though Figure 17-25 shows there was a spike registered for the Snapshot Delivered Cmds/sec and Snapshot:Delivered Trans/sec counters. The System Monitor registers data from the operating system point of view and does not provide any information at the granular level.

In contrast, the SQL Server Profiler capture the trace events of SQL Server, and we'll look at it next.

Using SQL Server Profiler

The SQL Server Profiler is a graphical tool that captures the trace events of SQL Server. You can use the Profiler to monitor and trace events for both the database engine and the Analysis server for SQL Server 2005. You can also use it to monitor SQL Server 2000.

First we will set up a trace template that can be used to gather information about snapshot replication. A template is essentially a file with a .tdf extension that contains the configuration for a trace, and SQL Server Profiler is a graphical interface to the trace. By using the traces, you will not only be able to monitor the system; you will see how SQL Server works internally and what stored procedures are called by what agents during replication.

It is not necessary to run the trace using the Profiler—you can instead use stored procedures to trace SQL Server and remove the overhead associated with running the Profiler. However, in this chapter I will use the Profiler to show you how to use templates to configure the traces.

Caution Due to performance costs, you should run the Profiler on a different machine from the one where SQL Server is running.

You can open the Profiler from SSMS by selecting Tools ➤ SQL Server Profiler. Once the Profiler opens, select File ➤ Templates ➤ New Template from the menu. This will open the Trace Template Properties window shown in Figure 17-28.

Note that you can select the server type. As mentioned earlier, you can also trace SQL Server 2000. Give the template a name, and check the "Base new template on existing one" box. If this box is unchecked, you will not be able to see the list of templates shown in the figure. When you do check the box, it automatically also checks the "Use as a default template for selected server type" box. I did not want to set a default template, so I unchecked that box, as you can see in Figure 17-28.

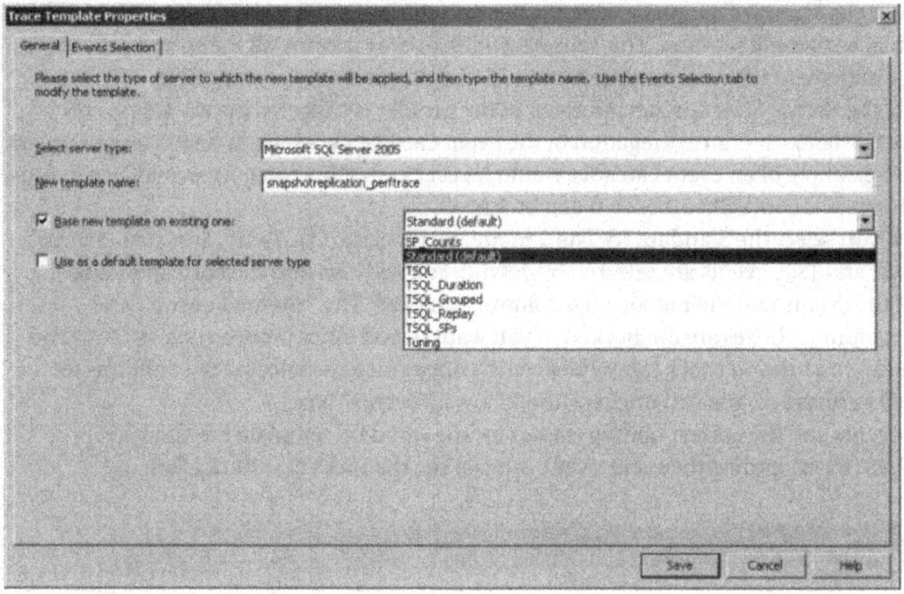

Figure 17-28. *Creating a new trace template*

There are several built-in templates located in the following directory for SQL Server 2005:
D:\Program Files\Microsoft SQL Server\90\Tools\Profiler\Templates\Microsoft SQL
Server\90. (There are separate folders for SQL Server 2000 and Analysis Server.) The templates
included for SQL Server 2005 are as follows:

- SP_Counts

- Standard

- TSQL

- TSQL_Duration

- TSQL_Grouped

- TSQL_Replay

- Tuning

- TSQL_SPs

For a description of each of these templates, refer to the SQL Server 2005 BOL.

Choose the Standard template, which is the default for tracing. We can add other trace objects to it, as you will see later. This template will not only capture all the stored procedures and T-SQL statements that are executed, but will also monitor the server activity.

Select the Events Selection tab. An *event* in the profiler is triggered by any actions of the SQL Server instance. It is an aggregation of the event categories, which in turn consist of event classes. An example of an event category would be Locks, and this category would be a collection of classes like Locks:Deadlock that can be traced.

When you select the Standard (default) template, the Security Audit, Sessions, Stored Procedures, and TSQL events are selected by default. You will also find the corresponding classes of the events and their associated columns checked. The "Show all events" and "Show all columns" boxes are unchecked. If you want to add other events, such as Locks and Performance, you need to check "Show all events"; once you have selected the columns for Locks and Performance, you can uncheck the "Show all events" box.

The events and the corresponding classes for the standard template are shown in Figure 17-29. By expanding the Locks event you can see the Locks:Deadlock class.

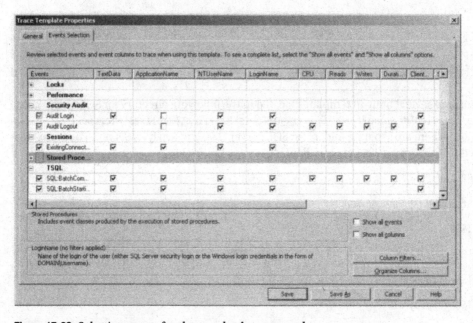

Figure 17-29. *Selecting events for the standard trace template*

I checked the NTUserName and LoginName boxes to run traces of the server in the background, in order to find out how Security Audit, Sessions, and Stored Procedure events, and different kinds of T-SQL statements, have been executed by the Windows user (NTUserName) and the name of the login of the user (LoginName). I unchecked the Audit Login and Audit Logout boxes for ApplicationName because I did not want to trace information on the client applications, such as SSMS and SQL Server Profiler. I also checked the box for "Show all events," which will display all the categories of SQL Server.

Other than the categories and classes that are checked automatically by the standard template, I selected the following categories and classes:

- `Database:Database File Autogrowth`

- `Database:Log File Autogrowth`

- `Errors and Warnings:ErrorLog`

- `Errors and Warnings:EventLog`

- `Errors and Warnings:Exception`

- `Locks:Deadlock graph`

- `Locks:Deadlock`

- `Locks:Deadlock Chain`

- `Locks:Released`

- `Locks:Timeout`

- `Performance:Showplan All`

- `Stored Procedures:RPC:Completed`

- `Stored Procedures:RPC:Starting`

- `Stored Procedures:SP:CacheHit`

- `Stored Procedures:SP:CacheInsert`

- `Stored Procedures:SP:CacheMiss`

- `Stored Procedures:SP:CacheRemove`

- `Stored Procedures:SP:Completed`

- `Stored Procedures:SP:Recompile`

- `Stored Procedures:SP:Starting`

- `Stored Procedures:SP:StmtCompleted`

- `TSQL:SQL:BatchCompleted`

- `TSQL:SQL:BatchStarting`

- `TSQL:SQL:StmtCompleted`

A sample of the events selected is shown in Figure 17-30.

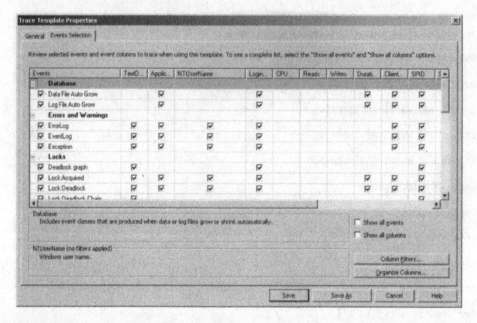

Figure 17-30. *Adding events in the standard template*

Save the template. If you then reopen the template, you will see that the new template, snapshotreplication_perftrace in this example, has the new events added to it as shown in Figure 17-30.

Now select File ➤ New Trace, and the SQL Server Profiler will ask you to connect to the server engine. After doing so, the Trace Properties window will open, as shown in Figure 17-31. Here you can specify how the trace will be saved.

In this case, I saved the trace both in file format and in a database table. Normally you will save it either as a trace file or in a table on a separate database. I created a separate database for storing the trace.

When you click the button beside the "Save to table" field, the Destination Table dialog box opens. Here you can select the destination database and table for the trace, as shown in Figure 17-32. Click OK to return to the Trace Properties window (Figure 17-31).

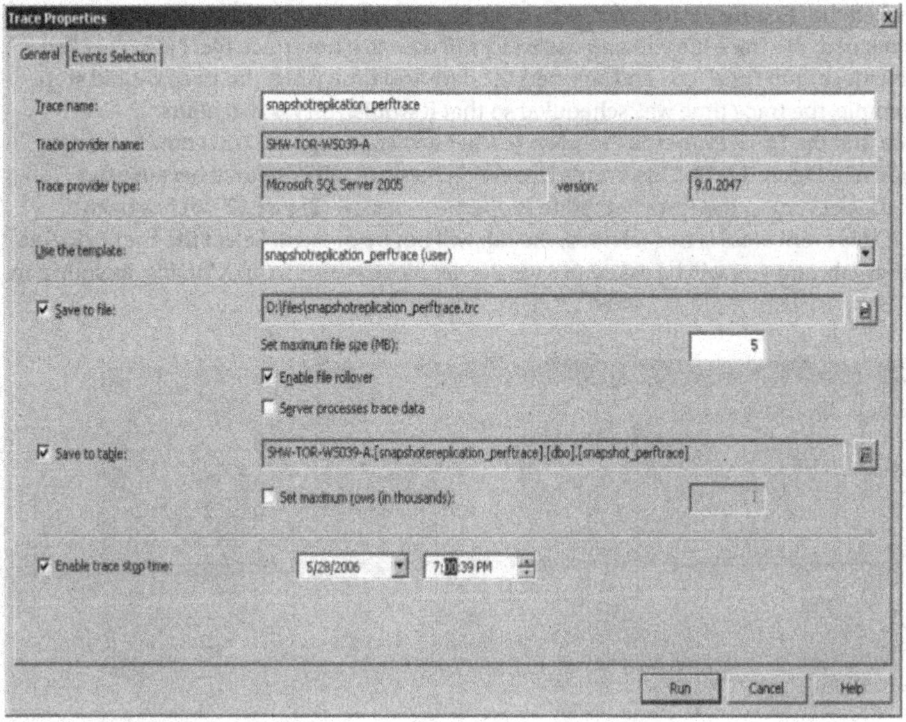

Figure 17-31. *The trace properties of snapshotreplication_perftrace*

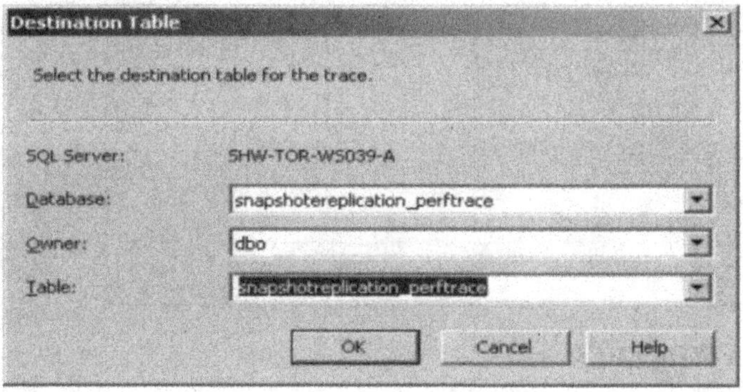

Figure 17-32. *Specifying a destination table for storing the trace*

I checked the "Enable file rollover" box. If the file exceeds the maximum file size of 5 MB, which I specified, the trace file will automatically roll over to a new trace file. I also checked the "Enable trace stop time" box and selected the date and time when the trace should stop. In this example, the trace time was scheduled so that it would run for two hours.

Notice that the Trace Properties window (earlier shown in Figure 17-31) now has a new tab, as shown in Figure 17-33. This Events Extraction Settings tab is created because the Locks:Deadlock event in the Trace Template Properties window (Figure 17-30) has been selected. If this event class is not selected, the tab will not be present. Select the Events Extraction Settings tab, and you will be asked to save the deadlock events in an XML file, as shown in Figure 17-33.

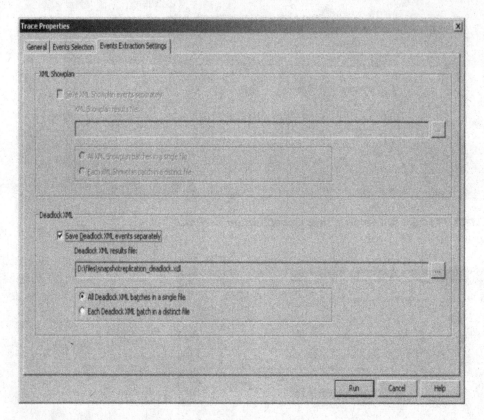

Figure 17-33. *Saving the deadlock file in XML format*

Now that we have finished setting up the trace, we will first use the System Monitor to run the counter log that we created while we configured the publication, subscriptions, and Distribution and the Snapshot Agents.

At the same time run the trace. While the trace is running, you can also stop it and read it. We will stop it and look at the trace to see whether the Snapshot Agent has started or is running. You can view the stopped trace by selecting File ➤ Edit and searching for sp_startpublication_ snapshot in the TextData column. This stored procedure is used to start the Snapshot Agent.

The trace output for the stored procedure is shown in Figure 17-34.

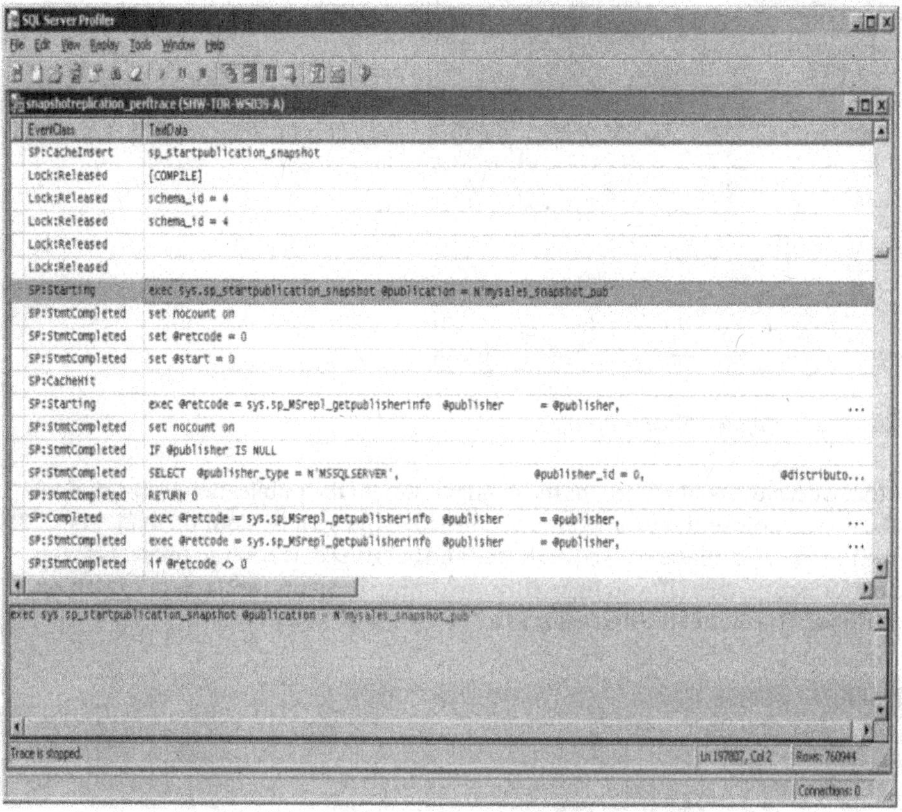

Figure 17-34. *Viewing trace output of the configuration of publication and push subscriptions for snapshot replication*

If you select the row that contains the stored procedure for starting the Snapshot Agent, you will see the code that was executed in the bottom pane. If you scroll down, you will be able to see the SPID, the client process ID, the name of the application, and the LoginName that started the Snapshot Agent.

You can step through the trace to view the steps involved in the execution of the Snapshot Agent and the time it took to execute. Similarly, you can see the stored procedures that need to be executed in sequence for the configuration of snapshot publication and subscriptions. You will find that procedures like sp_replicationdboption and sp_addpublication are in the trace. Notice that the trace is arranged in the same order as the columns in the Organize Columns dialog box shown in Figure 17-35.

You can open the Organize Columns dialog box by clicking the Organize Columns button in the Trace Template Properties window (Figure 17-30). You can rearrange the columns by selecting them and clicking the Up or Down buttons to move them in the list.

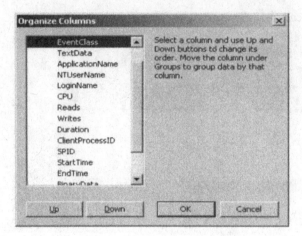

Figure 17-35. *Organizing the trace columns*

Now that we have seen the trace for the configuration of the publication, subscriptions, and agents, we will now see how the agents performed in the System Monitor. In Figure 17-36, you can see the spikes in the `Delivered Cmds/sec` and `Delivered Trans/sec` counters for the `snapshot` performance object. If you right-click on a line in the graph and select Properties, you can verify which counter the line belongs to.

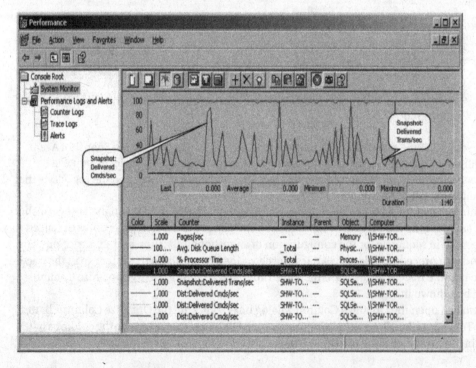

Figure 17-36. *Viewing the spikes in the Snapshot Agent counters*

We will now go back to the Profiler and open up the trace file that we saved. Select File ➤ Import Performance Data. This will open the Performance Counters Limit dialog box shown in Figure 17-37.

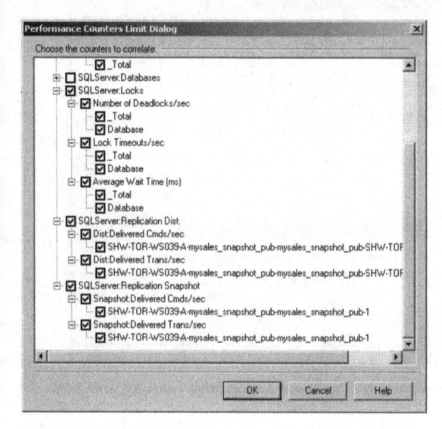

Figure 17-37. *Selecting the performance counters to correlate with the trace*

In this dialog box, select the performance counters you wish to use (I selected all but the SQLServer:Databases counter), and click OK. This will correlate the data from the System Monitor with that from the SQL Server Profiler and display it, as shown in Figure 17-38.

If you click anywhere in the graph, the Profiler will tell you the kind of event being called, and at the bottom of the screen it will show the T-SQL statement being executed. In this case, I clicked on the point where the vertical line is shown (at approximately 6:15 p.m.). You can see that the maximum value for the Average Wait Time counter for SQL Server:Locks is 151548.00 ms.

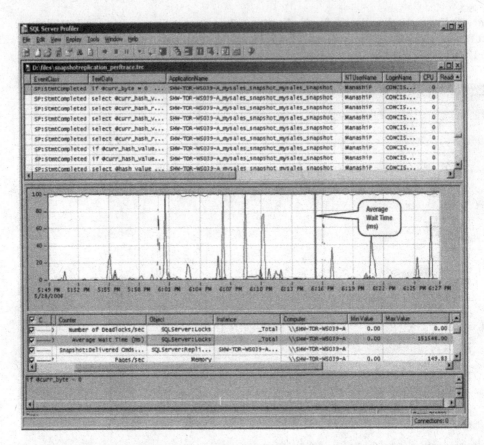

Figure 17-38. *Correlation of the System Monitor data with the trace file in SQL Server Profiler*

As you saw in Figure 17-32, the trace can be stored in a database other than the publication database. The table named snapshotreplication_perftrace is stored in the snapshotreplication_perftrace database. The SQL script that generates the table is shown in the following output:

```
CREATE TABLE [dbo].[snapshotreplication_perftrace](
    [RowNumber] [int] IDENTITY(0,1) NOT NULL,
    [EventClass] [int] NULL,
    [TextData] [ntext] COLLATE SQL_Latin1_General_CP1_CI_AS NULL,
    [ApplicationName] [nvarchar](128) COLLATE SQL_Latin1_General_CP1_CI_AS NULL,
    [NTUserName] [nvarchar](128) COLLATE SQL_Latin1_General_CP1_CI_AS NULL,
    [LoginName] [nvarchar](128) COLLATE SQL_Latin1_General_CP1_CI_AS NULL,
    [CPU] [int] NULL,
    [Reads] [bigint] NULL,
    [Writes] [bigint] NULL,
    [Duration] [bigint] NULL,
    [ClientProcessID] [int] NULL,
    [SPID] [int] NULL,
```

```
    [StartTime] [datetime] NULL,
    [EndTime] [datetime] NULL,
    [BinaryData] [image] NULL,
    [DatabaseID] [int] NULL,
    [DatabaseName] [nvarchar](128) COLLATE SQL_Latin1_General_CP1_CI_AS NULL,
PRIMARY KEY CLUSTERED
(
    [RowNumber] ASC
)WITH (PAD_INDEX  = OFF, IGNORE_DUP_KEY = OFF) ON [PRIMARY]
) ON [PRIMARY] TEXTIMAGE_ON [PRIMARY]
```

In this output, you can see that the SQL Server Profiler added the RowNumber column as the primary key, which is also a clustered index for the table. The rest of the columns are created in the same order as they were chosen in the Organize Columns dialog box (Figure 17-35). However, you can see that the EventClass column in the preceding script is an int data type, whereas in Figures 17-34 and 17-38, the output for EventClass shows as string. So, before we dig into the trace table, we need to relate the EventClass column with the EventClass in the SQL Server Profiler trace. This is done with the script in Listing 17-2.

Listing 17-2. *Relating Event Classes to Event Categories*

```
/*Execute this on the snapshotreplication_perftrace database */
use snapshotreplication_perftrace
go

select a.name as [EventClassName],
a.trace_event_id as [EventTrace],
b.category_id,
b.name as [Category],
b.type,
c.subclass_name
from sys.trace_events a,
sys.trace_categories b,
sys.trace_subclass_values c
where b.category_id=a.category_id and
a.trace_event_id=c.trace_event_id and
b.name in ('TSQL','locks','stored procedures')
go
```

This script uses three tables (sys.trace_events, sys.trace_categories, and sys_trace_subclass_values) to find out the name of the event class that corresponds to the event ID of the trace that corresponds to the EventClassName. We also need to find out which category the event class belongs to. The subclass_name column of the sys.trace_subclass_values table gives us the details of the event class, and the EventClass categories we want to find the integer values for are TSQL, Locks, and Stored Procedures.

Tip If you want to find out any other category values for the `EventClass`, just assign their names in the script where `locks` and `stored procedures` are placed.

The query returned 1,107 rows. Part of the output from the script in Listing 17-2 is shown in Figure 17-39.

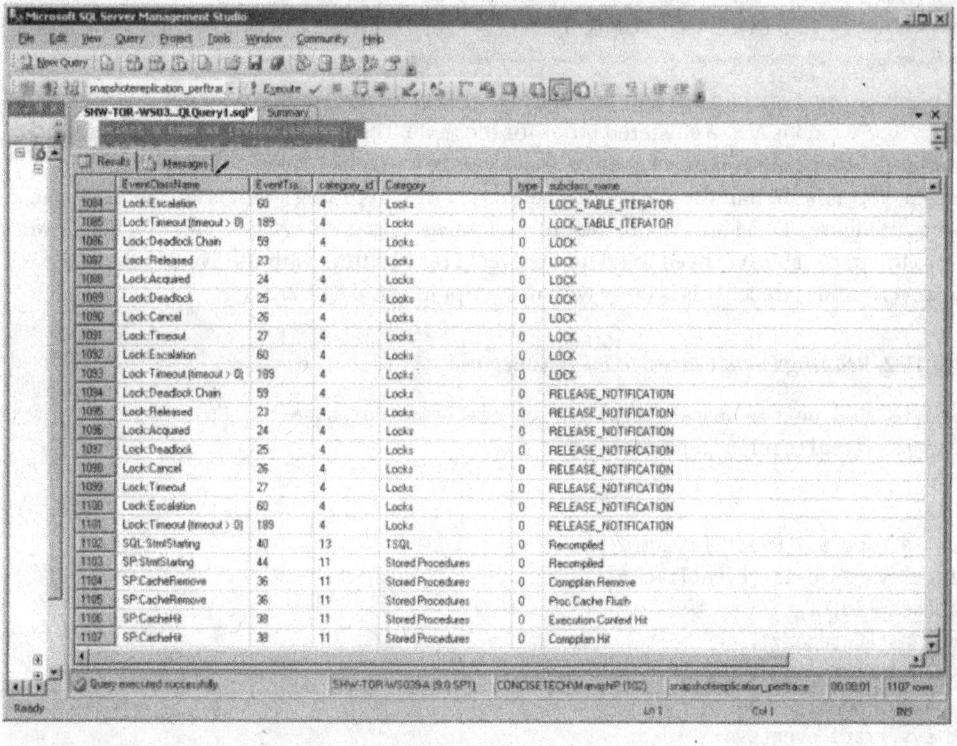

	EventClassName	EventTa...	category_id	Category	type	subclass_name
1084	Lock:Escalation	60	4	Locks	0	LOCK_TABLE_ITERATOR
1085	Lock:Timeout (timeout > 0)	189	4	Locks	0	LOCK_TABLE_ITERATOR
1086	Lock:Deadlock Chain	59	4	Locks	0	LOCK
1087	Lock:Released	23	4	Locks	0	LOCK
1088	Lock:Acquired	24	4	Locks	0	LOCK
1089	Lock:Deadlock	25	4	Locks	0	LOCK
1090	Lock:Cancel	26	4	Locks	0	LOCK
1091	Lock:Timeout	27	4	Locks	0	LOCK
1092	Lock:Escalation	60	4	Locks	0	LOCK
1093	Lock:Timeout (timeout > 0)	189	4	Locks	0	LOCK
1094	Lock:Deadlock Chain	59	4	Locks	0	RELEASE_NOTIFICATION
1095	Lock:Released	23	4	Locks	0	RELEASE_NOTIFICATION
1096	Lock:Acquired	24	4	Locks	0	RELEASE_NOTIFICATION
1097	Lock:Deadlock	25	4	Locks	0	RELEASE_NOTIFICATION
1098	Lock:Cancel	26	4	Locks	0	RELEASE_NOTIFICATION
1099	Lock:Timeout	27	4	Locks	0	RELEASE_NOTIFICATION
1100	Lock:Escalation	60	4	Locks	0	RELEASE_NOTIFICATION
1101	Lock:Timeout (timeout > 0)	189	4	Locks	0	RELEASE_NOTIFICATION
1102	SQL:StmtStarting	40	13	TSQL	0	Recompiled
1103	SP:StmtStarting	44	11	Stored Procedures	0	Recompiled
1104	SP:CacheRemove	36	11	Stored Procedures	0	Compplan Remove
1105	SP:CacheRemove	36	11	Stored Procedures	0	Proc Cache Flush
1106	SP:CacheHit	38	11	Stored Procedures	0	Execution Context Hit
1107	SP:CacheHit	38	11	Stored Procedures	0	Compplan Hit

Figure 17-39. *Part of the output from the script in Listing 17-2*

Suppose we want to use the trace table to find out which stored procedures executed during the configuration of both publication and push subscription were particularly CPU-intensive. We also want to find out how long it took to execute them. A value of 35 in the `EventClass` column of the snapshotreplication_perftrace table represents the completed execution of a stored procedure (identified in the SQL Server Profiler trace as `SP:Completed`). Finally, we want to get the description of the text (`TextData` column), the name of the application, and the SPID. The script in Listing 17-3 does this.

Listing 17-3. *Finding CPU-Intensive Stored Procedures and Their Duration of Execution*

```
/*Execute this on the trace database */
use snapshotreplication_perftrace
go
select eventclass,
```

```
textdata,
applicationname,
spid,
duration,
cpu
from snapshotreplication_perftrace
/* eventclass=35 corresponds to SP:Completed */
where eventclass=35
go
```

This script returned 750 rows. Part of the output is shown in Figure 17-40. In this case, none of the stored procedures were CPU-intensive, and the duration of the execution was negligible.

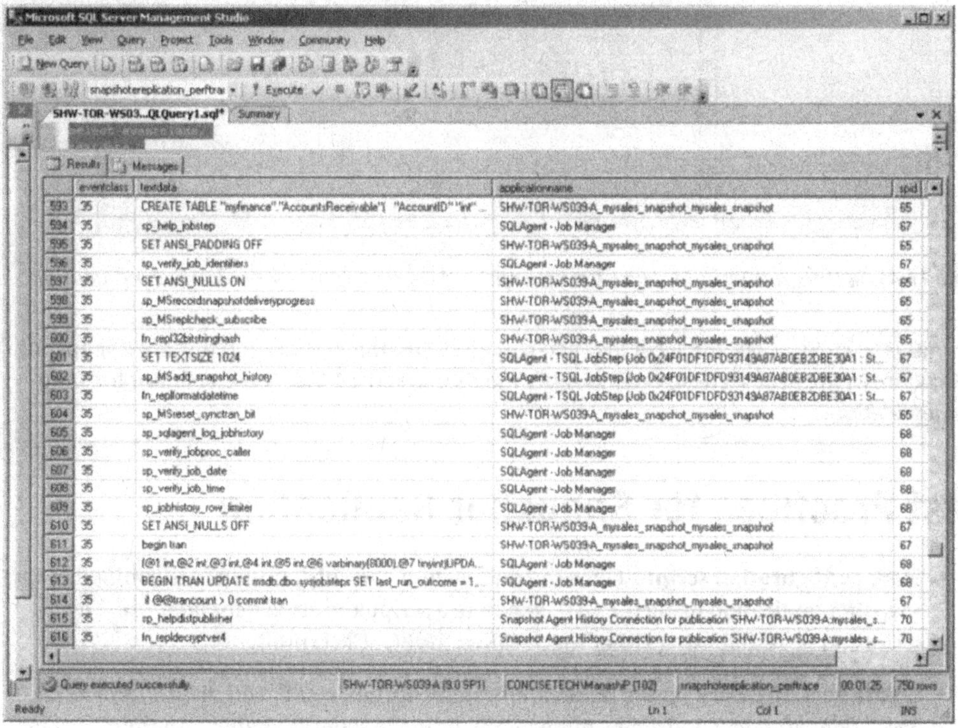

Figure 17-40. *Part of the output from running the script in Listing 17-3*

Now that the optimization process for snapshot replication has been completed, you can set up a threshold value; if the system exceeds that value, it can notify you of any actions that need to be taken. Open the Replication Monitor and, in the left pane, select the snapshot publication that you created, as shown in Figure 17-41. Select the Warnings and Agents tab. You can add to the warnings by clicking on the Configure Alerts button. In this example, I chose to be alerted if the subscription expires within the threshold of 80 percent. When the threshold is reached, an "Expiry soon" warning will be displayed for the status of the subscription.

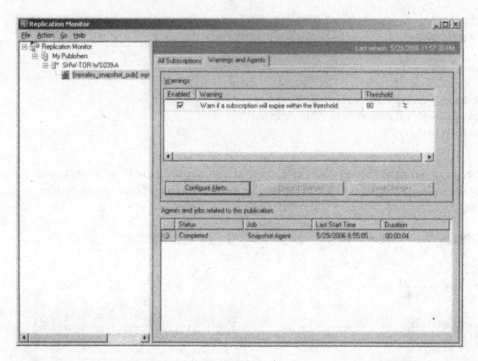

Figure 17-41. *Setting a threshold value for the expiry of a subscription for snapshot publication*

You now know about the tools that you can use to monitor, trace, and optimize snapshot replication. In the next section, I will identify the best practices that you can follow for snapshot replication.

Best Practices for Snapshot Replication

- **Store configuration scripts**: Once the publication and subscriptions are configured for snapshot replication using the GUI, generate a script and store it for later use. The script can be tested using either the SSMS or the SQLCMD utility.

- **Create backups**: Back up the publication, subscription, msdb, and distribution databases right after you add a new publication, or make schema changes on the publication. You should back up the msdb databases on the Publisher, Distributor, and Subscriber servers separately. Ensure that you have a backup and restoration script, and that you test it periodically.

- **Generate performance baselines**: Develop a baseline for the performance of snapshot replication on the server side for each of the server and hardware resources, like processors and memory, and the configuration of the Distributor. You should also develop a performance baseline for the client side for each of the filtering options, the agent parameters, the subscription options, the generation of the snapshot, and the settings of thresholds and warning.

- **Use data-modeling tools to design the database**: The physical data model (PDM) should at least be up to the third normal form. In designing the publication, add only the articles that are necessary. If you add articles the subscribing servers do not need, the Snapshot Agent will require more resources than necessary every time it runs. Consequently, use caution when adding indexes to the Subscriber server, as the creation of indexes other than the one on the primary key column can affect DML operations (refer to BOL).

- **Reduce contention**: Since latency is not an issue with snapshot replication, consideration must be made to reduce contention. This is particularly so between the activities of the user and the replication agent. Turning on the READ_COMMITTED_SNAPSHOT option for both the publishing and subscribing databases can reduce this.

Caution There is a double *T* in COMMITTED for the preceding option. There is another option called READ_COMMITED_SNAPSHOT, which, when set on, is used on the Transactional Isolation Level of read committed to provide statement-level read consistency by using row-versioning.

- **Consider using anonymous or pull subscriptions**: The Distribution Agent will reside on the Subscriber server, and not on the Distributor server, so using anonymous or pull subscriptions will reduce the workload on the Distributor server.

- **Schedule the snapshot carefully**: Generate the snapshot during off-peak hours and not during peak business hours, particularly if you have a slow network or low bandwidth.

- **Plan data locations**: Consider saving the data and the log files for the distribution database on a separate drive from where the snapshot is generated to reduce contention between the disks. Have the snapshot folder local to the Distributor server, since the Distribution Agent needs to access it to transmit the messages to the appropriate subscribing servers.

- **Assign permissions**: Ensure the right permissions are given to the snapshot folder on the Distributor server.

- **Use one snapshot folder**: Generate the snapshot only to one folder and not simultaneously to an alternate folder, as this requires the Snapshot Agent to write first on the default folder and then to the alternate folder. Instead, you could save the snapshot on some storage media and then transfer it physically to the subscribing server.

- **Consider compressing the snapshot**: Compressing the snapshot will make the transfer of files across the network easier and faster. Bear in mind, though, that more work needs to be done by the Snapshot Agent to generate the compressed snapshot and by the Distribution Agent to process the files, and this might have an adverse impact on performance.

- **Consider manual initialization**: Consider manually initializing subscriptions for snapshot publications containing a lot of data.

- **Minimize logging for initial synchronization**: During the initial phase of the subscription synchronization, have the subscribing database set either to the Simple or Bulk Recovery model. This will ensure that bulk inserts are logged minimally. Once the configuration is done, set it to Full Recovery. Do not set any of the databases to autogrowth mode, as this will lead to fragmentation and can degrade performance.

- **Adjust agent parameters**: Once you have configured snapshot replication, change the parameters for both the Snapshot and Distribution Agents, particularly -HistoryVerboseLevel and -OutputVerboselevel. Set -OutputVerboselevel to 0 so that only the error messages are logged. Set -HistoryVerboseLevel to 1 so that minimal history of the data is logged. Increase the -MaxBcpThreads parameter for the Snapshot Agent to 2 so that the bcp utility can run faster using parallel processing.

- **Use bulk inserts**: For the Distribution Agent use the -UseInprocLoader parameter, as this will cause the agent to use the BULK INSERT property instead.

Note You cannot use the -UseInprocLoader parameter if the data is in XML format.

- **Use the System Monitor**: System Monitor can trace the data for server-wide operations. Have separate counters for each of the operations that are monitored. For example, have separate counters for locks, Snapshot Agents, and Distribution Agents.

- **Use the SQL Server Profiler**: SQL Server Profiler can create a template to monitor the trace for snapshot replication. Save the trace in a file or a table in a separate database.

- **Set thresholds**: Use the Replication Monitor to set a threshold to warn when the subscriptions will expire.

Summary

In this chapter, I described how you can use the System Monitor to gather data on the performance of SQL Server. I also showed you how to use the templates provided by SQL Server to create a template that meets your business needs, and then save it in a file or as a table in a separate database. You should be able to read the trace and execute the required T-SQL to read the trace from the table. You should also be able to correlate data from the System Monitor with that of the SQL Server Profiler.

- Before deciding on the performance baseline of snapshot replication, consider latency, concurrency, throughput, and the duration of synchronization.

- Performance measurements should be taken regularly and consistently.

- Measurements should be taken both at peak hours and off-peak hours for query processing, replication agents and alerts, and snapshot generation.

- Measure the time it takes to back up and restore the replicated databases and system databases, such as the distribution and msdb databases.

- The System Monitor records the replication counters for the Replication Agents, Replication Dist, Replication Logreader, Replication Merge, and Replication Snapshot performance objects.

- For the Replication Snapshot performance object, the counters that you need to monitor are Snapshot:Delivered Cmds/sec and Delivered Trans/sec. The counters for the Replication Dist performance object are Dist:Delivered Cmds/sec and Delivered Trans/sec.

- The log files for the performance counters can be stored in CSV format and they can then be viewed using Microsoft Excel.

- You can use Excel's Chart Wizard to view the log in graphical format.

- Shared locks held on the publication can be seen using the Activity Monitor.

- The sys.dm_trans_locks dynamic management view can be used to view the locks held on the databases.

- SQL Server Profiler is a graphical tool that traces events. You can use the Profiler to trace events for SQL Server 2005, Analysis Server 2005, and SQL Server 2000.

- The standard trace templates are all located in the following directory for SQL Server 2005: \Program Files\Microsoft SQL Server\90\Tools\Profiler\Templates\Microsoft SQL Server\90. There are separate folders for SQL Server 2000 and Analysis Server.

- The different templates included for SQL Server 2005 are SP_Counts, Standard, TSQL, TSQL_Duration, TSQL_Grouped, TSQL_Replay, Tuning, and TSQL_SPs.

- You can save the trace either in a file format, such as with the .trc extension, or in a table in a separate database.

- You can correlate the data from the System Monitor on the SQL Server Profiler by importing the performance data by selecting File ➤ Import Performance Data in the SQL Server Profiler. Note that the start time and the duration must be set, or you will not be able to import the data for the System Monitor into SQL Server Profiler.

- You can use the sys.trace_events and sys.trace_categories catalog views to find the events for the traces, and the categories to which the traces belong.

- Use the Replication Monitor's Warnings and Agents tab to set the threshold for the optimization of snapshot replication.

- Use best practices for the administration of snapshot replication.

In the next chapter, I will focus on the optimization of transactional replication and will discuss the use of the Database Engine Tuning Advisor.

Quick Tips

- Prior to Windows NT 4.0, the name of the System Monitor was Performance Monitor.

- The counters can be saved in report format.

- Due to the performance costs incurred, you should run the Profiler from a separate machine from the server.

- Use the READ_COMMITTED_SNAPSHOT option to reduce contention between the user and the replication agent activity.

■ ■ ■

Optimizing Transactional Replication

This chapter focuses on optimizing transactional replication. I will describe the performance counters required for monitoring the Log Reader and Distribution Agents. I will also explain how to conduct a trace without using the SQL Profiler, and how to load the trace on the Database Engine Tuning Advisor. The chapter will conclude with a section on the best practices for the performance and tuning of transactional replication.

On completing this chapter, you will know all about the following:

- Tracing without using SQL Server Profiler

- The Database Engine Tuning Advisor

- The use of tracer tokens

- Best practices for optimizing transactional replication

Performance Considerations for the Transaction Log

As mentioned in Chapter 10, the transaction log is not only an essential component of the database structure but also of transactional replication. Data entries are written in the transaction log sequentially. Then the Log Reader Agent reads transactions marked for replication from the transaction log and sends them to the distribution database, which then sends them to the subscribing servers.

Note The internal workings of transactional replication are discussed in Chapter 10.

It is this dual processing of sequentially writing and then sequentially reading transactions marked for replication that incurs a considerable amount of I/O. While it is standard to write to the log file before a transaction is written to disk for all aspects of database processing (including snapshot and merge replication), reading from the log is only done for transactional replication. If the number of transactions is large, this dual processing can have a significant impact on the performance of the replicated database.

How the profile parameters and schedules of agents are set can also affect performance. For example, if the Log Reader Agent is running continuously, the agent is not stopped and restarted, and the downtime for that process can be averted. However, this can be offset if the time lag for the Log Reader Agent reading the transactions is high during periods of high transactions on the publication database.

However, before I discuss further those aspects of the agents that can be adjusted to improve performance, let's look at what we can do with the log to significantly optimize the process.

A transaction log consists of the logical log and the physical log file. The BOL states that the "transaction log operates logically as if the transaction log is a string of logical records." It is the logical log that keeps track of the log sequence number (LSN); any transactions entered in the log are identified by the LSN. In fact, both the restoration process and the transmission of replicated messages from the publication database to the subscription database are based on the LSN.

Every record in the transaction log is identified by the LSN, which is a unique number. The log records are stored sequentially as each record is added to the transaction log. Each of the log records in the transaction log is identified by the ID, and the log records contains the IDs for the transactions. They are arranged such that succeeding numbers are greater than the previous ones, and they are linked in a chain that points backwards to improve recovery speed (refer to the BOL). This is illustrated in Figure 18-1.

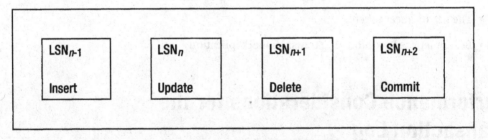

Figure 18-1. *The logical log containing the LSN that identifies the record of the transactions*

The physical log file is made up of a series of virtual log files (VLFs) that are dynamically created by the database engine itself. Depending on the size of the log file, the engine will create the requisite number of VLFs, although the engine strives to maintain a low number of VLFs.

When you start entering data, the logical log is created at the beginning of the physical log file. As subsequent log entries are made, the logical log keeps getting bigger and moves towards the end of the physical log file. Although you cannot configure the number of the VLFs, you can look it up by using the following command:

```
DBCC loginfo
```

The number of rows retrieved is the number of VLFs that you have. You can monitor the number of VLFs and keep the number as low as possible. For optimization purposes, keep the number of VLFs to less than 50.

Note If you want to find out how the number of VLFs affects the performance of SQL Server, see "Kimberly L. Tripp's Blog, immerse yourself in sql server," at http://www.sqlskills.com/blogs/kimberly/.

As the logical log progresses towards the end of the physical log, the portion of the logical log that precedes the minimum recovery LSN is truncated (removed). For replication, the MinLSN is the start of the oldest transaction that is yet to be replicated to the distribution database. The section of the logical log between the minimum recovery LSN and the logical log holding the last entered record is the active log. This is shown in Figure 18-2.

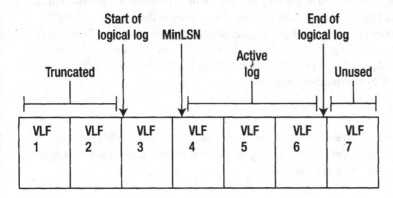

Figure 18-2. *The physical log, showing the VLFs, the logical log, and the active log*

Note Truncating the log means you are essentially truncating the logical log and not the physical log. Hence, the size of the physical log is not reduced. SQL Server merely reclaims space in the physical log for reuse by the logical log. To find more information about MinLSN, search for "Minimum Recovery LSN" in BOL.

You cannot truncate part of the active log, as it is used for recovering the database. Also, in replication it is the active log that contains the transactions marked for replication that have not been delivered to the distribution database. If the physical log becomes full, the portion of the logical log that is towards the end of the physical log reclaims the space in the physical log emptied by truncation and moves to the beginning of the physical log.

As long as you keep removing the old logical log files by truncating the log, the end of the logical log does not reach the beginning of the logical log, and this process is repeated until the end of the logical log reaches the beginning of the logical log. At this stage, two things can happen:

- If the growth_increment was specified for the FILEGROWTH option at the time of database creation, and disk space is available, new records are added to the logical log.

- If the amount of disk space available is less than the growth_increment specified, or if the FILEGROWTH option was not enabled, you will get a 9002 error message.

Note that the size set for growth_increment determines how many VLFs there will be. If the size of the increments is small, you will have a large number of VLFs. It is better to have a large value for the growth_increment and to set the size for the log file to a value close to the final value that you envisage. The default growth_increment for the log file is 10 percent.

Now that you know the structure of the log, let's look at how the data modifications are made. Data modifications are written to the log first, before being written to the disk. This is known as the write-ahead log (WAL). SQL Server uses this feature of the transaction log to ensure the ACID properties of the transactions are maintained. When data modifications are made, SQL Server retrieves the page from the buffer cache and makes the necessary modifications on the copy of the page. The data is not written directly to the disk unless a checkpoint is issued either manually or by the database engine.

Tip The CHECKPOINT T-SQL statement now has a checkpoint_duration option, which can help in the optimization process when a checkpoint is issued. Setting this option to a higher value makes the engine assign fewer resources than were it set to a lower value.

A modified data page that is held in the buffer but not yet written to disk is known as a dirty page. When modifications are made on the data pages in the buffer, entries are also made in the log cache, which is separate from the buffer cache of the data pages. If a commit is issued on the transactions, the log cache holding the modifications needs to be written to disk before the dirty pages are written to disk. SQL Server ensures that dirty pages are not flushed before the log cache is written to disk.

Using Tracer Tokens

As with snapshot replication, latency, throughput, concurrency, duration of synchronization, and hardware resources are the parameters that must be taken into consideration when you optimize transactional replication. While latency is not an important factor for snapshot replication, the low latency inherent in transactional replication makes latency crucial in determining the time taken to transfer committed transactions from the publication database to the subscription databases. For transactional replication, it is now possible to monitor the latency by using tracer tokens.

Note The optimization of snapshot replication is discussed in Chapter 17.

A token is a bit of data that is inserted in the publication log and is replicated from the publication database via the distribution database to the subscription database. It helps measure the time taken to transfer data from the publication to the distribution database and helps you to find the latency between the Publisher and Distributor servers.

The tracer token is picked up by the Log Reader Agent from the publication database and is transmitted to the distribution database. The latency between the distributing and the subscribing servers can also be found, because the Distribution Agent then transmits the tracer token to the subscription database. This way you can determine which Subscriber servers are performing well and which ones are waiting to receive data.

Before you insert a token into a publication database, you must ensure your system meets the following conditions:

- The Publisher server must be SQL Server 2005 or Oracle.

- The Distributor server must be SQL Server 2005.

- If you are running push subscriptions, the Publisher, Distributor, and Subscriber servers must be SQL Server 7.0 or later.

- If you are running pull subscriptions, the Publisher, Distributor, and Subscriber servers must be SQL Server 2005. Otherwise, you will not be able to track the messages from the Subscriber server.

There are a few other points to keep in mind about using tokens:

- The subscriptions must be active in order for them to receive the tracer tokens.

- Reinitializing subscriptions will remove the tracer tokens for those subscriptions.

- Republishing subscribing servers cannot send tracer tokens.

- Tracer tokens can be received by subscriptions only after initialization.

In order to insert a tracer token for a publication, open the Replication Monitor by right-clicking on the Replication folder in SSMS and selecting Launch Replication Monitor. Open Publishers in the left pane and select the publication for transactional replication that you want to monitor, as shown in Figure 18-3. In the right pane, select the Tracer Tokens tab and click the Insert Tracer button.

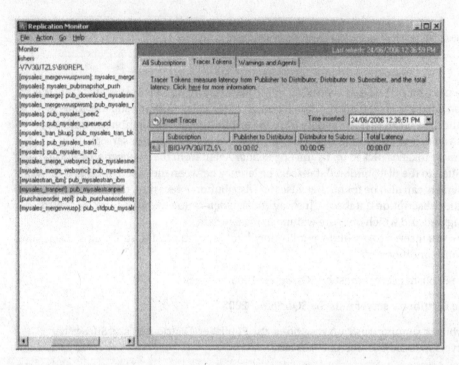

Figure 18-3. *Monitoring latency for transactional publication using tracer tokens*

Note that in this figure you can see the transfer time between the Publisher and Distributor servers and then between the Distributor and Subscriber servers. If the Subscriber or Distributor servers were waiting for the committed data to be received, it would show as pending. You can also view previously inserted tracer tokens by selecting the appropriate time from the "Time inserted" drop-down list.

Note If you select a snapshot publication in the Replication Monitor's left pane, the Tracer Tokens tab would not be displayed, since latency is not an integral factor in the optimization of snapshot replication. Also, if you use the tracer tokens for peer-to-peer transactional replication, there will be a delay, as all the nodes are equal. Hence, it is better not to use tracer tokens to determine latency in peer-to-peer replication.

While you can insert a tracer token and monitor the latency using the Replication Monitor, bear in mind that there is a performance impact when you use the monitor. To avoid this, you can use T-SQL to set the tracer token as shown in Listing 18-1.

Listing 18-1. *Setting the Tracer Token for a Transactional Publication*

```
:setvar logintimeout 120
:setvar server "BIO-V7V30JTZLZS\BIOREPL_PEER"
:connect $(server) -l $(logintimeout)
```

```
/*Execute this on the publication database */
use $(pubdb)
go

declare @tokenidoutput int;
exec sys.sp_posttracertoken @publication='$(pubname)',
@publisher= '$(server)',
@tracer_token_id= @tokenidoutput OUTPUT
go
```

This script uses the SQLCMD utility to insert the tracer tokens. The sys.sp_posttracertoken stored procedure asks for the name of the publication, the name of the Publisher server, and the ID setting of the tracer token. The @tracer_token_id parameter is the ID of the tracer token I inserted into the database, and it is an output parameter.

You can execute the script from the command prompt as follows:

```
SQLCMD -E -ic:\Inserttracertoken.sql -vpubdb="mysales_tranperf"
pubname="pub_mysalestranperf"
```

Note that you need to have active subscriptions for the publication when executing the script in Listing 18-1; otherwise you will get the following message:

```
C:\>sqlcmd -E -iC:\inserttracertoken.sql -vpubdb="mysales"
pubname="pub_mysales_tran2"
Sqlcmd: Successfully connected to server 'BIO-V7V30JTZLS\BIOREPL'.
Changed database context to 'mysales'.
Msg 21488, Level 16, State 1, Server BIO-V7V30JTZLS\BIOREPL,
Procedure sp_MSreplposttracertoken, Line 136
No active subscriptions were found. The publication must have active
subscriptions in order to post a tracer token.
```

The output of the script in Listing 18-1 is shown in Figure 18-4.

Figure 18-4. *Output of the script in Listing 18-1*

■**Tip** To find out whether the tracer token has been posted, you can execute sp_helptracertokens @publication='pub_mysalestranperf' on the publication database. The output will show you the values for the tracer_id and the publisher_commit columns.

We can then find the latency for the Distributor server by using the MStracer_tokens system table in the distribution database. This is shown in Listing 18-2.

Listing 18-2. *Determining the Latency of the Distributor Server*

```
/*Execute this on the distribution database */
Use distribution
Go


/* The time difference between the publisher_commit and the
distributor_commit is the distributor_latency */

Select a.tracer_id,
a.publication_id,
a.publisher_commit,
a.distributor_commit,
datediff(ms,a.publisher_commit,a.distributor_commit) as
distributor_latency,
b.publisher_db,
b.publication_type,
b.publication,
b.allow_push,
b.allow_pull
from MStracer_tokens a, MSpublications b
where a.publication_id=b.publication_id
go
```

This script finds the latency for the distributing server by first selecting the tracer_id, publication_id, publisher_commit, and distributor_commit columns from the MStracer_tokens system table. The difference in time between the publisher_commit and distributor_commit columns will give us the latency for the Distributor server. To ensure that the tracer tokens are indeed for transactional replication, the type of publication, the name of the publication, and the publication database are selected from the MSpublications system table in the distribution database. The two tables are joined with the publication_id.

■Note The system tables used for transactional replication are shown in Chapter 10, in the discussion of the internals of transactional replication.

The output of the script in Listing 18-2 follows:

```
Tracer_id       publication_id      publisher_commit
distributor_commit              distributor_latency
publisher_db        publication_type    publication
allow_push      allow_pull
```

```
-2147483645    36            2006-07-04 18:48:26.357
2006-07-04 18:48:27.630      1273
mysales_tranperf1    0                   pub_mysalestranperf1
1            1
```

Now that we know the latency involved in transmitting data from the publication to the distribution database, the next thing to do is find the latency between the distribution and the subscription database. This is shown in Listing 18-3.

Listing 18-3. *Determining the Latency for the Subscriber Server*

```
/* Execute this on the distribution database */
use distribution
go

/* The time difference between the distributor_commit in
the MStracer_tokens table and the subscriber_commit column in
the MStracer_history table is the subscriber_latency */

select a.publication_id,
a.publisher_db,
a.publication,
a.publication_type,
b.subscriber_db,
b.subscription_type,
d.distributor_commit,
c.subscriber_commit,
datediff(ms,d.distributor_commit, c.subscriber_commit) as
subscriber_latency
from MSpublications a,
MSdistribution_agents b,
MStracer_history c,
MStracer_tokens d
Where a.publication=b.publication
And b.id=c.agent_id
And c.parent_tracer_id=d.tracer_id
go
```

This script finds the latency for the subscribing server by using the MStracer_history table in the distribution database. It selects the publication name, the type of publication (which should be transactional), the name of the subscriptions, and the subscription types. To get all this information, the MSpublications table is joined with the MSdistribution_agents table.

As with the Distributor server latency, the time difference between the distributor_commit column in the MStracer_tokens table and the subscriber_commit column in the MStracer_history table will give us the latency for the Subscriber server. The output of the script in Listing 18-3 is as follows:

```
Publication_id       publisher_db          publication
publication_type     subscriber_db         subscription_type
distributor_commit        subscriber_commit          latency

36                   mysales_tranperf1     pub_mysalestranperf1
0                    mysales_remote5       0
2006-07-04 18:48:27.630    2006-07-04 18:48:28.340     710
```

You can obtain the overall latency by adding the Distributor server latency and the Subscriber server latency.

Using the System Monitor

In Chapter 17, I showed you how to add performance counters for the Snapshot and Distribution Agents for snapshot replication. Since latency and throughput are key factors in transactional replication, we will monitor the Log Reader and Distribution Agents in the System Monitor for transactional replication.

Note For the details of how to use the System Monitor, see the "Using the System Monitor" section in Chapter 17.

The counters that are monitored for the Log Reader Agent are shown in Figure 18-5.

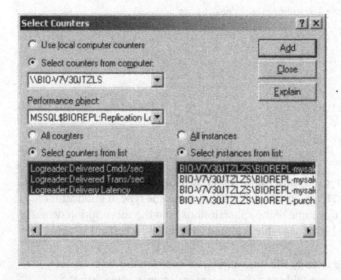

Figure 18-5. *Performance counters for the Log Reader Agent*

These are the three counters that I included for the Log Reader Agent:

- `Delivered Cmds/sec`: Indicates the number of commands per second that are delivered to the Distributor server

- `Delivered Trans/sec`: Indicates the number of transactions per second that are delivered to the Distributor server

- `Delivery Latency`: Indicates the time elapsed in milliseconds between when transactions were applied on the Publisher server and when they were delivered to the Distributor server

The counters for the Distribution Agent are the same as ones used for snapshot replication. This is shown in Figure 18-6.

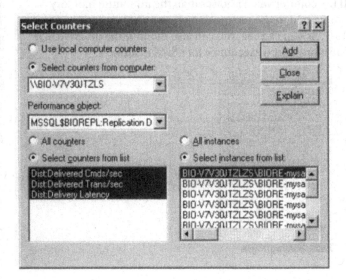

Figure 18-6. *Performance counters for the Distribution Agent*

Although the Snapshot Agent, as you are already aware, is used during the initial synchronization, I did not include counters for that agent since it does not often have any significant effect on performance. If you are transmitting large databases to different subscriptions, you might consider adding counters for the Snapshot Agent.

It can also be useful to monitor the total memory usage for SQL Server. As such, I included counters associated with the Process, Memory Manager, and Buffer Manager performance objects, as listed in Table 18-1.

Table 18-1. *Process- and Memory-Related Counters for SQL Server*

Performance Counter	Object Counter
Process	Working Set
Memory Manager	Total Server Memory (KB)
Buffer Manager	Page reads/sec
Buffer Manager	Page writes/sec
Buffer Manager	Total pages
Buffer Manager	Buffer cache hit ratio

The Working Set counter reveals the amount of memory used by a particular process; in this example it is SQL Server. If the counter value is lower than the minimum memory configured, the server has been configured to use too much memory, and you can change it accordingly, as shown in Figure 18-7. As you can see, you can also monitor the different SQL Server tools, such as the SSMS. The name of the executable for SSMS is SqlWb.

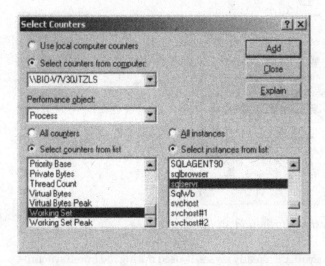

Figure 18-7. *Selecting the* Working Set *counter for the* Process *object*

The Total Server Memory counter for the Memory Manager performance object shows you how much memory is sought from the buffer pool.

The Page reads/sec and Page writes/sec counters for the Buffer Manager performance object indicate the number of physical pages that are being read and written every second. Since reading physical pages is an expensive I/O operation, it can be offset by adding the right indexes or by increasing the cache size.

The Total pages counter indicates the number of pages that are in the buffer pool. The Buffer cache hit ratio counter indicates how many pages are read without accessing the disk; this value should be as high as possible, although it usually tapers off after a while. The ratio is determined by dividing the total number of cache hits by the total number of cache lookups for approximately the last thousand pages. By increasing the memory, you can increase the ratio.

The performance counters added for the Buffer Manager performance object are shown in Figure 18-8.

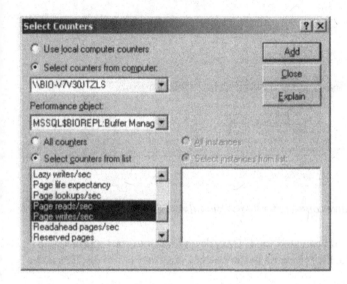

Figure 18-8. *Performance counters for the Buffer Manager object*

I also included the Number of Deadlocks/sec counter for the _Total instance of the Locks performance object, to find out whether there are any deadlocks when subscriptions are sent to different Subscriber servers.

Note The performance measurements should be taken at regular intervals, as mentioned in the discussion of optimizing snapshot replication (in Chapter 17). When performance measurements should be taken is discussed in the "Optimizing Performance" section.

For this example, I saved the counters in a text file and also saved them in HTML format so that they can be loaded on the Web if necessary. This is shown in Figure 18-9. If you select any of the counters, you will be able to see the counter moving across the page.

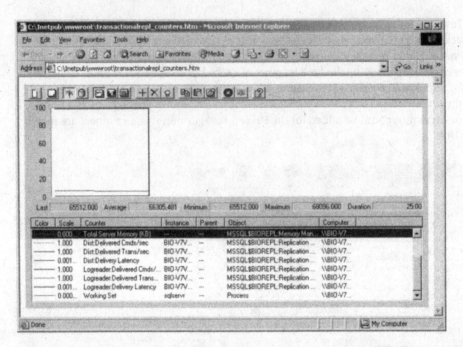

Figure 18-9. *Viewing the performance counters for transactional replication*

If the IIS is already running, you can load the HTML file and use it to start and stop the performance counters locally. The file is located in the wwwroot directory of the IIS. This is the HTML file created by the trace:

```
<HTML>
<HEAD>
<META NAME="GENERATOR" Content="Microsoft System Monitor">
<META HTTP-EQUIV="Content-Type" content="text/html;
charset=iso-8859-1">
</HEAD><BODY>
<OBJECT ID="DISystemMonitor1" WIDTH="100%" HEIGHT="100%"
CLASSID="CLSID:C4D2D8E0-D1DD-11CE-940F-008029004347">
    <PARAM NAME="_Version" VALUE="196611">
    <PARAM NAME="LogName" VALUE="transactionalrepl">
    <PARAM NAME="Comment" VALUE="">
    <PARAM NAME="LogType" VALUE="0">
    <PARAM NAME="CurrentState" VALUE="1">
    <PARAM NAME="LogFileMaxSize" VALUE="-1">
    <PARAM NAME="LogFileBaseName" VALUE="transactionalrepl">
    <PARAM NAME="LogFileSerialNumber" VALUE="1">
    <PARAM NAME="LogFileFolder" VALUE="C:\PerfLogs">
    <PARAM NAME="LogFileAutoFormat" VALUE="1">
    <PARAM NAME="LogFileType" VALUE="0">
    <PARAM NAME="StartMode" VALUE="2">
```

```
    <PARAM NAME="StartAtTime" VALUE="17/06/2006 11:04:41 PM">
    <PARAM NAME="StopMode" VALUE="0">
    <PARAM NAME="RestartMode" VALUE="0">
    <PARAM NAME="LogFileName"
VALUE="C:\PerfLogs\transactionalrepl_000001.csv">
    <PARAM NAME="EOFCommandFile" VALUE="">
    <PARAM NAME="Counter00001.Path" VALUE=
"\\BIO-V7V30JTZLS\MSSQL$BIOREPL:Buffer Manager\Buffer cache hit
 ratio">
    <PARAM NAME="Counter00002.Path" VALUE=
"\\BIO-V7V30JTZLS\MSSQL$BIOREPL:Buffer Manager\Page reads/sec">
    <PARAM NAME="Counter00003.Path" VALUE=
"\\BIO-V7V30JTZLS\MSSQL$BIOREPL:Buffer Manager\Page writes/sec">
    <PARAM NAME="Counter00004.Path" VALUE=
"\\BIO-V7V30JTZLS\MSSQL$BIOREPL:Locks(_Total)\Number of
Deadlocks/sec">
    <PARAM NAME="Counter00005.Path" VALUE=
"\\BIO-V7V30JTZLS\MSSQL$BIOREPL:Memory Manager\Total Server Memory
 (KB)">
    <PARAM NAME="Counter00006.Path" VALUE=
"\\BIO-V7V30JTZLS\MSSQL$BIOREPL:Replication Dist
.(BIO-V7V30JTZLZS\BIORE-mysales_tran_bkup-pub_mysales_tran_bkup-
BIO-V7V30JTZLZS\BIORE-27)\Dist:Delivered Cmds/sec">
    <PARAM NAME="Counter00007.Path" VALUE=
"\\BIO-V7V30JTZLS\MSSQL$BIOREPL:Replication Dist
.(BIO-V7V30JTZLZS\BIORE-mysales_tran_bkup-pub_mysales_tran_bkup-
BIO-V7V30JTZLZS\BIORE-27)\Dist:Delivered Trans/sec">
    <PARAM NAME="Counter00008.Path" VALUE=
"\\BIO-V7V30JTZLS\MSSQL$BIOREPL:Replication Dist
.(BIO-V7V30JTZLZS\BIORE-mysales_tran_bkup-pub_mysales_tran_bkup-
BIO-V7V30JTZLZS\BIORE-27)\Dist:Delivery Latency">
    <PARAM NAME="Counter00009.Path" VALUE=
"\\BIO-V7V30JTZLS\MSSQL$BIOREPL:Replication Logreader
(BIO-V7V30JTZLZS\BIOREPL-mysales_tran_bkup-5)
\Logreader:Delivered Cmds/sec">
    <PARAM NAME="Counter00010.Path" VALUE=
"\\BIO-V7V30JTZLS\MSSQL$BIOREPL:Replication Logreader
(BIO-V7V30JTZLZS\BIOREPL-mysales_tran_bkup-5)
\Logreader:Delivered Trans/sec">
    <PARAM NAME="Counter00011.Path" VALUE=
"\\BIO-V7V30JTZLS\MSSQL$BIOREPL:Replication Logreader
(BIO-V7V30JTZLZS\BIOREPL-mysales_tran_bkup-5)
\Logreader:Delivery Latency">
    <PARAM NAME="Counter00012.Path" VALUE=
"\\BIO-V7V30JTZLS\Process(sqlservr)\Working Set">
    <PARAM NAME="CounterCount" VALUE="12">
    <PARAM NAME="UpdateInterval" VALUE="15">
```

```
            <PARAM NAME="SampleIntervalUnitType" VALUE="1">
            <PARAM NAME="SampleIntervalValue" VALUE="15">
</OBJECT>
</BODY>
</HTML>
```

As with snapshot replication, you can correlate the System Monitor data with SQL Profiler. Now let's look at how to use the trace for transactional replication.

Using SQL Trace

SQL Profiler is a graphical interface to SQL Trace for monitoring the performance of both the SQL Server engine and the Analysis Server engine. However, the cost of using the graphical SQL Profiler is the overhead associated with it and the resulting effect on the operation itself. For this reason, it can be worthwhile to set up the trace using T-SQL stored procedures.

First, though, let's look at the benefits of using the trace:

- There is no overhead associated with trace.

- SQL Trace can monitor any event class.

- Traces can be received remotely.

- Events can be set up using the T-SQL stored procedures.

- If the SQL Server is stopped and restarted, the trace need not be restarted.

- Event data from the trace files can be queried programmatically.

■**Note** Programmatically querying event data from the trace files was shown in Chapter 17, in the discussion of optimizing snapshot replication.

In SQL Server, trace is enabled by default. If you execute the sp_configure stored procedure, you will see that the default trace enabled option is set to a value of 1, which indicates the trace is on; you can disable the option by setting it to 0. Since the trace is being run by default, you can also see the default trace file, which is located in the following directory: C:\Program Files\Microsoft SQL Server\MSSQL.1\MSSQL\LOG.

■**Note** You will be able to see the default trace enabled option only if you have show advanced options set to 1 for sp_configure.

You can find the name of the trace file by using the ::fn_trace_getinfo function, as shown in Listing 18-4.

Listing 18-4. *Locating the Default Trace File*

```
/*Execute this on the master database */
use master
go
select traceid,
property,
value
from
::fn_trace_getinfo(default)
go
```

This script retrieves the location of the trace file, which is in the value column of the ::fn_trace_getinfo function. The traceid gives us the ID of the trace for that particular property.

For a property of 1, a value of 2 means the trace file is enabled to roll over to a new file once the maximum size is exceeded. So if the original file is named log.trc, the name of the next file will be log1.trc. A property of 2 indicates the name of the trace file. The corresponding value gives us the name of the trace file. A property of 3 indicates that the maximum file size is 20 MB, which is shown in the value column. A property of 4 indicates the stoppage time of the trace. In this case, the value is NULL, which means that there is no stoppage time. A property of 5 indicates that the trace is currently running.

The output for the script in Listing 18-4 is follows:

```
Traceid property value
1        1        2
1        2        C:\Program Files\Microsoft SQL
Server\MSSQL.1\MSSQL\LOG\log_31.trc
1        3        20
1        4        NULL
1        5        1
```

Now that we have located the trace file, we can find out what's inside by using fn_trace_gettable. This function returns several columns, and the textdata column will tell us the kind of trace performed. This is shown in Listing 18-5.

Listing 18-5. *Reading the Trace File*

```
/*Execute this on the master database */
use master
go

/*Retrieve rows only for the mysales databases and where the
textdata column is not null */

select * from fn_trace_gettable
('C:\Program Files\Microsoft SQL
Server\MSSQL.1\MSSQL\LOG\log_31.trc',
```

```
default)
where textdata is not null
and databasename like 'mysales%'
go
```

The output of the script in Listing 18-5 is shown in Figure 18-10.

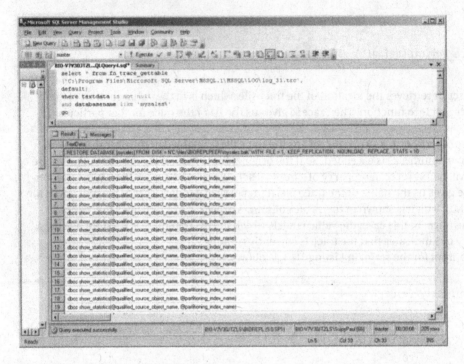

Figure 18-10. *Output for the script in Listing 18-5*

The script in Listing 18-5 specifies the filename and uses the default for the `number_files` parameter (the syntax for `fn_trace_gettable` is `fn_trace_gettable(filename, number_files)`). This makes the script read all the rollover files until it reaches the end of the trace file. In this example, I had five trace files.

I limited the textdata for all of the mysales databases. In Figure 18-10, you can see that the first statement executed was the restoration of the mysales database from the backup file; you can also see the options that were used during the restoration of the database.

Tip If you use the `select * from sys.traces` statement, it will return the pathname, the maximum size of the trace file, the maximum number of rollover files, and whether the rollover option is enabled or not. To retrieve the list of trace events and the corresponding IDs of the traces, you can execute `select * from sys.trace_events`. By using the `where` clause, you can filter out the name of the traces and the ID of the trace.

In order to run the trace using T-SQL, you need to execute the following stored procedures:

- Sp_trace_create to create the trace

- Sp_trace_setevent to add the events

- Sp_trace_setfilter to add the filters

- Sp_trace_setstatus to start, stop, and close the trace

You should keep in mind that when T-SQL stored procedures are used, the SQL Trace will actually trace on the server side and will capture all the events until the disk is full. Also, you can have an audit trail using either the SQL Trace or the SQL Profiler by using the standard C2 audit mode; in this case, it will run until the disk is full, at which point a write error will be generated and the SQL Server instance will stop.

I will show you first how to generate the T-SQL trace from the SQL Profiler, and then we will use the output to make the necessary additions.

First, open the SQL Profiler and create the appropriate trace template with the necessary events and their corresponding data columns, as shown in Chapter 17. Then start executing the trace and stop it.

Now, select File ➤ Export ➤ Script Trace Definition ➤ For SQL Server 2005, and save the file as an SQL file. SQL Profiler will generate the T-SQL code for the trace, as follows:

```
-- Create a Queue
declare @rc int
declare @TraceID int
declare @maxfilesize bigint
set @maxfilesize = 5

-- Please replace the text InsertFileNameHere, with an appropriate
-- filename prefixed by a path, e.g., c:\MyFolder\MyTrace. The .trc
extension
-- will be appended to the filename automatically. If you are
writing from
-- remote server to local drive, please use UNC path and make sure
server has
-- write access to your network share

exec @rc = sp_trace_create @TraceID output, 0,
N'InsertFileNameHere', @maxfilesize, NULL
if (@rc != 0) goto error

-- Client side File and Table cannot be scripted

-- Set the events
declare @on bit
set @on = 1
exec sp_trace_setevent @TraceID, 148, 11, @on
exec sp_trace_setevent @TraceID, 148, 51, @on
```

```
exec sp_trace_setevent @TraceID, 148, 4, @on
exec sp_trace_setevent @TraceID, 148, 12, @on
exec sp_trace_setevent @TraceID, 148, 14, @on
exec sp_trace_setevent @TraceID, 148, 26, @on
exec sp_trace_setevent @TraceID, 148, 60, @on
exec sp_trace_setevent @TraceID, 148, 64, @on
exec sp_trace_setevent @TraceID, 148, 1, @on
exec sp_trace_setevent @TraceID, 148, 41, @on
exec sp_trace_setevent @TraceID, 10, 7, @on
exec sp_trace_setevent @TraceID, 10, 15, @on
exec sp_trace_setevent @TraceID, 10, 31, @on
exec sp_trace_setevent @TraceID, 10, 8, @on
exec sp_trace_setevent @TraceID, 10, 16, @on
exec sp_trace_setevent @TraceID, 10, 48, @on
exec sp_trace_setevent @TraceID, 10, 64, @on
exec sp_trace_setevent @TraceID, 10, 1, @on
exec sp_trace_setevent @TraceID, 10, 9, @on
exec sp_trace_setevent @TraceID, 10, 17, @on
exec sp_trace_setevent @TraceID, 10, 41, @on
exec sp_trace_setevent @TraceID, 10, 49, @on
exec sp_trace_setevent @TraceID, 10, 10, @on
exec sp_trace_setevent @TraceID, 10, 18, @on
exec sp_trace_setevent @TraceID, 10, 26, @on
exec sp_trace_setevent @TraceID, 10, 34, @on
exec sp_trace_setevent @TraceID, 10, 50, @on
exec sp_trace_setevent @TraceID, 10, 3, @on
exec sp_trace_setevent @TraceID, 10, 11, @on
exec sp_trace_setevent @TraceID, 10, 35, @on
exec sp_trace_setevent @TraceID, 10, 51, @on
exec sp_trace_setevent @TraceID, 10, 4, @on
exec sp_trace_setevent @TraceID, 10, 12, @on
exec sp_trace_setevent @TraceID, 10, 60, @on
exec sp_trace_setevent @TraceID, 10, 13, @on
exec sp_trace_setevent @TraceID, 10, 6, @on
exec sp_trace_setevent @TraceID, 10, 14, @on
exec sp_trace_setevent @TraceID, 45, 7, @on
exec sp_trace_setevent @TraceID, 45, 55, @on
exec sp_trace_setevent @TraceID, 45, 8, @on
exec sp_trace_setevent @TraceID, 45, 16, @on
exec sp_trace_setevent @TraceID, 45, 48, @on
exec sp_trace_setevent @TraceID, 45, 64, @on
exec sp_trace_setevent @TraceID, 45, 1, @on
exec sp_trace_setevent @TraceID, 45, 9, @on
exec sp_trace_setevent @TraceID, 45, 17, @on
exec sp_trace_setevent @TraceID, 45, 25, @on
exec sp_trace_setevent @TraceID, 45, 41, @on
exec sp_trace_setevent @TraceID, 45, 49, @on
exec sp_trace_setevent @TraceID, 45, 10, @on
```

```
exec sp_trace_setevent @TraceID, 45, 18, @on
exec sp_trace_setevent @TraceID, 45, 26, @on
exec sp_trace_setevent @TraceID, 45, 34, @on
exec sp_trace_setevent @TraceID, 45, 50, @on
exec sp_trace_setevent @TraceID, 45, 3, @on
exec sp_trace_setevent @TraceID, 45, 11, @on
exec sp_trace_setevent @TraceID, 45, 35, @on
exec sp_trace_setevent @TraceID, 45, 51, @on
exec sp_trace_setevent @TraceID, 45, 4, @on
exec sp_trace_setevent @TraceID, 45, 12, @on
exec sp_trace_setevent @TraceID, 45, 28, @on
exec sp_trace_setevent @TraceID, 45, 60, @on
exec sp_trace_setevent @TraceID, 45, 5, @on
exec sp_trace_setevent @TraceID, 45, 13, @on
exec sp_trace_setevent @TraceID, 45, 29, @on
exec sp_trace_setevent @TraceID, 45, 61, @on
exec sp_trace_setevent @TraceID, 45, 6, @on
exec sp_trace_setevent @TraceID, 45, 14, @on
exec sp_trace_setevent @TraceID, 45, 22, @on
exec sp_trace_setevent @TraceID, 45, 62, @on
exec sp_trace_setevent @TraceID, 45, 15, @on
exec sp_trace_setevent @TraceID, 12, 7, @on
exec sp_trace_setevent @TraceID, 12, 15, @on
exec sp_trace_setevent @TraceID, 12, 31, @on
exec sp_trace_setevent @TraceID, 12, 8, @on
exec sp_trace_setevent @TraceID, 12, 16, @on
exec sp_trace_setevent @TraceID, 12, 48, @on
exec sp_trace_setevent @TraceID, 12, 64, @on
exec sp_trace_setevent @TraceID, 12, 1, @on
exec sp_trace_setevent @TraceID, 12, 9, @on
exec sp_trace_setevent @TraceID, 12, 17, @on
exec sp_trace_setevent @TraceID, 12, 41, @on
exec sp_trace_setevent @TraceID, 12, 49, @on
exec sp_trace_setevent @TraceID, 12, 6, @on
exec sp_trace_setevent @TraceID, 12, 10, @on
exec sp_trace_setevent @TraceID, 12, 14, @on
exec sp_trace_setevent @TraceID, 12, 18, @on
exec sp_trace_setevent @TraceID, 12, 26, @on
exec sp_trace_setevent @TraceID, 12, 50, @on
exec sp_trace_setevent @TraceID, 12, 3, @on
exec sp_trace_setevent @TraceID, 12, 11, @on
exec sp_trace_setevent @TraceID, 12, 35, @on
exec sp_trace_setevent @TraceID, 12, 51, @on
exec sp_trace_setevent @TraceID, 12, 4, @on
exec sp_trace_setevent @TraceID, 12, 12, @on
exec sp_trace_setevent @TraceID, 12, 60, @on
exec sp_trace_setevent @TraceID, 12, 13, @on
exec sp_trace_setevent @TraceID, 54, 7, @on
```

```
exec sp_trace_setevent @TraceID, 54, 8, @on
exec sp_trace_setevent @TraceID, 54, 64, @on
exec sp_trace_setevent @TraceID, 54, 9, @on
exec sp_trace_setevent @TraceID, 54, 25, @on
exec sp_trace_setevent @TraceID, 54, 41, @on
exec sp_trace_setevent @TraceID, 54, 49, @on
exec sp_trace_setevent @TraceID, 54, 6, @on
exec sp_trace_setevent @TraceID, 54, 10, @on
exec sp_trace_setevent @TraceID, 54, 14, @on
exec sp_trace_setevent @TraceID, 54, 22, @on
exec sp_trace_setevent @TraceID, 54, 26, @on
exec sp_trace_setevent @TraceID, 54, 3, @on
exec sp_trace_setevent @TraceID, 54, 11, @on
exec sp_trace_setevent @TraceID, 54, 35, @on
exec sp_trace_setevent @TraceID, 54, 51, @on
exec sp_trace_setevent @TraceID, 54, 4, @on
exec sp_trace_setevent @TraceID, 54, 12, @on
exec sp_trace_setevent @TraceID, 54, 60, @on


-- Set the Filters
declare @intfilter int
declare @bigintfilter bigint

exec sp_trace_setfilter @TraceID, 10, 0, 7, N'SQLProfiler'
exec sp_trace_setfilter @TraceID, 10, 0, 7, N'SQLAgent'
exec sp_trace_setfilter @TraceID, 10, 0, 7,
N'SQLServerManagementStudio'
exec sp_trace_setfilter @TraceID, 10, 0, 1, N''
exec sp_trace_setfilter @TraceID, 35, 1, 6, N'msdb'
exec sp_trace_setfilter @TraceID, 35, 1, 6, N'mysales_remote4'
exec sp_trace_setfilter @TraceID, 35, 1, 6, N'distribution'
exec sp_trace_setfilter @TraceID, 35, 1, 6, N'mysales_remote5'
exec sp_trace_setfilter @TraceID, 35, 1, 6, N'mysales_tranperf'
exec sp_trace_setfilter @TraceID, 35, 1, 6, N'mysales_tranperf1'
-- Set the trace status to start
exec sp_trace_setstatus @TraceID, 1

-- display trace id for future references
select TraceID=@TraceID
goto finish

error:
select ErrorCode=@rc

finish:
go
```

You can see that a queue is created in the preceding code. The trace architecture requires that events like SP:StmtCompleted that are captured in a trace definition be forwarded to a queue. It is from this queue that the trace information is either saved to a file or a database table.

The code then executes the sp_trace_create stored procedure. The @traceid parameter is generated by SQL Server, and the pathname for the output trace file is shown in the comments section. You can also see that the @maxfilesize parameter has been set to a default value of 5 MB. The value NULL indicates that there is no stoppage time for the trace until you manually stop the trace.

The code then adds the events by executing the sp_trace_setevent stored procedure, and it uses the traceid, the eventid, the id of the column that is added to the event, and a bitmap @on parameter that has been set to a value of 1, which means that the event is ON (if it were set to 0 the event would be turned off). The event names corresponding to the event IDs in the preceding code are shown in Table 18-2.

Tip You can look up the event names corresponding to the eventid values by retrieving the sys.trace_events table.

Table 18-2. *The Event IDs and Corresponding Event Names*

Event ID	Event Name
148	Deadlock Graph
10	RPC:Completed
45	SP:StmtCompleted
54	TransactionLog
12	SQL:BatchCompleted
35	SP:CacheInsert

The events in Table 18-2 are the ones I chose for tracing transactional replication. The Deadlock Graph event was chosen to see whether there are any deadlocks arising due to DML operations being carried out. The SP:StmtCompleted event will indicate which stored procedure execution was completed. The growth of the transaction log is being monitored because in transactional replication the Log Reader Agent needs to read the committed transactions in the publication database before it can send these transactions to the distribution database. Until the Log Reader Agent picks up the transactions, the log cannot be truncated, and the growth of the log can have an impact on the performance of the replication process. The SQL:BatchCompleted event has been added to monitor when the T-SQL batch statements are completed. The SP:CacheInsert event tells us when an item has been inserted in the procedure cache.

The column IDs and corresponding column names are listed in Table 18-3.

Table 18-3. *The Column IDs and Corresponding Column Names*

Column ID	Column Name
1	Textdata
51	EventSequence
3	DatabaseID
4	TransactionId
6	NTUserName
7	NTDomainName
8	HostName
9	ClientProcessID
10	ApplicationName
11	LoginName
12	SPID
13	Duration(milliseconds)
14	StartTime
15	EndTime
16	Reads
17	Writes
18	CPU
22	ObjectID
25	IntegerData
26	IntegerData
28	ObjectType
29	NestLevel
31	Error
34	ObjectName
35	DatabaseName
41	LoginSid
48	RowCounts
49	RequestID
50	XactSequence
51	EventSequence
55	IntegerData2
60	IsSystem
62	SourceDatabaseID
64	SessionLoginName

The code then filters out the data. The amount of data that SQL Trace or SQL Profiler returns can be daunting, so it is better to filter out those aspects you do not need and include only the ones you want to monitor. To do this, the sp_trace_setfilter stored procedure is used with following parameters: traceid, columned, and logical_operator (set to 0, meaning "add," or 1, meaning "or"). The comparison_operator has been either set to LIKE (value of 6) and NOT LIKE (value of 7). In this case, we do not want to trace applications like SQL Profiler, SSMS, and the SQL Agent while monitoring the distribution, msdb, publication, and subscription databases used for transactional replication.

Finally, the trace is started by executing the sp_trace_setstatus procedure, setting the status parameter to 1. A value of 0 will stop the trace, and a value of 2 will close the trace and delete it from the server instance.

Now that we have set the trace, we can schedule the tracing by setting a job and scheduling it job to run. This is shown in Listing 18-6.

Listing 18-6. *Scheduling the Job for the Trace*

```
BEGIN TRANSACTION
DECLARE @ReturnCode INT
SELECT @ReturnCode = 0

IF NOT EXISTS (SELECT name FROM msdb.dbo.syscategories
WHERE name='Database Maintenance' AND category_class=1)
BEGIN
EXEC @ReturnCode = msdb.dbo.sp_add_category @class='JOB',
@type='LOCAL',
@name='Database Maintenance'
IF (@@ERROR <> 0 OR @ReturnCode <> 0)
GOTO QuitWithRollback

END

DECLARE @jobId BINARY(16)
EXEC @ReturnCode =  msdb.dbo.sp_add_job
@job_name='mysales_perftrace',
@enabled=1,
@notify_level_eventlog=2,
@notify_level_email=0,
@notify_level_netsend=0,
@notify_level_page=0,
@delete_level=0,
@description='schedules the trace for transactional
replication of mysales database',
@category_name='Database Maintenance',
owner_login_name=N'BIO-V7V30JTZLS\SujoyPaul',
@job_id = @jobId OUTPUT
```

```
IF (@@ERROR <> 0 OR @ReturnCode <> 0)
GOTO QuitWithRollback

/* Step 1: Add the job step and start the trace:
 START THE TRACE */

EXEC @ReturnCode = msdb.dbo.sp_add_jobstep @job_id=@jobId,
@step_name='Start the trace ---tranperftrace',
@step_id=1,
@cmdexec_success_code=0,
@on_success_action=3,
@on_success_step_id=0,
@on_fail_action=2,
@on_fail_step_id=0,
@retry_attempts=0,
@retry_interval=0,
@os_run_priority=0,
@subsystem='TSQL',
@command=N'create procedure usp_mysalestranperf
as

/* Create a Queue */
declare @rc int
declare @TraceID int
declare @maxfilesize bigint
set @maxfilesize = 5

-- Please replace the text InsertFileNameHere, with an appropriate
-- filename prefixed by a path, e.g., c:\MyFolder\MyTrace. The .trc
extension
-- will be appended to the filename automatically. If you are
writing from
-- remote server to local drive, please use UNC path and make sure
server has
-- write access to your network share

exec @rc = sp_trace_create @TraceID output, 0,
N''C:\files\mysales_tranperf1.trc'', @maxfilesize, NULL
if (@rc != 0) goto error

-- Client side File and Table cannot be scripted

-- Set the events
declare @on bit
set @on = 1
exec sp_trace_setevent @TraceID, 148, 11, @on
exec sp_trace_setevent @TraceID, 148, 51, @on
```

```
exec sp_trace_setevent @TraceID, 148, 4, @on
exec sp_trace_setevent @TraceID, 148, 12, @on
exec sp_trace_setevent @TraceID, 148, 14, @on
exec sp_trace_setevent @TraceID, 148, 26, @on
exec sp_trace_setevent @TraceID, 148, 60, @on
exec sp_trace_setevent @TraceID, 148, 64, @on
exec sp_trace_setevent @TraceID, 148, 1, @on
exec sp_trace_setevent @TraceID, 148, 41, @on
exec sp_trace_setevent @TraceID, 10, 7, @on
exec sp_trace_setevent @TraceID, 10, 15, @on
exec sp_trace_setevent @TraceID, 10, 31, @on
exec sp_trace_setevent @TraceID, 10, 8, @on
exec sp_trace_setevent @TraceID, 10, 16, @on
exec sp_trace_setevent @TraceID, 10, 48, @on
exec sp_trace_setevent @TraceID, 10, 64, @on
exec sp_trace_setevent @TraceID, 10, 1, @on
exec sp_trace_setevent @TraceID, 10, 9, @on
exec sp_trace_setevent @TraceID, 10, 17, @on
exec sp_trace_setevent @TraceID, 10, 41, @on
exec sp_trace_setevent @TraceID, 10, 49, @on
exec sp_trace_setevent @TraceID, 10, 10, @on
exec sp_trace_setevent @TraceID, 10, 18, @on
exec sp_trace_setevent @TraceID, 10, 26, @on
exec sp_trace_setevent @TraceID, 10, 34, @on
exec sp_trace_setevent @TraceID, 10, 50, @on
exec sp_trace_setevent @TraceID, 10, 3, @on
exec sp_trace_setevent @TraceID, 10, 11, @on
exec sp_trace_setevent @TraceID, 10, 35, @on
exec sp_trace_setevent @TraceID, 10, 51, @on
exec sp_trace_setevent @TraceID, 10, 4, @on
exec sp_trace_setevent @TraceID, 10, 12, @on
exec sp_trace_setevent @TraceID, 10, 60, @on
exec sp_trace_setevent @TraceID, 10, 13, @on
exec sp_trace_setevent @TraceID, 10, 6, @on
exec sp_trace_setevent @TraceID, 10, 14, @on
exec sp_trace_setevent @TraceID, 45, 7, @on
exec sp_trace_setevent @TraceID, 45, 55, @on
exec sp_trace_setevent @TraceID, 45, 8, @on
exec sp_trace_setevent @TraceID, 45, 16, @on
exec sp_trace_setevent @TraceID, 45, 48, @on
exec sp_trace_setevent @TraceID, 45, 64, @on
exec sp_trace_setevent @TraceID, 45, 1, @on
exec sp_trace_setevent @TraceID, 45, 9, @on
exec sp_trace_setevent @TraceID, 45, 17, @on
exec sp_trace_setevent @TraceID, 45, 25, @on
exec sp_trace_setevent @TraceID, 45, 41, @on
exec sp_trace_setevent @TraceID, 45, 49, @on
```

```
exec sp_trace_setevent @TraceID, 45, 10, @on
exec sp_trace_setevent @TraceID, 45, 18, @on
exec sp_trace_setevent @TraceID, 45, 26, @on
exec sp_trace_setevent @TraceID, 45, 34, @on
exec sp_trace_setevent @TraceID, 45, 50, @on
exec sp_trace_setevent @TraceID, 45, 3, @on
exec sp_trace_setevent @TraceID, 45, 11, @on
exec sp_trace_setevent @TraceID, 45, 35, @on
exec sp_trace_setevent @TraceID, 45, 51, @on
exec sp_trace_setevent @TraceID, 45, 4, @on
exec sp_trace_setevent @TraceID, 45, 12, @on
exec sp_trace_setevent @TraceID, 45, 28, @on
exec sp_trace_setevent @TraceID, 45, 60, @on
exec sp_trace_setevent @TraceID, 45, 5, @on
exec sp_trace_setevent @TraceID, 45, 13, @on
exec sp_trace_setevent @TraceID, 45, 29, @on
exec sp_trace_setevent @TraceID, 45, 61, @on
exec sp_trace_setevent @TraceID, 45, 6, @on
exec sp_trace_setevent @TraceID, 45, 14, @on
exec sp_trace_setevent @TraceID, 45, 22, @on
exec sp_trace_setevent @TraceID, 45, 62, @on
exec sp_trace_setevent @TraceID, 45, 15, @on
exec sp_trace_setevent @TraceID, 12, 7, @on
exec sp_trace_setevent @TraceID, 12, 15, @on
exec sp_trace_setevent @TraceID, 12, 31, @on
exec sp_trace_setevent @TraceID, 12, 8, @on
exec sp_trace_setevent @TraceID, 12, 16, @on
exec sp_trace_setevent @TraceID, 12, 48, @on
exec sp_trace_setevent @TraceID, 12, 64, @on
exec sp_trace_setevent @TraceID, 12, 1, @on
exec sp_trace_setevent @TraceID, 12, 9, @on
exec sp_trace_setevent @TraceID, 12, 17, @on
exec sp_trace_setevent @TraceID, 12, 41, @on
exec sp_trace_setevent @TraceID, 12, 49, @on
exec sp_trace_setevent @TraceID, 12, 6, @on
exec sp_trace_setevent @TraceID, 12, 10, @on
exec sp_trace_setevent @TraceID, 12, 14, @on
exec sp_trace_setevent @TraceID, 12, 18, @on
exec sp_trace_setevent @TraceID, 12, 26, @on
exec sp_trace_setevent @TraceID, 12, 50, @on
exec sp_trace_setevent @TraceID, 12, 3, @on
exec sp_trace_setevent @TraceID, 12, 11, @on
exec sp_trace_setevent @TraceID, 12, 35, @on
exec sp_trace_setevent @TraceID, 12, 51, @on
exec sp_trace_setevent @TraceID, 12, 4, @on
exec sp_trace_setevent @TraceID, 12, 12, @on
```

```
exec sp_trace_setevent @TraceID, 12, 60, @on
exec sp_trace_setevent @TraceID, 12, 13, @on
exec sp_trace_setevent @TraceID, 54, 7, @on
exec sp_trace_setevent @TraceID, 54, 8, @on
exec sp_trace_setevent @TraceID, 54, 64, @on
exec sp_trace_setevent @TraceID, 54, 9, @on
exec sp_trace_setevent @TraceID, 54, 25, @on
exec sp_trace_setevent @TraceID, 54, 41, @on
exec sp_trace_setevent @TraceID, 54, 49, @on
exec sp_trace_setevent @TraceID, 54, 6, @on
exec sp_trace_setevent @TraceID, 54, 10, @on
exec sp_trace_setevent @TraceID, 54, 14, @on
exec sp_trace_setevent @TraceID, 54, 22, @on
exec sp_trace_setevent @TraceID, 54, 26, @on
exec sp_trace_setevent @TraceID, 54, 3, @on
exec sp_trace_setevent @TraceID, 54, 11, @on
exec sp_trace_setevent @TraceID, 54, 35, @on
exec sp_trace_setevent @TraceID, 54, 51, @on
exec sp_trace_setevent @TraceID, 54, 4, @on
exec sp_trace_setevent @TraceID, 54, 12, @on
exec sp_trace_setevent @TraceID, 54, 60, @on


-- Set the Filters
declare @intfilter int
declare @bigintfilter bigint

exec sp_trace_setfilter @TraceID, 10, 0, 7,''SQLProfiler''
exec sp_trace_setfilter @TraceID, 10, 0, 7,''SQLAgent''
exec sp_trace_setfilter @TraceID, 10, 0,
7,''SQLServerManagementStudio''
exec sp_trace_setfilter @TraceID, 10, 0, 1,''''
exec sp_trace_setfilter @TraceID, 35, 1, 6,''msdb''
exec sp_trace_setfilter @TraceID, 35, 1, 6, ''mysales_remote4''
exec sp_trace_setfilter @TraceID, 35, 1, 6, ''distribution''
exec sp_trace_setfilter @TraceID, 35, 1, 6, ''mysales_remote5''
exec sp_trace_setfilter @TraceID, 35, 1, 6, ''mysales_tranperf''
exec sp_trace_setfilter @TraceID, 35, 1, 6, ''mysales_tranperf1''

-- Set the trace status to start
exec sp_trace_setstatus @TraceID, 1

-- display trace id for future references
select TraceID=@TraceID
goto finish
```

```
error:
select ErrorCode=@rc

finish:
go
',
@database_name='master',
@flags=0
IF (@@ERROR <> 0 OR @ReturnCode <> 0)
GOTO QuitWithRollback

/* Step 2: STOP AND CLOSE THE TRACE */

EXEC @ReturnCode = msdb.dbo.sp_add_jobstep @job_id=@jobId,
@step_name='Stop and close the trace',
@step_id=2,
@cmdexec_success_code=0,
@on_success_action=1,
@on_success_step_id=0,
@on_fail_action=2,
@on_fail_step_id=0,
@retry_attempts=0,
@retry_interval=0,
@os_run_priority=0,
@subsystem='TSQL',
@command='exec sp_trace_setstatus @TraceID, 0
go
exec sp_trace_setstatus @TraceID,2
',
@database_name='master',
@flags=0

IF (@@ERROR <> 0 OR @ReturnCode <> 0)
GOTO QuitWithRollback

EXEC @ReturnCode = msdb.dbo.sp_update_job @job_id = @jobId,
@start_step_id = 1

IF (@@ERROR <> 0 OR @ReturnCode <> 0)
GOTO QuitWithRollback

/* Schedule the job */
EXEC @ReturnCode = msdb.dbo.sp_add_jobschedule
@job_id=@jobId, @name='mysales_tranperf1_schedule',
```

```
@enabled=1,
@freq_type=8,
@freq_interval=4,
@freq_subday_type=8,
@freq_subday_interval=1,
@freq_relative_interval=0,
@freq_recurrence_factor=1,
@active_start_date=20060627,
@active_end_date=99991231,
@active_start_time=0,
@active_end_time=235959

IF (@@ERROR <> 0 OR @ReturnCode <> 0)
GOTO QuitWithRollback

EXEC @ReturnCode = msdb.dbo.sp_add_jobserver @job_id = @jobId,
@server_name ='(Local)'

IF (@@ERROR <> 0 OR @ReturnCode <> 0)
GOTO QuitWithRollback

COMMIT TRANSACTION

GOTO EndSave

QuitWithRollback:
    IF (@@TRANCOUNT > 0) ROLLBACK TRANSACTION
EndSave:
```

The script first checks whether the job exists or not. If it does not exist, the job is categorized using the sp_add_category stored procedure. You can see the category, set with the @class parameter, is JOB, and it is going to run on the LOCAL server (@type). The category name (@name) specified is Database Maintenance.

Once the category is set, the job is added with sp_add_job. The name of the job is given by the @job_name parameter. The job is enabled by setting the @enabled parameter to 1, which is the default. The @notify_level_eventlog parameter is set to the default of 2, which means that if there is a failure, it will notify the Windows event log; the other possible values are 0 (the event log will not be notified), 1 (notifies if the job is successful), 3 (always notify). The @notify_level_email, @notify_level_netsend, and @notify_level_page parameters have been set to 0, which means that no messages will be sent by email, net send, or send to a page respectively upon completion of the job. The @delete_level parameter has been set to 0, which means that the job can never be deleted. The owner of the job is specified by the @owner_login_name parameter. The @job_id parameter is a unique job identification number that is created once the job is successful.

The next step in the code is to add the job step to start the trace. The sp_add_jobstep stored procedure does this. The @job_id parameter corresponds to the one obtained from sp_add_job. The name of the step is specified using the @step_name parameter. The name of the subsystem (@subsystem) is T-SQL, which is used to execute the @command parameter. A procedure, usp_mysalestranperf, is used to execute the trace. The @on_success_action parameter has been set to 3, which means that if the execution is successful, it will go to the next step. The @on_fail_action parameter has been set to 2, which will quit the job if there is a failure.

After step 1, which starts the trace, the script then performs step 2, which stops and closes the trace using the same sp_add_jobstep procedure. In this case, sp_trace_setstatus is initially set to 0, which stops the trace; then the trace is closed by setting the value to 2.

The job is then scheduled using the sp_add_jobschedule stored procedure. The frequency type (@freq_type) has been set to weekly (value is 8) and the job is scheduled to run every Tuesday (@freq_interval=4). This job is then scheduled to start on the local server using the sp_add_jobserver stored procedure.

We can now run the trace according to the schedule and collect the trace data. The trace data, as you know, can be saved to a separate table and then queried for proper analysis. For this purpose, I created a separate database and loaded the trace data into a new table in the database.

■**Note** You can load the trace file into a database table by using the SELECT INTO T-SQL statement from the fn_trace_gettable table.

Once the trace is done and the data is loaded into the table, we can explore the system performance based on the trace data. We can execute queries to find the longest running queries, the CPU utilization, or any locks.

■**Note** In the next section, the trace data will be used as a workload in the Database Engine Tuning Advisor.

First, we want to find out which stored procedures consume a high amount of CPU time. The code to do this is shown in Listing 18-7.

Listing 18-7. *Find Out Which Stored Procedures Are Consuming High CPUs Trace*

```
/*Execute this on the database where the trace data is stored */
use performance
go

select spid,
CPU,
(Duration/1000) as duration,
```

```
textdata,
reads,
writes,
objectname,
databasename
from mysales_tranperf1_trace
where CPU>(5000) and
textdata like '%sp%' and
order by CPU
```

This script selects the spid, CPU, duration, textdata, reads, and writes, along with the databasename, to find the stored procedures that are CPU-intensive. The duration is in microseconds and the CPU is in milliseconds.

The output of the script in Listing 18-7 is shown in Figure 18-11.

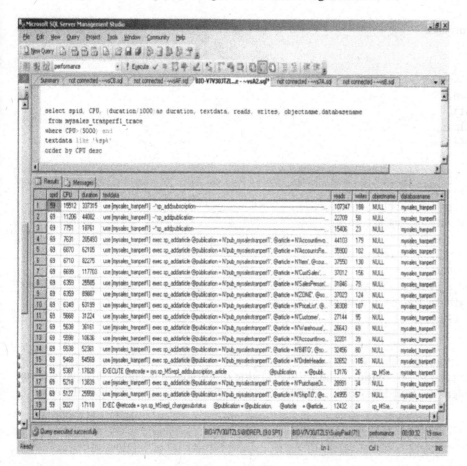

Figure 18-11. *Output of the script in Listing 18-7*

All the stored procedures that are CPU-intensive are in the mysales_tranperf1 database. You can see that there are a lot of I/O operations being carried out, since the reads column contains high values for each of the stored procedures being executed. You can also see that sp_addsubscription has the highest CPU utilization, at 15,512 milliseconds, and the corresponding number of reads is 107,347. The stored procedure that has the next highest CPU utilization is sp_addpublication, followed by sp_addarticle.

The sp_addsubscription stored procedure has a CPU utilization that is higher than 15 seconds, so it would be useful to determine the subclass name that corresponds to the eventclass. To get the event names and the corresponding subclass names for sp_addsubscription, you can execute the code in Listing 18-8.

Listing 18-8. *Retrieving Event Names and the Corresponding Subclass Names*

```
/* Execute this on the database where the trace data is stored */

use performance
go

select a.CPU,
a.duration,
a.textdata,
a.eventclass,
a.databasename,
a.reads,
c.name,
b.subclass_name
from mysales_tranperf1_trace as a,
sys.trace_subclass_values as b,
sys.trace_events as c
where eventclass in (10,12,45)
and CPU>15000
and c.trace_event_id=b.trace_event_id
and a.textdata like '%sp_addsubscription%'
order by CPU desc
go
```

The eventclass values selected are RPC:Completed, SQL:BatchCompleted, and SP:StmtCompleted. The output of the script in Listing 18-8 is shown in Figure 18-12. As you can see, the high CPU utilization for sp_addsubscription is for only for SQL: BatchCompleted.

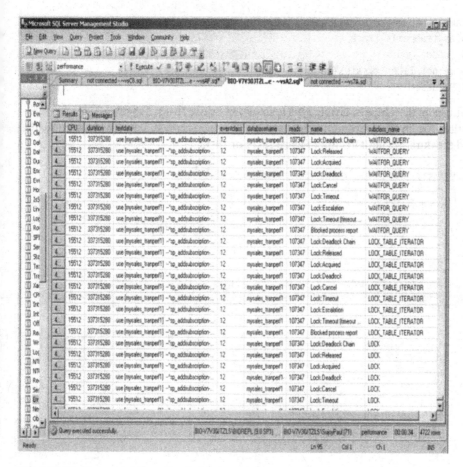

Figure 18-12. *Output of the script in Listing 18-8*

If you want to determine the CPU utilization of other databases involved in transactional replication, you can execute the code in Listing 18-9.

Listing 18-9. *Determining the CPU Utilization of Other Replicated Databases*

```
/* Execute this on the database where the trace data is stored */
use performance

go

select spid,
CPU,
(duration/1000)as duration,
textdata,
reads,
writes,
objectname,
```

```
databasename
from mysales_tranperf1_trace
where CPU>(4000) and
databasename not like 'mysales%'
order by CPU desc
```

The output of the script in Listing 18-9 is shown in Figure 18-13. As you can see, the highest CPU utilization in the distribution database is 4,937 milliseconds. The CPU utilization did not exceed the duration limit in either Figure 18-11 or 18-13.

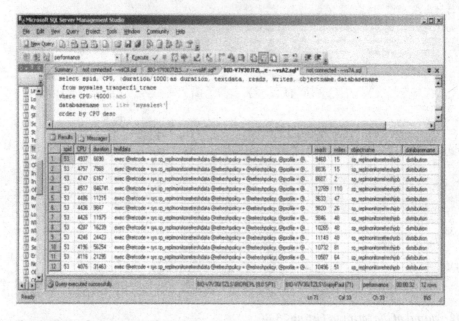

Figure 18-13. *The output of the script in Listing 18-9, showing the CPU utilization of the distribution database*

To find transactions where the CPU utilization exceeded the duration for event classes 10, 12, and 45, you can execute the code in Listing 18-10.

Listing 18-10. *Transactions Where the CPU Utilization Is Greater Than the* Duration of eventclass

```
/* Execute this on the database where the trace data is stored */
use performance

go
select spid,
CPU,
duration,
eventclass,
textdata,
reads,
```

```
writes,
objectname,
databasename
from mysales_tranperf1_trace
where CPU>(duration/1000)
and eventclass in (10,12,45)
order by CPU desc
go
```

The output of the script in Listing 18-10 is shown in Figure 18-14. You can see that the distribution database has the highest number of transactions where the CPU utilization exceeds the duration. You can also see a high number of reads associated with the CPU utilization. The eventclass associated with those transactions where the CPU utilization exceeds the duration is SP:StatementCompleted.

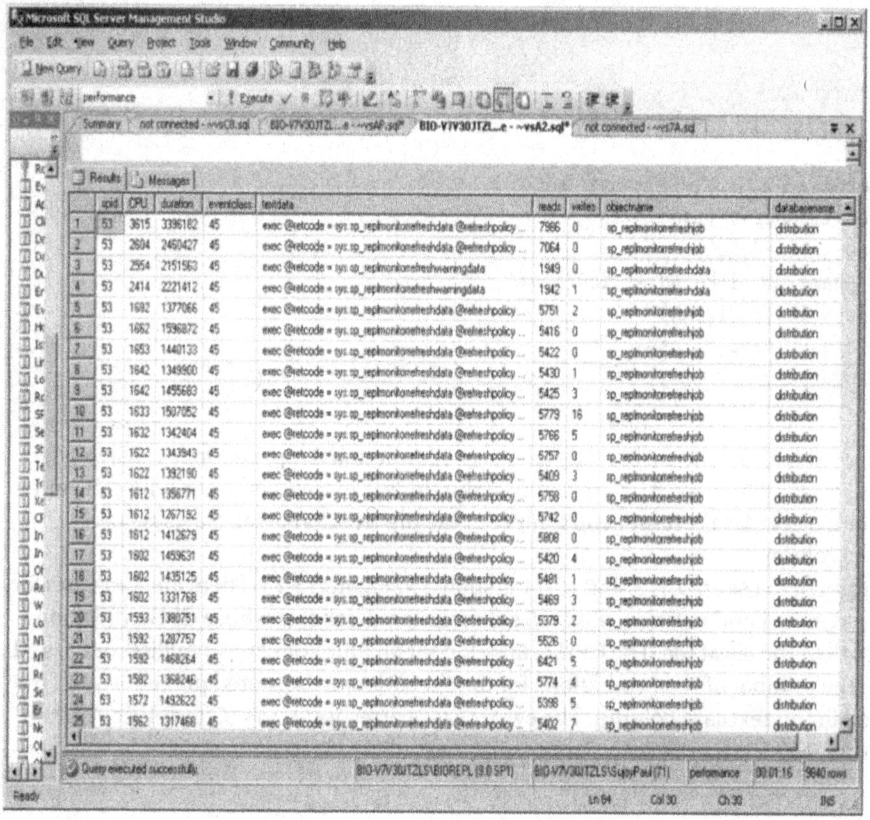

Figure 18-14. *Output of the script in Listing 18-10*

Since over 9,000 rows were returned, and most of them were associated with the distribution database, the next question is whether any of the insert statements had a CPU utilization that exceeded the duration. Executing the script in Listing 18-11 will tell us this.

Listing 18-11. *Finding Out Whether the CPU Utilization of* insert *Statements Exceeded the* duration

```
/* Execute this on the database where the trace data is stored */
use performance

go

select spid,
CPU,
duration,
eventclass,
textdata,
reads,
writes,
objectname,
databasename
from mysales_tranperf1_trace
where CPU>(duration/1000)
and databasename not like 'distribution%'
and eventclass in (10,12,45)
and textdata like '%sp_MSins%'
order by CPU desc
go
```

As you know by now, the insert statements of transactional replication are delivered using the sp_MSins_tablename. The preceding script finds transactions containing this stored procedure in the textdata column, and filters out the distribution database using the databasename column.

The output of the script in Listing 18-11 is shown in Figure 18-15. There are four rows for the mysales_remote4 and mysales_remote5 subscription databases whose CPU utilization were greater than the duration. The CPU utilization for all four lines are 10 milliseconds, and you can see the number of read operations for the execution of the stored procedure and the data inserted in the textdata column. The eventclass corresponds to RPC:Completed for the first three rows. The last row's eventclass corresponds to SQL:BatchCompleted.

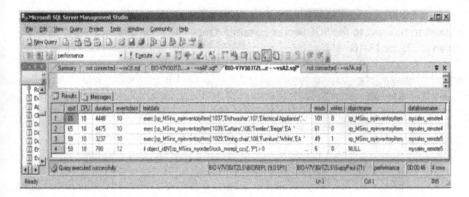

Figure 18-15. *Output of the script in Listing 18-11*

Now that we have some insight into the trace, we will see if the Database Engine Tuning Advisor can provide any recommendations to improve the process.

Using the Database Engine Tuning Advisor

The Database Engine Tuning Advisor (DTA) is available in GUI format and can also be executed using the command prompt. The name of the executable is dta.exe.

The DTA analyzes the performance of a workload in order to tune the statements; a workload is essentially T-SQL statements that are executed against one or more databases. Once the DTA has performed the analysis, it provides recommendations, which you can either apply or ignore. The DTA can also gauge the future performance of SQL statements, so that you can find out how a query or database configuration will perform on a test machine before you implement it on a production database.

In the previous section, I showed you how to perform a trace for transactional replication. You can use the trace from SQL Profiler as a workload for the DTA, or use the table where you stored the trace. If you do so, you must ensure that you included the T-SQL batch or RPC event calls, the event class, and the text data columns. We already included those columns in the previous section.

You should also make sure that the following conditions are met, regarding the workload:

- The trace table, when used as a workload, must reside on the same machine as the DTA. If it resides on a different server, you need to move the table.

- The tracing should stop before you load the trace as a workload.

- The trace files must always contain the rollover files for the DTA.

- If the trace contains the LoginName data column in the workload, ensure that the right permissions are given. The DTA impersonates the user identified in the LoginName, so if the right permissions are not given, the showplan requests that the DTA submits for tuning purposes will not be used.

You can open the DTA from SSMS by selecting Tools ➤ Database Engine Tuning Advisor. You will be asked to connect to the SQL Server instance. Once you have done so, the DTA will open, as shown in Figure 18-16.

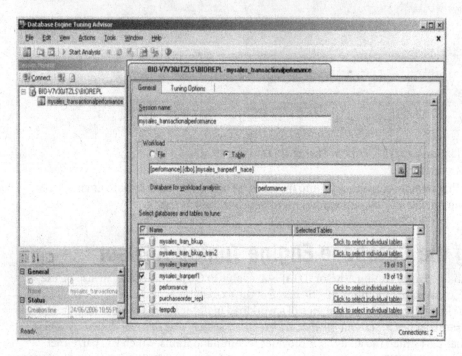

Figure 18-16. *The DTA showing the session name for the workload that will be used to tune the databases*

In the left pane, under the server name, you can name the session you want to tune. You can also clone the session properties.

In the right pane, you can provide a unique name for the session. This session name is identified by the ID, which you can see near the bottom of the left pane (under the General property). It also displays the start time, creation date, and status of the session. The information about the tuning session is stored in the msdb database.

In the right pane, under the Workload section, select the database where you stored the trace data. Then click the Table radio button and click the Select Workload Table icon. This will open the dialog box shown in Figure 18-17. Select the table containing the workload, and click OK to return to the DTA window (Figure 18-16).

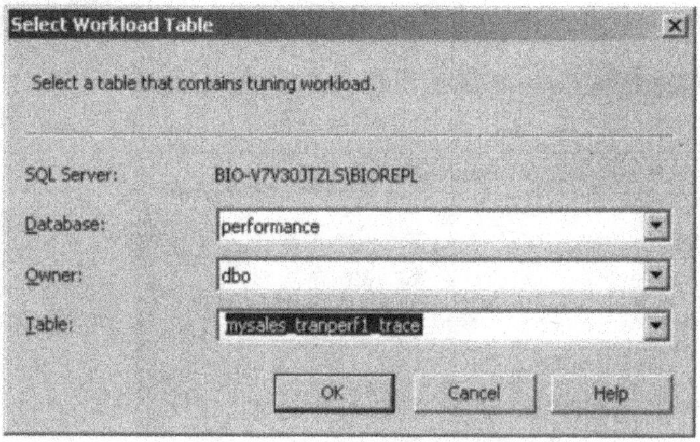

Figure 18-17. *Selecting the table for the workload*

In the bottom-right pane of the DTA (Figure 18-16), select the databases and tables you want to tune. In this example, I chose the distribution, msdb, mysales_tranperf, mysales_tranperf1, mysales_remote4, and mysales_remote5 databases. You can see the number of tables listed beside each of the databases you have selected.

If you click the down arrow beside the number of tables, you will see a window displaying the names of the tables and the corresponding schema, the number of rows, the projected rows, and the size, as shown in Figure 18-18.

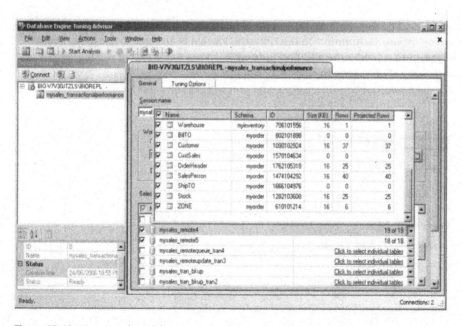

Figure 18-18. *Viewing the table names for the tuning of the mysales_remote4 database*

Now, click on the Tuning Options tab, as shown in Figure 18-19.

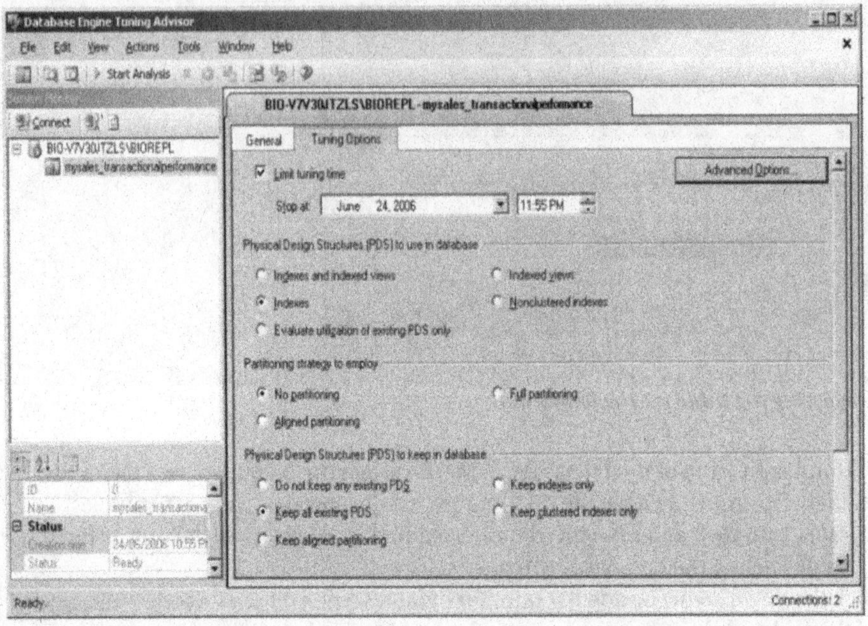

Figure 18-19. *Setting the tuning options for the session in the DTA*

In this example, I do not want the DTA to provide any recommendation on partitioning, since I am not using any partitioning; in the "Physical Design Structures to use in database" section, I only want to consider the addition indexes. Clicking the "Keep all existing PDS" radio button tells the DTA to keep the existing structures.

Now click the Advanced Options button, and you will see the window shown in Figure 18-20.

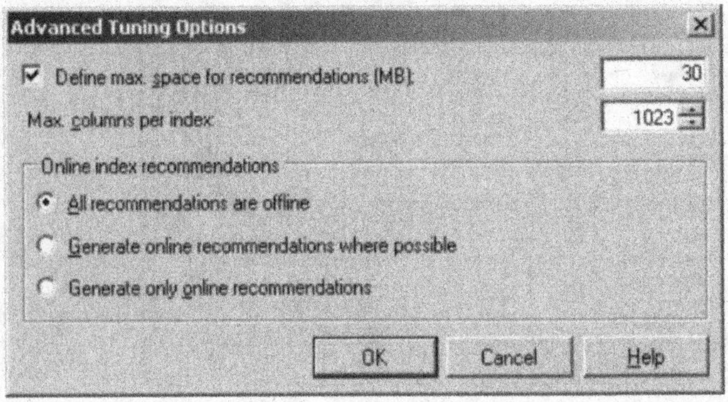

Figure 18-20. *Setting the advanced tuning options*

Here, I've asked the DTA to provide the recommendations offline. I have also checked the "Define max. space for recommendations (MB)" box and set it to 30. If the trace file or the table is large, you will need to set a value of at least 19 MB; otherwise you will get an error message when the DTA starts analyzing the workload. Click OK to return to the Tuning Options tab of the DTA (Figure 18-19).

Now we are ready to start the tuning. Click the Start Analysis button on the DTA toolbar. This will create a Progress tab, as shown in Figure 18-21. The Details section of the Progress tab shows the success or failure of the different actions taken to tune the workload.

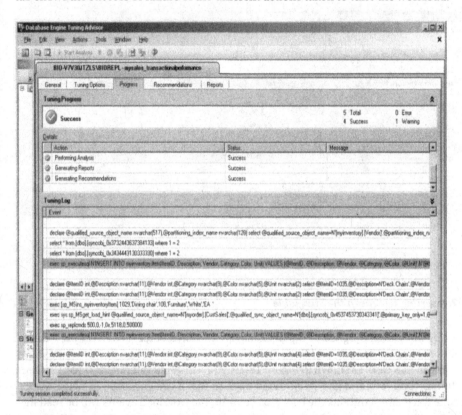

Figure 18-21. *Viewing the Progress tab containing the Tuning Progress and Tuning Log sections*

The Tuning Log section contains the Event column, and the two highlighted rows show how the INSERT statements are executed on the Item table. I had earlier inserted several rows for the Item table, as shown in Figure 18-22, and if I scroll down through the Tuning Log, I can see a series of INSERT statements being executed. Obviously, if you have a huge load of INSERT operations, performance can be impacted, since all the INSERT commands need to be committed on the publication database before the Log Reader Agent picks them up from the transaction log and sends them to the distribution database.

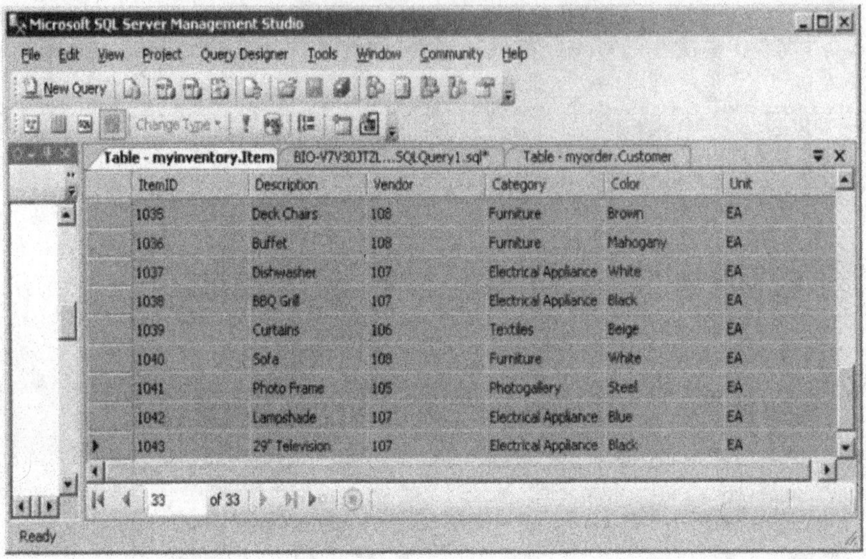

Figure 18-22. *Inserting records in the* Item *table*

Monitoring the tuning progress of the workload is expensive, since it analyses the workload, provides recommendations, and finally generates the reports. Although I have limited the tuning time in this case, as shown in Figure 18-19, you will get better results if you uncheck the "Limit tuning time" box and give it unlimited time, so that it can consume all of the workload. Since the trace table contains the Duration column, the workload events will be read in descending Duration order so that the events with the longest duration are analyzed first.

Once the tuning is finished, click on the Recommendations tab. You will see the results produced by the DTA, as in Figure 18-23. Click the "Show existing objects" box at the bottom of the window in order to see all the objects that have been tuned.

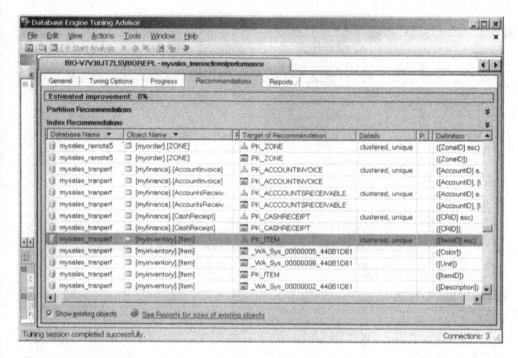

Figure 18-23. *Viewing the recommendations of the DTA*

In this example, the DTA did not make any recommendations. In Figure 18-23, you can see the type of indexes for some of the tables in the mysales_tranperf publication database; if recommendations were provided, you could either apply them immediately or schedule them to be applied later by selecting from the Actions menu. You could even save the recommendations.

Now click the Reports tab, as shown in Figure 18-24.

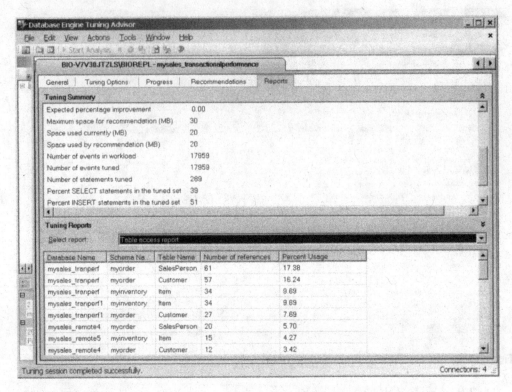

Figure 18-24. *Viewing the Tuning Summary and Tuning Reports in the Reports tab*

In the Tuning Summary section of the Reports tab, you can see the number of events that were included in the workload, and also the number of events that were tuned. It also shows the space that is used for recommendations (20 MB) and the space allocated for recommendations (30 MB), which is what I assigned in the Advanced Tuning Options window (Figure 18-20).

In the Tuning Reports section, you can select a report from the drop-down list. The Table Access Report provides information on each of the tables that have been referenced by the workload. The Database Access Report is similar, except that it lists the number of references the workload made to the databases, as shown in Figure 18-25.

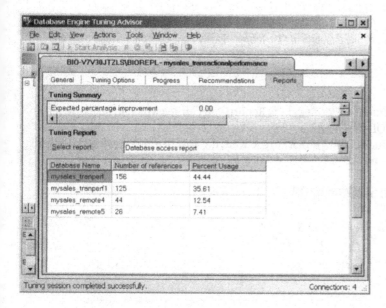

Figure 18-25. *Viewing the Database Access Report*

Now select the Index Usage Report, as shown in Figure 18-26. This report lists the names of the database, schema, table or view, and corresponding index that have been referenced, and the percent of usage.

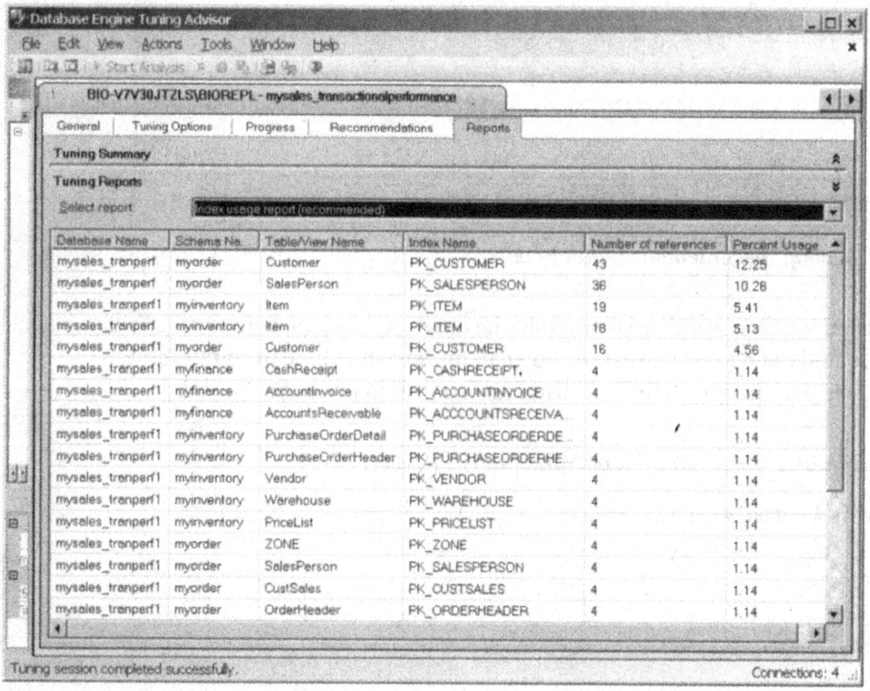

Figure 18-26. *Viewing the Index Usage Report*

Tip You can save the output of these reports in XML format. Simply right-click on the record set and select Export to File.

By selecting the Statement-Index Relations Report, you can see which indexes are referenced for a particular T-SQL statement.

Next, select the Statement Detail Report to see what the cost of executing the statements was. This is shown in Figure 18-27.

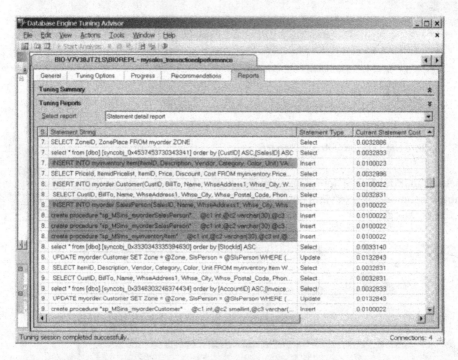

Figure 18-27. *Viewing the Statement Detail Report*

The session for each workload is saved in the dbo.DTA_input table in the msdb database. If you want to find the name of a session, you can retrieve the name from this table. Listing 18-12 shows you how to find out what tuning workload has been used.

Listing 18-12. *Finding Out What Kind of Workload Was Used*

```
/*Execute this on the msdb database *.

select sessionid,
sessionname,
tuningoptions,
logtablename
from msdb.dbo.DTA_input
go
```

This script will retrieve the names of the tuning sessions (sessionname) that have been used, the corresponding session IDs (sessionid), the options used for tuning the sessions (tuningoptions), and the names of the tables where the tuning is logged (logtablename) by querying the DTA_input table in the msdb database.

The output of the script in Listing 18-12 follows:

```
Sessionid     sessionname                              tuningoptions
logtablename


2             mysales_transactionalperformance
    <?xml version="1.0"...                                                    /
DTA_tuninglog
```

Here you can see the name of the session, the ID corresponding to the session, and the name of the table where the tuning log is stored. However, the output of the column name, tuningoptions, is in XML format, as shown here:

```xml
<?xml version="1.0" encoding="utf-16"?>
 <DTAXML xmlns:xsi="http://www.w3.org/2001/XMLSchema-instance"
xmlns="http://schemas.microsoft.com/sqlserver/2004/07/dta">
    <DTAInput>
        <Server>          <Name>BIO-V7V30JTZLS\BIOREPL</Name>
            <Database>          <Name>distribution</Name>
                <Schema>          <Name>dbo</Name>
                    <Table>              <Name>UIProperties</Name>
                    </Table>
                </Schema>
            </Database>
            <Database>          <Name>msdb</Name>
                <Schema>          <Name>dbo</Name>
                    <Table>              <Name>DTA_input</Name>
                    </Table>
                    <Table>              <Name>DTA_output</Name>
                    </Table>
                    <Table>              <Name>DTA_progress</Name>
                    </Table>
                    <Table>              <Name>DTA_reports_column</Name>
                    </Table>
                    <Table>              <Name>DTA_reports_database</Name>
                    </Table>
                    <Table>              <Name>DTA_reports_index</Name>
                    </Table>
                    <Table>              <Name>DTA_reports_indexcolumn</Name>
                    </Table>
                    <Table>
                       <Name>DTA_reports_partitionfunction</Name>
                    </Table>
```

```
<Table>
  <Name>DTA_reports_partitionscheme</Name>
</Table>
<Table>                    <Name>DTA_reports_query</Name>
</Table>
<Table>                    <Name>DTA_reports_querycolumn</Name>
</Table>
<Table>
  <Name>DTA_reports_querydatabase</Name>
</Table>
<Table>                    <Name>DTA_reports_queryindex</Name>
</Table>
<Table>                    <Name>DTA_reports_querytable</Name>
</Table>
<Table>                    <Name>DTA_reports_table</Name>
</Table>
<Table>                    <Name>DTA_reports_tableview</Name>
</Table>
<Table>                    <Name>DTA_tuninglog</Name>
</Table>
</Schema>
</Database>
<Database>              <Name>mysales_remote4</Name>
  <Schema>              <Name>dbo</Name>
    <Table>             <Name>sysdiagrams</Name>
    </Table>
  </Schema>
  <Schema>              <Name>myfinance</Name>
    <Table>             <Name>AccountInvoice</Name>
    </Table>
    <Table>             <Name>AccountsReceivable</Name>
    </Table>
    <Table>             <Name>CashReceipt</Name>
    </Table>
  </Schema>
  <Schema>              <Name>myinventory</Name>
    <Table>             <Name>Item</Name>
    </Table>
    <Table>             <Name>PriceList</Name>
    </Table>
    <Table>             <Name>PurchaseOrderDetail</Name>
    </Table>
    <Table>             <Name>PurchaseOrderHeader</Name>
    </Table>
    <Table>             <Name>StockItem</Name>
    </Table>
    <Table>             <Name>Vendor</Name>
```

```
        </Table>
        <Table>              <Name>Warehouse</Name>
        </Table>
    </Schema>
    <Schema>             <Name>myorder</Name>
        <Table>              <Name>BillTO</Name>
        </Table>
        <Table>              <Name>Customer</Name>
        </Table>
        <Table>              <Name>CustSales</Name>
        </Table>
        <Table>              <Name>OrderHeader</Name>
        </Table>
        <Table>              <Name>SalesPerson</Name>
        </Table>
        <Table>              <Name>ShipTO</Name>
        </Table>
        <Table>              <Name>Stock</Name>
        </Table>
        <Table>              <Name>ZONE</Name>
        </Table>
    </Schema>
</Database>
<Database>            <Name>mysales_remote5</Name>
    <Schema>             <Name>myfinance</Name>
        <Table>              <Name>AccountInvoice</Name>
        </Table>
        <Table>              <Name>AccountsReceivable</Name>
        </Table>
        <Table>              <Name>CashReceipt</Name>
        </Table>
    </Schema>
    <Schema>             <Name>myinventory</Name>
        <Table>              <Name>Item</Name>
        </Table>
        <Table>              <Name>PriceList</Name>
        </Table>
        <Table>              <Name>PurchaseOrderDetail</Name>
        </Table>
        <Table>              <Name>PurchaseOrderHeader</Name>
        </Table>
        <Table>              <Name>StockItem</Name>
        </Table>
        <Table>              <Name>Vendor</Name>
        </Table>
        <Table>              <Name>Warehouse</Name>
        </Table>
```

```
        </Schema>
        <Schema>              <Name>myorder</Name>
          <Table>             <Name>BillTO</Name>
          </Table>
          <Table>             <Name>Customer</Name>
          </Table>
          <Table>             <Name>CustSales</Name>
          </Table>
          <Table>             <Name>OrderHeader</Name>
          </Table>
          <Table>             <Name>SalesPerson</Name>
          </Table>
          <Table>             <Name>ShipTO</Name>
          </Table>
          <Table>             <Name>Stock</Name>
          </Table>
          <Table>             <Name>ZONE</Name>
          </Table>
        </Schema>
      </Database>
      <Database>            <Name>mysales_tranperf</Name>
        <Schema>             <Name>myfinance</Name>
          <Table>            <Name>AccountInvoice</Name>
          </Table>
          <Table>            <Name>AccountsReceivable</Name>
          </Table>
          <Table>            <Name>CashReceipt</Name>
          </Table>
        </Schema>
        <Schema>             <Name>myinventory</Name>
          <Table>            <Name>Item</Name>
          </Table>
          <Table>            <Name>PriceList</Name>
          </Table>
          <Table>            <Name>PurchaseOrderDetail</Name>
          </Table>
          <Table>            <Name>PurchaseOrderHeader</Name>
          </Table>
          <Table>            <Name>StockItem</Name>
          </Table>
          <Table>            <Name>Vendor</Name>
          </Table>
          <Table>            <Name>Warehouse</Name>
          </Table>
        </Schema>
        <Schema>             <Name>myorder</Name>
          <Table>            <Name>BillTO</Name>
```

```
        </Table>
        <Table>                <Name>Customer</Name>
        </Table>
        <Table>                <Name>CustSales</Name>
        </Table>
        <Table>                <Name>OrderDetail</Name>
        </Table>
        <Table>                <Name>OrderHeader</Name>
        </Table>
        <Table>                <Name>SalesPerson</Name>
        </Table>
        <Table>                <Name>ShipTO</Name>
        </Table>
        <Table>                <Name>Stock</Name>
        </Table>
        <Table>                <Name>ZONE</Name>
        </Table>
    </Schema>
</Database>
<Database>        <Name>mysales_tranperf1</Name>
    <Schema>            <Name>myfinance</Name>
        <Table>                <Name>AccountInvoice</Name>
        </Table>
        <Table>                <Name>AccountsReceivable</Name>
        </Table>
        <Table>                <Name>CashReceipt</Name>
        </Table>
    </Schema>
    <Schema>            <Name>myinventory</Name>
        <Table>                <Name>Item</Name>
        </Table>
        <Table>                <Name>PriceList</Name>
        </Table>
        <Table>                <Name>PurchaseOrderDetail</Name>
        </Table>
        <Table>                <Name>PurchaseOrderHeader</Name>
        </Table>
        <Table>                <Name>StockItem</Name>
        </Table>
        <Table>                <Name>Vendor</Name>
        </Table>
        <Table>                <Name>Warehouse</Name>
        </Table>
    </Schema>
    <Schema>            <Name>myorder</Name>
        <Table>                <Name>BillTO</Name>
        </Table>
```

```xml
          <Table>                    <Name>Customer</Name>
          </Table>
          <Table>                    <Name>CustSales</Name>
          </Table>
          <Table>                    <Name>OrderDetail</Name>
          </Table>
          <Table>                    <Name>OrderHeader</Name>
          </Table>
          <Table>                    <Name>SalesPerson</Name>
          </Table>
          <Table>                    <Name>ShipTO</Name>
          </Table>
          <Table>                    <Name>Stock</Name>
          </Table>
          <Table>                    <Name>ZONE</Name>
          </Table>
        </Schema>
      </Database>
    </Server>
  <Workload>
      <Database>
        <Name>performance</Name>
        <Schema>
         <Name>dbo</Name>
          <Table>
           <Name>mysales_tranperf1_trace</Name>
          </Table>
        </Schema>
      </Database>
  </Workload>
    <TuningOptions>          <TuningLogTable />
    <TuningTimeInMin>58</TuningTimeInMin>
    <StorageBoundInMB>30</StorageBoundInMB>
    <MaxColumnsInIndex>1023</MaxColumnsInIndex>
    <FeatureSet>IDX</FeatureSet>
    <Partitioning>NONE</Partitioning>
    <KeepExisting>ALL</KeepExisting>
    <OnlineIndexOperation>OFF</OnlineIndexOperation>
    <DatabaseToConnect>performance</DatabaseToConnect>
    </TuningOptions>
  </DTAInput>
</DTAXML>
```

Take a look at the end of this XML output, where you can see the TuningOptions element. This is where the configuration of the tuning is set, determining what you should be tuning, and how, for the workload. Also, note the Workload element and the kind of attributes that have been set in the workload. We can use this XML output to change the tuning configurations or even to change the workload settings, and then use the dta command-line utility to predict the performance.

Next, we can find out the recommended cost and current cost of executing the SQL statements, like the INSERT operations executed on the schema and the associated tables. The code in Listing 18-13 will do this.

Listing 18-13. *Determining the Recommended and Current Costs of Executing Different Statements*

```
/*Execute this on the msdb database */
use msdb
go

select a.schemaname,
a.tablename,
d.DatabaseName,
d.isdatabaseselectedtotune,
b.isclustered,
b.numrows,
b.recommendedstorage,
c.statementstring,
c.currentcost,
c.recommendedcost,
c.weight,
c.eventstring
from msdb.dbo.DTA_reports_table as a,
msdb.dbo.DTA_reports_index as b,
msdb.dbo.DTA_reports_query as c,
msdb.dbo.DTA_reports_database as d
where a.schemaname not like 'dbo' and
a.tableid=b.tableid and
c.sessionid=d.sessionid and
d.databasename like 'mysales%'
go
```

This script filters out any schemas owned by the dbo, and joins the tableid columns of the DTA_reports_table and DTA_reports_index tables. It also joins the sessionid columns of the DTA_reports_query and DTA_reports_database tables. The output of the script is shown in Figures 18-28 and 18-29.

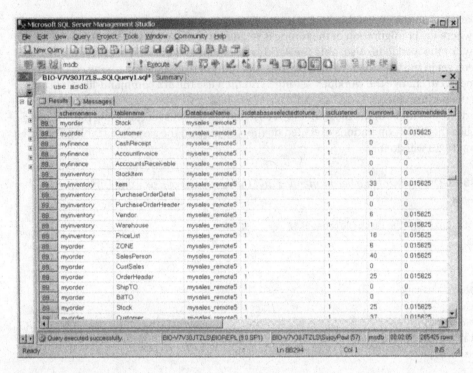

Figure 18-28. *The first part of the output from the script in Listing 18-13*

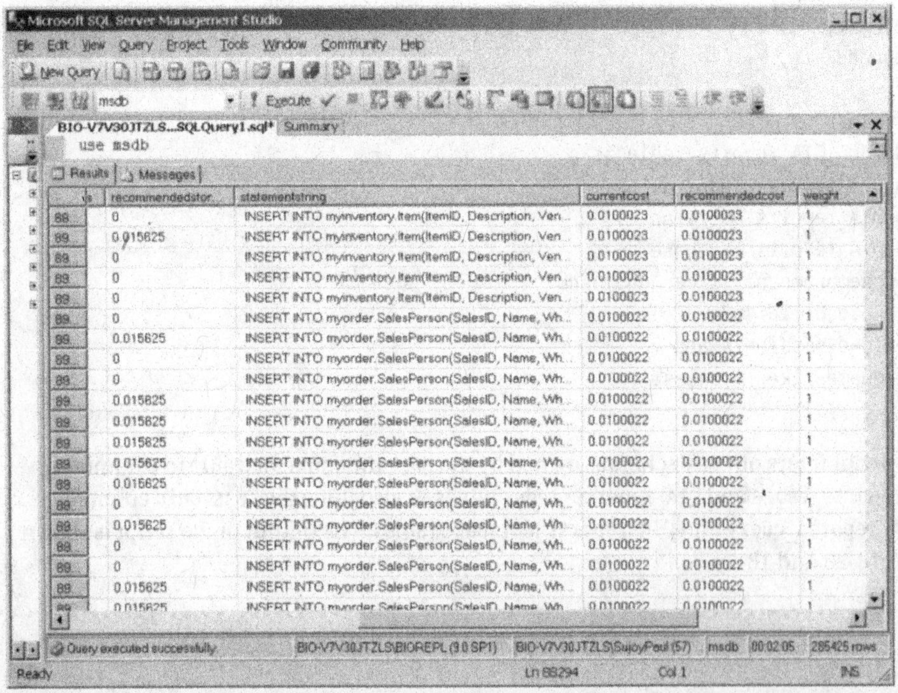

Figure 18-29. *The second part of the output from the script in Listing 18-13*

You can see that for each insert statement, replication creates a stored procedure to transmit the insert transactions from the publication database. Consequently, if you are transferring bulk insert statements in a batch, it is better to create a procedure that will incorporate all the insert statements, so that the next time you send the bulk inserts, only one stored procedure containing all the inserts will be executed.

If you want to find out what statements have not been tuned, and why, you can execute the code in Listing 18-14.

Listing 18-14. *Finding Statements That Have Not Been Tuned*

```
/* Execute this on the msdb database */

use msdb
go

select b.categoryid,
b.event,
b.statement,
b.frequency,
b.reason
from dbo.DTA_input as a,
dbo.DTA_tuninglog as b
where statement not like ' '
and a.sessionid=b.sessionid
and a.sessionname like 'mysales_transactionalperformance'
go
```

This script selects the categoryid, event, statement, frequency, and reason columns from the DTA_tuninglog table and matches the sessionid of DTA_tuninglog table with that of the DTA_input table. The DTA_input table contains the name of the session (sessionname) and the ID corresponding to the session (sessionid). It also contains a column called TuningOptions, which contains the tuning criteria set for the session.

The output for the script in Listing 18-14 is given in XML format, as shown in Figure 18-30. As you can see, the categoryid values listed are S001 and S003. These are indications of statement- or workload-level errors. S001 means that the statement does not reference any tables, S002 indicates that the tables that are referenced are not selected to be tuned, and S003 indicates that the statement references only small tables. You can also see the events that caused the errors, and the corresponding reasons.

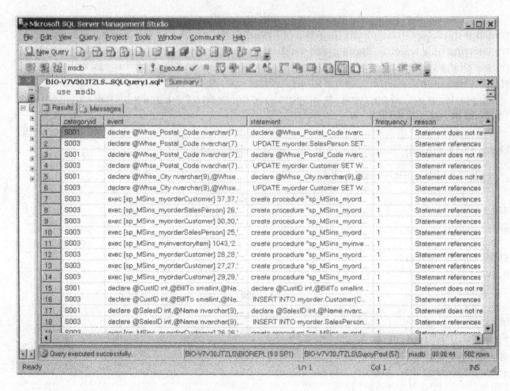

Figure 18-30. *Output of the script in Listing 18-14*

Best Practices for Transactional Replication

- **Save the scripts:** Once a publication and subscription are configured for transactional replication, store the script for later use.

- **Make regular backups:** Back up the publication, subscription, msdb, and distribution databases right after you add a new publication or schema changes are made on the publication. If you are using updatable subscriptions, back up the subscription database along with the msdb database on the Subscriber server. Periodically test the backup and restoration script. You should also back up the transaction log, since the Log Reader Agent transmits committed transactions from the log to the distribution database.

Note Chapter 15 discusses the backup and restoration of transactional replication.

- **Monitor disk space:** For each database involved in transactional replication, ensure that you have enough space for the transaction log. The log file is used not only as a write-ahead log; it is also being read sequentially by the Log Reader Agent to transmit committed transactions.

- **Consider autogrowth mode**: If you have situations where either the Log Reader Agent is not running or the distribution database is temporarily down, the transaction log will continue to grow until the transactions have been delivered. In such situations, it is better to set the log file to autogrowth mode.

- **Consider sync with backup**: Consider using the sync with backup option for the distribution database. This will ensure that the log file on the publication database is not truncated until the corresponding transactions have been backed up in the distribution database.

- **Validate the subscriptions**: After the backup and restoration of the databases used in transactional replication, you should validate the subscriptions using either the SSMS or the validate subscription script.

- **Check primary keys**: For tables used as publications in transactional replication, check to see that they have primary keys.

Note The configuration of transactional replication and the necessity of primary keys is discussed in Chapters 8 and 9.

- **Avoid truncating data**: For articles involved in transactional replication, be careful not to truncate the data, as truncated operations are not logged. Those changes will not be replicated to the subscribing databases.

- **Generate performance baselines**: Develop a baseline for the performance of transactional replication on the server side for each of the server and hardware resources like processors, memory, and the configuration of the Distributor. You should also develop a performance baseline on the client side for each of the filtering options, the agent parameters, the subscription options, the locks, the transaction log, and the settings of tracer tokens using the Replication Monitor. At the development stage of transactional replication, you should configure the publication design such that the business requirements are met. Ensure that you do not publish unwanted data, as this will have an impact on the distribution database, and keep the transactions to a minimum. You should also check that the right kind of indexes are created for the DML operations that you are going to use on the publication database. Keep row filters to a minimum, as they affect the throughput of the Log Reader Agent when it scans the transaction log of the publication database.

- **Save scripts for profiles**: Keep a script for the profiles for each of the agents used in transactional replication.

- **Use tracer tokens**: Since latency is an issue in transactional replication, monitor the latency using tracer tokens in the Replication Monitor.

- **Use data-modeling tools to design the database**: As with snapshot replication, design the database at least up to the third normal form. In designing the publication, add only the articles that you need.

- **Plan your replication use**: Transactional replication creates stored procedures on the database to perform DML operations, so do not use transactional replication as a stop-gap solution to provide real-time data for third-party applications. Plan well ahead, because insert, update, and delete operations use these system-generated stored procedures to monitor the changes in the database and then transmit them to the subscribing servers.

- **Plan for high-volume changes**: If you are going to use a high volume of inserts or updates (batch operations), write a stored procedure that will perform these operations. The stored procedure will be executed once to deliver inserts or updates. Otherwise, a system-generated stored procedure will be executed for each insert or update operation, which will have an impact on performance, since there will be a considerable amount of throughput involved.

- **Minimize the use of row filters**: Use row filters for articles involved in transactional replication with caution, since the Log Reader Agent will have to apply the filter to each row affected by the update. The Log Reader Agent will have to scan the log, which will slow down the performance of transactional replication.

- **Use the SQL Server queue**: When using queued updating subscriptions, it is better to use the SQL Server queue and not the message queue, as the latter will slow down the performance for queued updates.

- **Plan for how tables are published**: Remember that tables used for merge publication cannot be used for transactional replication with queued updating subscriptions.

- **Be careful updating keys**: Do not update the primary keys for transactional replication with queued updating subscriptions. This is because the primary keys are used to locate the records and updating them can lead to conflicts.

- **Consider resources required for subscriptions**: For immediate updating subscriptions, check to see that the MS DTC is installed and running. Remember that immediate updating subscriptions need to use the 2PC protocol, and this can be a drain on resources. Use it if it is a must for your business requirements.

Note Once the option for updatable subscriptions is enabled, you cannot disable it. You have to first drop the publication and then delete it.

- **Minimize conflicts**: Conflicts can occur in transactional replication with updatable subscriptions and peer-to-peer replication. Wherever possible, use data-partitioning strategies to minimize the level of conflicts and thus reduce the processing overhead associated with conflict detection and resolution.

- **Monitor conflicts**: If you need to set a conflict policy for updatable subscriptions, ensure that it meets the business requirements. Monitor the Conflict Policy Viewer to view the conflicts, and use them for troubleshooting purposes.

- **Prevent activity when altering schema**: When altering schema in updatable subscriptions, stop all the activities in the publishing and subscribing databases by putting them in quiescent mode. Ensure that all prior changes have been propagated before implementing the schema change.

- **Monitor delays in replication**: If there are delays in the delivery of transactions to the subscribing servers, consider reinitializing the subscriptions. Use the Replication Monitor to monitor the Undistributed Commands tab, which will show you how many transactions are still waiting to be delivered from the distribution database to the subscription database.

- **Match the schema for peer-to-peer transactional replication**: All the databases involved in peer-to-peer transactional replication must contain the same schema. The object names and the object schema, along with the publication name, must be the same in all nodes.

- **Use multiple distribution databases**: To eliminate a potential point of failure in peer-to-peer transactional replication, it is better to have the distribution database on each node.

- **Avoid identity columns in peer-to-peer replication**: Do not add identity columns to publications involved in peer-to-peer replication. If you do, you will have to manually manage the identity range.

- **Reduce contention**: As with snapshot replication, you can reduce contention by setting the READ_COMMITED_SNAPSHOT option on.

- **Monitor performance**: Use the SQL Trace function to trace the data and monitor the performance of transactional replication.

- **Schedule the traces with jobs**: You can create a job and schedule the traces. Create a separate job for each of the traces. Select only those event classes that you need, or the amount of information generated by the trace will be overwhelming. Check to see whether the C2 audit option is enabled on the server; enabling this option will cause the engine to capture everything.

- **Use the fn_trace_gettable function**: Do not save the trace directly from the SQL Profiler to a table in the database, as this will take an enormous amount of time.

- **Use the DTA**: Use the DTA to tune the trace data as a workload, and save the tuning sessions. Also tune the publication and the subscription databases using the DTA. Save the tuning session for the workload that meets the performance baseline on a testing environment and then export the requirements to other production servers.

- **Test the tuning**: Test the tuning of transactional replication on a test server before you export the requirements to a production server.

- **Monitor the DTA tuning**: Monitor the progress of the DTA so that if you are not satisfied with the tuning, you can stop before it eats into your valuable production time.

- **Review the DTA reports**: Use the DTA's Report tab to check the different kinds of tuning usage, like the index usage. Select the recommended reports to see the recommended and current costs for the tuning.

- **Assign a dedicated Distributor server**: Having the distribution database on a separate Distributor server will reduce the processing overhead on the Publisher server.

- **Consider anonymous and pull subscriptions**: As with snapshot replication, using either anonymous or pull subscriptions will reduce the workload on the Distributor server while shifting the processing to the Subscriber server.

- **Change agent parameters**: After the configuration is finished, change the parameters for the both the Log Reader and Distribution Agents. Set -HistoryVerboseLevel to 1 so that minimal history of the data is logged, and set -OutputVerboselevel to 0 so that only the error messages are logged. Increase the -MaxBcpThreads parameter for the snapshot agent to 2 so that the bcp utility can run faster using parallel processing.

- **Monitor the Log Reader Agent's latency**: Use the System Monitor to monitor the Log Reader: Delivery Latency and Dist: Delivery Latency counters.

- **Adjust the batch size for the Log Reader Agent**: Change the ReadBatchSize parameter for the Log Reader Agent. The default is 500 transactions, and the Log Reader Agent will process this number of transactions from the publication database in one processing cycle until all of them have been read. You should change this number of transactions to suit your needs.

- **Adjust the polling interval for the Log Reader Agent**: Increase the PollingInterval parameter from the default value of 5 seconds for the Log Reader Agent. Increasing the value for this parameter boosts performance by reducing the interference of the reads with the sequential writes in the transaction log. However, decreasing the polling interval will reduce the latency, as the Log Reader Agent will have to poll the log more frequently to deliver transactions from the publication database to the distribution database. You will have to balance latency and server processing by adjusting the PollingInterval parameter.

Note For more information on the effect of agent parameters on transactional replication, refer to "Tips for Performance Tuning SQL Server Transactional Replication," found at http://www.sql-server-performance.com/transactional_replication.asp. This article also mentions the CommitBatchSize parameter of the Distribution Agent.

- **Use the System Monitor**: As with snapshot replication, use the System Monitor to trace the data for server-wide operations, and have separate counters for each of the operations that are used to monitor the trace.

Summary

In this chapter, I described the use of tracer tokens to monitor the latency of transactional replication, and I discussed the difference between the inactive log and the active log while explaining the internal workings of the transaction log. For performance purposes, you should consider having the log file on a separate drive, if not on a separate disk.

I also showed you how to set up the trace, capturing the event columns using T-SQL and then loading the data on a table in a separate database. I then showed you how to use the data from the captured trace as a workload for tuning the databases involved in standard publication for transactional replication by using the Database Engine Tuning Advisor. I also described the system tables that are used in the msdb database for the DTA.

Finally, I outlined the best practices used in transactional replication.

- Consider latency, concurrency, throughput, and the duration of synchronization for both standard publication and updatable subscriptions for transactional replication.

- Performance measurements should be taken regularly and consistently.

- The three counters for the Log Reader Agent that need to be monitored in the System Monitor are Delivered Cmds/sec, Delivered Trans/sec, and Delivery Latency.

- The SQL Trace is enabled by default by SQL Server.

- By executing the fn_trace_getinfo function, you can locate and also determine the size of the trace file.

- The fn_trace_gettable function will help you load the trace file into a separate table on a database.

- You can create the trace, add the events, set the filters, and then start, stop, and close the trace by executing the sp_trace_create, sp_trace_setevent, sp_trace_setfilter, and sp_trace_setstatus stored procedures, respectively.

- You can create a job to run the trace using the sp_add_job stored procedure and then schedule the job using sp_add_schedule.

- Set the threshold warnings using the Replication Monitor.

- The Database Engine Tuning Advisor is used to tune the workload.

- The workload is a set of T-SQL statements that is used to perform tuning and analysis.

- Monitor the progress of the tuning session, and save the tuning session.

- The tuning session can be exported and used on another server.

- The Reports tab in the DTA will help you to see the recommendations made by the DTA.

- The tuning log can be configured in XML format, which can then be modified for testing other configurations.

- Measure the time it takes to back up and restore the replicated databases and system databases, like the distribution and msdb.

- The System Monitor records the replication counters for the Replication Agents, Replication Dist, Replication Logreader, Replication Merge, and Replication Snapshot performance objects.

- You can save the trace either in file format or in a table in a separate database.

- You can use the sys.trace_events and sys.trace_categories catalog views to find the events for the traces and the categories that the traces belong to.

- Use the Replication Monitor to set the tracer tokens for monitoring the latency of transactional replication.

- Use best practices for the administration of transactional replication.

In the following chapter, I will discuss the optimization of merge replication and will also discuss the use of the executable for the Database Engine Tuning Advisor.

Quick Tips

- The trace is enabled by default. You can determine that the trace is enabled by executing sp_configure with show advanced options set to 1 in the Query Editor of the SSMS.

- The sys.traces system table will return the path name of the trace file, its maximum size, its maximum number of rollover files, and whether the rollover option is enabled or not.

- The tuning log can be saved in XML format, which you can then use to change the configuration and tune the log.

- Save the trace in a table in a separate database using the fn_trace_gettable function.

- The sys.trace_events category view will list the trace events and the IDs of the traces.

■ ■ ■

Optimizing Merge Replication

Now that you have a fundamental understanding of SQL Server Profiler and DTA, I will focus on the optimization of merge replication. As in Chapters 17 and 18, this chapter will describe the performance counters required for monitoring the Merge Agent. Then I will show you how to use the trace that is generated to predict performance by using the dta executable. I will conclude with the best practices for the performance and tuning of merge replication.

On completing this chapter, you will know all about the following:

- Monitoring the merge replication counters using the System Monitor

- Tracing without using SQL Server Profiler

- Using the DTA utility

- Using the DTA to make an exploratory analysis

- Best practices for optimizing merge replication

Using the System Monitor

You can open the System Monitor by typing the following command on the command line:

Perfmon

Perfmon is the name of the executable that opens the System Monitor. The counters monitored for the Merge Agent are shown in Figure 19-1. Unlike snapshot and transactional replication, merge replication does not use the distribution database or the Distribution Agent, so there is no need to monitor their performance.

The three counters included in the list for the Merge Agent performance object, Replication Merge, are as follows:

- Conflicts/sec: This counter indicates the number of conflicts that occur during the merge process.

- Downloaded Changes/sec: This counter records the number of rows that have been replicated from the Publisher server to the Subscriber server every second.

- Uploaded Changes/sec: This counter is the opposite of the previous one; it indicates the number of rows that have been delivered from the Subscriber server to the Publisher server.

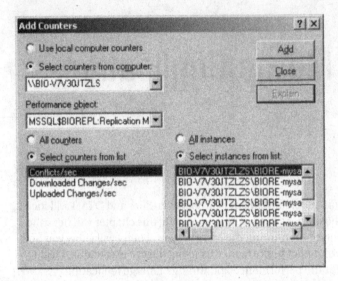

Figure 19-1. *Viewing the performance counters for the Merge Agent*

The counters for the Snapshot Agent in merge replication are the same as in snapshot replication, as shown in Figure 19-2.

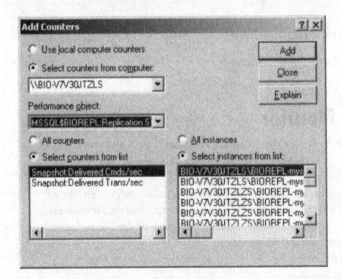

Figure 19-2. *Viewing the performance counters for the Snapshot Agent*

It is, however, possible to monitor all the agents involved in merge replication by selecting the Replication Agent performance object. I chose the "Select counters from list" option, as shown in Figure 19-3.

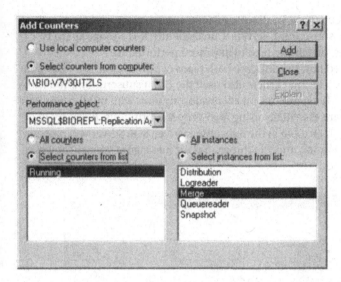

Figure 19-3. *Viewing the performance counters for all the agents*

Note Table 17-1 in Chapter 17 describes the performance objects available in replication and their counters.

The counter for the Replication Agent performance object is Running. I chose the Merge instance, since there are several Merge Agents currently running. You can choose the appropriate agents depending on your configuration.

The counters for the Replication Merge performance object are Conflicts/sec, Downloaded Changes/sec, and Uploaded Changes/sec. The Conflicts/sec counter will tell us the number of conflicts that are occurring every second during merge replication. The Downloaded Changes/sec counter will give us an indication of the number of rows that have been replicated every second from the Publisher server to the Subscriber server, and the Uploaded Changes/sec counter displays the number of rows that are replicated from the Subscriber server to the Publisher server every second.

You can save the counter logs as log files, as mentioned in Chapter 18, for each performance object, and then run each of the counter log files separately.

Using the SQL Server Profiler

As you know, in merge replication there are two kinds of publication: standard and download-only articles. Normally you would use publication with download-only articles when you want the articles to be read-only in the subscriptions.

There is no metadata to track changes for download-only articles, since update operations cannot be performed on the subscribing servers. Consequently, less storage space is required on the Subscriber servers, which can lead to improved performance.

In Chapter 11, which explained how to configure both types of publication, the Item table was used as the download-only article. That article also used the client subscription. You cannot execute INSERT, UPDATE, or DELETE operations on client subscriptions with publication with download-only articles. You are essentially using read-only subscriptions. If you try to perform INSERT operations on the Item table in the Subscriber server, SQL Server will prevent you from performing the DML operation and will throw an error message at you, as shown in Figure 19-4.

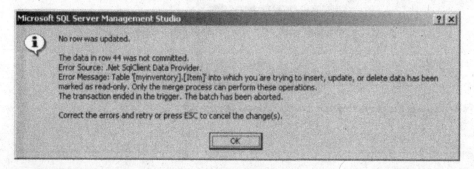

Figure 19-4. *Error message for inserting data in the* Item *table for a merge publication with download-only articles*

■**Note** The name of the database used in this example is mysales_tranperf1. This database is used for both transactional and merge replication, but the schema is the same as for other databases used throughout the book.

SQL Server Profiler, as you know, is used to monitor the performance of the server by tracing operations like stored procedures or triggers. In Chapter 18, I discussed how to set up a template to capture events in transactional replication. In this chapter, I will use the template created in the previous chapter and modify the events for merge replication to capture the trace.

Open the SQL Server Profiler and select the template for transactional replication, mysales_new_transactional_profile. We will add new events to monitor merge replication for publication with download-only articles.

Create a new trace. For this example, I've named the trace mysales_merge_downloadpub, and I saved it in a file and enabled file rollover. On the Events Selection tab, I added Lock: Deadlock to the Locks event, ShowplanXML to the Performance event, and SP:Recompile for the Stored Procedures event. This is shown in Figure 19-5.

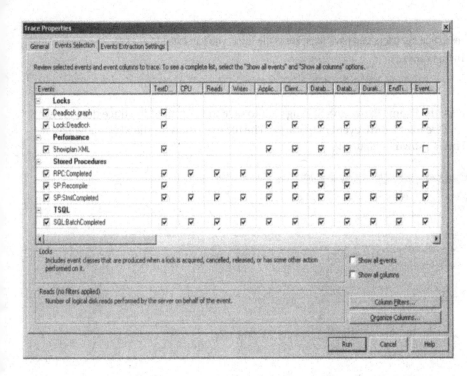

Figure 19-5. *Selecting events for merge publication with download-only articles*

Click on the Column Filters button to track the trace that you want, and to exclude unwanted data from the trace, as shown in Figure 19-6. In this case, I excluded rows that contain trace data for the applications like SQL Server Profiler, SQL Agent, and the SSMS.

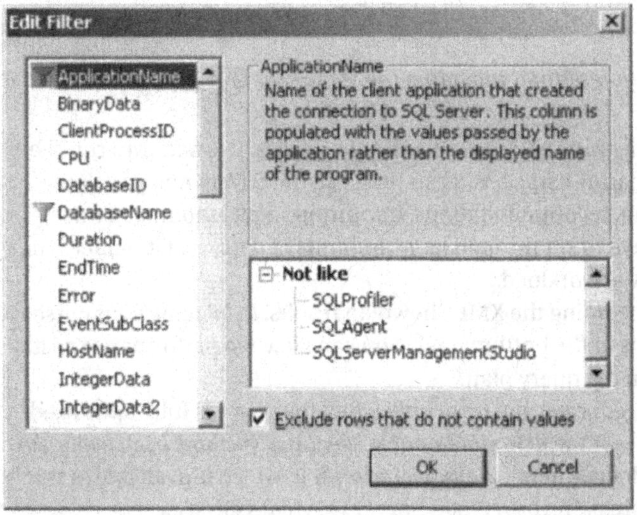

Figure 19-6. *Filtering out the applications that are not needed*

Tip In order to find the filters that have been set in the trace, you can execute `fn_trace_getfilterinfo(traceid)`.

Next, click the Events Extraction Settings tab to save the output of the trace data for XML Showplan and Deadlock XML events separately. The file extension for the XML Showplan is `.SQLPlan`. This is shown in Figure 19-7.

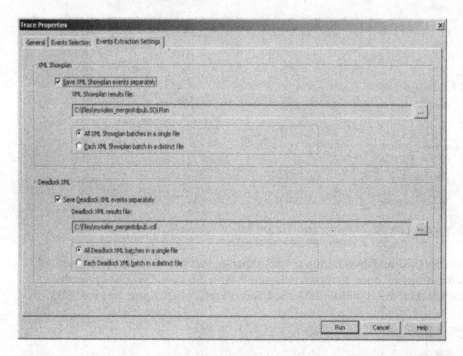

Figure 19-7. *Setting the event extraction settings including the Showplan XML events*

Now run the trace for the publication with download-only articles. It is better to run the trace for a small time and then restart the trace. You can then use the DTA to analyze all the queries and provide the appropriate recommendations. Capturing small amounts of trace helps the DTA, since it does not have to sift through large amounts of data, and it reduces the overhead cost associated with a large workload.

Figure 19-8 shows the trace, including the XML Showplan results. By placing your cursor beside each of the graphical objects in the bottom pane, you can view the performance cost associated with each of the steps in the query plan.

The `Showplan XML` event class generates the trace only when the query is fully optimized. This event class is displayed whenever the SQL statement is executed. It stores each event as an XML document, and a well-defined schema is associated with it, which is available in the following directory: `C:\Program Files\Microsoft SQL Server\90\Tools\Binn\schemas\sqlserver\2004\07\showplan`.

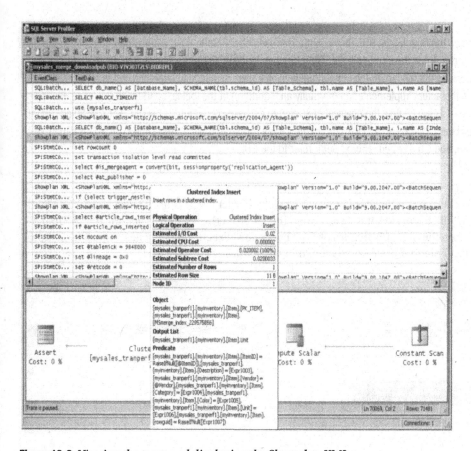

Figure 19-8. *Viewing the trace and displaying the Showplan XML*

Caution Using the Showplan XML trace event can have a significant impact on performance. Use it only for a short time to collect the samples, in order to minimize the overhead incurred.

In Figure 19-8, I selected the Clustered Index Insert operation. As you can see, this operation inserted rows for the Item table belonging to the myinventory schema into the clustered index from the input. You can also see the estimated I/O cost, the CPU cost, the object on which it is executed, and the predicate.

> **■Note** When tuning a query, SQL Server optimizer uses operators to build a query plan to perform the DML operation or return the desired result set. There are two kinds of operators: logical and physical. Relational query processing that occurs at the conceptual level is known as a logical operation, whereas a physical operation is the actual implementation (normally an algorithm) of the logical operator. In this case, the logical operation is an `Insert` while the physical operation is a `Clustered Index Insert`. For a detailed description of `Clustered Index Insert`, `Clustered Index Update`, `Clustered Index Delete`, `Clustered Index Scan`, and `Clustered Index Seek` refer to the BOL.

Right-click on the row in the trace and select Extract Event Data. It will ask you to save the query plan. Once you save it, you can open the file from the SSMS by selecting File ➤ Open ➤ File, and from the drop-down Files of Type list choose Execution Plan Files. Figure 19-9 shows the execution plan for the row selected in Figure 19-8.

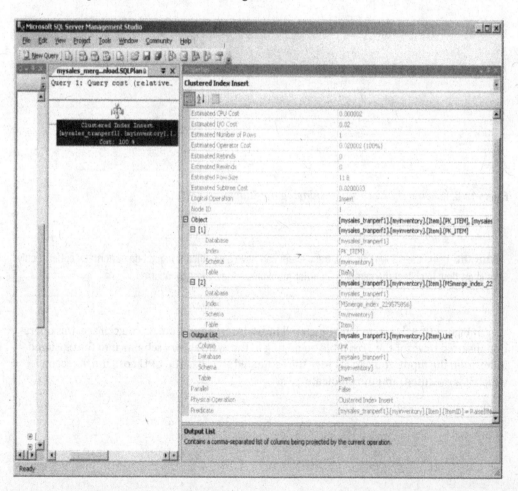

Figure 19-9. *Displaying the Showplan XML in SSMS*

Right-click on each of the query operations, and select Properties. This will display the properties in the right pane, as shown in Figure 19-9.

Note that it is possible to load the whole query plan of the Showplan XML event in the SSMS, as shown in Figure 19-10. The trace produced a total of 131 query optimization plans, as you can see. You can also see the query cost at the beginning of each query and the query plan subsequent to it. You can scroll through the plans, and as in Figure 19-8, you can view the in-depth cost information for each plan and save plans individually.

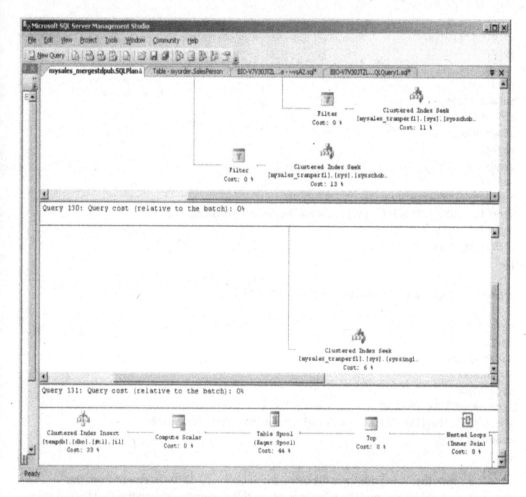

Figure 19-10. *Viewing all of the query optimizations for the trace*

Now that we have captured the Showplan trace, we will load it into the database as a separate table. Each of the events that we captured can then be loaded as a separate table and can be queried. This is shown in Listing 19-1.

Listing 19-1. *Capturing the Showplan Trace and Analyzing It*

```
/*Execute this on the trace database, performance */
use performance
go

/*Step 1: Load the data from the trace file for the
Showplan XML event */

select textdata,
spid,
cpu,
duration,
databasename,
objectname,
linenumber,
objecttype,
reads,
writes
into showplanmerge_down
from fn_trace_gettable('c:\files\mysales_merge_downloadpub.trc',
default)
where eventclass=122
go

/*Step 2: Query the showplanmerge_down table */

select spid,
textdata,
databasename,
objectname,
objecttype
from showplanmerge_down
where textdata like '%item%' and objectname not like 'dynamic%'
order by spid
go
```

This script first loads the trace file using the SELECT ... INTO statement from the fn_trace_gettable function. The table created by this statement is then queried for the spid, textdata (which shows the Showplan), objectname, and objecttype columns. In this example, it displays the Showplan for the Item table and filters out any dynamic SQL statements. The output for step 2 of the script is shown in Figure 19-11.

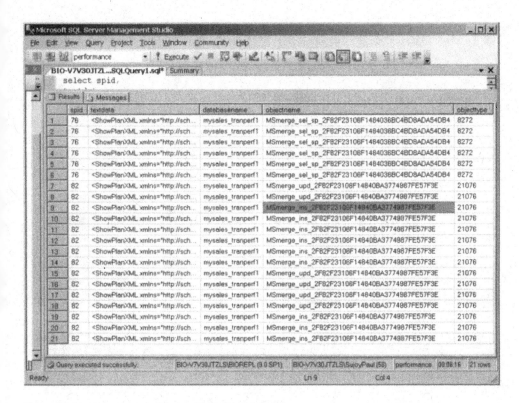

Figure 19-11. *The output of the script in Listing 19-1*

In this output, you can see the two SPIDs that produced the Showplan XML events. The objecttype values of 8272 and 21076 correspond to stored procedure and T-SQL trigger. For the trigger lines, you can see the INSERT and UPDATE operations that were carried out for the Item table while the triggers were replicating data for the merge publication of download-only articles.

Note For information on the possible values of the objecttype trace event column, see http://msdn2.microsoft.com/en-us/library/ms180953.aspx.

The insert and update triggers for the Item table are shown in Figure 19-12.

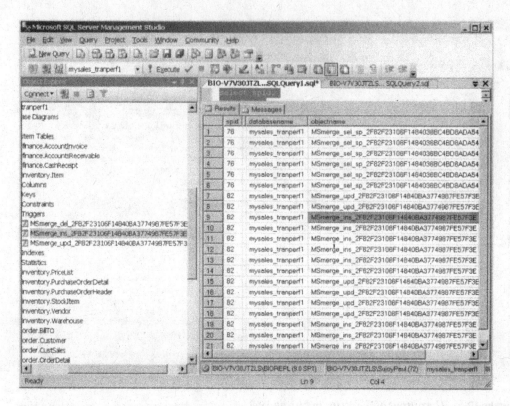

Figure 19-12. *The insert and update triggers in the left pane correspond to those in the right pane for the* Showplan XML *event trace*

To find out the performance cost for the execution of merge triggers, the code in Listing 19-2 can be executed.

Listing 19-2. *Determining the Performance Cost for Executing Merge Triggers*

```
/*Execute this on the performance database */
use performance
go


select spid,
cpu,
duration,
textdata,
databasename,
objectname,
objecttype,
reads,
writes
from mysales_tranperf_mergetrace
where textdata like '%trigger%'
```

```
and objecttype in (8272,21076)
order by cpu desc
go
```

This script chooses the `textdata`, `cpu`, `duration`, `reads`, `writes`, and `objectname` columns, and filters for data that contains only triggers. The output of this script is shown in Figure 19-13. You can see in the highlighted lines the duration and CPU usage for the merge insert and update triggers.

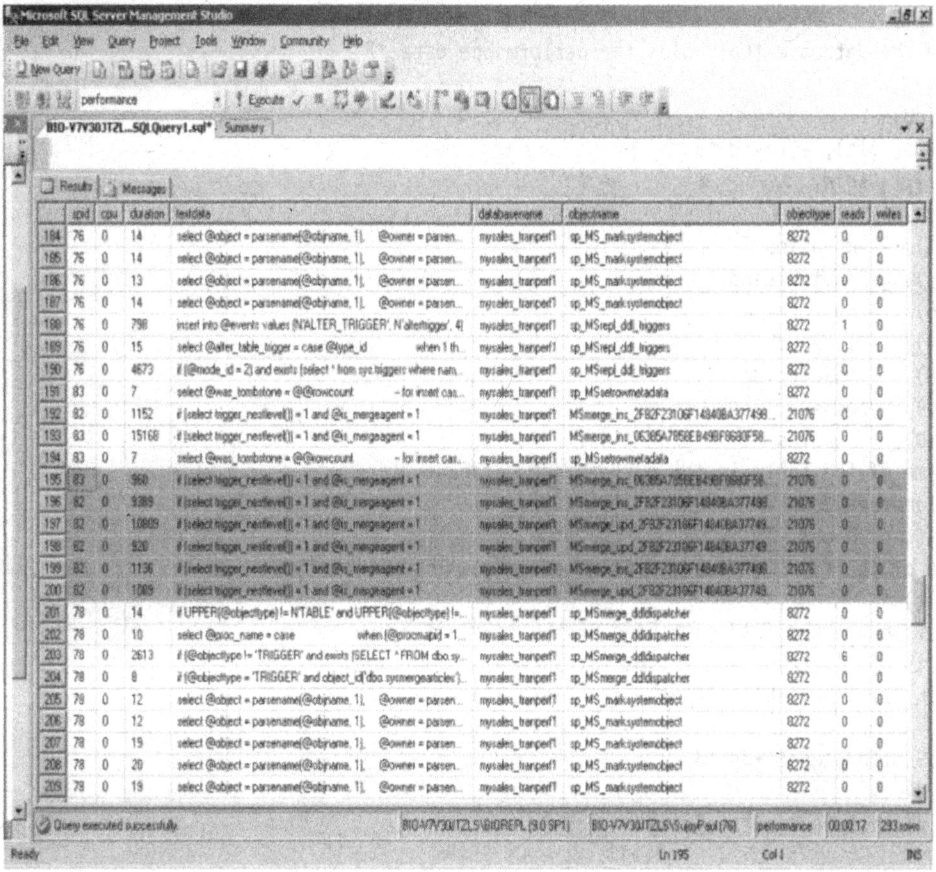

Figure 19-13. *The output of the script in Listing 19-2*

In Listing 19-2, all the trace data is loaded into a single table and then filtered by `objecttype`. However, it is better to create a separate table for each event class obtained from the trace, since this will make it easier to analyze the trace. So, for example, if you want to find out how the triggers are being used in merge replication, that information can be captured in the trace using the `SP:StmtCompleted` `EventClass` and then looking for the triggers in the `textdata` column.

Listing 19-1 can be adjusted to load trace data into separate tables according to the `EventClass`. Using the SQLCMD utility, you can do this as shown in Listing 19-3.

Listing 19-3. *Using SQLCMD to Generate Separate Tables for Trigger Trace Data*

```
/* Use the SQLCMD utility to execute this script */

:setvar logintimeout 120
:setvar server "BIO-V7V30JTZLZS\BIOREPL"
:setvar user "sa"
:setvar pwd "sujoy"
:connect $(server) -l $(logintimeout) -U $(user) -P $(pwd)

/* Use the database that holds the performance data */

Use $(db)
select $(col1), --textdata
$(col2), --spid
$(col3), -- cpu,
$(col4), ---duration
$(col5), --- databasename
$(col6), ---objectname
$(col7), ---linenumber
$(col8), ---objecttype
$(col9),---reads
$(col10), ---writes
 /* Name of the table in the performance database
showplanmerge_down */
into $(tablename)
/*Name of the file''c:\files\mysales_merge_downloadpub.t'c',
default) */
/* Just change the file extension if the trace file you are
using is of file type XML (*.xml) or SQLPlan (*.SQLPlan) */
from fn_trace_gettable('$(path).trc',default)

/* SP:StmtCompleted =45 */

where eventclass=$(eventclass)
go

select $(col2),
$(col1),
$(col5),
$(col6),
$(col8)
from $(tablename)
---showplanmerge_down
where textdata like '$(stringvar1)'
---'%item%'
and objectname not like '$(stringvar2)'
```

```
---'dynamic%'
order by $(col2)
go
```

You can add values to the column variables to suit your needs, or you can add extra column variables to load additional columns from the trace.

Running the workload using the DTA with the trace generated from the SQL Server Profiler produced the recommendations shown in Figure 19-14. You can see that the recommendations made by the DTA estimate an improvement of 35 percent. In this case, I asked the DTA to consider changes for the Physical Design Structure (PDS), but not changes in the partition.

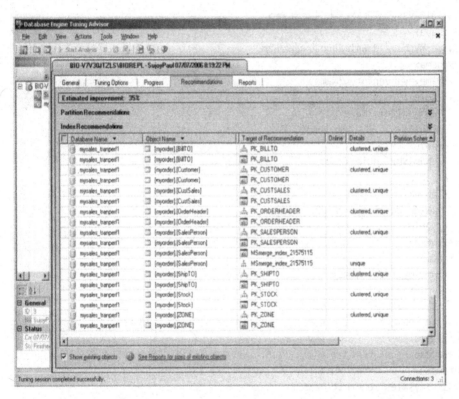

Figure 19-14. *Viewing the recommendations made by the DTA for the database involved in merge publication with download-only articles*

When I asked the DTA not to consider changes in the PDS, the DTA made recommendations that only provided for 5 percent improvement. Recall that in Chapter 18, the DTA did not provide any recommendations for the optimization of transactional replication. This is because of the large trace used as a workload in that chapter. The trace file contained more than a million rows, and it becomes difficult for the DTA to provide any recommendations. This is why you should collect traces for short periods of time.

Depending on the recommendations made, you can choose to apply the changes or discard them.

Now, in the DTA, double-click the session. From the menu, select File ➤ Export Session Definition. We can use this definition as a workload on another machine. The output can be saved in XML format, and it will look like the following:

```xml
<?xml version="1.0" encoding="utf-16"?>
<DTAXML xmlns:xsi="http://www.w3.org/2001/XMLSchema-instance"
xmlns="http://schemas.microsoft.com/sqlserver/2004/07/dta">
  <DTAInput>
    <Server>
      <Name>BIO-V7V30JTZLS\BIOREPL</Name>
      <Database>
        <Name>mysales_downloadpushsub</Name>
        <Schema>
          <Name>myinventory</Name>
          <Table>
            <Name>Item</Name>
          </Table>
          <Table>
            <Name>PriceList</Name>
          </Table>
          <Table>
            <Name>Warehouse</Name>
          </Table>
        </Schema>
        <Schema>
          <Name>myorder</Name>
          <Table>
            <Name>SalesPerson</Name>
          </Table>
        </Schema>
      </Database>
      <Database>
        <Name>mysales_remote1</Name>
        <Schema>
          <Name>myfinance</Name>
          <Table>
            <Name>AcccountsReceivable</Name>
          </Table>
          <Table>
            <Name>AccountInvoice</Name>
          </Table>
          <Table>
            <Name>CashReceipt</Name>
          </Table>
        </Schema>
```

```xml
<Schema>
  <Name>myinventory</Name>
  <Table>
    <Name>Item</Name>
  </Table>
  <Table>
    <Name>PriceList</Name>
  </Table>
  <Table>
    <Name>PurchaseOrderDetail</Name>
  </Table>
  <Table>
    <Name>PurchaseOrderHeader</Name>
  </Table>
  <Table>
    <Name>StockItem</Name>
  </Table>
  <Table>
    <Name>Vendor</Name>
  </Table>
  <Table>
    <Name>Warehouse</Name>
  </Table>
</Schema>
<Schema>
  <Name>myorder</Name>
  <Table>
    <Name>BillTO</Name>
  </Table>
  <Table>
    <Name>Customer</Name>
  </Table>
  <Table>
    <Name>CustSales</Name>
  </Table>
  <Table>
    <Name>OrderHeader</Name>
  </Table>
  <Table>
    <Name>SalesPerson</Name>
  </Table>
  <Table>
    <Name>ShipTO</Name>
  </Table>
  <Table>
    <Name>Stock</Name>
  </Table>
```

```
    <Table>
      <Name>ZONE</Name>
    </Table>
  </Schema>
</Database>
<Database>
  <Name>mysales_tranperf1</Name>
  <Schema>
    <Name>myfinance</Name>
    <Table>
      <Name>AccountInvoice</Name>
    </Table>
    <Table>
      <Name>AccountsReceivable</Name>
    </Table>
    <Table>
      <Name>CashReceipt</Name>
    </Table>
  </Schema>
  <Schema>
    <Name>myinventory</Name>
    <Table>
      <Name>Item</Name>
    </Table>
    <Table>
      <Name>PriceList</Name>
    </Table>
    <Table>
      <Name>PurchaseOrderDetail</Name>
    </Table>
    <Table>
      <Name>PurchaseOrderHeader</Name>
    </Table>
    <Table>
      <Name>StockItem</Name>
    </Table>
    <Table>
      <Name>Vendor</Name>
    </Table>
    <Table>
      <Name>Warehouse</Name>
    </Table>
  </Schema>
  <Schema>
    <Name>myorder</Name>
    <Table>
      <Name>BillTO</Name>
```

```
            </Table>
            <Table>
               <Name>Customer</Name>
            </Table>
            <Table>
               <Name>CustSales</Name>
            </Table>
            <Table>
               <Name>OrderDetail</Name>
            </Table>
            <Table>
               <Name>OrderHeader</Name>
            </Table>
            <Table>
               <Name>SalesPerson</Name>
            </Table>
            <Table>
               <Name>ShipTO</Name>
            </Table>
            <Table>
               <Name>Stock</Name>
            </Table>
            <Table>
               <Name>ZONE</Name>
            </Table>
         </Schema>
      </Database>
   </Server>
   <Workload>
      <File>C:\files\mysales_merge_downloadpub.trc</File>
   </Workload>
   <TuningOptions>
      <TuningLogTable />
      <TuningTimeInMin>52</TuningTimeInMin>
      <StorageBoundInMB>30</StorageBoundInMB>
      <MaxColumnsInIndex>1023</MaxColumnsInIndex>
      <DropOnlyMode />
      <KeepExisting>NONE</KeepExisting>
      <OnlineIndexOperation>MIXED</OnlineIndexOperation>
      <DatabaseToConnect>performance</DatabaseToConnect>
   </TuningOptions>
  </DTAInput>
</DTAXML>
```

In the preceding output, you can see the XML namespace associated with the root element of the output: DTAXML (Database Engine Tuning Advisor XML). The DTAInput category element is the input XML parent element for Server, Database, Schema, Table, Workload, and

TuningOptions. Since multiple databases are being tuned, you can see the list of databases under the Database element tag. For the TuningOptions element, you can see that the TuningTimeInMin element, which specifies the maximum length of tuning time in minutes, is set to 52.

■Note The DTA XML input file must conform to the DTAschema.xsd schema. It is located in C:\Program Files\Microsoft SQL Server\90\Tools\Binn\schemas\sqlserver\2004\07\dta\dtaschema.xsd.

You can export the results for the definition of a session by double-clicking the session in the DTA, selecting File ➤ Export Session Results, and saving it as an XML file. For brevity, I have only included a portion of the output here:

```xml
<?xml version="1.0" encoding="utf-16"?>
<DTAXML xmlns:xsi="http://www.w3.org/2001/XMLSchema-instance"
xmlns="http://schemas.microsoft.com/sqlserver/2004/07/dta">
  <DTAOutput>
    <TuningSummary>
      <ReportEntry>
        <Name>Date</Name>
        <Value>07/07/2006</Value>
      </ReportEntry>
      <ReportEntry>
        <Name>Time</Name>
        <Value>8:44:57 PM</Value>
      </ReportEntry>
      <ReportEntry>
        <Name>Server</Name>
        <Value>BIO-V7V30JTZLS\BIOREPL</Value>
      </ReportEntry>
      <ReportEntry>
        <Name>Database(s) to tune</Name>
        <Value>[mysales_downloadpushsub], [mysales_tranperf1],
[mysales_remote1]</Value>
      </ReportEntry>
      <ReportEntry>
        <Name>Workload file</Name>
        <Value>C:\files\mysales_merge_downloadpub.trc</Value>
      </ReportEntry>
      <ReportEntry>
        <Name>Maximum tuning time</Name>
        <Value>52 Minutes</Value>
      </ReportEntry>
      <ReportEntry>
        <Name>Time taken for tuning</Name>
```

```
        <Value>17 Minutes</Value>
      </ReportEntry>
      <ReportEntry>
        <Name>Expected percentage improvement</Name>
        <Value>35.72</Value>
      </ReportEntry>
      <ReportEntry>
        <Name>Maximum space for recommendation (MB)</Name>
        <Value>30</Value>
      </ReportEntry>
      <ReportEntry>
        <Name>Space used currently (MB)</Name>
        <Value>20</Value>
      </ReportEntry>
      <ReportEntry>
        <Name>Space used by recommendation (MB)</Name>
        <Value>12</Value>
      </ReportEntry>
      <ReportEntry>
        <Name>Number of events in workload</Name>
        <Value>2056</Value>
      </ReportEntry>
```

...

The results show the space used by the recommendations, and also the expected percentage improvement.

The exported XML schema definition can then be used for exploratory analysis with the command-line dta utility. Before we can run the utility, though, we have to add another XML element to the schema definition. We will use the schema definition from the preceding output and add the Configuration element. This element will help us explore a hypothetical configuration and give us direction about how the system would perform. The XML schema definition containing the Configuration element, which will then be used by the DTA utility for an exploratory analysis is shown in Listing 19-4.

Listing 19-4. *XML Schema Definition for the Exploratory Analysis Using the DTA Command-Line Utility*

```
<?xml version="1.0" encoding="utf-16"?>
<DTAXML xmlns:xsi="http://www.w3.org/2001/XMLSchema-instance"
xmlns="http://schemas.microsoft.com/sqlserver/2004/07/dta">
  <DTAInput>
    <Server>
      <Name>BIO-V7V30JTZLS\BIOREPL</Name>
      <Database>
        <Name>mysales_downloadpushsub</Name>
        <Schema>
          <Name>myinventory</Name>
```

```xml
      <Table>
        <Name>Item</Name>
      </Table>
      <Table>
        <Name>PriceList</Name>
      </Table>
      <Table>
        <Name>Warehouse</Name>
      </Table>
    </Schema>
    <Schema>
      <Name>myorder</Name>
      <Table>
        <Name>SalesPerson</Name>
      </Table>
    </Schema>
  </Database>
  <Database>
    <Name>mysales_remote1</Name>
    <Schema>
      <Name>myfinance</Name>
      <Table>
        <Name>AcccountsReceivable</Name>
      </Table>
      <Table>
        <Name>AccountInvoice</Name>
      </Table>
      <Table>
        <Name>CashReceipt</Name>
      </Table>
    </Schema>
    <Schema>
      <Name>myinventory</Name>
      <Table>
        <Name>Item</Name>
      </Table>
      <Table>
        <Name>PriceList</Name>
      </Table>
      <Table>
        <Name>PurchaseOrderDetail</Name>
      </Table>
      <Table>
        <Name>PurchaseOrderHeader</Name>
      </Table>
      <Table>
        <Name>StockItem</Name>
```

```
      </Table>
      <Table>
        <Name>Vendor</Name>
      </Table>
      <Table>
        <Name>Warehouse</Name>
      </Table>
    </Schema>
    <Schema>
      <Name>myorder</Name>
      <Table>
        <Name>BillTO</Name>
      </Table>
      <Table>
        <Name>Customer</Name>
      </Table>
      <Table>
        <Name>CustSales</Name>
      </Table>
      <Table>
        <Name>OrderHeader</Name>
      </Table>
      <Table>
        <Name>SalesPerson</Name>
      </Table>
      <Table>
        <Name>ShipTO</Name>
      </Table>
      <Table>
        <Name>Stock</Name>
      </Table>
      <Table>
        <Name>ZONE</Name>
      </Table>
    </Schema>
  </Database>
  <Database>
    <Name>mysales_tranperf1</Name>
    <Schema>
      <Name>myfinance</Name>
      <Table>
        <Name>AccountInvoice</Name>
      </Table>
      <Table>
        <Name>AccountsReceivable</Name>
      </Table>
      <Table>
```

```
      <Name>CashReceipt</Name>
    </Table>
</Schema>
<Schema>
  <Name>myinventory</Name>
  <Table>
    <Name>Item</Name>
  </Table>
  <Table>
    <Name>PriceList</Name>
  </Table>
  <Table>
    <Name>PurchaseOrderDetail</Name>
  </Table>
  <Table>
    <Name>PurchaseOrderHeader</Name>
  </Table>
  <Table>
    <Name>StockItem</Name>
  </Table>
  <Table>
    <Name>Vendor</Name>
  </Table>
  <Table>
    <Name>Warehouse</Name>
  </Table>
</Schema>
<Schema>
  <Name>myorder</Name>
  <Table>
    <Name>BillTO</Name>
  </Table>
  <Table>
    <Name>Customer</Name>
  </Table>
  <Table>
    <Name>CustSales</Name>
  </Table>
  <Table>
    <Name>OrderDetail</Name>
  </Table>
  <Table>
    <Name>OrderHeader</Name>
  </Table>
  <Table>
    <Name>SalesPerson</Name>
  </Table>
```

```
        <Table>
          <Name>ShipTO</Name>
        </Table>
        <Table>
          <Name>Stock</Name>
        </Table>
        <Table>
          <Name>ZONE</Name>
        </Table>
      </Schema>
    </Database>
  </Server>

<! --The name of the workload file; which can be xml or trc -->

  <Workload>
      <File>C:\files\mysales_merge_downloadpub.trc</File>
    </Workload>

<! --The tuning options -->
    <TuningOptions>
      <TuningLogTable />
      <TuningTimeInMin>52</TuningTimeInMin>
      <StorageBoundInMB>30</StorageBoundInMB>
      <MaxColumnsInIndex>1023</MaxColumnsInIndex>
      <DropOnlyMode />
      <KeepExisting>NONE</KeepExisting>
      <OnlineIndexOperation>MIXED</OnlineIndexOperation>
      <DatabaseToConnect>performance</DatabaseToConnect>
    </TuningOptions>

<! --The configuration options -->

<Configuration SpecificationMode="Absolute">
    <Server>
      <Name>BIO-V7V30JTZLS\BIOREPL</Name>
        <Database>
         <Name>mysales_merge</Name>
          <Schema>
            <Name>myinventory</Name>
             <Table>
               <Name>Item</Name>
                <Recommendation>
                  <Create>
                    <Index Clustered="true" Unique="false"
Online="false" IndexSizeInMB="873.75">
                      <Name>PK_Item</Name>
```

```
                </Index>
              </Create>
            </Recommendation>
          </Table>
        </Schema>
      </Database>
    </Server>
  </Configuration>
 </DTAInput>
</DTAXML>
```

The Configuration element contains an attribute called SpecificationMode. This attribute can have a value of either Absolute or Relative. When set to Absolute, as in this case, it means that the DTA will not consider the existing configuration and will evaluate it as a stand-alone configuration. However, if it were set to Relative, the DTA would analyze the specified configuration with the current one.

The names of the server, database, schema, table, and any recommendations that you want to configure are also specified. The Recommendation element contains a Create child element. Note, in this case, that the Recommendation element is meant for the hypothetical configuration.

If the XML file is not validated against dtaschema.xsd, you will get an error message. Consider the scenario where you have the following code:

```
<Configuration SpecificationMode="Absolute">
    <Server>
      <Name>BIO-V7V30JTZLS\BIOREPL</Name>
        <Database>mysales_merge</Database>
```

Notice that the Name child element for the Database parent element is missing. Suppose you tried to execute the preceding code from the command prompt as follows:

```
Dta -E -S BIO-V7V30JTZLZ\BIOREPL -s mysales_exploratory -ix
C:\files\mysales_mergedownload_tuning1_perfunct.xml
```

In this command, -E is the user trusted connection, -S is the server name, -s is the session name, and -ix is the input XML filename. The result of this command would be the output shown in Figure 19-15.

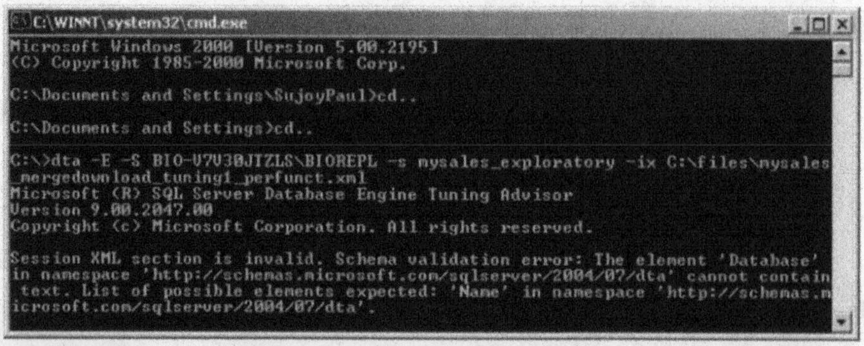

Figure 19-15. *The DTA showing a schema validation error for the* Database *element*

You can see in Figure 19-15 that the dta utility tells you that there is a validation error message for the Database element. In fact, it actually tells you that you need to incorporate the Name child element for the Database parent element. If you look at Listing 19-4, you can see that each of the input elements have a child element called Name, where you can specify text like that of the Item table.

The dta utility needs to be run from the command prompt, and the commands associated with it are shown in Figure 19-16.

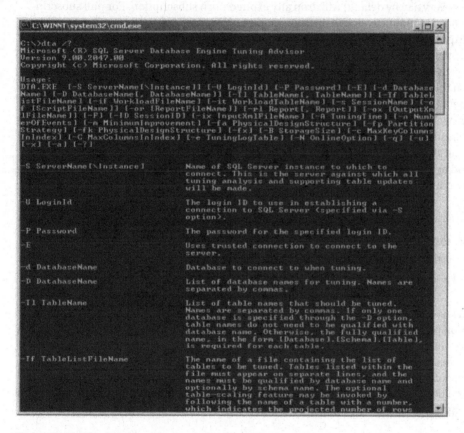

Figure 19-16. *Viewing the commands for the* dta *utility*

You can then use the following command to execute the script in Listing 19-4:

```
Dta -E -S BIO-V7V30JTZLZ\BIOREPL -s mysales_exploratory -ix
C:\files\mysales_mergedownload_tuning1_perfunct.xml -ox
C:\files\mysales_exploratory.xml
```

You now know how to use the DTA both as a GUI and a command-prompt tool. In the following sections, I will focus on the retention of publications, and the profiles and parameters of the Merge Agent that have an impact on performance.

Adjusting Publication Retention

When setting up merge publication, the retention period is set to 14 days by default. The subscription to merge publication must be synchronized within the stipulated retention period; if it isn't, the metadata for the subscription is deactivated or dropped by the Expired subscription cleanup job. If a subscription has expired, it needs to be reinitialized, since the metadata is not there. If you do not reinitialize the subscription, the Expired subscription cleanup job, which runs every day by default, will drop any expired push subscription. For pull subscriptions, you need to manually delete the subscription.

The Expired subscription cleanup job removes the metadata from the following system tables in both the Publisher and Subscriber servers: MSmerge_genhistory, MSmerge_contents, MSmerge_tombstone, MSmerge_past_partition_mappings, and MSmerge_current_partition_mappings. If the subscription is not synchronized frequently, these tables will grow in size, and the metadata cannot be cleaned until the retention period expires.

The growth of these tables can have a negative impact on the performance of merge replication. While you can manually remove the metadata by executing the sp_mergemetadataretentioncleanup stored procedure, you can also change the retention time period by using the @retention parameter with the sp_addmergepublication stored procedure.

Note The configuration of merge replication with T-SQL is discussed in Chapter 13. Listing 13-1 shows the retention period used when setting up merge publication.

If you know that subscriptions will synchronize regularly, you can reduce the value for the retention period and offset any negative impact this might have on performance. Bear in mind, however, that if you have republishing subscriptions, you should set the retention period for these subscriptions to a value that is either equal to or less than that of the original publication; otherwise you will have nonconvergence of data. (If you need to change the retention value of the publication, you will also need to reinitialize the subscription to avoid nonconvergence of data.)

Tip Consider staggering the synchronization schedule if you have a large number of subscriptions for merge replication.

Changing Merge Agent Parameters

In Listing 2-6 in Chapter 2, I showed you how to retrieve a list of profiles for each of the agents listed. In merge replication, the Snapshot Agent plays an important role during the initial synchronization, and then the Merge Agent is the most important agent in the replication process. (The Distribution Agent does not have any role in merge replication.)

Note Chapter 2 discusses the basics of replication and also discusses agent profiles.

The profile settings of these agents have a significant impact in the performance of replication. While the Snapshot Agent has a default profile setting, the Merge Agent has several profiles that can be used depending on the business requirements:

- Default agent profile

- Verbose history agent profile

- Windows Synchronization Manager profile

- Rowcount validation profile

- Rowcount and checksum validation profile

- Slow link agent profile

- High volume server-to-server profile

All these profiles use different values for the same parameters of the Merge Agent. For example, you can use the verbose history agent profile for troubleshooting purposes, or the slow link profile if you do not have a high volume network bandwidth or if your network is slow. The details of each of these profiles can be found in the BOL.

In order to view the list of agent profiles, right-click on the Replication object in SSMS, and select Distributor Properties. On the General page, click the Profile Defaults button and select the Merge Agents page. You will see the list of profiles for the Merge Agent, as shown in Figure 19-17. I chose Default Agent profile.

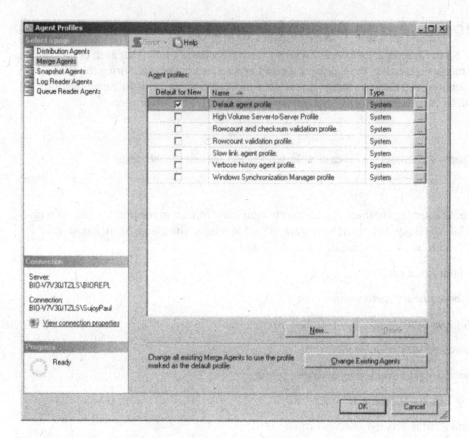

Figure 19-17. *Viewing the different Merge Agent profiles available*

As with the Snapshot Agent, you can change the Merge Agent's HistoryVerboseLevel parameter from a default value of 2 to 1 to minimize the effect on performance of logging historical data. You can change the OutputVerboseLevel parameter to 0 so that only error messages are logged. The default value is 2, which logs all error messages and progress reports. The UseInprocLoader parameter can be used if XML data is not being replicated; it enhances the performance of the initial synchronization by using the BULK INSERT command when applying the snapshot files.

Also, you can increase the batch sizes for both upload and download processing. These are the parameters that you can change to improve the performance of the batch processes:

- UploadGenerationsPerBatch: This specifies the number of generations that are processed in a single batch when sending changes from the subscribing server to the publishing server. A generation, by default, consists of 100 logical groups of changes for every article.

- UploadReadPerBatch: This sets the number of changes that need to be read when sending the changes from the Subscriber server to the Publisher server. The default value is 100.

- UploadWritePerBatch: This specifies the number of changes that need to be applied when sending changes from the Subscriber server to the Publisher server. Again, the default value is 100.

- DownloadGenerationsPerBatch: This is the number of generations that are processed in a single batch when sending changes from the Publisher server to the Subscriber server.

- DownloadReadPerBatch: This is the number of changes that need to be read in a single batch for changes being downloaded from the Publisher server to the Subscriber server. The default value is 100.

- DownloadWritePerBatch: This specifies the number of changes that need to be applied in a single batch for changes being downloaded from the Publisher server to the Subscriber server. The default value is 100.

■**Note** How the Merge Agent works is discussed in Chapter 14.

If you have a high volume of merge operations moving over a high-bandwidth network, consider using a new parameter that has been introduced in SQL Server 2005: ParallelUploadDownload. By setting the value of this parameter to 1, you enable parallel processing for the Merge Agent—it will upload changes to the Publisher server and download changes to the Subscriber server at the same time.

Snapshot Considerations

In merge replication, the Snapshot Agent generates the snapshot in the initial synchronization. The Snapshot Agent creates the snapshot containing the replication objects and the schema, and copies it to the snapshot folder. Then the bcp utility bulk copies the data from the publication database to the same snapshot folder. The Merge Agent then copies both the schema and the data to the required subscriptions.

As mentioned in Chapter 14, in the discussion of the internals of merge replication, each of the articles involved in merge publication generates its schema, trigger, and constraints, along with the index, data, system, and conflict table files. However, unlike snapshot replication, merge replication requires the addition of the rowguid column, which is a uniqueidentifier of 16 bytes. This column is used to track changes in merge replication.

■**Note** You can give the rowguid column any name, as long as the data type is uniqueidentifier. Figure 11-5 in Chapter 11 shows the uniqueidentifier column being added during the setup of merge publication.

If the rowguid column is not present in the articles, the Snapshot Agent needs to first add and then populate the column for each of the articles involved in merge replication. This negative impact on the performance of the initial synchronization can be alleviated by adding the rowguid column before generating the snapshot by using either the NEWID() or NEWSEQUENTIALID() functions.

Note The NEWID() function will generate a GUID that is different for each computer. If you use the NEWSEQUENTIALID() function, it is possible to predict the next GUID number.

Publication with parameterized filters is slightly different. The Snapshot Agent generates only the replication objects and the schema in the snapshot only for each partition. Then, for each partition, the bcp utility is used to generate the data in a separate folder if the "Pre-generate snapshots" or "Subscribers to request snapshot generation" options are enabled during the initial synchronization. The Merge Agent will then copy both the schema and the data for each partition to the appropriate subscriptions.

Note For more information on enhancements in merge replication performance in SQL Server 2005, see "Merge Replication Performance Improvements in SQL Server 2005," by Michael Blythe, at http:// www.microsoft.com/technet/prodtechnol/sql/2005/mergerepl.mspx.

You can also set up warnings for merge replication, just like the one that was set for transactional replication in Chapter 18.

Best Practices for Merge Replication

- **Save the configuration script**: Once the publication and subscription are configured for merge replication, store the script for later use.

- **Maintain regular backups**: Back up the publication, the subscription, and the msdb databases right after you add a new publication, or when schema changes have been made on the publication.

- **Optimize publication retention time**: Wherever possible, adjust the publication retention time to the minimum appropriate for your business requirements. This setting determines how long the tracking metadata is retained for the synchronization of the subscription, and hence how much disk storage is needed to hold the metadata.

- **Set the compatibility level**: Set the publication compatibility level to SQL Server 2005 so that the new features of merge replication are enabled.

- **Consider indexing when using filters**: When using row or join filters, consider indexing those columns involved in the filters. Indexing will speed up the merge replication process, since the engine will not need to read each of the rows involved in the filtration.

- **Use join filters when possible**: When using row filters for articles involved in merge replication, avoid complicated subqueries, since the Merge Agent will have to process data for each of the partitions. Use join filters instead, to make this process more efficient.

- **Minimize join filters**: Try to keep the number of join filters to fewer than five. Use join filters only for those tables that need to be partitioned among the subscribing servers.

- **Monitor synchronization performance**: Use the Synchronization History tab in the Replication Monitor to display statistics regarding uploading and downloading changes, history, error messages, and status.

- **Validate subscriptions after restoring**: After backing up and restoring databases used in merge replication, you should validate the subscriptions using either the SSMS or the validate subscription script.

- **Consider indexing metadata**: For optimizing purposes, consider indexing the `MSmerge_genhistory`, `MSmerge_contents`, `MSmerge_tombstone`, `MSmerge_past_partition_mappings`, and `MSmerge_current_partition_mappings` system tables, which store the metadata for merge replication.

- **Create performance baselines**: Develop baselines for the performance of merge replication on the server side for each of the server and hardware resources, like processors and memory. You should also develop a performance baseline for the client side for each of the filtering options, the agent parameters, the subscription options, the locks. You should also set up thresholds and warnings for each of the publication settings using the Replication Monitor.

- **Keep scripts for the agent profiles**: Keep scripts for the profiles of the different agents used in merge replication.

- **Use data-modeling tools to design the database**: As with snapshot and transactional replication, design the database at least up to the third normal form. In designing the publication, add only the articles that are necessary.

- **Plan for high-volume changes**: If you are going to use a high volume of inserts or updates (i.e., batch operations) write a stored procedure that will perform these operations. The stored procedure will be executed once to deliver inserts or updates. Otherwise, the system-generated stored procedure will be executed once for each insert or update operation, which will have an impact on performance because of the considerable amount of throughput involved.

- **Create conflict policies**: In merge replication, conflicts can occur. Set up an appropriate conflict policy to suit your business requirements. Use data partitioning strategies to minimize the number of conflicts and thus reduce the processing overhead associated with detecting and resolving conflicts.

- **Monitor conflicts**: Use the Conflict Policy Viewer to monitor whether the Merge Agent has detected any conflicts and resolved them to meet your business requirements.

- **Reduce contention**: As with snapshot replication, set the `READ_COMMITED_SNAPSHOT` parameter to on to reduce contention.

- **Prepare tables for replication**: For large tables, prior to the generation of the snapshot, create a `ROWGUID` column.

- **Use trace to monitor performance**: Use the SQL Trace function to trace the data in merge replication to monitor performance.

- **Save the trace**: Save the trace in a table on a separate database using the `fn_trace_gettable` function. Do not save the trace directly from the SQL Server Profiler to a table in the database, as this will take an enormous amount of time.

- **Use the DTA**: Use the DTA to tune the trace data as a workload and then save the tuning sessions. Also use the DTA to tune the publication and the subscription databases. Monitor the progress of the DTA, and cancel it if you are not satisfied with the tuning, before it eats into your valuable production time.

- **Save and test the tuning sessions**: Save the tuning session for workloads that meet the performance requirements, and then export the requirements on other servers. Test the tuning of merge replication on a test server before you export the requirements to a production server.

- **Review tuning reports**: Use the Report tab in the Database Engine Tuning Advisor to review the different tuning usage reports, like the Index usage report. Select the recommended reports to see what changes are recommended and the current costs for the tuning.

- **Adjust agent parameters**: After the configuration is finished, change the Merge Agent parameters. As discussed in Chapter 17, set `-OutputVerboselevel` to 0 so that only the error messages are logged. Set `-HistoryVerboseLevel` to 1 so that minimal history of the data is logged. Increase the `-MaxBcpThreads` parameter for the Snapshot Agent to 2 so that the `bcp` utility can run faster using parallel processing.

- **Monitor performance counters**: Monitor the counters for the Merge Agent by using the System Monitor. You can monitor the `Merge:Conflicts/sec`, `Merge:Downloaded Changes/sec` and `Merge:Uploaded Changes/sec` counters.

- **Adjust the batch size parameter**: Change the `ReadBatchSize` parameter for the Merge Agent. The default is 500 transactions, and the Merge Agent will process all these transactions from the publication database in one processing cycle until all of them have been read. Like the Log Reader Agent, you should change the number of transactions to suit your needs.

- **Trace with System Monitor**: As with snapshot replication, use the System Monitor to trace the data for server-wide operations, and have separate counters for each of the operations that are used to monitor the trace.

Summary

In this chapter, I showed you how to set up the trace for merge replication, capturing the event columns using T-SQL and loading the trace in a table on a separate database using the SQL-CMD utility. I also showed you how to generate the Showplan XML and use the dta utility to make an exploratory analysis.

I discussed the use of the dta command-line utility to perform tuning and also to make an exploratory analysis. I also described how you can adjust the publication retention, and the different merge agent profiles you can use. Finally, I outlined the best practices for merge replication.

- Consider latency, concurrency, throughput, and the duration of synchronization for merge replication.

- As with snapshot and transactional replication, performance measurements should be taken regularly and consistently for merge replication.

- The three counters for the Merge Agent that need to be monitored in the System Monitor are Conflicts/sec, Downloaded Changes/sec, and Uploaded Changes/sec.

- You can monitor the performance counters of all the replication agents in the System Monitor by selecting the Replication Agents performance object.

- Execute the fn_trace_getfilterinfo function to find the traces that are set.

- You cannot perform DML operations on client subscriptions to download-only articles.

- Only when the query is fully optimized will the Showplan XML event class generate the trace.

- The file extension for saving the Showplan XML is .sqlplan.

- Showplan XML will have a significant impact on performance; so use it with caution.

- Each event for the Showplan XML is stored as an XML document, and a well-defined schema is associated with each of them. They are available in the C:\Program Files\Microsoft SQL Server\90\Tools\Binn\schemas\sqlserver\2004\07\showplan folder.

- You can display the Showplan XML in both the SQL Server Profiler and the SSMS.

- Set the threshold warnings for merge replication using the Replication Monitor.

- You can monitor the merge triggers in the SQL Server Profiler, or trace them by using the SP:StmtCompleted and SP:Recompile event classes.

- The session definition and session results can be exported using the DTA. They can be saved in XML format.

- The dta command-line utility can be used to perform exploratory analysis.

- Lower the publication retention period to improve performance.

- The Expired subscription clean up job deletes expired push subscriptions but not pull subscriptions. You need to manually delete expired pull subscriptions for merge replication.

- The tuning log can be configured in XML format, which can then be modified for testing other configurations.

- Measure the time it takes to back up and restore the replicated databases and system databases, like the msdb.

- The Merge Agent contains the default, verbose history, Windows Synchronization Manager, rowcount validation, rowcount and checksum validation, slow link, and high volume server-to-server profiles.

- The System Monitor records the replication counters for the Replication Agents, Replication Dist, Replication Logreader, Replication Merge, and Replication Snapshot performance objects.

- Use best practices for the administration of merge replication.

So far, I have focused on the configuration and administration of all three types of replication where the Publisher and Subscriber servers are both using SQL Server. In the next chapter, I will discuss replication among heterogeneous databases. I will show you how to use an Oracle Publisher to replicate data to a SQL Server Subscriber.

Quick Tips

- Stagger the synchronizing schedule if there are a large number of subscriptions for merge replication.

- For troubleshooting purposes, use the verbose history profile of the Merge Agent.

- Remember that tables used for merge publication cannot be used for transactional replication with queued updating subscriptions.

- If you are using a slow network, consider using the slow link profile for the Merge Agent.

CHAPTER 20

■ ■ ■

Heterogeneous Replication

So far, I have demonstrated the three types of replication between SQL Server databases. The plethora of databases from different vendors residing on various platforms and serving different business requirements in a single company, makes it crucial to integrate data.

In this chapter, I will show you how to replicate data across heterogeneous databases. Specifically, I will focus on the replication of data from an Oracle Publisher server to SQL Server Subscriber servers. While all three types of replication can be carried out between SQL Server databases, you can only use snapshot and transactional replication between Oracle and SQL Server subscribing servers. On top of that, you can only use push subscriptions.

On completing this chapter, you will know how to do the following:

- Grant permissions to Oracle database objects

- Configure snapshot publication in an Oracle Publisher server

- Configure SQL Server subscriptions to an Oracle Publisher used for snapshot replication

- Configure transactional publication in an Oracle Publisher server

- Set up Oracle Publisher in the Replication Monitor to monitor replication

- Configure SQL Server subscriptions to an Oracle Publisher used for transactional replication

Snapshot Replication from an Oracle Publisher to a SQL Server Subscriber

I discussed snapshot replication in Chapters 4–7. In this section, I will focus on using snapshot replication between an Oracle Publisher server and SQL Server Subscriber servers.

Configuring an Oracle Publication for Snapshot Replication

To transmit data from an Oracle Publisher to SQL Server Subscriber servers using snapshot replication, you must ensure that you have already installed Oracle Database Server and that the default database is already installed.

Once you have installed Oracle, you can verify that the Oracle client connection can connect to the Oracle server. In this case, use SQL*Plus to test the connection. Open the command prompt, go to the root directory where Oracle is installed, and run the `sqlplus` command to establish a connection from SQL*Plus to the Oracle server, replacing `system` with the username and password:

```
Sqlplus system/system@orcl as sysdba
```

You can see the successful connection to the server in Figure 20-1.

Figure 20-1. *Connecting with SQL*Plus to the Oracle server*

Once SQL*Plus establishes the connection, you will see the `SQL>` prompt. You need to load the `oracleadmin.sql` file now, as shown in Figure 20-1. This script grants permissions to a specified user to configure the Oracle database on the Oracle Publisher for data publication using SQL Server replication. You will be asked for the name and password for the user and for the name of the default tablespace, which in this case is system. In Figure 20-1, the name of the user is sqlrepl. When you are finished, press Enter.

You will see the script file (SQL file) create users and triggers, as shown in Figures 20-2 and 20-3.

In Figure 20-3, you can see that permissions are granted to any trigger that is created. The triggers are used to track changes in the publication and are necessary for transactional replication. If you are only using snapshot replication, you can comment out the section of the script file that creates the triggers. Since I will be using both snapshot and transactional replication in this chapter, I allowed the creation of the triggers.

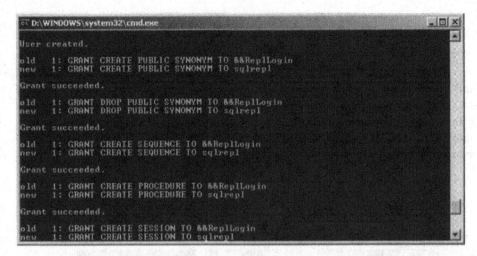

Figure 20-2. *Successfully granting synonym, sequence, procedure, and session permissions to sqlrepl*

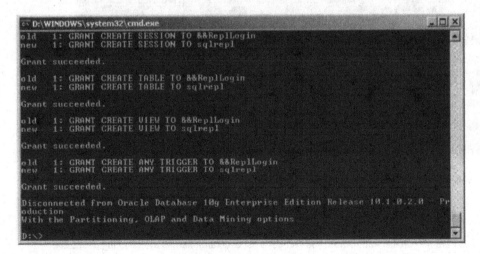

Figure 20-3. *Successfully granting table, view, and trigger permissions to sqlrepl*

Now that we have granted permissions to the user, the next step is to select the database objects in Oracle that will be published. Unlike SQL Server, you cannot publish all the Oracle database objects. These are the objects that you can publish:

- Tables

- Materialized views

- Indexes

- Index-organized tables

▓**Note** Materialized views are replicated as tables in SQL Server.

In this chapter, we will be using the default database that comes with the installation of Oracle. The OE schema and the corresponding three tables, Order_Items, Orders, and Product_Information, will be used as articles.

Before we start configuring the publication, however, we should first check whether the tables to be replicated contain any data. To do this, I executed the following code:

```
Select * from oe.orders
```

The preceding statement returned 105 rows, as shown in Figure 20-4.

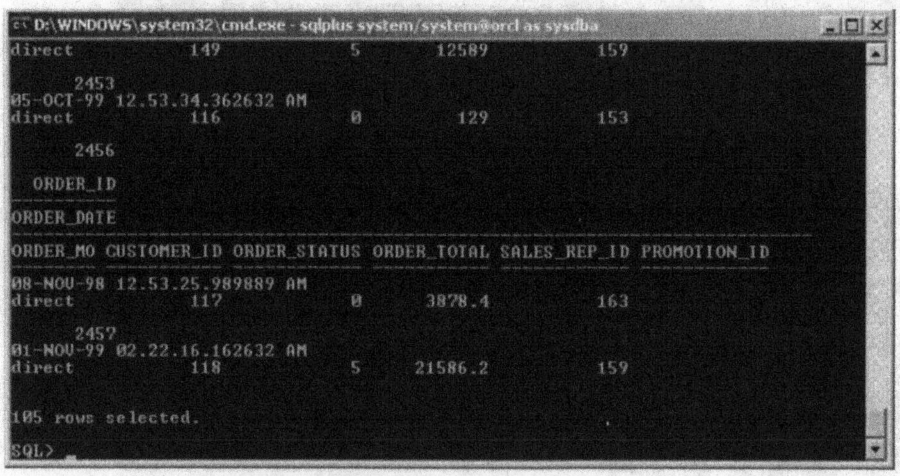

Figure 20-4. *There are 105 rows in the* Orders *table*

▓**Tip** If you are not familiar with Oracle, you can get a list of column names by executing describe oe.orders.

Now that we know the result set is in the table, we need to grant select permissions to the tables that will be used as articles. You can execute the following statement for each of the tables:

```
Grant select on oe.order_items to sqlrepl;
```

This is shown in Figure 20-5. Note that I have also granted insert and update permissions to the tables.

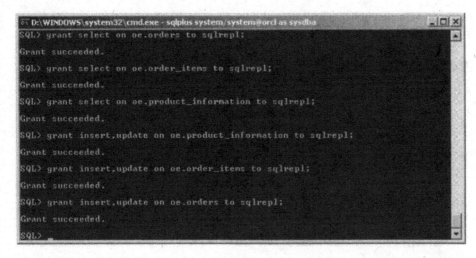

Figure 20-5. *Granting* select, insert, *and* update *permissions to the tables that will be used as articles*

Now open the SSMS. Right-click on Local Publications in the Object Explorer and select New Oracle Publication from the menu. This will start the New Publication Wizard and display the welcome message.

Click Next to select the Oracle Publisher, as shown in Figure 20-6. You can see that there are no Publishers listed for Oracle yet.

Figure 20-6. *No Oracle Publisher has been selected yet*

Click the Add Oracle Publisher button, and this will open the Connect to Server window shown in Figure 20-7.

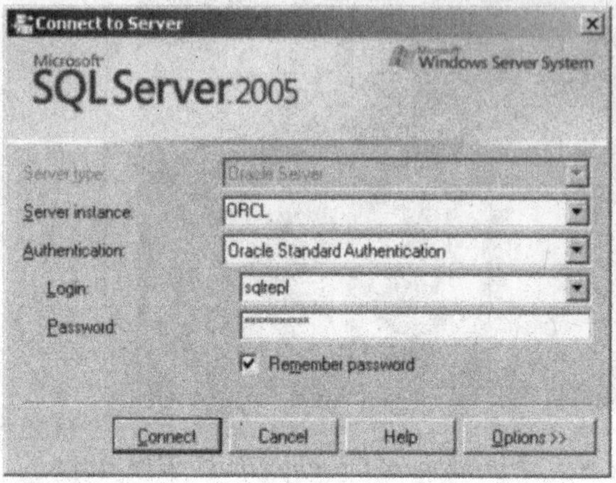

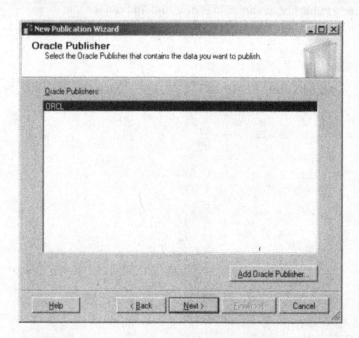

Figure 20-7. *Connecting to the Oracle server*

Click the Connect button, and the Publisher will be added in the Oracle Publisher window, as shown in Figure 20-8. Select the Oracle Publisher and click Next to select the articles.

Figure 20-8. *ORCL is added as the Oracle Publisher*

In the Articles page of the wizard, you will only see the list of tables to which you have granted select permissions, as shown in Figure 20-9. Check the tables that you want to select as articles.

Figure 20-9. *Selecting articles for the publication*

Click Next, and you will see the page where you can add filters for table rows if you wish, as shown in Figure 20-10. Click Next to continue.

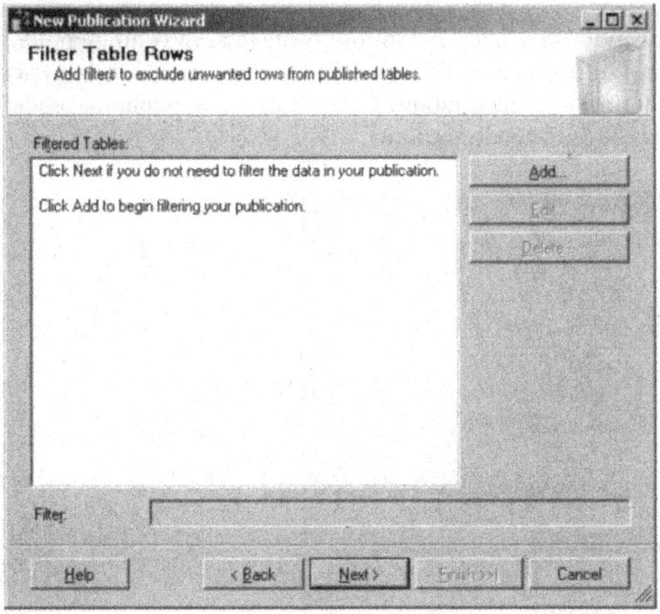

Figure 20-10. *The wizard page where you can filter table rows*

The next wizard page allows you to schedule the execution of the Snapshot Agent, as shown in Figure 20-11. Check the "Create a snapshot immediately and keep the snapshot available to initialize subscriptions" box. Click the Next button to continue.

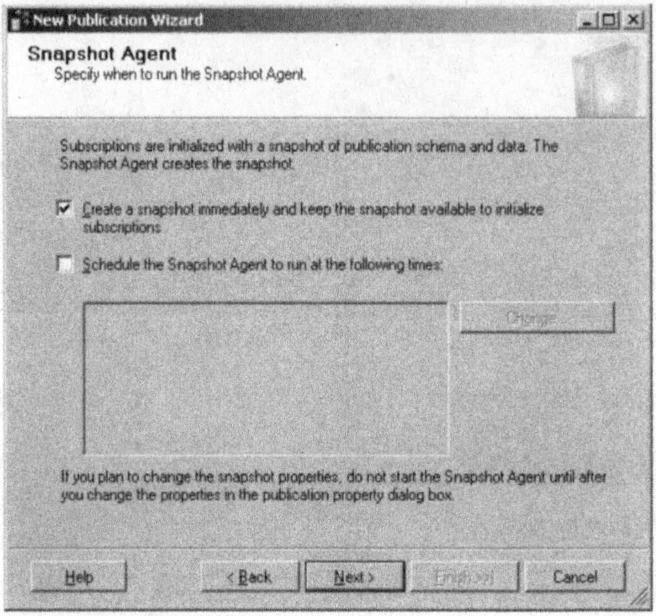

Figure 20-11. *Scheduling the Snapshot Agent*

The Snapshot Agent Security window is where you can specify the security settings under which the Snapshot Agent will run. I selected the SQL Server Agent service account, as you can see in Figure 20-12. I mentioned during the configuration of snapshot and transactional replication that it is recommended you use the domain account.

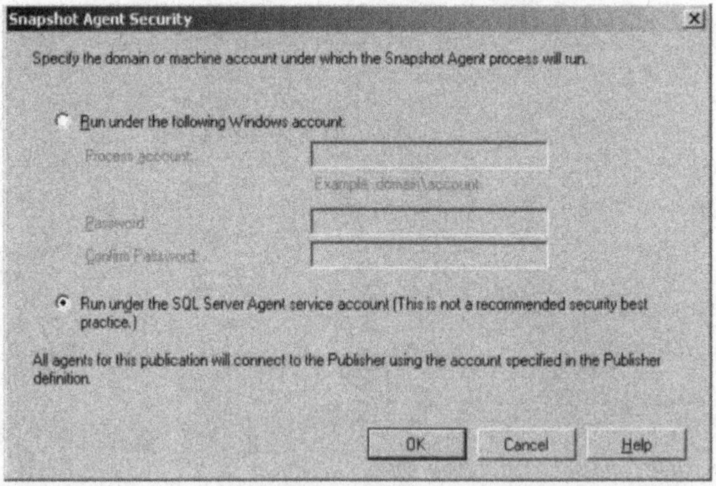

Figure 20-12. *Configuring security settings for the Snapshot Agent*

Click OK, and you will see the Agent Security page of the wizard, as shown in Figure 20-13. If the setting is correct, click Next.

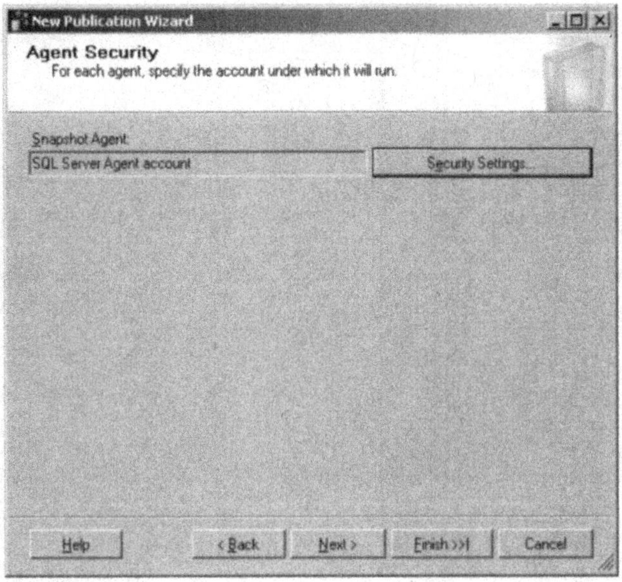

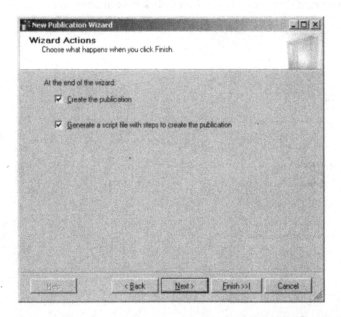

Figure 20-13. *Setting agent security*

You can now specify whether to create the publication and generate the script, as shown in Figure 20-14. Click Next to continue.

Figure 20-14. *Choosing to create the publication and generate the script file for the publication*

You can now specify the filename and the directory for the script file, as shown in Figure 20-15. Click Next to continue.

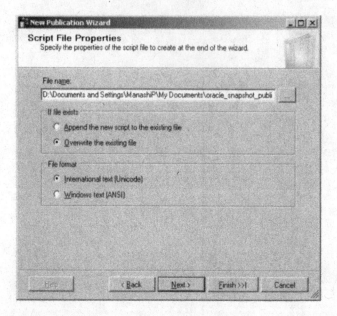

Figure 20-15. *Setting the script file properties*

In the Complete the Wizard page, enter a name for the publication, as shown in Figure 20-16. If you are not satisfied with the summary, you can click the Back button and make the necessary changes. However, if the summary is correct, click the Finish button.

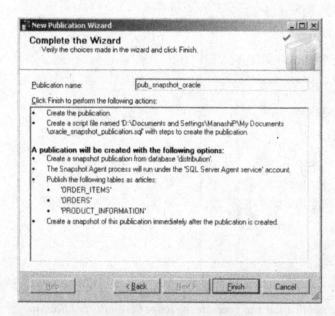

Figure 20-16. *Giving a name to the publication*

The wizard will show you whether the creation of the publication has been successful or not, as shown in Figure 20-17.

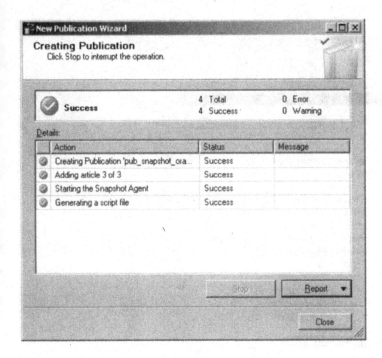

Figure 20-17. *Successful creation of the publication*

You can click the Report button to view more information about the creation of the publication, as shown in Figure 20-18, and you can save the report in a file for auditing or troubleshooting purposes. Click the Close button when you are done.

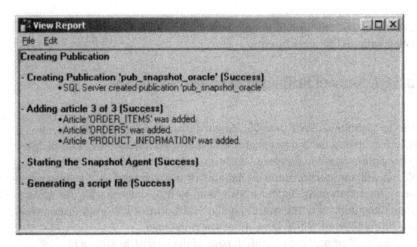

Figure 20-18. *Viewing the report on the creation of the publication*

Now click the Local Publications object in the Object Explorer, and you will see the publication, as in Figure 20-19. You can see the name of the Oracle server (ORCL) preceding the name of the publication.

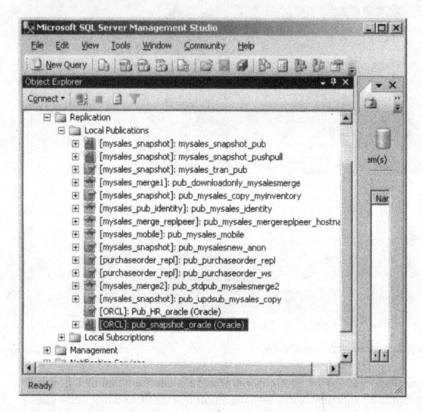

Figure 20-19. *The Oracle publication, pub_snapshot_oracle, is listed under Local Publications*

Now that we have completed the configuration of the publication for snapshot replication, I will show you how to configure the subscription.

Configuring a SQL Server Subscription for Snapshot Publication

The subscriber to the Oracle Publisher will be a SQL Server Subscriber. The SQL Server subscription that we will create in this section is a push subscription. As I mentioned earlier, this is the only type of subscription possible between Oracle and SQL Server.

For this example, we will assume the database has already been created on the Subscriber server, and the name of the subscription database is oe_snapshot. To start creating the subscription, right-click on the publication that you created in SSMS, and select New Subscriptions to start the New Subscription Wizard. Click Next on the welcome page.

You will now see the Distribution Agent Location page of the wizard, as shown in Figure 20-20. As you know, the Distribution Agent is located in the Distributor server for push subscriptions. Select the "Run all agents at the Distributor" option, and click Next.

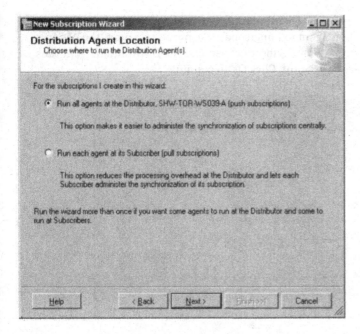

Figure 20-20. *Specifying that the Distribution Agent is located on the Distributor server*

The wizard will now ask you for the name of the SQL Server Subscriber and the database that you want to use as a subscription database. Check the box beside the Subscriber server, and from the Subscription Database drop-down list, select the name of the database, as shown in Figure 20-21. Click Next to continue.

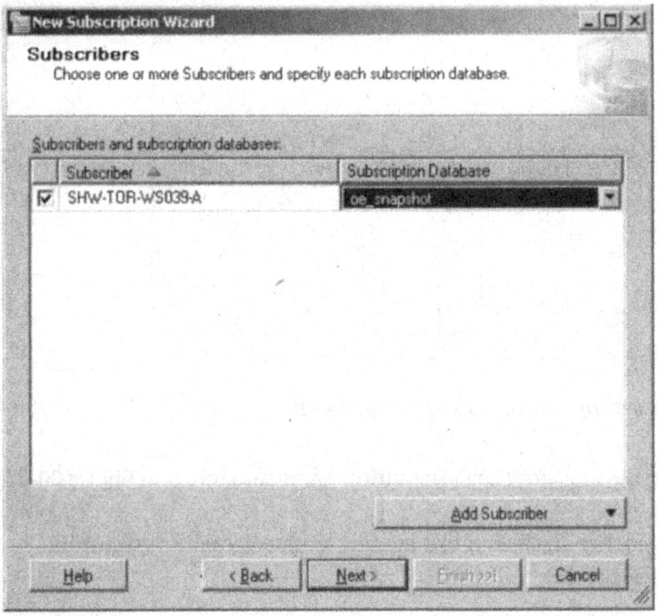

Figure 20-21. *Selecting the subscription database for the Subscriber server*

You can now set the security for the Distribution Agent, as shown in Figure 20-22. As you can see, I have set the Distribution Agent to impersonate the process account (the Windows account) to connect to the Distributor and Subscriber servers. The Distribution Agent runs under the SQL Server Agent service account. Click OK to continue.

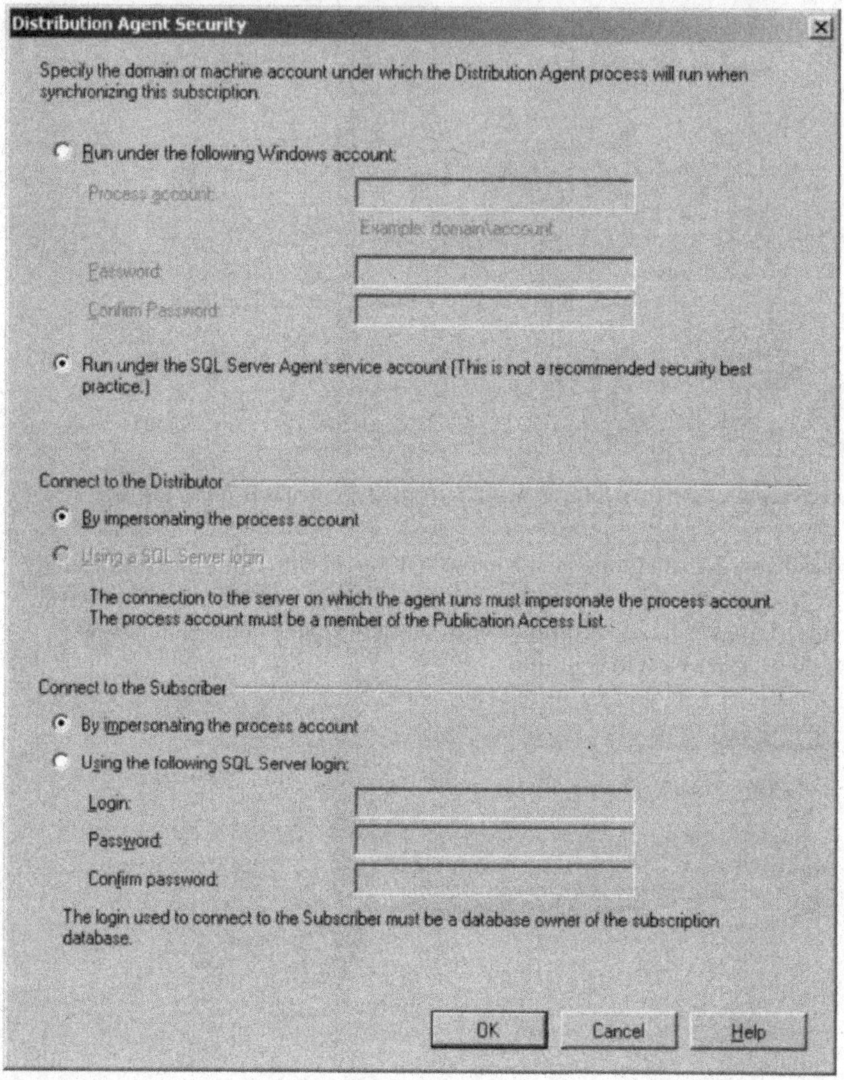

Figure 20-22. *Configuring security settings for the Distribution Agent*

You will now see the security settings for the Distribution Agent, as shown in Figure 20-23. Click the Next button.

Now you can schedule the synchronization of the agent. I set the agent to run continuously, as shown in Figure 20-24. Click Next.

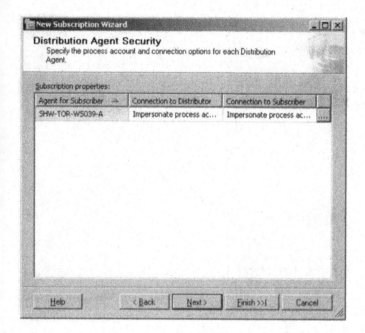

Figure 20-23. *Viewing the Distribution Agent security settings*

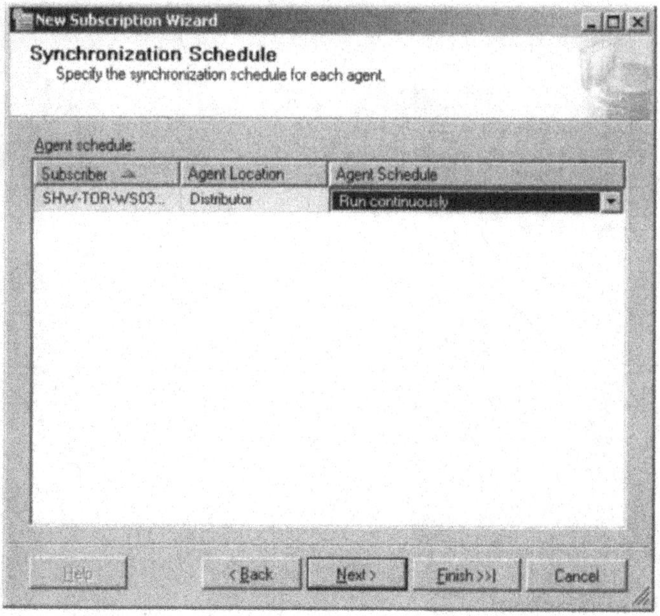

Figure 20-24. *Setting the synchronization schedule*

The next wizard page is where you initialize the subscription, as in Figure 20-25. From the Initialize When drop-down list, select Immediately and check the box in the Initialize column. Click Next to continue.

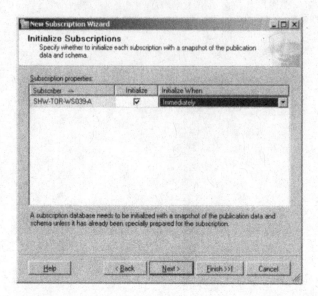

Figure 20-25. *Setting the subscription to initialize immediately*

Next, check the boxes to "Create the subscription" and "Generate a script file with steps to create the subscription." This is shown in Figure 20-26. Click Next when you're done.

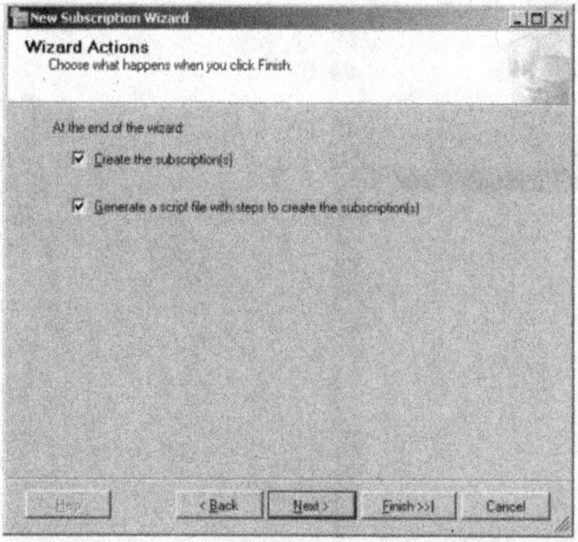

Figure 20-26. *Choosing to create the subscription*

The wizard will now ask you to enter a name for the file it will save the script in (as it did in Figure 20-15). Click the Finish button to move on to the Complete the Wizard page shown in Figure 20-27. If you are not satisfied with the configuration summary, click the Back button and make the appropriate changes. Otherwise, click the Finish button.

Figure 20-27. *Viewing the configuration summary for the subscription*

The wizard will create the subscription and generate the script, reporting its success as shown in Figure 20-28. Click the Report button to view or save the report, and click the Close button when you are finished with the wizard.

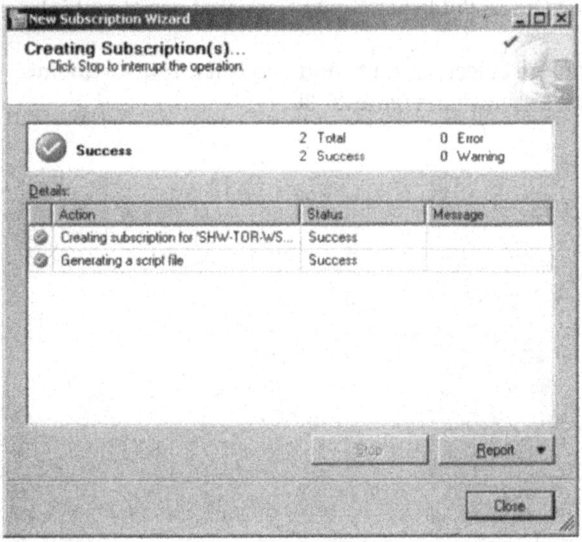

Figure 20-28. *Successful creation of the subscription*

If you now open the Oracle publication under the Local Publications object in the SSMS, you will see the push subscription that was created. Open the subscription database, oe_snapshot, and then open the Tables object. You will see that the Orders, Order_Items, and Product_Information tables are owned by the dbo schema and not by oe.

Right-click on the Orders table and select Open Table from the menu. The table will be displayed as in Figure 20-29. You can see that there are 105 rows for the Orders table.

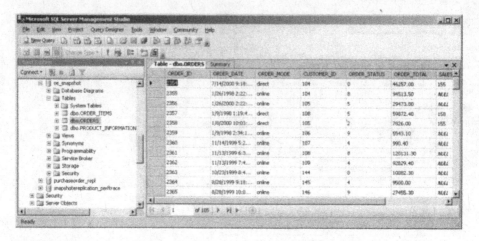

Figure 20-29. *Viewing the* Orders *table in the subscription database*

Monitoring Replication with Replication Monitor

As you know, you can monitor replication using the Replication Monitor, which displays SQL Server Publishers. You can also monitor replication for an Oracle Publisher and any associated Subscriber servers. In order to display the Oracle Publisher, though, you first need to add the Publisher in the Replication Monitor.

To do this, open the Replication Monitor. Select Action ➤ Add Publisher from the menu. This will open the Add Publisher window, as shown in Figure 20-30.

Figure 20-30. *Adding a Publisher to Replication Monitor*

Click the Add button, and from the drop-down list select Add Oracle Publisher. This will open the dialog box in Figure 20-31, asking you to identify the SQL Server Distributor for the Oracle Publisher. Click OK to continue.

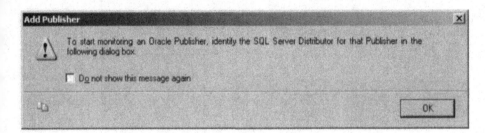

Figure 20-31. *Viewing a reminder about adding Oracle Publishers*

The Connect to Server window will now open, as shown in Figure 20-32. Click the Connect button.

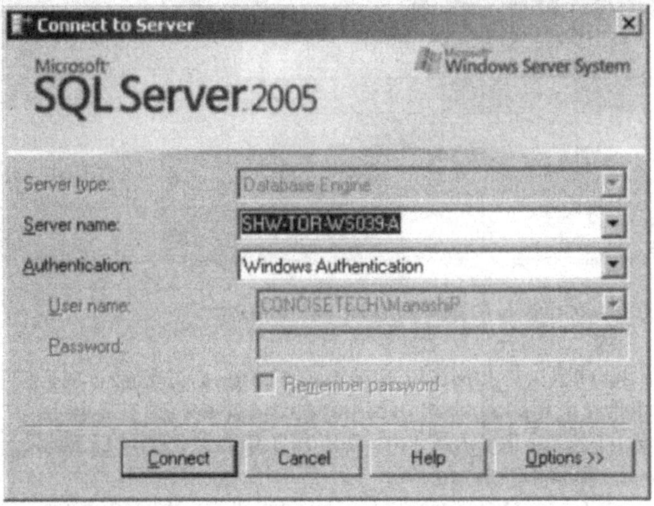

Figure 20-32. *Connecting to the SQL Server Distributor*

You will now see the names of the Oracle Publisher and the associated SQL Server Distributor in the Add Publisher window, as shown in Figure 20-33. Click OK.

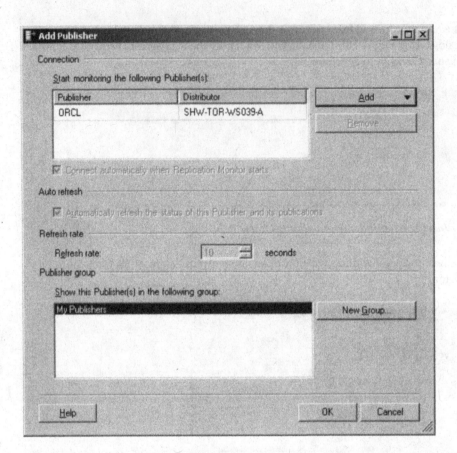

Figure 20-33. *Adding the Oracle Publisher, ORCL, to the Replication Monitor*

You will now see the name of the Oracle Publisher, ORCL, listed in the Replication Monitor. Expand the ORCL Oracle Publisher in the Replication Monitor, and select the snapshot publication that we just created. You will see the push subscription listed under the All Subscriptions tab in the right pane in the Replication Monitor.

Right-click on the push subscription that was created for the snapshot publication for Oracle and select View Details from the menu. This will open the window shown in Figure 20-34. As you can see, 105 rows of the Orders table were bulk copied. This is the same number of rows we saw in the subscription database, shown in Figure 20-29. Similarly, you can see that 665 rows of the Order_Items table and 288 rows of the Product_Information table were bulk copied.

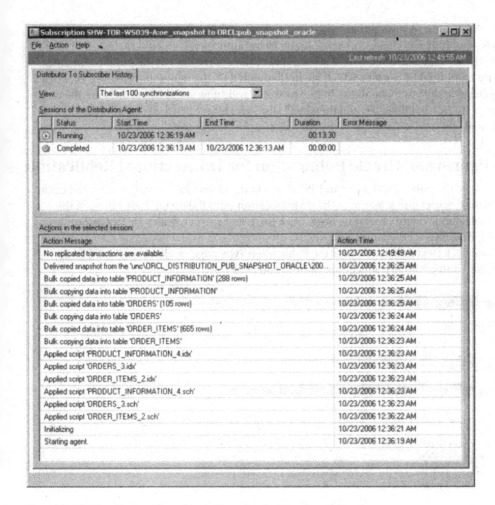

Figure 20-34. *Monitoring the subscriptions for the Oracle publication*

Transactional Replication from an Oracle Publisher to a SQL Server Subscriber

You already know that in transactional replication with SQL Server Publisher servers, the Log Reader Agent reads the transaction log on the publication database and sends only the committed transactions to the distribution database. However, when using an Oracle Publisher, the architecture for transactional replication is slightly different.

In this context, transactional replication still uses the Log Reader Agent to transfer the data changes from the Oracle Publisher to the Distributor server, and the Distribution Agent still sends the data to the Subscriber server. However, data changes in the publication database are monitored by triggers, which are implemented on the tables that are used as articles in the Oracle publication database. In this section, I will show you how to configure the publication for an Oracle Publisher, and then I will show you how the SQL Server subscription is configured.

Configuring an Oracle Publication for Transactional Replication

To configure the publication, open the SSMS and in the Object Explorer right-click the Local Publications object and select New Oracle Publication from the menu. This will open the New Publication Wizard's welcome page. Click Next, and you can select the Oracle Publisher as in Figure 20-8.

Then click Next again to display the Publication Type page, as shown in Figure 20-35. Select the "Transactional publication" option, and click Next.

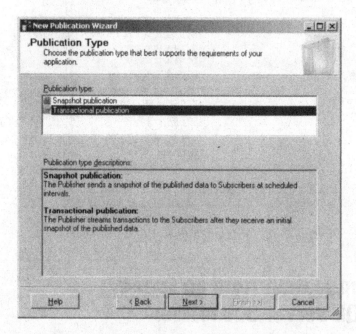

Figure 20-35. *Selecting the transactional publication type*

In the Articles page, shown in Figure 20-36, you need to grant select permission for the articles that will be included in the publication.

The articles I selected are Order_Items, Orders, and Product_Information. By selecting one of the articles, such as Product_Information, and clicking the Article Properties button, you can see the properties of the article, as shown in Figure 20-37.

Figure 20-36. *Selecting the objects to publish*

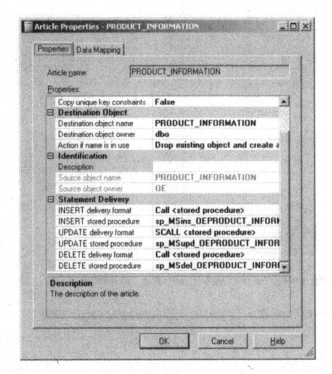

Figure 20-37. *Viewing properties of the* Product_Information *article*

You can see that the delivery format used for the insert and the delete operations is of the CALL format, while that for the update operation is of SCALL format. The stored procedures used by the CALL operation for insert, update, and delete operations are sp_MSins_<articlename>, spMSupd_<articlename>, and sp_MSdel_<articlename>, respectively. You can see that the schema name, OE, is added to the <articlename> in the stored procedure names. The destination object owner for the article is dbo.

Now click on the Data Mapping tab as shown in Figure 20-38. You can see that the Oracle data types do not always match the data types of SQL Server, and wherever possible, SQL Server actually maps the data types of Oracle to its data types. The number data type is mapped to the numeric data type, and you cannot change it to any other data type. The varchar2 data type has been mapped to the varchar data type. Select the default data types, and click OK to return to the Articles page of the New Publication Wizard (Figure 20-26), and click Next.

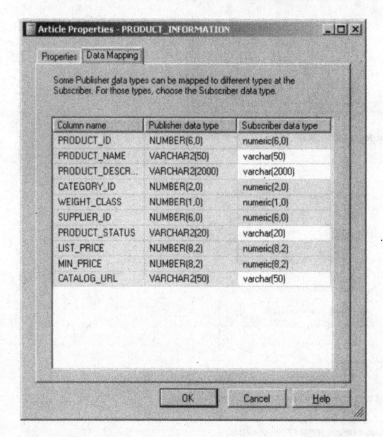

Figure 20-38. *Viewing the data mapping settings for the* Product_Information *article*

In the Filter Table Rows page, you can add filters if necessary, as shown in Figure 20-39. Click Next to continue.

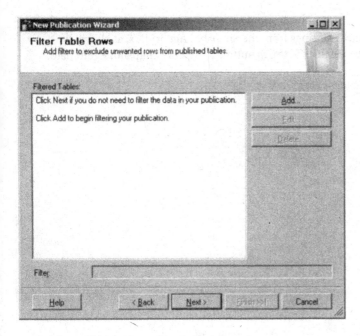

Figure 20-39. *The option to filter table rows*

In the Snapshot Agent page, check the "Create a snapshot immediately and keep the snapshot available to initialize subscriptions" box, as shown in Figure 20-40. Click Next to continue.

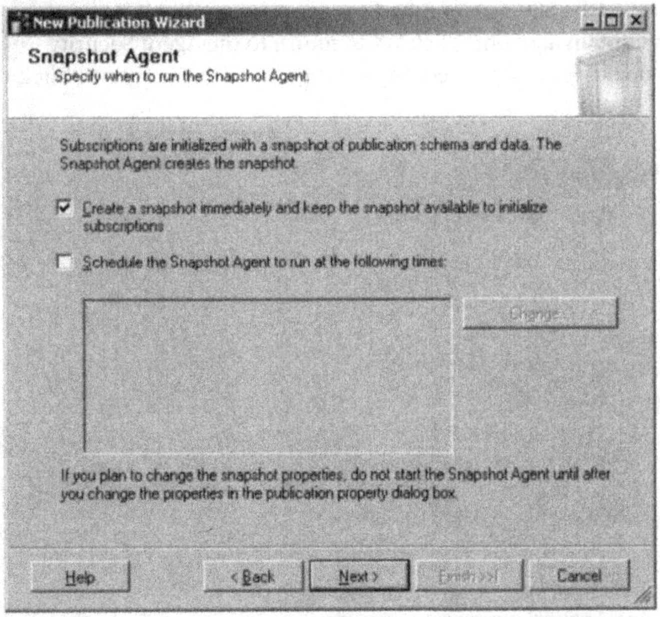

Figure 20-40. *Specifying the schedule of the Snapshot Agent*

In the Agent Security wizard page, the account settings for both agents will initially be blank. Check the "Use the security settings from the Snapshot Agent" box, as shown in Figure 20-41, and then click the Security Settings button beside the Snapshot Agent field.

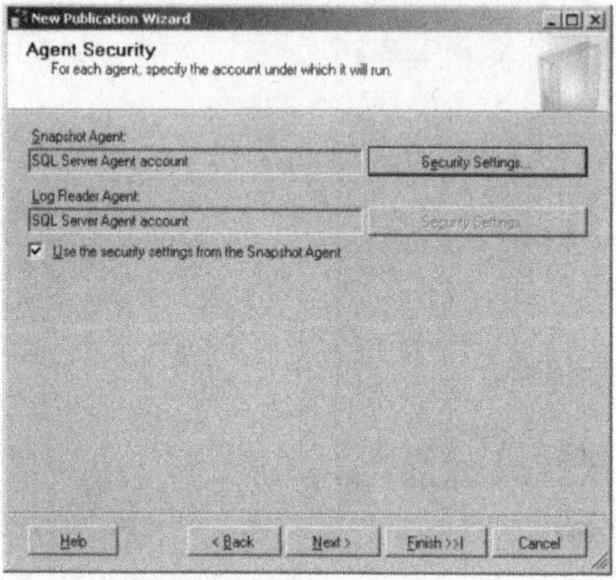

Figure 20-41. *Configuring security settings for the Snapshot and Log Reader Agents*

The Snapshot Agent Security window will open, as shown in Figure 20-42. As you can see, I set the Snapshot Agent to run under the SQL Server Agent service account, but it is recommended that you use a Windows domain account. Click OK to return to the Agent Security window (Figure 20-41), where you will now see the security settings for both the agents. Click Next to continue.

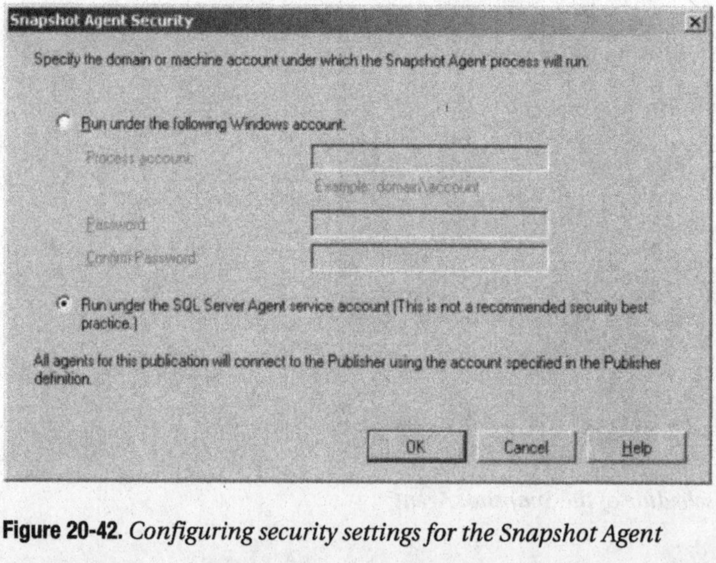

Figure 20-42. *Configuring security settings for the Snapshot Agent*

In the Wizard Actions page, shown in Figure 20-43, check the "Create the publication" box and click Next. I did not check the "Generate a script file with steps to create the publication" box, but doing so is recommended so that you will have a script for the configuration of the publication.

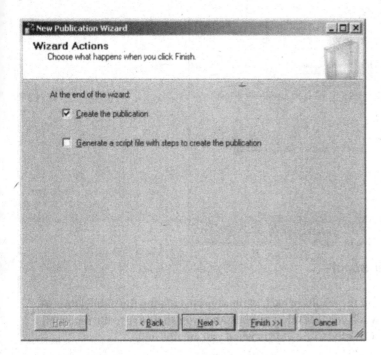

Figure 20-43. *Specifying the creation of the publication*

In the Complete the Wizard page of the New Publication Wizard, enter a name for the publication and review the summary, as shown in Figure 20-44. If you are not satisfied with the summary, click the Back button and make your changes. Otherwise click the Finish button.

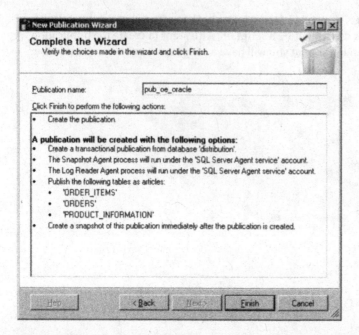

Figure 20-44. *Completing the wizard*

The wizard will show you the results of each of the steps in creating the publication, as shown in Figure 20-45. As when creating other publications, you should save the report for troubleshooting purposes. Click the Close button when you are finished.

Figure 20-45. *Successful creation of the publication*

Now that we have configured the publication in the Oracle Publisher server, our next step is to configure the SQL Server subscription for the Oracle publication.

Configuring a SQL Server Subscription for Transactional Publication

In the SSMS, right-click on the Local Publications object and select New Subscriptions from the menu. This will start the New Subscription Wizard. Click Next on the welcome page, and you will see the Publication page of the wizard, as shown in Figure 20-46. You can see the name of the Oracle Publisher (ORCL) and the names of the publications for the ORCL Publisher server. Select the publication, pub_oe_oracle, and then click Next.

Figure 20-46. *Selecting the publication from the list of publications*

In the Distribution Agent Location page of the wizard, select the "Run all agents at the Distributor" option, since this will be a push subscription. This is shown in Figure 20-47. Click Next to continue.

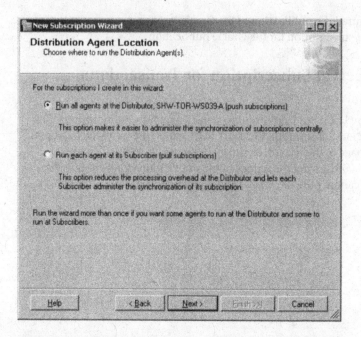

Figure 20-47. *Specifying the location of the Distribution Agent*

In the Subscribers page, shown in Figure 20-48, you will choose the Subscriber server and subscription database. Initially none will be displayed, so click the Add Subscriber button.

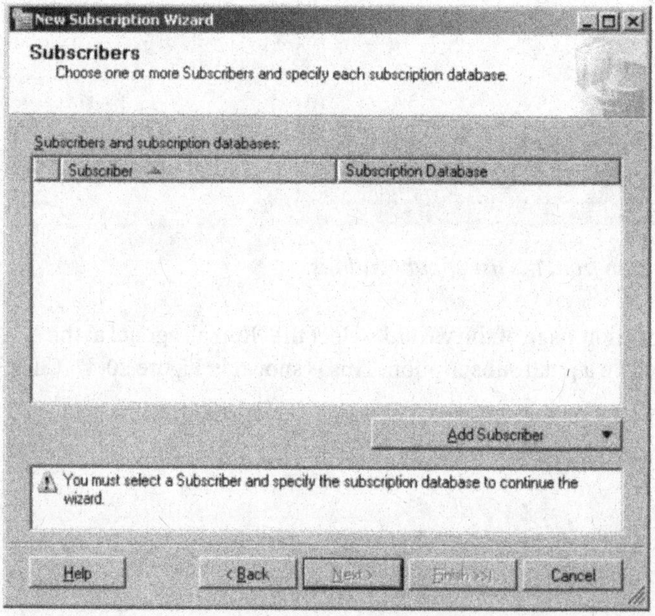

Figure 20-48. *Choosing subscribers and subscription databases*

The Connect to Server window will be displayed, as shown in Figure 20-49. Select the Subscriber server from the "Server name" drop-down list. (In my case the Publisher, Distributor and the Subscriber servers are on the same machine.) Click the Connect button.

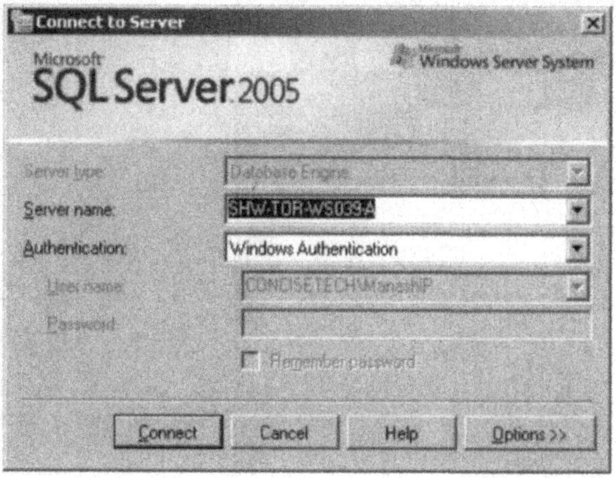

Figure 20-49. *Connecting to the SQL Server Subscriber*

You will now be returned to the Subscribers wizard page (Figure 20-48), and you will see the name of the Subscriber server listed. From the Subscription Database drop-down list, select the name of database, as shown in Figure 20-50. Click Next to continue.

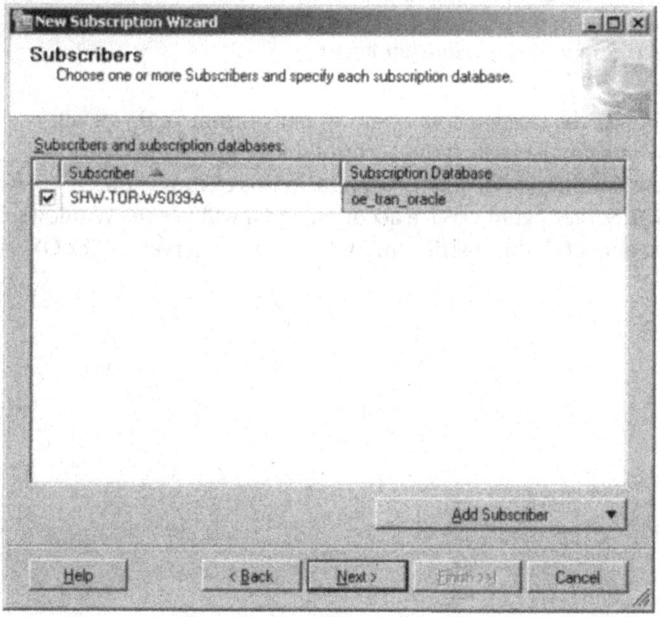

Figure 20-50. *Selecting the subscription database for the Subscriber server*

In the next wizard page, you can set the security settings for the Distribution Agent, as shown in Figure 20-51.

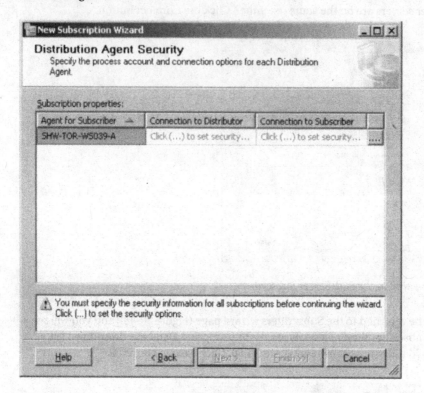

Figure 20-51. *Specifying security settings for the Distribution Agent*

Click on the ellipsis button beside the Connection to Subscriber column, and you will see the window in Figure 20-52 where you can select the account under which the Distribution Agent will connect to the Distributor and Subscriber servers. In this example, the Distribution Agent is using the SQL Server Agent service account, and it will use the Windows connection (process account) to connect to the Distributor and Subscriber servers. Click OK to continue.

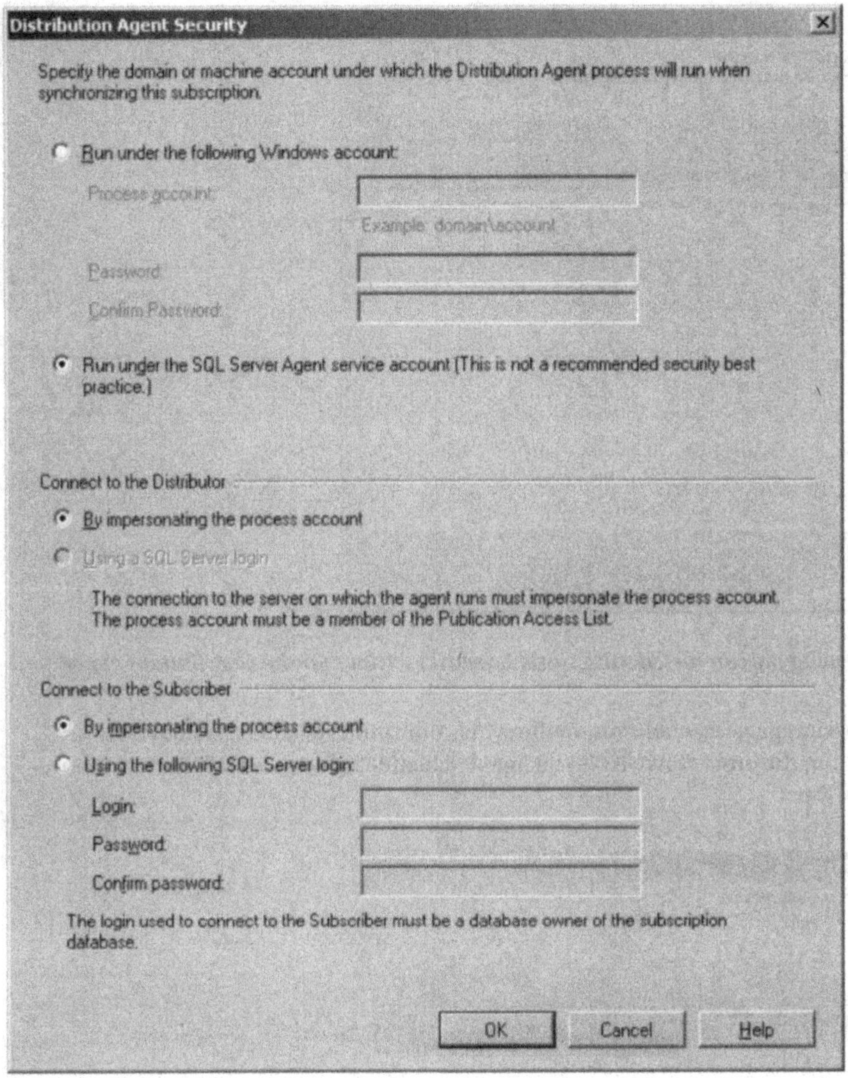

Figure 20-52. *Selecting the accounts under which the Distribution Agent will run and connect to the Distributor and Subscriber servers*

You will see the subscription properties completed in the Distribution Agent Security wizard page, as shown in Figure 20-53. Click Next.

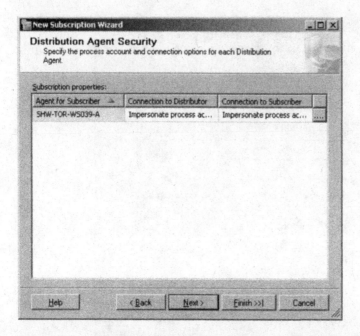

Figure 20-53. *Viewing the completed subscription security settings for the Distribution Agent*

The next wizard page is where you set the synchronization schedule, as shown in Figure 20-54. From the drop-down list in the Agent Schedule column, select "Run continuously' and click Next.

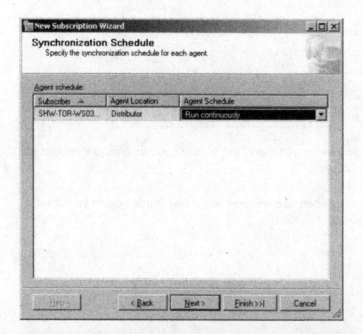

Figure 20-54. *Setting the synchronization schedule for the agent*

In the Initialize Subscriptions wizard page, check the box in the Initialize column, and from the drop-down list in the Initialize When column, select Immediately, as shown in Figure 20-55. Click Next to continue.

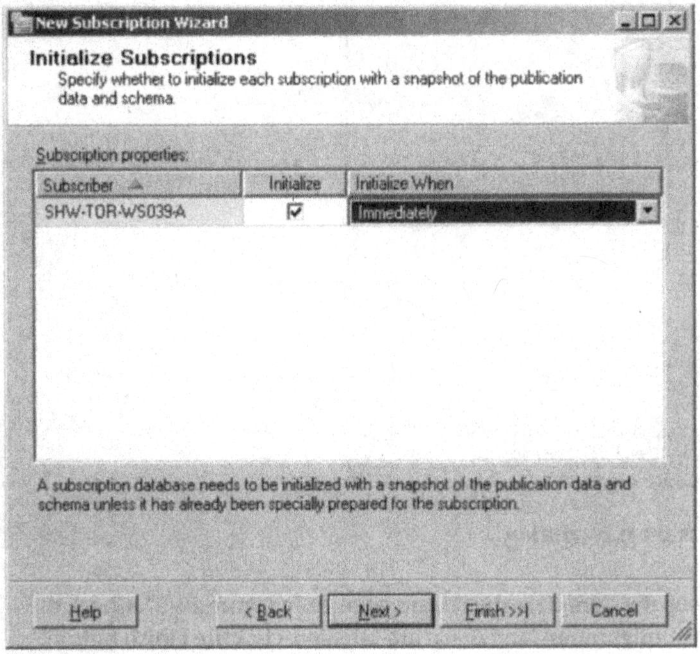

Figure 20-55. *Setting when the subscription is initialized*

Next, check the "Create the subscription" box in the Wizard Actions page to create the subscription, as shown in Figure 20-56. In this case, I did not check the "Generate a script file with steps to create the subscription" box. However, it is a good idea to generate the script for both the publication and subscription; if the publication and the subscription databases get out of sync in the future, you can use the scripts to restore the synchronization process.

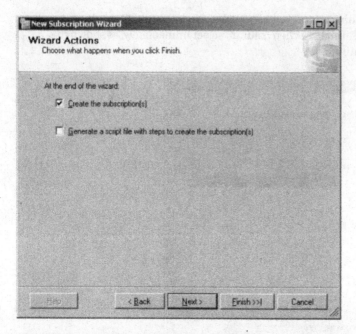

Figure 20-56. *Choosing to create the subscription*

Click Next, and you will see the Complete the Wizard page, as in Figure 20-57. Check the summary of the subscription configuration, and if you are satisfied, click the Finish button.

Figure 20-57. *Completing the wizard*

The wizard will show its success in creating the subscription, as shown in Figure 20-58. Save the report if you choose, and then click the Close button.

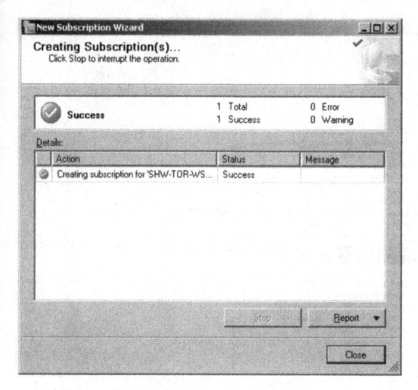

Figure 20-58. *Successful generation of the subscription*

Now open the publication in the SSMS, and the subscription that you just created for transactional replication will be displayed, as in Figure 20-59.

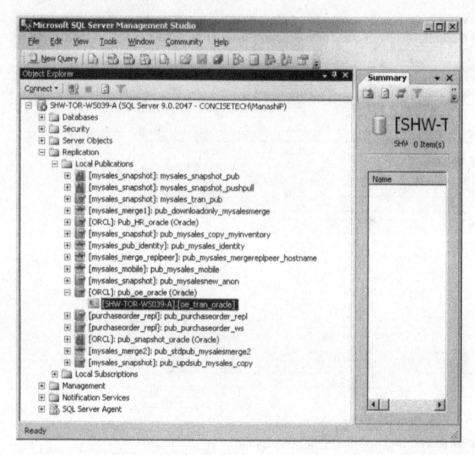

Figure 20-59. *Viewing the subscription for the transactional publication, pub_oe_oracle*

Summary

In this chapter, I discussed the configuration of both snapshot and transactional replication using Oracle as the Publisher server and SQL Server as the Subscriber server. I also discussed the granting of permissions on database objects before you can use them as articles in the Oracle publication database. You should be aware of which Oracle database objects can be included as articles in the publication, and the difference in data type mappings between Oracle and SQL Server. I also showed you how to set up SQL Server subscriptions.

- You can only use snapshot and transactional replication with an Oracle publication database. You cannot use merge replication.

- You need to run the `oracleadmin.sql` script file before you can configure replication with an Oracle database.

- You need to grant `select` permissions to those database objects that you want to include as articles in the publication database.

- You can only replicate Oracle tables, indexes, materialized views, and index-organized tables.

- Snapshot replication with Oracle as the Publisher server is similar to snapshot replication with SQL Server as the Publisher.

- The architecture of transactional replication with Oracle as the Publisher is different than when SQL Server is used as the Publisher.

- Triggers created in database objects in Oracle are used to track changes in transactional replication while the Log Reader Agent sends data to the Subscriber server.

- You can add an Oracle Publisher server to the Replication Monitor to monitor replication.

- In order to configure an Oracle publication, you need to select New Oracle Publisher from the menu in SSMS.

Quick Tips

- Use SQL*Plus to verify the connection between the Oracle client and the Oracle server.

- You can manually run the permissions stated in the `oracleadmin.sql` script file.

- Use the `DESCRIBE` statement to see which columns are included in the tables after the configuration of transactional replication.

■ ■ ■

E-R Diagram of the mysales Database

In this appendix, the E-R diagram for the mysales database is shown. The mysales database is used in all the examples discussed in this book, but with different names to match the type of replication. For example, while configuring merge replication in Chapter 11, I renamed the mysales database as mysales_merge.

There are three schemas in the mysales database:

- myfinance

- myorder

- myinventory

The tables for the myfinance schema are as follows:

- AccountsReceivable

- AccountInvoice

- CashReceipt

The myorder schema has the following tables:

- BillTo

- Customer

- CustSales

- OrderDetail

- OrderHeader

- SalesPerson

- ShipTo

- Stock

- Zone

These are the tables for the myinventory schema:

- Item

- PriceList

- PurchaseOrderDetail

- PurchaseOrderHeader

- StockItem

- Vendor

- Warehouse

The E-R diagram for the tables for the mysales database is shown in Figures A-1 through A-3.

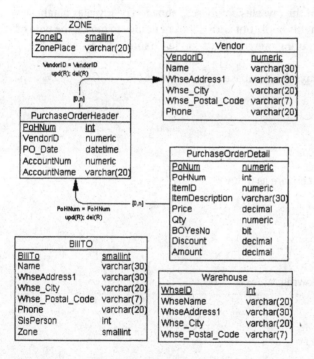

Figure A-1. *E-R diagram showing the* Zone, Vendor, PurchaseOrderHeader, PurchaseOrderDetail, BillTo, *and* Warehouse *tables of the mysales database*

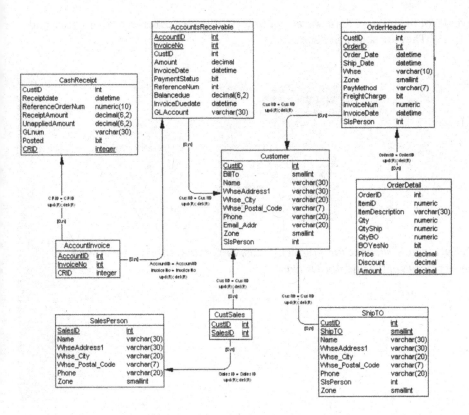

Figure A-2. *E-R diagram showing the* CashReceipt, AccountInvoice, SalesPerson, CustSales, Customer, AccountsReceivable, OrderHeader, OrderDetail, *and* ShipTo *tables of the mysales database*

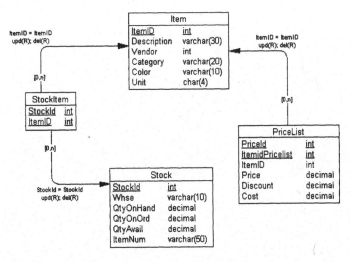

Figure A-3. *E-R diagram showing the* Item, StockItem, Stock, *and* PriceList *tables of the mysales database*

The views for the mysales database are vw_OrderStatus, vw_CustomerInvoiceStatus, and vw_ItemEnquiry. They are shown in Figure A-4.

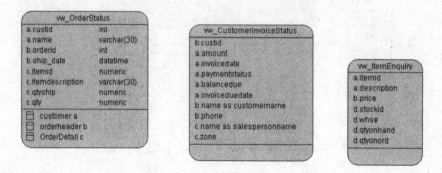

Figure A-4. *E-R diagram showing the* vw_OrderStatus, vw_CustomerInvoiceStatus, *and* vw_ItemEnquiry *views of the mysales database*

APPENDIX B

■ ■ ■

SQL Code for the Database

Listing B-1 contains the T-SQL code for the database that has been used in the book.

Listing B-1. *T-SQL Code for the Physical Database Structure*

```
/* ============================================================ */
/*   Database name:  Mysales                                    */
/*   DBMS name:      Microsoft SQL Server 2005                  */
/* ============================================================ */


/* ============================================================ */
/*   Schema: myorder                                                  */
/* ============================================================ */
create SCHEMA myorder
/* ============================================================ */
/*   Table: ZONE                                                */
/* ============================================================ */
create table [myorder].[ZONE]
(
    ZoneID            smallint              not null,
    ZonePlace         varchar(20)           null    ,
    constraint PK_ZONE primary key (ZoneID)
)


/* ============================================================ */
/*   Table: BillTO                                              */
/* ============================================================ */
create table [myorder].[BillTO]
(
    BillTo            smallint              not null,
    Name              varchar(30)           null    ,
    WhseAddress1      varchar(30)           null    ,
    Whse_City         varchar(20)           null    ,
    Whse_Postal_Code  varchar(7)            null    ,
    Phone             varchar(20)           null    ,
    SlsPerson         int                   null    ,
    Zone              smallint              null    ,
```

```
        constraint PK_BILLTO primary key (BillTo)
)


/* =========================================================== */
/*    Table: Stock                                             */
/* =========================================================== */
create table [myorder].[Stock]
(
    StockId             int                 not null,
    Whse                varchar(10)         null    ,
    QtyOnHand           decimal             null    ,
    QtyOnOrd            decimal             null    ,
    QtyAvail            decimal             null    ,
    ItemNum             varchar(50)         not null,
    constraint PK_STOCK primary key (StockId)
)


/* =========================================================== */
/*    Table: SalesPerson                                       */
/* =========================================================== */
create table [myorder].[SalesPerson]
(
    SalesID             int                 not null,
    Name                varchar(30)         null    ,
    WhseAddress1        varchar(30)         null    ,
    Whse_City           varchar(20)         null    ,
    Whse_Postal_Code    varchar(7)          null    ,
    Phone               varchar(20)         null    ,
    Zone                smallint            null    ,
    constraint PK_SALESPERSON primary key (SalesID)
)
/* =========================================================== */
/*    Table: Customer                                          */
/* =========================================================== */
create table [myorder].[Customer]
(
    CustID              int                 not null,
    BillTo              smallint            not null,
    Name                varchar(30)         null    ,
    WhseAddress1        varchar(30)         null    ,
    Whse_City           varchar(20)         null    ,
    Whse_Postal_Code    varchar(7)          null    ,
    Phone               varchar(20)         null    ,
    Email_Addr          varchar(20)         null    ,
    Zone                smallint            null    ,
```

```
    SlsPerson              int                       null    ,
    constraint PK_CUSTOMER primary key (CustID)
)



/* ============================================================ */
/*   Table: OrderHeader                                         */
/* ============================================================ */
create table [myorder].[OrderHeader]
(
    CustID                 int                    not null,
    OrderID                int                    not null,
    Order_Date             datetime               null    ,
    Ship_Date              datetime               null    ,
    Whse                   varchar(10)            null    ,
    Zone                   smallint               null    ,
    PayMethod              varchar(7)             null    ,
    FreightCharge          bit                    null    ,
    InvoiceNum             numeric                null    ,
    InvoiceDate            datetime               null    ,
    SlsPerson              int                    null    ,
    constraint PK_ORDERHEADER primary key (OrderID)
)



/* ============================================================ */
/*   Table: OrderDetail                                         */
/* ============================================================ */
create table [myorder].[OrderDetail]
(
    OrderID                int                    not null,
    ItemID                 numeric                null    ,
    ItemDescription        varchar(30)            null    ,
    Qty                    numeric                null    ,
    QtyShip                numeric                null    ,
    QtyBO                  numeric                null    ,
    BOYesNo                bit                    null    ,
    Price                  decimal                null    ,
    Discount               decimal                null    ,
    Amount                 decimal                null    ,
)



/* ============================================================ */
/*   Table: ShipTO                                              */
/* ============================================================ */
create table [myorder].[ShipTO]
```

```
(
    CustID              int                 not null,
    ShipTO              smallint            not null,
    Name                varchar(30)         null    ,
    WhseAddress1        varchar(30)         null    ,
    Whse_City           varchar(20)         null    ,
    Whse_Postal_Code    varchar(7)          null    ,
    Phone               varchar(20)         null    ,
    SlsPerson           int                 null    ,
    Zone                smallint            null    ,
    constraint PK_SHIPTO primary key (CustID, ShipTO)
)


/* ================================================================ */
/*    Table: CustSales                                              */
/* ================================================================ */
create table [myorder].[CustSales]
(
    CustID          int                     not null,
    SalesID         int             not null,
    constraint PK_CUSTSALES primary key (CustID, SalesID)
)
go


/* ================================================================ */
/*    Schema: myinventory                                        */
/* ================================================================ */
create SCHEMA myinventory


/* ================================================================ */
/*    Table: Warehouse                                          */
/* ================================================================ */
create table [myinventory].[Warehouse]
(
    WhseID              int                 not null,
    WhseName            varchar(20)         null    ,
    WhseAddress1        varchar(30)         null    ,
    Whse_City           varchar(20)         null    ,
    Whse_Postal_Code    varchar(7)          null    ,
    constraint PK_WAREHOUSE primary key (WhseID)
)
/* ================================================================ */
/*    Table: Item                                               */
/* ================================================================ */
create table [myinventory].[Item]
(
```

```
    ItemID              int                 not null,
    Description         varchar(30)         null    ,
    Vendor              int                 null    ,
    Category            varchar(20)         null    ,
    Color               varchar(10)         null    ,
    Unit                char(4)             null
        constraint CKC_UNIT_ITEM check (
            Unit in ('EA','BOX','DZ','PAIR')),
    constraint PK_ITEM primary key (ItemID)
)


/* ============================================================== */
/*   Table: Vendor                                                */
/* ============================================================== */
create table [myinventory].[Vendor]
(
    VendorID            numeric             not null,
    Name                varchar(30)         null    ,
    WhseAddress1        varchar(30)         null    ,
    Whse_City           varchar(20)         null    ,
    Whse_Postal_Code    varchar(7)          null    ,
    Phone               varchar(20)         null    ,
    constraint PK_VENDOR primary key (VendorID)
)



/* ============================================================== */
/*   Table: PurchaseOrderDetail                                   */
/* ============================================================== */
create table [myinventory].[PurchaseOrderDetail]
(
    PoNum               numeric             not null,
    PoHNum              int                 not null,
    ItemID              numeric             null    ,
    ItemDescription     varchar(30)         null    ,
    Price               decimal             null    ,
    Qty                 numeric             null    ,
    BOYesNo             bit                 null    ,
    Discount            decimal             null    ,
    Amount              decimal             null    ,
    constraint PK_PURCHASEORDERDETAIL primary key (PoNum)
)



/* ============================================================== */
/*   Table: PriceList                                             */
/* ============================================================== */
```

```
create table [myinventory].[PriceList]
(
    PriceId            int                 not null,
    ItemidPricelist    int                 not null,
    ItemID             int                 null   ,
    Price              decimal             null   ,
    Discount           decimal             null   ,
    Cost               decimal             null   ,
    constraint PK_PRICELIST primary key (PriceId, ItemidPricelist)
)


/* ============================================================ */
/*    Table: PurchaseOrderHeader                                */
/* ============================================================ */
create table [myinventory].[PurchaseOrderHeader]
(
    PoHNum             int                 not null,
    VendorID           numeric             not null,
    PO_Date            datetime            null   ,
    AccountNum         numeric             null   ,
    AccountName        varchar(20)         null   ,
    constraint PK_PURCHASEORDERHEADER primary key (PoHNum)
)


/* ============================================================ */
/*    Table: StockItem                                          */
/* ============================================================ */
create table [myinventory].[StockItem]
(
    StockId            int                 not null,
    ItemID             int                 not null,
    constraint PK_STOCKITEM primary key (StockId, ItemID)
)

go
/* ============================================================ */
/*    Scehma: myfinance                                         */
/* ============================================================ */
create SCHEMA myfinance
/* ============================================================ */
/*    Table: CashReceipt                                        */
/* ============================================================ */
create table [myfinance].[CashReceipt]
(
```

```
    CustID              int                 null    ,
    Receiptdate         datetime            null    ,
    ReferenceOrderNum   numeric(10)         null    ,
    ReceiptAmount       decimal(6,2)        null    ,
    UnappliedAmount     decimal(6,2)        null    ,
    GLnum               varchar(30)         null    ,
    Posted              bit                 null    ,
    CRID                integer             not null,
    constraint PK_CASHRECEIPT primary key (CRID)
)


/* ============================================================= */
/*    Table: AccountsReceivable                                  */
/* ============================================================= */
create table [myfinance].[AccountsReceivable]
(
    AccountID           int                 not null,
    InvoiceNo           int                 not null,
    CustID              int                 not null,
    Amount              decimal             null    ,
    InvoiceDate         datetime            null    ,
    PaymentStatus       bit                 null    ,
    ReferenceNum        int                 null    ,
    Balancedue          decimal(6,2)        null    ,
    InvoiceDuedate      datetime            null    ,
    GLAccount           varchar(30)         null    ,
    constraint PK_ACCCOUNTSRECEIVABLE primary key (AccountID, InvoiceNo)
)



/* ============================================================= */
/*    Table: AccountInvoice                                      */
/* ============================================================= */
create table [myfinance].[AccountInvoice]
(
    AccountID           int                 not null,
    InvoiceNo           int                 not null,
    CRID                integer             null    ,
    constraint PK_ACCOUNTINVOICE primary key (AccountID, InvoiceNo)
)
go


alter table [myinventory].[PurchaseOrderHeader] add constraint
FK_PURCHASE_RELATION__VENDOR foreign key (VendorID)
      references [myinventory].[Vendor](VendorID)
go
```

```
alter table [myorder].[OrderHeader] add constraint FK_ORDERHEA_REF_185_CUSTOMER
foreign key  (CustID)
      references [myorder].[Customer] (CustID)
go

alter table [myfinance].[AccountsReceivable] add constraint
FK_ACCOUNTS_REF_188_CUSTOMER foreign key  (CustID)
      references [myorder].[Customer] (CustID)
go

/*alter table [myorder].[OrderDetail] add constraint FK_ORDERDET_REF_233_ORDERHEA
foreign key  (OrderID)
      references [myorder].[OrderHeader] (OrderID)*/
go

alter table [myorder].[ShipTO] add constraint FK_SHIPTO_REF_220_CUSTOMER
foreign key  (CustID)
      references [myorder].[Customer] (CustID)
go

alter table [myorder].[CustSales] add constraint FK_CUSTSALE_REF_2432_CUSTOMER
foreign key  (CustID)
      references [myorder].[Customer] (CustID)
go

alter table [myorder].[CustSales] add constraint FK_CUSTSALE_REF_243_SALESPER
foreign key  (SalesID)
      references [myorder].[SalesPerson] (SalesID)
go

alter table [myinventory].[StockItem] add constraint FK_STOCKITE_RELATION__STOCK
foreign key  (StockId)
      references [myorder].[Stock] (StockId)
go

alter table [myinventory].[StockItem] add constraint FK_STOCKITE_RELATION__ITEM
foreign key  (ItemID)
      references [myinventory].[Item] (ItemID)
go

alter table [myinventory].[PurchaseOrderDetail] add constraint
FK_PURCHASE_RELATION__PURCHASE foreign key  (PoHNum)
      references [myinventory].[PurchaseOrderHeader] (PoHNum)
go

alter table [myinventory].[PriceList] add constraint FK_PRICELIS_RELATION__ITEM
foreign key  (ItemID)
```

```
        references [myinventory].[Item] (ItemID)
go


alter table [myfinance].[AccountInvoice] add constraint
FK_ACCOUNTI_RELATION__ACCCOUNT foreign key (AccountID, InvoiceNo)
        references [myfinance].[AccountsReceivable] (AccountID, InvoiceNo)
go


alter table [myfinance].[AccountInvoice]   add constraint
FK_ACCOUNTI_REF_861_CASHRECE foreign key (CRID)
        references [myfinance].[CashReceipt] (CRID)
go
*************************************************
view: vw_CustomerInvoiceStatus
*************************************************
create view [myorder].[vw_CustomerInvoiceStatus] as
select b.custid, a.amount, a.invoicedate, a.paymentstatus, a.balancedue,
a.invoiceduedate, b.name as customername, b.phone, c.name as salespersonname,
c.zone
from myorder.customer as b, myfinance.accountsreceivable as a,
myorder.custsales as d, myorder.salesperson as c
where a.Custid = b.custid
and b.custid = d.custid
and d.salesid = c.salesid
go


*************************************************
view: vw_ItemEnquiry
*************************************************
create view [myorder].[vw_ItemEnquiry] as
select a.itemid, a.description, b.price, d.stockid, d.whse, d.qtyonhand, d.qtyonord
from myinventory.item as a, myinventory.pricelist as b, myinventory.stockitem as c,
myorder.stock as d
where a.itemid = b.itemid
and b.itemid = c.itemid
and c.itemid = d.stockid
go
*************************************************
view: vw_OrderStatus
*************************************************
create view [myorder].[vw_OrderStatus] as
select a.custid, a.name, b.orderid, b.ship_date, c.itemid, c.itemdescription,
c.qtyship, c.qty
from customer a, orderheader b, OrderDetail c
where a.custid = b.custid
and b.orderid = c.OrderID
go
```

```
***********************************************************************
procedure: myorder.usp_GetCustomerInvoicePaymentDue
***********************************************************************
IF OBJECT_ID ( 'myorder.usp_GetCustomerInvoicePaymentDue', 'P' ) IS NOT NULL
    DROP PROCEDURE myorder.usp_GetCustomerInvoicePaymentDue;
go

CREATE PROCEDURE myorder.usp_GetCustomerInvoicePaymentDue
 @customername varchar(40)

AS
set nocount on

if(select paymentstatus from myorder.vw_CustomerInvoiceStatus)>0
begin
select custid,amount,customername,
case when datepart(dd,invoicedate)>datepart(dd,invoiceduedate)
then invoicedate end
from myorder.vw_CustomerInvoiceStatus
where customername=@customername
end

Select Sum(amount) as TotalAmount, Max(Amount) as MaxAmount,custid,customername
from myorder.vw_CustomerInvoiceStatus
group by amount, custid,customername
having custid>1
go


***********************************************************************
procedure: usp_InsertCustomerInvoice
***********************************************************************
IF OBJECT_ID ( 'myorder.usp_InsertCustomerInvoice', 'P' ) IS NOT NULL
    DROP PROCEDURE myorder.usp_InsertCustomerInvoice;
go

/* insert customer invoice in accountsreceivable table */
CREATE PROCEDURE myorder.usp_InsertCustomerInvoice
@accountid int,
@invoiceno int,
@custid int,
@amount decimal,
@invoicedate datetime,
@paymentstatus bit,
@referencenum bit,
@balancedue decimal(6,2),
@invoiceduedate datetime,
@glaccount varchar(30)
```

```
AS
set nocount on

INSERT myfinance.AccountsReceivable(AccountID, InvoiceNo, CustID, Amount,
InvoiceDate,
PaymentStatus, ReferenceNum, Balancedue, InvoiceDuedate, GLAccount)
SELECT
@accountid,
@invoiceno,
@custid,
@amount,
@invoicedate,
@paymentstatus,
@referencenum,
@balancedue,
@invoiceduedate,
@glaccount

/* if values are inserted then find the names of the customer and the identity of
the salesperson */
if @@rowcount<>0
select a.custid, a.name as Customername, a.phone, a.slsperson,
b.amount,b.invoicedate
from myorder.customer a, myfinance.accountsreceivable b
where a.custid=@custid
go


*********************************************************************
procedure: usp_GetItemAbovePremiumPrice
*********************************************************************
IF OBJECT_ID ( 'myinventory.usp_GetItemAbovePremiumPrice', 'P' ) IS NOT NULL
    DROP PROCEDURE myinventory.usp_GetItemAbovePremiumPrice;
go

/* find those items that are above average and will be sold to
premium customers*/
CREATE PROCEDURE myinventory.usp_GetItemAbovePremiumPrice
AS
declare @avgprice decimal
set @avgprice=(select avg(price) from myinventory.pricelist)
    select a.itemid, a.description,a.vendor,a.category,a.color,a.unit,
    b.price
    from myinventory.item a, myinventory.pricelist b
    where a.itemid=b.itemid and
    b.price>@avgprice
go
```

References

Blythe, Michael. "Merge Replication Performance Improvements in SQL Server 2005." Microsoft TechNet, October 2005. http://www.microsoft.com/technet/prodtechnol/sql/2005/mergerepl.mspx

Dorr, Bob. "SQL Server 2000 I/O Basics." Microsoft TechNet, January 2005. http://www.microsoft.com/technet/prodtechnol/sql/2000/maintain/sqlIObasics.mspx

Gray, J., P. Helland, P. O'Neil, and D. Sasha. "The Dangers of Replication and a Solution." In *Proceedings of the 1996 ACM SIGMOD International Conference on Management of Data.* Montreal, Canada, 1996.

Jones, Don. *The Definitive Guide to SQL Server Performance Optimization.* Realtimepublishers.com, July 2002.

Kacerek, Melanie. "Considerations for Deploying Peer-to-Peer Replication." http://www.quest-pipelines.com/pipelines/dba/archives/PeertoPeer_Replication2.pdf

Özsu, M. Tamer and Patrick Valduriez. *Principles of Distributed Database Systems,* second edition. Prentice-Hall, 1999.

SQL-Server-Performance.com. "Tips for Performance Tuning SQL Server Transactional Replication." www.sql-server-performance.com/transactional_replication.asp

Tom, Richard W., Kaushik Choudhury, and Qun Guo. "Well-Known Transactions in Data Replication." http://www.freepatentsonline.com/20050165858.html

Tripp, Kimberly L. *Immerse Yourself in SQL Server, Kimberly L. Tripp's Blog.* http://www.sqlskills.com/blogs/kimberly/

Weismann, M., F. Pedone, A. Schiper, B. Kemme, and G. Alonso. "Database Replication Techniques: A Three Parameter Classification." In *Proceedings of 19th IEEE Symposium on Reliable Distributed Systems (SRDS2000),* p. 206–15. Nürnberg, Germany: IEEE Computer Society October, 2000.

Index

Numbers and Symbols

(pound character)
  meaning of when preceding a credential name, 601
  preceding code comments with, 180
+ (plus) sign
  expanding list of tables with, 448
  in Performance window to view list of counters and objects, 766–767
20574 error message, registered in event of registration failure, 674
2PC protocol. *See* two-phase commit (2PC) protocol

A

Activity Monitor
  monitoring activity when database is idle in, 777
  shared locks held on database objects by Snapshot Agent, 109
  showing locks by objects, 167
  viewing locks held during synchronization process in, 108–110
  viewing locks held while publication is being configured, 778
  viewing filter settings for, 776
Add Counters window
  adding counters for SQLServer :Replication Dist performance object, 769–770
  adding counters for SQLServer :Databases object in, 771
  adding counters for SQLServer :Locks object, 770
  performance objects that indicate how replication is working, 767
  selecting counters for performance object in, 768–769
  viewing performance counters for Merge Agent in, 868
  viewing performance counters for Snapshot Agent in, 868
Add Data Partitions window, setting value for SUSER_SNAM() dynamic function in, 469
Add Filter page
  adding a filter to prevent replication of specific rows, 268
  adding a parameterized filter for SalesPerson table in, 460
  in New Publication Wizard, 94
Add Join to Extend Selected Filter option, in Publication Properties window, 461–462

Add Join window
  adding a join filter in, 461–462
  specifying logical record grouping in, 465
  using builder to build join filter in, 462–463
Add Objects dialog box, adding performance objects in, 773
Add SQL Server Subscriber button, in New Subscription Wizard Subscribers page, 115–116
Advanced page, selecting in Job Step Properties dialog box, 205
Advanced Tuning Options window, setting advanced tuning options in, 844–845
AdventureWorks, new sample database in SQL Server, 15
Agent Connection Mode
  Impersonate used by SQL Server to connect to Publishers, 37–38
  setting property for Publisher server in, 38
Agent history clean up, function of in snapshot replication, 223
agent profiles. *See also* replication agent profiles
  retrieving descriptions of, 59
  viewing different Merge Agent profiles available, 896
Agent Profiles dialog box, selecting new agent profile in, 241
agent security, setting in New Publication Wizard, 911
Agent Security page
  configuring security settings for Snapshot and Log Reader Agents in, 928
  in New Publication Wizard, 96, 259–260, 452
  security account under which Snapshot Agent will run, 96
agent timeouts, displaying, 125
agents, types and functions of, 25–26
anonymous subscriptions
  configuring, 157–158
  function of, 23
  as type of pull subscription, 112
article, any grouping of data to be replicated, 22
Article Issues page, in New Publication Wizard, 449
Article Properties window
  setting Item article's properties in, 257
  setting use of Interactive Resolver in, 469
  viewing properties of Product_Information article in, 924–925
article resolvers, for merge replication, 81–82

Q

You Need the Companion eBook

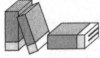

Printed in the United States
By Bookmasters